A Guiding Star

It is night. You are standing at a crossroads. You don't have a flashlight—but you do have the stars and planets to illuminate the path that you choose. Study them carefully; they will help you to choose wisely.

Horoscope for the New Millennium is a guiding star among the growing number of books regarding the new millennium. It offers an insightful look into the past and a provocative glimpse into the future. It is essential reading for anyone interested in the meaning of the great events of our time, and for people interested in how these events will affect their lives.

E. Alan Meece shares his positive vision of humanity's potential to create a great new age, starting *today*. Let the light of the planets illuminate your path to the New Millennium.

About the Author

Born in 1949, E. Alan Meece holds a Masters degree in philosophy from San Jose State University. He has written over thirty articles for *Welcome to Planet Earth*, an astrological magazine published in Eugene, Oregon. His articles have appeared in *American Astrology*, *The Mountain Astrologer* and the *A.F.A. Bulletin*. He was President of the South Bay Astrological Society (San Jose area) from 1994–96, and is producer of the annual New Age Renaissance Fair in San Jose (an art, health, and psychic expo).

His writings are the fruit of over twenty years of research, and are intended as gateways to help Humanity cross over into the New Age. He has also published an expanded version of this book called *The Horoscope of Humanity*, which describes in greater detail how planetary cycles reveal the pattern of history and the future.

He is the host of a radio program on KKUP-FM in Cupertino, California, called Mystic Music/Mystic Musings, where he interviews people who are experts in fields such as spirituality, the occult, music, philosophy, and religion. He has been interviewed often himself, and lectures on astrology, history, and prophecy at schools, astrology clubs, conferences, and New Age expos.

To Write to the Author

If you wish to contact the author or would like more information about this book, please write to the author in care of Llewellyn Worldwide, and we will forward your request. Both the author and publisher appreciate hearing from you and welcome your comments. Llewellyn Worldwide cannot guarantee a reply to all letters, but all will be forwarded. Please write to:

E. Alan Meece
c/o Llewellyn Worldwide
P.O. Box 64383, Dept. K461-8
St. Paul, MN 55164-0383, U.S.A.
Please enclose a self-addressed, stamped envelope or $1.00 to cover costs.
If outside the U.S.A., enclose international postal reply coupon.

Horoscope
for the
New Millennium

E. Alan Meece

1997
Llewellyn Publications
St. Paul, MN 55164-0383, U.S.A.

FIRST EDITION
First Printing, 1996

Cover design: Tom Grewe
Editing and interior design: Ken Schubert
Astrology charts generated using IO Edition software by Time Cycles Research,
27 Dimmock Road, Waterford, CT 06385

Library of Congress Cataloging-in-Publication Data

Meece, E. Alan (Eric Alan) , 1949-
     Horoscope for the new millennium / E. Alan Meece. -- 1st ed.
          p.   cm.
     Includes bibliographical references and index.
     ISBN 1-56718-461-8
     1. Predictive Astrology.   2. Horoscopes. 3. Twenty-first century– –Fore-
casts.   I. Title.
BF1720.5.M44 1997
133.5'890983—dc20   96-35825
                                                          CIP

Printed in the United States of America

Llewellyn Publications
A Division of Llewellyn Worldwide, Ltd.
P.O. Box 64383,
St. Paul, MN 55164-0383, U.S.A.

Contents

Foreword

AT THE EDGE OF A NEW MILL[...]

As we reach the magic year 2000 and cross over into the Tw[...]ty-First Century, we are hearing strange prophecies. This is the dawning of the Age of Aquarius! New continents will soon rise from the sea. The end of the world is due, and Christ is coming again. We'd all like a glimpse beyond the horizon, but what do these prophecies mean? Predictions abound, but does anyone really know what might happen in the next Millennium?

One thing is clear: the world is changing fast and people are worried. These kinds of prophecies are almost as old as the hills, but today the "end of the world" is a real possibility. Never before have these apocalyptic prophecies been so justified, nor followed by so many people with such breathless fascination. This is itself a sign of the times!

Among the sources of prophecy today are the psychics whose predictions we read in the gossip tabloids. Some have been startlingly correct. Jean Dixon, for example, foretold President Kennedy's assassination. By and large, though, these tabloid psychics have a low percentage of correct "hits." Then there are more powerful seers, like Edgar Cayce. In trance he was able to diagnose and prescribe treatments for people who were ill. For others he revealed their past lives, taking them back to the lost continent of Atlantis. His predictions were better than most. For example, he apparently foresaw the U.S. war with Japan and the racial turmoil in America in the '60s. He is perhaps most famous for predicting that California would fall into the sea and that new continents would rise at the end of the Twentieth Century. At this late date, these catastrophes seem pretty unlikely.

Then, of course, there's the Bible. Devoted Christians proclaim, as they have for two millennia, that the world will end soon and that Jesus is coming again. Millions listen as evangelists proclaim the good news that they will be saved from the fire if they believe in Christ; millions more flock to see apocalyptic movies like *The Omen* and *The Seventh Sign*. Ambitious writers such as Hal Lindsay use Bible prophecy to make detailed predictions. The return of the Jews to Palestine is the sign that "Armageddon" is approaching, they say. After Jesus defeats the "Anti-Christ," he will resurrect all "born again" Christians in "the rapture." There may be some prophetic insights in the fantastic visions from the Book of Revelation, but it seems to me that the basic purpose of all of this is to swell the ranks by playing to people's fear and uncertainty. After 2,000 years of waiting, I see virtually no chance that these apocalyptic events were meant to be taken literally.

i

ere's also a new kind of prophet on the scene. This species comes armed with sts of facts and figures printed on reams of computer paper. They too proclaim of the world," but on the basis of science instead of superstition. They detail the ways we are destroying ourselves: from overpopulation, toxic waste and depleted re- rces to global warming and a ruined ozone layer. These predictions seem most plausible f all. Not only are we contaminating our environment, but our social scientists confirm the conventional wisdom that our society is declining through mutual alienation, crime, and moral decay. We are facing the consequences of trying to be masters of the Earth and of hav- ing "eaten the fruit of the tree of knowledge," as Christians say.

At the same time, others who run the same computers and come out with opposite con- clusions. Visionaries like Peter Vajk announce that "Doomsday has been cancelled!" They be- lieve we can save ourselves by using the very same technology that threatens us. They paint exotic scenes of self-sufficient space colonies which beam abundant solar energy to Earth, where humans live happily with expanded intelligence and extended life spans in a peaceful global society. This view is just as plausible as the other one. After all, we've faced disasters before and overcome them, and we are freer and more technologically advanced today than at any other time in human history.

Still others believe we are being visited by beings from other worlds, who will soon help us to survive our present difficulties. Testimony of alien abductions, UFO sightings and evi- dence of their landings and crashes, telepathic communications with extraterrestrials, and the results of our explorations of outer space have convinced millions that "we are not alone."

Who's to say which view is right? No one knows, and meanwhile we remain as confused as ever. Most of us are totally ignorant of our place in history. Who are we anyway, and where are today's events taking us? Is a New Age dawning, or is the world coming to an end? Will our civilization survive? Are the glowing predictions for the New Millennium right, or are the prophets of doom correct instead? Are we entering Hell or Paradise? How can we find out?

Among the leading trends of our troubled time is the revival of mysticism and the occult. Ancient esoteric secrets, formerly the exclusive property of initiates, are now being made available to all. Spontaneous visionary awakenings have come to many people. And never before have such subjects as ESP, meditation, angels, life after death, and reincarnation been so popular. Among the occult practices now being revived is astrology, an ancient body of knowledge that has been used for centuries to understand the past and divine the future. It is also the source of today's well-known prophecy of the "dawning of the Age of Aquarius."

This book represents the first complete picture of human destiny as revealed in the stars. It gives us some exciting indications for the future, and also reveals the role each of us can play in the momentous events to come. It is a virtual road map of human destiny, showing the peaks and valleys, and the rough and smooth spots along the way. This kind of study lifts us out of normal awareness to a breathtaking view of the human journey. From it, we get a vivid picture of ourselves and the age we live in. We pinpoint our unique place in all of human evolution, and the lessons of history become crystal clear. We discover the remarkable future that lies in store for us, and we learn to face tomorrow without fear. We even discover how to find our own success and fulfillment in the new world to come.

We don't have to look at this map of destiny to find out what we most want to know, for the message of "the stars" is unmistakable. We are indeed at the dawn of a New Age. The old system of things must soon pass away, and a new one is rising to take its place, ushered in by a great new renaissance and revival of the human spirit.

To some this may seem like another outlandish prediction, but it is a middle ground between science and the supernatural. What we astrologers foresee are not fantastic, catastrophic events like the end of the world or the rise of new continents. Instead we predict something that has happened right on schedule many times before; a golden age, and a great leap forward for humanity. We have the historical facts and the planetary movements to back up our claim.

Therefore, let us consult astrology, the oracle of the ages! In it we shall find the answer to the riddle of our times. Today's renaissance in astrology is itself a part of the great renewal that we predict. Thus it may not only be an important contemporary trend, but one of the answers to the question, "where are we going?"

1

Introduction to Astrology:

OUR TOOL FOR MILLENNIAL PROPHECY

Astrology goes back many millennia. No one knows for sure when or where it began, but it was highly developed by the peoples of ancient Mesopotamia some three to five thousand years ago. They used it originally to predict the best times to grow and harvest their crops. They knew that the best time for planting would come when certain constellations were visible in the sky. Unlike most people today, the ancients were closely tied to the land and could see how the regular movements of the Sun and Moon were connected to the growth and decay of vegetation here on Earth. And the planets in the sky seemed much more imposing and powerful to us in the old days than they do now. Unlike today, when pollution and bright city lights block our view, people back then could actually see the stars!

This knowledge was so useful and important to the peoples of the ancient world that they soon extended it. Before long the Sun, Moon, and other planets were used to warn of imminent floods and other disasters or to determine the most auspicious times to act. Not only did astrology regulate the cultivation of the Earth, but their whole civilization. It became the chief means of understanding the world, a cornerstone of their culture. They believed it revealed the life-force that brought all things into harmony, and that the order observed in the heavens could be duplicated in our laws and social behavior here on Earth.

About 2,500 years ago, a great change of consciousness occurred—the Greeks discovered the rational individual. They were the most self-conscious people yet in history. They believed that their personal lives were important, and that people could conceive laws and social systems in their own rational minds. The Greeks were probably the first, therefore, to cast horoscopes for ordinary individuals as well as for kings. They contributed much to today's astrology. Despite their reliance on reason, horoscopes became one of the many oracles they turned to for guidance. Even Plato and Aristotle studied the heavenly bodies in order to discover the divine order which we should strive to duplicate in our lives.

As individualism increased, people saw less and less connection between the sky and their personal affairs. By Roman times, they were often as confused and alienated as we are today. As astrology continued to grow and flourish, it often degenerated into fortune telling. The traditional astrology we know today was largely developed at this time by the great astronomer

Ptolemy. In his astrology, the harmonizing life-force had vanished and the planets and "stars" had become separate, independent "influences" with set meanings.

The Christian church then rose to power and outlawed astrology as magic and superstition, but it continued to be practiced underground throughout the Middle Ages. Although branded as a heresy, it flourished because the people of those times still understood vividly that the divine eternal order above us is reflected in the world around us. It became a vital part of the secret wisdom of Hermetic magicians and alchemists in their quest for the "philosophers' stone," the symbol of self-knowledge. The Arabs further developed astrology and transmitted it to Christian philosophers like St. Thomas Aquinas, who broke the ban and made it an accepted part of Christian theology in the 13th Century.

Related practices were also being developed by other people, who observed that everything moves in cycles in a constant ebb and flow of change. The Celts of Northern Europe used various ways to symbolize the state of the universe at any moment in order to interpret the meaning of events, a practice called "divination." The Chinese also developed the classic system known as the I Ching, or Book of Changes, for this purpose. The Germans and Mayans both performed divination through rune stones, and ancient and modern European seers developed the series of mythical pictures known as Tarot cards. The rediscovery of these and other "archaic" practices in the Twentieth Century has revived our interest in divination and astrology, whose roots are found in our common heritage.

Astrology was as much a part of the "rebirth" of Europe 500 years ago as it is of the renaissance of today. Until the Seventeenth Century it played a prominent role in Western thought. It even inspired great astronomers like Kepler, who described the "music of the spheres" in the solar system and used astrology to help formulate its harmonic structure. The great scientific pioneers we think of as "fighting superstition," such as Copernicus and Newton, either believed in astrology or were astrologers themselves, but since the Seventeenth Century, when science and philosophy became more materialistic, humanity began to be separated from the universe. This eroded astrology's stature and influence, and since then, it has been regarded by many in our culture as an outdated superstition.

WHY ASTROLOGY WORKS

The next question is: how does astrology work, and what is it based on? Here we are not dealing with the *evidence* for astrology, but with the *theory* behind it. Admittedly, there is no "theory" in the strict scientific sense, but there are several definite principles that have been distilled through the centuries. These are the ideas on which astrology is based.

As Above, So Below. From the Babylonians comes the great Law of Analogy, known to us in the adage "as above, so below." This principle reflects their observation that the seasons and other events "below" on Earth correspond to the heavenly bodies "above." Astrologers further contend that the solar system and the galaxies constitute "greater beings," of which smaller beings like persons and nations are a part. We call the greater being the "macrocosm" and the lesser the "microcosm." By "reading" the planets, we can understand the will of the macrocosm; thus revealing the larger purpose hidden amidst the events of our lives. This principle of the greater reflected in the lesser went on to become central to Western thought, and was passed on to medieval mystics and Eighteenth Century rationalists. Ever since the Greeks opened astrology to the individual, each person could aspire to become a Microcosm containing the whole Universe in miniature—a goal perfected in medieval alchemy. The Jews had spoken of human beings as "created in God's image," and the followers of Jesus claimed that he personified our potential to become the "Son of God," truly uniting the microcosm with the macrocosm.

Unity of All Things. The second principle is closely related to the first—the idea that all things are interrelated. Astrology affirms that humanity is a part of the universe around us, and what happens in one part of it affects every other part. Heavenly movements have an impact on earthly or human ones—and vice-versa! Astrology rejects the stark dualism of heaven vs. earth or spiritual vs. physical, and sees the divine will working its way through the universe of people, planets and stars. This principle has not only been basic to Eastern philosophy and Western occult wisdom, it has been reaffirmed by modern philosophers and scientists such as David Bohm and Fritjof Capra. Quantum theory explicitly confirms it in Neils Bohr's principle of complementarity, as does Bell's theorem, which implies that events influence each other instantly although separated by vast distances.

Cycles. A third basic principle is that all events move in cycles. A movement is "cyclic" if it repeatedly returns to where it started. Furthermore, the length of time between each cyclic return is about the same, and is called its "period." Each cycle goes through stages such as the beginning, middle and end; but the end also leads on toward the beginning of the next cycle.

We observe that all events move in cycles every day. We each are born, live and die; and many believe we are reborn again and again. Nations and civilizations apparently follow the same course, as the following pages will demonstrate. Cycles encircle us everywhere; in fact our most important cycles are the ones used by astrology. We still regulate our lives by the hours of the day and the seasons of the year, and these are the basis respectively for the "houses" of the horoscope and the "signs" of the Zodiac. Time itself is circular, or why would we use circular clocks to measure it? We measure time based on the daily and yearly motions of the Earth, and astrology goes further, to assert that the Earth and planets are cosmic clocks which we can use to reveal the cycles we follow in our lives.

It might seem that to think cyclically denies our desire for progress. After all, we don't want to get caught in a "vicious circle." This is an illusion, because all cycles are contained within larger ones. Consider a graphic illustration of this point. To "get somewhere," we often travel in a car or another vehicle that moves on wheels. These wheels go round and round many times, always returning to the same point, but the car moves forward because the wheels have shifted their position on the roadway. The same is true with any cycle. It returns to the same point, but this point itself shifts as part of a larger movement. This also means that each succeeding cycle is unique, defined by its position in the longer cycle.

More and more people are thinking cyclically, seeing that "linear thinking" is false and limited. We are perfectly aware that "progress" doesn't move in a straight line, because so many of our optimistic projections have been disappointed over the years. The historical pendulum continues to swing back and forth, and yesterday's losers become tomorrow's winners. Long ago, the Chinese taught that whatever has reached a peak of power will soon begin to decline, because of the ever-repeating cycles of yin and yang. Today, we increasingly see the truth of this ancient principle. By thinking cyclically, we not only face facts better, we get a more complete picture of reality. The circle encompasses infinity, giving us a model of all possible experience. By placing ourselves on a cycle, we can see what's before and ahead of us—something we can't do while our point of view is restricted to a straight line.

Synchronicity. Our fourth principle is related to the worldwide practice of divination. At any moment, the universe will answer an earnest and urgent request for understanding through oracles, omens, or the chance behavior of coins, cards, or tea leaves. This idea is based on an alternate principle of causation, upheld in the East but rejected in the West since the Seventeenth Century. Unlike the modern Western view that material, mechanical forces cause effects to follow afterward in time, the Oriental view is that "like attracts like, and similar things happen together." In the 1920s, psychologist Carl Jung imported and redesigned the principle and gave it the name of "synchronicity." Jung himself used astrology to help his clients, and today many astrologers are also Jungian psychologists. According to synchronicity, events happen because they attract each other, causing "amazing coincidences" to occur that are significant to those who experience them.

This justifies astrology's claim that earthly events correspond to cosmic ones, when they coincide in a "meaningful" way. This is not causation in the usual sense. Most astrologers today don't claim that the planets "cause" or "pre-destine" events by exerting "physical" forces on us, as western science requires us to believe. Instead, great cosmic cycles are like omens that have a "vibrational sympathy" with, and reveal the meaning of, great events happening simultaneously on Earth. They are the momentous "signs of the times." If astrology works, it is not because it follows the limited laws of western science. On the contrary, it causes us to rethink those laws, giving us a larger picture of how events happen.

Holism. This, our fifth and last principle, encompasses all the others. It can be stated in the popular phrase, "the whole is greater than the sum of its parts." Nowadays, "holistic" subjects are becoming very popular, especially in medicine and psychology. Astrology also claims to be one of these "holistic" disciplines. This means it views things whole rather than piecemeal, unlike today's old-fashioned sciences.

A "whole" is one being; unified within itself, yet composed of many individual parts that are also wholes within themselves. Whole beings can be cells of the body, persons, nations, civilizations, cultures, planets, solar systems, and even periods of time. Astrology states that everything is a whole being, yet also part of a greater whole. Each whole is defined by its limits. It has boundaries, and a beginning and an end. It also has a unique identity—a particular tone or color that pervades it. Its role in the greater whole also helps to define this identity. Persons in astrology are therefore wholes, each having a "soul" or integral personality and consciousness. We must therefore treat our subjects of study, whether they are persons or cultures, with the respect due to whole, living beings. To understand them it is not enough to dissect and analyze their parts; everything must be seen in context.

So astrology sees the Universe as one, just as the Eastern sages teach, but it also sees free individuals. It blends the best from East and West. According to astrology, we are unique individuals, and a person is the whole cosmos seen from a particular point of view, yet our identity and vitality results from our unique connection to larger wholes, such as nation, planet, solar system, universe, the spiritual and the divine. These larger beings also have their own consciousness and identity as wholes.

ASTROLOGY FOR THE NEW MILLENNIUM

In reading *Horoscope for the New Millennium*, it is important to be fair and impartial, and to try to see things as they are. But it is useless for any writer to deny his or her biases, so I place myself unabashedly on the side of progressive forces, as I see them. In my view, to understand our destiny means to see how we are evolving. The significant trends of our time are not those that maintain business as usual or preserve the status quo. If we are to take a larger view of things, we cannot restrict ourselves to the perspective of the current ruling authorities. *The future is often on the side of those out of favor today.* Destiny rests not with the Establishment, but with the outcasts whose vision will reshape the world. The truth lies beyond conventional wisdom, although that's all most people are allowed to read and see. Although the drama of human evolution is played out in the oval office of the White House, in the halls of Parliament and in corporate board rooms, it's even more often to be found in streets filled with strikers and demonstrators, in small rooms occupied by impassioned, fanatical conspirators, and, above all, in the inspired minds of poets and prophets.

We all want to know what the future holds, but to know this we also need to study history. As Ken Burns (producer of the PBS series *The Civil War*) said, we can only know where we're going if we know where we've been. Or as Michael Wood (writer and host of *Legacy*) said, we will know our ends by our beginnings. This last statement is as fundamental a truth of astrology as any ever uttered. Predictions for the future will only be meaningful if they are seen *in context*, by placing them within the great cycles of time. The future arises out of the past and from the decisions we make today. By looking at cycles of the planets and correlating them to history and the future, we alter and expand our consciousness. Seen from this higher, longer view, the great meaning of events becomes clearer.

The planets and signs of astrology are powerful prophetic tools. By associating them with events and trends, we can bring them vividly to life. We feel intimately connected with the world in a way we never thought possible. We sense again that we belong, and are at home. We rediscover our souls as part of humanity's soul. At a time when people are confused, disoriented and adrift, *Horoscope for the New Millennium* provides us with the sense of purpose we need. We see our place and our role in the evolution of all humanity.

2

A Transcendental Trinity:

THE AQUARIAN AGE

No doubt most people, whether they believe in astrology or not, have heard that "this is the dawning of the Age of Aquarius." It is the most famous astrological prophecy. It is, at least, as good a name as any for the "New Age" we are predicting—but what exactly *is* the "Age of Aquarius"?

It means, say astrologers, that the next 2,100 years or so will have Aquarian characteristics. Aquarius is the sign of humanity (sometimes Aquarius is known as "The Water Bearer"; other times as simply "The Man" who holds an urn of water). Therefore, brother and sisterhood will spread across the planet, and humanitarian ideals will take hold. Democracy and respect for human rights will expand. Aquarius is the sign of groups and associations too, so corporations, nations, and international organizations will continue to become more powerful. Aquarius represents innovation, a perfect fit for our high–tech revolution. Most of all, Aquarius stands for knowledge, so New Age religions will be based on what people can know and experience for themselves, largely superseding the dogmatic and authoritarian religions of the preceding Age of Pisces, the sign of belief. Among the major religions of this era is Christianity, which was born about 2,000 years ago when the Age of Pisces began, and whose symbol was the fish. Aquarius, on the other hand, represents not only the "magic" of technology, but the "magick" that alchemists, gnostics, mages, druids, shamans, witches, and holy healers have practiced throughout the ages. It is the power to transform and transmute reality in accordance with the will. Aquarius is the sign of mind power.

The New Age sounds good. It is a wonderful myth to guide us toward the great renewal of humanity soon to come; a reason to be optimistic despite all of today's gloom and doom. However, most people don't even know why astrologers say that "this is the dawning of the Age of Aquarius." What *is* their basis for saying this?

THE PRECESSION CYCLE

The twelve *Ages*, of which the Aquarian is one, are twelve divisions of a 25,000-year-long motion of our Earth called the *precession of the equinoxes*. It is only one of three basic Earth cycles—the three most important in astrology. The first cycle is the year, in which the Sun appears to move through a belt of constellations called the zodiac. Aquarius is one of these constellations. The second cycle is the day, caused by the Earth turning on its axis every twenty-four hours, making the Sun appear to rise and set. The Earth also gradually wobbles backwards as its turns, as if it were a spinning top. This is the third Earth cycle. The "great wobble" causes the north pole to point to different stars at different times. By the year 2100, it will point exactly at Polaris, the star which we know today as "the north star." About 13,000 years ago, it pointed toward Vega, the brightest star in today's summer skies. It takes an average of 25,694.8 years for the Earth to complete one "wobble," so about 26,000 years from today, the north pole will again point to Polaris.

The seasons happen because the Earth's axis is tilted by about twenty–three degrees. During the summer (in the northern hemisphere) the pole is tilted *toward* the Sun, so the days are longer. During the winter it tilts *away* from the Sun, so the days are shorter. When the pole is exactly halfway between, so that the Earth's orbit is aligned with the Equator, the days and nights are equal. This is called the *equinox*. The apparent location of the Sun at the equinox also gradually shifts backwards along the ecliptic (the path of Earth's orbit) as the north pole wobbles. 2,100 years ago, when the zodiac of constellations was named, the Sun entered the constellation Aries at the beginning of spring. By now, the zodiac has shifted one-twelfth of the way backwards (almost thirty degrees), so today spring begins when the Sun is in the constellation Pisces.

It is a curious irony that the reason most often cited by skeptics that astrology is "false" is also the basis for the most famous prophecy ever made by astrologers. Many skeptics (though not all) claim that astrologers don't even know that the constellations have shifted, and are therefore using a zodiac that is off by thirty degrees! After all, they say, astrologers still maintain that the Sun enters the sign Aries at the beginning of spring! Yet astrologers also say that we are in the beginnings of the "Age of Aquarius." Why? Because the Sun's position at the Vernal Equinox will soon move from the constellation Pisces into Aquarius. If astrologers didn't know about this backward shift, why would they use it to make their most famous prediction?

What many skeptics (and even some astrologers) don't understand is that *astrology really has little to do with stars,* and that the zodiac is not a belt of constellations at all. As we've seen, astrology is a study of cycles and their relationship to our lives. The 360-degree circle of the zodiac is the path of the Earth as it travels around the Sun, and it is divided into twelve signs of thirty degrees each. The signs have the same names as the constellations, but they are not the same. The signs get their meaning from their place on the yearly cycle of the Earth, not from the shape of the stars in each of those twelve sectors.

The signs are the most accepted way of interpreting the meaning of the yearly cycle. Every cycle must have a beginning point, and for the zodiac, this is the Vernal Equinox— the start of spring in the northern hemisphere. It is the moment each year (around March 21) when the Sun enters Aries, the first sign of the zodiac. Most astrologers today use the zodiac of signs. They are called *tropical* astrologers (of which this author is one). Astronomers also use the zodiac of signs, not constellations, to locate stars on the "celestial sphere." Some astrologers continue to use the zodiac of constellations, although in fact they place little or no emphasis on them; they are called *sidereal* astrologers.

Yes—but wait a minute—something doesn't quite fit here. If most astrologers don't assign meanings to stars or constellations, why do they say the Aquarian Age is dawning just because the Vernal Equinox will soon occur in the constellation Aquarius? This can't be right. If constellations are just distant stars arbitrarily grouped together and given meanings by humans, if they are just a convenient way to locate stars, like street names on a map, then why should the constellation Aquarius have any influence when it's lined up with the Sun at Vernal Equinox time?

Knowing these facts, some astrologers today debunk the Age of Aquarius as just an enchanting fiction. I don't think it can be dismissed so easily, because the precession of the equinoxes and the polar wobble are based on an *actual motion* of the Earth. This cycle is just as real as the year itself is. Such a long cycle could help us a great deal in interpreting human history from the long view, so the study of cycles can and should include a study of the whole cycle of astrological "ages." As we've said, all cycles must have a beginning, and the trouble with the precession cycle is that nobody is sure just where it begins. If we rule out constellations as questionable reference points, what do we use?

In a later chapter (Cultural Shifts, Chapter 7) I will show that the "ages" have tremendous significance, particularly for the history of religion. For now, let's review some general evidence showing how past ages have corresponded to the precession cycle as astrologers describe it. In doing this, I refer to an idea put forward by philosopher–astrologer Dane Rudhyar. He points out that each Age can be divided in two parts; the first half will have the traits of the constellation at the Vernal Equinox, but the second half will have the sub–traits of the opposite constellation at the Autumn Equinox. These traits are at their peak about halfway through each sub-age. Here is how the cycle has shaped up throughout recorded history, using approximate dates:

2100–3200 will be the Age of Aquarius proper, meaning an age of knowledge, independent thought and demands for freedom and progress. The role of the individual and the organization will be coordinated into a humanitarian whole. From 3200 to 4200 the Age will be under a sub–influence of Leo, the opposite sign of Aquarius. The creative powers of the romantic individual will re–assert themselves.

1100–2100 was the second half of the Age of Pisces, under the sub-influence of Virgo. This now–ending age was one of science, intellectual analysis, and service to one's superiors, all traits of Virgo. Certainly the ever–increasing power of scientific and rational thought and the growing power of the secular state and bureaucracy in this period could reflect the Virgo influence.

0–1100 was the Age of Pisces proper, meaning an age of faith and religion, of dissolution and breakdown of structures, of devotion and compassion, and of escape into the "other world." This is a perfect fit for Christianity and similar religions worldwide that dominated the period. Some philosophers say that the denial of life and spirit, and the assault on nature that took hold under Virgo, were based on the escapist attempt to divorce spirit from the world that happened under Pisces.

1000 B.C.–A.D. 0 was the second half of the Age of Aries, under the sub-influence of Libra. This was the classical age of ancient Greece, an era when Libran values like the "golden mean" and beauty were worshipped. Even in India, the Buddha taught "the Middle Way." It was an age of intellectual accomplishments and of political inventions (also Libra fortes), demonstrated by Athenian democracy and the Roman Republic.

2100 B.C.–1000 B.C. was the Age of Aries proper, meaning an age of aggression and enterprise. The Aryan (Arian) invaders swarmed over and conquered the old world, and most civilizations of the age (such as the first Assyrian Empire, the New Kingdom of Egypt, the Trojans, the Mycenaeans, etc.) were dominated by warriors. Not long before the Age of Aries began, Sargon I created the world's first war–based Empire in Mesopotamia. The symbol of the Ram appears in the Ram's Horn so important to the Hebrews, whose aggressive religion began in this period. Since Aries is ruled by Mars, masculine, patriarchal values replaced the feminine values that flourished under the Venus-ruled Taurean Age which preceded it.

3100 B.C.–2100 B.C. was the second half of the Age of Taurus, under the sub-rulership of Scorpio. The earliest civilizations rose to greatness in this period. Scorpio is the sign of death and rebirth, and the Egyptians created the world's greatest funeral monuments and history's most remarkable death cult in this period. Their greatest symbols were the Scarab and the Hawk, similar to the Scorpion and the Eagle. Scorpio is an appropriate constellation for this time of great creative transformation and occult wisdom in which astronomy and astrology were developed.

4200 B.C.–3100 B.C. was the Age of Taurus proper. The Taurean traits seemed to display themselves most clearly in the second half of the Age during its sub-rulership of Scorpio, perhaps because written historical records do not begin until then. Certainly the pyramids, stone circles, and other great monuments of this entire age reflected the Taurean talent for building and architecture, and revealed the desire for permanent structure and security that gave rise to civilization in this period. It was also an age of fertility worship, a Taurean trait, and the bull was widely held sacred during this time.

This evidence is impressive, and other researchers have amassed even more facts. No doubt there are many things in history that don't fit the Age in which they occurred; for example, the Lion symbols in the sculptures of Mycenae and Assyria were made during the Age of Aries, not Leo—but generally, the sign of each Age and sub-age fits each period better than any other sign does.

Humanity has probably known of the precession cycle for millennia, but now we have access to other long cycles which have been unknown until our own century. They last long enough to be significant, yet are short enough to give us many more examples to study than the 2,000-year-long "ages" give us. Furthermore, many of us have had personal experience with them recently.

SOMETHING IN THE AIR— *AND* THE SKY!

Not so long ago, at least by cosmic reckoning, I was a young high school student growing up (I think!) in San Jose, California. It was not an entirely pleasant childhood, but I found refuge by studying science and other things. At that time, I believed science could explain everything, much as my parents did, but I could feel something mysterious happening around me. Suddenly I became intensely curious about life, and questions filled my adventurous young mind. What is the nature of mathematics? Why is music beautiful? Is there more to life than conventional paths? Then, in the early summer of 1966, I was overwhelmed with the beauty of things I had always seen and taken for granted before. I felt at one with the sky, and there seemed to be something magical and electric "in the air." The world seemed vibrantly alive, and love flooded through me. It came to me that somehow love was the answer to my questions. This, my "spiritual awakening," led me to radically change my attitudes toward science and religion. It started me on a philosophical quest that took me through Eastern and Western thought and, by the spring of 1968, to astrology.

I continued to wonder what this magical feeling was and where it came from. Surely, part of it was simply the feeling that exciting things were happening in the world. Only weeks and months after my own personal "awakening," I saw signs of a revolution exploding around me that had started a few months before in my own city, and in San Francisco, just fifty miles away. It was the youthful cultural explosion of the sixties, powered by the very same spirit that was simultaneously stirring inside me. By year's end, the Haight-Ashbury hippie scene was well established, and from there a whole counter-culture spread across the planet. At the same time the peace movement blossomed.

Many others testified to the strange feeling that "something was in the air" in the 1960s. The counter-culture was clearly not a deliberately planned phenomena. It was a spontaneous mass awakening whose origin was mysterious, and no one has ever really explained why it happened. What is even more remarkable is how many people of all ages had mystical experiences at the same time, and even in the same month, as I did, while others went through important personal life changes. You might know such people; or you might look back at your own life and notice what inspirations or drastic changes came to you in about 1966. Our whole culture was exploding and changing. Clearly, it was a time of spiritual awakenings that touched people everywhere.

After I began studying astrology and learned the meanings of the signs and the planets, I was able to predict what my own horoscope would be like. Very intrigued, soon I also began to wonder what rare and remarkable event might be going on out among the planets that would explain the explosive changes going on in the 1960s. I learned that in astrology the planets Uranus, Neptune, and Pluto stand for radical changes in consciousness and society—in fact, for everything strange, marvelous, eccentric, advanced, visionary, deviant, mysterious, occult, and out of the ordinary. I thought two or more of them must surely be forming what we call a conjunction, the most important planetary event (in which two planets line up exactly with the Earth). When I checked an ephemeris to verify my theory, I could not believe my eyes. Uranus and Pluto *were* in a conjunction. Then came an even more stunning discovery. I learned that the exact date of this Uranus-Pluto line-up was in late June 1966—*the exact time* of my own personal awakening, and that of so many others! Perhaps it was Uranus and Pluto we were resonating to—maybe it was the "electric" rays from Uranus that were "in the air."

THE KEYS TO OUR DESTINY

As the years passed, the revolutionary energy of the '60s waned. Some of the ideals of the "love generation" were discredited, and many of its dreams were literally shot down, but profound changes had taken place within society, and the goals were still important to many people. It seemed like just the beginning. So I wondered, did the conjunction of Uranus with Pluto mark the start of a whole cycle of revolutionary change, or were the movements of the sixties just passing fads? I thought history could answer this by showing whether revolutionary movements coincided with Uranus-Pluto conjunctions in the past. So I checked what happened during the dates of previous conjunctions, and I found convincing evidence that they do—as we'll see in a later chapter.

Meanwhile, I discovered that an even more rare and powerful conjunction had also occurred a relatively short time ago, at the turn of the Twentieth Century. This one involved Neptune and Pluto. If Uranus and Pluto together corresponded to the amazing, seemingly unexplainable events I witnessed in the '60s, surely this even rarer alignment should have coincided with even more remarkable events. And so it was. I found that this conjunction marked the end of one age of civilization and the start of another, and that previous such conjunctions had done so throughout history. The Neptune-Pluto conjunction further confirmed that a "New Age" was dawning in our time—the eve of a New Millennium.

The three outer planets, Uranus, Neptune and Pluto, emerged as the key to human destiny. What makes these planets and their cycles so interesting to study is the simple and profound fact that today is the first time we *can* study them. We are exploring virgin territory, because they have only been discovered in recent times. Invisible to the naked eye, they remained unknown until we gained the technical ability to explore the heavens. Unlike revelations based on 2,000-year-old texts, the cycles of Uranus, Neptune, and Pluto give us today's prophetic insights. Astrologers call them "the modern planets." They are a modern-day transcendental trinity. This is confirmed by the fact that the length of their orbits are in a three-fold relationship. Uranus revolves around the Sun once every eighty–four years, while Neptune takes about twice as long at 165 years, and Pluto takes three times as long at 248 years. It is the only such pattern in the solar system.

As the first generations to know these planets, we are the first to be able to truly chart the destiny of humanity. We have a further advantage today, for not only is a full study of astrology new, so is history itself. Before the Eighteenth Century, when Uranus was discovered, people believed that life never changes. The world was viewed as static, or as repeating in endless cycles. History consisted of the myths and legends of the culture into which you were born. No one thought of checking one's facts with historical research, and rarely was anyone concerned with cultures far away or long since vanished. Not until the late 18th Century, did a "romantic" interest in the distant past lead to a study of history as we know it. History became the vital chronicle of human progress and evolution. Thus, both history and the key to its interpretation became available to us in the late Eighteenth Century—the very time when Uranus, the first of the outer planets, was discovered.

♅ URANUS, THE MAVERICK (1781)

For historians, this moment represents the beginning of the modern age. Radical, sweeping changes have totally transformed the world since Uranus was first seen in 1781. All the ancient ways have been upset, and the pace of events has accelerated. Powerful new potentials have opened to us. We have taken a gigantic, terrifying, and irreversible leap into the future, and have begun to expand our consciousness. For astrologers, the discovery of Uranus in 1781 represents the start of this dramatic shift of awareness. Each new planet discovered represents further stages in our expansion of consciousness and human potential, for although the transcendental trinity has always influenced human history, until modern times it had only done so on an unconscious level for most people. Now their true significance is being fully revealed to all of us.

Revolutionary developments opened this age of expansion in the late Eighteenth Century. At the very time Uranus was discovered, the United States had just won its independence, and the sparks from that upheaval soon lit the fuse of a much larger one in France. The French Revolution of 1789 kindled the light of liberty and the flames of ferment over the whole world, while a quieter but even more drastic political and social transformation was reverberating through Britain. The industrial revolution also took off in the 1780s, mobilizing human and technical resources as never before. These two dramatic, explosive events that irreversibly changed our planet happened at practically the same moment that the astronomer Herschel discovered the new planet.

The Uranian wave was felt everywhere, and in many ways. In Germany, the revolution occurred in the realm of philosophy when Immanuel Kant published *The Critique of Pure Reason* in 1781 (exact year of Uranus' discovery), brilliantly demonstrating how knowledge depends on our own categories of thought. It was a declaration of independence for the mind. German and British writers unleashed an ecstasy of self–discovery called "the romantic movement," and asserted the creative freedom of the artist. For the French painter J. L. David, art became a means to arouse the people to revolt ("Oath of the Horatii," 1784). Our understanding of the infinite dimensions of the universe began to open up. Light was discovered beyond the normal visible spectrum to include ultraviolet and infrared. Discoveries in the fields of mathematics, electricity, astronomy, and chemistry in the 1780s and '90s eventually turned our knowledge of the physical world upside down.

It was clear from the start what Uranus would stand for in astrology. Its discovery in 1781 represents the end of the reign of Chronos (Saturn) in the life of humanity. It is the critical break from the past into the modern age of "progress." Its role is to free us from all conventional authorities and to drastically reform society along lines of truth and justice. It stands for our new awareness of individual freedom and liberty, and for "declarations of independence." Depending on other factors in force at the time, it can bring quick, beneficial reforms or violent, disruptive, destructive events. It is also associated with science and "enlightenment," and seeks to base authority on knowledge which we discover for ourselves. The planet of genius, Uranus constantly challenges us to look at things in a new way. It is sudden revelations and awakenings—the ruling planet of magicians, alchemists, and astrologers. The cosmic lightning bolt among the planets, its effects are always very striking, abrupt, and powerfully felt. It signifies charismatic leaders with enormous power. It stands for the modern dictator as much as the modern liberator. It is eccentric and unconventional, surprising, unusual, radical, outcast, and different from the norm. It represents all the inventions of the modern age and the skill to create and use them. It rules capitalism, "progress," and utopian expectations, and is one of the symbols of the "New Age." It is linked to Aquarius and the 11th House of the horoscope. Uranus represents the inner light—the creator from the invisible realms.

♆ NEPTUNE, THE MYSTIC (1846)

Astronomers soon realized that the new planet didn't behave as they expected (typical of Uranus, after all). Another planet was suspected farther out that would explain the strange perturbations in Uranus' orbit. By 1846, astronomers found it where LeVerrier and Adams predicted it would be. This new planet would turn out to be even more valuable in understanding human destiny than Uranus. It was named Neptune after the ancient god of the oceans, and its discovery coincided with the next expansion in modern consciousness.

When Neptune was discovered, the common people were sensing their power and identity as never before. The industrial revolution, until now largely limited to a few entrepreneurs and inventors in England, began to expand across the world. People started clustering together in vast urban conglomerations. Stripped from their roots and cut off from their old communities, they began identifying themselves with their nation, ethnic origin, or social class. The ties that bound the old society together began to decay and disintegrate, as famines and revolutions caused millions to migrate across the globe. Meanwhile, society was convulsed with idealistic, utopian movements. Kindness and compassion toward the less fortunate began to flourish on a mass scale for the first time. Dorothea Dix, Florence Nightingale, Clara Barton, and others promoted the new humanitarian ideal. Just two years after Neptune's discovery, Karl Marx and Friedrich Engels published *The Communist Manifesto*, launching a compelling, convulsive new movement toward human equality. Meanwhile, communal experiments spread across America, and the Mormons made their epic journey to Utah. A new religion sprang forth in Persia proclaiming the coming unification of humanity (the Bahai Faith). Interest in spiritualism and metaphysics mushroomed. Transcendentalist writers such as Thoreau, Emerson, and Whitman extolled non–conformity and the oversoul. Gas lighting spread through the cities, and anesthesia was applied to surgery. Ocean–going steamships made global commerce practical for the first time in history.

Neptune's character reflects these dynamic changes of the 1840s and '50s, and incarnates all the great movements of the Nineteenth Century. If Uranus represented freedom for the individual, Neptune stands for equality and the interests of collective society. It represents utopian social movements whose goal is to fairly distribute the world's resources. Neptune symbolizes compassion, kindness, and humanitarian concern. It rules hospitals, asylums, prisons, and big bureaucracies. More than any other planet, its movements represent the destiny and consciousness of humanity as a whole, and the "spirit of the times."

If Uranus is the transcendental mind, Neptune is the transcendental heart. It represents consciousness expanding until it encompasses all humanity and the entire universe. It is the symbol of everything intangible, mystical, imaginative, delicate and subtle, particularly as expressed through the most sensitive kinds of romantic, impressionist and visionary music and art. It is the urge to escape into a blissful state of ecstasy and reverie. It is life unrestricted by ordinary limits and boundaries, the transcending of all barriers, and the return to paradise and the golden age. Since it is so elusive and hard to pin down, Neptune also leads us into confusion, delusion and deception. Its talents are easily adapted by all who are in the business to deceive. It is the desire to escape from responsibility and to artfully and cleverly avoid facing reality. It frequently leads people and their leaders into involved and muddled affairs, and can signal floods, famines and diseases.

Since Neptune's discovery, the distribution of goods and services has increased remarkably. Neptune stands for all types of liquids, such as the seas, oils, solvents, and alcohol, as well as drugs and funguses. It represents decay and dissolution, but also the boundless, blissful state that results from the erasing of barriers. When fully expressed, Neptune is the beatific vision of universal, divine love and compassion for all beings. It is connected to the sign of Pisces and to the 12th House.

♇ or ♇ PLUTO, LORD OF THE UNDERWORLD (1930) $+80 = 2010$ $+40 = 1970$

One would think that with Neptune we have reached the ultimate; what could be higher than to connect with the infinite and the divine? But there is another planet, the necessary partner, shadow and complement to Neptune. For there is no heaven without hell, and no dissolution, decay, and death without the possibility of rebirth and new life. Astronomers soon found that, like Uranus, Neptune was wandering from its predicted path, so they began looking for "Planet X." This time the search was longer, but finally it was found in 1930 by Clyde Tombaugh. The name Pluto was taken from the initials of Percival Lowell, the man who predicted where the new planet would be found.

When Pluto was discovered, humanity was entering the deepest crisis in its history. The Great Depression was spreading; all the old values and authorities seemed to be crumbling. Hell on Earth loomed as the Nazis took over Europe. Gangsters and syndicates were becoming rampant, and big governments and corporations were taking control. Meanwhile, philosophers and psychologists such as Heidegger, Jung, and Reich were probing the human personality seeking sources of inner power, and physics was unveiling a whole new universe where uncertainty reigned supreme. Soon the atomic bomb confronted us with our own power to destroy all life on the planet.

Pluto, named for the Lord of the Underworld, is the symbol of death, destruction, drastic change, and complete transmutation. It leads us through the valley of the shadow of death and the dark night of the soul. Where Neptune offers forgiveness, compassion, and escape, Pluto ruthlessly confronts us with our responsibilities. Pluto is the probing detective, plumbing the depths and exploring beyond the edges to unleash new sources of power. It is the cosmic plunger seeking to eliminate anything that obstructs the flow of change. Where Uranus is the lightning flash, and Neptune the cosmic sea, Pluto is the atomic fire. With Pluto, we make ourselves more vulnerable so we can become more potent, as therapist Stan Dale puts it. Pluto is transcendental courage and guts. It gives us new life by forcing us to face death. It is the caterpillar shedding its skin to reveal the butterfly, or the phoenix rising from the ashes. It is the revelation of deep changes going on inside us. It destroys to rebuild, and it kills the old self that we may be born anew.

Pluto charts the rise and fall of all civilizations and power structures. It rules groups, syndicates, and all who pool their resources to boost their power. It can release undreamed–of wealth and opportunity. It is connected to all the movements of the Twentieth Century, such as existentialism, vitalism, totalitarianism, sexual revolutions, the rights of minorities and outcasts. What it touches it dismantles, rejuvenates, and reorganizes. Whereas Neptune insidiously dissolves and breaks things down, Pluto seeks to totally destroy and then rebuild them. Along with the Moon, it is connected to agriculture and all cycles of death and rebirth through its mythic connection with Persephone. It is sexuality and fertility worship, and represents the secrets of biology and the mysteries of creation.

In 1979, as Pluto's eccentric and elongated orbit took it inside Neptune's orbit, astronomers discovered that Pluto had a partner. They named it Charon (as opposed to Chiron, the comet-asteroid discovered at about the same time to be orbiting between Saturn and Uranus). It has now become clear that Pluto-Charon is a dual planet, each revolving around the other at the same rate so they are always facing each other. This represents the principle of complementarity, which Neils Bohr recognized at the heart of all things. It is thus not only the polarizing but the synthesizing planet, reconciling inner and outer worlds, male and female, bringing together the individual and the collective to form the creative. As our view of Pluto changes, it continues to bring forth new movements, such as ecology and feminism. Now "networking" and interdependence is replacing the older Plutonian ideal of totalitarian power. As the New Age dawns, we will discover that Pluto is *primarily* the planet that periodically brings new life and a renaissance of the human spirit. Pluto is linked to the sign of Scorpio and to the 8th house.

In the transcendental trinity of planets Uranus is the Lord of Light, Neptune is the Redeemer of Love, and Pluto is the Restorer of Life.

Some astronomers now say there may be another Planet X farther out. If so, it probably has an extremely long and eccentric orbit and has now moved deep into space, or astronomers would have spotted it by now. Some speculate that this new planet might be called Persephone and rule the sign Taurus or Libra. If so, we may expect to discover it in the Twenty–First Century; we may even find more planets or "planetoids" beyond it. Personally, however, I doubt this will happen.

The astrological nature of the planets of the transcendental trinity are reflected in the physical traits we are discovering about them. Uranus, for example, is surrounded by brilliant white clouds that seem to radiate energy from below them. Its axis it tilted by ninety–eight degrees relative to its orbit, symbolizing its independence and deviance from the norm. Like Saturn (co-ruler of Aquarius) it has a faint set of rings. Neptune is surrounded by deep, beautiful blue-green clouds that remind us of the sea. It has a giant spot similar to Jupiter's, the other planet traditionally linked to religion and the sign Pisces. Pluto's eccentric orbit gives it the aspect of the one who probes deeply into the unknown to bring back its secrets into the world. It too is tilted on its axis, making it as unconventional, radical, and deviant as Uranus is. Its nature as a dual planet (with Charon) represents the mysterious power of inter-relationship at the heart of life.

It is no accident that we have discovered the transcendental trinity in our time. The precession cycle places us at the cusp of the Ages of Pisces and Aquarius, signs ruled by transcendental Neptune and Uranus. Prior to this, we moved through the Age of Aries, which is ruled by transcendental Pluto. These three great astrological "ages," each ruled by a transcendental planet, are and probably will remain the only three complete ages we pass through in our history here on Earth, after which we may set sail for the stars or melt away into higher dimensions. The three great ages of the precession cycle, and the successive discovery of three outer planets one after another in modern times, reveal three stages in our quest to transcend ourselves—the assertive, innovative phase (Aries, Uranus), the escapist, compassionate phase (Pisces, Neptune), and (hopefully) the creative, integrative phase (Aquarius, Pluto).

3

The Prophetic Tool Kit:

THE BASICS OF ASTROLOGY

In this chapter, we review the basics of astrology. It may be helpful to know these principles in order to understand the astrological reasons for prophecies discussed in this book. On the other hand, many readers may already be familiar with them, and much of the book can be comprehended without referring to them. In that case, you may want to skip this chapter and go right on to Chapter 4, or refer to Appendix A for a summary of the basic meanings of the planets and signs.

All the tools of astrology are mythical symbols. By grouping many qualities under a common symbol, we understand the hidden connections between them. Astrological symbols allow us to comprehend the mysterious working relationship between all things. As we saw in the last chapter, the three basic cycles of the Earth itself, together with the three invisible planets, are the most important of these symbols in our quest to understand human destiny. Nevertheless, the other seven visible planets are also important. Like the outer planets in the transcendental trinity, each visible planet represents fundamental drives and functions within humanity. Their place in a horoscope shows where their energy is focused and directed in the life of a person or a nation.

THE SEVEN INNER PLANETS AND LIGHTS

☉ *The Sun* is the source of life for the solar system. It represents the conscious mind, will, ego, vitality, leadership, power, and authority. It rules important people, royalty, nobility, the head of state, the government, and the father. It signifies expressions of confidence such as sports, the theater, gambling, and romance. It stands for our genuine, authentic self, and our ability to radiate and shine. It rules the fifth sign Leo, and the Fifth House. Its cycle is equivalent to the Earth's year.

☽ *The Moon* is the complement of the Sun, reflecting its light onto the Earth and governing its tides and cycles. Seen from our planet, the two "lights" are equal in size. The Moon symbolizes our subconscious mind, habits, feelings, moods, instincts, reflections, and aspirations. It nurtures growth and protects life, and represents fluctuation, the feminine, the mother, the common people and their needs. It represents both the sea and the fertility of the land. It rules the fourth sign (Cancer) and the Fourth House. It orbits the Earth and the zodiac every twenty-eight days, and it completes one cycle between New Moons (one *lunation*) every twenty-nine and one-half days.

☿ *Mercury* is the fastest planet and one of the smallest. It is closest to the Sun. Named for the messenger of the gods, Mercury is inventive, restless, curious. It stands for communication, media, thought, mobility, writing, and education. It is the symbol of youth, students, workers, merchants, and civil servants. It rules the thirrd sign (Gemini), the sixth sign (Virgo), and the Third and Sixth Houses. It orbits the Sun every eighty-eight days— over four times a year.

♀ *Venus* is the brightest and loveliest planet. The Earth's closest neighbor toward the Sun, it represents our impulse to reflect, balance and evaluate. It brings love, peace, and harmony, and rules diplomacy, cooperation, and strategy. It stands for beauty, nature, the arts, affection, young women, social life, pleasure, and happiness. It rules wealth, money, and luxury goods. It rules the second sign (Taurus), the seventh sign (Libra), and the Second and Seventh Houses. It orbits the Sun every 225 days.

♂ *Mars* is the red planet, and the first leading us outward toward the stars, representing our desire to venture outward. Mars is energetic, impulsive, and active. It stands for enterprise, adventure, enthusiasm, missionary zeal, courage, athletic and mechanical skill, and sexual desire. It brings war, violence, quarrels, and accidents. It signifies machismo, the armed forces, pioneers, and agitators. It rules the first sign (Aries), the eighth sign (Scorpio), and the First and Eighth Houses. Its period of revolution around the Sun lasts almost two years.

♃ *Jupiter* is the largest planet, yet turns on its axis the fastest. As the first of the huge, gaseous planets outward from the Sun, it represents expanding opportunities and widening horizons. It stands for wisdom, the higher mind, prophecy, organized religion, universities, law, ceremonies, and rituals. It establishes far-ranging connections between people and ideas. It rules long-distance journeys, foreigners, diplomacy, treaties, publishing. It is the planet of abundance, prosperity, generosity, joviality, fortune, optimism, finance, and world commerce, but it tends to excess, over-confidence, self-righteousness, complacency and the resulting errors. It rules the ninth sign (Sagittarius), the twelfth sign (Pisces), and the Ninth and Twelfth houses. It orbits the Sun in just under twelve years.

♄ *Saturn* is the ringed planet that encloses and encircles what is within its realm. It is the highest authority in the visible world, defining limits, form, and structure. It represents caution, conservatism, realism, pessimism, orthodoxy, and old age. It brings depression, poverty, stagnation, restriction, and misfortune. It elicits depth of thought, ambition, perseverance, and the desire for status. It represents the State, the Establishment, politics, organization, and civil authority. It institutes discipline and repression, imposes order, and establishes justice. It signifies miners, land owners, farmers, officials, and administrators. Saturn represents the world and all its laws. It rules the tenth sign (Capricorn), the eleventh sign (Aquarius), and the Tenth and Eleventh houses. Its orbit lasts twenty-nine and a half years.

Many astrologers now say that Uranus is a higher octave of Mercury, Neptune of Venus, and Pluto of Mars. It is thought that Uranus also has a close relationship to Saturn, and that Neptune is closely related to Jupiter.

⚷ *Chiron* is a large, comet-like asteroid or small planetoid usually found somewhere between the orbits of Saturn and Uranus. Discovered in 1977, it is thought to act as a "key" or bridge between the visible and transcendental realms. It has been linked by some astrologers to the mythology of the centaur and the "wounded healer," and to the signs of Virgo and Sagittarius.

THE SIGNS OF THE ZODIAC

As we mentioned, the zodiac is the path of the Earth's orbit around the Sun, one of the three basic Earth cycles. The Sun appears to move through the zodiac as the Earth orbits around the Sun, and the planets follow the same path. For example, when Saturn is in the same place where the Sun appears around March 1, Saturn is said to be *in* Pisces. It takes on the meanings of that sign and transmits them to Earth. The functions of Saturn (government, limitation, etc.) are experienced by us in a Piscean way, and the traits of Pisces become more important in world affairs.

All twelve signs are thirty-degree segments of the zodiac. They are each associated with the four elements discussed by the Greek philosophers—fire, earth, air, and water. The elements are not "old superstitions," but equivalent to the "states of matter" known to science today—solid, liquid, gas, and conversion into energy. Not merely physical, they also represent the basic parts of the human soul.

The *Fire* signs are Aries, Leo, and Sagittarius. Fire sign natives are enthusiastic, creative, inspirational, enterprising, spirited, adventurous, proud, self-assertive, and self-confident. They are full of energy and vitality, and tend to be leaders. They are passionate, impatient, and easily angered. Fire signs are of the masculine gender (active, extroverted, yang), and are linked to the spiritual aspect of the psyche.

The *Earth* signs are Taurus, Virgo, and Capricorn. Earth sign natives are practical, reliable, cautious, plodding, pragmatic, careful, and sure-footed. They make all the enterprises of the fire people more useful, secure, and long-lasting. Earth represents the wealth and work of the world. Earth signs are of the feminine gender (passive, introvert, yin), and are linked to the body or physical aspect of the psyche.

The *Air* signs are Gemini, Libra, and Aquarius. They are intelligent, sociable, quick-witted, inventive, adaptable, diplomatic, and versatile. They are well educated, cultured, and full of new ideas. They open channels of communication and distribution. They can be fickle, flighty, or unpredictable. Air signs are masculine and linked to the mind.

The *Water* signs are Cancer, Scorpio, and Pisces. Water sign natives are emotional, sensitive, receptive and imaginative. They rely on their feelings, instincts and intuition, and are sympathetic, humane, and nurturing, but can be escapist or manipulative. The Water signs dissolve barriers and nourish new growth, and elicit mass group experiences and spiritual aspirations. Water signs are feminine and linked to the emotions.

Also important is a sign's *quality*. Each sign is cardinal, fixed or mutable. These are modes of behavior and action rather than basic substances of nature or psyche. They demonstrate the universal principle that all things unfold in three stages.

Cardinal signs are Aries, Cancer, Libra, and Capricorn. They are generating, initiating, enterprising, pioneering, creative, combative, and assertive. They represent the most active manifestation of their element. They have to do with new beginnings, but they don't always finish what they start.

Fixed signs are Taurus, Leo, Scorpio and Aquarius. Inclined to stability, they are organizing, perpetuating, single-minded, and dictatorial. They are stubborn, dogmatic, and concerned with economics. They can concentrate enormous power.

Mutable signs are Gemini, Virgo, Sagittarius, and Pisces. They are adaptable, adjustable, restless, curious, and democratic. They deal with travel, trade, distribution, and uncertain or chaotic conditions. They are "dual" signs, so they can be inconsistent or deceptive. They seek variety, knowledge, understanding and synthesis.

A table of correspondences is given below:

SYMBOL	SIGN	QUALITY	ELEMENT	GENDER	RULING PLANET(S)
♈	Aries	Cardinal	Fire	Masculine	Mars ♂
♉	Taurus	Fixed	Earth	Feminine	Venus ♀
♊	Gemini	Mutable	Air	Masculine	Mercury ☿
♋	Cancer	Cardinal	Water	Feminine	Moon ☽
♌	Leo	Fixed	Fire	Masculine	Sun ☉
♍	Virgo	Mutable	Earth	Feminine	Mercury ☿ / Chiron ⚷
♎	Libra	Cardinal	Air	Masculine	Venus ♀
♏	Scorpio	Fixed	Water	Feminine	Mars ♂ / Pluto ♇
♐	Sagittarius	Mutable	Fire	Masculine	Jupiter ♃
♑	Capricorn	Cardinal	Earth	Feminine	Saturn ♄
♒	Aquarius	Fixed	Air	Masculine	Saturn ♄ / Uranus ♅
♓	Pisces	Mutable	Water	Feminine	Jupiter ♃ / Neptune ♆

♈ *ARIES, the Ram.* First sign of the zodiac, March 21–April 20. Cardinal fire sign; ruler: Mars. Motto: "I am." Aries represents the first urge of life to manifest in the world. It is the sheer joy of activity. It seeks to initiate, aggravate, arouse, inspire, conquer, and command, and to set things in motion or explore virgin territory. It is endlessly creative, but too impatient to complete any task. Aries has a very strong sense of identity and an overweening attitude of "me first!" Since it is intolerant of obstacles, it frequently causes conflict and wars. It is not very sympathetic, for it hates weakness. It has missionary zeal as if possessed by a god. It is independent, self-reliant and full of new ideas. It has an endless thirst for experience and lust for life. It is the sign of the eternal warrior, often as the champion of the underdog. Aries is courageous, aggressive, energetic, optimistic, enterprising, pioneering, temperamental, fearless, headstrong, impulsive, rash, rude, reckless, rebellious, sporty, sensual, competitive, and combative. All signs rule a part of the body. For Aries, it is the head, since the Ram likes to butt its head against the wall (or other heads).

Famous Arians include: J.S.Bach, Pierre Baudelaire, Otto von Bismarck, Marlon Brando, Jerry Brown, Cesar Chavez, Chuck Connors, Clarence Darrow, Rene Descartes, James Garner, Vincent Van Gogh, Al Gore, Francisco Goya, Joseph Haydn, Henry II, Edmund Husserl, Thomas Jefferson, Nikita Khruschev, David Letterman, Eugene McCarthy, J.P. Morgan, Modest Mussorgsky, Napoleon III (Taurus cusp), Leonard Nimoy, Sandra Day O'Connor, Gregory Peck, Colin Powell, Diana Ross, Peter Ustinov.

♉ *TAURUS, the Bull.* Second sign of the zodiac, April 21–May 20. Fixed earth sign; ruler: Venus. Motto: "I have." Taurus steadies the originating impulse of Aries and gives it a secure and lasting foundation. Though it is less creative than Aries, it knows how to consolidate and put things to good use. Very resourceful, perceptive and alert for good business opportunities, it seeks to maximize profit through reliance on its own talents. It is fortunate with money, generates great wealth, and can be very materialistic and acquisitive. Taurus is stubborn, powerful, and determined—the strong, silent type. It has the strength of purpose to see a project through to the end as does no other sign. Sometimes it is cruel toward those who stand in its way. It produces excellent builders, architects, artists, and civil engineers. Its purpose is to implement order, placidity, peace, and plenty. Therefore it can be very stagnant, conservative, lazy, complacent, and traditional. It feels deep kinship with the earth. It is the sign of fertility rites and the pleasures of the flesh. Taurus is calm, patient, slow, sensuous, down-to-earth, affectionate, indulgent, and confident. Taurus rules the neck and throat. Consequently, the world's best singers are born under this sign.

Famous Taureans: Johannes Brahms, Georges Bracque, Buddha, Judy Collins, Oliver Cromwell, Bing Crosby, Salvador Dali, Leonardo da Vinci, Eugene Delacroix, Elizabeth II, Ella Fitzgerald, Sigmund Freud, Ulysses S. Grant, Adolf Hitler (Aries cusp), Saddam Hussein, Pope John Paul II, Immanuel Kant, Soren Kierkegaard, Vladimir Lenin, Jay Leno, Malcolm X, Karl Marx, George McGovern, Prince Metternich, Jack Nicholson, Maximilien Robespierre, Socrates, Benjamin Spock, Barbra Streisand, Tchaikovsky, Harry Truman.

♊ GEMINI, *the Twins*. Third sign of the zodiac, May 21–June 20. Mutable air sign; ruler: Mercury. Motto: "I think." Gemini coordinates the opposing forces of the two previous signs. It represents curiosity about the immediate environment, and the urge to learn and communicate. Gemini loves novelty, and is extremely versatile. It adjusts quickly to circumstance, and can juggle many things at once. It is quick-witted, restless, very inventive and mentally brilliant, but it lacks depth and can become a dilettante, "the jack of all trades and master of none." Gemini is the awareness of relationships and connections—the sign of synthesis. It has to do with travel, writing, education, schools, journalists, thought, ideas, trade, and networking. Geminis are sociable, cheerful, agile, energetic, flexible, youthful, loquacious, scattered, intellectual, logical, liberal, cultured, and objective. Gemini rules the arms, hands, shoulders, and lungs.

Famous Geminis: Raymond Burr, George Bush, Maurice Chevalier, Mario Cuomo, Dante Alighieri, Arthur C. Doyle, Bob Dylan, Ralph W. Emerson, Michael J. Fox, Judy Garland, Paul Gauguin, George III, Newt Gingrich, Bob Hope, Elbert Hubbard, Hubert Humphrey, Henry Jackson, John F. Kennedy, Henry Kissinger, Thomas Mann, Paul McCartney, Bill Moyers, Lawrence Olivier, Charles A. Reich, Oswald Spengler, Igor Stravinsky, Queen Victoria, Richard Wagner.

♋ CANCER, *the Crab*. Fourth sign of the zodiac, June 21–July 21. Cardinal water sign; ruler: the Moon. Motto: "I feel." Cancer introduces personal meanings and values into experience. It represents the urge to build a home and a secure refuge. It is the sign nurturing what is most intimate and unique. It is family, heritage, veneration of ancestors, nationalism, racism, and patriotism. Conversely, it also has a restless wanderlust and thirst for experience. This creates inner conflict and a desire to grow emotionally. Cancer is the sensitive underside of life, the subconscious mind, feelings, and instincts. It is very intuitive, imaginative, and illogical. Many poets and painters are born under this sign. It always seeks to conserve and preserve life, and to protect the rights of the individual, property, and the common people. It is talented at managing others and providing basic needs. Cancers are tenacious, emotional, timid, defensive, cautious, introverted, shy, sympathetic, sensitive, sentimental, humorous, sensation-seeking, acquisitive, economical, stingy, temperamental, subjective, nostalgic, cherishing, clinging, domestic, motherly, gentle, feminine, receptive, moody, and changeable as the tides. Cancer rules the stomach.

Famous Cancers: Les Aspin, Milton Berle, John Bradshaw, David Brinkley, Calvin Coolidge, Bill Cosby, Tom Cruise, Mary Baker Eddy, Gerald Ford, Stephen Foster, John Glenn, Merv Griffin, Henry VIII, Hermann Hesse, Helen Keller, Thurgood Marshall, Ross Perot, Rembrandt van Rijn, Jean Jacques Rousseau, Jean Paul Sartre, Red Skelton, Sylvester Stallone, Ringo Starr, Meryl Streep, Robin Williams.

♌ LEO, *the Lion*. Fifth sign of the zodiac, July 22–August 21. Fixed fire sign; ruler: the Sun. Motto: "I will." Leo expresses the confidence and power of the individual. Its purpose is to grow through testing itself against experience. Leos radiate warmth to everyone around them, and love to give and receive affection and adulation. They are dramatic, always enjoy being the center of attention, and their vibrant love of life is infectious. Their self-assurance and inward sense of nobility and grandeur make them great organizers and leaders, for people naturally feel confidence in them. Leos are stubborn, dogmatic, egotistic, and guard their rights and prerogatives tenaciously. Leo is connected to all activities of youth, self-expression and risk-taking, including theater, drama, sports, games, gambling, speculation, romance, education, entertainment, and recreation. Leos are proud, creative, complacent, loyal, stable, conservative, flamboyant, romantic, optimistic, dramatic, frank, inspirational, willful, and determined. Leo rules the heart and the spine.

Famous Leos: Neil Armstrong, Lucille Ball, Julius Caesar, Fidel Castro, Bill Clinton, Claude Debussy, Robert De Niro, Jerry Falwell, Henry Ford, Mata Hari, Dustin Hoffman, Herbert Hoover, Whitney Houston, Mick Jagger, Carl Jung, Norman Lear, Madonna, Benito Mussolini, Napoleon Bonaparte, Carroll O'Connor, Jacqueline Kennedy Onassis, Peter O'Toole, Robert Redford, Jason Robards, H. Norman Schwarzkopf (Virgo cusp), Arnold Schwarzenegger, George Bernard Shaw, Percy Shelley, Patrick Swayze.

♍ *VIRGO, the Virgin.* Sixth sign of the zodiac, August 22–September 22. Mutable earth sign; ruler: Mercury. Motto: "I analyze." Virgo refines the world of manifest form into perfection, and goes beyond Leo's pride to introduce a sense of duty to society. It takes care of all the details with which regal Leo can't be bothered. Virgo rules the "humble classes," workers, servants, and employees. It represents work and is connected to the military, civil service, and bureaucracy. Virgos are natural administrators. The Virgo desire for perfection and order makes it prudish, obsessed with purity and efficiency. It is also uncomfortable with the unknown. These qualities make it the sign of technology and scientific research, but often it is myopic, "missing the forest for the trees." Its nagging instinct for criticism can be directed toward changing society to help the poor, sick, and unfortunate, as it has a powerful need to heal or serve others. It is the sign of hygiene, health, and welfare. Virgos are self-effacing, helpful, witty, adaptable, analytical, industrious, reliable, conventional, conforming, pedantic, nervous, anxious, self-critical, and full of gossip. Virgo keeps things in good working order. It rules the intestines.

Famous Virgos: Shirley Booth, Stokely Carmichael, Sean Connery (Leo cusp), Jacques Louis David, Elizabeth I, Peter Falk, Alan Funt, Greta Garbo, Johann W. Goethe, Stephen Jay Gould, Georg Hegel, Michael Jackson, Lyndon Johnson, Gene Kelly, Charles Kuralt, Louis XIV and XVI, H. L. Mencken, Sam Nunn, Walter Reuther, Peter Sellers, Upton Sinclair, David Souter, Robert Taft, William H. Taft, Leo Tolstoy, George Wallace (Leo cusp).

♎ *LIBRA, the Scales.* Seventh sign of the zodiac, September 23–October 22. Cardinal air sign; ruler: Venus. Motto: "I balance." At Libra, life's outward thrust begins to yield and turn inward as it seeks wider and deeper relationships. Libra is permeated by the sense of form, harmony, and atmosphere. It is the most cultured, refined, artistic, and musical of the signs, representing the classical ideal of balance in all things. It has a strong sense of justice and fairness, and takes the initiative to bring reconciliation through negotiation. Libra rules partnership, marriage, divorce, relationships, diplomacy, open legal affairs, contracts, and alliances. It is the sign of war as well as peace. It becomes too dependent on others, and is apt to use them for its own ends. It constantly evaluates and sees both sides of an issue, but is often indecisive, artfully evading responsibility. Librans are charming, graceful, imaginative, idealistic, sociable, even-tempered, peaceful, lazy, discriminating, opportunistic, competitive, and calculating. Libra rules the kidneys and loins.

Famous Librans: Brigitte Bardot, Henri Bergson, Chuck Berry, Annie Besant, Jimmy Carter, Ray Charles, Dwight D. Eisenhower, John Kenneth Galbraith, Mohandas K. Gandhi, Art Garfunkel, George Gershwin, Rutherford B. Hayes, Martin Heidegger, Lee Iacocca, Jesse Jackson, Angela Lansbury, Timothy Leary, John Lennon, Franz Liszt, Groucho Marx, Bob Newhart, Friedrich Nietzsche, Eugene O'Neill, Richard III, Eleanor Roosevelt, Bruce Springsteen, Giuseppe Verdi, Barbara Walters.

♏ *SCORPIO, the Scorpion.* Eighth sign of the zodiac, October 23–November 21. Fixed water sign; rulers: Mars and Pluto. Motto: "I desire." Scorpio takes us deeper into the unmanifest. It is, according to Celtic mythology, the time of year when the boundary between this world and the next is the thinnest. Scorpio is the most passionate, turbulent and strong-willed sign. It seeks to penetrate beneath the surface, probe the mysteries, and uncover what is hidden. Keenly aware of death and its own vulnerability, it has unflinching determination and stamina. It is uncompromising in the struggle against its enemies and the quest of its desires, but it finds it must let go of these jealous obsessions and transform itself in order to attain its goals (whereupon it becomes the Eagle). In this way, it is the sign of spiritual rebirth. Scorpio is about restructuring, reorganizing and regenerating, consolidation and joint investment. It represents communion, where we lose our souls to find them in others. Scorpios are intense, combative, introspective, courageous, magnetic, dramatic, sensual, thorough, quiet, thoughtful, controlled, vengeful, critical, sarcastic, indomitable, suspicious, scheming, often sympathetic, and (at best) highly ethical. Scorpio rules the sex organs.

Famous Scorpios: Spiro Agnew, Marie Antoinette, Howard Baker, Alexander Borodin, Pat Buchanan, Richard Burton, Hillary Clinton, Richard Dreyfus, Michael Dukakis, Billy Graham, Katharine Hepburn, Robert Kennedy, Martin Luther, Charles Manson, Burgess Meredith, Claude Monet, William of Orange, Pablo Picasso, Dan Rather, Theodore Roosevelt, Carl Sagan, Grace Slick, Leon Trotsky, Oscar Wilde.

♐ *SAGITTARIUS, the Centaur.* Ninth sign of the zodiac, November 22–December 20. Mutable fire sign; ruler: Jupiter. Motto: "I see." Sagittarius seeks to expand its horizons widely in order to find wisdom. It is the sign of philosophy, the higher mind, higher education, publishing, the press, organized religion, the law, diplomacy, flight. It makes far-flung connections between people and ideas and travels to foreign lands. Well adjusted to society, it is buoyant, benevolent, and exuberant, but it also insists loudly on freedom for itself and others. It loves the outdoors and hates to be pinned down. Identified with humanity, it feels entitled to speak for it. Honest and outspoken, Sagittarius reveals the truth openly, regardless of consequences. The archer "cares not where it shoots its arrows." It thinks big, takes long chances and tends to exaggerate its achievements. Sagittarius is daring, adventurous, sociable, optimistic, idealistic, visionary, prophetic, impatient, careless, restless, argumentative, self-righteous, arrogant, snobbish, sporty, ambitious, and enterprising. It rules the hips and thighs.

Famous Sagittarians: Woody Allen, Ludwig van Beethoven, Hector Berlioz, William Blake, William F. Buckley, Andrew Carnegie, Winston Churchill, Charles De Gaulle, Walt Disney, Benjamin Disreali, Kirk Douglas, Dick Van Dyke, Francisco Franco, Theodore Gericault, Jimi Hendrix, Bette Midler, Rod Serling, Paul Simon, Alexander Solzhenitsyn, Strom Thurmond, Tina Turner, Mark Twain, Voltaire.

♑ CAPRICORN, *the Goat.* Tenth sign of the zodiac, December 21–January 19. Cardinal earth sign; ruler: Saturn. Motto: "I use." Capricorn steadies the far-ranging exuberance of Sagittarius. Its aim is to achieve status and solid worldly achievement. Capricorns are very good organizers, ambitious, and interested in politics. Conscientious and realistic, Capricorn meets many obstacles in its path and succeeds by overcoming them with patient, consistent, methodical efforts. It is very persistent and single-minded, and never likes to cut corners, since its aim is solidity rather than expedience. Capricorns prefer tradition, age, and experience. They have high integrity and can be relied on, unless and until they use or exploit others for their own ends. Often insensitive and impersonal, Capricorn looks only at results ("Winning isn't everything, it's the only thing"), yet its ultimate goal is to accomplish things for the good of society and humanity. It represents all large organizations and central authorities. Capricorn is practical, solitary, serious, conservative, fatherly, industrious, focused, sensual, strong, introspective, logical, rigid, dark, enduring, structured, obstinate, bigoted, and pessimistic. It rules the bones and knees.

Famous Capricorns: Conrad Adenauer, Muhammed Ali, Joan Baez, George Burns, Paul Cezanne, John Denver, Everett Dirksen, Ben Franklin, Barry Goldwater, Alexander Hamilton, J. Edgar Hoover, Howard Hughes, William James, Andrew Johnson, Janis Joplin, Martin Luther King, Rudyard Kipling, Mao Tse Tung, Walter Mondale, Mary Tyler Moore, Issac Newton, Richard Nixon, Louis Pasteur, Elvis Presley, Albert Schweitzer, Robert Stack, Joseph Stalin, Woodrow Wilson.

♒ AQUARIUS, *the Water Bearer.* Eleventh sign of the zodiac, January 20–February 18. Fixed Air sign; rulers: Uranus and Saturn. Motto: "I know." Aquarius shares and distributes knowledge on behalf of humanity. It challenges the prerogatives of authority and beckons us to embrace the new and unfamiliar. Very scientific, it seeks to understand the world so that it may re-invent it. Like Leo, it radiates a brilliant light, but one of knowledge and friendship toward all. Aquarians are very charismatic leaders and entertainers, masters of electronic media and group dynamics. It is the sign of fraternities and associations dedicated to idealistic causes. Aquarians are non-conformists, but not egotists. They are objective, detached and unemotional, yet expectant for a better tomorrow. They function spasmodically, and are very unpredictable. Aquarians are original, intellectual, independent, humorous, brilliant, magnetic, friendly, humane, eccentric, touchy, rebellious, perverse, abrupt, tactless, doctrinaire, dictatorial, contrary. Aquarius rules the legs and ankles.

Famous Aquarians: Alan Alda, Jack Benny, Lord Byron, Charles Darwin, Charles Dickens, Thomas Edison, Clark Gable, Galileo Galilei, Richard Gephardt, Jack Lemmon, Sinclair Lewis, Abraham Lincoln, Norman Mailer, Felix Mendelssohn, W.A. Mozart, Paul Newman, James A. Pike, Plato, Ronald Reagan, Franklin Roosevelt, Babe Ruth, Tom Selleck, Tommy Smothers, Paul Tsongas, Oprah Winfrey, Boris Yeltsin.

♓ *PISCES, the Fishes.* Twelfth sign of the zodiac, February 19-March 20. Mutable water sign; rulers: Neptune and Jupiter. Motto: "I believe." As the zodiac's "grand finale," Pisces seeks to understand and identify with the whole of creation and find ultimate redemption, sensing the undercurrents and underlying unity of life. In Pisces, the veil is lifted that we may gaze once more upon our original spiritual nature. It is fermenting chaos that incubates new birth. Chameleon-like, it wishes to be part of all, but not to define or enclose itself. It seeks escape from the limits of matter and form, and this gives it a large capacity to turn away from responsibility and deceive itself and others. It is the sign of scandal, delusion, decay, degradation, and self-undoing. Its compulsive empathy makes it the most compassionate, altruistic sign when its urge to escape becomes self-sacrifice. Unsure in this life, it has unwavering faith in the next, but its ideals can be tragically disillusioned. It is the sign of religion, fantasy, mysticism, imagination, surrealism, music, dreams, illusions, subtle theories, and abstract thinking. Pisces is "Macawber" or "the absent-minded professor." It is fluid, romantic, affectionate, spiritual, malleable, vacillating, versatile, adaptable, sentimental, and moody. It rules the feet.

Famous Pisceans: George Berkeley, William Jennings Bryan, Frederic Chopin, Billy Crystal, Albert Einstein, Mikhail Gorbachev, G. F. Handel, George Harrison, Rex Harrison, L. Ron Hubbard, Jesus of Nazareth (?), Ted Kennedy, Patrick McGoohan (Aries cusp), Michaelangelo Buonarroti, Daniel P. Moynihan, Ralph Nader, Linus Pauling, Maurice Ravel, Nicholas Rimsky-Korsakov, Bedrich Smetana, Elizabeth Taylor, George Washington.

Before we leave the subject of signs, let's cover a few more points. The first and last five-degree range of a sign is called the *cusp*. In this area, the traits of one sign merge with the next, modifying the meaning of both. The first four signs are concerned with primordial instincts, the second four with interpersonal (or international) relationships, and the final four with larger or universal matters. Each sign complements and contrasts with its opposite halfway around the zodiac, and also supplies much of what's missing in the previous sign.

The Sun travels one degree of the zodiac in about one day. Therefore, each of the 360 degrees of the zodiac is important, and each has its own peculiar meaning. I occasionally refer to the *Sabian symbols* to reveal the significance of each degree. They were developed by famed astrologers Marc Edmund Jones and Dane Rudhyar from a series of pictures given to Jones by a San Diego psychic, and published in Rudhyar's *An Astrological Mandala.*

ASPECTS

As the planets move around the zodiac, they also move in relation to each other, forming all possible angles between themselves. Certain of these angles are very basic and significant—they are called *aspects*. Aspects are probably the most important thing in astrology, particularly when analyzing or predicting events.

The most basic aspects are the New Moon and Full Moon, and the cycle of relationship between them is called the *lunation cycle*. The New Moon is a conjunction between Sun and Moon as seen from the Earth. At the New Moon, the cycle is just beginning, and new energy is stirring, but the Moon's light is hidden and withdrawn from us. As the cycle proceeds, the Moon's light gradually increases (or *waxes*) through the crescent, first quarter, and gibbous phases. At the Full Moon, the cycle climaxes and the Moon's light shines brilliantly and clearly. Afterward, it gradually decreases (or *wanes*) through its gibbous, last quarter, and balsamic phases, until the cycle completes at the next New Moon. In the case of an *eclipse*, the Sun and Moon are so closely aligned with the Earth that their light is blocked out. Eclipses are more important than other lunations, and their influence lasts far longer (for a solar eclipse, about the same length in years that the eclipse lasts in minutes).

All the planets go through phases with each other just like the Sun and Moon do. In the waxing phases, fortunes rise and new structures are built. In the waning phases, structures rigidify and decay, but ideas and group activities increase. The following are the most important aspects, or phases, in the cycles between planets:

The *conjunction* (0° angle) is like a New Moon. It is an alignment of planets, usually in the same sign. During important conjunctions, explosive events erupt spontaneously, and daring new initiatives are taken in fields represented by the two planets. Their energies are powerfully combined, concentrated and intensified. The aims and direction of the new cycle remain unclear, and often the most crucial changes unleashed by a conjunction remain hidden until later.

The *opposition* (180° angle, $1/2$ of the circle) is like a Full Moon, and planets are usually six signs apart on opposite sides of the Earth. It brings fulfillment of what began at the conjunction, but also a schism or polarization into two opposing sides. The opposition usually indicates major events in a very powerful and obvious way. People know clearly what they're doing and why, but may be locked in a frustrating stalemate.

The *square* (90° angle, $1/4$ of the circle) is like the first or last quarter phase. Planets are at right angles to each other, usually three signs apart in signs of the same quality. Together with the conjunction and opposition, the squares are the most critical phases of the cycle. The two planets are "squaring off" with each other, producing tension, crisis, conflict and dynamic activity. People stir up trouble, and important decisions must be made. Dangerous events tend to occur. Square and oppositions are also called "afflictions."

The *trine* (120° angle, $1/3$ of the circle) is like a gibbous phase. Here, planets are about four signs apart in signs of the same element. Under trines, events move quickly, and people are lively and confident. A flood of light and energy is released, and good fortune may result.

The trine gives us a wider perspective, but it often indicates that we are being frivolous, wasteful, or complacent.

The *sextile* (60° angle, $1/6$ of the circle) is like a crescent phase. In this aspect, the planets are two signs apart, usually in signs of the same gender. Like the trine, it tends to be a fortunate aspect. When it occurs, people are more creative, intelligent, and productive. It may indicate a crisis, but important events will generally move more smoothly.

The *semi-square* (45° angle, $1/8$ of the circle) is one half of a square. It is an aspect of friction and dynamic, constructive activity.

The *sesqui-square* or *sesqui-quadrate* (135° angle, $3/8$ of a circle) is a square plus one half. It also generates activity, and frequently brings upheaval. It is especially dangerous during a waning phase.

The *quincunx* (150° angle) may contribute to trials and tribulations that force us to make adjustments or confront uncomfortable karmic issues. In this aspect, the planets are usually five signs apart.

The *semi-sextile* (30° angle) puts planets one sign apart, and acts like a weaker sextile. It may show a phase of growth, or perhaps events that lead to larger ones at the time of the following sextile or conjunction.

Orbs. When exact, an aspect is at its peak of significance. Before exactitude, the forces and events it indicates are building up. After exactitude, the energy is released and distributed, bringing results and consequences. The orb, or amount of inexactness, allowed for lunations (such as Sun-Moon conjunctions) is at least twelve degrees. For conjunctions, oppositions, trines, and squares, it is up to ten degrees. For sextiles, allow up to seven. For semi and sesqui-squares, it is three degrees, and for semi-sextiles and quincunxes, use two degrees. The closer an aspect is, the more important it is. Astrologers don't always agree on allowable orbs.

Aspect patterns. Signs are always arranged counterclockwise around the edge of the circle. There are thirty degrees in every sign. Next to the symbol for a planet, there will usually be a number followed by a sign; this indicates which degree of a sign the planet is in. If the planet is in 2° Aries, for example, it is near the beginning of the sign. If it in 15° Aries, it is in the middle. In 29° Aries, it is near the end, and about to enter the next sign (Taurus). A good way to spot aspects is to notice which degrees the planets are in. One planet that is in nearly the same degree of any sign as another planet is making an aspect to that planet. At any given moment, there is more than one cycle unfolding, and thus more than one aspect going on. In fact, there is a whole pattern of them forming at all times. When a greater number than usual of important aspects are happening, it means the "cosmic weather" is more active; big events or the start of major trends can be expected! For example, below is the whole pattern of aspects that prevailed during the Bolshevik Revolution in Russia in November, 1917. You can see Saturn and Neptune in conjunction in Leo, with Uranus opposing them from Aquarius; while the Sun and Mercury in Scorpio square all three. This is un-doubtedly a powerful aspect pattern corresponding to an important event!

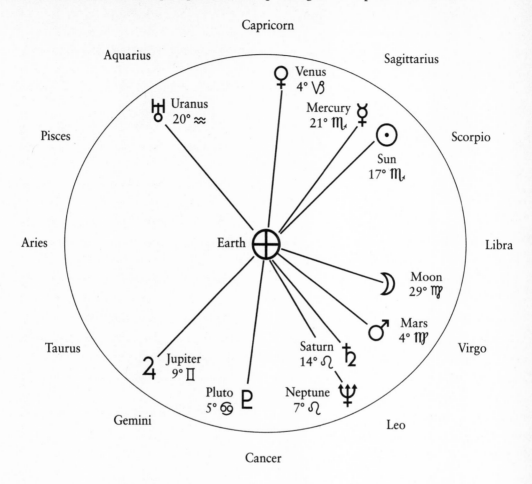

Planetary aspects during the Bolshevik Revolution. Chart data: November 10, 1917, 1:00 p.m. GMT.

FOCAL POINTS

In some cases, intense significance is focused on one key planet or several planets. The most important of these focal points happens when a planet passes closest to the Earth. At this critical moment it appears to turn *stationary,* and then move *retrograde* (backwards through the zodiac). Soon afterward, the planet turns stationary again and begins to move *direct.* When a planet turns stationary, its energy here on Earth is strongly intensified. While ret-rograde, its expression is inhibited and turned intensely inward toward the subconscious. The stations of Mars and Mercury are especially important, and events are often triggered shortly afterward. Retrograde planets are often marked "R" on a chart. "SR" means the planet is turning stationary-retrograde, and "SD" means stationary-direct.

Cyclic patterns are very significant in interpreting and predicting events, as we have already seen. Similar or related events will often occur when a planet returns to the same place it was in at the time of an earlier event.

Another very significant pattern is the *singleton*. In this case, a planet occupies over half the sky by itself. You can be sure that if one planet is on one side of the sky, and all the others are on the other side, it is highly significant. Everything is focused on the functions of that planet and the sign it's in. The illustration below shows Uranus in Pisces as a singleton in 1919 and the early 1920s.

Other focal points occur when several planets are grouped together in strong mutual aspects. The easiest of these patterns to spot is the *stellium*, where several planets are clumped close together, all in conjunction. A stellium always portends great events, but they rarely occur immediately because the energy of the planets is so tightly bound up. Whatever happens will strongly reflect the meaning of the sign in which the stellium occurred.

A very tense situation is indicated when one planet squares off with two others that are opposing each other. This is called a *T-square* and happened, for example, in the early 1930s. Even more rare and powerful is the *grand cross*, formed by two oppositions in square to each other. Three planets, each 120 degrees apart, form a *grand trine*, releasing keen, exhilarating energy that can bring great fortune but easily runs out of control or gets "carried away." The element in which the grand trine occurs is emphasized. A good example of a powerful grand trine happened in 1966-67 in the emotional water signs as the feelings and passions of the '60s were unleashed. Another grand trine in water signs happened during the "roaring '20s."

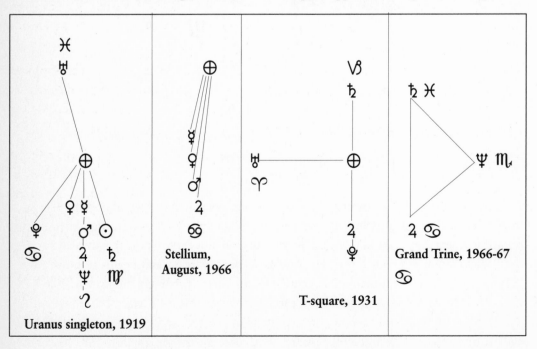

Examples of Significant Planetary Configurations in the Twentieth Century

READING HOROSCOPES: THE ANGLES

The word horoscope means "viewing the hour." A horoscope shows where the planets were at a particular time, allowing us to estimate the fortunes of a new enterprise or nation begun at that moment. For example, we can erect a horoscope for the U.S.A. for the time when the Declaration of Independence was signed on July 4, 1776, or we can focus on the personal horoscope of a current world leader. Watching when planets make aspects to (or "contact") the positions of planets in one of these important charts can tell us when events might occur that affect the nation or leader in question. Horoscopes can also be cast for the time of a lunation, eclipse, or conjunction. These help us to determine where events might occur, as well as to understand their long-range significance.

To read most of the horoscopes in this book, you only need to be able to locate the *horizon* and the *zenith*. The *Midheaven* (MH or MC) is synonymous with the zenith, and is the vertical line at the top of the chart. The *Ascendant* (Asc) is the horizontal line on the left and represents the eastern horizon. The opposing points to these are significant, too. The horizontal line at the right of the chart is the *Descendant*. It shows where the Sun and planets set. The vertical line running to the bottom of the chart represents the *Nadir* (IC), or the point directly beneath our feet. These points in the sky are called *angles*. Since they are the most important or "cardinal" points of the horoscope, any planets and signs that are located on or near these angles are considered the most significant and powerful in the chart.

The *Ascendant*, or eastern horizon, shows which forces are rising. It signifies the personality, health, and attitude of the individual or nation being represented. Planets there can represent daring actions or merely outspoken, aggressive, and violent behavior. The Ascendant corresponds to where the Sun is at dawn.

The *Midheaven*, or point overhead, stands for the authority in the "high" seat of power. Planets or signs there may indicate which trends are dominant at that location or show who or what has reached the zenith of fortune there. In a personal chart it represents career and worldly ambitions. The Midheaven corresponds to where the Sun is at noon.

The *Descendant*, or western horizon, may show what is on the wane. More often, it shows the other people or nations to be contended with, including a nation's enemies (whether real or perceived). Aggressive planets on the Descendant often stand for war or warlike attitudes, including civil war and divorce. It also represents diplomacy and efforts to adjust disputes. Planets here can signify people speaking out in public scandals. The Descendant corresponds to where the Sun is at sunset.

The *Nadir*, or low point, represents "the nadir of fortune." It indicates what is private and personal rather than public. It stands for the home, family heritage, and the land. In political terms, this means nationalism, racism, defense, "family values" or, in more advanced times, environmentalism. It stands for turning inward to spiritual life and rejecting the public world. Planets here can represent a sharp challenge to the ruling authorities. The Nadir corresponds to where the Sun is at midnight.

The vertical and horizontal axes of the horoscope divide it into hemispheres. The upper hemisphere above the horizon is objective, public, or concerned with wider issues, while the lower hemisphere is subjective, private, and more narrowly focused. The left side of the chart is self-assertive, independent, and rational, while the right side is concerned with relationships, and is oriented to feelings or sensations.

THE HOUSES OF THE HOROSCOPE

The horoscope figure is further divided into twelve "Houses," representing the twelve "departments of life." They are closely related to the twelve signs, and have corresponding meanings. The houses represent the "theater of activity" in which the planets interact.

The *1st House* takes its meaning from the Ascendant, and represents the self, the people, and their behavior (see "Ascendant" above). It is linked to Aries.

The *2nd House* represents all financial affairs, desires for stability, constructive talents, financial independence, and values. It is linked to Taurus.

The *3rd House* represents travel, communications, trade, journalism, the media, the mind, writings, intellectuals, education, youth, ideas, speech, neighbors, and relatives. It is linked to Gemini.

The *4th House* takes its meaning from the nadir (see above). It represents private institutions, home, family, ethnic pride, the personal and national soul, the land, and the weather. It is linked to Cancer.

The *5th House* represents self-expression, youth, romance, pleasures, financial speculation, sports, games, children, education, ambitions for power, imperial expansion, the Senate, royalty, and nobility. It is linked to Leo.

The *6th House* involves public health, welfare, work, civil and military service, bureaucrats, employees, labor unions, charities, volunteers, servants, and the service industries. It is linked to Virgo.

The *7th House* takes its meaning from the Descendant (see above), and rules international relations, diplomacy, politics, war, disputes, legal affairs, marriage, divorce, contracts, enemies, and public scandals. It is linked to Libra.

The *8th House* rules financial dealings, corporations, taxes, insurance, mortgages, inheritance, group management of funds, communes and communism, stock markets, and debts. It also stands for death, rebirth, rebuilding, renewal, and the occult. It is linked to Scorpio.

The *9th House* rules foreign affairs, trade, distant travels, higher education, philosophy, the law, the courts, the Church, and prophecy. It is linked to Sagittarius.

The *10th House* takes its meaning from the Midheaven (see above). It stands for the government, the executive, and public life. It is linked to Capricorn.

The *11th House* represents group cooperation, idealistic associations, the legislature (lower house), government finance, social programs, theater, friends, hopes for the future, and profitable inventions. It is linked to Aquarius.

The *12th House* rules personal and national karma, hidden forces, secret enemies, big institutions, prisons, asylums, monasteries, hospitals, occult interests, spirituality, exile, and the search for refuge and self-renewal. It is linked to Pisces.

SYMBOLS OF THE HOUSES

The signs have symbols. Even individual degrees have symbols. Why not houses, too? Here are my suggestions.

4

The Fortunes of Civilization:

THE NEPTUNE-PLUTO CYCLE

Far beyond the Sun's light, the two most distant planets of our solar system make their way slowly and serenely through the eerie, silent expanses of space. Within the vast panorama of planetary cycles, theirs is the one rhythm that underlies all the others. It is the base note of the cosmic symphony, and the drumbeat of all civilization. With it, we can chart the fortunes of humanity.

This is the rhythm of mystical, mysterious Neptune, and dark, potent Pluto. Every 493 years, they line up in conjunction. When they do, a new surge of cosmic energy is released to renew and transform the peoples of Earth. Old empires dissolve and ancient institutions crumble. Almost overnight, art, science, and religion take radically different directions, and people change their whole outlook on life. The world's political structure is revamped, and a new phase of civilization begins, which lasts until the next conjunction some 493 plus years later.

Although the first effects of the Neptune-Pluto conjunction are felt immediately, the new tone echoes across the landscape for decades afterward. A troubled "time of transition" begins that continues for 100 years or more. But then the magic moment arrives. It has never failed to happen—about 100 years or more after the conjunction, the pieces fall into place, and humanity celebrates a magnificent sunrise. Creative energy bursts forth, as the Earth blooms with spectacular spiritual worlds made visible. The phoenix has risen from the ashes; we have passed through the valley of death and reached the mountain top of new life. A great renaissance of the human spirit has begun.

Before reading on in this chapter, think for a moment. When have periods like this happened in history? You might even want to write down a list of these times of transformation. Verify for yourself if they correspond to the dates when Neptune and Pluto came together in conjunction, which are mentioned below.

Considering the shape of the world today, it should come as no surprise that we have recently been living through such a time of transition. The world wars in the first half of the Twentieth Century shook up a system that had lasted a thousand years. Every reigning empire was struck down during a nightmare of horror which has no precedent in human history. Technology has threatened to end all life on the planet. But the unsettled seas from this explosion have lasted for decades now. The most remarkable fact to consider is this: *the period of transition is over*. It is time for the dawn which follows the darkness, because the last conjunction of Neptune and Pluto happened over 100 years ago, in 1892. These planets have been sending us the unmistakable message that a vast change is happening. We must realize that we are in a new age—and act accordingly. A vast new cycle of civilization has begun that will last until the next Neptune-Pluto conjunction in 2385.

WHAT HAPPENED IN THE 1890s

The 1890s are an historical laboratory in which we can watch the yeasty forces of dissolution and transformation brewing and bubbling away. The people living in that remarkable decade witnessed the deepest and most pervasive change since ancient times. It was as if one world had begun, and another had passed away. This was the first Neptune-Pluto conjunction since either planet had been discovered, so it was more significant than ever. You can feel the process of metamorphosis emanating even today from the 1890s. Its upheavals still sweep through every corner of society, and deep into our own personal lives.

Just picture how drastically different our world is from the horse–and–buggy era of the Nineteenth Century. More inventions than at any time in history before or since radically transformed our planet in the 1890s. It was then, for example, that the world was set on wheels. Not only did we take to the air in the new airplanes, but with Marconi's invention in 1895, we began sending our thoughts through the air on radio waves. With the movie camera (1891), the modern newspaper, the telegraph, and telephones, we arrived in our mass media world.

The qualities of Neptune and Pluto pervaded all of society in the 1890s. Europe, for example, was caught up in the mood of "hypersensitivity and decadence." Others reveled in the imaginative clouds of the mind in an atmosphere resembling the drug culture of the 1960s. Artists, always the first to mirror changes in civilization, reached a watershed moment in the 1890s, as Cezanne, Gauguin, Van Gogh, and others broke from the 500-year-old Renaissance traditions of realism. Soon, the wildest forms and visions imaginable were appearing on their canvases. Old classic forms also tumbled in the music of Debussy and Ravel, and the spontaneous expressions of jazz and ragtime. Forests of skyscrapers spread from their breeding ground in Chicago in the 1890s, and soon they towered into the skies over every city. Other cultural earthquakes transformed the world of the mind. Isaac Newton's view of reality had stood for over 200 years, until Einstein and the quantum theorists overturned it. Psychological "certainties" were destroyed when Sigmund Freud opened up the subconscious in the 1890s and invented psychology as we know it. Thinkers like Bergson and Nietzsche simultaneously shattered our unquestioned faith in science and religion. The search for the "new paradigm" began.

The most noticeable world changes are usually political, and here too, the events of the 1890s were crucial. The Populist movement in America began in 1892 and ultimately led to the triumph of bureaucracy in the New Deal. Russia started on the road to revolution. In 1893, the war between China and Japan set these two nations on the road to become great powers, the first of many in the Third World to challenge the West.

In Germany, Kaiser Wilhelm II came to the throne in 1888, and soon afterward geared up his new war machine for action. An arms race ensued that led directly to the bloodbath which almost wiped Europe off the map. Probably no event in history did more to change the world than the first World War, marking the start of the crisis of modern times. What a list of imperial victims—the German, Austrian, Russian, and Turkish empires all fell. The World Wars were a form of mass suicide that discredited the ideals of the past. Afterwards, Oswald Spengler pronounced "the decline of the West." Since then, we have found many other methods of destroying ourselves.

Before the rude awakening in 1914, however, the world was on its way to new life. We must never forget the fact that a wonderful renaissance, begun in the 1890s, was growing before the Great Wars snuffed it out. It still continues, beneath the rubble of today's broken world. The Neptune-Pluto conjunction gives us the most basic insight into our times—an old world has died, and a new one is being born. Surely, it is accelerating as we cross into the New Millennium.

PRECEDENTS FOR A RENAISSANCE

The conjunction between Neptune and Pluto in 1892 is indeed a hopeful sign, but is one example enough to convince us that we live at a time of rebirth? If the fortunes of civilization really march in tune with Neptune and Pluto, then every such conjunction in the past should have coincided with similar radically transforming moments and times of transition. Every time, we should have emerged into a vibrant new renaissance.

From the Neptune-Pluto rhythm, we can draw the following pattern of dates stretching back from 1892: 1399, 905, 411, 83 B.C., and 577 B.C. When we investigate these dates, we see the course of our own history repeating itself and providing hopeful precedents for our own renaissance of today.

The Italian (and European) Renaissance started in Florence precisely during the conjunction of 1399–1400. Beginning with Ghiberti's design for the cathedral doors in 1400, artists like Donatello and Masaccio created a new style that emphasized our place in the world. Prophecies of doom spread across a land still recuperating from the devastating Black Plague. The Church was in the midst of a turbulent Great Schism out of which the Reformation developed. The rulers of all the major states of Europe and Asia began a struggle for power and national unity. In 1399, Henry Bolingbroke usurped the English throne, eventually provoking the Wars of the Roses that brought the powerful Tudor Dynasty of Henry VIII and Elizabeth I to power. In 1400, Tamarlane marched across Asia, and fifty years later his Turkish hordes captured Byzantium and founded the Turkish Empire. The Tsars of Russia arose and took over the mantle of fallen Byzantium. In the early Fifteenth Century, Portuguese sailors were making the first of those voyages of exploration that would soon make Europeans the masters of the Earth. Chinese navigators were also venturing out at the same time, but were stopped by their new Ming rulers—leaving their insular country open to eventual Western conquest. The Aztecs rose to power in Mexico around the time of the conjunction of 1400, only to be conquered themselves a century later by the Spanish invaders under Cortez.

One hundred years after the start of all this struggle and strife, Europe had literally entered a New World. Columbus' voyage of discovery opened fantastic opportunities. The famous Renaissance that had begun 100 years earlier now lifted the West out of the Middle Ages. Michaelangelo, da Vinci, Raphael, and Durer created humanity's greatest works of art. The Reformation gave new life to Christianity. The Renaissance quickly spread to France under Francis I, to Spain in the "Age of Gold," and climaxed in England under Elizabeth I. Ming China created fantastic painting, pottery and wooden sculpture, and in India, a great rebirth came in the mid-Sixteenth Century, almost simultaneously with the one in Europe. The new Mogul rulers brought peace and unity, and sponsored a temple architecture later made famous by the Taj Mahal. The Turks had their golden age under the enlightened secularist Suleiman the Magnificent (1520–1566).

The Renaissance came right on schedule. Is the time ripe now for us to open up "new worlds" too? If it happened once, it can happen again. In fact, it has happened again many times, just at the appointed hour.

If we go back another 493-plus years to 905 we come to the turbulent age in which the Catholic Medieval civilization was born. The invading Vikings, Saracens and Magyars were spreading fire and destruction across Europe, but right during the conjunction, new institutions were created to roll back the barbarian tide. In 911, Henry the Fowler founded the dynasty that built the Holy Roman Empire. In 910, the Cluniac reform movement began in the Catholic Church, spearheading a revival of learning and devotion. Soon, the churches were organized into a powerful coalition that became the greatest power in Europe. Around 900, Alfred the Great and his son founded modern England. Soon afterward, the royal dynasties of France were founded, as were those of Czechoslovakia, Hungary, and Russia. Around 900, after centuries of turmoil, the Byzantine Empire began a second great flowering. Elsewhere, in 907, the once powerful and prosperous Tang Dynasty collapsed in China, bringing a highly artistic culture to an end there, while half a world away, the great Mayan civilization of Guatemala was dying.

A hundred years later, a great rebirth was under way just as the masses of faithful feared "the end of the world," as many do today. With the support of their new political institutions, Tenth Century artists created the Medieval Christian styles of art and sculpture. By 1000, the Ottonian Renaissance flourished. The Romanesque style which spread from the Abbey of Cluny culminated in the great cathedrals. The once-dreaded Norse invaders were now becoming Europe's new rulers, and sailed to the shores of "Vinland," 500 years before Columbus! In China, the Sung dynasty arose to replace the Tang, and by the Eleventh Century its subtle landscape painting, its inventions (the compass, block printing, etc.) and its spiritual culture made the Sung period China's greatest golden age ever. A new Mayan Empire arose in 1027 in central Mexico, and, after centuries of chaos, the Tamils of Southern India produced some of their greatest sculpture and architecture at the very same moment. A great renaissance of faith in East and West had dawned. Once again, the world had destroyed and renewed itself.

Back another 493 years, we come to a date we all recognize as the Fall of Rome. In A.D. 410 (just one year before the exact Neptune-Pluto conjunction of 411), Alaric the Visigoth conquered the city. This huge catastrophe brought the great age of antiquity to an end and ushered in the Dark Ages. Government and cities collapsed and knowledge was forgotten. Immediately, St. Augustine wrote *The City of God* (413), which advised humanity to build its empires in heaven now that the eternal city had crumbled on Earth. It became the basis of Christian theology. Artists became other-worldly, turning away from classical styles and pursuing abstract ones instead. Almost simultaneously, the powerful Tsin Dynasty collapsed in China, and a similar religious revival ensued. A great African empire arose in Ghana.

Although in 410 most people thought civilization had ended forever, this didn't prevent a glorious new one from blossoming out of its eastern remains at Byzantium! Under Justinian, around 520, some of the world's most beautiful religious architecture and mosaic paintings were created at Ravenna (San Vitale) and Constantinople (Sancta Sophia). Byzantine art, law and culture inspired and dominated Europe for a thousand years, protected it from invaders, and helped transmit ancient culture to the modern world. Theodoric, Clovis and others set up new barbarian kingdoms around 500, and promoted Christianity. In 522, St. Benedict created European monasticism, a new way of life dedicated to spiritual, inward devotion. Hinduism revived in India, and Buddhism was brought to Japan. In the Americas, the great Mayan cities of Guatemala were rising even as the eternal city of Rome fell—their golden age began around 500. So even in the so-called "darkest hour of civilization," the pattern held magnificently and the world bloomed with a renaissance.

Another cycle brings us back to the riseof the Roman Empire which fell in A.D. 411. The dictator Sulla ended the faltering Roman Republic precisely at the stroke of the new cycle in 84–83 B.C. In the next few decades, Julius Caesar, Pompey, and Crassius carried out the famous bloody conquests which made Rome the world's greatest empire, one which laid the basis for all future Western civilization. It is no accident that historians have more information about the sixty turbulent years following the Neptune-Pluto conjunction of 83 B.C. than about any other period before modern times. It was a very crucial turning point!

The wars of conquest ended with the victory of Augustus, whose rule ushered in the Pax Romana. It was the longest period of world peace so far in history. The new Roman Empire became the closest thing to a universal state that has ever existed, and it extended the benefits of law and culture to all its citizens. The "Augustan Age" has come to stand for any classic or golden age in a nation's history. The renewal was made visible in sculpture in the Acra Pacis (Altar of Peace) in 8 B.C., and flowered in the literature of Virgil, Horace, Ovid, Livy and Seneca. This golden rebirth was vividly celebrated and impressed upon the people in a huge ceremony, the "Ludi Saeculares" or "Saeculum." Apparently, the Roman citizens had inside information about the then-still-invisible planetary cycle, for in their own occult tradition a saeculum is a 100 to 110-year period in which the entire human race is renewed—the same period described by the cycle of civilization![1] Even as the forums and aqueducts were being built during Rome's golden age, the pyramids of the Sun and the Moon were being erected half a world away in Teotihuaca, Mexico. Meanwhile, the new Funan empire was rising in Indochina.

While the Caesars and other emperors were celebrating their glory, a different sort of "kingdom" was being proclaimed. About 100 years after the conjunction of Neptune and Pluto, Jesus of Nazareth inaugurated the religion that would later take over the Empire. Christianity was the most successful of the many religions and cults that arose at this time to meet a spiritual hunger that would grow throughout the Roman Empire's 500-year reign. The same impulse stirred in the Orient too, where the *Bhagavad-Gita* was begun at about the time of the conjunction. A new sect of Buddhism also developed (Mahayana) which stressed personal salvation and faith much the way Christianity did in the West.

THE AXIS AGE AND THE TRIPLE CONJUNCTION

Tracing back one more cycle, we come to the greatest turning point of all. What happened during the years following the Neptune and Pluto conjunction of 577 B.C. has reverberated through the centuries, for this conjunction was an extra-special cosmic event. Around 575 B.C., it was joined by Uranus, symbol of enlightenment, making a spectacular triple conjunction of Uranus, Neptune and Pluto. It was an extraordinary union of all three planets of the transcendental trinity—*the first and only such alignment in history.* It was also the tightest conjunction of the three planets in tens of thousands of years.

Many of the momentous developments that followed this grandest planetary event in history are quite famous, but they emerged out of a turbulent time of transition, just like the other golden ages did. In the 580s and 570s B.C., the Greek city-state of Athens was a mere agricultural community ravaged by peasant revolt. Rome was under the heel of cruel Etruscan kings, and the Jews had been hauled off into exile by King Nebuchadnezzar, whose revived Babylonian Empire had run roughshod over the older states of ancient Mesopotamia. In India, the decaying Vedic culture was controlled by a corrupt Hindu Brahmin ruling class.

Already at the time of the conjunction, brilliant sages were appearing who blazed the trails of wisdom which humanity still follows today. At the exact moment when the three transcendental planets were lining up, the "seven wise men" could be found in ancient Greece. One of them, Thales, opened the great tradition of Western thought by proposing a single underlying principle of the world. An even greater advance was made soon afterward by Pythagoras, who was born during the triple conjunction. He sought that "first principle" in the miraculous power of numbers and proportions, and discovered that they were related to musical harmony. He not only founded a religion whose beliefs inspired great minds throughout the ages, but virtually created the mathematics that we know and use today. Another of the seven wise men, Solon, promulgated the laws of the Athens around 580. His legacy was so important that his name became a synonym for legislators everywhere for all time.

Once again, the world was coming to life in a renaissance about one hundred years after the conjunction of Neptune and Pluto—but *this* golden age was especially golden! In 490 to 479 B.C., almost exactly 100 years after the conjunction, Athens led the dramatic defense of Greece against the mighty Persian invaders. Buoyed by their great victory, the confident Athenians brought forth their genius in art, architecture, drama, and politics over the next fifty years. No golden age in history has ever been so widely celebrated as the first democracy under Pericles, when the Parthenon was built, and the writers Sophocles and Aeschylus, and the sculptor Phidias, produced their great works. It was at this time that Socrates began asking the questions out of which the Western search for knowledge and truth emerged. Another seminal republic began simultaneously in Rome.

The great awakening wasn't just limited to Greece. Simultaneously, the Celtic peoples of Northern Europe entered the period of their greatest independent power and creativity, when many of the myths were created which inspired later gothic and "fairy" tales. In the east, the Persian religion of Zoroastrianism consecrated the "battle of good and evil" that has influenced Western culture ever since. The Persian Empire rose to become the home of this new religion in 550 B.C. When the Persians conquered New Babylon, the Jews were able to return home. They brought the Holy Book back to Israel, in written form for the first time. The Bible kept the Jews united through over two millennia of wanderings and exile. Its authors, such as the prophets Isaiah and Ezekiel (influenced by Persian and Mesopotamian ideas while in exile), now they proclaimed that theirs was the One God of all peoples.

In India, the final and most mystical parts of the Upanishads were being written—the basis of Vedantic Hinduism. Their formula of Atman = Brahman became the fundamental principle of Eastern thought. A few decades later, Siddhartha Gautama, born to a Hindu king in 563 B.C., found enlightenment under the Bo Tree and set in motion the Buddhist "wheel of truth" that is still transforming the lives of people all across the world. The holy city of Benares became the center of culture and spirituality in India during its golden age. At the same time, Mahavira began the religion of Jainism in India, which teaches the sacredness of all life, while Confucius and Lao Tzu laid down the great religious and moral traditions of China.

It was a worldwide phenomenon, and the greatest age of enlightenment in human history. Most of the world's religions and philosophies were either founded or transformed in these years. Historians call it "the Axis Age," because so many of the world's greatest thinkers and teachers were alive at the same time. It was the great "hinge of history," when human thought and society changed in ways that still influence us today.

Five conjunctions of Neptune and Pluto were followed by five brilliant golden ages. Each time, we saw the old world pass away and a new one bloom in its place. Even before the Axis Age, the fortunes of civilization in Egypt, Crete, the Near East and China rose and fell according to the 500 year pattern, as you can see from the chart below. Clearly, we have every reason to expect that we, the heirs of the latest conjunction in 1892, can make it through today's time of transition (however belatedly) to a Sixth Renaissance and golden age in our time!

The charts on the following pages compare the rhythm of Neptune-Pluto conjunctions and oppositions with the beginnings and ends of great historical movements. Political, religious, artistic, intellectual, and economic structures rise and fall within the framework of this great planetary cycle.

THE RHYTHM OF CIVILIZATION
4033 B.C.–577 B.C.

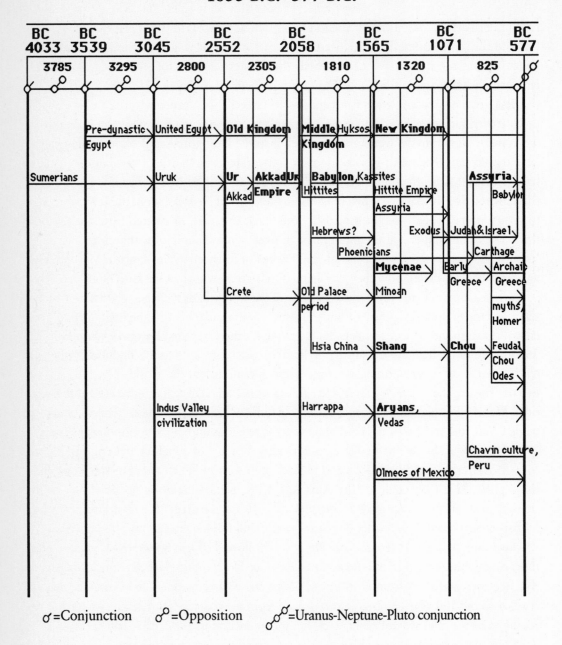

♂ =Conjunction   ♂° =Opposition   ♂°♂ =Uranus-Neptune-Pluto conjunction

THE RHYTHM OF CIVILIZATION
577 B.C.–A.D. 2385

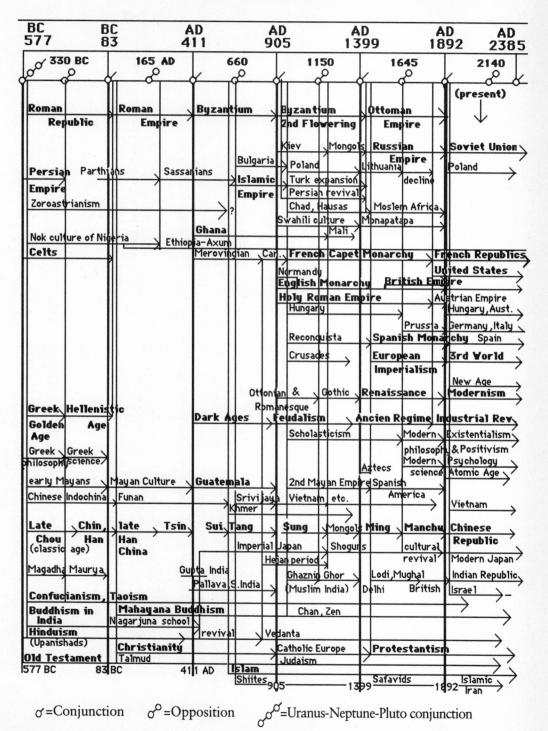

σ =Conjunction σ^{o} =Opposition σ^{oo} =Uranus-Neptune-Pluto conjunction

CONJUNCTIONS WHICH CORRESPOND TO CRUCIAL TURNING POINTS IN THE TIMES OF TRANSITION		GOLDEN AGE OR RENAISSANCE THAT FOLLOWS 100 YEARS AFTER THE CONJUNCTION	
1892	Modern art, atomic physics, fall of European empires	2000	New Age Renaissance, global and green awakening
1399	Early Renaissance, Great Schism, Turkish invasions, Aztecs	1500	Discovery of New World; High Renaissance of Michaelangelo, Da Vinci, Durer, etc.; Moguls, Suleiman, Ming China
905	Cluniac reforms, early European dynasties, fall of Tang Dynasty, fall of Mayans, Viking and Magyar invasions	1000	Ottonian and Byzantine Renaissance, Sung China, Tamil India
A.D. 411	Fall of Rome, fall of Tsin, barbarian invasions, Mayan cities, Ghana	520	Byzantine golden age, Mayan golden age, Hindu revival, Benedictine Order, Theodoric
83 B.C.	Sulla, Roman civil wars/conquests, Bhagavad-Gita	A.D. 10	Roman golden age, Sun pyramid, Mahayana sect, Christ
577 B.C.	Axis Age of enlightenment, Neo Babylonia, Celtic expansion	470 B.C.	Greek golden age, Greek and Roman Republics, Persian Empire, Buddhism, Benares, Chinese classic age
1071 B.C.	Fall of New Kingdom in Egypt, Dorian invasions, Israel and Judea founded, fall of Shang and rise of Chou dynasty	970 B.C.	Israeli golden age (David and Solomon), Assyria, Korea
1565 B.C.	New Kingdom of Egypt founded, civilizations of Mycenae and Minoan Crete began, Shang Dynasty, Aryan invasions in India, Olmecs	1470 B.C.	Cretean golden age (Minos), Egyptian golden age of Thutmose III
2058 B.C.	Middle Kingdom of Egypt founded, Fall of Ur to Semitic invasions, Old Palace Crete, Chinese Hsia Dynasty	1960 B.C.	Babylon, Rock tombs of Egypt built
2552 B.C.	Old Kingdom of Egypt, Ur & Akkad founded, Great Pyramids built	2460 B.C.	Ur golden age, Great Pyramid paintings
3045 B.C.	Narmer founded Egypt, Sumerian cities, Indus Valley civilization	2950 B.C.	Sumerian golden age

EMBRACING TODAY'S GOLDEN AGE

The only conclusion we can draw from the evidence is that, however strange it may seem, we live in a new golden age. Can we lightly dismiss a pattern which has held for 5,000 years? If we are not living up to the potential, it is only because we don't yet understand the pattern.

Most people don't believe a golden age is possible today. In fact, the most prevalent opinion (among those who care at all) is that a new dark age is looming. Clearly, there is much ground for gloom, with today's high crime rate, political gridlock, and manifold threats to the environment. Yet history shows that challenges like ours have called forth greatness in the past. As William McNeill pointed out, "Golden Ages of the past have always been times of vast and fundamental confusion... our age belongs in the high company of those times when people found themselves forced into far-ranging, fundamental creativity."[2] If ours is a time of dangers, it's also a time of opportunities. Despite George Bush's perversion of the term, we truly have entered a "new world order." As democracy breaks out around the world, we can divert our resources away from constant military confrontation if we choose to.

We live at the end of a time of transition when world wars and industrialism have left our culture spiritually shattered, however powerful it seems. Barbarians have always come in these transition times, and this time, they arose inside the gates, with their creed that money is "the bottom line" and what's beautiful is what sells. This shouldn't eclipse the fact that we have so much going for us, however. We are the first people in history able to know and understand all the world's cultures, past and present. More of us, whatever our race or gender, are free to unfold our talents. It's unthinkable that the Neptune-Pluto cycle could fail to bring a golden age at a time when humanity is actually aware of these planets for the first time. Don't ever let it be said that we are "too poor" or "too busy" to create a renaissance. Other peoples in history have done greater things than we, despite fewer resources and much less comfort than we have. All we need is to remember what time it is, and to put an end to business as usual. The greatest goal of life is to manifest our creativity and vision, and now is the best time ever to do it.

That this new golden age will dawn somewhere seems inevitable. Rebirth follows death as surely as the Twenty-First Century follows the Twentieth. The only question is whether you and your society will participate. The fact for those of us in the United States is this: every great nation and civilization has had its golden age, and we have not yet had ours. So far, we have produced only a few brilliant artists and writers, along with fantastic weapons of war and enormous mountains of garbage. Will Americans be remembered a thousand years from now for their wise and inspired contribution, or only for their bad TV, technical gimmicks and toxic pollution? As a dawning world culture, we must ask what our place in history will be. Europe has yet another chance for revival, while the nations of the Far East are poised on the edge of a new prosperity that may enable them to unfold their full potential.

The golden age has already begun, but the opportunity it presents may soon pass us by. So look now and decide what contribution you can make. Are you an artist, musician, poet, philosopher, or patron and promoter of the arts? Above all, are you a dreamer? No great civilization was ever built out of cynical skepticism. A new vision or "paradigm" is unfolding today, based on the knowledge that we are one humanity composed of individuals who have the universal, divine, creative spirit within us. Let's dream now of what's possible in this new global, holistic culture; and then make it happen. Open your heart to the vibrant, pulsing, playful energies of our dawning renaissance and New Earth Awakening. The facts are clear—if we don't dedicate our lives *now* to fulfilling our place on the great cycle of civilization, we will be cheating ourselves of our destiny.

PHASES OF THE CYCLE: THE KEY TO CIVILIZATION'S FUTURE

When Neptune and Pluto join together in conjunction, they begin a cycle that lasts for 493 years. It is like a "New Moon" of civilization, and just like the Moon does, Neptune goes through "phases" in its cyclic relationship to Pluto. As these phases come and go, civilization develops, reaches full flower, and decays. Our New Age which began in 1892 will also follow these phases. Since, in the past, civilization has followed them in a quite astounding way, they should give us a good idea of what is to come over the next 400 years.

Each of these phases is indicated by aspects which Neptune makes to Pluto during the 493-year cycle. The conjunction is only the beginning—the originating impulse that sets the cycle going. Afterward, there are seven other main phases. The first three are "waxing," when Neptune is "increasing in light," and civilization is building its creative power. The last three are "waning," when Neptune is "decreasing in light," during which civilization is either declining, becoming fixed in its ways, and/or releasing "seeds" that will only bloom in the next cycle. In between is the opposition, which is civilization's "Full Moon"—its climax and full flowering. The details of the events corresponding to these phases throughout history are shown in Appendix D.

Following the conjunction, the first phase is the waxing sextile, when Neptune has moved two signs ahead of Pluto. It is like a Crescent Moon phase. These are the creative golden age or renaissance periods when the new civilization overcomes obstacles to its further growth and clearly expresses itself for the first time in serene and classic forms. The Golden Age of Greece, the Augustan Age of Rome, the High Renaissance of Da Vinci and Columbus, and the turn of the New Millennium in our own age, are examples of the waxing sextile phase.

By the time of the waxing square phase, Neptune has moved three signs ahead of Pluto. This is like a First Quarter Moon. It is a time of crisis which tests the foundations of the New Civilization, such as when the Peloponnesian War ended the Golden Age of Greece. We can expect this phase of crisis to arrive again in the years 2065–70. Environmental destruction, ethnic clashes, or epidemics could endanger our new Millennial civilization then. We will have to meet and defeat the "ghosts" of the industrial age, such as corporate greed and excessive demands for individual freedoms.

The next phase is the waxing trine, which is like a Gibbous Moon. This is the time when civilization is confidently expanding and moving toward its climax, as when Trajan and

Hadrian brought the Roman Empire to its greatest power in its brilliant "silver age," or when the First Crusade in 1095 mobilized the Christian Medieval world. The dynamic cathedral art and sculpture of this "Romanesque" era around A.D.1100 is often compared to the Baroque style 500 years later. The next waxing trine is scheduled for about 2090. We can expect our new science and art to move ahead confidently, leaving the "old paradigm" forever behind. Earth-centered spiritual ideals will increasingly predominate over the older ideas of "progress." We will move rapidly toward a fully high-tech Aquarian Age culture integrated with the cosmos, but we could also see a rising "crusade mentality" in the following years that may cause a too-aggressive attitude.

When Neptune opposes Pluto across the heavens, it is like a Full Moon of civilization, which now attains its greatest power and expression. During the opposition a culture's ideals are most clearly and scientifically defined. Afterward, however, civilization may start to split apart or rot from within, or else encumber and rigidify itself with too many rules and structures. For example, at the time of the opposition of 323 B.C., Alexander the Great died at the height of his power. His empire crumbled practically overnight, and Greek culture began to decline in the "Hellenistic" Age. Similarly, in the mid-Seventeenth Century, Louis XIV the French "Sun King" brought classical European Renaissance culture to its height, but then it began to rigidify into the "Ancient Regime" that later collapsed in war and revolution. Greek scientists like Euclid, Roman ones like Ptolemy, and the modern scientific revolution of Descartes and Newton that separated Matter from Spirit, all belong to this Full Moon/opposition phase. The next opposition is due in 2140. We can expect our high-tech, spiritual and Earth-centered Aquarian Age culture to reach full flower and a new architecture to refashion our cities, but some of our new worldwide institutions may expand too far and attain too much power. These global structures may start to become rigid after 2140, and today's "new paradigm" may become too well-defined and formalized in the following years.

During the waning trine, the beliefs and ideas of the new civilization are disseminated, distributed, and institutionalized. The dissemination of Buddhism through Ashoka's empire in India, the establishment of Christianity by Constantine, and the spread of "rational" Enlightenment ideas by the Eighteenth Century "enlightened despots" illustrate this phase. This is usually a happy, light, or decadent period, so we can expect the Twenty-Third Century during the next waning trine to be relaxed and peaceful but complacent. We can expect that the "powers that be" on Earth, or even missionaries from other planets, will be actively sponsoring and disseminating liberating New Age ideas and lifestyles to the people. Global religious institutions may appear.

The period leading up to and during the **waning square** is a dramatic, powerful, final climax of the cycle. It is like a Last Quarter Moon, and represents the "last glory" of civilization. Usually a powerful leader, such as Ashurbanipal, Constantine, Charlemagne, or Napoleon creates a great empire, but it seldom lasts for long. Hopes of a New World (as in the French Revolution) soon fade, yet the seeds of new ideas are planted which will bloom in the civilization of the future. This turbulent, emotional period will arrive again in about

A.D. 2300. Powerful seers will then help us glimpse the coming "Age of Light," due to arrive after the next conjunction of Neptune and Pluto in 2385. However, the illumination of these prophets will not yet be bright enough or free enough from the traces of our Earthbound, corporate, technological society. We will at this time only dimly see this coming New Age of Light—an era when we will truly be able to transform ourselves into Light Beings and embark for the far galaxies and the etheric dimensions. By then, we will no longer be held back by our unfinished business on Earth, or by our rationalistic Twentieth/Twenty-first Century methods. The strong leaders of 2300 will try to prepare us for this bright future, but the hopes they promise for us will fall short of realization.

Instead, if the pattern holds, a period of dissolution or disintegration will ensue. This is the waning sextile, equivalent to a Balsamic or "Dark Moon" phase. Typically, it is marked by peasant or worker revolts and by barbarian invasions, such as those of the Huns and Vikings. It's also sometimes a highly inventive period when new economic arrangements are developed. When the next waning sextile arrives around 2340 we know something of what to expect: much revolt, migration, plague, famine, and atomic and/or ecological catastrophe. New methods of keeping track of value could replace the monetary system and allow us to trade with other galaxies and dimensions. We can expect today's "new paradigms" (the fundamental beliefs and world views now emerging) to start to unravel in a time of skepticism, controversy and fanaticism. If we are ever invaded by a race from another planet, this could be the moment, though we can expect such "barbarian aliens" to be held at bay until then. In any case, it may be the time when the barriers between our Earth civilization and those of other planets and planes begin falling at an unprecedented rate.

CHAPTER 4 ENDNOTES

1. Dudley, Donald, *The Civilization of Rome,* p. 130.
2. McNeill, William, "Epilogue" from *Great Ages of Man: Twentieth Century* by Joel Colton and the editors of Time-Life Books, p. 172.

5

The Cosmic Clock of Civilization

What will the New Age be like? What does fortune hold for our civilization in the next 400 years? We can get even more information on this question by watching the Cosmic Clock of Civilization. As we mentioned, every cycle, no matter how long, takes place within a longer one. Just as an ordinary clock has a minute hand and an hour hand, the Cosmic Clock has a shorter cycle and a longer one. This is how it works: every 493 years, Neptune and Pluto return to their conjunction in about the same place in the zodiac. The last two conjunctions have occurred in Gemini, and the ones before that happened in Taurus; but Uranus shifts its position backward almost forty-five degrees at the time of each conjunction. It takes 3,940-plus years (about 4,000), or eight Neptune-Pluto conjunctions for Uranus to shift all the way back to the same place it started.

A spectacular event inaugurates a Great Cycle. As Uranus, Neptune, and Pluto light up the sky with a brilliant triple conjunction, an enormous turning point in human evolution is reached. We are not at such a moment today: ours is just one in a series of cycles that have followed from the previous triple conjunction. That happened, as we said, around 575 B.C. It coincided with a great awakening that girdled the globe, and has never been equaled in the history of humanity. It was so powerful that its reverberations have continued ever since. It set in motion the great cycle that Buddha called "the wheel of truth." Each subsequent cycle of civilization since then has been an echo or ripple from that first impulse, when the greatest artists, seers, and sages in history set in motion all the changes of the last 2,500 years. This radical shift ended the archaic ages, a time when human culture and society were fully embedded within cycles of visible nature and restricted to the domain of tribal gods and kings. The Sixth and Fifth Centuries B.C. were the world's classic age, one which could only have come during the most rare and sublime of planetary events. For the first time, we beheld transcendental realms and became conscious of ourselves as free rational and spiritual beings. As Plato would say, we began to venture beyond the cave. We began our quest to understand and control nature, and to reorganize society according to universal moral and spiritual ideas. We embarked on a bold, dangerous experiment whose possibilities and consequences are still being played out today, and won't be complete until the next triple conjunction, almost 4,000 years afterward. This is still quite distant for us—it will occur around the year 3370.

When Uranus aligned with Neptune and Pluto in 577 B.C., the great triple conjunction (the closest and most powerful in tens of thousands of years) opened a vast cycle of time in which we are still involved. Each of the smaller 500-year cycles between Neptune and Pluto can be seen against the backdrop of this larger, more inclusive one. It puts them all in context and allows us to interpret the meaning of each one, including our own. By shifting clockwise almost forty-five degrees at each succeeding conjunction of Neptune and Pluto, Uranus divides the 4,000-year cycle into eight smaller cycles of civilization. Uranus acts as the "hour hand" on the cosmic clock of civilization, showing the place which each period occupies in the larger cycle. You may recognize forty-five degrees as the semi-square, an aspect of friction and dynamic, constructive activity. With the great cycle moving to this rhythm, it's no wonder people have called it "the march of progress" or "civilization's march through history." We certainly haven't been "waltzing" through time—the struggles to build our civilization have brought much change and conflict. So far, we haven't been able to "march forward" without marching soldiers into battle.

Although Uranus shifts "backward" through the signs, I find it clearer and more logical to conceive Uranus as moving "forward" through the twelve houses, since we are describing a cycle, and all astrological cycles take place "on the wheel." Uranus was therefore in a "first house" phase in relation to Neptune and Pluto at the triple conjunction, so the first cycle (and thus the first great age of civilization in this series) had the traits of the First House and its ruling sign Aries. During the next conjunction (83 B.C.), Uranus had shifted back almost forty-five degrees into the Second House, giving the second age the traits of that house and its ruling sign, Taurus. At the next conjunction (A.D. 411), Uranus had shifted back another forty-five degrees, making a total of ninety degrees since the triple conjunction. Uranus was therefore at the cusp of the Third and Fourth Houses, giving this third age of civilization the traits of those houses and their ruling signs (Gemini and Cancer). By the time of the fourth conjunction in the series (A.D.905), Uranus had shifted back 135 degrees into the Fifth House (Leo), and by the fifth conjunction in 1400, it had shifted back almost a full 180 degrees from its original position in 577 B.C. Thus, it was in opposition to the conjunction, marking a halfway point in the 4,000-year cycle. The period took on the traits of the Sixth and Seventh Houses, which are related to the signs Virgo and Libra. This happened just before 1400 A.D., marking the beginning of the Renaissance.

That brings us to our own age, which began with the Neptune-Pluto conjunction of 1892. Ours is the sixth cycle in the series, and Uranus has shifted back 225 degrees into an Eighth House or Scorpio-like position. Our age takes on the traits of that sign of death, rebirth and transformation, and of its potent ruling planet Pluto, discovered in our own century. The seventh age starting in 2385–86 will bring us to the Midheaven and the Ninth and Tenth Houses. We can expect the traits of Sagittarius and Capricorn to come to the fore. The eighth and final cycle starting in 2879 will be the grand climax of the whole series. Since Uranus will be in the Eleventh House, this period will take on the traits of that house and Aquarius, its ruling sign. We can therefore predict that the "Aquarian Age" will come into full flower in that time.

The diagrams on the following pages show the 4,000-year Cosmic Clock of Civilization plotted into a horoscope. The house in which Uranus is located at the time of each conjunction gives us the meaning of each 493-year period.

FIRST HOUSE PHASE: 577 B.C.–83 B.C.

The First House Phase was the Classical Age. Since Uranus was in the First House and on the Ascendant, the period had the traits of Aries, the cardinal fire sign. It was an age of new beginnings. In fact, so many bold departures were made that it will take the entire 4,000-year cycle to fully realize them. Never was an age more original or creative. Dramatic plays and sculpture, great literature and architecture, new philosophies and religions laid down the classic models for all the world's civilizations. Buddha set the great wheel of truth in motion. New cities, states, and an entire new system of democracy were founded. We've always looked back to the prophets and visionaries of this age to inspire and guide us, but the practical details were left for future ages. The people of the First House phase kept their heads in the clouds of the mind. The Greeks conceived the ideal Republic, but could not successfully rule themselves. They discovered the laws of nature, but didn't think of ever applying them. The Jews remained the "people of the book," and the sages of the East could not change the world. The Roman Republic failed, and the Celts could never stop fighting each other long enough to consolidate their power.

Aries rules the head and the ego; its motto is "I am." Therefore the great oracle during the First House Phase was "know thyself," not "build the Earth" or "love God." In fact, it was the Greeks who invented the notion of the "individual." As their magnificent art records, the Greeks celebrated themselves and the glory of their own minds and bodies. Success became a matter of personal achievement and fame, and "man" himself became "the measure of all things." The Buddhists also concentrated on the self, although their purpose was to extinguish it. Their approach was equally self-centered, for just as the Greek philosophers conceived absolute truths using only their own minds, the Buddhists monks meditated alone to reach their own private Nirvana.

During phase one, people were active, assertive, and aggressive in the Aries way. Masculine traits were emphasized and feminine ones suppressed. Individuals, cities, and finally states became competing rivals until one state emerged victorious. As is true of all periods that begin with Uranus at the angles (the Ascendant, Nadir, Descendant and Midheaven), this one was unstable and full of wars. Although it was an age of competing equals, some were more equal than others. The masses remained largely separate from the upper classes, as is generally true during all the cycles ruled by cardinal or mutable signs. In Rome, the patricians dominated the plebeians, while India developed its caste system, and most Greek cities were dominated by privileged aristocrats.

SECOND HOUSE PHASE: 83 B.C.–A.D. 411

The Second House phase was the Imperial Age. Uranus in the second house bestowed the traits of fixed earth sign Taurus. This was a time of building and consolidation. The age of empires

THE GREAT 4,000-YEAR CYCLE OF URANUS

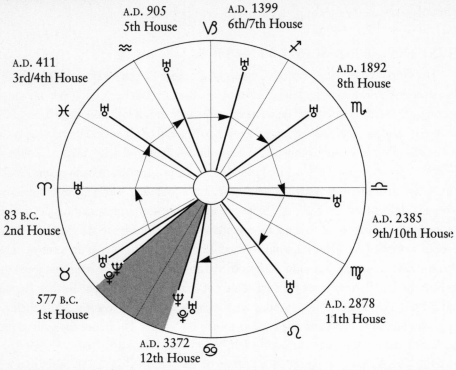

A.D. 905
5th House

A.D. 1399
6th/7th House

A.D. 411
3rd/4th House

A.D. 1892
8th House

83 B.C.
2nd House

A.D. 2385
9th/10th House

577 B.C.
1st House

A.D. 2878
11th House

A.D. 3372
12th House

THE COSMIC CLOCK OF CIVILIZATION: CURRENT CYCLE

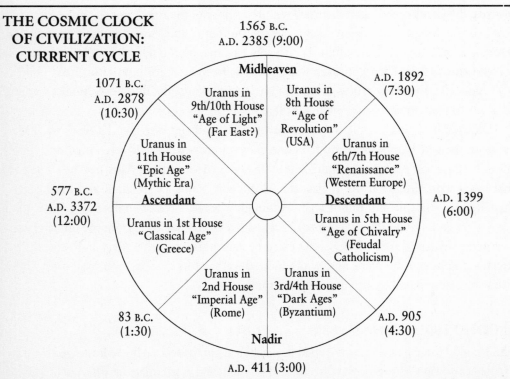

1565 B.C.
A.D. 2385 (9:00)

Midheaven

A.D. 1892
(7:30)

1071 B.C.
A.D. 2878
(10:30)

Uranus in
9th/10th House
"Age of Light"
(Far East?)

Uranus in
8th House
"Age of
Revolution"
(USA)

Uranus in
11th House
"Epic Age"
(Mythic Era)

Uranus in
6th/7th House
"Renaissance"
(Western Europe)

577 B.C.
A.D. 3372
(12:00)

Ascendant

Descendant

A.D. 1399
(6:00)

Uranus in 1st House
"Classical Age"
(Greece)

Uranus in 5th House
"Age of Chivalry"
(Feudal
Catholicism)

Uranus in
2nd House
"Imperial Age"
(Rome)

Uranus in
3rd/4th House
"Dark Ages"
(Byzantium)

83 B.C.
(1:30)

A.D. 905
(4:30)

Nadir

A.D. 411 (3:00)

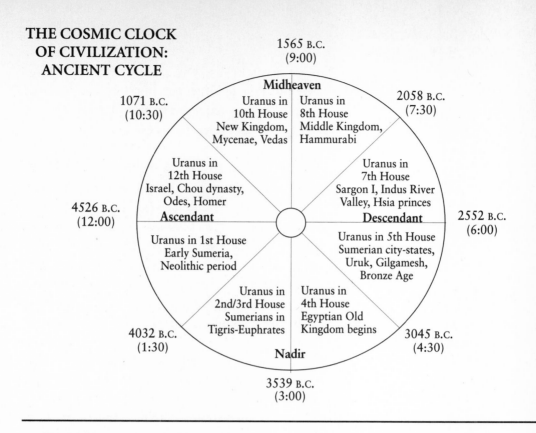

THE COSMIC CLOCK OF CIVILIZATION: ANCIENT CYCLE

1565 B.C. (9:00)

1071 B.C. (10:30)

2058 B.C. (7:30)

4526 B.C. (12:00)

2552 B.C. (6:00)

4032 B.C. (1:30)

3045 B.C. (4:30)

3539 B.C. (3:00)

Midheaven

Uranus in 10th House New Kingdom, Mycenae, Vedas

Uranus in 8th House Middle Kingdom, Hammurabi

Uranus in 12th House Israel, Chou dynasty, Odes, Homer

Uranus in 7th House Sargon I, Indus River Valley, Hsia princes

Ascendant

Descendant

Uranus in 1st House Early Sumeria, Neolithic period

Uranus in 5th House Sumerian city-states, Uruk, Gilgamesh, Bronze Age

Uranus in 2nd/3rd House Sumerians in Tigris-Euphrates

Uranus in 4th House Egyptian Old Kingdom begins

Nadir

CURRENT CYCLE

Year	Estimated Position: ♆☌♇	Estimated Position: ♅	House Position: ♅
577 B.C.	12° Taurus	6° Taurus	1st
83 B.C.	17° Taurus	29° Pisces	2nd
A.D. 411	23° Taurus	24° Aquarius	3rd/4th
905	28° Taurus	20° Capricorn	5th
1399	3° Gemini	15° Sagittarius	6th/7th
1892	8° Gemini	4° Scorpio	8th
2385	12° Gemini	20° Virgo	9th/10th
2878	17° Gemini	2° Leo	11th
3372	22° Gemini	28° Gemini	12th

ANCIENT CYCLE

Year	Estimated Position: ♆☌♇	Estimated Position: ♅	House Position: ♅
4526 B.C.	1° Aries	8° Pisces	1st
4032	7° Aries	2° Aquarius	2nd/3rd
3539	12° Aries	29° Sagittarius	4th
3045	17° Aries	27° Scorpio	5th
2552	21° Aries	17° Libra	7th
2058	26° Aries	5° Virgo	8th
1565	1° Taurus	18° Cancer	10th
1071	7° Taurus	12° Gemini	12th

55

arrived to complement the age of the classics. In the West, there was Rome. In China, somewhat earlier, there was the Han Dynasty. In India, somewhat later, the Gupta Empire arrived. In Mexico, there was the first Mayan Empire. The creative energy that blossomed in the first phase became power to be harnessed by the empire builders of the second. The restless, competing peoples of the Classical Age were gathered together into a few orderly and magnificent states. The boundless majesty of the Pax Romana replaced the bitter wars between rival city-states and war lords.

Where the First House phase originated, the Second House phase consolidated. Idea became reality and theory became practice. Civilization was put on a solid foundation that enabled it to survive the storms of succeeding ages. The second phase of any great cycle always seeks to pacify, perpetuate, and make practical the unbridled impulses of the first phase. Without the Roman Empire, the glory of Greece would have been lost to the ages, and Christ's words would have remained in the wilderness. Instead of creating new ideas, Rome borrowed and developed them. It embodied the Greek culture and bequeathed it to the world, and later did the same for the Judeo-Christian tradition. In the East, Confucian morals would never have been put into practice without the creation of the Chinese state under the Han Dynasty.

Under earthy Taurus, people took their heads out of the clouds and planted them on solid ground. The Romans were a practical, down-to-earth people, less assertive and creative than the Greeks. They didn't make their castles in the air, as Plato and Confucius did, but in the real world. They were great builders and administrators, not inventors or imaginative thinkers, but what they built was made to last. Roman architecture, in which the first arches and domes were developed, was a great engineering advance. Their own artistic styles were notable for being realistic, especially in the remarkable portraits of ordinary people. As in our day, practical motives dominated artistic ones.

The consolidating ages under fixed signs tend to favor the common people as much as the privileged. For example, although Rome was an empire, her citizens were equals before the law, and racial and class distinctions declined. Slavery diminished and serfdom didn't exist yet. Individual lives became more important than the nation's, since citizens could not identify themselves with the vast empires of that time as easily as with the city-states of Greek times. Like the consolidating age we live in today, Rome was a mass society. Art and culture reflected the needs and tastes of the crowd instead of the philosopher-aristocrat. We need only compare the chariot races and gladiator fights in the Coliseum with our own sports stadiums and horror movies. The arts and fashions of this era reflected personal feelings and tastes, and we get the term "romantic" from Rome.

Religion changed with the times as well, becoming more realistic and worldly. No longer did the spiritual path lead merely to a solitary salvation. In Mahayana Buddhism and Christianity, the new goal was to serve others. Nature regained its divine status in this period, especially in Oriental religions, while cults involving fertility rites and sex rituals proliferated in Rome. In East and West alike, religion responded to the needs and emotional problems of the masses and promised them salvation through the sacrifice of a personal savior. The Buddhist bodhisattva could not rest until every sentient being in the universe was free from the endless wheel of suffering. As religion recovered, philosophy declined. To love became more important than to know, and charity became more valuable than wisdom. In many ways, the Second House phase perpetuated and consolidated the first, but in some ways it was also an antithesis of and reaction to the first. It's interesting, by the way, that Uranus during the conjunction in 83 B.C. was located at the cusp of the signs Pisces and Aries, just as (many astrologers believe) we moved from the Arian to the Piscean Age in which religious faith became dominant. As we'll see, this was also the place of the "Star of Bethlehem" in Jesus' chart.

THIRD/FOURTH HOUSE PHASE: 411–905

With phase three, we arrived at the Nadir, or cusp of the Third and Fourth House. That means the age was ruled by restless Gemini and introverted Cancer. With Uranus at the Nadir, where the Sun is at midnight, it is no wonder that we called this period the Dark Ages. Despite the compelling momentum unleashed by the Classical Age, most of the history that followed seemed like a long decline. People gradually lost the buoyant faith in themselves that had been the source of Greek genius. It was as if the sunlight dimmed and night decscended as we moved toward the dark Nadir of the chart. Life became more burdensome and oppressive, and society turned decadent. Finally, as the Dark Ages opened, many governments just collapsed. Cities became empty and knowledge was forgotten as barbarians trampled through the land.

With Uranus at the Fourth House cusp in the year 411, people turned inward toward spiritual life. St. Augustine pronounced the world and all its pleasures evil, and now the human body once worshipped by the Greeks was considered sinful. Culture was found mostly within the protected sanctuary of the monastery, where the monks could carry on, safe from the turbulence outside. There in typical Fourth House, Cancerian style, they nurtured the growth of a civilization that one day would recover and grow beyond the walls.

These were also the aims of the brilliant new civilization at Byzantium that dominated the age. Here, monuments as majestic as those of the Acropolis in Athens were created, but they evoked awe of the spiritual world instead of celebrating the order and proportion of the natural. At Ravenna, Italy, we see the enlarged eyes of Byzantine mosaic figures gazing inward as if in a trance, their features transformed into monumental symbols. Not until the Renaissance did the natural human figure fully return into art. The Byzantine emperors, patriarchs of a unified church and state, surrounded themselves with the aura of awesome grandeur and Oriental mystery in order to isolate and create a vast distance between themselves and their subjects, who were intensely loyal and patriotic (typically Cancerian). These "Caesaro-papists" of Byzantium were like the ancient emperors of Mesopotamia, Egypt, and China. Like the monks, the Byzantines protected classical civilization and helped keep it alive for future ages. At the same time, the frightened people of the countryside found protection inside the castle of their Lord. The constant threat from invaders, as well as re-curring palace revolutions, kept them in a continuous state of fear and paranoia (a mood they passed on to their Russian and Soviet successors).

Alhough the Nadir represents a low point, it also stands for a "new start."At the bottom we also immediately begin to ascend. Fittingly, we entered the right or western half of the chart just as "Western Civilization" began, though East and West were still marching in lock-step at this time. Devotional Buddhism captured the Orient just when Christianity swept over the West. Both preached mystic contemplation, withdrawal from the world, the renouncing of desire, love and gentleness, and salvation of the soul through faith.

Where phase one originated and phase two perpetuated, phase three dispersed and distributed on a huge scale. The third phase of any cycle always means movement. In this case, we saw the greatest folk migrations and wanderings in history throughout the whole period. As the people moved, they acquired and spread the religion of the dying classical world. With cardinal and mutable signs dominant, people were restless and unsettled, and there was constant war. Kenneth Clark compared the Dark Ages to an American western movie that ran too long—they fought so much of the time that they forgot they had nothing to fight over. Meanwhile, the common people lost everything, and their lot became one of unremitting toil and fear.

Each of the first three phases saw the birth of a major Western religion. Following the usual astrological progression of the "modes" (cardinal, fixed, and mutable signs), the Jews were the originators, and thus by nature cardinal. In the first phase they became the "people of the book," creating the basic moral principles and ideas. The Christians gave them a solid, fixed foundation through the "incarnation" of Jesus and a powerful state church. Thus, the Christians were fixed by nature. The Moslems distributed these things worldwide through their conquests in the Seventh Century, and transmitted ancient civilization to the future through their scholarship. Islam was the mutable religion in this great series.

FIFTH HOUSE PHASE: 905–1399

The Fifth House phase was the Age of Chivalry. It was dominated by the hierarchical Order of Feudalism and the Catholic Church. Uranus in the Fifth House gave the age the glory, pageantry, and romance of the sign Leo. Momentum shifted as the barbarian peoples organized themselves and rapidly reduced chaos to order. Peace and stability returned under consolidating, fixed sign Leo, as people in both East and West found their place in the social order under a universal church (Catholicism in the West, Islam in the Middle East, and Buddhism in the East). A definite role was prescribed for each person, and everyone stayed within the bounds of the village, manor, and church district into which they were born. In return, society gave each person specific rights through feudal contracts and charters, and the prosperous and growing cities offered many new opportunities.

This phase demonstrated beyond any doubt the cultural influence of the Fifth House and Leo. The code of Honour and Chivalry, developed by the epic poets and troubadours portraying the exploits of knights in shining armor seeking the Holy Grail, is the signature of this age. During this era we find the famous English king Richard I, known as *Coeur de Lion*—the "Lion Heart." Leo's creative potential was revealed by the greatest religious art and architecture ever created. Fifth House sports and gamesmanship was certainly reflected by jousts, tournaments, and competitions for the favor of a lady's hand. In fact, the troubadours gave us our first glimpse of the ideal of romantic love, which has become so important to us. Its mythic tales, wizardry and heraldry make this age the one most attractive to fantasy buffs today. The Leo tendency toward romance is also expressed in the cult of worship for that most lovely of ladies, the Virgin Mary. The many religious cults and pilgrimages in which the faithful millions participated certainly shows how, in this fixed-sign period, the common people had a powerful effect on the culture, as they did in Roman times. If Leo's pride was too often expressed in the willful ambitions of kings and bishops, it was also reflected in the traditions of every Western family, whose name and heritage originates in this era.

The Fifth House phase continued to emphasize the same spiritual and otherworldly interests that dominated the previous phase, just as the Romans perpetuated Greek rationalism. However, the "light of the world" began to return as we passed the Nadir and moved up toward the horizon again. The wondrous colors beaming through the beautiful Rose Windows of medieval cathedrals were meant to convey God's presence in the world. Medieval philosophers sought to reconcile reason and faith. Toward the end of this phase, the exaggerated heights of Gothic architecture leveled off, while the more worldly ambitions of politicians and bankers expanded. The Black Plague cast doubt on whether religion alone could help the people cope with their suffering. St. Francis proclaimed our brother and sisterhood with nature, and it was to nature that the philosophers of the next phase would turn (although unlike St. Francis, they would not be teaching the spiritual practice of poverty!)

This phase completed the first half of the 4,000-year Great Cycle between triple conjunctions, synthesizing the previous three ages. The Medieval synthesis brought church and state, God and Nature, inspiration and intellect, and even classic and romantic, into a precarious balance not attained before or since. We look back to this period as the shining source of civilization as we know it today, with its now-decaying institutions, customs and traditions. The radiance of Leo could be seen in the cultures of almost every people on Earth, from the second flowering of Byzantium and the epic poems and exotic minarets of Islam, to the wonderful works of the Sung Dynasty in China. The Sung period was the greatest and still-unsurpassed synthesis of Chinese culture, as its many inventions and wonderful tapestries demonstrate. Although there was much to fear in the world of those days, this was indeed a great "age of faith" worldwide—a wonderful climax of civilization.

SIXTH/SEVENTH HOUSE PHASE: 1399–1892

The houses in the upper half of horoscope, which begin at the Descendant, always extend the range of their opposite houses in the lower half. With the Sixth/Seventh House phase we came to the halfway point of the cycle, as Uranus opposed Neptune and Pluto a few years before they joined in 1399. In effect, we emerged back above the horizon into the light of the world. This phase was also closely related to the opposite First House phase, each opening one-half of the Great Cycle. Both were periods of "new beginnings." This was the era of the Renaissance, which claimed to be the "rebirth" of classical times. Since Uranus was in the Sixth House near the cusp of the Seventh, this phase was linked to both Virgo and Libra. Like Aries, which ruled the Classical Age, Libra is a cardinal sign.

Renaissance humanists, like the classical Greeks, celebrated the glory of human beings who were endowed with the power and intelligence of the gods and could "do all things if they will." Humanity began shifting its focus away from the supernatural and the spiritual, and back toward material achievement, success, and glory on Earth. Just as in Greek times, the natural human figure re-emerged to replace the stiff, monumental forms of the old religious style. Architects made sure that their buildings evoked a human and worldly scale and expressed balance, harmony, and mathematical proportion (the traits of Libra). Religious rebels declared that the light of God could be found in the human heart through study of His word, now that the printing press made it possible for all believers to read the Bible for themselves.

Since the Descendant is the Western horizon, civilization centered in the West during this phase far more than during others. As soon as it began, European explorers boldly ventured westward by land and sea to explore "beyond the far horizon," while the Chinese pulled back into their cocoon. Since the Descendant also rules "the other," the West sought to "discover" and conquer other peoples and places. Uranus in the Sixth House bestowed the traits of scientific Virgo, as the voyages of discovery stimulated our ability to test, experiment with, and analyze the world. Knowledge continued to expand as we increasingly questioned authorities and superstitions.

The characteristics of harmonious Libra were reflected in the growth of classical music and art, and in the period's emphasis on politics and diplomacy. Society again became elitist, as political power concentrated in the central royal bureaucracies that replaced "feudal anarchy," and these competing kings and aristocrats became the patrons and arbiters of what was defined as "art" and "culture." Even so, enterprising and daring men (though not yet women) could find great success and fame. Like the ancient Greeks whom they emulated, the "Renaissance men" of this cardinal/mutable phase were individualistic and aggressive, and the great kingdoms they created became competing "great powers." Unlike the Classic Age, however, the Renaissance did not turn inward on the self. Instead, it was eager to experience, discover, and master the outer visible world. It was not so much an original or creative civilization as it was inventive. It was able to expand on and apply ideas in very useful and profitable ways.

EIGHTH HOUSE PHASE: 1892–2385

Our own phase bears the traits of the Eighth House and its sign, Scorpio. Just as the Renaissance revived the Classical Age, so ours has seen the building of new empires, with the

United States (and perhaps eventually a global government) as the new "Rome." The U.S. and its former adversary Russia are, in fact, historically descended from the Western and Eastern parts of the Roman Empire which split in two at the end of the second phase in A.D. 411. Despite the Scorpio-like turmoil at the start of our age, Scorpio is a fixed sign, so this will be a phase of increasing stability, much as the Pax Romana followed the struggles of the early Caesars. The new age of peace is emerging from the crucible of conflict, just as the phoenix of new life rises from the ashes of death.

Unlike the Romans, who were ruled by the opposite sign Taurus, we are not laying down foundations for future ages, but uprooting the foundations of the past in an Age of Revolution. Under Scorpio we are probing, questioning, or destroying everything we have received from previous ages so we can transform and revitalize ourselves. Our times are a "purification by fire," in which humanity faces annihilation unless it learns to live together. The life-threatening results of our Scorpionic greed will force a transformation through vivid spiritual experiences connecting us to each other and the planet. We are called not just to meet and conquer other peoples, as in the previous phase, but to renew ourselves by joining them in true interdependence. Our task in fixed sign Scorpio is to revitalize the original ideals of the "Axis Age" 2,500 years ago. To do this, we must eliminate those aspects of our legacy from the classical age which now inhibit and block us. Another great Scorpionic quest of our time is to explore the unexplained mysteries of life and spirit. Our Scorpio traits are doubly emphasized by the fact that Uranus in 1892 was not only in an eighth house phase on the Cosmic Clock of Civilization, but was actually transiting the sign Scorpio as well-- and in an exactly corresponding degree! In effect, as the forward motion through the signs (the transits) and the backward motion through the houses (on the Cosmic Clock) meet each other, we are learning to press forward and fall backward at once. Our challenge is to merge inner and outer, past and future, yin and yang, male and female, East and West.

With Uranus in the financial Eighth House, practical and economic motives dominate our lives as they did in Roman times. Our Eighth-House ability to share and pool resources has created our enormously successful corporate economy. Even more than the Romans, people today have many rights and legal protections. It's almost as if Rome has been magnified a thousandfold and spread across the whole planet. Ours is a mass culture that caters to the needs and desires of the people, but frequently descends into mediocrity and consumerism as a result. We feel alienated from the huge institutions that run our lives, but the Scorpio ability to penetrate to the roots gives our age an enormous creative potential. When we look beyond the economic "bottom line," we moderns sense the powerful mystery and wonder at the heart of all creation. As the poet Baudelaire wrote, "modern is romantic." As natives of the fixed water sign, emotional satisfaction is as important to us as our technical power, and our deepest goal is to transform ourselves. Our alienation won't end until we can all tune in to the vibrant energy of our whole planet (or the "noosphere," as Teilhard de Chardin called it). As in Roman times, once again our only "salvation" is to identify ourselves with a larger Being, just as the Romans eventually gave their souls to Christ.

NINTH/TENTH HOUSE PHASE: 2385–2878

With Uranus in the Ninth House near the cusp of the Tenth, in 2385 we will have arrived at the Midheaven, where the Sun is at Noon. That means the next period of civilization could be one of great illumination, for if Uranus at the Nadir was the Dark Ages, Uranus at the Midheaven will be the Age of Light.[1] Since the Ninth and Tenth Houses are linked to Sagittarius and Capricorn, and represent the highest parts of the horoscope, we will seek the light of the spirit not by retreating into the monastery or the castle, but by expanding out into the universe in all its dimensions. Once again we will be under mutable and cardinal signs, so the times will be restless and unstable, and there could be a huge migration of peoples. This probably means we will move out into the solar system and the galaxy in this period. We can expect to emerge from our transformation on planet Earth under Scorpio renewed and ready to explore the vast realms of inner and outer space. This time, perhaps Eastern peoples will lead the way (instead of retreating, as in 1400).

Under Sagittarius, we can expect people of the Ninth/Tenth House phase to be wise and well traveled. New forms of expression will emerge that celebrate our all-encompassing vision of the cosmos, but many people may be left behind by all the change and dislocation. An effort will be needed if the new opportunities are to be made available to all. Since the ninth and tenth houses will be combined, we will see Church and State come together again as they did in the Middle Ages, but in an open, global society. Humanity will conceive new principles of how to live together and relate to others in the galaxy, as our social maturity finally catches up with our technological prowess.

ELEVENTH HOUSE PHASE: 2878–3372

The Eleventh House Phase will be the final consummation of the preceding seven ages—perhaps a wonderful, glorious expression of the "Age of Aquarius," since the Eleventh House is linked to that fixed air sign. Certainly, if the "new age" ever arrives, it will have done so by then. Uranus in the Eleventh House will expand the "code of chivalry" of the corresponding Fifth House phase into a "code of friendship and association" in which all people will act as brothers and sisters. The benefits of the new society will be distributed widely so that all may share in them. We can expect great feats of construction that surpass anything we can imagine today (even the great cathedrals), and brilliant epic poets who, as in the days of Homer, will express the significance of the whole human adventure. Earth will arrive at a stable and peaceful grand synthesis and prepare itself for the new 4,000-year cycle that will begin with the triple conjunction in A.D. 3370. The transition to the new cycle in 3370 may be difficult, though, since humanity will face still more karma from its activities over the past 4,000 years.

EAST AND WEST

Uranus in astrology represents "breaks and estrangements." It happened that when Uranus joined Neptune and Pluto at the beginning of the 4,000-year Great Cycle in the Sixth Century B.C., the world's culture began to break into East and West. At first, however, the great awakening on both sides of the world had much in common. Socrates and Confucius both sought the basis for a moral life and a just society, and both Plato and Buddha taught us how to transcend desire. Skeptics undermined old beliefs everywhere, and great teachers spoke of humanity as the spiritual essence of a universal God. Nature was still thought of as a living organism in both cultures.

It was in the Sixth Century B.C., however, that the historical current began separating into two streams. In the West, beginning with Greek philosophers such as Pythagoras and Aristotle, science and mathematics began to move toward the mastery of nature, and "enlightenment" meant discovering the underlying rational principles of all things. The West also became teleological, propelled by the messianic faith of the "chosen people" in the "Second Coming," and later by the Protestant ethic, while God stood above and outside nature and human beings, ruling over the universe from Heaven. The West moves aggressively toward an ultimate goal. It is the masculine, yang, left brain of world culture; always on the move and rarely at peace. With its all-conquering science and technology, Western culture has mastered the outer world and inspired other peoples with its adventurous spirit, but it knows little of its own soul, and faces moral and spiritual bankruptcy as a result. The West is the culture most specifically linked to Uranus as it marches through its great 4,000-year cycle, forming dynamic, discordant squares, semi-squares and oppositions to Neptune and Pluto on its way.

The East, on the other hand, is the feminine, yin, right brain of the world mind. Starting with the Upanishads and the Buddha, Eastern "enlightenment" has always meant inner awakening, not outer knowledge. God is the divine nature within each human being, and the universe is conceived as a harmonious whole. The East became an exotic, Neptunian Shangri-La, quietly and serenely refining its exquisite culture. Although it fell behind the West technologically, its psychology became far more advanced. While Western crusaders marched noisily across the world, Eastern sages calmly pursued their quest into the profound mysteries and powers of the psyche. They mastered the soul, but neglected the world, so the culture stagnated and left itself vulnerable to eventual Western conquest.

The center of Western culture has moved steadily westward throughout its history. From its origins in Mesopotamia, it moved through Egypt, Crete, and Palestine to Greece, Rome, Germany, France, Spain, and England. When Uranus reached the western horizon in the Renaissance, Western Civilization ventured across that very horizon—sailing its ships over the Atlantic to America. Today (as we'll see later) it is centered in California, reaching out once more towards the sea. Now (as World War II established) there's no land left for the West to grab, and as we launch ourselves onto the boundless Pacific seas, we are meeting the current flowing eastward. For as the West has moved east, the East has moved west—for example, witness the travels of Buddhism from India through China to Japan. As the currents meet, the West discovers the wisdom of the mystic East, as the East adopts Western industrialism and capitalism.

THE HORIZONTAL AND VERTICAL AXES

We can get vital information on the past and the future from the Cosmic Clock of Civilization by considering the two axes of the horoscope diagram. At the horizon, or east-west axis, we find ourselves on the same level with the world. From this vantage point, things are seen on a human scale, and we expand ourselves along the plane of the Earth. We believe we humans are "equal" to the world's tasks, and movements toward human equality begin. The horizon is therefore the *humanist axis,* and the 1,000-year periods that begin when Uranus is at the horizon are humanist and worldly. This was the case with Greece and Rome, and also with the Renaissance and modern times. It's interesting that the Greeks went due east to conquer Persia and India, while Europe went due west to conquer America.

At the vertical meridian, or North-South Axis, we are either looking up from or down to the world. We expand into other planes of experience rather than across the earth plane, and we seek a deeper source of divine strength. Humanity stands in fearful awe of the supernatural, translating its visions into legendary stories and lofty works of stone. Society is organized vertically into a hierarchy of unequals. The meridian is therefore the *otherworldly axis,* and so ages of civilization that begin when Uranus is at the Nadir or Midheaven are otherworldly and/or spiritual. The Middle Ages cowered in fear before the Almighty and built towering monuments toward heaven. There was also an otherworldly "dark age" in Greece before classical Greek times, and a simultaneous "feudal age" in China before Confucius. The Greek myths, Homeric stories, Chinese odes, Indian Vedas, and huge Egyptian temples of the thousand years before the Sixth Century B.C. have their counterparts in the later Medieval cathedrals and legends of chivalry. Today, we are moving toward a future age beginning in 2385 that will also be otherworldly, but where Medieval Humanity looked up from Earth to a God in the sky, future Humanity will look down from the sky to the God/Goddess on Earth. Society will be organized in a true hierarchy of spiritual attainment.

Whether we are moving up or down in the Great Cycle seems to affect our view of history. We have been moving upward from the Nadir since A.D. 411, so we have come to believe in "progress," as opposed to the ancients of Greek and Roman times who were moving downward from the heights of the Midheaven, and thought of their world as declining. They looked back to a lost arcadian "golden age," while we see it coming in the future. By 2385, however, we will have arrived back at the top of the wheel. Perhaps then "progress" will end and paradise will return, only to be succeeded by another "decline," or perhaps by then we will have outgrown these deceptive myths!

Using this same Cosmic Clock, we can see the cycle (popularized by Joseph Campbell) in which the great Western civilizations have risen and declined through three stages—spiritual, political, and economic. In his view, a new civilization is full of creative energy, inspired by vibrant spiritual and religious experiences. Myths and imagery guide and uplift the people. As the culture begins to lose touch with its original vitality, however, political motives take over. Finally, the spirit is lost altogether and the culture is concerned only about economic security. On the other hand, power and opportunity are given to more people as time goes on. In this sense there is "progress" as well as decline. Campbell pointed out that each of these stages was demonstrated in Western history by which kind of building dominated the urban landscape. In the medieval town the first thing you saw when you entered it was the cathedral, while in the Renaissance town it was the palace, and in the modern city it is the bank or commercial office building.

We can trace this process more or less repeating itself three times in the history of Western civilization, corresponding to the 2,000-year movement up and down the vertical axis of the Great Cycle. Western European culture began in the Dark Ages at the otherworldly angle of the Nadir in 411. Spirituality dominated while Uranus was in the Fourth and Fifth Houses of the Great Cycle. When it passed into the Seventh House of "relationships" in the Renaissance, politics and diplomacy became dominant, while our own times are ruled by the economic concerns and corporate power of the Eighth House of "shared resources."

The same pattern happened with Greek and Roman cultures, which began at the Midheaven in 1565 B.C. In their first thousand years as Uranus passed through the Tenth and Twelfth Houses, the Greeks created their great myths and stories. When Uranus reached the assertive First House in 575 B.C., political power became all important in the affairs of both cultures. Economic concerns took first place in the Roman Empire when Uranus reached the Second House of money.

We see the same in the ancient Near East. Five thousand years ago, the vibrant cities of Sumeria were religious centers where the first great myth (the Epic of Gilgamesh) was born. The Sumerians built great temples during the thousand years when Uranus was moving up from the Nadir of 3539 B.C. After Uranus reached the Descendant in 2552 B.C., the first great law codes were created at Ur, and aristocrats increasingly took power from the priests. Warfare increased (Seventh House) and the first empire (Sargon I) appeared. As Ur fell to Babylon (Eighth House, the parallel to our times), increasing disorder and uncertainty caused people to depend more and more on money and possessions for security. The wars had dispersed the land and wealth among the people, and this stimulated the growth of commerce.

THE FOUR QUADRANTS

The horoscope is divided into four quadrants, which mirror Jung's four psychological functions. Intuition (or conception) is linked to the lower east quadrant, feeling to the lower west, sensation to the upper west, and thinking to the upper east. When we tie these meanings of the four quadrants to the Cosmic Clock of Civilization, we find that they reveal the way in which people of the various periods understood and functioned in their world. (See the diagram below.)

The houses below the horizon (the humanist axis) are subjective and personal, while the houses above the horizon are objective and interpersonal. The eastern half of the horoscope is self-reliant and self-aware, while the western half is in relationship and aware of others. The first or lower-east quadrant is subjective self awareness (which means intuition), and the second or lower-west quadrant is subjective awareness of others (or feeling). The third

THE QUADRANTS AND THE COSMIC CLOCK

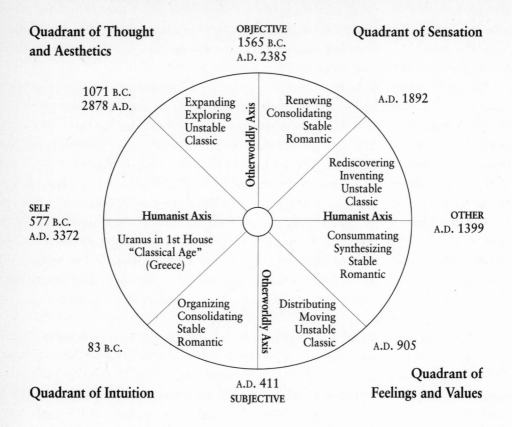

**Quadrant of Thought
and Aesthetics**

OBJECTIVE
1565 B.C.
A.D. 2385

Quadrant of Sensation

1071 B.C.
2878 A.D.

A.D. 1892

Expanding
Exploring
Unstable
Classic

Renewing
Consolidating
Stable
Romantic

Otherworldly Axis

Rediscovering
Inventing
Unstable
Classic

SELF
577 B.C.
A.D. 3372

Humanist Axis

Humanist Axis

OTHER
A.D. 1399

Uranus in 1st House
"Classical Age"
(Greece)

Consummating
Synthesizing
Stable
Romantic

Organizing
Consolidating
Stable
Romantic

Otherworldly Axis

Distributing
Moving
Unstable
Classic

83 B.C.

A.D. 905

Quadrant of Intuition

A.D. 411
SUBJECTIVE

**Quadrant of
Feelings and Values**

or upper-west quadrant is objective awareness of others (sensation), while the fourth or upper-east quadrant is objective self-awareness (thinking). The horizon represents immediate, direct experience (intuition on the east, sensation on the west). The meridian or vertical axis represents indirect experience and interpretation (feeling at the Nadir, thinking at the Midheaven).

The first quadrant from 577 B.C. to A.D. 411 (the classical world), extending from the Ascendant to the Nadir, functioned by intuition. Certainly, that describes the meditating Buddha and his followers, who gained intense, direct experience of four "noble truths." The Greeks were intuitive in a different way, seeking knowledge for its own sake and the first principles underlying all things. They arrived at their ideas not by experiment, but by conceiving. The Pythagorean theorem, Plato's forms, Archimedean mechanics, and Confucian sayings are examples of intuitive first principles that illuminated the entire world.

The Medieval world from 411 to 1399 (from the Nadir to the Descendant) fell into the quadrant of feeling. In this age, religions like Christianity reigned supreme over human minds. Certainly, "feeling" describes how emotionally devoted the Christians were to their savior and to the saints and relics of their faith, and how they cowered in fear and terror before God's judgment. No longer content with mere first principles, Medieval Christians used them in their emotional judgments of people as good or evil. Although the Greeks and Jews had conceived moral principles, Augustine and his successors from 413 onwards converted evil into "sin." Medieval philosophers took over the classical ideas and built on them an elaborate system of categories with which to interpret and order their lives.

Our modern world from 1399 to 2385 (from the Descendant to the Midheaven) certainly functions by sensation. As the light of Uranus came over the horizon in the West in Renaissance times, philosophers and scientists announced that "seeing is believing." Explorers promptly ventured forth to discover the external, visible world. The scientific method depends on sensation for evidence to prove its claims. Modern thinkers rigorously stick to the facts of experience on which subsequent analysis is based. We seek all kinds of sensations and experiences for their own sake, and the media creates "sensational" cult heroes. Unlike the ancients, we do not depend on our own minds alone for the truth. Ancient principles were static and based on truths supposed to be eternal. Modern principles are dynamic and must be tested and put into practice within the laboratory of experience. Our quadrant is the most worldly and pragmatic of all, applying the results of our experiments to generate material benefits on a scale never before imagined.

In time, our vivid personal experiences and practical knowledge will lead us back to a new age of faith, due when we reach the Midheaven in 2385 and enter the quadrant of thinking. This will not be the kind of thinking we know today, however, because the Midheaven is otherworldly and indirect as well as objective. The new type of thinking will revive the mythic, interpretive approach that is based on hidden, subtle truths rather than obvious ones, suggesting and evoking its conclusions instead of directly stating them. The epics, odes, and Vedas of pre-classical times that fell in the same quadrant are examples of this kind of thinking. As in Medieval times, we can expect elaborate systems of thought that interpret the *meaning* of the experiences that our modern world has so thoroughly observed and analyzed. The new Holistic thought will embue knowledge with significance; it will be richly and deeply symbolic of spiritual ideas and magical rites, like the mythologies of old.

We of the Eighth House or Scorpio period bear a special responsibility to transform ourselves so that this process of evolution can continue. As Dane Rudhyar has suggested, at the beginning of our Great Cycle, when the Greeks rejected the old myths and gods in favor of rational knowledge and abstract ideals, we lost our instinctive sense of quality. We became separate individuals and began to destroy the collective sense of community which more "primitive" peoples possess. We divided God from nature and began losing our sense of the Earth as sacred and alive. If we are to further our original quest to become free, conscious human beings in a universally valid moral order, we must go back to our roots 2,500 years ago, heal these rifts within us, and rediscover the sacred in all things.

Chapter 5 Endnotes

1. Thanks to Professor Marie Fox for the phrase "Age of Light" to describe this period.

6

The Three Revolutions:

THE URANUS-PLUTO CYCLE

Neptune and Pluto are our guides to the growth and decay of civilizations on planet Earth, but inventive, eccentric Uranus has a crucial part to play too, as we've seen. Besides being the "hour hand" on the cosmic clock of civilization, it helps us understand the great revolutions that happen periodically in our society.

Uranus aligns with Pluto every 110 to 130 years or so (127 on average). This is a loud signal to humanity that an earth-shaking, revolutionary transformation has begun. Uranus was discovered late in the Eighteenth Century during the American, French, and Industrial Revolutions. It has come to signify revolutionary events. Pluto, discovered just as the Great Depression broke, has come to represent deep, explosive social transformations and the power of "the group." Therefore, when these two planets come together, a great revolution begins that not only topples governments, but starts a whole movement, one which shapes the goals of all subsequent revolutions. Whenever Uranus and Pluto join forces, the status quo is seriously threatened. People jump ahead decades or even centuries and boldly experiment with radically different ways of being and living together. Afterward, they are brought "back to reality" to gradually try to make the new ideals work under the existing conditions.

Many of us remember the Uranus-Pluto combination vividly, when these planets last joined together during the turbulent 1960s. As I said previously, I wondered what in heaven could explain the extraordinary social changes and the spontaneous, spiritual awakenings that so many of us experienced simultaneously at this time. After learning the meaning of the three outer planets, I concluded that at least two of them must then be lining up, and when I checked I discovered I was right—that Uranus and Pluto were conjunct.

People who oppose the great cultural and social movements of the '60s say they were just passing fads at best, and the root of current moral decline at worst, but the Uranus-Pluto conjunction of that era means that these movements are actually just the beginning of a decades-long cycle of revolution that will eventually transform all of society. So in a sense these critics are correct—the old values *are* being undermined, as they *always are* under this influence. We should never forget that in our modern times today's "Establishment" is always due to the efforts of yesterday's "revolutionaries."

Uranus-Pluto conjunctions contrast sharply with Uranus-Neptune, as we'll see in the next chapter. Whereas the Uranus-Neptune conjunction often resolves and unifies (or confuses), Uranus-Pluto unleashes new creative impulses. Let's look back in history and see whether it's really true that society is transformed when Uranus and Pluto come together.

In ancient times, Uranus-Pluto conjunctions coincided with such events as the outbreak of the Peloponnesian war, the death of Alexander the Great (after which his empire broke up), the Roman slave revolt of Spartacus, and the founding of Constantinople. Five years after the conjunction of 1090, Pope Urban suddenly and dramatically announced the First Crusade in 1095, opening an inspired, creative age of European expansion. Soon after the conjunction of 1343–44, the Black Death of 1346–49 wiped out half of Europe and eroded the foundations of feudal Catholic society. The following conjunction in Leo in 1455–56 coincided with the invention of printing, which gave all future revolutionary movements their prime weapon. Two years before, in 1453, Constantinople succumbed to the same conjunction under which it had been founded, as the city fell to Turkish invaders. Scholars fleeing west then propelled the Renaissance into high gear. During the Uranus-Pluto conjunction in Aries in 1597–98 Baroque art and music were invented, and Galileo opened the scientific revolution. French King Henry IV ended the Wars of Religion in his country by freeing the dissident Huguenots in the Edict of Nantes.

THREE GREAT REVOLUTIONS

The Uranus-Pluto conjunction at the end of Leo in 1710–11 was the first of three great revolutions whose impact has dominated modern history. The first revolution opened with the first incendiary works of Voltaire around 1711. The authorities were so incensed at him that they locked him up in the infamous Bastille prison, thus turning him into the great hero of liberty. Freemasonry began a few years afterward, spreading revolutionary ideas through secret societies. Some of the greatest minds of the Eighteenth Century joined them, including many of America's "founding fathers." In 1715 Louis XIV died, immediately setting off a reaction against the absolute rule of the Bourbons. Something similar happened in England in 1714, when George I was brought over from Germany to succeed Queen Anne.

It became easier to question authority in this new, more irreverent atmosphere. The Baroque phase of culture passed into the Rococo, typified by the more relaxed, sensuous, elegant style pioneered by the painter Watteau in 1712. Signs of even more disruptive upheavals came when iron smelting and the Newcomen steam pump were invented the very same year. The Industrial Revolution was on the horizon.

The goal of the Enlightenment and the first great revolution that began with the Uranus-Pluto conjunction of 1711 was individual liberty. The leaders of the movement, such as Voltaire, wanted to overthrow the Kings who claimed power by divine right, and replace them with governments whose rule depended on the consent of the governed. They wanted to protect free speech, free inquiry, and other human rights against the capricious power of Church and State, and to destroy the unfair privileges of the priests and nobility. In fact, most of our modern conceptions of a free, democratic state are based on their works. Representing the rising power of the bourgeoisie and merchant classes, they also protested against institutions, tariffs, and regulations that restricted free enterprise, but the nobility reasserted its power and successfully blocked the efforts of the reformers. A great confrontation seemed inevitable. Many leaders of the movement were born during the conjunction, such as the encyclopedist Diderot (1713), the skeptical philosopher Hume (1711), and above all Jean Jacques Rousseau (1712).

After every conjunction comes the Uranus-Pluto opposition, about halfway through the cycle. Its impact is often as great or greater than the conjunction. In fact, when Uranus stands opposite to Pluto in the heavens, the revolutionary movement reaches its peak. We are at the Full Moon of the movement, and the light of this "Full Uranus" lasts over an entire generation. This pattern took hold most noticeably from the Renaissance onward. For example, right after Uranus opposed Pluto in 1395, Henry Bolingbroke led a rebellion against King Richard II of England. A similar upheaval took place in France. Henry IV took power in England, but when the next conjunction came along in 1455, another rebellion broke out (the Wars of the Roses), leading to the Tudor takeover.

Another great revolutionary full moon came in 1649, the year Charles I met his fate at the hands of Oliver Cromwell and the Great Rebellion. The absolute rule of the English kings was forever overthrown and gradually thereafter replaced by today's parliamentary system. Puritans and other religious dissidents challenged the Church of England and gained their freedom. Simultaneously, the Fronde revolt in France challenged Louis XIV, although this attempt eventually failed. At the same time Descartes was expanding the scientific revolution begun by Gallileo.

This brings us back to the movement that started in 1711. By the 1780s it was moving toward its "Full Moon"—the most awesome one of all. Charles I lost his head in England during the Uranus-Pluto opposition of 1649, and Louis XVI lost his head in France during the Uranus-Pluto opposition of 1793. The first great modern cycle of revolution came to its climax in the French Revolution. Aristocratic power was smashed, and bourgeois power took its place. A great charter of liberties was proclaimed, inspired by the American revolution a few years before. The French revolution set into motion that "engine of liberty" which transformed the nations and peoples of the world, making them fiercely loyal not to their king or even their God, but to their revolution and their nation. Its slogan of "liberty, equality and fraternity" not only encapsulated its own aims, but the goals of all three modern revolutionary movements, each in turn.

Just as Oliver Cromwell seized the reins of the Great Rebellion and became a despot, the French Revolution was seized by the "despotism of liberty" and the Reign of Terror. Napoleon took power soon afterward. The opposition is always the climax of the revolutionary movement, but it brings conflict and schism, too. In our modern revolutionary age, old tyrants are often replaced by new ones. The old revolution becomes the new despotism, and new rebels arrive to challenge the revolutionary power of the old rebels.

The first great revolution unleashed the tyranny of Napoleon, but more importantly, it created the tyranny of the bourgeoisie. The commercial and business interests that rose to power in the French and Industrial Revolutions eventually became even more oppressive than the aristocrats they had replaced. The new capitalist industry dehumanized and practically enslaved millions of workers. This was an intolerable situation for the heirs of the Revolution, and inevitably, socialism emerged to challenge the power of capitalism.

The people moved into action during the next Uranus-Pluto conjunction in 1850, at the cusp of Aries-Taurus. This movement erupted at virtually the same moment as Neptune's discovery in 1846, the planet that came to represent self-surrender and compassion. The second great revolution was launched, and its goal was not liberty, but equality. The movement's leaders wanted to overthrow not only the king, but also the capitalists by taking control of the "means of production." They saw that individual freedom alone often just allows the strong to oppress the weak, so they wanted to use the state to break the power of the business class and put it in the hands of the working class. They wanted to protect society from the greed of the individual; they exalted cooperation and collective identity above the competitive spirit. The masses rose up in revolutions throughout the European continent in 1848, and in China in 1850 in the Taiping Rebellion (the most massive uprising in history). Also in 1848, Karl Marx described the aims of the new movement in *The Communist Manifesto*. Social realists like Engels, Courbet, Millet, and Dickens vividly portrayed the plight of poor workers, and humanitarians demanded proper treatment of the sick and downtrodden for the first time in human history.

The new socialist movement was easily crushed at first, but Marx saw that as industry and capitalism expanded, the proletariat would become stronger. Each succeeding crisis of "boom and bust" would bring the revolution close. So even as the movement was crushed in 1850, the industrial machine went into high gear. Greed went unchecked, and society became ever more divided along class lines. The second great cycle reached its climax at the opposition at the turn of the Twentieth Century (1901), when labor unions and socialist parties expanded as they never have before or since. A more violent labor movement (syndicalism) exploded at the same time, while the "muckrakers" aimed their pens at the evils of capitalism and launched the progressive movement. European imperialism suffered a black eye around 1901 through the Boer War, the Chinese Boxer Rebellion and elsewhere, and "anti-imperialism" became an integral part of the Communist program.

In 1902–03, Lenin's Bolsheviks split from the other Russian Communists and took over the movement. In 1905, the Russian revolution against the Tsar went into high gear, and exploded in the greatest socialist upheaval yet. In 1917, Lenin founded the Soviet Union, which institutionalized socialism. Once in power, the Communists unleashed their own "reign of terror" that was far longer and deeper than the French one. Instead of the "despotism of liberty," they created the "dictatorship of the proletariat." The turn of the Twentieth Century thus represented another generation of revolutionary change that corresponded to the "full moon" or opposition of Uranus and Pluto in 1901.

Throughout the remainder of the second revolutionary cycle, socialism and communism advanced relentlessly, and half the world came under the "red" sway. Even in "democratic" countries, socialism made gains. The communist and democratic-socialist movements succeeded in making people more equal in wealth and improved living standards, but in so doing, it reduced the individual to an anonymous cog in the industrial machine. As industry advanced, it destroyed the quality of life in many ways. It also threatened all life on Earth for the first time ever. Once again, a new tyrant had replaced the old; this time the tyrant was not only the greedy capitalist, but also the machine itself, and the monolithic, corporate, communist state which had swallowed individual identities. Since 1850, scientists and politicians alike had divided humanity into warring classes, races and nations, and the free spirit of the person was forgotten.

This is the background of the third great revolution, the movement of our own time. The next conjunction arrived in 1966 in the sign Virgo. The American military-industrial complex went haywire, as bureaucratic blindness and inertia caused the U.S. to stumble into the disastrous war in Vietnam. Youth turned to drugs and the occult and dropped out of industrial society, and authority and conformity were challenged at all levels. The U.S. was rocked by massive protests against the war, and by minority groups asserting their civil rights. Revolutions attempted to overthrow the state in France and Czechoslovakia, and the worldwide student movement shut down universities and blocked military activities everywhere. In China, the Red Guard hit the streets. The long-term result of the "cultural revolution" excesses of the Red Guard in 1966 was to discredit Chairman Mao and his brand of communism. This, coupled with the Czech movement, would eventually inspire radical reforms in China and throughout the Communist world.

What do the revolutionaries of the third movement want? Its political aims can be summed up in three words: peace, ecology, brother/sisterhood. We who believe in this revolution want an end to war. We want to save the planet from destruction. We want all people to join together as brothers and sisters in one common family, a true human "fraternity." We ask you to "imagine," as John Lennon did, a world without rigid borders of race, sex, creed or nationality.

In order to have true peace outside, we must also gain peace inside. Therefore, the third revolution is not only political, but cultural and spiritual, too. We want to discover the life and spirit within us and to explore psychic and spiritual dimensions. We want creative freedom to pursue our own life and career path and to "follow our bliss," as Joseph Campbell said. We want to get off the industrial treadmill and live according to our true values. We declare, as Patrick McGoohan's television character in *The Prisoner* did in 1966, that "I am not a number, I am a person;" that no dehumanizing system or institution shall entrap and enslave us. Culturally, the '60s opened up new styles which are still developing, such as "visionary," "psychedelic," "New Age," and "World Fusion." Womens' Liberation (Uranus-Pluto in Virgo, the Virgin), is also dramatically transforming our culture (N.O.W. formed in 1966). Just as they and others we call "minorities" empower themselves, so we all are also throwing off outdated social roles and recovering the "feminine," less domineering side of their nature.

The new movement has superseded the old ones, though the goals of the first two revolutions remain. Wherever human rights and liberty are denied, there is the place for the first revolution. Wherever the working class remains in poverty and subjection, there is the place for the second. The vanguard of change now rests with the third revolution, however. Its aims underlie all movements from the 1960s on. The two older movements still dominated political parties in most nations as late as the 1990s, but their ideals are now as much a part of the past as a part of the future—as much a part of the problem as a part of the solution. In the New Millennium, the ideals of the third revolution will increasingly come to dominate our politics, and many of its goals, such as saving the planet, building peace and bringing the creative spirit back into our public life, will gradually be achieved.

Marx believed that *his* movement was the synthesis of previous movements, since he couldn't conceive of another one beyond it. In fact, the *third* revolution is the new synthesis. The first revolution exalted liberty for the individual (and still does). The second revolution (Marx's) exalted equality and society's rights over the individual (and still does). The third revolution exalts fraternity, or the individual in interdependent, creative relationship to society and the planet. It proposes unity within diversity. It's ultimate symbol is ecology, the union of all life which enhances the quality of life of each individual. The "green revolution" answers the crying needs of our time—survival of the planet, and of our own humanity. Thus, green replaces red as the new radical color.

The dual planet Pluto in its higher phase of renewal is the planet of this cycle (its lower phase of death was fascism, which erupted after its discovery in 1930). The asteroid/planetoid Chiron, discovered in 1977, is the symbol of the "wounded healer." It moves between Saturn and Uranus, and is also linked to the third movement. It represents the "keys" to help us access transcendent or invisible realms and integrate them into our lives on Earth. These include such things as holistic and New Age techniques and information technology.

Despite the attempts by reactionaries to stem the tide, time is on our side. The third revolution is only starting; it will have over 100 years to succeed. The opposition may desperately try to reconstruct the walls that have held down the human spirit: fixed roles, racial division, fanatic religion, warring nations, oppressive corporations, a polluted environment, and denial of our own spirit. They may even seem to grow stronger, just as the aristocrats did before they crumbled in the French Revolution. In the end, it's inevitable that the walls will fall, just as the Berlin Wall did—it's "in the stars." Whether they fall easily, or whether we fall into a worse tyranny (i.e. apathetic self-indulgence, or excesses in any of our goals) is up to us.

The climax of the new movement will come in the middle of the next century. It will bring down many of the big institutions that harm the environment and block our creativity, and will further shift our lifestyles toward inclusiveness and mutual respect. After that will come further movements. If 1966 represents a new Renaissance, as did the conjunction of 1456, then the next Uranus-Pluto conjunction in 2103 will bring a new "baroque" phase.

There are so many ways to participate in today's Revolution and Renaissance. Find yourself, and share your new life with those around you. Work for peace on Earth. Find a way off the industrial treadmill. Stand up for your rights, and those of others. Support organizations helping to save the planet. Already, we saw the movement make its mark in Germany in the early 1980s with the Green Party (interestingly, the first socialist parties also gained strength in Germany). Now similar parties are springing up everywhere, as I predicted they would, but their original inspiration all came from the movements here in the U.S. in the 1960s. Those who propose a third party or a new politics in America or elsewhere coild do no better than to adopt the name and program of the Green Party. However you participate, *now* is the time. The new revolution is happening, and you can help to shape it.

URANUS-PLUTO CYCLE.
Virtually all revolutions in modern history correspond to the aspects between Uranus and Pluto. Below is a list of past events and future predictions, corresponding to their contacts

Date	Aspect	Revolutionary Events
1711	Conjunction	Freemasonry, rococo reaction, Voltaire's writings
1730	Semi-square	No known correlation.
1759–60	Square	Seven Years War, which led to "enlightened despotism" in Prussia
1776	Sesq-square	American Revolution (this aspect appears in the U.S. horoscope)
1793	Opposition	Height of the French Revolution
1808	Sesq-square	Risings in Germany and Spain against Napoleon
1820	Square	Unrest in Britain and revolts in Europe and South America
1830	Sextile	Revolutions in France, Belgium, Poland, first British Reform Bill and attendant disturbances (Uranus also in Aquarius)
1834	Semi-square	Mass worker uprisings in France and England
1850	Conjunction	Revolutions in Europe (1848-51); Taiping Rebellion (China)
1863	Semi-square	Great uprising in Poland against Russian rule
1867–68	Sextile	Series of government reorganizations in Europe and the U.S.; overthrow of the Shoguns in Japan
1876	Square	Massive revolts against Turkish rule in the Balkans
1889	Sesq-square	Strikes and farmer-labor unrest
1901	Opposition	Boxer Rebellion, Philippine revolt, Progressivism, Bolshevism
1917	Sesq-square	Russian Revolution creates Soviet Union; Arab revolts against the Turks, etc. (Uranus also in Aquarius)
1933	Square	Fascist revolution in Germany; New Deal
1943	Sextile	During World War II
1949	Semi-square	Communist revolution in China

1966	Conjunction	Cultural Revolution, Black Power, peace and ecology movements
1986	Semi-square	Philippine "people's revolt" against Marcos
1996	Sextile	Latin American and Asian liberation movements; corporate crisis in America (Uranus in Aquarius)
2012–13	Square	Major revolts in the wake of economic/ecological disasters and refugee problems; "crossover" into the New Age (Mayan calendar)
2032	Sesq-square	Turbulent reorganizations and ethnic upheavals shake America, Asia, nations ruled by Cancer (Saturn conjunct Uranus
2047	Opposition	Climax of the third revolution

THE THREE REVOLUTIONS AND THEIR GOALS

Revolution	Dominant in	Ruling planet	Emphasis	Ideal:
1st Revolution	1711–1850	Uranus	Ideas, innovations	Liberty
2nd Revolution	1850–1966	Neptune	Productive forces	Equality
3rd Revolution	1966–2103	Pluto/Chiron	People, spirituality	Fraternity

Original form in the 1790s	Core value	Class	Color(s)
Political	Individual	Bourgeoisie	Red, white, blue
Industrial	Collective	Proletariat	Red
Romantic	Creative	Outcasts	Green

Government	Economics	Philosophy	Religion
Democracy	Capitalist	Rationalist	Deist
Communist	Socialist	Materialist	Atheist
Cooperative	Ecological	Spiritualist	New Age

WHAT THE NEW REVOLUTION WILL MEAN FOR YOU

The years surrounding 1966 brought personal crisis and discovery for many people. What changed in your life in the mid-'60s? What does the Uranus-Pluto conjunction and the third revolution mean for you today?

Every time any two of the outer three planets come together, a radical shift happens in society. It is as if we've entered a whole new world. The conjunction leaves its firm imprint on all of our lives. Wherever the most recent conjunction of its kind falls in your own horoscope shows its meaning in your life. It may also show what role you have to play in the continuing social and cultural trends it represents. Wherever the Uranus-Pluto conjunction of 1966 happened in your chart shows how you are responding to the challenge of today's revolutionary movement, and how you might contribute to it.

Were you born between the fall of 1962 and the fall of 1969? If so, the revolutionary Uranus-Pluto conjunction in Virgo appears in your own horoscope and is very significant in your life. You can become an inventive genius, a brilliant scientist, a computer engineer, an inspired poet, a social critic, a charismatic revolutionary leader, or a skilled creative artist. You can set the trends for many decades to come, unless you let your cynical attitudes lead you to apathy and self-destruction.

The conjunction remains in force until 2103, and applies regardless of what year you were born. Reading the paragraph below for your birthday will give you some immediate clues. In general, those born closest to the dates specifically mentioned below will have felt the conjunction strongest. For example, those born on September 9 will have felt the strongest impact. Those born at the beginning of any period (for example, near August 9) will also need to read the next paragraph (e.g., late Cancer, early Leo). Since you're on the "cusp," it may also apply—and very strongly, too!

In the listings below, "early" means before the middle of a sign; "late" means after it. For example, "early Aries" means Aries between 1–16 degrees, or where the Sun is between March 21 and April 6. If you know your rising sign (Ascendant) and degree, you may also want to read the paragraph for that sign and combine what it says with the other paragraph. If you know your birth time, you can consult Appendix B to see approximately how close your Ascendant is to 16 degrees of any sign. If it was close, the conjunction was very significant in your life.

August 9–September 9 (late Leo, early Virgo birthdays): The conjunction of 1966 happened in conjunction with your Sun in a "First House" position. It has stimulated you to express the creative energies of the New Revolution through your forceful, charismatic personality. Because of your passionate desire to serve others, you may be a leader in today's social and cultural movements. You also may have found a successful avenue for your heightened creative abilities. You are called on to burst through all inhibitions and fully share the essence of who you are. You can transform yourself through intense self-awareness, involving not only meditation, but especially more active physical movement trainings such as Feldenkrais, the Alexander technique, martial arts, sports, dance, etc. You should make your voice, body and appearance a vehicle for today's revolutionary styles of expression. You are becoming a pioneer who can show the way for others into the future.

July 9–August 8 (late Cancer, early Leo): The conjunction happened in a "Second House" position in relation to your Sun. You are called on to "declare your independence" from subservience to others and follow your own methods of making a living through developing your original talents. Finances will continue to be unstable for you, but the more creative you are, the better luck you'll have. You'll need to reassess your attitude to money and property and make sure it doesn't become the "bottom line" of your life. You can transform yourself by developing personal resourcefulness and learning to profit from any situation. The arts are an excellent avenue for you to express your response to the revolutionary energies of our times.

June 8–July 8 (late Gemini, early Cancer): The conjunction of 1966 happened in a "Third House" position in relation to your Sun. You are called upon to transform yourself through improving your communication skills. Writing and speaking will be your best avenue to express the ideals of the third revolution and help them (and yourself) to succeed; the more original your thoughts and ideas, the more success you'll have. Your beliefs changed radically in the '60s, and may go on changing—you may even violently disagree with the ideas you held just the year before. If you find that you are too full of thoughts, and that your mind has become radical or unstable, then some type of meditation practice should help you to focus. Your inventive talents could be quite profitable. Seek to meet and learn from many different people as long as possible. The revolution for you is a mental gymnasium and a kaleidoscope of educational wonders.

May 8–June 7 (late Taurus, early Gemini): The conjunction squared your Sun in a "Fourth House" position. You have probably undergone many changes in your home and family life. They may have been disrupted by the turbulent '60s, and you are now struggling with the issue of "family values." You can transform yourself by gaining greater knowledge of your personal roots and deepening your relationship to the land and the Earth. You have undergone profound changes in consciousness. You can learn to tap the growing power of your subconscious mind, which has become linked to the collective unconscious through Uranus and Pluto. Record your dreams, use a journal or hypnosis to access these hidden powers, and your success will multiply. New talents have unfolded, and your life has taken new directions since the '60s. You are used to scurrying after money and/or scattering your energies, but now you wish to find a quiet place inside yourself and a loving, supportive family or social network to restore your spirits. Express the "new renaissance" by getting involved with efforts to protect our fragile planet.

April 7–May 7 (late Aries, early Taurus): The conjunction trined your Sun in a "Fifth House" position. This means that many favorable opportunities will keep coming to you for personal expression. The "revolution" encourages you to stay young and enjoy life as much as possible. Sex and romance are wonderful avenues to transform yourself, and theater or the arts are good outlets to express your response to the creative impulses of the times. Your natural self-reliance will encourage you to design a successful career path which allows you to follow your heart. Working with children through education or recreation is a great way for you to promote the new ideals. Sudden disaster could come through gambling and speculation, so look before you leap into risky ventures.

March 8–April 6 (late Pisces, early Aries): The conjunction happened in a "Sixth House" position in relation to your Sun. You are called upon to help through dedicated service to others. You are keenly aware of all the issues we need to face and are deeply involved in the social movements of our time and with organizations dedicated to helping people. Fitness, diet, and how human nutrition affects other living things may also concern you, since you are probably interested in health and animal rights. You can transform yourself through self-analysis, volunteer efforts at helping others, and submitting to the regimen of a training program or the help of a spiritual teacher. You are finding it increasingly useful to retreat from the world periodically so you can restore yourself and reflect on your ideals. Of course, if you are an Aries, you will be eager to get back into the fray and push hard for the things you believe in.

February 6–March 7 (late Aquarius, early Pisces birthdays): The conjunction of 1966 happened opposite your Sun in a "Seventh House" position. Your marriage or other close relationships may have been disrupted in the '60s, and you continue to meet many creative and strange people who inspire you to move in new directions. You will need to work hard to keep the destabilizing influence of today's revolutionary currents from disrupting your relationships, and it may be good to experiment with unusual parnerships and "open relationships." You have been called to share your creative, imaginative, and visionary talents in a more public way. You may often find yourself involved in controversies or personal clashes over issues related to today's revolutionary movement.

January 7–February 5 (late Capricorn, early Aquarius): The conjunction happened in an "Eighth House" position in relation to your Sun. Your financial arrangements with your spouse or partners may have been disrupted by the turbulent effect of the '60s revolution on your marriage and family life. You may have had continuing challenges involving your mortgage, loans, taxes or inheritance. You can find a route toward transformation through joining communes or forming joint creative business ventures. Intimate communion with others has become more important to you. Your natural ambition to wield power in order to change society may be frustrated, forcing you to alter your approach. Your ability to penetrate occult wisdom and develop magical powers may have been stimulated, and you may have had strong mystical or near-death experiences.

December 9–January 6 (late Sagittarius, early Capricorn): The conjunction trined your Sun in a "Ninth House" position. It may have stimulated you to travel widely and learn from other cultures. You can see how the revolutionary trends and shifting values of our time may affect the future. You also find that you are having to transform your own values to find real success or fulfillment in your career. Transformation can come through higher education or organized religion. Your dreams and visions are very vivid, and your interest in philosophy or higher thought is keen. You identify with all of humanity and its struggles for liberation around the world.

November 9–December 8 (late Scorpio, early Sagittarius): The conjunction squared your Sun in a "Tenth House" position. It has probably stimulated your ambition. It may be your role to directly challenge the powers-that-be as a revolutionary activist, or (if you are a conservative) to champion and wield authority against today's currents of change. Your career may have been disrupted in the '60s and continues to be unstable. However, you could transform your life and gain fame and status through developing your own original ideas, especially if you can get the financial support of others. You could be someone who's working to change the power structure to allow more people to participate in decision making. You definitely need to discover and follow the path that matches your inner drives and desires.

October 10-November 8 (late Libra, early Scorpio): The conjunction happened in an "Eleventh House" position in relation to your Sun. This means you can apply the wealth you are gaining through your profession to benefit your friends and ideals. Personal transformation comes through group activities and associations dedicated to causes aligned with today's revolutionary movement, and through sharing your musical, theatrical, and other creative talents. You meet many exciting people who inspire you to expand your life. You can become a visionary whose utopian fantasies and elaborate plans become models for the society of the future. You can inspire others to keep going because you are so filled with hope and optimism.

September 10-October 9 (late Virgo, early Libra): The conjunction happened in a "Twelfth House" position in relation to your Sun. It has stimulated you to analyze and uncover the hidden, karmic sources of the problems in your life. You are called on to improve your spiritual and physical health, and free yourself from fears due to past social rejection. You can transform your life by becoming a spiritual seeker and developing your psychic or mediumistic powers, and by sharing your heightened sensitivity through your craftsmanship or artistic talents. Psychedelic drugs may appeal to you, but approach them very carefully. Your compassion may lead you into medicine or service work for humanitarian causes, or you may become a reclusive hermit in order to explore the inner dimensions of your being. You may rebel against big bureaucracies that destroy personal identity. You may also get involved in secret conspiracies within giant institutions, but if you skirt the law or your own sanity, you could end up in a big "institution" yourself.

URANUS-PLUTO ON THE ANGLES

If you know the time you were born, consult Appendix B to find out if the Uranus-Pluto conjunction happened on one of the *angles* of your horoscope (the Ascendant, Midheaven, Descendant, or Nadir). If so, it has had a particularly powerful impact on your life, and may continue to do so. If "16° Virgo" is listed under one of the angles for your birth time (within thirty minutes or so), Uranus-Pluto was on that angle in your chart. The closer it is, the stronger it is! If Uranus or Pluto was located on one of the angles of your own natal horoscope when you were born, the conjunction has stimulated the meaning of these planets in your life from 1966 on.

Uranus-Pluto on your Ascendant: Your personality has undergone radical change, and you have experienced a dynamic spiritual awakening of consciousness. You have become more magnetic and expressive. You made important new departures in 1966 and struck out on a new, independent, perhaps reckless course. You are a leader in (or enemy of) the social or cultural movements that began in the sixties. You have become intensely concerned to unfold yourself and your creative abilities and have made great progress. You may have some extraordinary inventions or new ideas to share with the world.

Uranus-Pluto on your Midheaven: Your career has undergone radical change. You probably lost your job or found a new one in 1966, and you may have embarked on a totally new profession. Your career has become a vehicle for advancing the ideals of the '60s or other great causes you believe in. It has become your personal mission to transform the world, and you want to do it in the spotlight. Your original ideas can lead to success and fame.

Uranus-Pluto on your Descendant: Your relationships have undergone radical change. You may have divorced in 1966 or shortly thereafter, and may have married and divorced again many times since. You have met so many eccentric and unusual people that your life has become a virtual kaleidoscope of strange experiences. Some of these people are intensely disturbing, but others have inspired you to take creative new directions or awakened your spiritual path. You are a public leader in (or opponent of) the movements begun in the '60s or other causes, but you have encountered staunch opposition. You may have experimented with alternative lifestyles.

Uranus-Pluto on your Nadir: Your home life has undergone radical and continuous change. You may have split from your parents or family, or perhaps declared an independent course of which they disapprove. If you occupied a powerful career position before 1966, you may have lost or transformed it. The conjunction struck the foundations of your soul and awakened your subconscious mind. You gained a new sense of communion with your community or the land and became connected to the "collective unconscious." Intense inner experiences in 1966 brought a major turning point in your life, reorienting your career goals and your life purpose. This earthquake at the core of your being has left you confused, forcing you to reorganize your whole approach to life, drop older interests and unfold new talents.

URANUS-PLUTO ON YOUR PLANETS

Are the Sun, Moon, or any of the planets in your horoscope located within five degrees of 16° Virgo? If so, they've been radically stimulated by the revolutionary rays of Uranus-Pluto. To find out where your planets are, you will need to consult an ephemeris for your birthdate or have a natal chart cast by an astrologer or chart service, since it is beyond the scope of this book to list all the dates.

Sun: You suddenly became a forceful, expressive, charismatic leader in spite of your Virgo reserve. You experienced dramatic awakenings of consciousness around 1966. You have embarked on a courageous, ambitious path of self-unfolding. You can be a revolutionary leader. Also read the section above for August 9–September 9 with special attention.

Moon: Your emotions and psychic abilities were awakened. Your home life and relationship with parents were altered. You manifest the revolution through unfolding your sensitivities. Also read the section above for May 8–June 7.

Mercury: Your mind and communication skills have been powerfully awakened. You have developed strikingly original ideas and can unfold magical or occult proclivities. You are keenly interested in the less fortunate. Your mushrooming scholarly and intellectual abilities are your best tools to advance the revolution.

Venus: Your artistic talents were awakened. You have endlessly analyzed your love life as a path toward personal growth. Your relationships keep changing. Contribute to the new renaissance by sharing your exotic, creative craftsmanship.

Mars: Your energies have been super-stimulated. Your keen and critical mind has been honed on all the tough issues of the '60s. You have continually broken through old limits and begun many new enterprises. You may have become a radical, passionate, outspoken champion of the oppressed; an unyielding foe of all authorities. You are intensely interested in health and fitness and have delved deeply into all of life's mysteries. Your intensity may have led you into crime, violence, sexual perversity or nervous breakdowns.

Jupiter: Your generosity and outlook have drastically expanded. Fortunate surprises have come your way. You have traveled extensively and made discoveries about other cultures. You pursue the revolution through your persinal largesse and thirst for wisdom.

Saturn: You have been stimulated to challenge old authorities or confront blocks within yourself. Your career path has been radically transformed. Ego defenses or parental fixations may block your goals, but your inner struggle with them has made you more creative. Your special task is to make the revolution an organized, working reality. Your contribution will be long-lasting.

Neptune: Your creative imagination was stimulated enormously. You became a revolutionary spiritual seeker and prophet. You can remold the world into your own image through your visionary musical and poetic talents, or by transforming big institutions. Meditation, hypnosis, or psychedelics may be found along your path, too.

7

Cultural Shifts:

THE URANUS-NEPTUNE CYCLE

Uranus and Neptune are the two planets that represent the most lofty and inspired experiences of humanity. Unlike Uranus-Pluto, which we covered in the previous chapter, conjunctions between Uranus and Neptune occur in a very regular cycle—every 171.4 years or so. This is three times more often than the conjunction between Neptune and Pluto, which has to do with the "fortunes of civilization." "Culture" generally has a more restricted meaning than "civilization," so I assume that this shorter cycle between Uranus and Neptune has to do with "culture."

An alignment between these two giants, which rule the two most humanitarian and idealistic signs of the zodiac (Aquarius and Pisces), is very significant. The word "culture" describes very well what the Uranus-Neptune conjunction means to us. It mostly boils down to four things. First, it stands for important creative developments which we usually call "cultural"—namely, the high peaks of achievement in the arts. Second, it profoundly affects the course of international affairs; the relationships between different cultures or nations. Third, in modern times the major Uranus-Neptune aspects bring revolutions, though these are less drastic than those which occur under Uranus-Pluto contacts. Finally, Uranus-Neptune conjunctions challenge and alter our most dearly-held beliefs and ideals, and mark the times when great religions are born. We could say that Uranus and Neptune bring spiritual or religious revolutions as well as political ones.

RESHAPING THE WORLD ORDER

A conjunction of Uranus and Neptune has been happening during most of my work on this book. Becoming exact in 1993, it lasted from about 1988 to 1998. Under it, we have witnessed the birth of a "New World Order," as President Bush named it—a major change in the relationships between nations. I foresaw that this would happen, having studied occurrences around the time of the previous Uranus-Neptune conjunction in 1821. A similar new world order was born then, after the defeat of Napoleon. Since these two conjunctions occurred in Capricorn, the sign of politics, the political effect has been even greater than usual.

When Uranus and Neptune join together, they combine the transcendental mind and heart of humanity. This indicates a chance to make giant leaps forward in our relationships with one another, on both the personal and international level. It is a splendid chance to look beyond the apparent (or "visible") realities around us, to rediscover the most profound truths of our lives, and to rededicate ourselves to fulfilling our deepest beliefs. Some have pointed out that this conjunction meant a "mid-life crisis" for the "baby boom generation" (born in the late 1940s and 1950s), but in reality, it has had this significance for all generations. When a great conjunction like this happens, it means humanity has come to a "fork in the road." It is a chance to start over after the slate has been wiped clean— a moment of decision when we must choose a path to destruction or a path of renewal. This is the key to the events of the 1990s. The end of the Cold War forced us to shift the direction of our lives and our society. Whether we move toward a peaceful, sustainable way of life that allows us to express our creative potential, or simply allow the destructive, depersonalizing, corporate, military-industrial society to continue, is the great issue we confront in the years after this great conjunction.

Uranus and Neptune have to do with whole peoples and cultures. The aspects between these two planets bring peoples and their governments into contact and (usually) conflict. Research shows that Uranus-Neptune has its most obvious and powerful impact on international affairs. The Uranus-Neptune conjunction represents a period when one set of international conflicts comes to an end and another one begins. Disputes are resolved that have disrupted relations between nations for decades, and a whole new structure is arranged that lasts for decades to come. In ages past, before the "democracy" of today, a new order was usually created by a powerful ruler or rulers who organized or restored a great empire or major kingdom. These enduring empires (principally in Europe and China) were the most influential in world history and did the most to advance civilization.

Neptune has to do with endings and conclusions, which is why this conjunction seems to wrap things up that have been unsettled for decades. Apparently though, shifting the international furniture around just allows new conflicts to surface that have been buried beneath the old ones, due to our insatiable appetite for acrimony. Whenever Uranus-Neptune aspects are in force, there are always major international tensions which may explode into war when Mars, Saturn and Pluto indicate the time is ripe. On the other hand, under Uranus-Neptune trines and conjunctions there is also always great opportunity for international cooperation.

Here is how Uranus-Neptune has shifted world order throughout history. The Peloponnesian War (which had begun under a Uranus-Pluto conjunction) ended in 404 B.C. during the Uranus-Neptune conjunction. The conjunction of 232 B.C. occurred in the last years of Ashoka's rule in India, which established the first Buddhist Empire. At the same time, Shih-huang-ti embarked on his campaign to build the first Chinese Empire (the Ch'in dynasty), which laid the basis of all succeeding empires and gave China its name. Under the conjunction of 61 B.C., Julius Caesar, Pompey, and Crassus formed the first Roman triumvirate, leading the way to the Roman Empire. In A.D. 112, the emperor Trajan established the Roman Empire's greatest extent of power. In 282, Diocletian restored the empire from collapse with a series of drastic reforms and reorganizations that prepared the way for the establishment of Christianity as the state religion under Constantine.

It was just a few years before the Uranus-Neptune conjunction of 623–24 (in 618) that the elegant new Tang Dynasty ended centuries of a splintered China. The Khmer Empire in Cambodia began about the same time, and Mohammed's flight from Mecca in 622 soon led to the Islamic Empire. Charlemagne established the Holy Roman Empire at the time of the conjunction of 794. He was crowned Emperor by Pope Leo on Christmas day, in the year 800. Otto the Great restored this empire in 962 after the Viking raids. Two years earlier, the Sung Dynasty restored the Chinese empire. Both these events happened just a few years before the Uranus-Neptune conjunction of 965. The conjunction of 1307 happened when King Philip the Fair of France made his kingdom more powerful than the Catholic Church. The conjunction of 1479 saw the decades-long Wars of the Roses come to an end, after which the Tudor Dynasty restored peace and order to England. Other European rulers like Ferdinand and Isabella of Spain consolidated their power around the same time. Under the conjunction of 1650, Louis XIV became the great "Sun King" and established French supremacy in Europe.

The Uranus-Neptune conjunction of 1650 (also opposed to Pluto and Saturn) was a perfect example of one international order superseding another. The Treaty of Westphalia in 1648 ended the Thirty-Years War and the wars of religion, and opened an era of wars among competing great powers. These wars revolved around the conflict between France and England. During the following square (around 1700), Louis XIV tried and failed to defeat England. During the opposition (around 1740), they fought with their allies over the royal succession in Austria, and during the square around 1780 they fought over the American Revolution. The conflict finally ended with the defeat of Napoleon in 1815, just before the next great Uranus-Neptune conjunction in 1821. The Vienna Conference of 1815 resolved all the disputes of the past and created a settlement that lasted for decades, but the treaty contained within it the seeds of all the conflicts of the following years, because it left unanswered the questions of national rights and boundaries.

The first of these conflicts was the war for Greek independence from the Turkish Empire, which broke out during the conjunction of 1821. This vast empire ruled over virtually the entire Middle East, and its decline precipitated troubles which continued through the Twentieth Century, and have disturbed world peace over and over again. During the square of the late 1860s came the German wars of unification, igniting Franco-German border tensions unresolved since Charlemagne. Both of these vexing problems exploded in the First World War, which closely followed a set of crises that began in Bosnia during the opposition of 1908, and soon brought the Soviet Communists to power in Russia. During the square of the early to mid-1950s, the United States confronted the Soviets during the height of the Cold War. Israelis and Arabs also clashed during the Suez crisis in 1956.

The next conjunction in 1993 resolved the Cold War conflict and eased Middle East tensions.. Unfortunately, plenty of new conflicts surfaced beneath the old ones of the Cold War.

Just as a crisis in Bosnia in 1908 under Uranus opposite Neptune led to World War I a few years later, so the crisis there that began in 1992 under Uranus conjunct Neptune may explode just before the New Millennium.

Ethnic conflicts have become the bane of the New World Order. To surmount them, we must learn to identify with the whole Earth instead of one race, culture or nation. At this time, the still-fledgeling United Nations represents the best hope for making this effort, despite nationalistic opposition and the intransigence of some member nations. The next Uranus-Neptune square (in 2037) and the next opposition (in 2078-2080) will mark times when our ability to learn these lessons will be tested again. If we fail, then soon after 2080 another Balkan or Austrian conflict could again threaten world peace.

SUMMITS OF ARTISTIC CREATION

Uranus and Neptune are the brightest lights within our inner cosmos. Uranus pours out a steady stream of genius into the minds of all would-be creators, allowing them to see the truth beyond conventional wisdom. Neptune is that reservoir of infinite intelligence and compassion which allows the hearts of all would-be saints and poets to feel the profound love and unity that transcends all apparent chaos. It is no accident, therefore, that when Uranus and Neptune come together, artists and writers produce many of their greatest works. Here, as in politics, the Uranus-Pluto conjunction (and sometimes the opposition) initiates sudden and startling new ideas and trends, but the Uranus-Neptune conjunction often consummates them.

For example, the trial and death of Socrates in 399 B.C. (soon after the conjunction of 404 B.C.) inspired Plato to write his great dialogues. The column of Trajan in A.D 111. marked the beginning of Rome's "silver age." This was when when the Pantheon was built—the inspired masterpiece of Roman architecture. Even while Rome was being sacked by Vandals during the conjunction in 453, the first great cathedral of Byzantine art was being built at Galla Placidia. Charlemagne restored art and culture from the clutches of the Dark Ages around the time of the conjunction of 794.

Under the alignment of 1136 (also opposite Pluto), Medieval culture soared to its height under the influence of Gothic architecture and philosophy. The great artist Giotto anticipated the coming Renaissance under the conjunction of 1307. The conjunction of 1479 just preceded the High Renaissance of DaVinci and Michaelangelo. The conjunction of 1650 inspired the greatest Baroque artists like Bernini, Rembrandt, Vermeer and others. The conjunction of 1821 marked the height of Romanticism, including composers such as Schubert and Beethoven, the painters Delacroix and Turner, and poets like Byron and Shelley. Now, after the conjunction of 1993, we await the works of artists and musicians who will bring the visionary arts opened up in the 1960s to full expression, and hope for a cultural renaissance that alone can create the "New Age." Perhaps artists unknown in the 1990s are working whose greatness will later be recognized, although they may be using media which is not yet understood as "art."

REVOLUTIONS

Significant aspects to Uranus, the solar system's lightning rod, are bound to bring political revolutions. When paired up with Neptune, which represents our compassion for all beings and resentment against restrictive boundaries, powerful upheavals are likely. Uranus-Pluto conjunctions initiate revolutionary movements, but Uranus-Neptune often brings them to fruition and success.

For example, the German Reformation erupted into peasant revolt in 1522 exactly as Uranus squared Neptune. The conjunction of 1650 coincided with the great rebellion of Cromwell in England and with the French Fronde revolt. The American revolution was fought during the square of 1777–83. The conjunction of 1821 saw revolutions erupt throughout southern Europe (Greece, Romania, Italy, Spain) and the Americas (Mexico, Brazil, Chile, etc.). The following square around 1870 witnessed the famous Paris Commune celebrated by Karl Marx. Under the great opposition around 1908, successful revolutions happened in China and Mexico. Earlier in 1905, the Russian Revolution began. During the square of the mid-1950s came the first group of revolts against Soviet communism in Eastern Europe (East Germany, Poland and Hungary). They failed, but were signs of things to come. Successful communist revolutions also broke out in Cuba, Vietnam, and Iraq that would later haunt the United States. Then in 1989 another great conjunction began, and communist control of eastern Europe evaporated in the most successful series of revolutions ever seen.

Some successful revolts also happened in this same period in U.S. satellites such as South Korea, the Philippines and Chile. This may mean that more changes are due in the capitalist as well as in the communist world. Let us hope they come, for social transformation is as necessary as a new world order if we are to move into the promised renaissance. If the industrial world merely congratulates itself on winning the Cold War, and ignores the growing divisions and injustices within, it does so at its own peril. Even the world's last superpower can't withstand a crumbling foundation, and the solution is not to impose its will on the world to protect the rich, but to make a renewed commitment to Liberty, Equality, and Fraternity.

Combining the findings in this section with those in the previous chapter leads us to a startling conclusion. Almost all revolutions (as opposed to wars, civil wars, disturbances, or great reforms) break out during Uranus-Pluto aspects (conjunctions, squares, oppositions, sextiles, and semi/sesqui-squares) and/or Uranus-Neptune aspects (conjunctions, squares and oppositions). Perhaps only the Iranian and Nicaraguan revolutions in 1979 were exceptions to this rule.

THE RELIGIOUS CYCLE AND THE AQUARIAN AGE

In a series of brilliant articles in *The Encyclopedia of Astrology*, Charles Jayne revealed his research on the planetary cycles. Among his findings was a 600-year cycle of the world's great religions.[1] Every 600 years, he said, a new religion is born, and at each of those times Uranus is either aligned with or opposing Neptune. Here are the dates:

575 B.C.: Births of Buddha and Pythagoras; careers of Lao-Tzu, Mahavira and Confucius. Babylonian captivity of the Jews. Final Upanishads written.

A.D. 25: (opposition) Mission and crucifixion of Jesus Christ.

624: Flight of Mohammed from Mecca in 622 A.D.; birth of Islam.

1222: (opposition) Founding of Franciscan and Dominican Orders in Catholicism; career of St. Thomas Aquinas; a peak in the Age of Faith.

1821: Births of the co-founders of the Bahai Faith; Joseph Smith's conversion (Mormonism); birth of Mary Baker Eddy (Christian Science, Unity, etc.), births of Thoreau and Whitman (American Transcendentalism); founding of the American Unitarian Association.

(This was also the time when Marx and Engels were born, suggesting that this cycle represents socialism as a religion, while the Uranus-Pluto conjunction of 1850 represents socialism as a revolutionary movement. Its career as the former may thus long outlast its history as the latter.)[2]

2420: (opposition) The next great religion is not due until then. It may incorporate the essence of the Aquarian Age, as Christianity did for the Piscean. It could be a new sect within an already existing religion.

We can further speculate that the previous opposition of 1176 B.C. may have coincided with Moses or Zoroaster, the conjunction of 1778 B.C. with Abraham, and the conjunction of 2980 B.C. with Krishna.

Uranus-Neptune conjunctions and oppositions are also linked to the great precession cycle of 25,000-plus years, which defines the great Ages: the Piscean, Aquarian, etc. After twenty-five conjunctions, Uranus and Neptune make a conjunction in exactly the same place in the sky. This takes 4,285 years, which is almost exactly the length of two astrological "Ages." To complete six of these returns takes 25,710 years, which is very close to the average precession cycle of 25,694 years. For the foreseeable future, every astrological age will begin during a conjunction or opposition of Uranus-Neptune in the same location in space.

Clearly, both Uranus-Neptune and the precession have to do with religion, so the two cycles are linked. As we saw above, Uranus opposed Neptune in Capricorn at the time of Christ, in A.D. 25 In 1821,1,800 years later, the two planets made a conjunction in Capricorn. In twice this time (3,600 years), the conjunction or opposition always returns to virtually the same degree of the same sign (not the same constellation, which takes 4,285 years). This is why the religious cycle is 600 years long; it is exactly one-sixth of the time between Uranus-Neptune conjunctions in the same degree of the zodiac. Since the conjunction of 1821 happened at such a significant time, one-half of the 3,600-year cycle since Christ, the new religions of the Nineteenth Century (Bahaism, Transcendentalism, Unitarianism, Christian Science, New Thought, Socialism, etc.) may be important progenitors of the religions of the future.

There are also significant cosmic events in our time (the turn of the third millennium) that mark the oncoming Aquarian Age. For example, the galactic center is now close to right angles to the equinox, at the very moment when we are reaching out to the stars and outer space. At the time of Christ, in 25 A.D., Jupiter in Libra and Saturn in Aries made a grand cosmic cross with Uranus in Cancer and Neptune in Capricorn. On January, 1910, virtually the same cosmic cross occurred, as Uranus in Capricorn opposed Neptune in Cancer, with Saturn (and Mars) in Aries once again opposing Jupiter in Libra. Three years after the cross of 25 A.D., Christ was crucified. Four years after 1910, humanity made its own sacrifice, as millions died in the Great War so that a new unified world could be born under the League of Nations (forerunner of today's United Nations).

By the way, the great 493-year Neptune-Pluto cycle in the fortunes of civilization (see Chapter 4) may also be linked to the precession of the equinoxes (the 2,000-year "Ages"). A Neptune-Pluto conjunction returns to the same place in about 50,000 years, equal to two precession cycles.

THE HOROSCOPE OF JESUS OF NAZARETH

Various proposals have been made of a chart for Jesus: I have one, too. Many historians agree that the "three wise men" referred to in the Bible were astrologers, and that "the star" they followed was a conjunction of planets which indicated to them that a new avatar (or Christ figure) would be born. The only great conjunction in the period of Jesus' birth was that between Jupiter and Saturn in Pisces in 7–6 B.C. (conjunctions with Uranus would have been unknown to astrologers at that time). This would be an appropriate symbol for the prophet of the Piscean Age.

The Bible story lends credence to the notion that Jesus was born in springtime. This could have meant the spring of 7 B.C., when the conjunction first formed and was opposed by Mars in Virgo, or (as I prefer to think) it could have been in late February of the following year, when Mars lined up with the conjunction in Pisces soon before it ended. The astronomer Kepler also thought this triple conjunction was the "star." Legend has it that Jesus was thirty-three years old when he was crucified, and that this happened three years after he began his ministry, which the great cross indicates was in A.D. 25. A stationary Mars in Scorpio opposed Saturn in Taurus in April of A.D. 28. This is a potentially very violent figure that also occurred during the French "reign of terror" when the new modern "religion" of nationalism was "crucified." Also in A.D. 28, the expansive religious planets Jupiter and Neptune joined in Capricorn—an eloquent symbol of the resurrection. If Jesus was born in 7 B.C.,though, he would have been nearly thirty-five when his ministry ended. It seems more likely, therefore, that he was born a year later, so that he would have just turned thirty-four when he died in April of A.D 28.

All this is just speculation, but putting the date of Jesus' birth at February 25, 6 B.C., gives us an interesting horoscope. It makes Jesus himself a Pisces, as well as putting the "star of Bethlehem" in that sign. The Sun that day was aligned with Uranus (the spiritual revolutionary), and trine Neptune in Scorpio. These aspects are common in the charts of great spirits who initiate vast movements and enterprises. Venus in Capricorn, in sextile to the

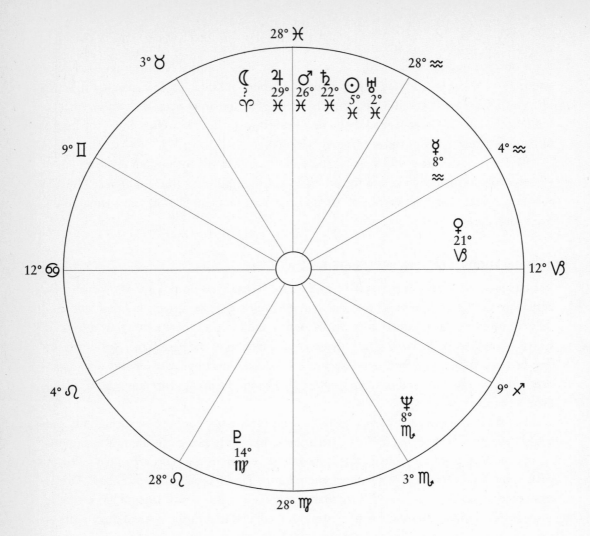

Jesus of Nazareth

This is a speculative chart for Jesus' birth, showing the "Star of Bethlehem" stellium in Pisces, as described by Johannes Kepler. Chart data: February 25, 6 B.C., 2:00 P.M., Bethlehem, Judea.

"star" in Pisces, could represent Jesus' ability to accept defeat and turn it into victory. The Sabian symbol for its degree on Feb. 25 reads, "A defeated general gives up his sword with noble dignity; a spiritual victory." Mars joined with Jupiter and Saturn emphasizes the importance of blood in Christian mythology, the fact that death and sacrifice (Mars in Pisces) were necessary for salvation. Mars-Jupiter represents the evangelist and preacher. The star was widely opposed by Pluto in Virgo ("loaves and fishes").

If we put the "star" or stellium of Mars, Jupiter and Saturn in Pisces on the Midheaven, it makes the birth time about 2:00 P.M. This puts 12° Cancer on the Ascendant, which carries the Sabian symbol "a babe surrounded by a divine halo." The Sun and Uranus occupy the Ninth

House of religious philosophy, while Mercury in Aquarius is in the Eighth house (death and resurrection) squaring Neptune (poetic imagination). The reforming planet Pluto in the Third House of communications reminds us of Jesus as a youth, arguing with the rabbis in the temple.

THE URANUS–NEPTUNE CYCLE

Date	Aspect	Sign	Major Events (5-year orb on each side of aspect)
B.C.			
575*	Conj.	Taurus	Birth of Buddha, Pythagoras; Lao Tzu, Confucius; time of Thales, Solon
404	Conj.	Gemini	End of Peloponnesian War; death of Socrates
232	Conj.	Gemini	End of Ashoka's reign; start of Ch'in Empire
61	Conj.	Cancer	First Roman triumvirate
A.D.			
25*	Oppos.	Canc/Cap	Ministry and crucifixion of Jesus
111	Conj.	Cancer	Victories and column of Trajan
282	Conj.	Leo	Reforms of Diocletian
453	Conj.	Leo	Defeat of Attila; Galla Placidia built
624*	Conj.	Virgo	Founding of Islam; Tang Dynasty
794	Conj.	Virgo	Charlemagne founded Western Civilization
965	Conj.	Libra	Ottonian Empire; Sung Dynasty
1136	Conj.	Libra	Beginning of Gothic culture
1222 *	Oppos.	Scorp/Taur	St. Francis, St. Thomas Aquinas
1307	Conj.	Scorpio	Philip the Fair, Papal controversy, Giotto
1479	Conj.	Scorpio	High Renaissance began; Wars of Roses end
1522	Square	-	Peasant revolt of German Reformation
1565	Oppos.	Sag/Gem	Height of religious wars
1650	Conj.	Sagittarius	Louis XIV defeats Fronde; Great Rebellion; Treaty of Westphalia; Baroque Art summit
1698	Square	-	Wars of Louis XIV
1737	Oppos.	Sag/Gem	War of the Austrian Succession
1781	Square	-	American Revolution; Industrial Revolution
1821*	Conj.	Capricorn	Concert of Europe; revolutions in Greece, Italy, Spain, Latin America; Mormonism
1869	Square	-	Franco-Prussian War; Paris Commune
1908	Oppos.	Cap/Canc	Bosnian Crisis leading to First World War; modern art and music
1954	Square	-	Cold War; Mid-East Suez crisis; revolutions in eastern Europe, Cuba

Date	Aspect	Sign	Major Events (5-year orb on each side of aspect)
1993	Conj.	Capricorn	End of Cold War; New World Order; New Age/Green Renaissance? Bosnian Crisis II
2037	Square		Crisis in the New World Order, probably involving Germany and/or France
2080	Oppos.	Cap/Canc.	World tensions, war in central Europe
2126	Square		Possible religious crusade or space war
2165	Conj.	Aquarius	Aquarian Age cultural summit

* Corresponds to Jayne's 600-year religious cycle

PHASES OF THE CYCLE

Whenever Uranus and Neptune line up with each other, a whole cycle or period begins that lasts 171 years. The conjunction is like the New Moon, the beginning of the cycle. The opposition is the Full Moon and fulfilling climax halfway through the cycle. Other important phases begin at the First and Last Quarters, when the two planets are in square or ninety degrees apart. We can divide this significant cycle into twelve equal phases in all, each one beginning with an aspect or important angle between Uranus and Neptune, such as an opposition, square, sextile, etc. (Because of the slight eccentricity of orbits, the exact aspects often come a few years after the actual phase begins.)

These twelve phases can always be described in terms of the twelve houses or signs. The first fourteen-plus years of the cycle is the First House phase, the next fourteen is the 2nd, etc. A house phase is also only slightly longer than the time which Neptune itself spends in one sign (fourteen years). Other important cycles are always going on, so none of these phases can be considered in isolation from other meaningful cosmic events. If we bear this in mind, we can use these twelve phases to help us understand the past and forecast the future.

First House phase (1821–1835): This is the house of self-assertive, creative new beginnings (or New Moon phase, which began when Uranus was conjunct Neptune). In this phase many of the inventions were made that powered the new industrial age, such as applied electromagnetism and railroads. The people asserted themselves in mass democratic and nationalist movements, and the middle class gained lasting political power. Artists and composers developed the Romantic style. Socialist ideals were first articulated by Saint-Simon (1820). This was phase one in a great Uranus-Neptune cycle in which Industry rose to power, and the People repeatedly rose up to take power within it.

Second House phase (1835–1850): This is the house of money and wealth. Industrial enterprises expanded during the "roaring '40s" railroad booms in Britain. The gold rush exploded, and the Industrial Revolution expanded to France, Germany, and the U.S., where Manifest Destiny was declared.

Third House phase (1850–1865): This is the house of travel and communication. During this time the trans-Atlantic cable was laid, the trans-Alpine tunnel was made, and international shipping mushroomed. There were mass migrations from Ireland and Europe to America and elsewhere. Many governments liberalized toward the end of the period.

Fourth House phase (1865–1879): This is the "house of home," and it's amazing how many nations reorganized themselves on the home front in these years. Reconstruction occurred in America after the Civil War, and Germany, Austria, France, Canada, and Britain also went through their own "reconstructions." The "wild west" was conquered and settled. The Fourth House is acquisitive, and it was at this time that the robber barons and money swindlers were the most active. The Fourth House and its sign Cancer are very patriotic, so nationalism expanded in the age of Bismarck. This was the First Quarter phase, corresponding to Uranus' square to Neptune in the late 1860s. By coincidence, Uranus also entered the sign Cancer in 1865.

Fifth House phase (1879–1893): Under this house of youth, pleasures, and speculation came the free-wheeling "belle époque" commemorated by impressionist artists in France. Neo-romantic decadence began. Education was made available to all children in these years. This is an economic house; and the industrial economy was reorganized in this period to make it less competitive. Trusts, monopolies, and tariffs mushroomed; prosperity resulted.

Sixth House phase (1893–1908): This is the house of labor and health. Labor movements flourished and strikes reached epidemic proportions in these years. Health concerns showed up in campaigns by progressives like Upton Sinclair to clean up the cattle stockyards, improve our food (Pure Food and Drug Act), improve working conditions, and conserve the land. At the start of the Sixth House phase came Neptune's conjunction to Pluto and the Panic of 1893. From then on, Industry was forced to start recognizing its duty to society.

Seventh House phase (1908–1922): This is the house of relationships, but also of war and divorce. After forming great alliances, industrial nations slaughtered each other in World War I, carrying out national rivalries begun in the Fourth House phase. Then came the Treaty of Versailles and the League of Nations. This is the climactic opposition or "Full Moon" phase, so Romantic art fulfilled itself in Modern Art. Revolutions occurred all over the globe, most notably in Russia as socialist ideals reached their peak of influence.

Eighth House phase (1922–1937): This is the house of death and transformation. Certainly, this was the moment of death for European culture in the Great Depression, Russian gulags and Nazism. Reactionaries and dictators rose to power everywhere throughout this period. This is also another economic house, ruling the sharing of resources, so the industrial economy transformed and socialized itself in the New Deal (and less benignly, in Communist Russia and Nazi Germany). Resources were shared through the Social Security system. Pluto, which rules the Eighth House, was discovered in 1930.

Ninth House phase (1937–1951): This is the house of wide travel and foreign affairs, and once again (as in the Seventh House phase) its worst possible meaning was played out—this time in the unprecedented destruction (often via long-range bombing campaigns) of World

War II, followed by Cold War hysteria. Nevertheless, there were also peace conferences, new alliances and the United Nations. The war enormously advanced long-distance air travel (jet planes, radar, rockets).

Tenth House phase (1951–1965): This is the house of power and status, and this period marked the industrial economy's apex in the form of the American and Soviet assumption of "Superpower" status. The corporate state and the military-industrial complex expanded, and its bureaucrats lost touch with how their decisions affected people and the environment. The American and Soviet goal was to preserve and extend their power, status, and control at all times. This phase is also called the Last Quarter, since Uranus squared Neptune in the early to mid-1950s.

Eleventh House phase (1965–1979): After the peak, the fall begins. The industrial economy began to decline in this period. Uranus joined Pluto at the stroke of the new phase in 1965–66, marking the last two houses in the 171-year cycle as the momentous final stages of industrial power. America's defeat in Vietnam and the oil embargoes of the 1970s shifted economic power away from the West. This is an economic house, but it indicates a time when individuals and small-scale business first reassert themselves. Post-industrial high technology appeared. The Eleventh House represents high ideals and causes, so social movements exploded in the mid and late 1960s. This is a "house of pleasures" like the Fifth; a good symbol of the hedonistic, psychedelic counter-culture that dawned as the hippies celebrated "peace and brother/sisterhood." (The French Revolution also came in the Eleventh House phase of the previous cycle.)

Twelfth House phase (1979–1993): This is the house of spirituality, self-undoing, delusions, plagues, and hidden enemies. The old civilization stalled and lost its way, and politics declined. The industrial economy, especially in the U.S. and the Soviet Union, began sabotaging itself. The rise of the Ayatollah in Iran and the consequent destruction of Carter's presidency paved the way for Reaganomics and massive debt. Secret, illegal wars and corrupt government activities were revealed (Iran-Contra and other scandals). Christianity flexed political muscle in the U.S., while New Agers brought meditation, creative visualization, and alternative healing into the mainstream. Karma seemed to rebound on the sexual revolution and the counter-culture (AIDS, Jonestown). In previous cycles, this phase saw destructive wars (Thirty Years war, Napoleon) which led to new international arrangements.

THE NEW CYCLE

With Uranus joining Neptune again in 1993, a new cycle has begun. Despite today's looming planetary crisis, astrological indications point to smoother and more constructive times in the Twenty-First Century. Of course, if we fail to clean up our environment by altering our civilization, we may not survive to enjoy it. Combined with other cycles, we can estimate the trends ahead:

First House phase (1993–2008): The fall of totalitarian communism, many new democracies, the end of the Cold War, and Clinton's ascendancy all marked the new beginning around 1993. Many environmental inventions, new spiritual technologies, and political revolutions are being made. Artistic creativity is unfolding in new forms and great artists are appearing. Catastrophic events in the 1990s and around 2008 will diminish corporate power and transform our institutions. Around the year 2000, spiritual movements will explode and a new Golden Age may dawn. The new cycle thus represents a chance to develop a global, green, spiritually oriented, post-industrial, peaceful New World Order. On the other hand, the decline of socialism may mean an era in which we ignore our responsibilities to our fellow citizens.

Second House phase (2008–2022): This period will see environmental catastrophes such as floods, famine, disease, and mass migrations from the Third World. Economic and political structures will have to adjust to the new global realities. Many governments could be toppled (Pluto enters Capricorn, 2008; Uranus- Pluto- Saturn T-square in 2010). People may be disillusioned, causing them to retreat again into conservatism. Later in the Second House phase an environmental "post-industrial" revolution will get going. High-tech, green-conscious, and New Age businesses will prosper.

Third House phase (2022–2037): Extreme political activity and reorganization will bring justice to the people and the possible breakup of the United States. A horde of new inventions, ideas, controversies, and pioneers will appear. More spectacular breakthroughs will be made in communications, plus links to the solar system and beyond. Humanity will recover its youthful, expressive confidence and boldly burst forth into the new era.

Fourth House phase (2037-2051): More environmental disasters will lead to new ideas about how to use the land properly. Agriculture and diet will be totally transformed. Nationalist movements may flourish. The power of green, feminist, and/or libertarian politics will reach a revolutionary climax (Uranus-Pluto opposition, 2047). France and Europe may lead the way toward reorganizing governments into a world great society. As usual, revolutionaries may go to extremes and become dictatorial. Attempts to hoard the wealth or cut property taxes may lead to depression and/or revolution.

Fifth House phase (2051–2066): The 2050s will be a progressive, inventive and optimistic time. Green businesses will become larger and linked together, and government help may be important again. Hedonism and romanticism will return, and so will the danger of population growth. People will still be obsessed with new ideas and gadgets (Neptune in Gemini). Economic and international problems may quietly increase in the 2060s, as the basic conflicts of the era come to the surface again (Neptune squares Pluto in about 2065).

Sixth House phase (2066–2080): Labor practices will be reorganized on a global scale. Depression or disease may lead to reforms or forced population control. Radical green politics will reassert itself around 2073 (Uranus square Pluto), as will ethnic rivalry or separatism. Research will help reshape science according to new realities. Conservation and health engineering will come of age. The common people will reassert their rights.

Seventh House phase (2080–2095): This will be the "Full Moon" opposition and climax of the new Uranus-Neptune cycle that began in 1993. Earth-centered spiritual ideals will become highly influential, leading to radical political change. Humanity will declare the "end of progress" in its old form. Artistic trends begun at the turn of the Twenty-First Century will reach full flower. Many innovations in music, the mystical arts and spiritual technology will occur in this and the following phase. Although these years will be very optimistic and creative, the viability of the new international structure developed during the Twenty-First Century will be tested severely, as Twenty-First Century conflicts reach their climax.

Eighth House phase (2095–2109): Institutions or cultures not adjusted to the new world economy may collapse with dizzying speed (Uranus conjunct Pluto, 2103). Attempts to share the wealth could return. The post-industrial economy will face severe challenges, and power may be dispersed or reorganized into new bureaucracies. A surge of spiritual creativity could emerge if we have done our duty to protect the Earth. If not, civilization as we know it may end in this period.

Ninh House phase (2109–2123): A very expansive, exotic time,when we may be forging links to other planets or spiritual dimensions. Unfortunately, growing reformist and missionary zeal may lead to warlike crusades toward the end of this phase. If civilization has collapsed, the mounting unrest and chaos will lead to fierce tribal and/or religious wars by then.

Tenth House phase (2123–2137): Some of the new worldwide institutions (or religious and environmental authorities) may become dictatorial and remote from the people. Wherever the focus of power has developed in the world (the Pacific Rim, perhaps) will experience its peak of influence. The economy will prosper due to large organizations of shared power. Confidence will be expanding among the people, who will push for their full share in material and spiritual abundance. The ideals of the 1990s and 2000s may be the rising power in the land. Radical youth will be questioning authority and exploring strange literary and scientific ideas (Uranus in Virgo square Pluto in Gemini, 2130).

Eleventh House phase (2137–2151): This should be a very creative, progressive time with many groups dedicated to wisdom and the common good becoming influential. Many important reforms will be made, but cracks will appear in the institutions and nations which recently enjoyed so much power. New ideals will be expressed which may dominate the next Uranus-Neptune cycle.

Twelfth House phase (2151–2165): Many powerful institutions of the world will now decline and decay, and old international alignments will disappear. Many people will pursue psychic exploration, expressed in highly creative endeavors. There may be scandal, delusion, secret wars, or escapism. The decks will be cleared for the new civilization to continue expanding, and humanity will be made ready for the new spiritual impulse beginning with the next Uranus-Neptune conjunction in 2165. Another New World Order may be established that will reorganize nations and peoples according to the Aquarian ideals of the interactive global culture. Earth's civilization may be linked with those in other galaxies or dimensions. Great temples could be built to honor the new spirituality.

WHAT THE NEW CULTURE WILL MEAN FOR YOU

As in the last chapter, we now need to enter the personal level and see how the Uranus-Neptune conjunction of 1993 will affect each individual. The house position in your chart where this significant event occurred shows how you might contribute to the new culture that is emerging today.

Were you born between 1988 and 1998? If so, the Uranus-Neptune conjunction in Capricorn is very sigificant in your own horoscope. You will experience powerful visions and strive to realize them. You can establish new cultural trends and achieve great things in the arts, politics, or religion. The need to save and preserve the planet will inform all of your activities. You feel keenly that "you are the world," and that it is your personal responsibility to help it to survive and advance. Your generation is extremely successful, ambitious, and dedicated to helping the community. Your organizational powers are greater than those of previous generations. You will leave society in better working order than you found it and make New Age ideals into workable realities. If the conjunction appears on one of the angles of your horoscope (see Appendix B), your abilities can approach the level of genius.

The conjunction remains in force until 2165, and is significant to everyone regardless of his or her year of birth. Read the paragraph indicated below for your birthday. In general, those born closest to the dates specifically mentioned will have felt the conjunction strongest. Those born at the beginning of each period will also need to read the following paragraph—it may also apply very strongly to you. If you know your rising sign (Ascendant) and degree, you may want to read the paragraph for that sign too. ("Late" means between nineteen and twenty-nine degrees of a sign.)

December 12–January 10 (late Sagittarius, early/mid Capricorn): Uranus and Neptune aligned with your Sun in a "First House" position. That means you became more inspired and creative in the 1990s. You have broken from old ideas and traditions and have struck out on a radically new path. You are called on to unfold your personality to the utmost and make yourself the mouthpiece for today's new cultural trends. Apply your great determination to unfolding your full potential. Of course, some of you may get yourselves in trouble with drugs, crime, jails, hospitals, or eccentric and rebellious behavior, but others of you can exercise your leadership and organizing skills to get things moving in your community. From the 1990s on, your role in the New Culture is to transform yourself into something more than you ever dreamed of being before.

November 12–December 11 (late Scorpio, early/mid Sagittarius): The great conjunction happened in a "Second House" position in relation to your Sun. You probably went through financial troubles and changes in the '90s. Take stock of your life and see what you have done in the past that has led to your present plight. New chances for success will come from unusual and eccentric sources and from your own inventive ideas. Self-reliance is the best path from the 1990s on; become financially independent and you will make it. Don't be a slave to the corporate world that is crumbling, because it doesn't care about you or anything else but the bottom line. Be open to the sudden chance, and be as free as you've always wanted to be from the financial and institutional ties that bind you.

October 13–November 11 (late Libra, early/mid Scorpio): The conjunction happened in a "Third House" position in relation to your Sun. This is the time to open the floodgates of ideas and feelings you have kept inside. You are in a good position to benefit by networking and sharing knowledge with others. Opportunities and ideas will be flowing your way, so put your thinking cap on, use your penetrating detective powers, and come up with an invention or scheme that will change the world. Get out of your rut, explore everything new, and unleash your powerful, compelling magnetism and charisma. Use it not only to attract new love, sex and/or wealth into your life, but to help reshape the world according to your convictions. You are probably right about what you believe needs to be done in the world, so get busy and be an agent of the great renewal of spirit happening all over the planet.

September 13–October 12 (late Virgo, early/mid Libra): The conjunction squared your Sun in a "Fourth House" position. You have gained sensitivity to beauty everywhere, especially in your immediate environment. You are very impressionable and able to tap your deeper feelings. Continuing changes in your finances and home life are likely. You may have become suddenly wealthy, or you may be altering your home and family or making them the center of your creative interests. All this could lead you to reorganize all of your affairs. At the same time, your idealism is being stimulated, and you may have plunged into community action to support the environment, the arts, peace, women's rights, etc. You may be less tolerant than usual of other people's opinions. What doesn't measure up to your ideals has to be opposed or rejected, in your view. That's true at home, too, when things are less peaceful and harmonious than you'd like—meaning they aren't going your way! Meditation and study of your subconscious mind may help you to realize your high ideals and dreams.

August 13–September 12 (late Leo, early/mid Virgo): The conjunction happened in a "Fifth House" position in relation to your Sun. It opened up your creative abilities. Since the 1990s, you have been more romantic, confident, and buoyant. Go out into the world, meet new people, and find new opportunities. Learn to take more risks, especially in your romantic and social life. Take up creative hobbies like writing, poetry, drama or arts and crafts. You are naturally youthful and childlike, and you can make a big difference in the lives of children, and vice-versa. Take a lesson from them in learning to shake off your inhibitions! The world needs to see more of the joy and color in life, so look beyond the ordinary, drab ways of the world and express this richness for all to see.

July 12–August 12 (late Cancer, early/mid Leo): The conjunction happened in a "Sixth House" relation to your Sun. The cultural changes of today are affecting your health and your work. You may have revised your view of success and learned to limit your proud ambition. It's time to consider the needs of others now instead of just your own dreams. You have a duty to society and your community, and you will gain happiness through helping and healing others. You may also find that you need to heal yourself after being burned out by your fruitless quests to become top cat in the jungle. You can no longer gamble with your fortunes or those of others. Self-discipline is what you need. Find a spiritual teacher, enroll in a yoga class, begin a diet or fitness regimen, analyze the demons within you, and then share what you learn. If you have lost your job, find another which may be less remunerative but contributes more to the betterment of your fellows.

June 11–July 11 (late Gemini, early/mid Cancer): The Uranus-Neptune conjunction opposed your Sun from a "Seventh House" position. Chances are you have been on a roller coaster ride since the 1990s began, financially and emotionally. You may have moved, divorced, or spent much time in court quarreling with your enemies. There is much potential for romance, but also disappointment if you expect too much from lovers. Other people puzzle you, just as you puzzle them (and seem to enjoy it!). Don't be taken in by people who promise you things that seem too good to be true. Maintain your natural tenacity, and don't depend too much on others. Your mood swings have been as wild as the shifting tides of your external affairs. Steady your nerves and don't let worries sap your energy. Avoid drugs and alcohol, and don't test the limits of the law. Honesty is the best policy for you! Channel your anger into action rather than blaming others for your own problems. Creative power may be unfolding for you, especially in poetry, painting, or performing. Take the time to explore your feelings, and help to nurture others. If you are attuned to the higher vibrations of Uranus and Neptune, you will find a more fulfilling path than you have ever known. Remember, don't despair—what goes down must come up again—that's how roller coasters work!

May 11–June 10 (late Taurus, early/mid Gemini): The conjunction happened in an "Eighth House" relation to your Sun. The mid-1990s were probably a period of some-painful adjustments for you. You were forced to change some ideas and see things in a new way. Old idols and false securities have fallen for you. Look at your past investment practices and the financial habits of the partners you have trusted. Look at your job and your relationships, too. If they are genuinely working for you, keep them. If they're not, junk them. Live your life as if you were going to die tomorrow. Connect deeply with those you truly care about, and transform yourself by becoming more healthy and serving others. If you feel confused or discouraged in today's hard times, remember your ability to learn anything quickly, including a new job skill. If you get disillusioned with yourself or others, it's no excuse to be cynical and throw out all your values and ethics altogether. You can't trick or scheme your way around all the changes happening today, so learn to confront them directly.

April 10–May 10 (late Aries, early/mid Taurus): The conjunction trined your Sun from a "Ninth House" position. This means you can see better than most the true situation around you and in the country as a whole. From the mid-'90s on, you became something of a prophet and a visionary. Take advantage of this by traveling more and improving your education. If you get out, see the world, and break out of your rut, you may find it financially rewarding as well as refreshing. Take advantage of any sudden changes in your financial situation—what appears to be a bad break may be a good opportunity in disguise. Expand your consciousness, study your dreams, and renew your spirit. Then share your new visions with the world.

March 11–April 9 (late Pisces, early/mid Aries): The conjunction squared your Sun from a "Tenth House" position. The conjunction stimulated your drive to work hard and succeed. Use your leadership abilities to light the fires under those around you! Politics could be a good avenue for you, or perhaps you may be moving up inside your company. From now on, your career must become something you truly believe in, not just something to pay the bills. You probably have great ideas about how your world could be improved, so decide what you want changed and then get moving. Rely on your natural independence of spirit, and be careful with drugs or weird superstitions. You can accomplish great things by thinking big, but don't get discouraged if there are delays, and don't cut too many corners. Increasingly, you are going off on your own and breaking with those who have held you back. From now on, the old rut and the second best aren't good enough. Your mission now is to make a real impact on the world, and you shouldn't settle for less.

February 9–March 10 (late Aquarius, early/mid Pisces): The conjunction happened in an "Eleventh House" relation to your Sun. This means you are called upon to make idealism the basis of your life. You can wed your values to your work in the world and join your hopes to real possibilities. Get involved in organizations and societies that are working to restore our nation to its true priorities. Look to your friends for help and opportunity, and offer your friendship to others. You may be able to gain benefits through travel, or by helping to bring distant people and places together. In the years after 1993 you will be able to enjoy financial rewards from your past career. Share your love and concern for your fellows and feel your hopes coming true as never before. Find a new outlet to express your artistic and performing talents, and enjoy the people and places that you love the most.

January 11–February 8 (late Capricorn, early/mid Aquarius): The Uranus-Neptune conjunction happened in a "Twelfth House" relation to your Sun. This is mainly a spiritual influence for you, affording many chances in the years ahead to go within and clean out the old cobwebs of your mind. Expose the remains of past bitterness and resentment and heal the hidden wounds from those who have hurt you, and then open up to psychic, intuitive powers that go beyond your usual scientific, left-brain notions. The problems of the world concern you deeply; take time to contemplate and re-evaluate them. You may be comfortable working inside a corporation or institution, since you feel you can make more changes within the traditional structure than without. You may be quite successful, since your new intuitive powers can help you make good decisions—unless the unresolved problems in your deeper psyche intrude and make you emotionally unsuited to your tasks. Power struggles with authority may also wear you down and exhaust you. Then another kind of institution (the ashram, asylum, monastery, hospital, or psychiatrist's office) may be where you need to be. If you were born on or shortly after January 11, also go back and read the first paragraph (for late Sagittarius and early Capricorn).

URANUS-NEPTUNE ON THE ANGLES

If you know your birth time, consult Appendix B to find out if the Uranus-Neptune conjunction happened on one of the angles of your horoscope (the Ascendant, Midheaven, Descendant, or Nadir). If so, it has had a particularly powerful impact on your life, and may continue to do so. If "19° Capricorn" is listed under one of the angles for your birth time (within thirty minutes or so), Uranus-Neptune conjoined on that angle in your chart in 1993. The closer it was, the more important it is—and will continue to be!

Uranus-Neptune on your Ascendant: You are becoming personally more magnetic and alluring. You may experience a dynamic spiritual awakening. You are called upon to break from past traditions and go in uncharted, original directions. Don't let fear of authorities hold you back: become more independent and creative. You are now a charismatic leader and a pioneer who can blaze a trail for others. You have a greater sense of self than you ever dreamed possible before, and perhaps more original ideas than you know what to do with. Put them to use to benefit humanity and you will reap great rewards.

Uranus-Neptune on your Midheaven: Your career is becoming a vehicle to change the world. You will gain ever-greater power and status as the years go by if you stick to your ideals. Your original inventions could lead to success and fame. Trust your awakened intuition to make the best decisions. You could find yourself in a position to vastly improve other people's lives. If you merely follow your selfish ambition, however, you could suffer a sudden downfall. Redirection of your whole life will follow.

Uranus-Neptune on your Descendant: Your relationships will be subject to constant change in the years ahead. You'll demand that they meet your highest ideals. Still, others may deceive you, or vice-versa. You are becoming much more public on behalf of the causes you believe in, and you'll encounter much opposition over them. You will meet many unusual and spiritual people who will transform your life in undreamed of ways. Widen your horizons, and be open to many opportunities.

Uranus-Neptune on your Nadir: Your home and inner life will be unsettled. Deep spiritual or mystic experiences may expand the powers of your subconscious mind. Cultivate these through hypnosis or dream work. The 1990s represent a crucial new departure in your life. You may break away from family or parents. Old interests will end and new talents will unfold, and your beliefs and goals may totally change. You will feel a powerful new kinship with the land, your community, and the Earth. You may need to develop a new career more in tune with your own interests. Go within often to heal the confusion caused by all these new beginnings.

URANUS-NEPTUNE ON YOUR PLANETS

If the Sun, Moon, or any planets in your horoscope are close to 19° Capricorn, the conjunction may have stimulated you in very dynamic ways. Consult your natal chart or ephemeris to find where your planets are, since we don't have space to list all the dates here.

Sun: You have become much more magnetic, dynamic, and creative. You now have the power to realize your deepest dreams. Original ideas and mystic feelings flow through you. You will make drastic new departures from past traditions. Relations with father or sons may be altered. You'll feel the need to forge a new career that represents your highest ideals and become a leader in movements to change the world. Read the paragraph above for December 12–January 10 with special attention.

Moon: Your sensitivities have been awakened. Your ambition is now to help humanity. Many changes are due in your home, family life, and career. Advance by cultivating a new self-image. Use your psychic talents and your subconscious mind to succeed in business.

Mercury: You suddenly became full of inventive ideas in the 1990s. Your task is to travel and learn as much as possible and open new networking channels. You are a spokesperson for today's cultural movements, with strikingly original thoughts about how to restructure organizations. Your thinking may sometimes become too radical and eccentric.

Venus: Relationships could become more deeply spiritual, or just more unusual or unstable. Your artistic talents may unfold and your inventive career plans may bring you wealth. Love and spiritual beauty have touched you deeply. New emotional habits and aspirations have become set since the 1990s. You seek now to live only by the highest truth.

Mars: A volcano of energy has erupted inside you. You are becoming an enterprising and organizational genius. Engineering or athletic talents may unfold. You can exercise your leadership abilities on behalf of great social causes. You will have many conflicts with authority in the years ahead. You are setting off in radically new and ambitious directions.

Jupiter: Become a philosopher and prophet of the New Age. Your attitude regarding organized religion is being altered. Make the most of major opportunities for success and prosperity, especially in the 1990s. Develop the full powers of your higher mind and share your original ideas. Discover life's possibilities, widen your horizons, and boost your faith.

Saturn: Transform your career to accord with your highest purposes, or you could lose it. You must defeat external authorities, internal blocks, and ego defenses. You may be subject to paranoia, exaggerated ambitions, or delusions of grandeur. Develop your elaborate plans to reorganize your community or institution. You have been granted a high political or artistic vision that will take many years to achieve, but if you succeed, the highest worldly status could be yours.

CHAPTER 7 ENDNOTES
1. Jayne, Charles, "Cycles" from *Encyclopedia of Astrology*, p. 80
2: Consult article by Graeme Jones in *Welcome to Planet Earth*, Scorpio-Sagittarius 1992, for more information on the Uranus-Neptune cycle and Marxism.

8

The Planetary Ark and the Phoenix

As we stated earlier, the three outer planets not only move in a mutual relationship to each other, forming conjunctions, oppositions and squares; they also move around the Sun individually in their own cycle through the zodiac. Called transits, these cycles are highly significant prophetic tools. One transit in particular stands out—the cycle of Neptune. In recent years, whole books have been devoted to this cycle alone. It is very long: Neptune takes over 164 years to go once around the zodiac.

NEPTUNE IN THE SIGNS

This planet represents the masses of common folk. It is the ocean liner or "Planetary Ark" carrying with it the soul of all humanity as it cruises among the stars through the vast ocean of space. The sign that Neptune occupies at any time is the index to the current state of mind of the people and the "spirit of the times," past, present, and future. It is amazing how often the years when Neptune moves from one sign to the next correspond to major events which cause great shifts in world affairs.

1778–1792: Neptune was in Libra. This sign's high ideals of justice and balance were embodied in the U.S. constitution, the Bill of Rights, and the French Declaration of Rights. The thought of Thomas Jefferson and the music of Haydn and Mozart epitomizes this Neptune-in-Libra period.

1792–1806: Neptune was in stormy, passionate Scorpio, reflected in the turbulent French Revolution and its deep transformation of society. The period began in 1792 as an aroused French people overthrew their king. In the arts, the balance of Libra was overthrown in favor of the passion and ecstasy of the romantics.

1806–1820: Neptune was in Sagittarius, sign of travel and the higher mind, during the adventurous age of Napoleon. It was a period of religious revival ("the great awakening") and of idealistic philosophers like Hegel. Among the great romantic artists of this expansive time were the poets Byron and Shelley and the composer Beethoven, a Sagittarian who embodied the spirit of his times.

1820–1834: Neptune was in authoritarian, conservative sign Capricorn, symbol of the reactionary movement that gripped Europe after Napoleon fell. Metternich and the Concert of Vienna kept the lid on world revolution. In the 1820s, central authority strengthened and industrial progress was slow. In America, Chief Justice John Marshall's decisions increased the power of the federal government.

1834–1848: Neptune was in inventive, progressive Aquarius, when humanitarian and utopian ideals were conceived and attempted throughout the world. Legions of reformers campaigned for idealistic causes such as the fight against slavery, and technological progress picked up steam.

1848–1861: This oceanic planet entered its natural sign of Pisces, the compassionate, dissolving, escapist, and chaotic water sign, soon after its discovery in 1846. After the Irish Potato Famine (caused by a fungus), people migrated by the millions, just as they had during the last Pisces transit in the 1680s. The industrial revolution expanded widely, accelerating the collectivization of humanity. Passivity and escapism prevailed during much of the period, which was marked by such muddled and chaotic affairs as the Crimean War. Humanitarian concerns led to improvements in the care of the insane, the sick, and the wounded. The widespread use of ocean-going steamships greatly increased world commerce, and Pasteur's studies of fermentation improved the making of beer and wine.

1861–1874: Neptune was in assertive Aries. Aggressive individualism peaked in the age of Darwin, as the "struggle for survival" became the model for human behavior. Nations embraced liberalism in a rush of reforms. Germany and Italy were allied in a series of wars in which Bismarck demonstrated the virtues of "blood and iron." The bombing of Fort Sumter began the U.S. Civil War on the day Neptune entered Aries.

1874–1887: Neptune was in acquisitive, sensuous Taurus. The rush of greedy go-getting under Aries ended when Neptune entered earthy Taurus, as the failure of Jay Cooke and Co. precipitated a depression. Economic transformation followed, as companies merged (Neptune) into giant cartels. The new U.S. President, Rutherford B. Hayes, asked America to "calm down" after civil war and reconstruction troubles, and a deceptive stability soon reigned everywhere. The sensitive art style of impressionism developed (another sensitive style, rococo, had developed during the previous transit in the early 1700s).

1887–1901: Neptune was in restless, mobile, mercurial Gemini. The U.S. Interstate Commerce Commission was founded in 1887, prompting businessmen to seek overseas markets. Increased world trade resulted. Multitudes of new ideas and inventions appeared, captivating the public. The car put the world in motion, and the radio and the movie camera improved communication. The yellow press stirred up the masses, and adventurers traveled the globe, fueling the aims of imperialism.

1901–1915: Neptune was in sensitive, defensive Cancer. Patriotic nationalism and ethnic conflicts flared as the world careened towards war, and nations protected themselves behind political and military alliances. Freud opened awareness of the subconscious mind, and Teddy Roosevelt rode a wave of interest in conservation and protecting the rights of the common people against big business.

1915–1929: Neptune was in flamboyant Leo. In World War I, soldiers gave their lives heroically for a "noble cause." Flaming youth of the jazz age broke through taboos to self-expression and romance, while sports and games became big business. Business itself went on a binge of boosterism and speculation, as Americans became proud and overconfident throughout the "roaring 20s." Flamboyant art styles like Dada appeared.

1929–1942: Neptune was in self-effacing Virgo. Just as in 1874, when Neptune entered earth sign Taurus, the boom times ended in a bust—this time caused by the stock market crash in 1929. Greed and pleasure were renounced in favor of service to society and concern for the common man/woman. Bureaucracy and conformity mushroomed in New Deal America, Nazi Germany, and Soviet Russia, among other places.

1942–1956: Neptune was in diplomatic Libra. Halfway through the zodiac from Aries in 1861, America was again thrust into war by another bombing, this time at Pearl Harbor (December 1941). Liberal ideals returned to Europe after the Allies won the war and organized the United Nations. A period of equilibrium and economic equality set in under Libran President Eisenhower. Classical music experienced a revival.

1956–1970: Neptune in secretive Scorpio, sign of "shared resources" and turbulent transformations, brought civil rights struggles and anti-war protests, as well as growing interest in spy mysteries, the occult, and the intense experiences of sexual and spiritual union. In 1960, JFK asked America to get moving again—just the reverse of 1876 in Taurus. The expanding corporate economy generated boom times. The rapid urban growth and hot-tempered controversy of this era were similar to that of a century earlier under Neptune in Aries—a sign also ruled by Mars. People became aware of threats to all life from environmental and nuclear destruction for the first time under Scorpio, the "sign of death."

1970–1984: Neptune was in outspoken Sagittarius. The boom times ended, as the destructive effects of war and overexpansion were felt on the economy. The Pentagon Papers revealed the secrets of the Vietnam War, and the Watergate scandal fueled a boom in investigative reporting as well as an increase in cynicism. Another religious revival occurred, and spiritual interests expanded in the New Age movement. Fitness and outdoor sports became the rage as joggers filled the streets. Global trade expanded, and the diplomacy of Metternich during the last transit in the 1810s found an echo in the diplomacy of Kissinger (detente) and Carter (Camp David accords) during this one.

1984–1998: Neptune transits Capricorn. The sentiment that "we are the world" took hold in this most universal of earth signs. As famine swept Africa, artists and musicians organized worldwide efforts to help the starving millions, as well as American farmers who were being evicted from their land. Politically, however, Capricornian reaction and conservatism prevailed worldwide. Powerful governments and empires (Capricorn) dissolved (Neptune) into rival ethnic cultures.

1998–2011: Neptune is in the utopian, humanitarian sign of Aquarius. The "New Age" may blossom during this period, as great achievements in the arts and sciences set trends lasting hundreds of years. Ideals of brother/sisterhood will be put into practice, social reforms will be made throughout the world, and many groups will be formed to promote the common good. However, deceptive ideals of utopia will also appear, and toward the end of the period an earth-shattering catastrophe may occur.

2011–2025: Neptune in mystical, chaotic Pisces will bring deep spiritual movements, mass psychic experiences and great migrations of starving peoples. Efforts of social revolution may fail, bringing great disillusionment, apathy and escapism, but hope returns toward the period's end. Many institutions will disappear or face upheaval. Humanity will first become fully linked together in one consciousness and one economy.

2025–2038: Neptune is in energetic Aries. This will be an extremely active period when pioneers appear over every hill and "progress" will resume. People will be in a confident, enterprising mood and plunge ahead with rebuilding a good society. Many reckless wars might break out, especially in America and Europe. The U.S. itself might break up or suffer revolution in this period, as it did during the previous Aries transit.

2038–2052: Neptune is in placid, complacent Taurus. This may be a new "gilded age" like the 1870s, as people dream again of getting rich, but the economy, overheated during the previous transit under Aries, may be unstable. This could result in uncertainty and disillusion that could fuel the "Green Revolution" (which climaxes in this period). Our whole economic and spiritual relationship with the planet will change, as people once again rediscover the sacredness of Mother Earth. Art styles will become sensitive and delicate.

2052–2065: Neptune is in inquisitive, inventive Gemini. This should be a positive, cheery, progressive era when humanity expands its vast network of communications. At the end of this period, however, look for much unrest. Health, economic, and religious problems, along with widespread migrations, put our New Age society at risk. Many deceptive, strange ideas and controversies will add to the uncertainty, and people could be wondering just what to believe.

2065–2079: These problems will continue in the early years of Neptune's Cancer transit. They could lead to ethnic, conservation, and libertarian movements and international crises. The definition of "family" and "home" will expand.

2079–2092: Neptune will be in confident Leo as we launch enthusiastically into a creative, revolutionary, expansive time. A new idea of "progress" will take us beyond technology to spiritual innovation and missionary zeal.

PLUTO IN THE SIGNS

Pluto produces significant transformations corresponding to the nature and areas of life symbolized by the sign it transits.

1577–1608, 1822–52, 2067–2096: In Aries, Pluto has signified the age of pioneers and of such missionary attitudes as the American "Manifest Destiny." England (which is traditionally ruled by Aries) prospered under Queens Elizabeth I and Victoria. In 1095, under Uranus and Pluto in Aries, Pope Urban announced the First Crusade. New "crusades" will be proclaimed in the 2080s and '90s.

1608–1640, 1852–84: In Taurus, Pluto has signified the generation of materialism, realism, and the "gilded age." From Galileo, Francis Bacon, and Descartes, to Charles Darwin and

Karl Marx, scientists tried to prove indestructible matter as the first cause of all things. In Gemini (1640–69, 1884–1914), it has signified the age of invention and mobility, when colonists and imperialists traveled the globe to fulfill the "white man's burden," and science and technology progressed by leaps and bounds.

1669–93, 1914–38: In Cancer, Pluto has signified national conflicts and intolerance (Salem witch trials, 1692, and Nazi takeover, 1933). Around 1700, Louis XIV started wars against his neighbors, the karma for which returned in 1914. Enormous upheaval came to the domestic affairs of nations (the New Deal, Stalinism, Hitler, Spanish Civil War, etc.).

1693–1712, 1938–57: As Pluto transited Leo, the last (we hope) World War was fought. Great leaders reshuffled the balance of power (Peter the Great, William of Orange, Louis XIV, Hitler, Stalin, FDR, Churchill).

1712–1725, 1957–71: In Virgo, Pluto represented the age of technology and social protest. The Newcomen pump and iron smelting (1712), the communications satellite, the integrated circuit, and the computer chip were invented. The civil rights movement, the Theater of the Absurd, beatniks, hippies, and Rococo sensualists challenged established culture.

1725–37, 1971–84: In Libra, Pluto has represented a generation of peace. The U.S withdrew from Vietnam. Stagnation and placidity prevailed, and diplomacy advanced. Musicians were creative and fertile.

1491–1503, 1737–49, 1984–95: With Pluto in Scorpio, its ruling sign, great discoveries, or world transformations have occurred, such as Columbus' voyage in 1492, the discovery of Pompeii around 1740, and the fall of the Soviet Empire in 1991. In the mid-1980s, sex and death became linked through the AIDS crisis.

1503–1516, 1749–62, 1995–2008: In Sagittarius, Pluto has represented enlightenment. Jesus and the Greek philosophers of Athens emerged during this transit, as did Diderot's *Encyclopedia* and Rousseau's *The Social Contract*. Our own golden age should reach its height in this period, as New Age prophecies inspire new ideas.

1516–1531, 1762–78, 2008–2024: In Capricorn Pluto has signified reformation of existing institutions. Martin Luther initiated the Reformation, Americans declared and won independence. In ancient Greece, Pericles led the way for America with the world's first democracy.

1531–53, 1778–98, 2024–43: In Aquarius, Pluto has a powerful impact, signifying an age of revolution. Philip the Fair and Edward I weakened feudalism. Henry VIII shook up England and broke with Rome. The French Revolution transformed the world. Charlemagne saved Europe from the Dark Ages, and Constantine institutionalized Christianity. Look for similar drastic changes after 2024!

1553–77, 1798–1822, 2043–67: In Pisces, Pluto brought disillusion, a quest for the sublime, and religious wars and controversy. Defeat and destruction have caused painful disillusionment and sorrow. Around 1798, "romantic" poetry and painting began, and the religious "great awakening" happened. Pessimism and disillusion followed the conquests and defeat of Napoleon in 1815. The previous transit saw Bloody Mary and Queen Elizabeth take turns putting Protestants and Catholics to death. The Pope gained power over the Emperor in the 1070s. Socrates was put to death in 399 B.C., leading to the visionary pessimism of Plato and Euripides.

PLUTO'S "FERTILIZATION" OF NEPTUNE

Pluto's orbit around the Sun is by far the most eccentric in the solar system. It ventures far out into space to a distance twice as far from the Sun as Neptune, then swoops back and "surfaces" above the God of the Oceans to spend twenty years inside Neptune's orbit. For this brief period, Pluto is actually nearer to the Sun than Neptune. This is called Pluto's perihelion passage, when it reaches its closest point to the Sun and Earth.

This is an enormously vivid cosmic symbol, and has become well known because it's happening in the 1990s. Every time Pluto returns inside Neptune's orbit, it is as though he is sending Persephone back above ground to bring new life to the world. The phoenix rises from the ashes. Before its perihelion, Pluto spends many decades wandering in the darkness, searching and exploring silently the depths of the unknown, only to return later on above the orbit of Neptune to share its new powers and discoveries with humanity.

Pluto's most potent perihelion passage is the one following its conjunction with Neptune, about 100 years before. This is another reason a renaissance happens at these times. Despite its reputation as the "planet of death," Pluto has never failed to bring new life at these times (marked * below). Pluto's other perihelion passage, coming 100 years after its opposition to Neptune, also brings important alterations to society and culture, although these changes remain mostly hidden for decades.

PLUTO'S PERIHELION PASSAGE SINCE THE AXIS AGE:

Date	Major Events
489 B.C.*	The Battle of Marathon, making possible the Greek Golden Age.
241 B.C.	The time of Ashoka, the Buddhist "philosopher-king" of India. Rome's defeat of Carthage put the future Roman Empire in the ascendant.
A.D. 7*	The Age of Augustus, close to the time of Christ's birth.
255	The time of philosopher Plotinus, and of Emperor Valerian who brought order out of chaos in Rome and who first joined sacred to secular power there.
503*	The time of Theodoric, and just prior to Justinian.
751	Pepin the Short founded the Carolingian Dynasty.
998*	The Ottonian Renaissance was at its peak.
1246	Height of the Gothic Age.
1492*	Columbus "discovered" America, and the High Renaissance began.
1741	The Enlightenment went into high gear, and the classical style of music was created. The Roman city of Pompeii was discovered beneath volcanic lava. This aroused interest in ancient societies, which fueled the democratic and romantic movements.

1989*	Democracy came to Eastern Europe in the most successful series of peaceful revolutions ever seen. World peace became possible with the end of the Cold War.
2237	Today's spiritual and green ideas will change how we live in society.
2484*	The next "rebirth" during the "Age of Light" will see illumination from the cosmos flooding the planet and reveal our place in the "galactic federation." The Earth itself will become transformed and bathed in Light.

9

High Times on the Time Lines

Many of us remember the turbulent decade of the 1960s. In the previous chapter, we pointed out that during this time, Neptune passed through Scorpio, sign of death and resurrection. In this revolutionary decade, John Kennedy called us to action, and Martin Luther King gave us a new dream. We heard about the dawning of the Age of Aquarius and the revival of spirit among a new generation. Under Scorpio we were reborn and regenerated; our intense experiences were a gateway of spiritual initiation. We once more became a people who could reach toward "the unreachable star."

Death precedes rebirth, though, and our hopes and dreams were literally shot down with our visionary leaders. Yet all the new possibilities continued to echo inside us. Before Dr. King left us, he said that "we as a people will get to the promised land," and however disillusioned we have become, however empty the promise may seem, one thing is clear—the planetary cycles support his prophecy. We saw in Chapter 6 how the '60s were just the start of a revolutionary cycle that aims to create a restored and peaceful planet. In Chapter 4 we learned that throughout history a golden age has always come one hundred years or so after Neptune joins Pluto in conjunction. We reached that landmark in 1992, which means that we can create a renaissance right now if we seize the opportunity.

In this chapter we unveil still more evidence for this rebirth, then weave everything together into a grand vision of history. First of all, consider again the movements of Neptune, the planetary "ark of humanity." Tracing back one cycle to 165 years before the sixties, we see another period of "spiritual initiation" very much like our own—the turbulent times of the French revolution. The Woodstock generation finds its historic echo in the generation of the romantics 165 years before, and though they were just as disillusioned as we (if not more so), they did not let their inspiration die. They channeled it into some of the greatest creative works in human history. Neptune was in virtually the same place in the sky in 1823 when Beethoven wrote the heaven-storming sounds of the "Ode to Joy" as when Leonard Bernstein played them to celebrate the opening of the Berlin Wall in 1989.

We have passed this way many times before. It is part of an amazing cyclic pattern which has never before been discussed by astrologers, to my knowledge. Each time Neptune transits

Scorpio, our spirit and vitality is once more restored to us. We are put in touch again with that creative intelligence that empowers and enriches our lives. Then Neptune carries us still higher toward an awesome summit in the sign of the Winter Solstice, Capricorn (equivalent to the house of the Midheaven). A brilliant and dazzling culmination follows as Neptune transits Aquarius, sign of the golden age. Whenever Neptune is in these "higher signs" of Scorpio through Aquarius, international relations improve, great discoveries are made, and artists become more creative. I call these periods the "High Times" or the Golden, Silver, and Copper Ages of Neptune.

There have been sixteen transits of Neptune through these four high signs since the Great Mutation or "Axis Age" in the Sixth Century B.C., and in each 493-year cycle of civilization there have been three. The first period is the Golden Age, when the creative forces of the new civilization are first expressed in a classic period or renaissance. The confidence of the age is reflected in serene and eloquent new forms of art. The Golden Ages are marked (G) in the text below.

The second Neptunian High Time is the Silver Age. It occurs in the middle of the cycle near the time when Neptune opposes Pluto (the "full Neptune"). It is a culminating climax, when civilization reaches full flower and gains the confidence to expand and conquer. Art becomes more dynamic, and wondrous temples are built. Scientific thought of great clarity often emerges. These periods have been even more impressive during more recent centuries, when Uranus has also joined Neptune in the high signs. The Silver Ages are marked (S).

The third and final Neptunian High Time is the Copper Age. This "last glory" of a waning civilization is a "proto-renaissance" and an emotionally charged "romantic age" that plants the seeds for the next cycle. Though very creative, this dramatic "high time" turns out to be a "false dawn," and it soon falls before the oncoming forces of disintegration. The Copper Ages are marked (C) below.

Now, let's follow these High Times throughout history.

THE HIGH TIMES OF NEPTUNE

501–446 B.C.: Benares enjoyed its golden age in India during the early days of Buddhism. The Greeks defeated the Persians around 480, giving them the confidence to create the first and greatest of the golden ages since the Great Mutation. In Athens, the great tragic dramas of Aeschylus and Sophocles were written, the philosopher Socrates appeared, and the Parthenon was built. Democracy was born under the leadership of Pericles (G).

337–282 B.C.: Alexander the Great expanded Greek power and influence across much of the ancient world. Aristotle brought Greek philosophy to its climax and paved the way for the great Greek scientists like Euclid and Archimedes. The library of Alexandria was founded (S).

173–118 B.C.: Rome gained control of the Mediterranean and was influenced by Greek culture. The first great Roman playwrights appeared. Pergamum in Asia Minor became the center of an advanced culture after turning back Celtic invaders in a replay of the Greek defeat of the Persians. Brilliant sculpture was created there for the dramatic "Altar of Zeus" (C).

10 B.C.– A.D. 46: Rome enjoyed its classical age under Augustus. Latin literature reached its peak in the works of Virgil, Horace, Livy, Ovid, and Seneca. The great sculpture of the "Acra Pacis" celebrated the Pax Romana. Jesus of Nazareth preached love and forgiveness, and inspired a religion that would span the world. Half a world away, the Mayans built magnificent pyramids at Teotihuacan (G).

155–210: Roman civilization reached its height under its last great emperors. Marcus Aurelius became Rome's "philosopher king." Ptolemy developed a system of astronomy and astrology that was gospel for 1,500 years. Civil wars began when this period ended (S).

319–374: This era included the last years of Constantine the Great, who created the first Christian Empire. The basilica of St. Peter in Rome set the pattern for future church architecture. Constantinople was founded, and the Gupta Empire was established in India. In 374, the barbarian invasions of Rome began, ending this "last glory" of the Roman Empire (C).

483–537: Byzantium enjoyed its brilliant golden age under Justinian. The most inspiring religious architecture and mosaics ever seen were created at Sancta Sophia, Sant Apollinare, and San Vitale. Theodoric restored civilization in Italy (later destroyed by Justinian's invasion in 536). Pseudo Dionysius and Boethius wrote the most inspiring and influential spiritual literature of the Dark Ages. The Mayans began building their great cities and temples in Guatemala (G).

646–701: The merging of Celtic and Christian civilizations in Northumbrian England would later spark a renewal on the continent. Here, the brilliant Lindesfarne gospels and similar elaborate designs were made, and the Venerable St. Bede created the first great history and literature of the West. Meanwhile, the Muslims established their empire, and the graceful and elegant culture of the Tang Dynasty in China was in its heyday. The Mayans reached their peak, and soon afterward began their decline (S).

810–865: Inspired by Byzantine grandeur and Northumbrian missionaries, the Christian conqueror Charlemagne initiated a great European cultural revival (although after 840 his heirs could not hold his fragile empire together). The new Islamic Dynasty of Harun al Rashid and al-Mamun in Baghdad brought Muslim science, literature, medicine, astronomy, and architecture to its brilliant peak, which sowed the seeds of Western European culture. The mystical Islamic sect of Sufism opened a universal path to the Spirit. In India, Shankara became the greatest Hindu Vedantic philosopher (C).

974–1029: Otto the Great turned back barbarian invaders and founded the Holy Roman Empire. The Abbey of Cluny spearheaded a great spiritual revival which created the new Romanesque (or "Cluniac") style of the first great cathedrals. The themes of medieval art were enunciated in the brilliant Ottonian Renaissance. The first cathedral schools initiated scholastic philosophy. China enjoyed its most brilliant golden age under the Sung, and Tamil sculpture and architecture in southern India rivaled the best Western art (G).

1138–1193: The troubadours created the first poetry of romantic love. The Romanesque cathedrals of the 1130s were followed by the luminous, graceful Gothic style invented by Abbot Suget of St. Denis in the 1140s and perfected in the cathedral at Chartres. Peter Abelard, St. Bernard, Giselbertis and Hildegard of Bingen were among the great philosophers and artists of this inspired period. As Neptune entered Pisces in 1194, the fervent townspeople of Chartres united to rebuild the world's most beautiful building after it was damaged by fire. Halfway around the world, the Orient's most splendid temple was erected at Angor Wat (S).

1301–1356: Giotto opened the "Proto-renaissance" in Italy with the most dramatic paintings seen since ancient times. The inventive poet Dante summed up Medieval culture in *The Divine Comedy*. The Lorenzetti brothers highlighted the great artistic school at Siena, and Petrarch enunciated the first humanist philosophy. At the end of this "false dawn," as Kenneth Clark called it, the Black Plague sucked the life out of Europe and accelerated the destruction of the medieval world (C).

1465–1520: The High Renaissance began in the 1460s under Lorenzo de Medici. The world's greatest sculpture was created, from the last works of Donatello to Michaelangelo's masterpieces, as were classic paintings by Raphael, Durer, and Leonardo daVinci. Columbus and Vasco daGama opened up new worlds to Europe. It was the time of great humanistic poets like Erasmus and the beginning of the Reformation. This "golden moment," as Kenneth Clark called it, came to an end with the deaths of Raphael and daVinci in 1519–20 and the peasant revolts in 1522 (G).

1629–1684: The buoyant Baroque style of architecture was created by Bernini and Borromini. Christopher Wren built the fabulous St. Paul's Cathedral in London, and the Taj Mahal was completed in India. Baroque painting reached its summit in the art of Rubens, Velasquez, and the Dutch masters (Rembrandt, Ruisdael, Vermeer). Painters Claude Lorrain and Nicholas Poussin and playwrights Moliere and Racine highlighted French classicism under "Sun King" Louis XIV. Literature reached a summit in *Paradise Lost* by John Milton, this period's equivalent of Dante. Descartes opened the way for modern science and philosophy in a "revolution" that climaxed in the physics of Issac Newton (S).

1792–1848: This was the Age of Revolution and Romanticism, beginning with the fall of the French Monarchy to the volunteers singing La Marseillaise, and ending with the climactic, continental uprising in 1848, whose failure dashed the Romantic dreams. Blake, Wordsworth, and Coleridge created romantic poetry, and Byron, Shelley, and Keats personified its youthful adventure. Goethe, Pushkin, Balzac, Dickens, and the Brontë sisters brought new breadth and sensibility to literature, while Turner, Constable, Delacroix, and Friedrich expressed the Romantic spirit in painting. The German idealists from Kant to Hegel stretched the limits of philosophy, while Lavoisier, Dalton, and Volta vastly expanded the range of science. Beethoven, Chopin, Schubert, and Mendelssohn expressed romantic ideals in the world's most inspiring and heroic music (C).

1956–2011: Once again, the great patterns of history (in this case the "high times" of

Neptune) indicate that ours is a "golden age." It is the first age of inner and outer space, beginning with Sputnik in 1957. In the coffee houses of San Francisco, "beat" poets like Lawrence Ferlinghetti and Allen Ginsberg launched a "renaissance" in 1956, which expanded into the "hippie" psychedelic culture ten years later. The great achievements in space exploration such as the Moon landing in 1969 have inspired artistic movies like 2001, and have resulted in incredibly rapid advances in technology, which are helping to open new art forms in electronic and computer media. Nam June Paik pioneered video art, and Brian Eno used a palette of electronic tools to resculpt sound into "ambient music." The Internet has made a worldwide exchange of ideas possible Meanwhile, the revival of occultism and spirituality and the new thrust to bring science and religion together offer opportunities to explore "inner" space, and other great composers have created "space music" that expands our awareness. But much more needs to be done. We'd better not wait for the famous "end of the Mayan Calendar" in 2012 to express our full creativity, because today's "golden age" may start to wane after then (G).

2120–2175: This High Time of Neptune should be an expansive, dynamic Baroque phase that brings today's new trends to their culmination, the Silver Age of the current cycle of civilization. Great temples will celebrate our new cosmic, inner Earth wisdom, and it's quite likely that people will begin settling in outer space. The new paradigm of science and religion will be fully developed (S).

2283–2339: This "romantic time" will climax our age and contain the seeds of the "Age of Light." Many brilliant prophetic visions will be expressed (C).

On our first "time line" (on the next two pages), I have placed the dates of "noted" painters and sculptors (as defined by the *World Almanac* in 1993) from their twentieth year to their death, and compared them with the dates for the High Times of Neptune. I have also added the dates for the High Times of Uranus and Pluto. The artists are represented on the top part of the chart, while you will find the planets' high periods shown along the bottom. As you can see, the correspondence with Neptune is striking. The number of artists during the Renaissance High Time was nineteen, compared with only three during the late Mannerist phase. Then it rose to eleven at the peak of the Baroque High Time, after which it fell to only one at the turn of the Eighteenth Century. Then it slowly rose again, jumping way up in 1800 and reaching twenty-three at the height of the Romantic High Time in 1820. Thence forward, the rise in population and the factor of nearness to the present inflates the number of artists in the Almanac. The number of "noted" artists working in 1510 during the Renaissance "High Time" was over six times the number in 1580–90, during the late Mannerist phase, and nineteen times the number in 1690–1700, during the late Baroque. Notice also that artistic momentum increased in the years following the Neptune-Pluto conjunction—that is, in the Fifteenth Century and the 1890s–1900s.

ARTISTS AND THE TIME LINES
1260–1740

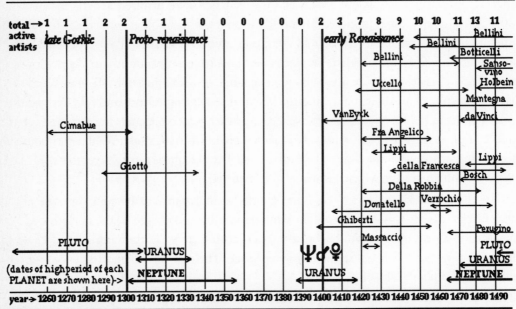

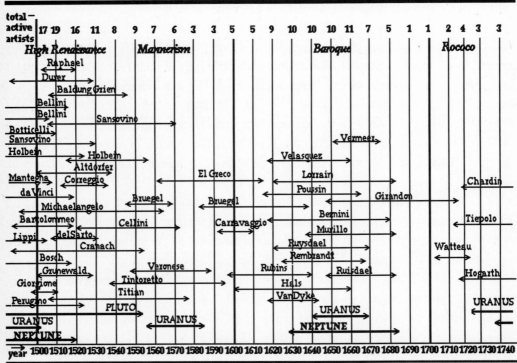

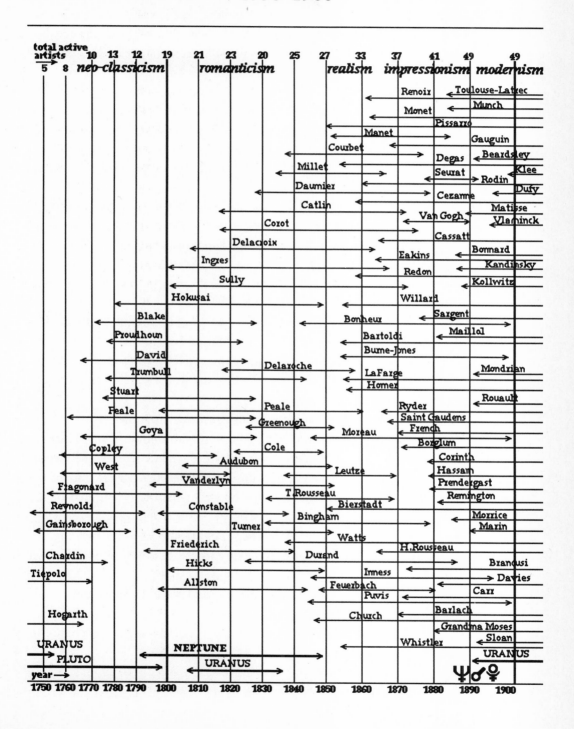

THE HIGH TIMES OF URANUS

The High Times of Uranus are also significant. Here are the dates for the High Times of Uranus during the current and previous two 493-year cycles of civilization:

970–998: The Ottonian Renaissance and the Sung Golden Age began.

1053–1082: This period is often called a "turning point," when the thrust of the new European awakening accelerated. Norman Romanesque architecture appeared, as did musical polyphony and the first troubadours.

1137–1166: The Romanesque era climaxed, and the Gothic style began.

1221–1249: This was the "High Gothic" Age when Amiens and Reims Cathedrals were built. The radiant Rayonant style of architecture appeared, and St. Thomas Aquinas brought Medieval scholastic philosophy to its summit.

1305–1333: Giotto painted the Arena Chapel, and Dante wrote *The Divine Comedy*. The Lorenzetti Brothers spearheaded the Siena school of painting.

1388–1417: The Renaissance began in Florence. The dome and minaret of the mosque appeared in India. Geoffrey Chaucer wrote *The Canterbury Tales*

1472–1501: The Renaissance reached its heights in the paintings of Botticelli and the early works of daVinci and Michaelangelo. The classical revival was in high gear.

1556–1584: This period spanned Mogul Akbar the Great's reign in India and the earlier years of Elizabeth I in England. Spain's Age of Gold.

1640–1668: Baroque Art reached its apotheosis in the works of Bernini, Rembrandt, and Poussin. The Taj Mahal was built. The Scientific Revolution began.

1724–1752: This was the period of the early Enlightenment led by Voltaire and Diderot. Baroque music reached a summit with Bach and Handel, and Rococo architects like Neumann dazzled the world with their delicate designs.

1807–1835: This was the summit of Romantic painting, music, and poetry.

1891–1919: This period opened with Gauguin's voyage to Tahiti and the artistic revolution by Cezanne, and ended with the demonstration of Einstein's Theory of Relativity. Freud, Jung, Bergson, Picasso, Matisse, Kandinsky, and deChirico were among the many other illustrious names of this creative "new dawn," which was shattered by the First World War.

1975–2003: Uranus was still in the midst of another "High Time" as of this writing. An accelerating stream of change presents an opportunity to create a new Global Golden Age of Aquarian culture.

2058–2087: This will be the next High Time of Uranus, another chance for good political leadership to encourage new movements in the arts.

2142–2170: This will mark the summit of the current cycle of civilization; a chance to fully express the ideals of our new Aquarian Age.

Other Uranus High Times will occur in the years 2226–2254 and 2310–2338.

THE HIGH TIMES OF PLUTO

Potent, powerful Pluto can also help to lift civilization to its greatest heights. Pluto travels through the high signs of Scorpio through Aquarius twice in one 500-year cycle of civilization, once during and after Neptune's Golden Age (thus extending it) and once during and preceding its Copper Age (so that the preceding years are building toward it).

481–407 B.C.: This was the Greek Golden Age from the defeat of the Persians to the defeat of Athens in the Peloponnesian War.

234–162 B.C.: Roman culture absorbed the Greek, and Pergamum fully expressed Hellenistic art. The Chin and Han Dynasties established the unified Chinese Empire.

A.D. 13–84 : This was the time of Jesus, St. Paul, the Stoic philosopher Epictetus, and the poet Seneca. Architectural glories were built in Rome and Teotihuacan.

259–329: Diocletian and Constantine gave the Roman Empire its last great days. Christianity was established. Neo-platonic philosophy appeared.

505–573: The glorious Byzantine cathedrals and Mayan temples were built. Justinian reunited the Roman Empire, and Buddhism arrived in Japan.

752–818: Pepin the Short and Charlemagne created the Carolingian Empire and rescued Europe from the Dark Ages. The Abbassid Dynasty lifted Arab culture to its heights in Baghdad.

998–1064: Romanesque culture began in Europe. The Sung and Tamil golden ages began. Arab scholarship permeated Europe.

1244–1308: The Gothic Age reached its height, and the Proto-renaissance began. Marco Polo traveled to the East.

1491–1553: Columbus discovered America and Copernicus transformed our view of the cosmos. The High Renaissance and the Reformation occurred.

1737–1798: This was the Age of Enlightenment and the American and French Revolutions. Major discoveries made in electomagnetism, chemistry, and mathematics.

1984–2043: Once again, our age fits the pattern. New possibilities have opened for our current Golden Age, now that world peace has become possible with the end of the Cold War. Our view of the cosmos will be expanded and spiritualized in these years.

2230–2288: Psychic powers and high technology will be applied to social change as never before. A new "enlightenment" will set off sparks for the "Age of Light."

DOUBLE AND TRIPLE STIMULATION

If any one of the outer planets in the high signs can stimulate such startling advances in civilization all by itself, just think how powerful two of them together are. It stands to reason that the more planets are in the higher signs, the higher human culture soars. If two planets are high, the signs are very propitious—but imagine the effect of all three of the creative outer planets in the highest signs. Surely, these must be the greatest ages in human history.

Judge for yourself. All three outer planets were high between 1491, when Columbus was preparing for his voyage of discovery, and 1501, when Michaelangelo carved his statue of David, and Leonardo daVinci was working on the Mona Lisa at the peak of the

High Renaissance. What better example could you find of civilization at its height! Here were our most celebrated artistic triumphs, combined with the immense opportunity of the New World. Looking back further, we find the other most celebrated period in history, the peak of the Greek Golden Age from 455–446 B.C., when Pericles ruled Athens as the noble philosopher-democrat, when the sculptor Phidias and the dramatist Sophocles created their great works, and when Socrates first walked the streets beneath the Acropolis, where the columns were rising for the Parthenon. These two rare moments, when Uranus, Neptune, and Pluto skirted the heights of the zodiac for some of the longest periods ever, are the two undisputed, unsurpassed moments of triumph for the creative spirit, the fairest days of the human adventure! All three planets were also high between A.D. 319–329 when the foundations of Christian culture were laid, including the first cathedral of St. Peter, between 810–818 when Charlemagne lifted Europe out of the Dark Ages and Arab culture soared to its glittering heights at Baghdad, and between 1305–1308 when Giotto created his awesome, dramatic works in the Arena Chapel and Dante wrote *The Divine Comedy*.

Such striking evidence is breathtaking, but what is most amazing is what this pattern says about *our* times. Pluto entered Scorpio in 1984, and all three outer planets are in high signs for the first time since 1501. This condition lasts until Uranus leaves Aquarius in 2003, making it by far the longest such period so far in recorded history. What a different picture astrology gives us of our time than the usual business-as-usual or gloom and doom. If these indications are right, there will be startling changes in the years ahead, but no collapse of civilization and no nuclear, natural, or supernatural Armageddon. We will not only survive our current troubles; we will rise up to create the greatest Renaissance and Golden Age in recorded history!

The opportunity will not last for long, however. The planets give us no guarantees, for the Golden Age will not unfold all by itself. Now is the time for each of us to share what we have to offer. Today's Renaissance will be whatever we make it. Ours can be an age of discovery, creativity, increasing world unification and spiritual renewal. Whatever schemes you have been harboring for the advancement of humanity or the celebration of the springtime of peace, now is the time to act. The New World is being born within the cracks of the dying civilization all around us.

Here is a list of the dates of Double and Triple Stimulation in each cycle of civilization from the Axis Age to A.D. 2600 so you can check the "height of civilization" during these times for yourself. Also listed are the lowest periods when none of the three outer planets were high.

HIGHEST PERIODS (Three planets high)
455–446 B.C.   A.D.319–329   810–818   998   305–1308   1491–1501
1984–2003   2477–2502

HIGH PERIODS (Two planets high)

Cycle 1:

481–455 B.C.	446–426 B.C.	288–282 B.C.	204–175 B.C.	173–162 B.C.	121–118 B.C.

Cycle 2:

10–7 B.C.	A.D. 13–46	48–78	155–161	299–319	329

Cycle 3:

483–496	505–537	550-573	646–664	802-810	818–831

Cycle 4:

974–998	998–1029	1053–1064	1138–1166	1244–1249	1301–1305
1308–1333					

Cycle 5:

1472–1491	1501–1520	1640–1668	1737–1752	1792–1798	1807–1835

Cycle 6:

1975–1984	2003–2011	2142–2170	2230–2254	2283–2288	2310–2338

Cycle 7:

2476–2477	2502–2505

LOW PERIODS (No planets high)

Cycle 1:

593–539 B.C.	509–501 B.C.	407–371 B.C.	342–337 B.C.	258–34 B.C.

Cycle 2:

91–37 B.C.	A.D. 84–132	210–216	245–259	374–383

Cycle 3:

412–467	580–634	701–718	747–752	865–886

Cycle 4:

915–970	1082–1137	1193–1221	1356–1388

Cycle 5:

1417–1465	1553–1556	1584–1629	1684–1724	1848–1891

Cycle 6:

1919–1956	2043–2058	2087–2120	2175–2226	2339–2394

Cycle 7:

2422–2447	254–2561

(At all other times one planet was high. These were usually "medium" periods.)

THE TIME LINE OF CIVILIZATION

By combining the various astrological factors we've mentioned so far and putting them all on a point system, I've developed a time line which graphically portrays all the ups and downs in each period. This is based on a sampling of the cosmic forces in play at the beginning of each decade, for the years 600 B.C.–A.D. 2600. It measures the "height" of civilization, meaning the level of cultural creativity and political viability of civilization worldwide, although with a somewhat greater emphasis on the West.

It's necessary to further clarify what I mean by "high" and "low" times. In high periods, which score the most points in our astrological "system," people are genuinely inspired by spiritual or humanistic ideals. Artists, scientists, and philosophers are more numerous and creative than during low times. Peace, freedom, and/or political order are developing. People are optimistic, and many new ideas and attitudes are afoot.

By contrast, during low periods people tend to be materialistic, close-minded, fanatic, or superstitious. There may be exciting technological progress, but science and philosophy are dominated by dangerous, questionable, materialistic doctrines. War, terror, murder, and destruction prevail to a much greater degree than during high times. People are pessimistic, and conformity and mediocrity predominate.

Of course, these are generalizations. You can find creative artists during low times, and war and destruction don't come to an end during high times. In addition, on any point system there are inaccuracies due to rigidity in the rules. Most of these inaccuracies, however, can be explained by two regular patterns. First, the period of the "Baroque Trine" (about 200 years after each Neptune-Pluto conjunction) should have a score of about ten to twenty points higher than the point system allows, because civilization is then moving toward its climactic half-way point in the "Silver Age." Second, the Triple Conjunction of 577 B.C. and the conjunction/opposition in the 1390s seemed to propel civilization higher during the following 100 years than is reflected in the point system.

DETAILS OF THE POINT SYSTEM

Neptune's sign: For Sagittarius, Capricorn, and the first nine years of Aquarius, add fifteen points. For Scorpio, fourteen points. For the last five years of Aquarius, thirteen points. Libra and Pisces, three points. Aries, Cancer, Leo, and Virgo, one point. Taurus and Gemini, zero points.

Uranus' sign: For Scorpio, Sagittarius, Capricorn, and Aquarius, add six points. For Libra, two points. For Virgo and Pisces, one point. For other signs, zero points.

Pluto's sign: For Scorpio, Sagittarius, Capricorn, and Aquarius, add eight points. For Pisces, three points. For Libra, two points. For Aries and Virgo, one point. For Taurus, Gemini, Cancer, and Leo, zero points.

Four points are added to the year nearest Pluto's perihelion. Two synergy points are added to the score for years in which all three planets are in high signs.

Points for aspects between the outer planets: If a Neptune-Pluto conjunction occurred within five years, add twelve points. Within ten years, add six points, and within fifteen years, four points. If a Neptune-Pluto opposition occurred within three years, add eight points. Within six years, add four points. Add ten points to the year closest to the waxing Neptune-Pluto trine. If the years are equidistant, add five points to each. Add six points to the year closest to the exact waning trine(s). During years of a continuous waning trine, add three points; and if the trine is within orb but never becomes exact before leaving orb, add two points. For a continuous or exact waxing sextile, add four points. If the sextile never becomes exact before leaving orb, add three points. For a Neptune-Pluto square, add two points. For the waning Neptune-Pluto sextile, add zero points.

If a Uranus-Neptune conjunction occurs within three years, add eight points; within six years, add four points. If a Uranus-Neptune opposition occurs within three years, add six points; within six years, add three points. If a Uranus-Pluto conjunction occurs within three years, add six points; within six years, add three points. If a Uranus-Pluto opposition occurs within three years, add four points; within six years, add two points. In 1770, two points were added for a close grand trine between the outer planets. In 1780, 1850, and 1930, one point was added for the discovery of a new planet.

Creative energy builds after Neptune's conjunction to Pluto, but wanes later on. Therefore, points are added as follows, using the nearest decade to the conjunction:
First 100 years after a Neptune-Pluto conjunction: four points.
100–150 years after a conjunction: five points.
150–250 years after a conjunction: four points.
250–300 years after a conjunction: three points.
300–400 years after a conjunction: two points.
400–430 years after a conjunction: one point.

It usually takes from ten to thirty years for creative and powerful people to absorb and work out the inspired impulses coming from the outer planets during a high decade. Therefore, I have added "momentum points." Using only the total raw score so far (not scores to which momentum has already been added), momentum points have been added as follows: For a raw score of fifteen to nineteen points, add two points to the following decade's score. For twenty to twenty-four points, add four points to the next decade, and two points to the decade after next. For twenty-five to twenty-nine points, add six points to the next decade, and four points to the decade after next. For thirty or more points, add eight points to the next decade, five points to the decade after next, and three points to the third decade.

In addition, special momentum is added for periods when more planets are in high signs than are reflected in the raw score (for example, two planets were high between 1244 and 1249, and this was not reflected in the score for 1240 or 1250—years when only one planet was high). Add two points to the next decade, and if three planets were high (as in 1305–1308) add four points.

On the next few pages are time-line graphs of "The Height of Civilization," relating human history to the high and low times of of Uranus, Neptune, and Pluto, as described above. Using our point system, we follow corresponding important events and significant historical figures decade-by-decade for the years 600 B.C. through A.D. 2600. In this way, we take a broadly defined measure of the cultural creativity and political activity in civilization worldwide. Now, check the time line charts to see how the scores for each decade match up with the record of history!

TIME LINE: "THE HEIGHT OF CIVILIZATION"
600 B.C.–A.D. 280

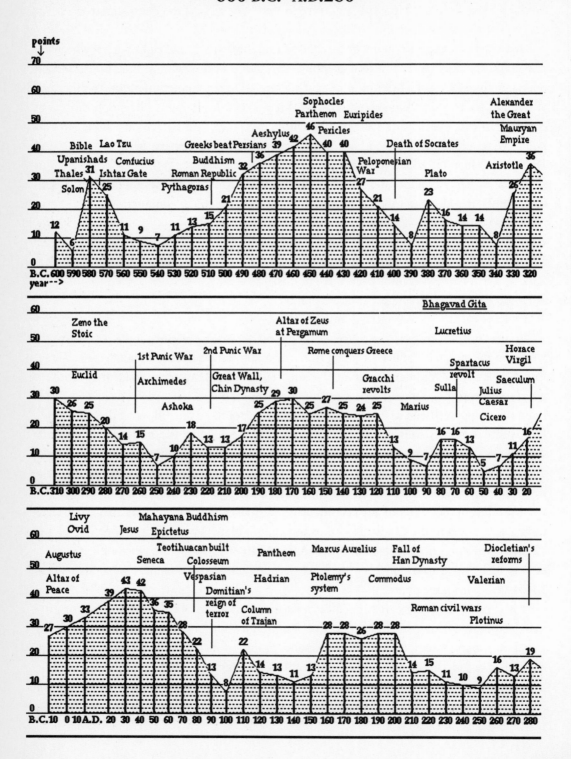

TIME LINE: "THE HEIGHT OF CIVILIZATION"
A.D. 290–1130

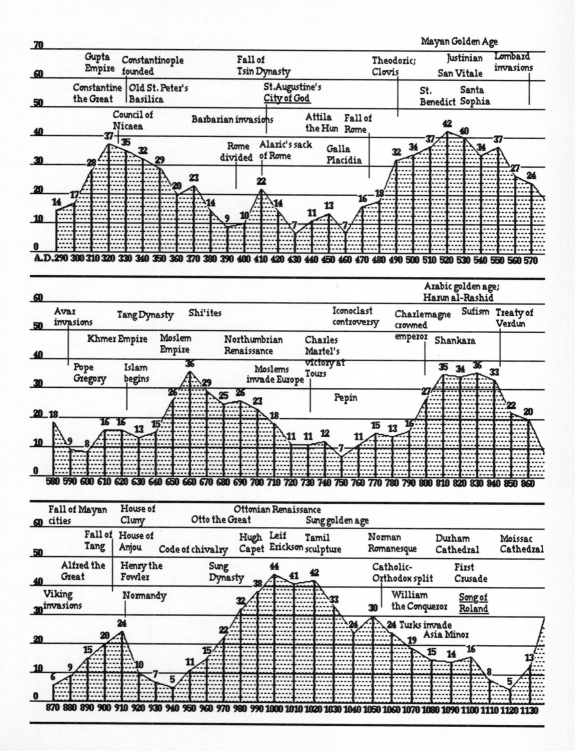

TIME LINE: "THE HEIGHT OF CIVILIZATION"
A.D. 1140–1880

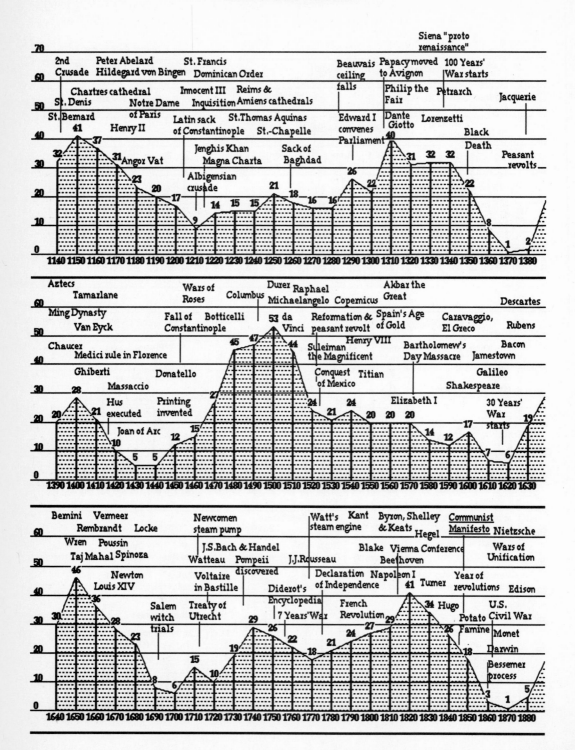

126

TIME LINE: "THE HEIGHT OF CIVILIZATION"
A.D. 1890–2600

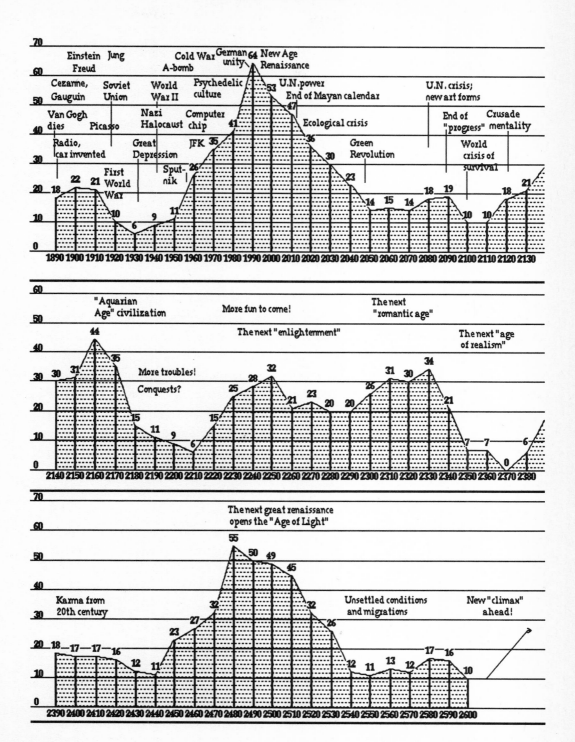

As you can see, the highest scores on the Time Line are remarkably consistent with the highest ages of civilization. But can you believe it? The 1990s are the highest decade of all time. Can this be true? Is our Time Line totally skewed, or do we have some awesome potential which we haven't yet realized? Is something going on that hasn't yet received the attention it deserves? Let's interpret this message from the cosmos correctly. If the 1990s have the highest score in history, this does not validate what we are already doing; it is an invitation (perhaps even a command) to do much more. We should take heart, because ours may be the best opportunity in all of history to be super-creative, if we open our eyes to the awesome possibilities around us. In the 1990s, we have already witnessed the most amazing breakthroughs ever seen toward world peace and freedom. We also seem to be getting stimulus from paranormal realms. As Pluto reached its perihelion in 1989–1990, a sudden increase occurred in the number of those strange and wonderful "crop circles" that have been appearing. More "unexplained" events (like sightings of angels and the Virgin Mary) are happening today than ever before. All this is a "message from the beyond" to those of us alive on the planet today that we can unleash our creativity and shift our concerns toward saving the Earth and rediscovering the Spirit.

Nothing from our culture so far can be remotely compared to other high-scoring periods of history, though. We have exciting new tools, but we aren't yet using more than a fraction of their potential. In fact, the technological mass media seems to be the chief enforcer of mediocrity and consumerism, as opposed to creativity and citizenship. Perhaps we should be amazed that anything of artistic significance makes it through the hoops and barriers of our commercial culture. But we have a long way to go to fulfill our destiny, and not much time. Further decline is the only alternative now to a great creative advance. So let's take advantage of this great opportunity of a more free and peaceful world to build a golden age.

Each person can do their part. Some of the other chapters in this book contain clues about the most successful paths for you, but a New Renaissance won't happen unless enough of us dedicate our lives to making it happen now. This means courageously "following your bliss" by unfolding your creative talents, and by doing work that fulfills your dearest ideals—at whatever cost. It means a commitment by our society as well as by individuals to bring this New Age about. It means expressing our deepest inspirations in brilliant, collective public works and in powerful artistic and social movements, as all the previous "highest" ages on the Time Line have done. The score stays very high for several decades after the 1990s, and some of the "momentum" from the cultural movements of the sixties and seventies (and perhaps from the still-hidden impetus of the 1990s) is still there too.

Looking ahead on the Time Line, we can get a good idea of the ups and downs to come. As our new Golden Age continues, we can look forward to increased reliance upon the United Nations, which for the first time has become an effective peace-keeping body since the end of the Cold War in 1989. This will happen despite many crises and the resulting resistance from "isolationists" and conservatives in the U.S. While I don't foresee a monolithic world government, a global structure is the only alternative to wars and "great power" rivalries. As the score on the Time Line declines after 2012, ecological disasters, global inequities, and refugee crises (major problems in the Twenty-First Century) will impel us toward a new Earth economy and a Green Revolution at mid-century. Although much progress in organizing a "great world society" will be made, the accompanying disruptions will cause greater chaos and unsettlement in the ensuing years. Toward the end of the Twenty-First Century, as we reach the waxing trine and other key configurations, creativity will rise again despite international crises and further catastrophes. We shall move into the Twenty-Second Century with increasing enthusiasm, though an evangelistic "crusading mentality" could lead to wars. By mid-century, we will be in the midst of the next "high period"—the climax of today's age of civilization. The new science and art will be thoroughly developed, and contact with extraterrestrial peoples will expand our culture. Global political and economic structures will solidify.

As usual, a decline will follow. This one will occur around 2180, as our urge to expand becomes overconfident, and intolerance and ethnic strife grows. Afterward, the Twenty-Third Century will see a continuing momentum toward reform and the spread of new ideas within existing institutions. Problems will level out, and a positive mood will prevail. As the Twenty-Fourth Century begins, great leaders and prophets will lay the foundations for the coming "Age of Light." Around 2340, however, some kind of catastrophe will open up a long period of troubles, as we face the "karma" from all the misdeeds of our technological, corporate lifestyle. We can expect wholesale dissolution and destruction of the old ways, and resulting discomfort and disorders. Economic insecurity and earth changes will force us to transform our money system. We may be unable to sustain the equalized, global economy built on "doing what you love" that had been developed earlier.

Eventually, things will be gradually sorted out. Out of the darkness, as so many times before, will arise the next renaissance. It will be perhaps the greatest one ever, as we are propelled at the end of the Twenty-Fifth Century into the "Age of Light" (described in the chapter "The Cosmic Clock of Civilization"). Humanity as a whole will become illuminated, and for the first time ever, we will learn to manage our society according to spiritual principles.

10

The Generations, A to Z

People who are born and grow up in roughly the same period of history share many characteristics. Their attitudes are formed by common experiences. These are the "generations," and we can paint a miniature portrait of each of them by using the outer planets as "brushes." The signs occupied by Uranus, Neptune, and Pluto in the birth charts of each group reveal major traits and potentials, as do the aspects between them.

The youth of the 1990s are famous as "Generation X." Counting backward, we can give each generation a letter in the same series. Since a "generation" like Generation X is supposed to last about twenty years, and the positions of the outer planets usually change faster than that, there are also sub-groups within each generation which I have called, for example, Generation X-a, Generation X-b, etc. The last Generation A would have been born about 500 years ago. The sequence of modern generations starts in 1885 with Generation T, a group very similar to Generation X—in fact, it was the previous "lost generation." Before Generation T, however, there was an inventive, idealistic generation that shaped modern culture. Let's start our list with them.

"The modernists," 1878–84 (Generation S-c,) (Uranus in Virgo trine Neptune in Taurus; Pluto in Taurus). These people could also be called the first of Generation T. Most of the modern artists and scientists of the early Twentieth Century, and many of its most visionary political leaders, came from this creative group. They were idealistic, yet practical. Examples: Mustapha Kemal (Ataturk), John Barrymore, Georges Bracque, Pierre Teilhard de Chardin, Albert Einstein, W. C. Fields, James Joyce, Henri Matisse, Benito Mussolini, Pablo Picasso, Sam Rayburn, Franklin Roosevelt, Oswald Spengler, Joseph Stalin, Igor Stravinsky, Leon Trotsky, Harry Truman.

"The seekers and founders," 1885–1897 (Generation T-a) (Neptune conjunct Pluto in Gemini; Uranus in Libra and Scorpio). These courageous people laid the political and cultural foundations of today's world, often following the course begun by the previous, more inventive Generation S. Very sensitive, they loved to explore life's mysteries, but they had to be sharp, ruthless, and adaptable in a collapsing world. Many of them died in the Great War. Others experienced the upheaval of the Twentieth Century to its fullest. Examples: Jack Benny, Neils Bohr, Pearl Buck, Chiang Kai Shek, Charles De Gaulle, Will Durant, Jimmy Durante, T. S.

Eliot, Dwight D. Eisenhower, William Faulkner, F. Scott Fitzgerald, Francisco Franco, David Ben Gurion, Martin Heidegger, Adolf Hitler, Ho Chi Minh, Aldous Huxley, Nikita Khruschev, Sinclair Lewis, Huey Long, Mao Tse Tung, Groucho Marx, Jawaharlal Nehru, Eugene O'Neill, Juan Peron, Dane Rudhyar, Josip Broz (Tito), J.R.R. Tolkien, Arnold Toynbee, Grant Wood.

"The flaming wits," 1898–1904 (Generation T-b) (Uranus in Sagittarius opposite Pluto in Gemini; Neptune in Gemini and Cancer). Many revolutionaries come from this group, along with many free-wheeling spirits. They were the "flaming youth" of the roaring twenties. Quite irrepressible, they made great actors and writers. Examples: Louis Armstrong, Humphrey Bogart, Chou En Lai, Gary Cooper, Bing Crosby, Thomas Dewey, Marlene Dietrich, Walt Disney, Enrico Fermi, Clark Gable, Cary Grant, Ernest Hemingway, Heinrich Himmler, Alfred Hitchcock, Bob Hope, Ayatollah Khomeini, Andre Malroux, Margaret Mead, Wayne Morse, Aristotle Onassis, George Orwell, Linus Pauling, Benjamin Spock, John Steinbeck, Adlai Stevenson, Strom Thurmond, Spencer Tracy.

"The organization men (and women)," 1904–1913 (Generation U-a) (Uranus in Capricorn and early Aquarius, opposite Neptune in Cancer; Pluto in Gemini). Bold and adventurous, many of these people were also emotionally unstable, secretive, extreme, or fanatic. Though often dissatisfied with their lot in life, most remained conservative and traditional. They were experts at rising within the ranks, and interested in business and civic projects. Those born 1912–13 border the next group. Examples: Spiro Agnew, Leonid Breshnev, Warren Burger, Albert Camus, William Casey, Norman Cousins, Richard J. Daley, Henry Fonda, Gerald Ford, John K. Galbraith, Barry Goldwater, Dag Hammarskjold, Rex Harrison, Katharine Hepburn, L. Ron Hubbard, Howard Hughes, Hubert Humphrey, Lyndon Johnson, Marshall MacLuhan, Joseph McCarthy, Richard Nixon, Lawrence Olivier, Tip O'Neill, Ronald Reagan, Nelson Rockefeller, Dean Rusk, Jean Paul Sartre, Robert Young.

"The techno-altruists," 1914–1919 (Generation U-b) (Uranus in Aquarius, Neptune in Leo, Pluto in Cancer). This group is similar to the previous one, but is more intellectual and more dedicated to social ideals. They were very charismatic, and provided most of the corporate technocrats. They were the knights of Kennedy's "Camelot." Examples: Leonard Bernstein, Walter Chronkite, Jackie Gleason, Paul Harvey, John F. Kennedy, Eugene McCarthy, Robert McNamara, Howard Metzenbaum, Edmund Muskie, Gregory Peck, William Proxmire, Anthony Quinn, Anwar Sadat, Arthur Schlesinger, Pete Seeger, Sargent Shriver, George Wallace, Mike Wallace, Alan Watts, Caspar Weinberger, Orson Welles.

"The warm souls," 1920–1929 (Generation V-a) (Uranus in Pisces, Neptune in Leo, Pluto in Cancer). This group is inwardly secure and confident. They are typically conventional, warm-hearted, and sensitive, and are subject to strange mystical experiences. Though humanitarian, they have made generally poor political leaders. Many excellent actors and poets come from this group. Examples: Marlon Brando, David Brinkley, Richard Burton, George Bush, Johnny Carson, Jimmy Carter, Fidel Castro, Judy Garland, Allen Ginsberg, John Glenn, Alexander Haig, Joseph Heller, Lee Iaccoca, John Paul II, Robert Kennedy,

Henry Kissinger, Timothy Leary, Jack Lemmon, Norman Mailer, George McGovern, Don Rickles, Rod Serling, Sen. Paul Simon, Elizabeth Taylor, Gore Vidal, Kurt Vonnegut.

The last part of this group (1927–29) has Uranus in Aries; thus it is more rebellious, activist, and individualist: Cesar Chavez, James Garner, Che Guevara, Martin Luther King, Patrick McGoohan, Walter Mondale.

"The rebels without a cause," 1930–35 (Generation V-b) (Uranus in Aries square Pluto in Cancer; Neptune in Virgo). This is an unpredictable, sometimes wild and explosive group that provided the leaders of the "Beat Generation." They make innovative, caring leaders, but often lack specific goals and are insecure or unsure of their direction. It is the first generation born after Pluto's discovery, so it and succeeding groups are sometimes less wedded to ancient traditions. Examples: Mario Cuomo, James Dean, Michael Dukakis, Mikhail Gorbachev, Dick Gregory, Jack Kemp, Ted Kennedy, Ken Kesey, Paul Krassner, Charles Kuralt, Jerry Lee Lewis, Shirley MacLaine, Charles Manson, Bill Moyers, Ralph Nader, Leonard Nimoy, Peter O'Toole, Ross Perot, Dan Rather, Carl Sagan, Robert Anton Wilson, Boris Yeltsin, Andrew Young.

"The silent generation," 1935–1939 (Generation V-c) (Uranus in Taurus, Neptune in Virgo, Pluto in Cancer). With all three planets in passive signs, they tended to be shy, quiet, conforming, moody, dreamy, sympathetic, and introspective. The one subject on which they can become outspoken is their desire to help others, and like the previous group, they can be quite unpredictable. Examples: Bruce Babbitt, Warren Beatty, Jerry Brown, Pat Buchanan, Judy Collins, Jane Fonda, David Frost, Gary Hart, Dustin Hoffman, Barbara Jordan, Jack Nicholson, Robert Redford, Sam Nunn, Ted Turner.

"The war babies," 1939–1946 (Generation W-a) (Uranus in Taurus/Gemini, trine Neptune in Virgo/Libra; Pluto in Leo). This group provided the leaders of the '60s "counterculture." They are outspoken, visionary, and unconventional, but they burned up much of their energy in their youth (Gemini). Impulsive, confident, spontaneous, and restless, they are rebels with a cause and can become great leaders. Perhaps they have been too fickle or adaptable to remain true to the great ideals of their youth. This group and the next are very musically talented. Examples: Muhammed Ali, Joan Baez, The Beatles, Joseph Biden, Chevy Chase, Robert DeNiro, John Denver, Bob Dylan, Richard Gephardt, Newt Gingrich, Tom Hayden, Jimi Hendrix, Jesse Jackson, Mick Jagger, Janis Joplin, Ted Koppel, Oliver North, Pat Schroeder, Tom Selleck, Pete Townshend, Paul Tsongas.

"The baby boomers," 1946–1956 (Generation W-b) (Uranus in late Gemini and Cancer, square Neptune in Libra; Pluto in Leo). This populous group is famous for its idealism and provided the "shock troops" for the '60s rebellions. These "flower children" are outgoing, warm, adventurous, confident, outspoken, and exhibitionist, but less original than the war babies. Born to prosperous but uncertain times, they were called "spoiled" and "impatient." Although they dropped out as "hippies," some also became the first "yuppies" (young urban professionals). They insist on their creative autonomy (Leo), but also long for union with others (Libra), so some of them are emotionally insecure or inconsistent. Examples:

Cher, Bill Clinton, Kevin Costner, Billy Crystal, Al Gore Jr., Jay Leno, David Letterman, Joe Montana, Jane Pauley, Arnold Schwarzenegger, Bruce Springsteen, Meryl Streep, John Travolta, Robin Williams, Oprah Winfrey.

"The baby boomers, part two," 1957–62 (Generation W-c) (Uranus in Leo, Neptune in Scorpio, Pluto in Virgo). This group was too young for the sixties, and so are more conventional in their approach to life. They are talented investigators or analysts, and provide many computer professionals. Most in this group are self-contained, shrewd, secretive, careful, tenacious, calculating, and capable. They are more thoughtful, hesitant, reflective, and unsure than the elder boomers, but often no less outgoing and exhibitionist (Uranus is in Leo). In fact, many in this group have already made quite an impression in the show business world. Examples: Scott Baio, Matthew Broderick, Katie Couric, Tom Cruise, Michael J. Fox, Woody Harrelson, Michael Jackson, Madonna, Demi Moore, Eddie Murphy, Donny Osmond, Sean Penn, Prince, Tim Robbins.

"The techno-punks," 1963–1969 (Generation X-a) (Uranus conjunct Pluto in Virgo; Neptune in Scorpio). It was said that the "punks" were the hippies of the eighties. This group is free-wheeling, impulsive, clever, and resourceful, but more hard-nosed and cynical than the baby boomers were. They grew up in a declining society with little moral direction, and so have been called "the new lost generation." They were labeled "Generation X" because they were so unsure of their identity or purpose. Despite having to grow up as "brash, pragmatic, suspicious, skeptical, selfish, sharp-eyed survivalists," this group has enormous creative potential once they find something to believe in. The first children of the computer age, they will undergo many personal upheavals and changes. Great scientists, artists, and revolutionary political leaders could emerge from this group. Examples: Lisa Bonet, Kurt Cobain, Wesley Snipes, Rob Lowe, Marlee Matlin, Sinead O'Connor, Luke Perry, Jason Priestley, Kieffer Sutherland.

"The mellow ones," 1970–1974 (Generation X-b) (Uranus in Libra, Neptune in Sagittarius, Pluto in Virgo/Libra). This group is mostly seen as a friendly, easygoing, confused, indolent group of "slackers," but it has great potential in music and diplomacy. Not so fanatical and less cynical than their elder brothers and sisters, they are often wise, generous, and mature. This group needs to motivate and discipline itself, and make up for its often poor educational background. Once it does, some very talented artists, writers, philosophers, and teachers may come from this sub-generation. Examples: Christina Applegate, Kirk Cameron, Neil Patrick Harris.

"The explorers," 1975–1981 (Generation X-c) (Uranus in Scorpio, Neptune in Sagittarius, Pluto in Libra). This group is more intense, exuberant, and disciplined than the previous one. They are "mellow," but also very cynical. Relationships and sex are important to this generation, like other recent ones. Many children of the seventies and eighties feel the need to fill the cultural void in their lives by exploring the extremes and traveling widely. They see the lurking danger to their future, so the best of them are driven to investigate the roots of our problems, although others may act out their alienation destructively. Examples:

Macauley Culkin, Fred Savage, Shannon Miller, Melissa Joan Hart.

"Explorers, part two," 1982–84 (Generation X-d) (Uranus and Neptune in Sagittarius, Pluto in Libra). Temperamentally, this exuberant group is more like the "mellow ones," but they are also definitely "explorers." They are undisciplined and unfocused, but very positive and mature otherwise. This transitional sub-generation will be a great source of visionaries, adventurers, humorists, storytellers, writers, and philosophers, but don't look for too many great political leaders.

"The benevolent entrepreneurs," 1984–88 (Generation Y-a) (Uranus in Sagittarius, Neptune in Capricorn, Pluto in Scorpio). This is a more ambitious and well-disciplined group. It will include many far-seeing leaders and entrepreneurs. Though most will probably be on the conservative side, many will organize great projects for the public benefit. They feel a great duty to society and humanity.

"The committed ones," 1988–1995 (Generation Y-b) (Uranus conjunct Neptune in Capricorn, Pluto in Scorpio). This is a group with outstanding potential. It is a very precocious generation, but won't burn itself out in youth. They are steady, persistent, determined, ambitious, and passionate. They have great talent in the arts, politics, and organization, and they may be the great leaders who lay down lasting foundations for a new age of civilization. On the other hand, some might consider them too cold, calculating, rigid, worldly, or obsessed with their own goals.

"The flame throwers," 1996–2003 (Generation Y-c) (Uranus in Aquarius, Neptune in late Capricorn and Aquarius, Pluto in Sagittarius) This will be a very outgoing, irrepressible, exuberant generation, quick to question authority and convention. They will be brilliant intellectuals, inventors, reformers, and propagandists.

"The universal free spirits," 2003–2010 (Generation Z-a) (Uranus in Pisces, Neptune in Aquarius, Pluto in Sagittarius/early Capricorn). Their successors will be similar, but more easygoing, sensitive, and poetic. They will follow the paths laid down by the previous two generations, but will show greater brilliance in the imaginative arts. As the first of Generation Z, they will teach compassion for humanity as we all reach the "omega point" of universal human awareness after 2012.

"The lonely rebels," 2011–2018 (Generation Z-b) (Uranus in Aries square Pluto in Capricorn; Neptune in Pisces). This group will be similar to those born in the early 1930s. Like them, they will be confused rebels or lonely seekers in their youth. Growing up in times of crisis, they will insist on breaking free from authorities and blazing their own path, however unsure of where it might lead them. Highly visionary, in later years some of them will be able to adapt and find a powerful leadership position within society.

"The silent searchers," 2018–2025 (Generation Z-c) (Uranus in Taurus, Neptune in Pisces, Pluto in Capricorn). This generation will be similar to the "silent generation" of the late 1930s. Confused seekers like their elder brothers and sisters, they will keep many of their hopes and dreams to themselves until later in life, when they will effectively act on their desire to help others. Many will be acquisitive and conformist due to their strong desire for security.

"Green pioneers," 2025–2032 (Generation A-a) (Uranus in Gemini trine Pluto in Aquarius; sextile Neptune in Aries) With this generation, we start our letter count over again and arrive back at "A" (the last generation A having lived about 500 years ago). Like the "war babies" of the 1940s, this will be a highly idealistic, inventive, dynamic, and creative group determined to change the world. Instead of "dropping out" or protesting against society as their grandparents did, these people will be intensely active and goal-oriented. They will be the young leaders of the "Green Revolution" at mid-century, intent on transforming the world no matter how disruptive it may be to the peace or the status quo.

GENERATIONS IN AMERICA

William Strauss and Neil Howe wrote a best seller titled *Generations: The History of America's Future*. They have no knowledge of astrology as far as I know; nevertheless, this book has become quite famous in the astrological community. Why? Because the length of the "generational cycle" they describe is eighty to ninety years: the same as the time Uranus takes to travel around the zodiac (eighty-four years). The authors described a repeating pattern of generations whose characteristics largely determined American history, and therefore, the future. We are the children of the times in which we grew up; we carry that signature through our lives, and influence history in turn. Strauss and Howe (themselves baby boomers) traced a cycle of four types of generation (each about twenty years long) which have reappeared five times since 1584: Idealist, Reactive, Civic, and Adaptive (akin to fire, earth, air and water). Each is built around the periodic "great American worldly crisis" that corresponds with the transit of Uranus in Gemini every eighty-four years: King William's War (1689–97), the Revolutionary War (1774–81), the Civil War (1861–65), and World War II (1941–45). About twenty-five to forty years later, a "spiritual awakening" comes. American history oscillates between these two poles.

The cycle works something like this: the Idealists grow up indulged in a prosperous but spiritually impoverished world which has successfully navigated the great crisis, and comes of age propelled by a spiritual awakening. They become elder leaders during the next crisis. The Reactives grow up during a spiritual awakening when institutions are being questioned or destroyed. Their elders desert them to pursue religious or personal growth, so they become alienated risk-takers and mature into pragmatic managers. Next, the Civics grow up under Idealist parents who give strong moral guidance. In youth, they give themselves dutifully to help in the great crisis, brought on by the mounting neglect of secular problems. Afterward, they build powerful institutions, only to be criticized as "too worldly" by the next wave of Idealists. Finally, an Adaptive generation grows up ignored and "suffocated" by the great crisis. Sensitive and sympathetic, they emulate and conform to their elders, but in mid-life pursue personal growth and social concern during the next awakening. Interestingly, Strauss and Howe predict another great American crisis for the 2020s, just as astrologers do. Among groups described above, Generations S (modernists), W (war babies and baby boomers) and A (green pioneers) are Idealists; Generations T (seekers) and X (techno-punks and explorers) are Reactives; Generations U (organization men/women and techno-altruists) and Y (entrepreneurs, committed ones and flame throwers) are Civics; Generations V (the rebels without a cause and the silent generation) and Z (the free spirits and lonely rebels) are Adaptives.

Various astrologers have tried to link these traits with the sign Uranus occupies when the generations are born. What they often forget is that this is purely a cycle of American history. The key to this cycle is Uranus' karmic return to Gemini, which signals the "great American crisis" every eighty-four years. It is also the time when the first idealists are born. However, Howe and Strauss sometimes "stretched forward" the generations to conform with events. The Romantic Movement, for example, was so powerful that this "spiritual awakening" had the effect of postponing the reactive generation for over twenty years. In fact, Strauss and Howe had to eliminate one entire Civic generation to make room for their extended "Idealist" generation, born from 1792 to 1822. If we make the cycle regular, however (with some minor "stretching forward," depending on other aspects), we can say in general that Idealists are born with Uranus in signs near the Summer Solstice (Gemini, Cancer, Leo, which corresponds to the period when the war babies and baby boomers were born: 1942–1962). These signs have the "narcissistic" and "inward-turning" qualities supposed to characterize the Idealists. Civic generations thus have Uranus in the opposite signs of the Winter Solstice (Sagittarius, Capricorn, Aquarius), which are directed outward toward institutional success. The other generations are born with Uranus near the equinox; they "mediate" between the Idealists and Civics.

11

The Continents and "The Creation of Man"

The destiny of humanity is written in the stars—but what about the Earth, whose shape at first sight seems so haphazard? With the important events happening upon it, shouldn't they be reflected in the current shape of the continents?

It is now known, thanks to verification of Wegener's theories, that the continents "drift," or gradually move their positions, and that this is the cause of earthquakes, volcanoes and other disasters. In recent geologic times the American continents broke away from Eurasia and Africa, whereas once all three were joined in one huge super-continent. Couldn't this symbolize the subsequent emergence of human beings and their break (and consequent alienation) from nature and God?

Get a good, illustrated book on art history and turn to "The Creation of Man" by Michelangelo. This great work was executed during the Renaissance, soon after America was discovered: a time when Humanists celebrated the powers of "the individual." I believe that Michelangelo, among the most inspired artists of all time, actually recorded the destiny of humanity in his great masterpiece, even as he illustrated the Biblical story of creation. Perhaps his work was divinely directed—certainly it was the fruit of his own godlike powers. Little did he know that an important chapter in "the creation of man" was happening at the very time he worked. Or maybe he did know!

Observe the painting, then observe a world map. Isn't there a resemblance? Doesn't America, erect from North to South, look vaguely like a human being? Isn't the shape of Eurasia similar to God's in the painting? In this context, Central America is Adam's waist, South America his legs, and North America his chest and head. (The waist is awfully thin, but who more than Americans are concerned about their waistline?) At the top left of this innocent, newly created continent is Alaska. It resembles a man's hand, although it has three fingers instead of four; the thumb is the Aleutian Peninsula. It is reaching out to receive the "spark of electricity" from the hand of God that will endow the first man (Adam) with God's light and life. As you can see, it is now Russia touching the United States, the two greatest nations of the world. You can see the outstretched finger of God, through which the spark will pass, separated from Alaska only by the Bering Straits. Russia, once the seat of the revolution of collectivism, and the United States, home of the capitalist, democratic revolution, meet at their extremes, although their capitols are actually closer to each other from the opposite direction.

Now observe the shape of Europe, the birthplace of these revolutions and of Western philosophy, science, and "rational, enlightened thought." Does it not also resemble a brain? There is another person in Michelangelo's painting sitting by God's cloak; this is Eve, soon to be created from Adam's rib. Just as Eve caused the "fall" by eating the fruit of the tree of knowledge, so it has been Western and European thought and science which has now endangered the continued survival of humanity on this planet because of the technology it has created. Eve looks suggestively toward Adam in Michelangelo's painting. Already, says Kenneth Clark, one feels she is a "source of mischief." That's a good characterization of Europe too, I think!

Africa, on the other hand, resembles the shape of a heart instead of a brain. The birthplace of humanity, it is home to the black race, noted for their "soul" and closeness to nature, in contrast to the white race of Europe, noted for their "reason" and alienation from nature. In the painting we see Africa as the largest infant, who sits beneath Eve and symbolizes today's "developing" peoples. Europe represents humanity's intellectual and inventive powers, and Africa our emotional and physical energies. Asia represents our vast intuitive resources—the divine within us.

The ongoing "creation of man" came to a milestone in the French Revolution. Lightning (Uranus) struck, followed by thunder (Neptune and Pluto). All European peoples demanded freedom from their ancient tyrannies, but those in Western Europe got it faster; causing a split with the East whose effects linger today. This political and industrial "progress" in the West resulted in insanity—literally the loss of its head—in the French Revolutionary period. You could also say that in the Nineteenth Century Europe fell sick. Where did this "sickness" begin? In the neck, soon after the Revolution in which people lost their heads—severed from their body by the guillotine. As Europe dominated the world it began to break down, according to the old law that if you gain the world you lose your soul. Lose touch it did, in the neck—the Balkans and the Middle East.

Look at the Balkan Peninsula. Doesn't it look like a neck that is severed from Asia Minor? And the Aegean Islands are the drops of blood! It was Greece, after all, which began the turn away from God and instinct to reason and democracy—where the whole began to be lost among the parts. Greece was also the scene of the War of Independence from Turkey in 1821, which led directly to many more Balkan and Middle East Crises over the next 170 years. It sent the Turkish Ottoman Empire on the road to dismemberment and collapse. For this reason, it was thereafter known as "the Sick Man of Europe." Interestingly, both the neck and Turkey are traditionally ruled by the sign Taurus.

Western Civilization, as we said, was always a westward movement. The Balkan peoples, such as the Slavs, were "backward" in the Nineteenth Century. The western part of Europe had gone too far forward without keeping in touch with the rest of "the body," which wasn't yet ready for democracy and "progress." The growing break between the "head" in Western Europe and "the body" in the Middle East was also a break between conscious and subconscious, which caused the schizophrenia and hysteria diagnosed by the Austrian psychologist Sigmund Freud by the century's end.

Each European nation's place in Eve's "head" represents its function in European culture. Looking closely we see that Spain is the chin, audacious and culinary France of course is the mouth, and Brittany is the nose. Musical Austria is the ear, artistic Holland the eyes, inventive England the forebrain and thoughtful Germany the central cortex itself. Operatic Italy could be the voice box. The Urals could be seen as the border (or crease) of God's cloak as it shelters and protects the unborn Eve emerging from beneath Him.

Humanity broke from God and came to America. The chains of ancient institutions were too tight in the motherland. We declared "independence," but notice—God is touching Adam from the opposite direction in the map from that seen in the painting—from the East. This means we could be seeing the back of Michelangelo's painting as we look up toward the Sistine Chapel Ceiling, as if God had engraved it from above. However you look at it, it's clear that America must reverse its direction, twisting and turning toward the East to receive the charge of life from God. This also means turning inward, and toward the Earth as well.

What is the charge? It is the interaction between East and West now happening in the "Third Revolution." Since the 1960s we have seen detente and the end of the Cold War. America, the individual freed from God, is turning in the opposite direction to find union with Russia, or the divine collective.

Dane Rudhyar compared Europe and Asia to a small orange growing on the skin of a larger one, rather than to Eve and God in Michelangelo's painting. He noticed that in many ways Europe is a miniature version of Asia. The three peninsulas of Spain, Italy and Greece, for instance, are similar to Arabia, India, and Indochina; and they have similar historical and cultural functions. Greece and Indochina are home to great artists, Italy and India are the seat of great religions, and Spain and Arabia host peoples of missionary zeal. Above India we see the Himalayas as a nearly flat crescent pointing upward, allowing the energies of the divine to be received, while above Italy we see the Alps as a sharp crescent pointed downward, cutting off the spiritual from the human. Persia corresponds to France, China and Mongolia to Germany, and seafaring Japan (from reverse positions) to England. Throughout history, warriors have come down from the North and become civilized in the South.

This parallel can be extended to America. Florida and the Southeast is another version of Greece and the Balkans, close to creative centers on the Gulf Coast like New Orleans. Baja California is like another version of Spain, while wine-growing California itself is comparable to France and Palestine ("the Holy Lands") complete with vineyards. Mexico is not a peninsula like Italy, but is joined to all of South America. Like Italy and India, however, it is the seat of influential religions and great ancient empires and civilizations. North America, by contrast, is a land of warriors like Germany and Mongolia, and was conquered by materialistic and greedy industrialists from Europe. The Americas have a chain of mountains running north to south, instead of the crescent shape in Europe and Asia, symbolizing Adam's backbone. It represents America's desire to become independent and whole.

As America finds reunion with God, its peoples must also get together. Blacks came to America too, but as slaves from Africa who have had to fight for their rights. Many live in the Southeast portion of the U.S.—equivalent to the Balkans (also a scene of ethnic conflict) and to Indochina. Since the Third Revolution began in the 1960s, the U.S. has had to confront its problems with both Blacks and Vietnamese. The Balkans themselves are now also a source of trouble for America (in Bosnia, for example). If the United States of America is to truly be the "new Rome" and fulfill its destiny of "equal justice for all," it must also integrate itself with the Latin peoples south of the border.

12

The Horoscope of Modern Humanity

In this chapter we take a good hard look at ourselves in these times. We begin with a brief glance at the natal (or birth) horoscope for the United States of America, then focus in on a very special defining moment: the Horoscope for Modern Humanity.

Many birth dates have been suggested for America, including the dates for the Constitution and the Articles of Confederation. Most astrologers, however, use the traditional Independence Day of July 4, 1776 (as I do), but even many of those who agree on the date disagree on the time. The chart accepted for many years put Uranus in Gemini on the Ascendant, which seemed to accord well with America's image as the home of liberty—but for that chart to be accurate, the Declaration of Independence would had to have been signed at 2:17 A.M. This is highly unlikely, and in any case, Thomas Jefferson is said to have remembered it being signed in the late afternoon. Pictured here is the chart put forward more recently by Barry Lynes. Dane Rudhyar and C. E. James have also proposed similar versions. These charts are all based on a birth time for America of about 5 P.M.

As Rudhyar pointed out, Sagittarius is a far more appropriate rising sign for America than the traditional Gemini. Sagittarius represents perfectly the high-spirited, exuberant, cavalier and self-righteous American personality. It shows both our love of liberty and our respect for conventional authority. It reveals our constant desire to expand and our tendency to be sociable "joiners." The Barry Lynes version of the chart puts Uranus in Gemini almost exactly on the Descendant angle, an eloquent symbol not only of our love of liberty, but the fact that the nation began by "divorcing" itself from England. Since the Descendant is the cusp of the Seventh House of war, this explains why when Uranus returns to Gemini every eighty-four years, a great war happens that becomes "a struggle for the very existence" of the country. These included the Revolution (1774–81), the Civil War (1861–65) and World War II (1941–45). The next "great struggle" is due in about 2025.

The Descendant in the Lynes chart is at the same degree (within three minutes) in which Neptune and Pluto conjoined in 1892, inaugurating our current Cycle of Civilization. This connects the United States closely with the major events of the Twentieth Century. Victories in the World Wars and the invention of nuclear weapons lifted America to superpower status. Uranus in Gemini also shows the great transportation, communication, and information networks that have arisen here since Neptune and Pluto joined it in 1892.

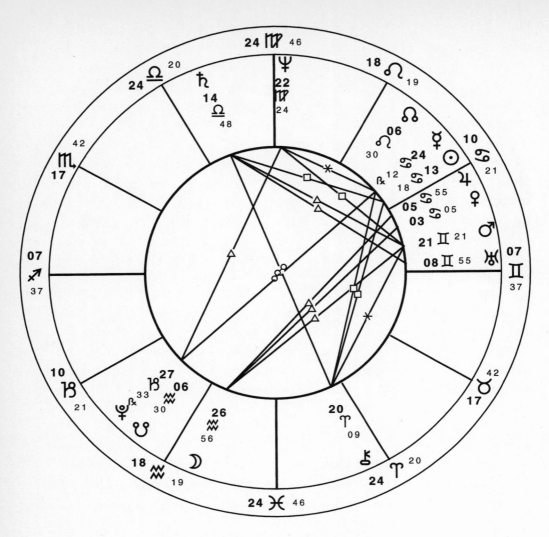

United States of America

This is Barry Lynes' version of the horoscope for America, cast for July 4, 1776, at 4:47 P.M.
However, I have used the Placidus house system instead of the Koch system originally used by
Lynes. Chart data: July 4, 1776, 04:47 P.M. LMT, Philadelphia, PA, U.S.A., 39W57, 75N10.

Four planets in the 7th house show Uncle Sam's tendency to get involved in wars and
throw its weight around. This is a characteristic of America which those who prefer the Gemini rising version perhaps don't like to admit. Uranus in the 7th house shows our tendency to
project our fears onto other nations who are undergoing revolutionary upheavals. Whenever major planets transit through late Taurus, Gemini, and early Cancer, and thus pass through
the Seventh House of the U.S. horoscope, America usually goes to war. This is especially true
not only of Uranus but also of Jupiter, which is the ruling planet of America's rising sign, and

is also located in the Seventh House. Whenever Jupiter returns to its degree of 6° Cancer in the natal U.S. chart, America often in some way fights for independence all over again.

Another place to watch in the U.S. chart is aggressive Mars at 21° Gemini, squaring Neptune at 22° Virgo in the Ninth House (delusions in foreign affairs). The U.S. is involved in muddled international events whenever outer planets reach these positions, or whenever they are located near 21° Sagittarius or 22° Pisces (opposing the U.S. Mars or Neptune).

The Sun in motherly, patriotic Cancer represents America as "the land of apple pie and motherhood." Pluto in Capricorn in the Second House is a perfect symbol of American plutocracy, and Mercury opposing it in self-centered Cancer represents the ongoing American struggle of "the little guy" against big business and big government (Capricorn). Saturn in the Tenth House also shows the power of executives in this country (whether in government or business), and in Libra it is the perfect symbol of the enduring power of our Constitution with its system of checks and balances. Neptune near the Midheaven shows the (often latent) high idealism and spirituality of the American people.

THE HOROSCOPE OF MODERN HUMANITY

In this section, I describe the one horoscope figure which I believe represents humanity today. It is not only an accurate mirror of ourselves and our times, but is another key to understanding our past and a very useful tool for predicting the future.

However long the human species has been around, the age we live in could be described as the birth times of humanity. It was only about 10,000 years ago that we emerged from caves, according to most archeologists. And it is just in the last 200 years that we have thrown off the shackles of bondage to authority, tradition and custom and begun to become truly ourselves. New power and knowledge has been released to us in our time. In astrology, all this is symbolized by the discovery of the outer, invisible planets in the last 200 years. In a real sense, then, we are being born today. And the birth has been difficult. We are still children, and the Earth has trembled and shuddered at this strange new human power that has been released upon her. Humanity could yet be stillborn if we do not soon begin to grow and mature. The real question for us today is not "will we survive?" but "will we even be born?" or perhaps, "will we survive infancy?"

If we are being born today, we should be able to cast a horoscope for the birth. I've looked at various possibilities, but none of them represent who we are today better than the chart I call the Horoscope of Modern Humanity. It may prove to be more important than the horoscope of any nation, person, or planetary event. In a sense, we can say that humanity has been reborn over and over, just as a person reincarnates again and again. The horoscope for today's birth of a new humanity, then, will be the horoscope for this incarnation; the unique chart for our age.

The way I validated astrology for myself was not by predicting future events in my life, but by largely predicting in advance what my own horoscope would be like. I thought about my own life and personality, then compared this to what I knew about the planets and signs.

For example, I predicted correctly that Uranus in Cancer would be on my Ascendant by analyzing my personality traits. We can all do the same thing with the Horoscope of Modern Humanity. Knowing the meanings of the planets, signs, and aspects, and knowing our times and our behavior as a people, we can speculate what our horoscope should be like. If the horoscope matches our expectations, then we know it's valid, and we help to validate astrology for ourselves.

I invite you now to think about the age we live in. Take a piece of paper and make a list like the one below. Take a look around you. What are the salient traits of our times? What are we like as a people today? What are our preoccupations? What dominates our lives? Bear in mind we are not just talking about yesterday's news, but the persistent traits of our age. After you have a list of about ten to twenty nouns or adjectives, think about the signs of the zodiac, and what they mean, then write the symbol for the sign which most accurately corresponds to each word on your list. Important: do not look ahead to the next page!

Traits of our age   **Corresponding signs**

_____   _____

_____   _____

_____   _____

_____   _____

_____   _____

_____   _____

_____   _____

_____   _____

_____   _____

_____   _____

Notice which signs come up most often. These should be the most prominent signs in the Horoscope of Modern Humanity. These should be the signs which the planets occupy in the chart. Perhaps you can even guess which planets are in these signs. Then, think about the aspects, and which ones might be in the chart. If you can, write a few of these down too next to the words on your list above.

I have done this several times at meetings of astrologers. I asked people in the audience (all of whom knew something of the meaning of the signs and aspects) for a list of words to describe our age, and for the signs corresponding to them, and wrote them on the blackboard. Most people were amazed at how closely the signs we wrote down matched the signs which are prominent in the chart I propose as the Horoscope of Modern Humanity.

On April 26, 1892, a total solar eclipse occurred which forms the basis for this remarkable chart. Solar eclipses are not unusual; as a matter of fact, they happen every year or so. But in this case, within days of this eclipse in 1892 there was a conjunction between Neptune and Pluto. This conjunction only happens once in 493 years. These are the two outermost planets in the solar system, so the conjunctions between them are the most rare. What happened in 1892 was spectacular. I don't know another major conjunction that happened so close to a total solar eclipse. We can use the time of this eclipse to cast the Horoscope of Modern Humanity.

Many astrologers would use the time and day of the Neptune-Pluto conjunction itself as the basis of the chart, but I think it's impossible to know exactly when a conjunction between two such slow-moving planets occurred. We can be fairly certain, on the other hand, exactly when an eclipse happened. A new moon is often used to interpret or predict events during the following month; an eclipse is even more significant. Today's authorities say that the conjunction of Neptune and Pluto happened on April 30, 1892, just four days after the eclipse. Older accounts put the conjunction on April 25, just one day before. In any case, it is a profoundly unusual coincidence that such a rare conjunction happened on virtually the same day as a total eclipse of the Sun.

Let's look at the chart for the solar eclipse and great conjunction on April 26, 1892 (our "birthday"). First, see if the list of adjectives and matching signs below agrees with those that you came up with, and then check which signs are prominent in the actual chart.

It's not hard to think of adjectives and nouns to represent our world today. Some of the words that people came up with at my lectures include: money, greed, materialism, power, technology, mass media, bureaucracy, controversy, war, superficiality, novelty-seeking, restlessness, organization, change, movement, revolution, sexual liberation, struggle between haves and have-nots, science, space travel, invention, commercialism, anxiety, hedonism, questioning authority, alienation, loneliness, pragmatism, deception, domination, destruction, and confrontation with death.

That's a pretty good list. How does it square with yours? Now, which signs rule these characteristics? Well, for money, greed, materialism, commercialism, pragmatism, hedonism, and sexuality: obviously Taurus. For power, organization, domination, and again, materialism: Capricorn. For war, restlessness, controversy, how about Aries? Technology, science, bureaucracy, anxiety? That could only mean Virgo. Superficiality, change, novelty, restlessness, mass media, movement, invention? How about Gemini! Confrontation with death? Sexual liberation? Sounds like Scorpio. For invention, questioning authority, revolution: maybe Aquarius. Which signs came up for you most often? Were they these? For some of the aspects, how about a Sun affliction with Uranus for revolution? A Venus affliction Saturn for alienation? What other aspects did you come up with?

Now let's look at which signs are prominent in the actual chart. Obviously, if the eclipse occurred on April 26, that gives us a Taurus Sun, with the Moon in Taurus too for good measure. Ours *is* an age of greed and materialism, and we *are* preoccupied with money. In fact, we have more material wealth, ease, and comfort than our ancestors ever dreamed of having, but we are still unsatisfied, nor is the wealth shared equally. Why? The Sun/Moon conjunction is violently opposed by Uranus in Scorpio—here we see the struggle between the established "haves" (Taurus, "I have") and the revolutionary "have-nots" (Scorpio, "I desire"), which has dominated politics since the 1890s. In this aspect we see reflected the constant upheaval that marks our times. In the modern world, no custom, no tradition, no authority has been left unchallenged, and the battle between capitalists (Taurus) and communists (Uranus, Scorpio), has led us to the brink of annihilation (Scorpio) in a hundred ways. Ours is the time of radical transformation. We are challenged to "live together or die."

Next in importance to the positions of the Sun/Moon and Uranus is the grouping of Saturn, Mars, Venus, and Mercury. Saturn in Virgo comes first. Always we look to Saturn to find the most difficult lessons we must learn, the cross we must bear. Saturn is our Achilles heel; our weakest point. Saturn in Virgo shows us up magnificently! Our age has been titled the Age of Analysis, also the Age of Anxiety. What slaves to Virgo we are. We have accumulated and analyzed so much data that we have long since passed "information overload." We are so specialized, so attentive to detail that we have completely lost the broader view. Our skepticism, our narrowness, our deference to the "experts," our over-caution knows no bounds; nothing is valid in our age of "science" unless it is verified with rigorous testing. We worship technology and efficiency, those hallmark traits of Virgo; everything is subservient to the needs of the machine. So we must conform and keep pace with the "rat race." Saturn shows us by its position in our chart *where the power is* in society. Under Saturn in Virgo, we today live under the rule not of the king or the priest, but of the expert, the scientist, the technocrat, and the bureaucrat.

What is the chief preoccupation of these rulers? Well, look which planet is most strongly aspected to Saturn. Mars in Capricorn is almost exactly trine, and in Saturn's own sign. As President Eisenhower said, "We must guard against… the military-industrial complex. The potential for misplaced power exists, and will persist." The God of War here in the sign of organization and power is its symbol.

Mars trine to Saturn in practical earth signs shows our huge and easy success with technology, our giant industrial plants and information systems, our bold feats of engineering. "Heroic Materialism" is the title which historian Kenneth Clark gave our age. But we gained the world only to lose our own souls. The only thing that matters to "the system" is the bottom line. We are pragmatic; we want results. Winning isn't everything, it's the only thing. What counts is status, power, worldly success and fame, or so we think—but in our Capricorn quest for outward success, we too often forget the opposite sign of Cancer, the symbol of the private self and the feelings. Ours is the age of "the lost self" and "the lonely crowd." We live in a standardized, public world; a mass society. Inwardly barren and bankrupt, we look to externals to fill the void, or we escape into drugs or alcohol (Neptune sesqui-square Mars). We are caught up in the runaway Capricornian system which has no purpose and no soul of its own. The needs of the system take over, and with Mars trine to

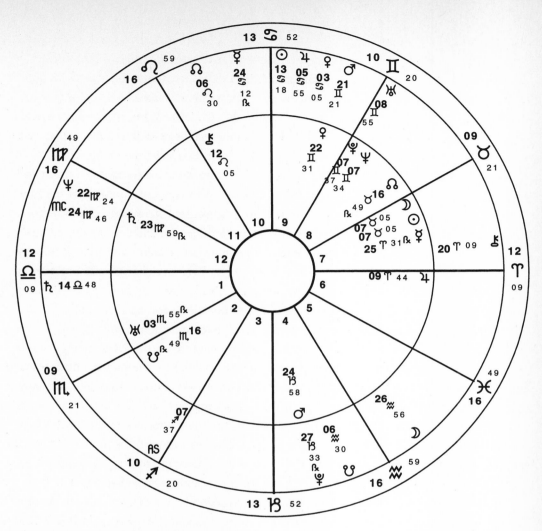

The Horoscope of Modern Humanity (the chart for the age we live in)
This chart for the total solar eclipse of April 26, 1892, serves as the chart for the conjunction of Neptune and Pluto, usually dated April 30, 1892. Local sidereal time: 7:00:37. IN OUTER CIRCLE: Positions of the planets in the horoscope for the United States of America, July 4, 1776, at 4:47 P.M.

Saturn, this means we are often led by the bureaucrats into war. In Orwell's vision of 1984, it is constant war which keeps the system going. That has been our fate in America since the 1940s, and Europe's fate since the 1890s.

Look at the amazingly close and violent square by Mars to Mercury in Aries. This completes a tight trinity of the planets Mercury, Mars, and Saturn grouped together, each in a sign ruled by one of the others. Mercury square Mars, the closest aspect in the whole chart, seems to confirm the image we get of our times from the TV and the newspapers (Mercury = the media) as one of rampant crime and violence (Aries). It pinpoints our pressing need to steady our nerves and quiet our minds (Jupiter, also a symbol of the mind, is also in Aries). As Saturn in Virgo also showed us, we are supremely powerful intellectually. We can solve any problem or discover any fact, but we too seldom relax and listen to another person's point of view. We mentioned "war" and "controversy" above; here we see the constant battle of ideas and ideologies which yield more heat than light. We said we live in a restless age always on the move; Mercury, Mars and Saturn together symbolize the automobile, as well as all the other mechanical gadgets that have entered our lives since the 1890s.

Mercury is also the ruler of Gemini, the sign which represents the restless movement and superficiality of our times that we mentioned. Sociable Venus is in Gemini, showing how easily we make contacts through our miraculous communication technology, and how good we are at public relations. On the surface, at least, we are cheerful and easy-going. But deep and lasting relationships are not the Gemini forte. Our very mobility and love of novelty only deepens our feelings of transience and rootlessness. Even our charm and good humor is mostly used for commercial purposes (we are Sun Taurus, after all). Notice that Venus is closely square to Saturn. This is the prime symbol of our alienation and loneliness. The famous astrologer C. E. O. Carter describes the Venus-Saturn affliction as "serious," with such meanings as "loneliness," "depression," and "parental fixations." The quality of our relationships to each other and to the environment is defiled by the violent, mechanical forces represented by Saturn, Mercury, and Mars. Caring and conservation take a distant back seat to self-interest and the profit motive. Venus, the chart's ruler, is joined in Gemini by the conjunction of Neptune and Pluto, magnifying all these indications at least ten-fold.

So there you have it: all the signs we mentioned! The Horoscope of Humanity paints an accurate if uncomfortable picture of ourselves. It is even more interesting to see how it affects the United States. When we cast the chart for the time the eclipse happened in Washington, D.C., it shows Libra rising, with Uranus (symbol of liberty) appropriately in the first house (representing the "liberty-loving" identity and character of America). Saturn in Virgo in the Twelfth House (and right over the U.S. Neptune!) shows even more clearly the hidden and insidious power of our big, bureaucratic institutions (the secret government).

This "Horoscope of Modern Humanity" from 1892 is indeed at least as important as the chart of the United States itself. And yet, it is amazing how the two charts are linked. This confirms once more the significance of this birth date for Modern Humanity, April 26, 1892. It is the United States that has dominated our age, and it is only to be expected that the chart of our age should confirm this. For starters, the Neptune-Pluto conjunction itself occurred at 8° Gemini, just where Uranus is located in the horoscope for our country. This amazing triple alignment of the three outer planets shows how the U.S. could lead the radical transformation of Humanity in our times if it chose to. Second, Venus is at 22° Gemini, within one degree of Mars in the U.S. chart. Notice where Mars is in the Horoscope of Modern Humanity—25° Capricorn, just two degrees shy of a conjunction to America's Pluto, and exactly opposing the U.S. Mercury. Finally, notice that Saturn in 24° Virgo is closely aligned with America's Neptune. Half the planets in the 1892 chart are aligned with U.S.

planets! But there's more. The Ascendant at 12° Libra is very close to the U.S. Saturn position, and the chart really shines the spotlight on the United States by putting the U.S. Sun at 13° Cancer on top at the Midheaven.

The Horoscope of Modern Humanity also reveals the role other nations play in our age. For example, the Far East countries have signs rising that are at the beginning of the zodiac (Vietnam, Aries; China, Taurus; Japan, Gemini), meaning they have embarked on an aggressive course of new beginning and development. India (Pisces rising) has lagged behind and remained the country with the most venerable religious tradition. Europe shows Sagittarius rising, meaning it has undergone deep transformation in the recent past (Scorpio, the previous sign), and is now at a mature stage of development. America (Libra rising) still has turbulent change ahead under Scorpio.

Even more revealing is where the Neptune-Pluto conjunction was at the time the eclipse happened in each country. It was on the Descendant (or exactly setting) in Western Europe, showing the "decline of the West" since the World Wars. The U.S. (especially the West Coast) has the conjunction on the Midheaven, symbolizing American dominance in our age, but the conjunction is on the Ascendant in Japan, showing its ascendency along with other nearby "Pacific Rim" countries. The Middle East and Central Asia, where the Neptune-Pluto conjunction is at the Nadir, is revealed as the original source of the Western civilization (and of its oil) that has now reached its peak in California.

Although our horoscope paints a drab and disturbing picture of humanity today, that is only what we should expect. As we grow and mature, the more positive aspects of these positions in our horoscope will come out. We can use our enormous engineering skill and intellectual power to save our threatened world as well as to destroy it. The strong focus on earth signs may signify not only our need to achieve wealth and power in the world, but also our increasing awareness of the beauty and value of the Earth itself and the need to preserve it. There are also some indications of change in the chart itself. We are as much born under Scorpio as under Taurus—probably more so—and no sign has as much potential to transform itself, or to explore the depths of the human spirit. With old certainties gone, our "encounter with nothingness" forces us from time to time to wipe away our illusions and seek out the unknown. Scorpio loves a mystery, and nothing shows this more than the popularity of our TV detective shows and horror movies. In this time of ultimate peril, we relish the challenge of impending death. Indeed, courting danger is almost a moral tenet today. Nothing entices us more than a cheap thrill. And of course, Uranus in Scorpio represents "sexual liberation." Then there's the fact that Mars is on the cusp of Aquarius, representing change and transformation. Mars in Aquarius is the same symbol as Uranus in Scorpio, with sign and planetary rulers reversed.

Mars will loom even larger in the next chapter. There we will "progress" the Horoscope of Modern Humanity, or move the positions of the planets forward (or backward) at the rate of one day after April 26, 1892, for each year of history. This progressed horoscope also contains profound symbols of our times. Mars is one of these, because in the progressed chart it not only moved into Aquarius, but turned powerfully stationary there at some point during our age (perhaps now you might want to guess when). And this is only one of the powerful tools the progressed chart of 1892 gives us for understanding our past and predicting our future.

The two other great conjunctions of outer planets in the Twentieth Century—Uranus' alignment to Pluto in 1966, and Uranus' alignment to Neptune in 1993—also show the great transformation of our times. America is once again at the center of it all, since in 1966 Uranus and Pluto lined up right over the U.S. Neptune (and 1892 Saturn), while in 1993, Uranus and Neptune aligned over the U.S. Pluto (and 1892 Mars). Of course, Neptune and Pluto themselves joined together with the U.S. Uranus in 1892. In effect, this makes three triple conjunctions of the outer planets in the U.S. horoscope in our age. Does this mean a great change is coming to America, or is the sky blue? I don't believe we have fully understood the impact and meaning of these three conjunctions on the U.S.A., but they certainly indicate much more change in the future.

For now, since you now know the birthday of Modern Humanity, please join me in wishing us all a belated happy 100th birthday!

YOUR PLACE IN TODAY'S WORLD

Your own birthday may indicate the distinctive contribution you can make to this New Age now emerging. By finding the paragraph below for your sign, you can "orient" yourself to the currents of the times. The conjunction's "house position" in relation to your Sun sign shows this. Also read the paragraph for your rising sign; this may also be important. "Early" means the first eight days of each sign (for example, March 21–28 if you are an Aries). If you were born soon after the eighth day of a sign, read both paragraphs for that sign, as they may both apply to you.

Pisces, early Aries (first eight days): Neptune and Pluto joined in a "Third House" position. Your role in our unfolding new civilization is to be a writer, student, teacher or orator with pioneering new ideas. You are stimulated to travel, learn, and share what you know. Your brothers and sisters could help you in important ways to further your goals.

Aries, early Taurus: Neptune-Pluto was in a "Second House" position. You can contribute as an architect or builder of new structures, or as an artist, musician, or vocalist. You could profit from financial ventures which further the growth of today's new culture. You can help people develop self-reliance and self-esteem.

Taurus, early Gemini: Neptune-Pluto was in a "First House" position. You can contribute most to the New Age by unfolding your powers of self-expression. Becoming a more authentic and enlightened person will help you communicate and share knowledge. Exploring mysticism and the occult will help you develop your talents. You could be an important leader or pioneer in shaping today's world.

Gemini, early Cancer: Neptune-Pluto in a "Twelfth House" position means you can work behind the scenes to transform and personalize today's institutions, and bring to light the "dirty laundry" that corrupts our efforts. You can also contribute to the new world by se-cluding yourself in order to follow a spiritual path. Renew yourself by discovering the hid-den secrets of reality; then help others to do so.

Cancer, early Leo: Neptune-Pluto was in an "Eleventh House" position. Your role is to help others enjoy life, and to open channels for people to get together and cooperate with one another. You can inspire people to transcend boundaries of race, creed and sex. You can suc-ceed and foster new ideas as a charismatic media personality.

Leo, early Virgo: Neptune-Pluto was in a "Tenth House" position. Your place in today's world is as an administrator. You can become an executive of organizations dedicated to serving Humanity. Your work can be a vehicle for your ideals. You may need to psycho-an-alyze your relationship with your parents and other authorities.

Virgo, early Libra: Neptune-Pluto was in a "Ninth House" position. Your role could be as a philosopher and prophet. Study and travel widely in order to expand the connections and networks between ideas, peoples and cultures. The church, the law, the university, or spiri-tual movements are good outlets for you.

Libra, early Scorpio: Neptune-Pluto was in an "Eighth House" position. Study the mysteries of life and transform yourself by penetrating to the center of your being. You can restore hu-man community by deepening your relationships and helping others do so. Profit by co-in-vesting in financial ventures and joint efforts that further the growth of the new civilization.

Scorpio, early Sagittarius: Neptune-Pluto was in a "Seventh House" position. You can help build the new world as a citizen or government diplomat, strategist or peace activist. You may contact important currents of change through your marriage or business partner. You could excel in public relations and international networking.

Sagittarius, early Capricorn: Neptune-Pluto was in a "Sixth House" position. You could help to organize new ways of work that are more satisfying or which better serve people, and restructure bureaucracies and institutions so this can happen. You can develop ways to help people improve their health. Your volunteer work can be a vehicle for change.

Capricorn, early Aquarius: Neptune-Pluto was in a "Fifth House" position. You can use your natural talents as a charismatic personality to propagate new ideas and inspire people to unfold their creative potential and self-confidence. You can help reorganize society so that individuals can shine and romance can flourish.

Aquarius, early Pisces: Neptune-Pluto was in a "Fourth House" position. As you transform your early conditioning, you can foster a creative approach to family life in the New Age. You can encourage reverence for the land and environment and participation in local affairs. You can teach people to appreciate their nation and explore their cultural and racial history.

Which of the three great conjunctions of our age will be the most significant for you? Prob-ably the one closest to the same degree of any sign that your Sun or Ascendant are in. If ei-ther or both the Sun or Ascendant are near eight degrees of your sign, then the interpreta-tions above for Neptune-Pluto will most strongly apply. If near sixteen degrees, then the indications in Chapter 6 for Uranus-Pluto will be most significant. If near nineteen degrees, then Uranus-Neptune (Chapter 7) will be most significant. Whichever of these conjunctions closely aspected a planet in your chart will also be strongest in your life.

If a planet in your chart is within five degrees of 8° Gemini, or strongly aspecting this point, then you have an important role in giving birth to the new age. This may involve a special gift or talent indicated by the nature of the planet.

Sun: Vitality, radiance, and organizing powers (John F. Kennedy)

Moon: Emotional, nurturing instincts (Sigmund Freud)

Mercury: Writing, speaking, learning, teaching (Oswald Spengler)

Venus: The arts, diplomacy, romance, finance (Paul Gauguin, Bob Dylan)

Mars: War, sports, engineering, pioneering, new enterprises (Benito Mussolini)

Jupiter: Philosophy, ideas, commerce, diplomacy, law (Thomas Edison)

Saturn: Executive leadership, organizational abilities (Harry Truman)

Uranus: Electronics, inventing, social action, radical politics (W. J. Bryan)

You may also have a special role to play if one of the planets in your own horoscope is within roughly one degree of any of the other planets in the Horoscope of Modern Humanity. Your influence on the times is shown by which planet in your chart is involved. I found in a statistical study that famous people have planets in these degrees at a rate approaching twice that of chance. Besides the degree of the conjunction itself (8° Gemini), the most powerful connection you can have with the Horoscope of Modern Humanity is if a planet in your birth chart is conjunct with the eclipse (7° Taurus) or the Uranus degree (4° Scorpio).

4° Scorpio planet: You embody in some way today's passionate quest for renewal. Examples: Theodore Roosevelt (Sun), Harry Truman (Moon), Robert Kennedy (Mars), Marshall MacLuhan (Jupiter), Mahatma Gandhi (Mercury), Dwight D. Eisenhower (Moon), Hubert Humphrey (Jupiter), Jimmy Carter (Saturn), Hillary Clinton (Sun).

7° Taurus planet: You are especially fitted to help set the New Age on a realistic foundation. Examples include: Pablo Picasso (Saturn), Franklin Roosevelt (Saturn), Theodore Roosevelt (Pluto), Joseph Stalin (Neptune), Henry Kissinger (Venus), Ludwig Wittgenstein (Sun), Saddam Hussein (Sun), James Baker III (Sun).

25° Aries planet (aligned with Mercury in our chart): You are an activist, propagandist, or pioneer in literature or education. Famous examples include: Adolf Hitler (Mercury), V .I. Lenin (Mars), Sigmund Freud (Venus), Annie Besant (Pluto), Oswald Spengler (Saturn).

25° Capricorn planet (aligned with Mars in the chart): You can turn your vast organizational talents to help Humanity. You are part of the vibrant forces of change, and can move with them successfully. Examples: Alexander Solzhenitsyn (Mars), Martin Luther King (Sun), Marshall MacLuhan (Uranus), Ronald Reagan (Uranus).

22° Gemini planet (aligned with Humanity's Venus): You can be an intellectual leader or artist with a unique fascination. Examples: Elbert Hubbard (Venus), Bob Dylan (Mercury), Hermann Hesse (Mercury), Theodore Roosevelt (Jupiter), George Bush (Sun).

9° Aries planet (location of Jupiter in the 1892 chart): You can be a vigorous leader and prophet of the age. Examples: Al Gore Jr. (Sun), George Bernard Shaw (Jupiter), Eugene McCarthy (Sun/Jupiter), Joseph Stalin (Saturn), Lyndon Johnson (Saturn), Charles De-Gaulle (Moon), Vincent Van Gogh (Sun).

24° Virgo planet (degree of the 1892 Saturn): You identify with either the public bureaucracy or with scientific and technical achievements, and can apply them to help people. You may be an expert on the anxiety engendered by modern life. Examples: Harry Truman (Uranus), Timothy Leary (Saturn), Bob Dylan (Neptune), Karl Jaspers (Moon/Uranus), Henri Bergson (Mars).

13

The Progressed Chart:

THE FUTURE OF OUR AGE

The Horoscope of Modern Humanity, cast for the solar eclipse and Neptune-Pluto conjunction of April 26, 1892, reflects an image of ourselves in the celestial mirror. It's not a very comforting sight, but just as an individual person does not remain the same throughout life, neither does humanity as a whole. The Horoscope of Modern Humanity can be progressed, just like a personal horoscope, to represent our continued development as we grow and mature in the years following birth. The technique of progressions is based on the maxim: "a year is a day in the life of the Lord." This refers to the fundamental influence in our lives of the two great cycles of time, the day and the year; and to the two basic elements in any horoscope which are based on them, the houses and the signs. In progressing a chart, each day following birth is used to represent one year of life. Thus, if the birth chart is like a mirror of ourselves frozen in time, the progressed chart is like a home movie, chronicling our development.

Progressions are not the same as transits. The transits are the current positions of the planets, especially the outer ones, and their relationship to the original positions in any horoscope. The progressions (mainly by the inner planets) show how we rise to the occasion to meet events indicated by the transits. Nevertheless, the progressions in the Horoscope of Modern Humanity are so revealing that they should be considered just as important as the current transits are. This progressed chart is so powerful that it is as though we were all still living in 1892 today. The 492 days after April 26 are a microcosm of the 492 years after 1892. What is truly amazing is this: the progressed positions correspond not only to events that happen, but often to the actual transits of the time too! In other words, the progressed positions in the chart are similar to the transits. For example, transiting Neptune in Aries in the 1860s corresponded in time to the progressed Sun's square to Mars, the ruler of Aries, in 1864. The collective soul of humanity (the progressions) is, as it were, resonating to the world and the universe (the transits).

We can run the movie backwards as well as forwards. We can "precess" the chart back from April 26, 1892, to watch the "prenatal" development which led up to our birth, and this is just as revealing. Saturn, for example, turned stationary at 0° Libra, the sign of law and balance, just as our founding fathers wrote the constitution in 1787. (Planets are most powerful when stationary; that is, when they appear to stand still and change directions.) Saturn in Libra is a perfect symbol of the ideals of justice enshrined in the U.S. government's system of checks and balances. Saturn is also in Libra, of course, in the U.S. horoscope, but in the progressed Horoscope of Modern Humanity, Saturn soon went back into pragmatic Virgo. This represents our continuing struggle to make these ideals of justice a reality. As Saturn continued to move retrograde during the days corresponding to the Nineteenth Century (February–April, 1892), the ideals of the Revolution were often corrupted by the growth of corporate and state power. The retreat culminated when conservative Saturn turned stationary again in 1923. This is an incredibly symbolic moment, the time when fascist and totalitarian dictators rose to power and politics everywhere turned sharply to the right. Yet nowhere is there an astrological explanation for this incredible coincidence of events worldwide except the stationary Saturn in the progressed Horoscope of Modern Humanity. The nightmare peaked in 1940 with the following solar square to Saturn as World War II began. This aspect left its mark deeply on the lives and outlook of the war generation. Soon Saturn was moving forward again, and so fascism was defeated. By 2017, Saturn will reach Libra again. By then we can expect the dream of justice to be fulfilled to a much greater degree than today.

In 1815, the rebel planet Uranus also turned stationary and began to move retrograde. The revolutionary upheavals of the previous thirty-five years came to their climax as Napoleon was defeated at Waterloo and the Concert of Vienna restored the old authority. Here again, there is no other astrological symbol that so clearly explains this landmark event. The revolutionary movement was arrested and distorted in the years after 1815 as Uranus moved backwards, and the original ideals of liberation were increasingly submerged in the growing militarism and worship of the machine. In 1966, progressed Uranus finally turned stationary and began moving direct again. There was a new urge to liberation in the '60s, and suddenly new magic appeared in the midst of our dusty industrial world. Since Uranus was in Scorpio, its powerful station in 1966 coincided exactly with Uranus' conjunction to Pluto (Scorpio's ruler) in the transits that same year. Uranus became the signature of the "new generation," as Saturn had been of the old; and liberation continues to move ahead today around the world.

Mars is probably the most important progressed planet. The movements of Mars clearly define the times. Going back to the late Eighteenth Century, we find Mars was in intense Scorpio during the Revolution, coinciding with Neptune's transit in Scorpio. Both emerged into Sagittarius in the early Nineteenth Century. The works of the romantic artists aptly illustrated the Sagittarian spirit of those times. Beethoven, for example, was a Sagittarian, as was the poet William Blake, and great romantic painters like Gericault and Delacroix often portrayed the exuberant wild horse. It was a time of religious "great awakenings" and idealistic philosophers. Then at mid-century came a great divide and a major turning point. Mars entered Capricorn in 1848, the year of revolutions and *The Communist Manifesto*. Disillusion followed the failure of the revolutions, and romanticism was replaced by realism

(Capricorn). Instead of expanding consciousness and adventure, people now pursued wealth and power as ruthlessly as they could, thus launching our famous obsession with worldly success. The romantic ideals of liberation for the whole person got lost. 1848 saw the rise of "realistic" politicians like Bismarck, leading directly to Hitler and Stalin.

People became even more aggressive in the 1860s, as the progressed Sun entered Aries. It formed an exact square to warlike Mars (ruler of Aries) in 1864 during the worst battles of the U.S. Civil War, and during the first War of Unification in Germany. The precessed chart mirrored the transits, since Neptune was in Aries (a sign ruled by Mars) during the 1860s. Aggression culminated in the First World War in 1914. This great catastrophe came suddenly and explosively, and there is no better symbol for it anywhere than the violent T-square between Mars, Mercury and Uranus during the war years in the progressed chart. It position in the early fixed signs shows the four-year stalemate on the Western front.

In 1902, just before the Great War, Mars entered inventive Aquarius, and Mercury turned stationary. Transiting Pluto was in Gemini (Mercury's sign), opposing Uranus. Immediately the Twentieth Century threw off the restraints of the Nineteenth. People everywhere became boldly experimental, led by inventive artists and scientists (Picasso, Einstein, etc.). "Progress" and innovation went into high gear, and "progressives" attacked all the evils of the day. A half century of revolution began.

In 1963, just as all this "progress" reached its crest, Mars turned stationary in 17° Aquarius—and began moving backwards. This is perhaps the most powerful symbol of our times, and nothing like it can be found anywhere except in this chart. President Kennedy was assassinated. Our drive for progress and control of the environment was arrested. From then on, it seemed that we were powerless to change our external circumstances. Progress lost its appeal, and politics hit a dead end. Although this symbol is found nowhere else, it was loudly echoed by the transits. 17° Aquarius is exactly where the famous Aquarian eclipse and conjunction involving the seven visible planets occurred in February 1962, and exactly where Saturn was in November 1963 when Kennedy was shot. Notice, however, that soon after Mars in Aquarius turned retrograde, Uranus in Scorpio turned direct. Each planet was in the other's ruling sign. In effect, the initiative was transferred from the masculine and macho Mars to the enlightened and transcendental Uranus, a perfect symbol of the kind of liberation that is primarily needed today. Mars stationary and Uranus stationary in Scorpio corresponded to Neptune's transit of the martial sign Scorpio in the 1960s. This station of Mars has accelerated the "dawning of the Age of Aquarius" in the late 20th Century. By the way, if you have a planet in your chart within a degree of 17° Aquarius, it may indicate a special talent which you can share to help humanity enter the Aquarian Age.

Next to Mars in importance is the progressed position of the chart-ruler Venus. Not only has Mars been retrograde, Venus has too, and this tells us that we have been revamping our emotional lives, as Venus has been in Cancer (sign of feelings) since the turn of the century. Venus rules diplomacy, peace, and war, so when Venus turned stationary-retrograde in defensive Cancer in 1945, the world wars ended, the U.N. was founded, the Cold War began, and the defense establishment was erected. (Notice the correlation with Neptune again, which at that time was transiting Venus' ruling sign Libra.) Progressed Sun and Mercury also entered Cancer in 1947. In 1966 the progressed Sun conjoined Venus, and this new defense machine went haywire in Vietnam. This was also the year that "peace and love" was preached by the "flower children" (Venus/Sun); it was also the start of women's liberation. By the way, this progressed conjunction of Sun-Venus occurred in President Johnson's own Venus degree at the very time he escalated the war in Vietnam!

By 1989, Venus turned stationary-direct in 10° Cancer (the very same degree where the powerful transiting Jupiter turned stationary in the Fall of 1989 during the revolutions in Europe, and Jupiter's degree in Gorbachev's chart). Just as in 1945, the diplomatic picture was reshuffled. Peace "broke out" around the world. The Cold War, begun when Venus turned retrograde in 1945, ended; and the defense establishment began to wane. Meanwhile, nationalism (Cancer) revived, as I predicted it would back in 1976 (*A.F.A. Journal*). Venus stationary also indicated that in 1989–1990 we were recognizing the value (Venus) of our Earth home (Cancer), as I also predicted would happen.

Indeed, I said that this would be a "glorious" time, as the liberation around the world in 1989 proved—but the cultural renaissance begun at the conjunction of Sun-Venus has not yet come fully into bloom. The last great Renaissance of the Fifteenth Century began in central Europe, and didn't fully reach the English-speaking world until the Elizabethan Age a century later. Perhaps Europe will lead the way again.

The progressed Sun opposed Mars in 1991–92, right during the great Uranus-Neptune conjunction. Ethnic conflicts again threatened to tear Europe apart, and the Middle East was still exploding. A "holy war" could be in our future too, because Jupiter will be turning stationary retrograde in 25 °Aries in 2001, squaring Mars' position in the original 1892 chart. We could also see a religious revival, breakthroughs in travel (a space odyssey?), UFOs, and other Jovian phenomena. Mercury will be stationary in Virgo in 1999. Science and literature will leap ahead; and today's health crisis will climax, leading to new breakthroughs. The Sun's trine to Jupiter in 2005 may be the sign of new optimism that our golden age is unfolding.

The Sun's opposition to Mars in Aquarius in 1991-92 highlighted a new progressive era in the 1990s, as we confronted the results of our thirty-year political deadlock. It also highlighted the "battle of the sexes," as revealed in the Clarence Thomas hearings. Mars retrograde could dash our hopes again, though, just as they have been dashed over and over these last twenty-nine years. The futility of American politics continues as Americans seem to be paralyzed by that seemingly all-powerful retrograde Mars. Still, a turn-around must come sooner or later, unless America wishes to keep declining. Some writers believe the Age of Aquarius will begin in 2025. This is close to the year (2023) when the progressed Mars in Aquarius turns stationary and begins moving forward again—just as transiting Neptune enters Aries and Pluto enters Aquarius. We can assume that "progress" will resume then. Will America have to wait until then to get moving again, or can enough of us shake America out of its fog of disillusionment and apathy so it can join the rest of the world's revival before then? We'll know soon enough.

What we must never forget amidst all of today's chaos is this—we have recently celebrated the 100th birthday of humanity. Neptune's conjunction to Pluto over 100 years ago launched us into a new age. Since history began, a renaissance or golden age has never failed to come in about 100 years after this conjunction. The golden ages of Greece, Rome, Byzantium, China, India, Christian Europe, the European Renaissance, the Mayans, and many other cultures all testify to this. Today, we are suddenly no longer troubled by many of the walls and conflicts of the past. Our resources have never been greater. If we fail to grasp this glorious opportunity, we will have wasted our potential and missed our destiny.

Jupiter stationary in 2001 and its trine to the Sun in 2005 could signify a new faith in this rebirth. Let's not wait; let's make the new age happen now. Taking care of business is important, but more important is the role we all have to play in the birth of a new humanity. Find your role now, and play it; in this lies your greatest personal fulfillment.

THE PROGRESSED LUNATION CYCLE

Another important tool in the progressed Chart of 1892 is the Lunation Cycle, and its New and Full Moons. At the New Moon the Moon is dark. Since the Moon represents the common people, they are, in a sense, also in the dark during a progressed New Moon. They are in retreat, inactive and uninvolved, and in the resulting chaos powerful people take the initiative in a spirit of "everyone for themselves." Nevertheless, a new era in human affairs is beginning, and new forces are astir. By the time of the Full Moon, when the Moon is at its brightest, the common people have come alive and are full of revolutionary and reforming zeal. They are aware of problems and solutions and take conscious action to solve them. As the Full Moon wanes the people increasingly spread their energy in different directions, and the progressive movements begun during the Full Moon become institutionalized.

The lunation cycle lasts twenty-nine and a half days, which corresponds to twenty-nine and a half years in a progressed chart. This is exactly how long it takes Saturn to travel around the zodiac. Each cycle confirms and strengthens the other; the Moon showing the mood of the people, and Saturn the attitude of institutions. As the New Moon happens in the progressed 1892 chart, Saturn enters Virgo and begins a phase of "power dispersion." This is the period when the ideal of deregulation and laissez-faire competition ("everyone for themselves") is paramount. When the Full Moon happens in the progressed chart, Saturn is in Pisces in the middle of a "progressive" phase, when new political ideas emerge and revolutionary reform movements are strongest. In modern times, the Full Moon has also corresponded closely to strong revolutionary aspects between Uranus and Pluto.

In 1951, for example, a New Moon happened as Republicans took over in America and the Conservatives returned to power in Britain, opening a period famous for its drift, stagnation, and conformity. What was "good for General Motors" was "good for America," and the people of the "silent generation" wore "gray flannel suits" and "kept up with the Joneses." By the mid-'60s, though, the Moon had become full, and people were in the streets demanding peace and civil rights, and "dropping out" of "the rat race" to create a new culture. In 1966 not only was a Full Moon happening, but Saturn in Pisces opposed an exact conjunction of Uranus and Pluto. Uranus also turned stationary in the progressed chart! No wonder there was "something in the air!" As the progressed Moon's light waned in the 1970s, energy dissipated and the new institutions increasingly lost touch with the people. By the time of the next New Moon of 1981 the people were in full retreat, so they elected Ronald Reagan to bring back the '50s and allow the "unregulated free market" to operate, creating cut-throat competition, speculation, massive debt and greed just like in the 1920s.

In the future, the difficult Uranus-Pluto aspects (conjunctions, oppositions, and squares) will not happen during the progressed Full Moon, so these "progressive" periods will be less cataclysmic. Instead, they will correspond to the easier Uranus-Pluto trines and sextiles. Such was already the case in the early and mid-1990s. Instead of radical, catastrophic change followed by savage reaction, social "progress" will be more constant and continuous. Revolutionary changes may be made by a powerful few, while constructive and lasting reforms may be accomplished by the people themselves acting together. During the next New Moon (in 2010), revolutionary changes may be carried out by a few powerful leaders while the common people are "asleep" or deceived, and there is danger that the changes made will not really be to their benefit. During the next Full Moon in 2025, however, the awakened masses of people will work together to bring about very beneficial changes—even though America will be facing partition.

One further interesting fact about the progressed lunation cycle: the Full Moon in the Horoscope of Modern Humanity happens within two years of the New Moon in the progressed chart of the U.S.—and in the same degree. This confirms again how closely the destiny of America is linked to the destiny of humanity in these times.

MORE PREDICTIONS: 2020–2120

When Mercury went from Leo into Virgo in 1982, the spirit of the '60s was dampened by fears of AIDS (Virgo, health sign), and was replaced by the desire to get ahead in a world dominated by high technology. The new generation was more cynical, supporting America's wars instead of marching against them. In 2017 Mercury re-enters Leo and turns stationary there in 2024, and the exciting changes of the 2020s (Mars stationary direct) may restimulate the youth culture and make the young people of this period more optimistic and assertive. Israel may face dangerous conflicts in this period. Venus also enters Leo in 2026, showing a new romantic expressiveness in our culture. People will not hold their feelings inside as much as they do today under Venus in Cancer.

The year 2028 (Venus sextile Saturn) may see an economic recession caused by ecological damage and concerns over the environment. The period 2033–35 will see important confrontations. It will be a time of readjustment to the changes of the 2020s, and the conflicts they caused. Although progress resumes in 2023, its direction will be reevaluated again in 2033. Ethnic quarrels may cause distrust or xenophobia among peoples, and China is certain to erupt. A quieter period will start in the late 2030s. Under the New Moon in 2040 and the Sun's conjunction to Saturn in 2044, the early 2040s could be quite conservative. There could also be austerity programs to help the environment. Because Sun and Saturn will be in Libra, big constitutional reforms may happen in many nations, and Europe could be reorganized. Active idealism will reawaken as Mars trines Neptune and the "Green Revolution" unfolds around 2047. Venus trine Jupiter in 2048 may signal returning prosperity and generosity by the government. Expect more constitutional reforms in 2049–50 as progressed Mercury conjuncts Saturn.

According to many aspects in the progressed Horoscope of Modern Humanity, the 2050s will be active, idealistic, innovative and optimistic. There will be heroic exploits (reminiscent of Lindbergh's flight) and explosive advances in travel and communication—but in the 2060s, some kind of financial scandal could trigger a conflict over basic values in society. It will be another decade of "malaise" in which we must come to terms with the results of our past mistakes. Like the 1960s, it may also be a time of escalating drug use and new sensitivity and/or debauchery that causes health problems. This phase of uncertainty will not lead to apathy, as in the 1970s and '80s, but toward increasing revolt and activism in the 2070s, culminating in the revolutionary years of 2077–78 (Sun conjunct Uranus).

The Lunar eclipse of 2084 in Taurus may indicate some kind of economic, ecological or international catastrophe this year, or perhaps a trend toward overindulgence in pleasure and money. Mercury square Mars the same year may show a confrontation between peoples, plus more uprisings and revolutions. The eclipse may also signal a basic speeding up of our "vibration" as physical bodies on Earth. The mind of a reawakened humanity may become grounded in our lives on Earth. In 2089, Mars enters Pisces. This could be a critical turning point away from preoccupation with science and progress, marking the start of a great religious, spiritual, or cultural revival. Depression or disillusionment may trouble people in these years (Venus conjunct Saturn, 2090), but people will regain their confidence in the middle and late 2090s, as they gain a sense of stability, fulfillmen,t and accomplishment through discovering new ways of rebuilding society and serving other people.

The Twenty-Second Century will begin on a note of hopeful change (Mars trine Uranus, 2103). We will move forward confidently, but realistically. There could be explosive growth in spiritual building and construction, and a desire to make lasting visionary changes (Saturn trine Neptune, 2105). Our relationship to the Earth could be drastically reorganized, restructuring our whole society. If we play our cards right, we will have solved our ecological problem by 2110 and can move ahead fully focused on rebuilding Earth as a holy place revered as Goddess. By 2120 or 2130, we may also be able to begin moving out into space.

As the Sun opposes Neptune and Pluto in 2111, individuals and nations will develop new ways of relating to each other. In the 2110s through the 2130s, people will be enthralled with the possibilities of exploration and travel to other dimensions, and with inventions to help us get there. As the year 2120 approaches, the new religious enthusiasm and desire to venture and explore may lead to crusades and conflicts (including with aliens), as the Sun in expansive Sagittarius squares Mars in spiritual Pisces. Religious Jupiter turns stationary in warlike Aries at the same time. It could indicate another holy war, or perhaps exploding confidence sweeping us into the new Aquarian Age civilization of global interaction and creativity.

See Appendix E for a full listing of the precessed and progressed positions in the 1892 Horoscope of Modern Humanity. More details on the Twenty-First and Twenty-Second Centuries can be found in the final chapters of this book.

14

The Modern Spirit's Journey:

PART ONE: 1762–1892

Now we narrow our focus from the full panorama of time to concentrate on our own historical epoch. It is an era of ever-widening freedom and possibility, when Modern Humanity is throwing off its shackles and beginning to create its own destiny. The decisions we have made and continue to make in these times will determine our evolution for centuries to come, for we live at the gateway to a dawning tomorrow.

The movements of the three outer planets, Uranus, Neptune and Pluto, outline for us a neat and well-defined period of 200 years, which is the heart of our story. At the beginning, Uranus made a dynamic opposition to Pluto in 1792–93. This corresponded to the great French Revolution when we burst through our cage, took responsibility for our destiny, and began our journey to a new world. This was conception, the seed from which everything grew in our modern age. 100 years later came Neptune's conjunction to Pluto in 1891–92. This was our birth moment for which we cast the Horoscope of Modern Humanity in Chapter 12. It is the centerpiece of our story, defining our age as a time of transition. Finally came the conjunction of Uranus to Neptune in 1993, completing our journey to youthful maturity. We confronted our destiny as one free humanity on one planet, and as mature human beings who must live with the consequences of our actions. Conception of a new spirit in 1793, birth in 1892, and young maturity in 1993. That in brief is the outline of modern history up to the 1990s.

THE TIMEKEEPERS: JUPITER AND SATURN

As we followed the grand rhythm of the ages in previous chapters, the three outer planets (Uranus, Neptune and Pluto) were our guides and timekeepers. As we focus on modern times we rely on the two largest planets, Jupiter and Saturn, to keep the beat. The aspects between these two giants, especially when they conjoin and oppose each other, reveal the fortunes of "the Establishment." The significance of Jupiter-Saturn has been brought home forcefully to Americans by the fact that it corresponds to the deaths of U.S. presidents in office every twenty years, at least from 1841 until Ronald Reagan escaped his fate "by inches" in 1981. Into this fast-moving rhythm of Jupiter-Saturn are poured the sweeping melodies of Uranus, Neptune, and Pluto. They are the creative outsiders that challenge the authority of Jupiter and Saturn. The counterpoint between the Dynamic Duo of the Establishment (Jupiter and Saturn) and the Transcendental Trinity of the Creative (Uranus, Neptune, and Pluto) allows us to set the modern story to the "music of the spheres." Each twenty-year period reaches its climax when Jupiter and Saturn reach opposition. The most dramatic events usually happen at this point. The whole direction of events shifts, often taking a 180-degree turn.

CROSSING THE VALLEY OF TRANSITION

Imagine a valley of time stretching between two great mountain peaks—the *valley of transition*. The peaks represent two peak experiences in the life of modern humanity. The first happened over 200 years ago; the second is unfolding as I write. The journey between them has taken us through the shadows of deepest darkness as we moved from one great age of civilization to another.[1]

This 200-year voyage to a new world has been the most rapid period of change in human history, and our collective engines have been revved into high gear. One mighty cry reverberates from the sound of these engines of history—"liberation!" For over 6,000 years we have endured war, poverty, and domination by the few over the many. We bowed to kings and priests because we did not dare to believe we could take charge of our own lives. Then came the breakthrough; the great earthquake within humanity. The bonds of tradition were broken, and for the first time we tried to improve our lives by our own efforts. We discovered that evolution had been unfolding since the time of creation, and that we humans were now in the vanguard. What we embarked on 200 years ago was not just evolution—it was revolution!

To understand the scope of this revolution, consider what the world was like over 200 years ago. Kings and emperors ruled the land by "divine right" from one side of the world to the other. Beneath their exalted authority stretched a pyramid of rigid social classes in which everyone's place was given to them by birth, and could rarely be exceeded by effort or merit. The priests (or Brahmins, mullahs, etc.) were the ultimate spiritual authorities who sanctioned the established order, provided some education, defined social and cultural rules, dispensed charity, and supported the arts. The nobles and aristocrats (along with many priests) were the lords of vast estates. They protected the people from danger and provided "justice" in exchange for tolls and tributes. The Church and clergy (Jupiter) and the State and nobility (Saturn), though sometimes at odds with one another, were closely linked and stood together at the center of people's lives. Beneath them were the bourgeoisie or middle class (Uranus), who tended to grow in importance as time went on. These were the great financiers and merchants, followed by professionals, traders, craftsmen, and shopkeepers further down the ladder. At the bottom of the pyramid were the peasants and laborers (Neptune), the people we today would call farmers and workers. By far the largest and poorest group, the peasants spent long days in the fields cultivating the soil with archaic methods, and were subject to constant threats of famine, drought, and disease. Most did not own their own land. Although sometimes there were rebellions and food riots, it never occurred to most people to question their place in this divinely-ordained social order.

Though enjoined by God and by their social contracts to be fair and just, the authorities often abused their status and subjected their people to many indignities. Unfair laws and punishment by torture were common in many places. Most people lived within the narrow bounds of their local village and could never rise above the status into which they were born; but they did live closer to the rhythms of nature, preserved a strong sense of community, and had the support and guidance of the authorities. Men dominated family and society, and after Columbus "discovered" America in 1492, the white European races increasingly imposed their rule over other ancient cultures worldwide. As the great Revolution grew closer, the elite everywhere tightened its grip on power even more.

We broke through our shell in 1781 when we discovered Uranus, the first invisible, transcendental planet. Today we know Uranus as the flash of lightning, the inventive genius that allows us to see the unexpected. The coincidence of that discovery with the flurry of shocking events in the 1780s and 1790s gave Uranus its reputation. By discovering electricity and the electromagnetic spectrum, and by rediscovering the occult (as in Mesmerism), we expanded our awareness beyond the naked eye. The Industrial Revolution unleahed the power of machines and transformed the nature of labor, disrupting our whole relationship to Earth and to one another. Romantic artists declared their independence from the Academy. And colonists in America made the Old Regimes of Europe tremble on their thrones by achieving independence at Yorktown, just months after Uranus' discovery in 1781.

The shot fired at Lexington in 1775 was truly "heard 'round the world." From that moment until the last shots at Waterloo in 1815, humanity experienced its liberation—and its awesome expectations. These years of awakening contained much of modern history in microcosm. After the French-inspired American Revolution came the American-inspired French Revolution, and the world was never the same. Tremendous human forces were released and the pace of events accelerated.

The French Revolution was a peak experience—a sudden and complete revelation of liberty. Astrologically, it was a "peak," because Neptune and Pluto were at this time skirting the heights of the zodiac; in other words, traveling through the "high" signs of Scorpio through Aquarius. These years in the late Eighteenth and early Nineteenth Centuries, as we saw, were among the most inspired in history. Romantic artists, poets, composers, and philosophers celebrated "liberty, equality and fraternity" and awakened us to our new creative possibilities. The summit was marked by the vivid, dramatic planetary symbol of Uranus in Leo opposing Pluto in Aquarius in 1792, the very year French citizens established the first true national Republic. At that moment the great struggle for freedom began. We left the finite, structured, familiar Saturn-ruled world of the past, where everyone knew their place, and ventured off into the unknown. We and most historians look back to this peak experience as the origin of all the succeeding events. From that time to this stretches our valley of transition—a valley of the deepest darkness, terrors and trials. We've been making this hero's journey for over 200 years now, but the signs say that we are now reaching another shore and ascending another peak.

This great journey of transition represents the birth of the Modern Spirit. We today are different from the people who lived dutifully under the Old Regime of the past. As children of the Enlightenment, we question authority and all inherited traditions. We believe that "we the people" are the ultimate authority, duty-bound to restructure society according to the laws of nature. Voltaire and other Enlightenment "philosophers" of the Eighteenth Century instilled in us the myth of "progress" (our belief that things always get better and better), thus setting our modern times in motion. Thanks to the Industrial Revolution, which erupted at about the same time as the French Revolution, we also believe we can reshape the world for our own convenience and are no longer bound to the soil. We can improve our status and economic position, and we are moving toward a classless society.

At its deepest heart, the modern spirit is romantic. The Romantic movement grew up along with the political and industrial revolutions; it is the third aspect of this "Triple (not just dual) Revolution" of modern times. Without it we moderns have no soul, for political "liberty" and industrial "progress" alone leave us dehumanized and alienated from ourselves, each other and the Earth. The godfathers of the modern spirit were the romantic poets and artists, but everyone is a romantic who believes in the infinite creative potential of human beings and who seeks out the unfamiliar and the unknown. As children of the outer three invisible planets discovered since 1781, we modern romantics are moving beyond the visible towards developing our creative imagination and—most of all—rekindling our sense of wonder. Foolishly perhaps, we are perpetually hopeful, since we can glimpse (however dimly) the awesome possibilities opening up before us.

Before the French Revolution people waited for God's grace to usher in the new millennium. Now we know that the divine is acting through us too, and that we have become co-creators. Indeed today a "New Millennium" is literally upon us: the year 2000. It could be the gateway to heaven on Earth; certainly we have now passed through the valley and into a new kind of world. Only those romantics who are awake to its possibilities will be able to take part in building it.

THE STORM BUILDS

Many loud rumblings preceded the revolutionary eruption, as the light of Uranus grew brighter while approaching its opposition to Pluto in 1792–93. Other great cosmic alignments corresponded with the key events as the great storm grew. In 1762, for example, Jupiter, Saturn, and Uranus lined up closely in Aries, sign of "new beginnings." It was indeed a great new beginning for humanity, when the end of the Seven Years War launched the career of the "enlightened despots" who tried to enact some of the Enlightenment program. The same year the greatest spiritual father of the Revolution, Jean Jacques Rousseau, provided the rocket fuel for the modern takeoff by arguing in *The Social Contract* that beneath all the conventions of traditional society we humans are pure and uncorrupted. "Born free, yet everywhere in chains," we have the right to shake off our shackles and build a new society closer to the state of nature, based on a free contract among all its members.

In 1770, the outer three planets grouped together to form a momentous, ringing prophecy of a New World on Earth. For the first time in recorded history, they formed a grand trine, with all three planets in earth signs. Just then the "back to nature" cult exploded, as tales from Captain Cook's voyage to Tahiti seemed to validate Rousseau's ideas of "natural man" and the "noble savage." And yet ironically even as Western Humanity began to appreciate and glorify nature and her beauties, the industrial technology was being created which we would use to assault Mother Earth on an unprecedented scale. James Watt's steam engine dates from 1769, and Arkwright's spinning frame dates from the same year. So the grand trine in earth signs signaled our new ability to master as well as to worship nature. Indeed, it seems we often appreciate something more when we are about to lose it— or to become "liberated" from it. In 1770, the Boston Massacre in America and King Louis XV's battle with his own nobles in France ignited the revolutionary movements in each country, as events across the oceans moved in tandem. Old King Louis was himself one of the prophets of the new era that would succeed him. "After me," he would often say, "comes the deluge."

With Uranus' discovery in 1781, which happened while Uranus was in square to Neptune, the flood waters rose. A wave of electricity swept over the Western world in the wake of America's independence and Britain's industrial takeoff. In the summer of 1786 Saturn joined Pluto in Aquarius: the explosive time-bomb among the planets that was just about to blow. Immediately King Louis XVI had to confront the costly results of helping the American rebels kick out his British rival King George; his kingdom was now broke. He called an assembly of notables to make the rich French aristocrats pay their fair share of taxes. (On September 18, 1787, the nobles forced the king to back down.) That same summer of 1786, Shay's Rebellion in Massachusetts scared some American aristocrats into calling the Constitutional Convention. By September 17, 1787, as Jupiter in Gemini, Saturn in Aquarius, and Neptune in Libra formed a magnificent grand trine in the intellectually able air signs, the U.S. Constitution was completed—the basis of the durable federal system which some say was originally designed to protect the interests of rich Americans.

By the spring of 1789, just as George Washington became the first U.S. president, the French king was forced to call the Estates General, a representative body that had not met for almost 200 years. The rebellious nobles who helped bring this about assumed they would keep their old monopoly of power in it. For until now the First Estate (the clergy) and the Second Estate (the nobles) could always outvote the Third, which represented ninety-six percent of the people but had only one-third of the votes—but the confident bourgeois leaders of the Third Estate, the ideals of the Enlightenment in their minds, broke away on June 20 and declared themselves the lawmakers for the nation. Generous, optimistic Jupiter joined idealistic Uranus in Leo that summer of 1789, just as they had joined in 1776 (year of the American Declaration of Independence). When the King gathered his forces and tried to shut down this new National Assembly, the people rose up to defend it in one of the most heroic and legendary events of all time—the Fall of the Bastille.

On July 14, 1789, as Venus joined Jupiter and Uranus in conjunction, a group of citizens-in-arms and national guards invaded and conquered this old fortress where Voltaire had been held, and which was rumored to be packed with weapons and political prisoners. The Bastille's fall convinced the timid King Louis XVI to give in and recognize the Revolution—at least for the moment. He donned the new national colors, the red and blue of Paris combined with the royal white, which National Guard leader and American hero Lafayette was parading around the city. Citizens promptly staged similar events in towns all across France. The wildest enthusiasm gripped the land; it was the great dawn of liberty. So much so that July 14 is still fondly celebrated as the French National Day, just like the American Fourth of July. Patriots, artists, and intellectuals everywhere acclaimed the Revolution of 1789, and were encouraged by it to fight for liberation in their own lands. The great legend was born that the masses had risen in their majesty to overthrow despotism. The people of Konigsberg knew something important had happened when Immanuel Kant, whose habits were so regular they could set their clocks by him, failed to appear on his daily walk at exactly 3:30 P.M.. The old scholar was saluting the arrival of liberty.

More miraculous uprisings followed. French peasants, suffering from the worst harvest in memory that year, followed the lead of their fellow "citizens" in the towns and rose in revolt, forcing the Assembly to abolish centuries-old feudal dues and titles in a single frenzied night. At the same time the legislators drafted a Declaration of Rights which became a "national catechism," and the center of the world's political debate for a century—the first written charter of specific human rights decreed by a national government. Then on October 5, as Mars joined Jupiter and Uranus, the people marched to the King's villa at Versailles and demanded "bread," whereupon probably came Queen Marie Antoinette's fabled advice to "let them eat cake." The people's response was to kidnap the King and Queen and bring them back to Paris where they could be watched.

The people and their new representatives did not stop there. Citizens reveled in their new freedom, as clubs and newspapers multiplied. We know it would take over 200 years for us to cross the valley to the New Millennium, but the French in 1790 wanted to get it all done in 200 days! Quickly the Assembly confiscated church property (Saturn was in Pisces, showing repression of religion), sold it to the peasants, established a new currency, created a fair tax system, reformed the penal code and set up a "pyramid" of elected officials. During this feverish activity, Mars and Jupiter turned stationary as they continued to conjunct in Virgo, much as they would later do during another famous "100 Days" (the New Deal). France became a true "participatory democracy," with so many local councils that required so many meetings and elections that the people soon got sick of them.

As Uranus drew ever closer to its catastrophic rendezvous with Pluto (its 1793 opposition), the growing revolutionary storm got so forceful and out of hand that it threatened all the new reforms. The move to put the State in charge of Church affairs so angered the King that he decided on June 20, 1791, to flee France and rally his fellow Kings abroad to support him. He was recaptured, but the people never forgave this act of treason. Nor did they forgive their bourgeois leaders who massacred fifty people circulating a petition to overthrow him. Meanwhile, the economy, which had recovered, went sour again. Bread prices soared, and tempers soared commensurately. The common people of Paris became militant rebels, demanding not only democracy but price controls, welfare measures and the execution of all traitors—including aristocrats and financiers. These red-capped and red-bonneted "sansculottes" (so called because they refused to wear culottes, the pretentious knee-breeches worn by rich people), soon became the heart, soul, and muscle of the Revolution and the most formidable mass movement the world had ever seen—forerunners of all subsequent populist movements on behalf of "little people."

What really whipped the Revolution into a hurricane were the threats against the new nation from foreign kings responding to Louis XVI's appeals. The plucky French idealists, led by a new group of bourgeois legislators called Girondins (because most came from the Gironde Department on the west coast), beat them to the punch and declared war on April 20, 1792, just as Mars turned stationary at 17° Virgo. At the same time, Jupiter in Libra opposed Saturn in warlike Aries, meaning that the twenty-year period begun at their conjunction in 1782 had now reached its climax. The French Revolution became the World Revolution, because the French offered help to any nation "seeking to recover its liberty." The war of peoples (Mars in Virgo, a sign of commoners) against kings had begun—the first great "ideological" war.

The Girondins forgot one thing, however—they had no army! The French generals were still loyal to the King and refused to fight, and even Lafayette turned traitor and fled the country. Meanwhile the Prussians and Austrians advanced and threatened to burn Paris to the ground. France responded with a frenzy of revolutionary patriotism that lasted for two years. Spearheaded by some angry, brave volunteers who had marched all the way from Marseilles, the people invaded the palace on August 10 and forced the Assembly to overthrow the King. As the volunteers marched into the capitol they were singing a powerful song written at the time war was declared, music which Carlyle called "the most fortunate musical composition ever promulgated" which even today can "make the blood tingle."[2] Now called "La Marseillaise," it became the French national anthem.

Watching it all was the young poet Wordsworth, who quickly wrote the words that became the seed and essence of romantic poetry, just as all romantic musical compositions are variations on "La Marseillaise":

Mighty were the auxiliars which then stood
Upon our side, we who were strong to love!
Bliss was it in that dawn to be alive,
But to be young was very heaven![3]

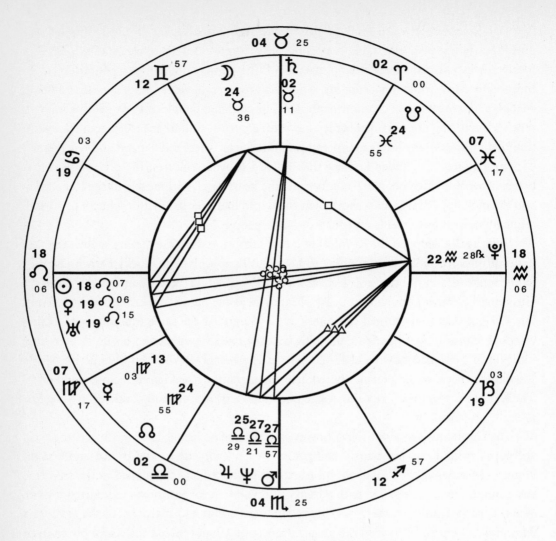

The Second French Revolution

On this day, the people captured the Tuileries palace and dethroned the king. Among the most awesome events in history, it happened "to the tune of" one of the most remarkable planetary figures ever. Mars, Jupiter, and Neptune in conjunction became the "Marseillaise planets." Venus was conjunct Uranus, as on Bastille Day. Saturn opposite Neptune in late 1792 and early 1793 represents the growing paranoia of the French people. Among those born around this time was the poet Percy Shelley, on August 4, 1792. Chart data: Sunrise chart for August 10, 1792, 4:31:13 A.M. LMT, Paris, France 48N52, 02E20.

For over a decade, Rousseau, Blake, Schiller, and other romantics had summoned "natural man" and the "common folk" to throw off the restraints of reason and outdated tradition. "The tigers of wrath are wiser than the horses of instruction," said Blake.[4] Wordsworth now saw how his own generation had become the kind of natural men and women who had once existed only on distant enchanted islands. The youth of France were transforming themselves to shake off "ancient corruption." Among their "mighty auxiliars" were certainly the planets, as they formed some of the most remarkable alignments ever seen. Strong in love they were, these first romantics, as the planet of love (Venus) aligned in the sign of love (Leo) with brilliant Sun and Uranus, and opposed potent, passionate Pluto. What sounds ever issued forth from the music of the spheres to equal Neptune, Jupiter, and Mars together in melodious Libra during this revolutionary march! From this time on, whenever they joined again, they brought back that transforming moment of August 1792 when humanity breached the limits of the Old Regime and "went to confront the infinite."[5]

The euphoria didn't last for long, though. Now that the Revolution rested in the hands of the unleashed forces of nature, down what sublime and terrible paths would it take us? As Neptune, Jupiter, and Mars entered stormy Scorpio, a "reign of terror" unfolded. In early September, mobs invaded the prisons and massacred inmates indiscriminately, afraid that "traitors" inside might break out and attack the people. If the "natural men" of France were not yet safe from themselves, they also proved too much for the "ancient forces of tyranny." The new citizen-soldiers under General Kellerman, singing as they fought, turned back the Prussians at Valmy—a miraculous victory which the poet Goethe, an eyewitness, called the beginning of a "new era in the history of the world."[6] Two days later, on September 22, 1792, delegates to the new National Convention celebrated by declaring it the first day of "Year One of the Republic."

THE WINDY MOUNTAIN TOP

"Seven hundred forty-nine human individuals never sat together on our earth under more original circumstances," said Carlyle about the new Convention.[7] Almost immediately this most audacious parliament in history became the scene of a murderous power struggle. Its effervescent, uninhibited debates were life-and-death matters for the nation—and for the Convention's members. All of them knew they could be toppled at any time by another stormy insurrection. The chart for the new Republic shows all this, with violent Mars in turbulent Scorpio T-squaring the revolutionary planets Uranus and Pluto.

The Convention quickly split into factions of Left, Right, and Center. These familiar terms date from these first modern parliamentary battles during the French Revolution, when those who wanted to push further sat on the left of the hall and those who wanted to slow things down sat on the right. Until the "reign of terror" unnerved it, this first revolution veered ever leftward, while those who wavered were shoved aside. The party of the left had become the party of the right, to paraphrase Pete Townsend. The rich, bourgeois Girondins, once the starry-eyed idealists of the movement, became the laggards of the Convention and sat on the right. Their radical opponents, members of the huge Jacobin political club, sat in the upper tier of seats on the left and so became known as the Mountain. They championed the demands of the "sansculottes" of Paris for price controls and taxes on the rich, which the Girondins resisted. In between them sat the shifting

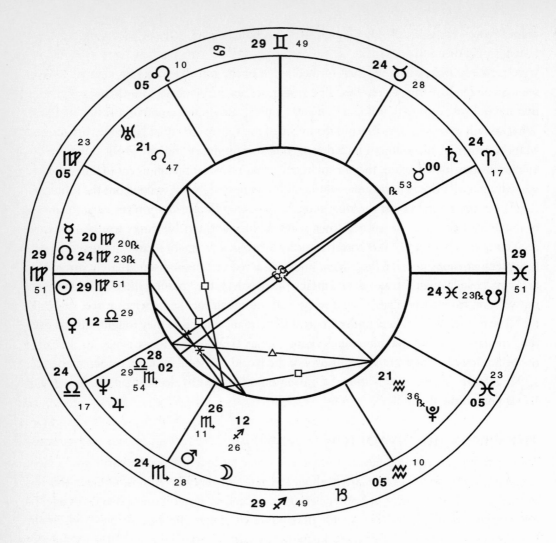

Proclamation of the Republic

On September 22, 1792, the National Convention proclaimed the first day of "Year One of the Repub-
lic". In this "birth chart" for the "new world" ("seed moment" of our age), when the First French Re-
public was proclaimed, the religion (Jupiter conjunct Neptune) of the nation-state (opposite Saturn)
emerged. The masses (Neptune) overwhelmed the government (Saturn), as they would do again in
1989, under almost identical and equally powerful aspects. The Mars-Uranus-Pluto T-square shows the
revolutionary fever at its height. Saturn at 1° Taurus is pregnant with karmic meanings of future "ter-
rors." Two days before, on September 20, the Battle of Valmy made the new world possible; on the next
day, the National Convention convened. Chart data: Sunrise chart for September 22, 1792, 05:52:08
A.M. LMT, Paris, France, 48n52, 02E20.

mass of uncommitted delegates called the Plain, which held enough votes to control the balance of power.

Their first great battle was over the fate of King Louis XVI. The Mountain gained favor with the Paris masses by demanding immediate execution. They prevailed by one vote, and Louis Capet was decapitated on January 21, 1793, as Mars joined deadly Pluto and opposed radical Uranus, and as Jupiter in Scorpio (meaning death of a prominent person) squared off with all three planets.

It was the "war against kings" that sealed the fate of the Girondins. They were the first democrats to understand and practice a cardinal rule of modern government: if your citizens are restless and unhappy, you can always divert their attention to the foreign foe. But both the Girondins and the king learned another modern principle the hard way: that wars are unhealthy to the fortunes of rulers who start them! As long as the war went well, the Girondins maintained their leadership and kept the reign of terror in check. Then in February, the British threatened war over the recent French conquest of Belgium. Soon, the Prussians and Austrians invaded France again, and a counterrevolution broke out in the west. France faced world war and civil war all at once. No government, not even a democratic one, could have mastered this extraordinary situation without some economic and political controls—but the Girondins stubbornly resisted, calling their opponents on the Mountain criminals and arresting radical leaders. The Mountain prevailed anyway, taxing the rich and fixing prices in May just as four planets in fixed earth sign Taurus formed a grand cross with Jupiter, Uranus, and Pluto. Finally, the Girondins were banished from the Convention in a huge insurrection by 80,000 sansculottes and the National Guard on June 2, 1793.[8] Those Girondins who escaped promptly joined the counterrevolution.

Now securely in power, the Mountain went political mountain-climbing during this peak experience of humanity. Marat, their most popular and fiery leader, had declared that "the time has come to organize a brief despotism of liberty in order to crush the despotism of kings,"[9] summing up the Revolution's greatest irony. He soon fell victim to his own methods. He was assassinated in July in his bathtub by a Girondin sympathizer, and immediately became the Revolution's cult hero. The Convention quickly followed his advice by setting up the Committee of Public Safety with emergency powers. It also sold the lands owned by nobles and "traitors" to the people at cheap prices, and abolished slavery in French colonies. It declared a radical democratic-socialistic constitution, but it never went into effect, because the Committee declared that the government was revolutionary (that is, beyond the law) until the peace—which never came until Napoleon fell at Waterloo, long after the Jacobin idealists had fallen off their "Mountain."

The Grand Committee mobilized for the first time an entire nation at war. In August 1793 all loyal French citizens, already the first frenzied devotees of the new religion of patriotism, were summoned to defend liberty "according to their means."[10] The Old Regime's antiquated forces were no match for the vast revolutionary armies, composed of citizens whose hearts burned with the fervor of the new religion and whose officers rose through the ranks by courage and talent alone. On the home front, the Committee, led by dogmatic, feisty idealist Maximilian Robespierre, imposed wage and price controls, rationed supplies and gave help to the needy, thus anticipating later state-planned economies. From atop their "Mountain," they made startling leaps into the future, decreeing social security, unemployment benefits, and medical relief.[11] Robespierre also declared "the Republic of Virtue," setting up a new religion recognizing the "Supreme Being." The Republic's red-bonneted and red-capped citizens enforced civic virtue with watch committees and suspect lists. Virtue also meant the first public education, support for scientific research, the metric system—and even a new calendar which started with Year I at the New World's "birth" on September 22, 1792. Since this was the Fall Equinox, the new months corresponded with the signs of the zodiac (an interesting signal of destiny!), and they were given poetic names to honor the cycle of nature (the month of meadows, the month of flowers, etc.). Perhaps we could call this the calendar of the modern spirit, which is now over 200 years old.

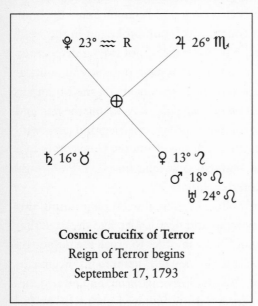

Cosmic Crucifix of Terror

Reign of Terror begins
September 17, 1793

Unfortunately, terror grew along with virtue. "The guillotine has been fasting too long," shouted the sansculottes,[12] as lustily cheering crowds and haughty knitting women watched the blade come down on the heads of aristocrats, financiers, traitors, and other suspects. Authoritarian Saturn T-squared Uranus and Pluto in 1793–94, potentially the most tense and dangerous of all cosmic configurations, as the ironic program of the despotism (Saturn) of liberty (Uranus) was played out in the reign of terror. Robespierre justified it by saying state executions were better than random killings like the massacres of September 1792. In September of 1793, Mars, Venus, and Jupiter joined the T-square to form a cosmic crucifix, as terror became official policy. In spring 1794 (or Germinal, the month of buds, Year II), as Mars reached Scorpio, turned stationary and opposed Saturn, the Revolution began eating its own children, acting out the Greek myth of Saturn. First the Committee eliminated their enemies on the left, led by Hebert, then their enemies on the right, led by the patriot Danton, who in 1792 had helped organize the overthrow of the King and the defense against the royal invaders (he and his followers were now thought to be fraudulent speculators). "Robespierre will follow me," warned Danton, as the guillotine came down on his ferocious head.[13] His prophecy came true in August (Thermidor, the month of heat), when Robespierre and his followers were overthrown and executed as the sansculottes, upset by the death of Hebert, failed to support him. By then, the mighty revolutionary armies had beaten back the Republic's enemies and the reign of terror suddenly seemed unnecessary. During all these climactic events in 1794, stationary Mars joined Neptune, just as during the Marseillaise march of 1792; the same conjunction appeared in the charts of both Robespierre and Danton, among others.[14]

THE VIRGIN REPUBLIC FALLS TO ITS PROTECTORS

The "Thermidorian Reaction" followed, which gave the political term "reaction" its meaning, as events now moved in the opposite direction. The rigid controls of the Terror were ended and the nation relaxed. Among the prisoners miraculously saved from the knife were General Kellerman, hero of Valmy; Rouget de Lisle, composer of "La Marseillaise"; and even Dr. Guillotin, promoter of the "humane" head chopper.[15] The Neptunian dreams fell victim to the blood of Mars, and cautious disillusion increasingly squelched the revolutionary flame. We fell off the mountain and began descending into the valley of transition. But the Jacobin fire kept burning in the hearts of all who continued to fight for freedom and justice, and the red, bloodstained Neptunian dreams would live again once the Second Revolution got going.

Tensions relaxed in the skies as well, as Saturn and Uranus shifted from stubborn and powerful fixed signs (Taurus and Leo) into flexible and easygoing mutable ones (Gemini and Virgo). Generous, war-generating Girondins under cardinal signs had been replaced by the rigid doctrinaires of the Mountain under fixed signs; now they in turn yielded to the moderate, adaptable, shifty "Thermidorian" schemers and profiteers under mutable signs. The same mutable signs showed how the Revolution was now being dispersed, as the army overthrew feudal lords and instituted the efficient revolutionary system in all the lands they conquered. This is why the French Revolution was the start of a world liberation movement that continues today.

Women became prominent again after 1794, as Uranus transited through Virgo the Virgin. In this First (or "virgin") Republic, the banal, bourgeois popular culture we know today appeared in an early form for the first time, as the people completed the Revolution by expropriating the Old Regime's pleasures for themselves. Ancient palaces were converted into public theaters where female "stars" revealed their bodies as well as their minds.[16] Made possible after Robespierre relaxed the divorce codes, this sensuous, permissive society echoed the earlier aristocratic Rococo reaction to Louis XIV's death in 1715, and anticipated both "La Belle Epoque" in the Paris of the 1880s and the counterculture and feminism of 1960s America—also under Uranus in Virgo.

The Terror's end led to economic and political instability. Prices soared after controls ended, bringing starvation to the masses and more revolts in April 1795, as Mars opposed Neptune. After suppressing these revolts, the Thermidorian leaders of the Virgin Republic shifted from left to right in order to hold on to power by fair means or foul—usually foul. On October 5, 1795 (13 Vendemiaire, month of vintage, Year III), they called upon a young general named Napoleon Bonaparte to help beat back a royalist uprising. Mars was in Virgo, conjunct Uranus. After a "red scare" in May of 1796 (caused by Babeuf's first Communist revolt), the royalist right wing rebounded and won new elections. The Thermidorians, now led by a "Directory" of five members, decided to protect this first "constitutional" bourgeois Republic by becoming its dictators in the "coup of Fructidor" (fruitful month, September 1797). Once again it was orchestrated by Napoleon, as Mars returned to Virgo and conjoined Uranus again. In the sign Virgo, where it was when the "war against kings" began in 1792, Mars symbolized the Virgin Republic's ultimately fatal dependence on war and the armed services.

Mars was also in Virgo in the chart of the man who was to deliver the fatal blow: Napoleon. He was already a legend after conquering Italy in the same month of the "red scare" on May 10, 1796.[17] The "unleashed forces of nature" had now been harnessed by France's greatest warrior. In his next adventure, this seemingly superhuman hero opened the European imagination to the exotic east by sailing off to conquer Egypt as Pluto and Mars entered picturesque, watery Pisces in 1798. It was as if he was becoming the "ancient mariner," a poetic character conceived that very year, as its author Coleridge, along with writers Wordsworth and Schlegel, officially launched the Romantic Movement. On the same trip, the Rosetta Stone was discovered, which decoded the ancient Egyptian language. Napoleon defeated the local warlords at the Battle of the Pyramids in July 1798.

Napoleon's Egyptian Odyssey mobilized a new coalition of foreign despots against France, which in turn aroused a new Jacobin revolutionary spirit at home. After more coups and counter-coups, Napoleon emerged in the public mind as the only leader who could master the situation he himself had helped to cause. On 18 Brumaire (the foggy month), Year VIII (November 10, 1799), the lion took charge after some complicated and deceptive maneuvers. On that day, stationary Saturn in Leo testified eloquently to the rise of the proud, enlightened despot whose very name contained within it the name of his own noble sun sign. Quickly, Napoleon the Leo announced that the Revolution was "finished"; then proceeded to institute a bureaucracy that extended into every corner of the land, and which still endures today. Uranus demonstrated its power in bureaucratic Virgo, as it would do again in 1882 (birth of the U.S. Civil Service) and 1965 (Johnson's Great Society). The Constitution of the Year VIII and the Code Napoleon, which became law in 1804 (Saturn stationary in legal Libra), safeguarded the Revolution's principles and those who benefited from them by stabilizing society. Something similar happened in the U.S., where after his "revolutionary" election victory in 1800, Thomas Jefferson protected American liberties but also strengthened federal authority. Napoleon then marched off against his foreign foes with a brilliant flanking move across the Alps, a journey which the great revolutionary painter J. L. David glorified in his famous romantic image of the young conqueror on horseback. As Napoleon left, Mars returned to the sign of his Egyptian Odyssey (Pisces) and joined Pluto there again. But he needed help from General Kellerman, the old hero of Valmy, to prevail at Marengo on June 14, 1800, as Mars crossed into Aries and opposed Uranus. With some relief, Napoleon then quickly made peace with his enemies.

THE VAST SEA OF THE "STORMY SUBLIME"

As we mentioned, Jupiter and Saturn mark off twenty-year periods by their conjunctions. In 1802, the next conjunction in Virgo exactly opposed romantic Pluto in Pisces, and this symbolized the mood and spirit of these new times. Our liberation from the restrictive security of the past had left us like castaways in an uncertain and stormy sea, too vast for anyone to master—except perhaps a godlike emperor. Yet Napoleon himself admitted he was just a "pawn of destiny." Now our task was not to gain freedom to control events, but to step back and surrender in rapt awe and wonder before greater powers—to what the romantics called "the sublime."

Schopenhauer, a leading philosopher of the time, defined the "sublime" as the magnificent experience of seeing huge and terrible events from a point of view beyond our personal interests.[18] William Blake described it vividly as "the roaring of lions, the howling of wolves, the raging of the stormy sea and the destructive sword...portions of eternity too great for the eye of man."[19] "Mock on, mock on, Voltaire, Rousseau," Blake wrote in about 1803; "mock on, mock on, 'tis all in vain! You throw the sand against the wind, and the wind blows it back again."[20]

Romantics like poet Lord Byron taught us how to revel in the sublime. "Once more upon the stormy waters," he wrote. "Welcome to their roar! Swift be their guidance, wheresoe'er it lead!"[21] The planets themselves had embarked upon the seas too. Never in history did they better reflect the spirit of the times, as passionate Pluto swam through oceanic Pisces, and watery Neptune simultaneously sailed through stormy Scorpio in a potent mutual reception—a double cosmic statement! Unfortunately, many of the romantic "pilgrims of eternity" (like Byron) succumbed to the tempest of these times, and died young. One who survived was an artist who pictured the sublime in paint the way Byron captured it in words: J. M. W. Turner. In 1802 he made it to shore in a rowboat through a perilous storm and, sketchbook in hand, created the first great romantic painting. Others like Gericault and Delacroix followed his lead.

Turner, Byron, Schopenhauer, and others were called "pessimists" because they realized that humanity could not control events; recent history had shown that revolutions would be hijacked by tyrants and that the people would bring terror upon themselves. We faced the results of our own liberation, as we still do today. In 1813 Mary Shelley, second wife of the poet, created in *Frankenstein* the ultimate statement of how our own unleashed powers can create a monster; meanwhile the great artist Goya painted austere documents of disillusion by showing the Devil triumphant and Saturn eating his children. Another portrait of unrestrained power was Goethe's *Faust,* the first volume of which was completed in 1807, which told of the romantic dream of making a bargain with the Devil to gain eternal youth. Schopenhauer stated that at the root of all life was a relentless, ruthless, insatiable will to live that was perpetually in conflict with itself, and that the only alternative was to surrender to the sublime and mystical All.

Beethoven and Hegel, however, saw beyond disaster to the New World's hopeful possibilities. Both were born under the great prophetic grand trine in earth signs around 1770, as were Wordsworth, Coleridge, and Napoleon himself. In 1808, Beethoven finished his own musical rendition of "storm and stress" in the first movement of his Fifth Symphony, the most famous composition of all time. It is a perfect portrait of Schopenhauer's dire description of "the will." Schopenhauer himself said that music was the supreme art because it "reveals the will" most directly.[22] When asked the meaning of the famous opening four-note phrase from which the symphony develops with a relentless logic, he was supposed to have replied, "fate knocking at the door" (number four is the number of Saturn, and thus of "fate"). But by the end, as in all his symphonies, Beethoven reaches a glorious victory. In 1821, when Uranus and Neptune joined in conjunction at the heights of the zodiac (early Capricorn), Beethoven was writing the most eloquent prophecy of the New Age ever made in his "Ode to Joy" from the Ninth Symphony. In this music, the planets truly sang out the harmonious "music of the spheres" from the grand trine in his horoscope. But his victory was (as J.W.N. Sullivan states in his "spiritual biography" of the composer) a triumph over himself, not external circumstances; a submission to the mystical power of grace. His vision of "the will" was not so different after all from Schopenhauer's. Beethoven's music is the supreme portrait of our modern spirit as it struggles to be born.

The philosopher Hegel, also born in 1770, showed how the inevitable conflicts of "the will" as described by Schopenhauer and fellow German philosopher J.G. Fichte would reach an ultimate synthesis. His view of history as a meaningful series of stages unfolding through conflict arose naturally out of the experience of his times. Hegel helped shape our idea of history as an ongoing drama involving all humanity.[23] By 1820, when he wrote his influential *Philosophy of History* during the Uranus-Neptune conjunction, he saw history as "the progressive unfolding of ever-greater freedom." But by saying in 1807 that this "freedom" was exemplified by the newly reformed Prussian state, he fell in line with the pessimism of the times. To be "free" meant to surrender to the greater power of the state, and thus Hegel's romantic dialectic paved the way for Marx's scientific and communist one in 1848, when Neptune followed Pluto into Pisces during a time of even greater disillusion.

It was in July-August 1802, during the Jupiter-Saturn conjunction, that Napoleon steered all humanity onto the sublime and stormy path to disaster being described by the romantics. That month, he made himself dictator ("first consul for life") and began expanding abroad. Carried away by his compulsion to conquer, symbolized by aggressive Mars joined to his grand trine, by 1805 his actions had aroused the alarmed foreign despots against him again. As the French armies marched off once more to meet the coalition of kings in 1805, Jupiter and Neptune joined together as they did in 1792 during the march of the "Marseillaise." In the Fall, during the decisive battles, Saturn and Uranus joined too, just as they would during the next bid for world conquest in 1941–42.

Napoleon rode to imperial glory by skillfully using the revolutionary citizen armies, whose size, mobility, and morale fitted them for reckless mass attacks and lightning-fast strikes (the signature of newly-discovered Uranus, exactly trine to Mars in Napoleon's chart). On December 2, 1804, he followed his model Charlemagne (two 500-year cycles before), and had himself crowned Emperor. Only this time Napoleon took the crown from the pope's hands and put it on his own head, symbolizing his arrogant, revolutionary boast that he had created his own power. Exactly one year later, he overwhelmed his royal enemies in his "masterpiece of battles" at Austerlitz, after which he demolished Charlemagne's Holy Roman Empire. More fabulous victories followed. "We have met the Prussian army, and it no longer exists," he told his wife Josephine after the Battle of Jena in October of 1806.[24] Then he defeated the Russian Tsar in a bloody battle at Eylau, just after Mars turned stationary in Virgo again (February 8, 1807). Finally, as Mars returned to the same place, he forced the Russians and Prussians to surrender at Friedland on June 14, 1807.

Napoleon conquered Europe for the Revolution. His easy victories discredited the Old Regime, which was quickly replaced in his new empire by fairer taxes, efficient administrations, and his new legal code. Uranus in 1807 entered Scorpio, thus reaching the very place where Neptune in 1792 symbolized the "Marseillaise" march to freedom. Since Uranus is in the same place in our Horoscope of Modern Humanity (Chapter 12), it shows how Napoleon's revolution laid down seeds for our times.

However, Napoleon was also a tyrant who mercilessly exploited the lands he conquered, and the subject peoples now used French ideas to fight against her. In 1807–1808, when Beethoven finished the Fifth Symphony, fate knocked on Napoleon's door, as a new "patriotic national spirit" arose in Beethoven's land. One day this heroic new German spirit would bear the ugly fruit of another, less benevolent world conqueror. In October 1807, as Mars joined Neptune, it led Chief Minister Stein of Prussia to end feudalism, set up democratic assemblies and—most importantly for Napoleon—build a revolutionary citizen army. A week later, trouble began in Spain too—a nation ruled by religious sign Sagittarius, the sign Neptune had just entered. In May 1808, the people rose up defiantly against Napoleon after he deposed their royal family. Napoleon struck back on October 29, 1808 by invading Spain as Mars returned to Virgo and T-squared both Neptune and Jupiter. He won, and promptly performed a lasting service to humanity by abolishing the Spanish Inquisition on December 4, but the traditional, devoutly Catholic Spanish remained a stubborn thorn in his side.

Born under the grand trine in earth signs, Napoleon was master on land, but he was unable to beat the British on the seas, because they had sunk his fleet in the Battle of Trafalgar in October 1805 (Mars was conjunct watery Neptune on that day too!). "Like the tiger and the shark,"[25] each power was supreme on its chosen element but couldn't get at the other. So they used economic weapons such as trade embargoes. The Americans, already the leading neutral trading nation, were caught in the middle and fought back with embargoes of their own. In 1812, Jupiter in Cancer opposed Saturn in Capricorn, just like in 1991. The Gulf War of 1991 was not the first time war could have been avoided if "sanctions had been given more time to work"; the British had already lifted their embargo against the U.S. in June 1812 when the Americans declared war on them!

In this "Second War of Independence" the American national spirit awakened. The American "Marseillaise," "The Star Spangled Banner," was written on September 13, 1814 when Mars was at 17° Virgo—the same degree as in April 1792 when the French national anthem was composed! With Pluto still in watery Pisces and opposing the U.S. Neptune, America got its taste of sublime glory not on land, as the French did, but at sea. "We have met the enemy, and they are ours!" exclaimed Commodore Perry after a naval victory on Lake Erie.[26] "Pogo" later revised the slogan to read, "We have met the enemy, and it is us!" That would have made more sense in the first place, considering how divided America was about the war and how poorly it was fought. Pluto, which opposed Neptune's place in Virgo in the U.S. horoscope in 1814, brought home the same lesson in the 1960s in Vietnam when it conjoined America's Neptune.

The age of the "stormy sublime" reached its titanic climax in the War of 1812, as Jupiter opposed Saturn and the storm's winds shifted direction again. The twenty-year war of peoples against kings now became the war of peoples against peoples. The Americans rebuffed the British invasion; but when Napoleon invaded Russia simultaneously, on the pretext that it wasn't observing his embargo against Britain, he stepped into a quagmire. He beat the Russians in another "sublime and terrible" victory at Borodino, as Mars returned to Virgo; but he couldn't capture the elusive Russian army and had to retreat. Most of his troops never made it back to France. Napoleon summed up his sad journey home and the destiny of his times by coining a now-famous phrase. "From the sublime to the ridiculous is but a step," he said.[27] Emboldened, the other peoples then rose up against him in the "War of Liberation," as warrior Mars turned stationary in liberating Aquarius, and defeated him at Leipzig in October 1813 in the huge "Battle of the Nations." In June 1815, as Mars returned to watery Pisces and joined Pluto, like during his Egyptian Odyssey, Napoleon finally "met his Waterloo" and was beaten by British and Prussian forces.

BACKWARDS AND FORWARDS

The Great Revolution was over, but its glory still hung in the air as Uranus and Neptune soared through lofty Sagittarius. America basked in its "era of good feelings," while European soldiers and students dreamed of further achievements. The peak experience was over; now it was up to us to slowly work out its goals and implications. The fondest desire of the Old Regimes that regained power after Napoleon was a return to peace and order, though, and not more change. Led by Prince Metternich of Austria, who had Sun, Venus, and three other planets in stabilizing Taurus, they met in Vienna and created the Concert of Europe. It was revolutionary in its own right, for it was the first time the Great Powers had joined in a common association to preserve world peace—a forerunner of today's United Nations. Showing convincingly how outer planets in the "high signs" (Scorpio through Aquarius) contribute to an international perspective, the statesmen of the Concert respected agreements and the rights of other nations and created a durable "balance of power" that lasted at least until Neptune left Aquarius in 1848.

They also disappointed the hopes of reformers by restoring old thrones and boundaries. To the titled aristocrats meeting at Vienna, the Revolution of 1789 was an "errant aberration" that revealed the "insolent arrogance" of human nature that would bring "chaos" if not suppressed, so they tried to sweep the Revolution under the rug and turn back the clock. They kept the lid on pretty well until 1848, but the modern spirit continued bubbling underneath and burst out periodically. Although the great war ended, the revolution really didn't, and some kind of uprising occurred every couple of years. There were three great waves of revolution, each more serious than the last. Each wave corresponded to a powerful planetary aspect by revolutionary Uranus: its conjunction to Neptune in 1821, its opposition to Saturn in 1830, and its conjunction to Pluto in 1850.

The first wave under Uranus-Neptune began with unrest among the poor in Britain, which climaxed in August 1819, when veterans of Waterloo fired on their own citizens at a rally at St. Peter's Field in Manchester (The "Massacre of Peterloo"), just as Mercury, Mars, Saturn, Uranus, and Pluto all formed a violent grand cross. Soon afterward, Britain began following a path of reform, but the other powers of the Concert, united in a "Holy Alliance" to preserve divine authority, blindly opposed all change for fear of fomenting revolution. "I will have no innovations!" cried Emperor Francis of Austria.[28] The idealistic students of Germany resisted by staging a mammoth rally in October, 1817, on the anniversaries of Martin Luther's Reformation and the Battle of Leipzig. The Jupiter-Uranus conjunction of 1789 returned in Sagittarius (sign of universities), while stationary Mars in Gemini (students) opposed visionary Neptune. When a reactionary poet was assassinated two years later, Metternich moved to destroy the student movement and ended all reforms in Germany, and in 1821 the Vienna Powers stamped out bold outbreaks of revolution in Portugal and Italy.

Two areas escaped their reactionary grip, however: Greece and the New World. In 1821, the revolt led by Simon Bolivar liberated all of colonial Latin America. Two years later, the self-anointed bully boys of Vienna restored the King of Spain, overthrown by revolution in 1820, and promptly threatened to give him back his colonies in America. The British navy stood in their way, as did President Monroe, who declared that henceforth the U.S. would defend any nation in the western hemisphere against outside attack. In this audacious Monroe Doctrine, which thoroughly annoyed the helpless Vienna despots, the U.S. declared independence again; only this time it applied to the whole western hemisphere over which we had assigned ourselves as "protectors." In 1823, Jupiter returned to early Cancer where it had stood in 1776, 1788 (Constitutional Convention), 1799 (U.S. navy created in battles with France), and 1812 ("Second War of Independence"). The cycle continued in 1823 when Stephen Austin was granted land in Texas for settlement by the Mexican government, which then owned the territory. When Jupiter returned again to Cancer in 1835, these restless pioneers followed their grandfathers' example and "declared independence." Soon they wanted to join the U.S. too, so during the next return in 1846 America conquered Texas and the whole southwest in its war with Mexico. Stay tuned; this pattern of Jupiter returning to Cancer continues today—especially in regard to Latin America!

The Greeks rose up against the Sultan of Turkey in 1821— a huge revolt that aroused frenzied sympathy all over the world for the overly romanticized Greeks. Even Lord Byron fought and died for their cause. The war was full of atrocities like the 1822 Massacre of Chios, ignited by a huge Mars station and singleton in Leo and commemorated by the romantic painter Delacroix. I thought this war would be a sign of things to come when Uranus joined Neptune again in the 1990s. This prediction was fulfilled in nearby Bosnia, also once part of Turkey. After more massacres in Greece in 1824–26, even the Russian Tsar was forced to take the rebel side to defend his fellow Orthodox Christians there. In 1827, six years after Uranus joined Neptune, Britain, France, and Russia formed an alliance and defeated the Turks. In 1914, six years after Uranus opposed Neptune, the same three powers united to defend nearby Serbia. Perhaps another alliance will restore order in Bosnia six years after Uranus' latest conjunction to Neptune in 1993. By the way, when Neptune returned to the same degree of Capricorn in 1991 that it occupied in 1827, another "Allied Coalition" acted to rein in another Mid-East tyrant (again, much as I predicted).

The second wave of revolution broke out after Uranus entered futuristic, electric Aquarius in 1828 and opposed Saturn in 1829–1830, joined by Jupiter. Progress now seemed to accelerate, especially in England, much like the new railroad engines that opened up new industries. Tycoons and inventors emerged, like Faraday, creator of the first electric generator in 1831. The Romantic vision stirred again, too. Political sparks flew when the French threw out their last Bourbon tyrant, restored after Napoleon's fall by the Vienna boys, in the "July Revolution" of 1830, which inspired Delacroix's painting "Liberty Leading the People." The French rising ignited more revolts in Belgium, Germany, Italy, and Poland the same year. "Saddle your horses, gentlemen," shouted the Tsar. "Revolution rides again!"[29] The Concert of Europe had its way once more in the east, but was forced to leave Belgium and France alone. The fires spread to England too, where the old Tory rulers were thrown out and the Parliament was forced by a near-revolution to make democratic reforms. The wave even washed up in America, where President Jackson made the U.S. the world's first true democracy, and the movement against slavery got going. In 1831, Nat Turner led the first slave revolt as Mars conjoined Saturn in Virgo (action by the humble classes).

The Bourgeoisie took power again in the Western countries in 1830, but the people soon discovered that they cared only about protecting their profits. The new romantics of France like Victor Hugo pilloried and satirized the new rulers, while in Britain Charles Dickens railed against the grim industrial world they were creating:

> *"You saw nothing in Coketown but what was severely <u>workful.</u> If the members of a religious persuasion built a chapel there, they made it a pious warehouse of red brick... Fact, fact, fact everywhere; what you couldn't show to be purchaseable in the cheapest market and saleable in the dearest, was not, and never should be."*[30]

Many people now saw what Blake had warned against in his poem about "satanic mills" in the 1790s; the new industry was quickly becoming a monster. British workers rebelled against their bourgeois bosses who had herded them into slimy, dangerous factories where they and their children worked for long hours for low pay. First they organized a National Union, but this was suppressed in April 1834 during another wave of revolt that also spread to France. Afterward, as Uranus left visionary Aquarius, the rebels went back to their old strategy of demanding more democracy, and in May 1839 (as Mars turned stationary in Virgo) they presented their first "Charter" to Parliament. The bourgeois stand-patters rejected it without debate, and violence followed (repressive Saturn square rebel Uranus).

By the mid-1840s Neptune was about to leave Aquarius. The romantic flight was coming in for a landing, as poets and artists increasingly turned away from mysticism toward the mounting problems of the new industrial society. Before they woke up to "reality," though, under Neptune's influence in Aquarius many of them spun wistful utopian dreams that became seeds for tomorrow. In America, there were so many visionaries that Emerson, himself the great prophet of "non-conformity," said that "there wasn't a reading man who didn't have a utopian scheme in his waistcoat pocket."[31] Experimental communes and reform movements proliferated worldwide.

In 1846, astronomers discovered the planet Neptune. The planet of unity and the collective ideal came into human consciousness in the midst of all this social idealism and concern. At that very moment, the great crisis broke which was to generate the third and greatest of the major revolutionary waves and open the Socialist Revolution. The catastrophic Irish potato famine brought starvation and depression throughout Europe. Anxious observers thought they saw "vapors rising from the earth" that caused the Irish potatoes to rot; scientists meanwhile discovered that a previously-unknown life form, the fungus, was to blame. Whichever explanation you believed, it was symbolized by watery Neptune's discovery and represented the dissolution and decay of Western society that now accelerated. The potato fungus was almost literally a mold growing profusely on the decaying, agriculture-based Old Regime, while reformers and prophets like Emerson were openly calling for righteous crusades that would "rise like vapors" to crush society's corruption. Marx and Engels wrote late in 1847 of the "spectre of communism haunting Europe."

Even they were surprised at the size of the visitation that came just a few months later. By now, the Old Regimes were so vulnerable that they were like a row of dominoes waiting for the first one to fall; the Neptunian fungus had rotted their foundations. Early in 1848 the long-awaited Revolution erupted, as the rising vapors became an exploding geyser. On February 22, the very day Neptune left the "high signs" and crossed into watery Pisces (square Mars), the French rose again and overthrew their middle class "citizen-king" Louis Phillippe and his reactionary minister. France was the model and inspiration for revolt; where she led, other nations followed. Within a month of the French collapse, Old Regime governments in Germany, Austria, Hungary, and Italy fell in the greatest series of revolutions the world would see until 1989. Metternich himself was humbled, as was his boss. "Are they really allowed to do that?" cried the incompetent Austrian Emperor Ferdinand as workers invaded his palace.[32]

THE DESCENT INTO REALISM

The dominoes of the Old Regime lay strewn about the land, trampled on by the "emerging masses" of Europe—aware for the first time of their political power and national identity. Women awakened too, especially in America. In July 1848 (as Mars in Virgo "The Virgin" opposed Neptune), they staged the first "Women's Rights Convention" at Seneca Falls, New York. Marx's "revolutionary proletariat" was also rising, and the "red flag" was seen everywhere in the 1848 revolutions.

The workers had not yet "lost their chains,"though. If the rapid fall of so many apparently powerful repressive governments was shocking, their rapid recovery in the "counter-revolution" was even more so. In the process, they transformed themselves from royal absolutists who cooperated with each other to keep peace and order into pragmatic, ruthless adventurers who sought to build the power of their own state by any means. The first examples of this new *realpolitik* were the ministers under the new Austrian Emperor Franz Joseph, who got Russian help to crush the Hungarian revolt in 1849. They ruthlessly betrayed their old allies a few years later by helping to strip them of territory at the peace conference after the Crimean War.

Realpolitik was only one of the many kinds of cynical "realism" that took hold after all the high hopes of 1848 were crushed—the crash landing of romanticism. Jupiter opposing Saturn represented this climactic "change of direction" from idealism to realism in 1850–51. The powerful disillusion that shook all the beliefs of the past was shown by Neptune entering dissolving Pisces in 1848 and by radical Uranus and Pluto joining in early Taurus (sign of realism and materialism) in 1850–51. This conjunction was a great signpost in the sky. Past this point, our descent into the Valley of Transition, gradual until now, suddenly got quicker. A great pattern of history was repeating itself. Every 500 years God seems to take a vacation and turn out the lights. Grace gradually leaves us in our conduct and beliefs, as our old familiar world loses its bearings. We are led through the valley of the shadow of death, a deep gorge astrologically symbolized by Neptune's and Pluto's descent together into the "lower" signs as they approach their dark "New Moon" phase of conjunction. At the peak of 1792–93, we were given a sparkling vision which seemed tantalizingly within our reach from across the mountain tops. But we had not yet reached the new world; our new liberty had been a mirage. We descended into a valley wider and deeper than we had suspected. As we descended, we lost the vision possible only from the peak. Our viewpoint narrowed as the Old Order decayed to make room for the new. We were on our way to the other side, but first we had to traverse the canyon.

After 1850, we began to embrace strange and indecent notions. Inspired by expanding industry and all the prosperity and "success" it brought, which contrasted sharply to the 1848 Revolution's failures, young people who once thought of imitating Napoleon or Robespierre now dreamed of getting rich in the new "gilded age." Scientists gave support for their new dreams from 1850 on by declaring matter to be the first cause of all things. Nature, once viewed as sacred and alive, became just material for us to use. Readers of the 1850s eagerly grabbed up books that reduced life to chemistry. "Is life worth living? It depends on the liver!" ran a popular joke.[33] We started defining ourselves according to our race and social class; in the new "sociology" (Comte's *Treatise on Positivism*, 1851), individual freedom was reduced to the mere plaything of circumstances. Theories of racial superiority based on human physical traits appeared (for example, Gobineau's *Inequality of Human Races*, 1853). Artists and writers followed the realist trend (Courbet, Millet, Eakins, Flaubert, Zola, Hardy, etc.). Meanwhile, reality mirrored our new beliefs. Huge industries dehumanized our lives, declared war on our planet's finite resources and reduced millions to want even as they enriched a few. The misery of those who worked in their factories fueled a Second Revolution to challenge the First. Its leaders, Marx and Engels, authors of *The Communist Manifesto* (1848), stopped dreaming of utopias and proposed "scientific" proof that the workers would win the inevitable "class struggle." Meanwhile, the cause of liberty for all nations taken up by the First revolutionaries in 1792 was transformed into an armed struggle for national power by the realpolitikers. At the same time, the physical barriers between humanity began to break down, as we increasingly migrated throughout the planet and lumped ourselves together in cities. And as the Old World lost its outlines, the decaying Neptunian humus created a yeasty brew in which new ideas could grow. The Modern Spirit entered its cocoon.

The Uranus-Pluto conjunction, which symbolized all these events and trends of mid-century (1848–52), was joined at the beginning of June 1851 by Saturn, Mars and Venus at the cusp of Aries-Taurus in a mammoth planetary pile-up or cosmic trigger that graphically represented all the violent forces of the following years. As the planets moved together from fiery, impulsive Aries into fixed, earthy Taurus, it was as though an irresistible force (Aries) had hit an immovable object (Taurus). The result was "matter-in-motion" on a gargantuan and deadly scale. The momentum of sixty years of romantic, revolutionary idealism, unleashed in the French Revolution, would henceforth be transferred to gigantic cam-wheels, smokestacks, cranes, turrets, machine guns, goose-stepping armies, and screaming masses of jingoists[34] who believed in Social Darwinism and "survival of the fittest." Certain facts confirm the enormous significance of this "planetary pile-up" in the years after 1851. Lenin was born on April 22, and Hitler on April 20; both therefore had Sun in early Taurus aligned with this conjunction. They were prime, archetypal examples of what it meant for humanity. Also born on April 20 was Napoleon's nephew Louis, who became President of France in 1848 and Emperor Napoleon III in 1851–52 after a bloody coup.

THE HEYDAY OF AGGRESSION: WARS FOR NATIONAL UNITY

Napoleon III's very name was a challenge to the "peace and order" of the Vienna concert; so was the new movement to unify Germany. In 1850, urged on by revolts among the German people, Prussian King Frederick William IV tried to accomplish the German unification, but he was frustrated by the Austrians ("the Humiliation of Olmutz"). If he hadn't backed down, war might have erupted in 1850 instead of 1866.[35] The debacle led one Prussian statesman,

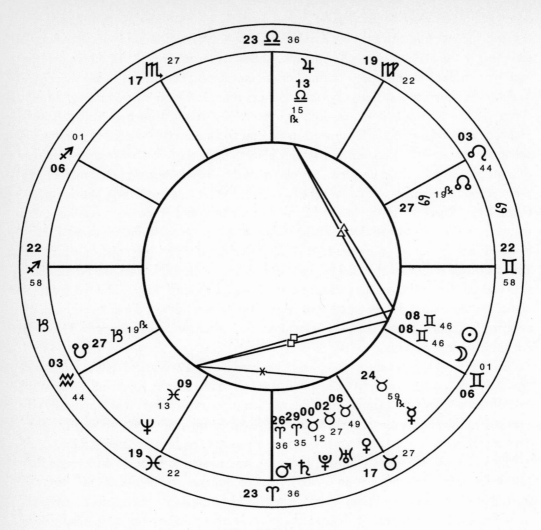

Matter in Motion

The "planetary pile-up" of Venus-Mars-Saturn-Uranus-Pluto at 0° Taurus, June 4–7, 1851. This is the chart for the previous New Moon, on May 30. In eastern France the planets were at the Nadir (nationalism); in the U.S. the pile-up appears in the Seventh House of war and divorce (Civil War). The New Moon is conjunct the U.S. Uranus (breaks, estrangements). Note the Jupiter singleton representing the confident, over-optimistic "jingoism" that unfolded after 1851. Jupiter was also stationary at this time! Jupiter in Libra represents Bismarck's diplomacy (he also had Jupiter in Libra). Sun/Moon square Neptune symbolizes the era's growing delusion, mass hypnosis, and decay, plus oil as the fuel for the ensuing industrial world conquest. Chart data: May 30, 1851, 08:47 P.M. GMT, Paris, France, 48N52, 02E20.

Otto von Bismarck, to conclude that war with Austria was inevitable. Prince Bismarck, along with Napoleon III, was one of the "realist" politicians who rose to power amid the turmoil of the 1848–50 revolutions. Another was Camilo Cavour, the new Prime Minister of Piedmont in northern Italy. Cavour made it his mission to strengthen his tiny kingdom so that it could lead the struggle to unify Italy, much of which (like Germany) was still under Austrian control. In 1858–59 he and Louis Napoleon pulled off a scheme to trick Austria into war; they defeated the ancient empire easily, after which Cavour and the patriot Garibaldi led the people of Italy to unity. At this point, Saturn and Pluto, aligned as part of the "cosmic trigger" in 1851, reached their waxing or opening square. These Saturn-Pluto cycles became the prime symbol (along with Mars-Saturn aspects, and Mars stationary) of major wars and confrontations between states in the modern age.

The Uranus-Pluto-Saturn line-up in 1850–51 was a watershed; the prevalence of revolutionary waves and outbreaks was succeeded by a long series of wars that culminated in the Twentieth Century. The first one developed from a religious dispute in the Holy Land in 1851 between Catholic and Orthodox Christians. Their respective champions, Britain and France on the one hand and Russia on the other, fought each other in the Crimean War starting on March 28, 1854 (Stationary Mars, exactly squaring Saturn). The attitude of the belligerents, especially the poorly trained, rusty British army, was summed up in the phrase made famous by Tennyson: "Ours is not to reason why, ours is but to do or die!" It became the virtual motto of the next 110 years, in which society and its soldiers followed their leaders blindly into trenches and tank battles to die by the millions. It was as if the decaying, Neptunian fungus was dissolving the rational restraints of the human mind (much like LSD, which is made from a fungus that grows on rye plants). The disastrous failures of the Crimean War (like the "Charge of the Light Brigade") did cause the leaders of many nations to begin to think rationally, however—about how to update their armies to make them even more efficient tools in the struggle for power.

The new realist leaders recognized that their nations could only be rich and powerful if they encouraged the new industry, and by the 1860s they realized that liberal policies were good for business. In late 1860 and early 1861, as Neptune crossed into aggressive, individualist Aries, all the countries of Europe began embracing the liberal ideas they had crushed in 1848. "Daring to bring liberty out of order," Napoleon III of France started liberalizing his regime. Tsar Alexander II of Russia emancipated the serfs and reformed the courts. Even Emperor Franz Joseph of Austria promised to respect civil liberties and develop a constitution.

Neptune's start of a whole new 164-year cycle through the zodiac in 1861, magnified by a new Jupiter-Saturn conjunction in Virgo aligned with Mars the same year, coincided with breakthroughs and new beginnings in cultural fields too. Russia's liberalization was a welcome relief after decades of reaction; it was their first *glasnost*. In this freer atmosphere, new nationalist composers like Mussorgsky and Rimsky-Korsakov of the "Russian Five" emerged, while novelists Tolstoy and Doestoevsky wrote about the implications of the new reforms. Aggressive, "nihilist" youth were the "Generation X" of their time. Neptune's "springtime" in Aries in the 1860s was truly a "Russian Easter," and the overture to the coming Revolution was being written. In France, Manet's shocking painting of a nude lady having a picnic in the grass inaugurated the whole Avant Garde school of art. Manet's work paved the way for Impressionism by making "bright light" the real subject of his painting, according to historians. Meanwhile, physicists measured the speed of light itself, and Maxwell's study of light opened questions that would lead to the new physics.

It was Charles Darwin who created the biggest scientific uproar in the 1860s. His *Origin of Species*, published in 1859, proposed that living species (including humans) had been "naturally selected" by their inherited traits to survive the rough "struggle for existence." Aggressive realism and materialism now had its charter. As Neptune entered Aries in 1861, the age of aggression quickly unfolded and provided "proof" of Darwin's theory, especially when applied to human society. Prussia led the way, where the liberals also gained power in 1861 but were soon outwitted by the new King William I and his Chief Minister, Prince Bismarck (himself an Aries). Appointed in 1862, Bismarck announced that Prussia's key to success was "blood and iron." His scheme was to co-opt the liberals' cause of German national unity and achieve it by force, thus building the prestige of the crown, the aristocracy, and the military. When the liberals would not approve his huge new army budget, the ruthless, realistic Bismarck simply ignored them. He built the most efficient military machine in Europe, and baptized it with a war on Denmark in 1864. A quarrel with the Austrians over this war enabled him to provoke them into war in 1866, as Pluto and Mars opposed Saturn (the climax of the war cycle begun in 1851).

After his victory over Austria, Bismarck proceeded with a mammoth reorganization of the new Germany in 1867. Other nations reorganized at the same time. Defeated Austria became dependent on the Hungarians to survive and became the Dual Monarchy of Austria-Hungary. Under this marriage of desperate convenience, the home of Freud became truly schizoid—and increasingly neurotic. In Britain, Prime Ministers Disraeli and Gladstone led a successful campaign for more democratic reform, while the United States and China faced painful reconstructions after their civil wars.[36] Uranus in the sign Cancer always represents unsettled, emotional times of domestic reconstruction after major wars, especially in America; witness the era of the Articles of Confederation after the Revolution and the Age of Anxiety after World War II. McCarthyism in the early 1950s echoed the "Age of Hate" in the late 1860s, during which the Ku Klux Klan was founded and Yankee "carpetbaggers" punished and exploited Dixie. In 1867, Saturn in Scorpio, sign of regeneration, opposed Pluto, adding to these indications of turbulent "reconstruction" worldwide.

A quarrel over who would succeed to the Spanish throne provided Bismarck the chance to goad France into war and complete his new Germany. He doctored the telegram of King William's negotiations with the French to make it sound like an angry exchange. The French responded as he expected, and the Franco-Prussian War was declared on July 19, 1870, as Jupiter and Venus joined in Gemini (communication), all opposing Saturn:

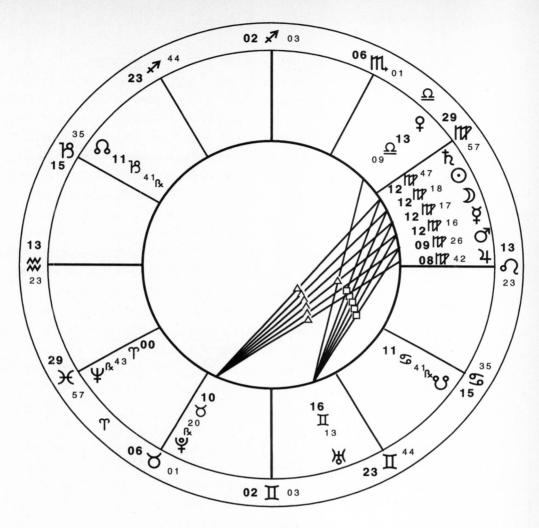

Age of Aggression

This is the chart for a New Moon preceding the Jupiter-Saturn conjunction in Virgo on October 21. Here Mars, Mercury, Moon, and Sun join Jupiter and Saturn in the Seventh House of war and divorce in the U.S. as the Civil War gears up. This mammoth conjunction struck the Nadir in the chart for Central Europe, just like the 1851 pile-up did. Chart data: September 4, 1861, 10:12 P.M. GMT, Washington, D.C., 38N54, 77W02.

a perfect symbol for a war begun by telegram. With Jupiter opposing Saturn, the Age of Aggression fully unleashed in 1861 had reached its climax. These mirrored the aspects of 1812, when another war humbled another Napoleon. This time, Napoleon III's forces were rolled over by the German machine in just a few months, and the German Empire (or Second Reich) was proclaimed at Versailles in January 1871. Afterward, as Mars turned stationary in 18° Virgo, the working people of Paris tried to stage another revolution. The

Paris Commune was bloodily suppressed, but was celebrated by Marx as a great episode in the "class struggle."

Germany's conquest of Alsace-Lorraine fueled anti-German hatred in France. After the wars, there was the usual "change in direction" (Jupiter opposite Saturn). Bismarck announced in 1871 that he was now a guardian of peace, and pursued liberal policies, but the wars created a growing climate of fear, nationalism, and militarism that took us deeper into the canyon. The masses were taught to view other nations as their enemies by their teachers and journalists. "No person who has not read through the literature produced between 1871 and 1914 has any idea of the extent to which it is one long call for blood."[37] The Neptunian decay of the Old World, begun twenty years before, now took the form of growing war clouds. Sinister forces lurked on the horizon.

A similar change occurred in America: a rural, religious, divided country full of idealists became a unified industrial giant captivated by greed. Bismarck himself probably learned a thing or two from President Polk's war against Mexico in 1846, in which Polk goaded that country into war and then took half its territory. Saturn conjoined Neptune that year, often a fateful configuration in American history. When the two planets reached opposition in 1862–63, the defeated Mexicans could only console themselves with the thought that America's attack on them had led the Americans themselves disastrous civil war.

Many disillusioned "forty-eighters" from Europe's Revolution became "forty-niners" the next year in the California Gold Rush. Such a frenzied, electric event could only have come under a planetary lineup like the Uranus-Pluto conjunction in Aries (rush) and Taurus (gold). It also made California, just conquered from Mexico, ripe for statehood. This issue touched off the debate between North and South over the relative power of free and slave states. Before it was resolved by the great Compromise of 1850, several states of Dixie threatened to seize New Mexico, and President Taylor was ready to march against them. Had he not died on July 9, the Civil War might have erupted in 1850 instead of 1861.[38] As with Prussia and Austria, 1850 (when Uranus joined Pluto in a rare conjunction) was the watershed year when confrontations began that later erupted into wars.

Uncle Tom's Cabin was published during the "cosmic trigger" conjunction in June,

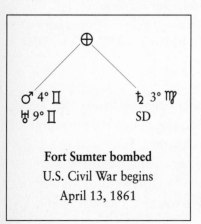

Fort Sumter bombed
U.S. Civil War begins
April 13, 1861

1851. Proving convincingly that the pen can be more incendiary than the sword, the book inflamed hatred of slavery. When Lincoln later met author Harriet Beecher Stowe he said, "So you're the little woman who made this great war."[39] In May 1856, under a T-square of violent Mars-Saturn with righteous Jupiter, war broke out between abolitionists led by the fiery John Brown and pro-slavery men in Kansas territory. The same week, a southern congressman beat a northern senator to the floor with a cane right in the Senate hall! In October 1859, with Mars in Virgo opposing

Neptune (mass action by the humble classes), John Brown tried to spark a slave revolt at Harper's Ferry, Virginia, but was captured by Robert E. Lee and hanged. His sensational trial made him the North's martyr, and a new song was heard which became the Yankee "Marseillaise." Months later the words to "John Brown's Body" were transformed by Julia Ward Howe into the "Battle Hymn of the Republic."

The Civil War broke out on April 13, 1861, when Neptune entered Aries. Saturn also squared Uranus and Mars that day, and Uranus returned to the exact degree it occupied when the colonies declared independence. Now Dixie did the same thing, as America met its karma and the Confederacy was born. Southern General Robert E. Lee repulsed the first Yankee march in 1862, then advanced on Washington.[40] A great turning point was at hand; the South had to be stopped, or they might have gotten French and British help (after all, the French had helped in the *first* revolution). Lee was halted at Antietam in one of the war's bloodiest battles in mid-September, as Mars stood stationary in Aries with Neptune. President Lincoln now felt able to make the war officially a crusade against slavery, not just a battle to preserve the Union, and issued the Emancipation Proclamation on September 22. Exactly seventy years after the start of "Year I" in France, this date was indeed the key moment in the "age of aggression," as Mars' position showed; Prince Bismarck (himself an aggressive Aries) became Chief Minister of Prussia on the same day!

The Confederates stopped the Union march south again, but Lee's second attempt to advance on Washington was defeated at Gettysburg, as Uranus reached 22° Gemini (Mars' position in the U.S. horoscope). This time, the North succeeded in its next long march on the valiant South, despite stout and bloody resistance. The next Mars station (also in 22° Gemini) corresponded to Sherman's conquest of Atlanta late in 1864, which broke a long stalemate. Lee's capture in April 1865 finally ended America's deadliest war. For the black men, women, and children to whom life in America was the antithesis of freedom, it was truly a war of liberation—an epic moment in the emergence of the modern spirit of freedom for all humanity. Can we redeem the war's high cost by continuing that liberation today?

The U.S. Civil War and the Reconstruction were as much a "war of unification" as those which unified Germany and Italy. The North conquered Dixie in a triumph of industrial "blood and iron." North and South became one. Simultaneously, so did East and West. Just as Sherman was setting fire to Georgia under the Mars station in 22° Gemini in November 1864, Native Americans were being massacred at Sand Creek, Colorado. The conquest of the American West in the age of cowboys and indians also reflected the Heyday of Aggression under Neptune in Aries, and other indigenous peoples were conquered at the same time all around the world. For example, the Russians conquered their own "wild west" tribes in the south and east, and Britain beat down the Maoris of New Zealand.

THE AMAZING CENTURY-TO-CENTURY PARALLELS

The American Civil War had been over for only five days when "The Great Emancipator" was gunned down by John Wilkes Booth at Ford's Theater. The nation was in shock and grief for many months. Lincoln immediately became a martyr to the Union, and before long was considered the nation's greatest president. His loss was substantial, because without his wise and moderate leadership all chance for quickly healing the wounds of war vanished.

More recently, the American nation experienced a similar shock when yet another president was martyred to the same cause, with the same results to the domestic peace. No astrologer can ignore the extraordinary signs of destiny that surrounded the death of President Kennedy on November 22, 1963. Most amazing were the famous pattern of "coincidences" between him and Lincoln—a pattern that underscores the importance of these two men and their times.

In case you have forgotten the amazing Lincoln-Kennedy coincidences, I will repeat them here. The last names of both Lincoln and Kennedy contain seven letters. Both presidents were shot in the back of the head, and in the presence of their wives. Both were shot on a Friday. The names of the alleged assassins, John Wilkes Booth and Lee Harvey Oswald, contain fifteen letters. Booth was born in 1839; Oswald was born in 1939. Booth shot Lincoln in a theater and was captured at a warehouse. Oswald shot Kennedy from a warehouse and was captured at a theater. Both assassins were themselves assassinated before they could be brought to trial.

Lincoln had a secretary named Kennedy who warned him not to attend Ford's Theater; Kennedy had a secretary named Lincoln who warned him not to go to Dallas. Each man had relatives who held the same positions in government, including Mayor of Boston, Senator and Attorney General. Both Lincoln and Kennedy lost children while in the White House. Both began their careers in Congress a century apart: Lincoln in 1847, Kennedy in 1947. Both ran unsuccessfully for vice president in '56 and were elected President in '60—a century apart. Both engaged in famous debates: Lincoln against Douglas, and Kennedy against Nixon (who was also in Dallas on November 22, 1963, by the way). Both presidents were succeeded by southern Democrats named Johnson who had served in the Senate. Andrew Johnson was born in 1808, Lyndon Johnson in 1908. Their first and last names contain thirteen letters. Both Kennedy and Lincoln had premonitions of their own deaths.[41]

Such astounding "coincidences" as these cry out for an astrological explanation. The most famous is the twenty-year Jupiter-Saturn cycle, which links not only Lincoln and Kennedy, but other presidents. From 1841 to 1961, the president who took office during a Jupiter-Saturn conjunction in an earth sign died while still in office. In 1850, Zachary Taylor died during the first opposition between Jupiter and Saturn that followed the first conjunction in the deadly series.

In 1841, William Henry Harrison died shortly before the Jupiter-Saturn conjunction (Capricorn) of January 1842. In 1865, Abraham Lincoln was assassinated after the 1861 Jupiter-Saturn conjunction (Virgo). In 1881, James Garfield was assassinated following that year's Jupiter-Saturn conjunction (Taurus). In 1901, William McKinley was assassinated soon after a Jupiter-Saturn conjunction (Capricorn). In 1923, Warren G. Harding died following the Jupiter-Saturn conjunction (Virgo) of 1921. In 1945, Franklin D. Roosevelt died after the 1941 Jupiter-Saturn conjunction (Taurus). In 1963, John F. Kennedy was assassinated after the Jupiter-Saturn conjunction (Capricorn) of 1961.

In 1981 Ronald Reagan escaped assassination "by inches," because the Jupiter-Saturn conjunction of 1981 occurred in the early degrees of Libra—an air sign instead of an earth sign. No wonder Nancy Reagan began consulting the stars soon afterward! In 2000, the conjunction again occurs in an earth sign. It may be handy knowledge then that most presidents who have died in office did so in the first year of a term, and that all (except Taylor) have died in odd-numbered years.

However amazing this twenty-year pattern is, it doesn't quite explain why Lincoln and Kennedy stand out in an amazing destiny link spanning a century. The fact that two cycles of the newly discovered asteroid Chiron equals 100 years may be important. Certainly, the horoscopes of Lincoln and Kennedy make it clear they were both marked men at the time of their deaths. Both had Mars in the Eighth house (death), which was afflicted by Saturn at the time. Both had Saturn conjunct Neptune in their charts (as did Franklin Roosevelt). The *real* answer, however, emerges from a startling fact—the Lincoln-Kennedy coincidences are just the centerpiece of further century-to-century parallels that last throughout the decades of the '60s and beyond.

The 1860s and 1960s were remarkable decades, filled with unrest, rising expectations, and massive change. In the 1860s, America fought a civil war which was followed by a turbulent reconstruction. In the 1960s, it intervened in a civil war abroad which brought about near-civil war conditions at home. In both cases, Neptune was in a Mars-ruled sign throughout the period: Aries in the 1860s and Scorpio in the 1960s. Another parallel is the major conjunction of each era. The Jupiter-Saturn conjunction of 1861 occurred in 17° Virgo, and the Uranus-Pluto conjunction of 1966 occurred in the same degree—which is also the degree of President Kennedy's natal Moon. In 1866, Saturn and Pluto were in opposition, just as they were in 1966, marking the decisive dividing moment in each decade. In 1867, Neptune was in Aries, and Saturn was in Scorpio, while in 1967, Saturn was in Aries, and Neptune was in Scorpio.

The century-to-century parallels, unlike the Lincoln-Kennedy coincidences, are not known at all. They begin with April of '61, the opening of crisis in both decades. In April 1861, Fort Sumter was bombed, opening the Civil War. In April 1961, the Bay of Pigs in Cuba was invaded, re-opening the Cold War. In the fall of '62 crucial turning points were reached in the Lincoln and Kennedy administrations: the Battle of Antietam in September 1862, and the Cuban missile crisis in October 1962.

In 1863, the Emancipation Proclamation was issued. In 1963, the Civil Rights bill was proposed. Slavery was abolished by the Thirteenth Amendment in 1865. The Voting Rights Act and Great Society programs were approved in 1965. The names of the losing candidates for president in '64, Goldwater and McClellan, each contain nine letters. Shortly after both President Johnsons took over, they were opposed by "radicals" in Congress and the nation. In the Fall of '66, each Johnson lost ground in Congressional elections. In both cases, their brusque and awkward personalities added to their problems. Both Lincoln and Kennedy were born under air signs (erudite, charming, flexible), which made an unhappy contrast to the Johnsons, both born under earth signs (more stubborn, down-to-earth). Uranus (rebellion) in Cancer exactly opposed Andrew Johnson's Sun in Capricorn in 1865. Uranus was in conjunction with Lyndon Johnson's Sun in Virgo in 1965.

In 1867, the white South was put under military rule. In 1967, black ghettos were under martial law. Andrew Johnson was impeached in March 1868. Lyndon Johnson announced he would not seek re-election in March 1968. The Democratic conventions of 1868 and 1968 were each torn by terrible dissension. Each Johnson was succeeded in '69 by a Republican. whose names (Ulysses S. Grant and Richard M. Nixon) each contain thirteen letters. Both were also earth sign natives. Grant and Nixon both narrowly beat candidates named Horatio: Horatio Seymour and Hubert Horatio Humphrey. When Grant took office, he said, "Let us have peace." When Nixon took office, he promised to "bring us together."

In 1868, Prague was put under martial law by the Hapsburg Empire. In 1968, it was invaded by Soviet Russian tanks. The French autocratic hero Napoleon III fell in 1870. De Gaulle, also an autocratic hero, resigned in 1969 and died the following year. The two decades were capped by great technological transportation and travel achievements. The first transcontinental railroad and the Suez Canal were completed in 1869. Two men landed on the Moon in 1969. Blacks were finally given the vote in 1870; eighteen year-olds were given the vote in 1970.

The parallels continued into the '70s and '80s. The administrations of both Grant and Nixon were rocked by huge scandals in '72 and '73 (though only Nixon had to leave office). Both achieved redeeming success in foreign affairs with the help of their foreign minister (Secretary of State Fish opened detente with Britain in 1871: Secretary of State Kissinger opened detente with China and Russia in 1971). A great depression, brought on by international grain competition, opened in 1873. Another depression, brought on by an international oil embargo, opened in 1973. Both Grant and Nixon faced a "liberal revolt" in the '72 election, but won by a landslide anyway. Then the Democrats won big victories in Congress in both 1874 and 1974. The presidents succeeding Grant and Nixon came into office with a cloud over their titles; Hayes because of the deal by which he was given the White House in exchange for ending reconstruction; Ford because he pardoned Nixon a month after succeeding him (Nixon had appointed Ford vice president during the scandal).

Presidents Hayes (1877) and Carter (1977) promised to end corruption. Both were Libra natives. In 1878, a great conference hosted by the world's leading statesman, Prince Bismarck, settled Middle East disputes at Berlin. In 1978, President Carter, leader of the "free world," did the same at Camp David. In 1879–81, a conservative trend was evident worldwide. In 1979–81 the same was true. The farm crisis of the 1880s paralleled the farm crisis of the 1980s. Politically, the nation saw mediocre leadership in the 1870s and '80s. I dare say the same was true in the 1970s and '80s.

The early 1890s saw another depression, plus the rise of progressive movements like the Populists. These trends have already proved somewhat true of the early 1990s. As I predicted might happen, 1992 saw the defeat of a one-term Republican president, just as 1892 did. Both elections saw powerful Third Party campaigns (the Populists and Ross Perot). The great conjunction of 1892 signaled a new American thirst for world empire. The great conjunction of 1993 symbolized (again, as I predicted) American leadership in "the new world order" (as President Bush called it). In an earlier version of this section, I asked whether Gorbachev would fall in 1990, bringing new instability, just as Bismarck's fall in 1890 did. Well, Gorbachev fell in 1991, and it *has* brought instability. Progressive politics should predominate in the first decade of the new century, if the parallel holds. Revolution in China may occur in 2000, as it did in 1900.

Although these century-to-century parallels are unprecedented, they are not new. For example, in both 1688-89 and 1789, revolutions in Europe led to major international wars which ended in 1715 and 1815. A similar revolution-to-war process took place between 1886 and 1919. Months before the revolutions broke out in Europe in 1989, I wrote that it "may happen again from 1989 to 2012."[42]

COMBINATION AND DISSOLUTION

The terrible depression that began when Neptune entered conservative Taurus in 1873–74 cooled off the individualist, liberal fever of Aries and caused increased demands for government regulations (an idea which today we usually call "liberal"). In addition, people of all classes banded together to protect themselves against the Social Darwinism of the age. Around 1880, the "liberal center" of politics began to decline and the extremes of left and right asserted themselves. The swing to the right in 1879–1881 was the most noticeable. It corresponded to Uranus' entry into cautious Virgo in 1879, recalling the first political "reaction" in the mid-1790s, and to the huge line-up of planets (including Jupiter, Saturn, and Neptune) in conservative Taurus in April-May 1881. In 1879, both German Chancellor Bismarck and Austrian Emperor Franz Joseph broke their alliances with liberal parties and embraced conservative ones. In 1881, British Tory Prime Minister Disraeli died, after which his ruling party swerved sharply to the right. That year in Russia, liberal Tsar Alexander II (the "great reformer") was assassinated; cruel repression followed (including wholesale massacres of Jews).

At the same time, the right sometimes cooperated with the left in an "alliance against the liberal center." This trend first appeared in 1874 in Disraeli's "Tory Democracy" in Britain, in which conservative aristocrats joined with labor to pass regulations on business. After cracking down on socialists and liberals, Bismarck co-opted them in 1881 and instituted the first-ever social insurance program (national accident and sickness coverage, etc.). Inspection of industry laws were passed in Austria in 1883, and even in Russia anti-child labor laws went hand-in-hand with repression and censorshipin 1882. After white supremacy was restored in the South in 1877, the dominant Republican Party became conservative (and has remained so since). Even so, it created the U.S. Civil Service in the Pendleton Act in 1883.

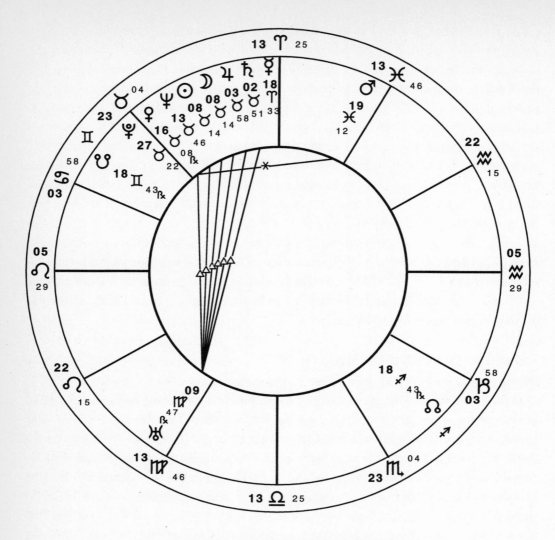

The Generation of Materialism

This is the chart for the New Moon following the Jupiter-Saturn conjunction in Taurus on April 18, 1881. Seven planets in Taurus represent the "generation of materialism" as described by Carlton Hayes. Venus retrograde, conjunct Neptune shows the "corrosion and dissolution" of materialism, the economic and diplomatic trend toward "combination," as well as the era's impressionist art style that "climaxed and dissolved" renaissance realism. Note Mars in Pisces, symbolizing the increasing submersion of the individual into the mass. Born near the time of this mammoth conjunction was scientist and philosopher Teilhard de Chardin. Chart data: April 28, 1881, 10:24 A.M. GMT, London, England, 51N30, 00W10.

The two trends were part of an overall increase in planning and bureaucracy (Uranus in Virgo) and the collectivizing (Neptune) of the economy (Taurus, money sign). Around 1880, the two planets trined (or "combined and cooperated with") each other. The first business combinations (monopolies, trusts and cartels) reduced competition and regulated production, starting in the U.S. with Standard Oil in 1879. At the same time, labor increasingly combined into unions (progressive Uranus in Virgo: labor sign). The Federation of Organized Trades was formed in America in 1881, and the Fabian Society inaugurated the British Labor movement in 1883. The first "boycott" occurred in 1880, named after the Irish landlord who was the first target of one. Meanwhile, political nationalism under Neptune in Aries was replaced by economic nationalism under Neptune in Taurus. Old feudalistic landowners and new industrial giants ("the big rye–big steel alliance") reversed the liberal trend toward free trade in 1879 with a new tariff. Soon, nations were becoming like Medieval fortresses with walls and moats (tariffs) behind which the new cartels and trusts flourished, often with state support.

Germany led the way in developing this corporate national state. The name "National Socialism" is no accident—the new state-run economies were models for later totalitarian societies as well as for our own corporate state.As the Second Revolution proceeded, the individual was increasingly swallowed up into the collective. Society began to reek of decay as we neared the canyon floor in our journey of transition. Left and Right became even more polarized; yet both remained unconscious agents of Neptune, dissolving persons into nations, races and classes. Socialists as well as nationalists increasingly preached racism and anti-semitism as well as "survival of the fittest," and the materialistic "science" justifying all this insanity proliferated.

Under Neptune in Taurus, the need for security predominated, not only economically but internationally. The new tariff wars only increased this climate of fear among nations,.So they formed alliances just as companies were forming combines, and here too Germany led the way under Prince Bismarck (Neptune was now crossing his own Venus in Taurus at Midheaven). In 1875–76, under a tense T-square of Saturn, Uranus and Pluto, and just as Neptune crossed the "cosmic trigger" point in early Taurus, the Balkan volcano erupted with more anti-Turkish revolts. In bloody trench warfare, the Russians defeated the Turks and then sponsored several new Balkan nations. The alarmed Austrians quarreled bitterly with the Russians over the region, and after Bismarck settled things at his Congress of Berlin, the Russians were steaming mad at him. He felt compelled to make a secret anti-Russian alliance with Austria in October 1879, on the day stationary Mars joined Pluto in Taurus.

Then the wily, deceptive double-dealer (his Mercury was square Neptune) made a pro-Russian alliance at the same time by reviving the old Holy Alliance, getting Russia to join Austria and Germany in a Reinsurance Treaty (on the exact day diplomatic Jupiter joined Neptune, June 18, 1881). Bismarck had found security for his new Reich, but it turned out to be a deceptive security (Neptune in Taurus).Only four years later, another Balkan dispute broke out over Bulgaria, and soon afterward Europe became as polarized internationally as it was becoming domestically.

Carlton Hayes called these times the "generation of materialism." By the 1880s, industrial "progress" was proceeding steadily, and science continued to build on its paradigm of matter as first principle. European culture was reaching its final consummation in splendid illusions of material progress and worldwide colonial domination. In the arts, realistic paint-ing climaxed in the delicate style of impressionism, which coincided with Neptune's transit of artistic, sensuous Taurus from 1874 to 1886. This "soft-focus" style revealed the hidden, Neptunian dissolution of the times perfectly. For example, Monet's paintings of railroad sta-tions perfectly reflected the evanescent, ever-changing industrial world. The closer the im-pressionists observed external nature in the 500-year-old Renaissance tradition, the more it melted into shimmering light before their eyes. The faceless people in Manet's "Bar of the Folies Bergere" seemed to be melting away. Similar dissolutions were occurring in music, as the grand but meandering music of Wagner led toward the impressionism of Debussy, who was inspired by the dreamy "symbolist" poets like Mallarme. In physics, the "anomaly" raised by the issues of light and electricity remained unresolved. The world of the 1880s *seemed* stable, but beneath the veneer the confident world of materialism was dissolving and corroding. The Renaissance-Enlightenment civilization dominated by Europe was in its final days, and its ideal of "progress" would suffer many reversals in the new century.

CHAPTER 14 ENDNOTES

1. For more details on modern events and their astrological correlations, see my forthcoming book , *The Horo-scope of Humanity.*

2. Thomas Carlyle, *The French Revolution,* 444.

3. Kenneth Clark, *Civilization,* 296.

4. William Blake, *A Selection of Poems,* 97.

5. Clark, *op. cit.,* 296.

6. Carlyle, *op. cit.,* 515.

7. Carlyle, *op. cit.,* 528.

8. Furet & Richet, *The French Revolution,* 181.

9. Ibid, 177.

10. Leo Gershoy, *The Era of the French Revolution,* 156.

11. Will & Ariel Durant, *The Age of Napoleon,* 79.

12. Furet & Richet, *op. cit.,* 190.

13. Will & Ariel Durant, *op. cit.,* 78.

14. For example: Napoleon, Lenin, Stalin—and John Lennon. Robespierre and Danton's conjunctions were in mid-late Leo, right where Uranus stood during the Revolution. Napoleon's was in Virgo.

15. Rene Sedillot, *An Outline of French History,* 273; Furet & Richet, *op. cit.,* 231.

16. Furet & Richet, *op. cit.,* 336-345, 351-354.

17. Jenner developed the smallpox vaccine the same day; Mars was trine inventive Uranus in Virgo, sign of medicine.

18. Will Durant, *The Story of Philosophy,* 337.

19. Blake, *op. cit.,* 97.

20. Ibid, 67.

21. Clark, *op. cit.*, 293.

22. Will Durant, *op. cit.*, 337-38.

23. William Langer, et al. *The Expansion of Empire to Europe in the Modern World*, 355.

24. Will & Ariel Durant, *The Age of Napoleon*, 209.

25. Thomas Bailey, *The American Pageant*, 194.

26. Ibid, 207.

27. Will & Ariel Durant, *op, cit.*, 711.

28. Gordon Craig, *Europe 1815–1914*, 52.

29. Ibid, 28.

30. Charles Dickens, *Hard Times*, 31.

31. Bailey, *op. cit.*, 346.

32. Craig, *op. cit.*, 128.

33. Langer et al, *op, cit.*, 416.

34. "Jingoists" referred originally to the phrase "by jingo," used in a British war song during the 1878 crisis.

35. George Fasel, *Europe in Upheaval: The Revolutions of 1848*, 165.

36. The massive Taiping Rebellion had begun in China in 1850, even before the European Revolution of 1848 had subsided, showing that similar events *do* happen in widely different places under similar planetary conjunctions (in this case, Uranus-Pluto).

37. Jaques Barzun, quoted in *The Expansion of Empire to Europe in the Modern World*, 419.

38. Bailey, *op. cit.*, 381.

39. Ibid, 394.

40. Many important Civil War battles occurred during Mars squares and oppositions to Saturn, including Forts Henry and Donelson, Fredericksburg, Chancellorsville, and Cold Harbor.

41. Recounted from Joseph Goodavage, *Astrology: The Space Age Science*, 186.

42. See *Welcome to Planet Earth* magazine, Libra, 1989.

15

The Modern Spirit's Journey:

PART TWO: 1892–2000

In 1892, we reached the bottom of the canyon in our journey across the Valley of Transition as Neptune and Pluto joined in their dark "New Moon." Oppositions to each planet by Uranus soon followed. As we waded through the muddy rivers of watery Neptune and Pluto at the canyon floor, we realized we were crossing a boundary between two worlds we could never bridge again. We awoke for a moment from our deepening illusions to notice that something was dying and something was being born. As historian Oron Hale said, "One era had ended and another had begun."[1] A germination began within us as the Plutonian "seed" began to sprout within the great "cosmic incubator" of Neptune, and we were baptized into a new view of the world.

Thinkers like Spengler and Nietzsche announced the "decline of the West" and the "revaluation of all values." Everything now came into question. From the 1890s on, scientists like Einstein and Heisenberg redefined the physical universe so that the world we thought we knew became relative and dependent on the observer. Psychologists like Freud and Jung and occultists like Gurdjieff and Crowley opened new horizons of the mind. Symbolist writers and post-impressionist artists lost themselves in the watery mists, overcome by "hypersensitivity and decadence." When they surfaced, they brought with them strange new crystallized forms that left the Renaissance behind. Cezanne, for example, "painted nature in cylinders, spheres and cones," leading other artists like the cubist Picasso toward abstract art. Gauguin and Van Gogh transmuted *im*pressionism into *ex*pressionism, pouring their own feelings onto the canvas. Inspired but confused, some of the new prophets (Bergson, Nietzsche, Richard Strauss) portrayed the coming "sunrise," while others (Munch, 1893) pictured a silent but blood-curdling "scream." In Tchaikovsky's last symphony (also 1893), the old civilization seems to run out of gas and fall over the edge right before our ears! Disoriented within the dissolving void in this "end of the century" mood, we entered The Age of Anxiety. The Old World had ended, but the New World was but a new born babe.

Malaise and decadence spread over Europe and the world like a deep fog—the fog of Neptune and Pluto in conjunction. Poets and playwrights made the mood respectable, and sex books became big sellers in European cities. Despairing youth abandoned themselves to reckless enjoyment, much as many have done ever since, including the "grunge" culture of

100 years later. The psychedelic poster art of the 1960s was said to have revived the buoyant, organic "art nouveau" style that dominated art, architecture, and design in the 1890s under similar astrological circumstances.[2] Art Nouveau was a kind of over-rapid growth stimulated by the heavy rains of Neptune and Pluto, and showed our thirst to re-admit nature into the civilized world. Toulouse-Latrec captured this new culture (the direct ancestor of our own) in Paris, recording and satirizing the extraordinary characters he found in the city's bars and brothels. In Vienna, capital of the "Schizoid Empire" where decadence and cultural neurosis were most prevalent, writers like Sigmund Freud observed it firsthand. Freud did to his clients what Toulouse-Latrec did to his subjects: "dissected" them to reveal their "moral and psychological nakedness."[3] Neptune and Pluto were dissolving the illusions of Western society, and imperial Europe would soon have no clothes.

Economic depression contributed to the malaise of the early 1890s, as strikes spread across the industrial world and socialist politics expanded as never before or since. By 1896, the populist movement had taken over and reoriented the Democratic Party in the United States, making it the champion of a watered-down socialism that it has been ever since. In Russia, things were rapidly gearing up for the Revolution after the weak Tsar Nicholas II ascended the throne in 1894. As domestic politics polarized between the socialist left and the nationalist right, international politics in Europe also split into two rival blocs. The new Emperor Kaiser Wilhelm II didn't want the "iron chancellor," at the willhelm, so he fired Bismarck in 1890 and destroyed his precarious diplomatic system. As Pluto squared Saturn and opposed Mars, the Kaiser broke off the "alliance" with Tsarist Russia in 1890, which in turn formed an astonishing new one with republican France in 1894. Britain later joined this "Triple Entente," first with France in 1905 (exactly when Mars reached the 0° Taurus trigger point) and then with Russia in 1907 (Saturn square Pluto again). The "Triple Entente" now faced the "Triple Alliance" (Germany, Austria, Italy). And in 1892, the year Neptune joined with Pluto, German General Schlieffen began developing his famous "plan," which committed the Germans to attacking France first if any war broke out with Russia, guaranteeing that a Balkan dispute between their Austrian allies and Russia would cause a European war![4]

The turn of the Twentieth Century marked the end of European imperial dominance. The last rush of colonial expansion in Africa and Asia during the Neptune-Pluto conjunction in Gemini (1884–1896) was like a final vacation for Europe before retirement. This time, new powers arose to challenge Europe just when it was preparing to destroy itself. Japan, which entered the modern age in 1867 as European nations were reorganizing themselves, now became a world power by attacking and defeating China (1893–94). This aroused the mighty Dragon from its slumber, and soon afterward it ousted both the European exploiters and the Manchu emperors who protected them (1911). The U.S. expanded into the Pacific, buying Hawaii in 1893 and conquering the Philippines from Spain in 1898. That year and the next, as Saturn opposed Pluto, several other wars and confrontations broke out that reversed 500 years of European expansion, most notably the Boer War, which aroused the worldwide anti-imperialist movement. In 1902, Lenin made anti-imperialism a part of his Communist Party program.

Even the American Eagle got its wings clipped, as the Filipinos revolted against their new masters in 1899. After the American Indians made their last heroic stand at Wounded Knee in December 1890 (Mars square Saturn, opposed Pluto and Neptune), the westward expansion within the United States was over too. The end of the frontier meant there was no more escape valve. New and old immigrants would now have to live together. After 500 years of exploration and conquest, Europe had created a global culture, and we crossed the threshold in the 1890s into an age of consolidation. The world began "imploding" into the "global village," and what Teilhard de Chardin called the "noosphere" (the sphere of thought). In 1892, the new "world soul" for which I cast the "Horoscope for Modern Humanity" was born. Within this emerging global mind and society, cultural barriers are falling, and no one religion or philosophy can legitimately claim to be "the only way." European science and technology dissected and conquered nature, but since the 1890s it has been increasingly forced to discard its notion (or "paradigm") of an "external, objective world" and to integrate its views with the thoughts of wise ones from distant times and places. In our time technology has also begun to threaten as well as help us, and since 1891–92 (Sierra Club founded; first national forests) we have become just as interested in preserving Earth as in conquering and exploiting Her.

RITES OF SPRING AND RITUAL SACRIFICE

Jupiter and Saturn joined again in 1901, signaling a new era. Around that time, the fog of malaise lifted and Humanity felt a surge of vital optimism at the dawn of the new century. In their great conjunction, misty, dissolving Neptune had passed the baton of destiny to potent, explosive Pluto. Like two giant ocean liners passing in the night, Neptune carried one age of Humanity to its grave and Pluto carried another to its cradle. Neptune brought decay and dissolution in the Nineteenth Century, and Pluto, the third invisible planet to be discovered, brought death and new life in the Twentieth. Intoxicated again by the idol of "progress," we confidently began our ascent up the other side of the valley. Inventions multiplied under Neptune and Pluto in mobile, inventive Gemini. We built skyscrapers to give us a better view of the peak ahead, and cars and airplanes to get us there faster.

As revolutionary Uranus opposed radical Pluto in 1901, in the signs of writing and journalism (Sagittarius-Gemini), the muckrakers aimed their pens at all the evils of capitalism and launched the Progressive movement. More violent socialist movements erupted simultaneously, such as the Syndicalists, Bolsheviks, and Social Revolutionaries. With his "big stick," Theodore Roosevelt, the "trust-buster," personified the energetic, belligerent liberal leaders who emerged in many nations in 1901. Even as he was turning politics into energy, the Fauves ("wild beasts") exhibition turned art into "outbursts of pure emotion on canvas" in 1905— the same year Einstein's Special Theory of Relativity revealed matter as energy. This new "cocksure" onward and upward mood in all fields was captured nowhere better than in the finale to French composer Louis Vierne's First Organ Symphony (1899), in which the Romantic modern spirit seemed to "gallop" across the valley of transition into tomorrow.

At first, our new vitality was aggressive and violent, like a rebellious, unruly child. A huge, violent revolution broke out in Russia in 1905 as Uranus reached the Winter Solstice (0° Capricorn), opposing Pluto and Neptune. Revolutions had broken out in many of the same places (Latin America, Portugal, Romania) the last time Uranus reached this point (conjunct Neptune) in 1821; they also erupted when Uranus returned there in 1989 (also conjunct Neptune). More revolutions followed 1905, as Uranus continued to oppose Neptune, and by the time it reached electric, rebellious Aquarius in 1912, strikes and riots had reached epidemic proportions. In 1910, French artist Delaunay painted a striking portrayal of the Eiffel Tower exploding; in 1913 the premiere of Stravinsky's frenzied celebration of humanity's springtime in "The Rite of Spring" not only gave a foretaste of what began the next year with a ritual human sacrifice, but also provoked a riot in the concert hall itself between supporters and opponents of the revolutionary work.[5] Petrified autocrats trembling on their thrones remembered a way to escape this turbulent public temper: if your subjects are unhappy, divert their attention to the foreign enemy. It wasn't hard for them to arouse the nationalist passions and racist hatreds of the age.

Demonic forces had assembled amidst the dark shadows of the canyon, and the new industrial technology had given them greater tools for destruction than ever before. The death knell of the Old World had been sounded by Neptune and Pluto in 1892, and now it continued to resound ever louder. A crisis over Bosnia in October 1908 occurred while Mars was in late Virgo, and as Uranus opposed Neptune and squared Saturn. This ignited a series of confrontations leading to the Great War. In 1911, a tiff over Morocco came as Mars reached the "trigger point" at 0° Taurus and formed a virulent grand cross with Mercury, Jupiter, Uranus and Neptune. Two small wars in the Balkans followed: the first in October 1912,

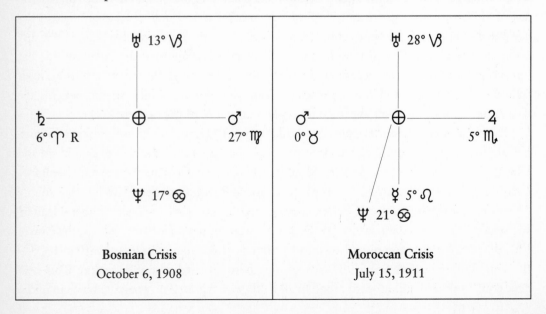

Bosnian Crisis
October 6, 1908

Moroccan Crisis
July 15, 1911

when Mars hit 0° Scorpio, and the second in June 1913, when Mars returned to early Taurus. The assassination of the Austrian imperial heir Francis Ferdinand on June 28, 1914 by Serbian extremists finally brought the two great European power blocs to blows. World War I was declared on August 1, 1914, as Mars returned to its exact degree in late Virgo during the Bosnian Crisis, and squared Saturn and Pluto as they made their next potent and dangerous conjunction.

Catastrophe followed. We discovered that the climb ahead of us out of the canyon was too steep; millions fell off the cliffs to their deaths. A solar eclipse in August of 1914 signaled the debacle. The Schlieffen Plan failed in the Battle of the Marne, so the two armies got stuck in the muddy trenches along the western front. After another solar eclipse in February 1916, conjoining cataclysmic Uranus and opposing a stationary Mars in Leo (remember Chios?), half a million men were cut down by machine guns at the Battle of Verdun. A million more fell at the Somme as Mars returned to late Virgo. The price of each inch of real estate gained was measured in gallons of blood. By 1917, the stalemate had become a bottomless pit into which tumbled the lives, wealth, and power of Europe. Formerly neutral America now stepped in to tip the balance, as Pres-

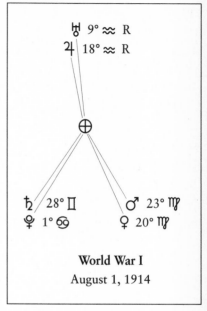

World War I
August 1, 1914

ident Wilson declared war on the Central Powers (now Germany, Austria-Hungary, Turkey, Bulgaria) in order to "end all war" and "make the world safe for democracy." America and the Allies mobilized themselves to a fevered pitch the same way the French First Republic had done in 1792–93 (both times there were many planets in the stubborn, powerful, doctrinaire fixed signs). America's victory in 1918 in the Argonne forest came very near the place where the "New World's birth" had been secured at Valmy.

The cataclysm cleared away the weight of old anachronisms. The ancient European empires toppled to make way for the potential of world peace and liberation in our time. The Russian Tsars fell with the greatest thud, as the Bolsheviks seized power and instituted Communism in the Soviet Union. It was the rise of this and other dictatorships in the 1920s that proved the world was not yet safe for democracy, after all. The "war to end war" became the seed of most of the wars that have happened since (for example, the Turkish Empire's demise triggered wars over the liberated territory in the Middle East). The world's hope for peace lay in the League of Nations, founded as diplomatic planet Jupiter conjoined Neptune in 1919–1920. The same conjunction had accompanied the first disarmament conference at the Hague in 1907, and returned when the United Nations was founded in 1945. But in 1920, America rejected the League sponsored by its own President. We thereby kicked the fruits of this costly victory under the table,

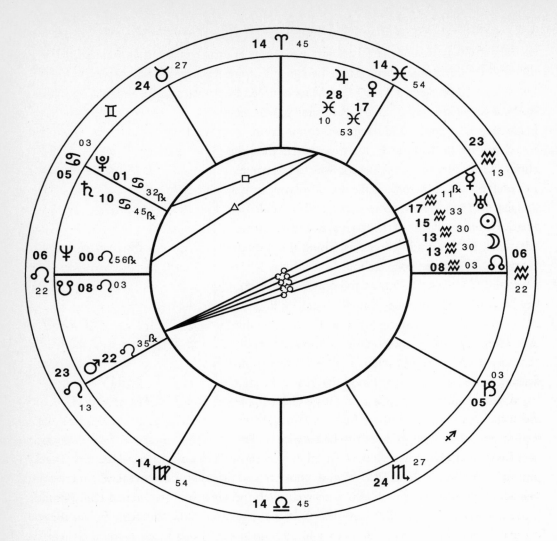

1916 Solar Eclipse

This "catastrophic" total eclipse in Aquarius, conjunct Uranus and opposite Mars, preceded the outbreak of the Battle of Verdun on February 21. Chart data: February 3, 1916, 04:05 P.M. GMT, London,
England, 51N30, 00W10.

and abdicated our responsibility to "win the peace." Still, coming so close after the great
Neptune-Pluto conjunction which separates our time from the past, the League of Nations
will undoubtedly be seen as the seed of the global community of nations which it is our
primary destiny in this age to build.

The generation that died in the First World War gave their lives in an enormous ritual
sacrifice to a world without war; only if we learn the futility of war and nationalism will
they not have died in vain. We learned from the Great War that humanity is not immor-
tal, that we can destroy ourselves with our machines and our hatreds. The horror did not

end, though; the First World War was the direct cause of the Second, which in turn released the nuclear genie. As we saw in Chapter 5, our times are ruled by Scorpio, sign of death and rebirth; this means we must become reborn as one people or face extinction together.

MISCHIEF AND MISERY BETWEEN THE WARS

The war shattered all of humanity's ancient moral certitudes, leaving us in the existential abyss. Since it failed to end war or save democracy, it also generated a great wave of disillusion in the 1920s as Uranus (now a super-powerful singleton) left visionary Aquarius and entered unhappy Pisces. The disappointments of 1800 and 1848 returned. In America, this caused the defeat of "high and mighty" Wilson by the Republicans under Warren G. Harding, who promised a "return to normalcy." This was just the kind of escapist talk that an age dominated by Uranus in Pisces wanted to hear. Another new and different period had begun, as Jupiter joined Saturn in 1920–21. Harding, who was elected on his birthday, had Pisces rising and embodied the gullibility and moral laxity of his times. Unable to tell the difference between a convivial friend and a conniving fiend, he fell victim to a bribery scandal generated by his Interior Secretary (the Teapot Dome Affair). This was just the tip of the iceberg in these fishy and swampy Piscean times in which the phrase "I've got some swamp lands in Florida you might be interested in" was born in the Florida land swindles.

Americans could be just as enthusiastic as cynics as they had been as patriots, as could Europeans after they recovered from their catastrophe. In the 1920s, their new goals were wealth and pleasure, as provided by all the new inventions from the turn of the century that now became available everywhere (cars, radios, movies, etc.). Electric Uranus, powerfully perched in decadent, disillusioned Pisces, and nebulous Neptune (the Piscean ruler), now positioned in proud, hedonistic Leo, combined to generate the shockingly crass, "low-brow," modern mass urban culture that we know today, with its cigars, "sex appeal," cosmetics, commercialism, and glamorous sports and movie heroes. It got another boost from the potent solar eclipse in 1923 that opposed the shocking Uranus in Pisces and joined pleasure-loving Venus (see the chart on the next page). In the "jazz age" of the 1920s, the "decadence" of the 1890s came into its own, as "flaming youth" and female "flappers" challenged the prudish customs of the past and shattered sexual taboos.

The entertainments and pastimes of the people suddenly became as influential as the plunderings of politicians. Only Neptune in gaming sign Leo can explain this sudden fascination with recreation and frivolity. Scores of ordinary people befuddled the pundits by playing with oriental tiles and crossword puzzles all day long and ballroom dancing all night, while more daring dabblers took nonsense to new heights by climbing the new skyscrapers, "flagpole sitting" or "barnstorming." Critics decried this new conformity, but the fads also represented the creativity of our new group mind in our "noospheric" age. Like the "hundredth monkey" syndrome, a fad takes hold when a "critical mass" is reached and people eagerly get on board and ride the next wave until the advent of tliberating experience.

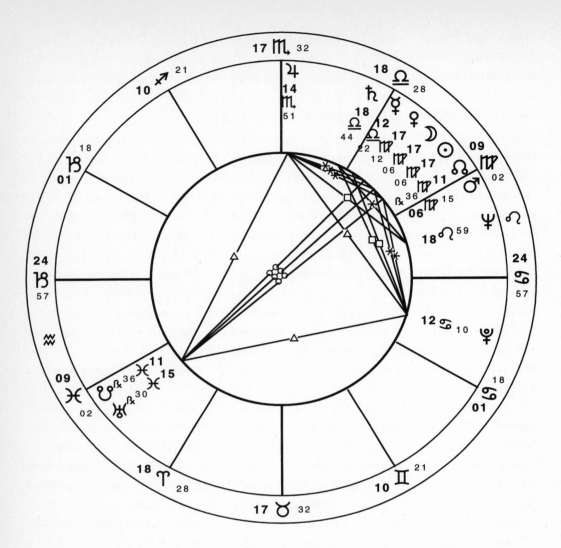

1923 Solar Eclipse

*The "Roaring '20s." Notice Jupiter at the Midheaven (optimism) in the sign of investment (Scorpio).
Venus opposite Uranus in the 2nd house means money through electric gadgets, and along with Neptune
in Leo in the 7th shows the dissolving of social taboos. The Jupiter-Uranus-Pluto grand trine in water
signs shows how carried away people got with "carrying on" during this revolutionary, alcoholic joyride
in the 1920s. Chart data: September 10, 1923, 08:53 P.M. GMT, Washington, D.C., 38N54, 77W02.*

Uranus in Pisces is inspired as well as disenchanted, so the times also produced a brilliant group of "high-brow" hedonists and cynics. F. Scott Fitzgerald, T. S. Eliot, Ezra Pound,
Theodore Dreiser, Sinclair Lewis, and others wrote of their desire to escape the meaningless
conformity of post-Great War America. This was actually the century's most fertile period
in U.S. literature (e.e. cummings, William Faulkner, Ernest Hemingway, etc.). America's

greatest playwright, Eugene O'Neill, wrote vivid portrayals of Americans caught between painful reality and their false dreams (Pisces). In Europe, Surrealist painters (Magritte, Tanguy, Klee, Dali) made shocking juxtapositions (Uranus) between the normal world and the realm of the imagination (Pisces). As always, these and other artistic achievements of the 1920s were remembered long after the fads were forgotten.

Fitzgerald was an alcoholic, as were many of the faddists and flappers. Alcohol was the fuel that made the twenties "roar." The grand trines in water signs which Jupiter in 1923 and Saturn in 1925 made to Uranus and Pluto shows how "carried away" people got with "carrying on." At the decade's start, Saturn in puritanical Virgo tried to dry up the nation with prohibition by opposing Uranus in alcoholic Pisces, but that only made drinking the favorite way for cynical youth to flout authority and gave the new gangsters a vast market. Saturn in Virgo opposing Uranus in Pisces in 1919–1920 symbolized the raging conflict between the new prurient urban culture and its rural puritan opponents, expressed in such sensational events as the Red Scare, the Sacco and Vanzetti trial, and the Scopes "Monkey Trial." The Ku Klux Klan revived in this intolerant atmosphere, and lynchings occurred.

More conservative city dwellers had their own new religion called Boosterism. This was truly the age of bread and wine (Virgo and Pisces), except that the new converts worshipped at the altar of Money and Success. Their champion in the White House was Calvin Coolidge, whose famous motto was "the business of America is business." Elevated to the presidency upon Harding's death in 1923, he and his successor Herbert Hoover suppressed unions and lowered taxes and regulations on corporations, believing that prosperity would "trickle down" from the generous fat cats as they feasted on the American pie atop their skyscrapers. Sound familiar? It should: this "trickle-down" theory was resurrected sixty years later as "supply-side economics" when Saturn returned to the same signs it occupied in the 1920s.

A thirty-year Saturn cycle became clear; starting with McKinley's victory in 1896, conservative, pro-business Republicans returned to power in the 1920s, 1950s, and 1980s. These conservative trends extended worldwide in the 1920s as they did in the other decades. Before the 1890s, the time of the "great sea change" in politics as in so much else, what is now called "conservative" was called "liberal." The old "liberalism" was converted into a justification for unregulated greed.

The roaring twenties reached its highest decibel levels in 1927, as cynical escapism was transformed into a mania for sports heroes (Babe Ruth, Bobby Jones, Jack Dempsey, etc.) No feat was celebrated more than that of Charles "Lucky Lindy" Lindbergh, who made the first solo flight across the Atlantic Ocean. Jupiter (flight and travel) and Uranus (technology) joined at the beginning of sporty Aries that year. Forty-two years later, they joined at the exact opposite spot of the zodiac in early Libra when another "Eagle" landed on the Moon. Saturn trined the two planets in 1927 from Sagittarius, sign of long travels, the same sign it occupied when the golden spike completed the first transcontinental railroad in 1869, and when Sputnik opened the Space Age in 1957. Sagittarius is

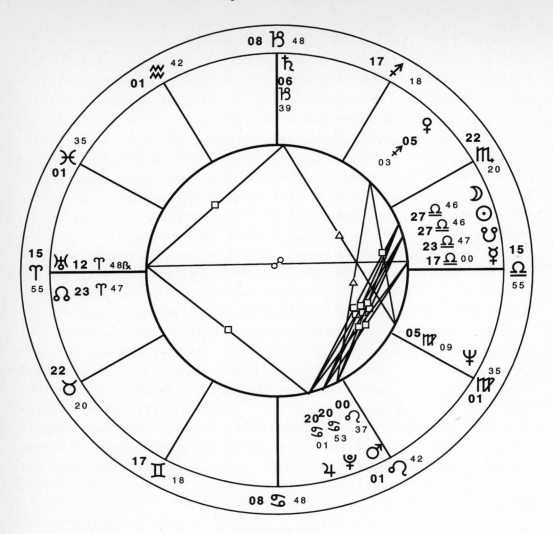

1930 Solar Eclipse

Depression times. Saturn in Capricorn at Midheaven (depression; big government) squares Uranus rising (public discontent). Venus square Neptune means dissolving finances. Chart data: October 21, 1930, 09:48 P.M. GMT, Washington, D.C., 38N54, 77W02.

also a diplomatic sign, and it was Lindbergh who flew to Mexico in 1927 to bridge the ocean of animosity between that country and America. Europe seemed to be making peace, too. The next year, all nations got together and solemnly pledged to "outlaw war" in the Kellogg-Briand Pact.

These and other confident illusions crashed to the ground in 1929, when Neptune left confident Leo and fell to earth in humble Virgo. After a frenzied wave of speculation in stocks bought "on margin" (with borrowed funds), the bubble burst and the Stock Market crashed in October. The following year, a singleton Saturn in gloomy Capricorn brought home the reality of depression. President Hoover said that prosperity was "just around the corner" and asked for voluntary cooperation, hoping that the loans he made to Big Business would trickle down to the people. But the slide was so intractable that it discredited his philosophy of self-reliance. From this point on, people would become ever more dependent on the programs of the federal government (Saturn in Capricorn).

The noose tightened as Saturn made a catastrophic T-square with Uranus in Aries and Pluto-Jupiter in Cancer in 1931. This is the most difficult planetary figure of the century. Certainly this Jupiter-Saturn opposition was a "change of direction." By 1931, the Great Depression had spread to Europe, where the major banks of Austria and Germany failed in May and June. "With the shock of a delayed effect ... the full consequences of the First World War came to the surface."[6] Our load lightened with the weight of old empires and customs gone, we had tried to pick up the pieces late in the 1920s and continue our ascent. But we were still so dazed and confused by the recent war's upheaval that when the Great Depression came we fell back down again and remained mired within the canyon walls. The gathering demonic forces of industrial, racist, bloodthirsty national socialism reached their nightmarish climax in the Holocaust.

In 1930, Uranus reached the exact point in Aries it had occupied in 1846 when Neptune was discovered (during another depression, and two years before the revolutions of 1848). Pluto, planet of the underworld, was discovered in 1930 as the Great Depression hit. More revolutions followed; they were the climax of the Second revolutionary movement that began in 1848. Uranus and Pluto had joined then, and in 1933 they reached their closing (or waning) square in the same great cycle. The two branches of the socialist movement—the left-wing communist/democratic-socialist branch, and the right-wing nationalist/fascist branch—had developed side by side since 1848–50. In the 1880s the two wings had been "allies against the liberal center"; now they were about to fight to the death for world supremacy. Around 1930, Joseph Stalin launched his catastrophic five-year plan to forcibly collectivize and industrialize the Soviet Union, followed by massive "purges" of supposed state enemies ("the Red Terror"). This doctrine of "socialism in one country" sounded similar to national socialism, the rival branch that took over in Germany. These were, after all, two branches of one great movement.

The Nazis were like disturbed, earthbound spirits of a bygone age unable to part this world. In 1933, they transformed Germany into an elemental force of rabid robots demonically possessed by the black magic of their charismatic leader, Adolf Hitler. Brainwashed by him into believing a distortion of Darwinian theory that all human races were locked in a fight to the death for the "survival of the fittest," Germans were hell-bent on avenging their defeat in 1918 and proving that they were the elite members of the superior Aryan race.

A history teacher once told me about a pet German theory that the Nazi "revolution" was a "German 1789." I thought it was more like a German 1793. The same T-square that accompanied the Reign of Terror (Saturn-Uranus-Pluto) had returned in the early 1930s. Hitler idealized the State and the Wagnerian Teutonic heroes from the Dark Ages, but not

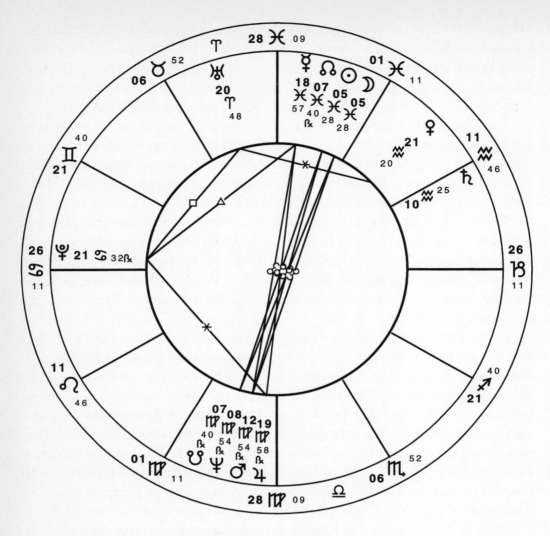

1933 Annular Eclipse

This solar eclipse happened just 3 days before the Reichstag fire in Germany, and 8 days before FDR took office as U.S. President. The planets of the fascist revolution, Uranus in Aries square Pluto in Cancer, were on the angles in Berlin. Notice the three "Marseillaise planets," Mars, Jupiter, and Neptune, conjunct in Virgo (sign of bureaucracy) opposite Mercury (ruler of Virgo) in Pisces. Chart data: February 24, 1933, 12:44 P.M. GMT, Berlin, Germany, 52N30, 13E22.

the liberties of the French Revolution. His movement was the antithesis and the ironic, karmic repeat of that earlier "great storm." The infamous one-arm Nazi salute with its "Seig Heil" chant was the same salute seen in J. L. David's "Oath of the Horatii" which the French revolutionaries had used to swear allegiance to liberty. Some say Hitler was Napoleon reincarnate; he climaxed the Second Revolution just as Bonaparte had fulfilled the first, and the Nazis were the distorted (and perhaps inevitable) result of the nationalist faith begun in

France in 1789.[7] Pluto in Cancer squaring radical Uranus in Aries in 1933 symbolized this hellish nationalism of the Third Reich, just as Uranus in Cancer squaring Neptune in Aries represented the aggressive nationalism of Bismarck's Second Reich in 1871. After becoming chancellor in January 1933 through some clever political maneuvering, Hitler ordered his brown-shirted bullies to set fire to the Reichstag (parliament) building, then used it as an excuse to assume dictatorial powers. A solar eclipse on February 24 lit up the skies three days before the fire, and opposing it were the same three planets (Mars, Jupiter, and Neptune) that had aligned in 1792 during the "Marseillaise" march. The Nazis proceeded to cure the depression by putting people to work beating plowshares into swords for the upcoming global battle.

The same eclipse signaled the rise of another great leader in America. Elected after Hoover ordered General MacArthur to shoot some unemployed veterans camped out at the White House, Franklin Roosevelt assured his nation that everything would come out "Roosey" declaring "the only thing we have to fear is fear itself." He administered alphabet soup to his sick country, as Congress passed major reforms and set up three-lettered bureaucratic agencies to put people to work and cure the depression. During this famous first "100 days" of his administration, Mars lingered over Jupiter and Neptune in Virgo, as if America were being treated in the emergency room (Virgo is sign of health and bureaucracy). In August 1935, Venus did the same thing over Neptune in Virgo, as Congress passed the landmark Social Security Act, and Mars was conjunct Jupiter again (in Scorpio this time, sign of shared resources). The New Deal was like a gigantic Hoover Dam across the deep chasm between the wars that allowed America to continue the climb to liberation. It was life-saving medicine for America, repairing the morale of a broken people. But it didn't quite cure the patient; as in Germany, only when the U.S. rearmed itself for war did it fully recover. Military spending became an all-consuming addiction, and the question became whether the cure was worse than the original disease.

As the "winds of war" began to blow, Americans dreamed of a future beyond the depressing dangers of the 1930s. They went to the 1939 New York World's Fair, where they gazed longingly at the "streamlined world of 1960." They went to the movies in their golden age, where they could escape to past troubles and glories in Gone with the Wind, or watch Dorothy travel over the rainbow to Oz on a cyclone. Soon they would be borne high on the winds of a real storm, and over its rainbow in the future lay a technological "Oz" fashioned in the fiery furnace of conflict. On our journey of transition, we have gained a new brain (the scarecrow, Uranus the inventor), a new heart (the tin man, or Neptune the giver of compassion), and new courage (the lion, or Pluto the seeker of new life). By the 1940s, we had the wizard-like power to create our dreams, but now, like Dorothy, we must "come home" from our battles with wicked witches in the east and west (like Japan and Germany) to the "home" within ourselves, and to our precious and endangered Earth home.

The first storm clouds gathered in 1931, the climactic "change of direction" year, when Japan attacked Manchuria as Saturn opposed Pluto and Jupiter. Hitler's first move didn't come until 1935 when, as Mars turned stationary on his own Ascendant degree and opposed Uranus on his solar degree (the "cosmic trigger" point of 0° Taurus), he defiantly resumed the military draft and expanded his navy. A year later, he marched his troops west into the Rhineland. His fellow dictator Mussolini of Italy rolled over the world's oldest nation, Ethiopia (then known as Abyssinia), and annexed it in October 1935. This became the death blow to the feeble League of Nations, which imposed sanctions against Italy, and then meekly withdrew them. The two dictators then tested their new war toys in the Spanish Civil War, which broke out as Francisco Franco led his armies in revolt against the five-year-old republic. This occurred one month after a solar eclipse in June 1936 which was conjunct Mars, square Saturn, and opposed Jupiter in Spain's sign of Sagittarius. The war generated the kind of enthusiasm for an idealistic republican cause not seen since the Greek War of Independence, but the Fascists won anyway. The Spanish republican matador lost to Taurus the Bull in the person of Hitler, who celebrated with Mussolini by forming the Rome-Berlin Axis.

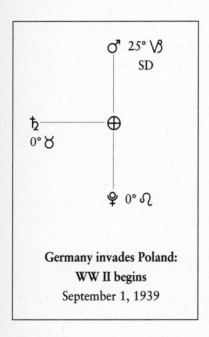

Germany invades Poland:
WW II begins
September 1, 1939

Declaring himself ready to "fight for the self-determination of the German People," Hitler marched his armies into Vienna in mid-March 1938 as Mars crossed his "trigger degree" and united Austria with Germany. The enthusiastic citizens of Vienna welcomed him with open arms as a conquering hero. Austria was no longer schizophrenically divided, but was it sane?

The Western nations had become too confused and demoralized to resist. In September 1938 came the event now famous as the Munich Appeasement. British Prime Minister Chamberlain and French Premier Daladier gave Germany part of Czechoslovakia, as Hitler promised to make no further territorial claims. Appeasement meant we would give the dogs of war a piece of meat now and hope they would never get hungry again. Judge Chamberlain let the criminal out on parole before he was rehabilitated, but Winston Churchill rendered his own judgment. "You had a choice between war and dishonor. You chose dishonor; you shall have war."[8] The disastrous failure of the Munich Appeasement has been used ever since to justify military action against possible aggressors before they get too strong. Thus has Hitler shaped foreign policy for over sixty years and counting. In September 1938, Mars was in Virgo (where it was when both the Soviets and the Nazis assumed power), and now the former symbol of the French Virgin Republic's fatal dependence on war became the symbol of the Munich Doctrine.

Shorn of their fortifications in the lost Sudetenland, the Czechs were easy victims to Hitler when he shattered the illusion of peace and took the rest of the country in March of 1939. On August 23, as Mars stood stationary on its degree in the "Horoscope of Modern

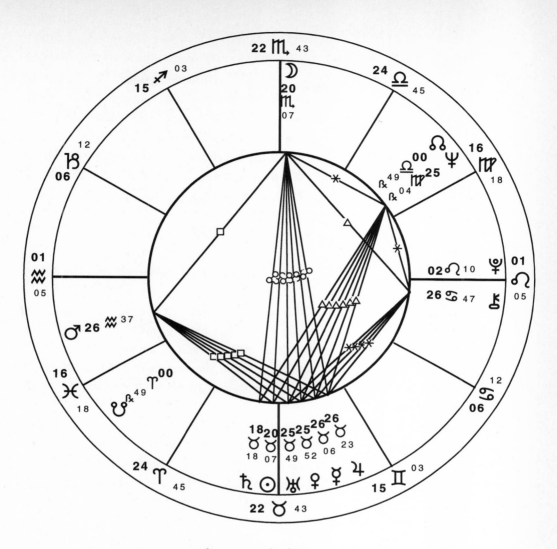

The Arsenal of Democracy

This is the chart for the Full Moon of May 11, 1941, that followed Jupiter's conjunction to Uranus on May 8. At about the time of this mammoth conjunction in Taurus, America became the "arsenal of democracy," and thereby the world's leading industrial power. Russia was invaded soon afterward on June 22. The Full Moon and the Taurus planets were all squared by aggressive Mars, and atomic Pluto was on the Descendant (war) in the U.S. Chart data: May 11, 1941, 05:15 A.M. GMT, Washington, D.C., 38N54, 77W02.

Humanity," opposing Pluto and squaring Saturn at the 0° Taurus "trigger" degree, Hitler and his rival dictator Stalin made a pact not to attack each other. The world knew instantly what this meant. A week later the Germans stormed into Poland in a *blitzkrieg* (lightning war). Hitler was surprised when the British and French finally stood up to him and declared war. The Second World War had come.

THE EARTH WAR

Even then, the Allies could only muster up a "phony war"—a *sitzkrieg* or defensive posture while Hitler and Stalin divided up Poland and the Baltic countries. In April 1940 (after another solar eclipse), the Germans conquered Scandinavia and most of western Europe. As Jupiter and Saturn made their next conjunction in July–August 1940 (square Mercury-Mars-Pluto), Hitler attacked Britain from the air—but like Napoleon, Hitler the Taurus was out of his earthy element, and the heroic British air forces gave him his first defeat. "Never had so many owed so much to so few," said the new Prime Minister, Winston Churchill.[9] Ironically, during the turning point in the battle on September 7, Mars returned to the same degree it occupied at the Munich Conference. Instead of an illusory peace, Britain now had a victory in its "finest hour." The "winds of war" were changing direction; after the August 1940 conjunction, things would not be such a breeze for the dictators.

Checked in the west, Hitler expanded in the east, attacking Greece and the Soviet Union. His mammoth invasion of Russia on June 22, 1941, came exactly 129 years after Napoleon's (about one Uranus-Pluto cycle of revolution); and just one month after Jupiter, Saturn, and Uranus lined up in Taurus with three other planets and squared Mars. This enormous conjunction in Taurus, similar to the "new beginning" conjunction in Aries in 1762, with which our story of the Modern Spirit began, also represented the vast material resources marshaled for the war, which made America the "arsenal of democracy," and thus the world's leading industrial nation.

Convinced the war was won, Hitler now implemented his "final solution" to the "Jewish problem." The Jews were, from the beginning, the scapegoat on which the Nazis projected all their demonic fears. They and other "misfits" were executed, used as slave labor, or tortured and exterminated in concentration camps. Six million were killed simply for being Jewish, a completely unprecedented horror. The scientific materialism of 1851, adopted by racists who twisted it to their hateful ends, had reached its ultimate conclusion. Parallel events happened in America, where Japanese-Americans were sent to camps for "protection" during the war.

It was the actions of the Japanese that got the United States into the war to begin with. The attack on Pearl Harbor on December 7, 1941 came as Mars stood stationary in Aries and Jupiter returned to Gemini, on top of the U.S. Mars. These were virtually the same positions under which America entered the First World War. Japan began overrunning southeast Asia the same day, including America's colony in the Philippines. "I shall return," vowed General MacArthur after being forced to flee in March 1942.

I call World War II the "Earth War" because it was history's only truly world-wide war. The name is also a takeoff on "Star Wars," referring to the enormous boost the war gave to air and space flight. The air element was so pronounced in these "winds of war" because Saturn, Uranus and Neptune were all in air signs during most of the war, at least from 1942 on. By then the Soviet Union and the United States were allies with Britain against the Axis powers, and the balance was tipped in the Allies favor. Now that the Soviet Union and the United States were Allies with Britain against the Axis powers, the balance was tipped in the Allies' favor. As this happened, Neptune crossed into airy Libra ("the Balance"), and Uranus returned to Gemini, always the signal for American entry into a great war. The exact conjunction of Saturn and Uranus in May 1942 marked the turning point. That month, the U.S. stopped Japan's advance at Corregidor. On June 7, they crippled the Japanese navy at the Battle of Midway. In October, after a see-saw battle (Neptune on the cusp of Libra "the Balance") in the North African desert, the British under Montgomery drove German Field Marshall Rommel back at El Alamein. In November, as four planets in turbulent Scorpio squared Pluto, the Russians stopped the Nazis at the horrendous, epic Battle of Stalingrad.

In July of 1943, as Mars crossed Hitler's "trigger point" of 0° Taurus and squared gargantuan Jupiter and explosive Pluto in fiery Leo, huge firestorms lit up the skies. Hitler attacked Russia again, but was beaten back in the most gigantic tank battle in history. The Allies avenged the bombing of London by setting off a huge conflagration at Hamburg, Germany. After driving the Axis out of Africa, they invaded Sicily in July and Italy in September. Interestingly, both Jupiter and Uranus now occupied the same sign positions they did in 1859; through this second "war of unification," Italy was getting another chance to become a whole, truly civilized nation as Fascism died in the streets. In November 1943, with Mars in 22° Gemini stationary over Mars in the U.S. Horoscope, the U.S. began its move on Japan by attacking in the Gilbert Islands. Finally, at Stalin's urging, the Allies opened a second front in Western Europe, led by General Eisenhower. "D-Day" came on June 6, 1944, as Uranus (with Venus) reached 9° Gemini, its place at the Declaration of Independence and the start of the Civil War. This time America was liberating the world as well as itself, and repaying their French liberators from two cycles of Uranus back.

This Allied invasion at Normandy was a masterful, determined effort to ascend the very cliffs from which so many had fallen before: this time, it succeeded, as other "cliffs" were conquered in campaigns around the globe. The French in Paris were liberated on August 25, as Mars passed through Virgo (symbol of the Virgin Republic) and joined Neptune, Mercury, Venus, and (widely) Jupiter in a great planetary line-up approximating the "Marseillaise" conjunction of 1792. Despite desperate counterattacks, the Fatherland was caught in the Allied pincers from east and west, and surrendered on May 7, 1945. Meanwhile, Hitler had gone back to Hell.

The Americans island-hopped their way to the Philippines where MacArthur "returned." As Saturn moved into watery Cancer and squared Neptune in October 1944, they sank the Japanese fleet in Leyte Gulf in the greatest naval battle in history. In bloody fighting, they conquered Iwo Jima (scene of the famous flag raising) and Okinawa, which allowed them to rain terror and death from the Japanese skies.

Before Japan could surrender, the U.S. unleashed a horror almost as inconceivable as that caused by her enemies. On August 6, 1945, our Plutonian catharsis called "Hell on Earth" reached its infernal climax with the detonation of an atomic bomb over Hiroshima.

Three days later, the target was Nagasaki. Although this event is really beyond any possible symbolic representation, we can mention that Mars stood conjunct to Uranus and its natal degree in the U.S. Horoscope, also near the degree of the Neptune-Pluto conjunction of 1892, which coincided with our discovery of the atomic worlds.

The Fascist jungle-world of "survival of the fittest," ugly fruit of a century of materialism and decay, had now been cleared away by the Allied soldiers. We owe to them our chance to build a new world. Without their efforts we might not be here today. We must not forget the Russian contribution to this effort. They bore the brunt of the Nazi attack and achieved the greatest victories, and they performed a lasting service to humanity by wiping out the East Prussian aristocracy that had led Germany into conquest so often before. The Americans did the same kind of thing in Japan. After the war, the U.S. and Soviet Union redeemed their failure to support the League of Nations, which might have prevented a second world war. The United Nations opened for business on October 24, 1945, under the same Jupiter-Neptune conjunction during which the League began. This time it was in diplomatic Libra and joined by its ruling planet Venus. These were better signs of success.

The Earth War is the cautionary tale of our modern age. Even today, we still have our "ghettoes," named after the walled-off communities where Jews were kept before being sent off to die. The Nazis were just an extreme example of the kind of evil that stalks our society today whenever people submit to unquestioned authority and reduce themselves and others to objects. In a memorable moment from the TV series "Holocaust," a Jew asked his Rabbi, "How can you any longer believe in God?" "How can you any longer believe in Man?" was the reply. All faiths were shattered in the Holocaust; the dark shadows of the canyon still surrounded us, and the famous religious "problem of evil" now had its ultimate example for all time. But the problem has a solution. We can all find meaning by resisting this evil wherever it appears. We can stand up to the opressors of the human spirit and resist the scapegoating of groups that can lead to genocide. French philosopher and resistance leader Jean Paul Sartre wrote that he and his comrades "were never more free than during the German occupation." We can unleash the growing modern spirit inside us, instead of bowing to despair and false prophets of doom. The Nazis made a monumental attempt to keep us from making our climb out of the Valley; horrors like this generally occur only during or near these uncertain "times of transition." That they were able to erect Hell on Earth for twelve years shows we must be ever-vigilant to the demons within and around us. We must never forget the horrors of Hitler's Hell.

As the smoke cleared, we began to count the cost. Fifty-five million people had been killed; millions more were left starving and displaced amid an entire civilization in ruins. Saturn in Cancer (deprivation of resources) symbolized this time of "austerity." Mammoth rebuilding efforts lay ahead, as the power vacuum at the center was filled by the tides rushing in from east and west. Though there was physical and political rebuilding, the culture left standing after the Holocaust was still empty, shorn of its faith, and lacking a spiritual compass. Still largely under the spell of materialism, we had not yet climbed very far out of the Valley of Transition. Europe's creative fires had burned out, to be replaced by the commercial wasteland of American culture and the dribble of Communist slogans from Russia.

The war had ended the Depression and boosted technology, creating an unheard-of prosperity in America. Having escaped the destruction of its homeland, the U.S. was now the unchallenged military and economic superpower. The "American Decade" began, and the triumphant Americans became fat, happy, and complacent; especially their corporate leaders, who began to create huge organizations built on the model of the pyramidal military command structure.

Soon to be rivals, the two new dominant societies in America and Russia were really not so different. Western capitalism had become a huge bureaucracy in which faceless people worked in offices and factories for faceless managers. Post-war America was commercial communism in all but name; a world of the organization man in the gray flannel suit.[10] Employees were loyal and did what their company asked; in return they got the pensions and health benefits of "welfare capitalism." One did one's best to "keep up with the Joneses" and get ahead in the "rat race." "Little boxes made of ticky-tacky" went up on the suburban hillsides in which alienated "nuclear families" consumed the new plastic products (and, it was later said, became "plastic" themselves). Soldiers came home, then moved away to raise families of their own, and women returned from their work opportunities during the war to resume their roles as housewives and mothers. Uranus in domestic Cancer from 1948–1955 could represent this wave of "domesticity"[11] and the resulting "baby boom." In the evening, you could relax and watch the "vast wasteland" on your new TV set. Its escapist programming was designed to reach a wide audience so advertisers could sell cars, soap, and orange juice, as the mass, commercial culture of the 1920s found a new outlet.

Our era is amazingly unique; remarkable for its extreme wealth and extreme poverty. Though our crass culture and lifestyle has divorced us from Earth and Spirit, we are nevertheless the first-born inheritors of the legacy of all humanity. Beneath the rubble and monotony of our broken world lies a soil richly fertilized with all the nutrients needed for the most luxuriant creative growth ever seen. Only recently recovered by archeologists and scholars, this once-buried legacy (symbolized by our 8th house phase in the Cosmic Clock of Civilization) now lies at our fingertips in our media, schools and libraries. To nurture this new spiritual and global culture is the greatest task facing us in the wake of history's greatest war.

WORLD WAR THREE: THE COLD WAR

The original liberal Revolution had at last triumphed in Europe. The struggle for basic liberation achieved there, it shifted elsewhere. But as so often before, the liberators became the oppressors. The United States of America, the First revolutionary nation that had taken Western and Central Europe out of the depths and up over the cliffs in World War II, now competed for world dominion with that other "evil Empire," the once equally revolutionary Soviet Union, carrier of the Second Socialist Revolution. The one had liberated people

221

from royal tyranny, the other had tried to free us from economic tyranny. The tense "Cold War" between them happened as the symbols of each Revolution (Uranus, representing the revolution of liberty, and Neptune, the revolution of equality) passed in square to each other in the 1950s on their way to their unifying conjunction to come in the 1990s. The world's division into two power blocs continued, except that an East-West rivalry now replaced a dangerous and unruly Center. Much the same had happened around 1820 when Napoleon was succeeded by a British-Russian rivalry.

Just as international tension sparked an arms race in the 1870s, when Uranus squared Neptune, and again before World War I, as it opposed Neptune, it did the same in the late 1940s and 1950s, as Uranus squared Neptune again. I call the Cold War "World War III" because the allies and surrogates of the two sides waged wars all over the world, and the Armageddon we feared (usually called "World War III") would have happened if the nuclear arms race had continued. Caught in the middle were the colonized peoples of the "Third World," who struggled against the Old Empires (British, French, Dutch) and the New Empires (American and Soviet).

With Neptune now transiting at the top of its horoscope, the U.S. became obsessed with maintaining its new world leadership. It was Winston Churchill, though, who identified the West's new enemy: "From Stettin in the Baltic, to Trieste in the Adriatic, an Iron Curtain has descended across the Continent." This phrase defined the post-war world. As he spoke in Fulton, Missouri, in March 1946, Mars turned stationary over fearful Saturn in defensive, nationalist Cancer. After Munich, the U.S. could not risk ignoring Churchill, however much it wanted to return to its isolationist ways. His views were supported by American expert George Kennan, who wrote that Russia harbored an ages-old "inherent need to expand." The Soviets didn't see themselves as aggressors; they wanted a buffer zone in Eastern Europe against another "capitalist" invasion from the west like the one that had just destroyed half their nation and killed twenty-seven million of their people. At first, the nations of Eastern Europe believed Soviet promises that they were being liberated from the rich, but Stalin made his neighbors into little carbon copies of Soviet Russia, and soon they suffered from the same tyranny and terror that he had imposed on his own people.

When the Red Tide rose in Turkey and the Balkans, where the World Wars had arisen after a century of troubles, the Cold War began in earnest. Four score and four years before, Uranus had aligned with the U.S. Mars at 22° Gemini during the Battle of Gettysburg. As it returned there in March 1947, President Truman echoed Lincoln by declaring the world

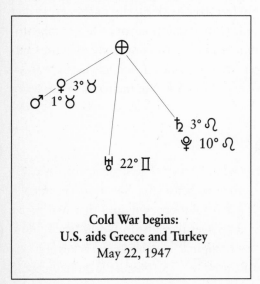

Cold War begins:
U.S. aids Greece and Turkey
May 22, 1947

half-slave and half-free, and that it was America's duty to "contain" the Soviet enslavers. On May 22, aid was approved to Greece and Turkey, just as Mars and Venus crossed the "trigger point" at 0° Taurus. (As we saw in our chapter on geography, this is also a Middle East trigger point.[12]) In square to Venus and Mars were Saturn and Pluto in conjunction, opening the next modern war cycle. It was a cosmic figure remarkably like that seen at the outbreak of World War I (and very similar to one in Hitler's horoscope). The Greek Civil War of the late 1940s was the first of those surrogate wars between puppets of East and West, of which the last ended in Central America in the early 1990s. As Mars stood stationary over Saturn/Pluto in Leo in March 1948, the U.S. declared economic war by shoring up its threatened western allies with the Marshall Plan. The Arabs and Israelis also became pawns in the Cold War game: beginning in May they fought the first in a series of wars.

The U.S. was talking tough about "preventing another Munich," but they couldn't stop Czechoslovakia from falling into Stalin's hands in February 1948. Just a few weeks before, Mars had turned stationary in Virgo (the sign it occupied as Czechoslovakia was sacrificed to Hitler at Munich). When Mars returned to Virgo in June, Stalin tried to starve Berlin into submitting to the Communists, who controlled the surrounding area. The West defeated his blockade with an airlift (Mars square flighty Jupiter and Uranus), after which Germany was split into East and West.

As the Red Tide continued to rise, many shocks and surprises followed, including President Truman's upset victory for re-election on November 2, 1948. But it didn't surprise astrologers, who knew that a total solar eclipse, which represents sudden and unexpected events, had happened the day before the election! The biggest jolt to America came in the Fall of 1949, as Mars conjoined Pluto in Leo (as during D-Day), which was then exactly over Mars in the President's horoscope. Americans panicked as Mao Tse-Tung's communist revolution took over China, and, even worse, it was learned that Russia had the bomb. Suddenly, the U.S. was vulnerable and needed an even bigger bomb. The nuclear arms race was off and running, and the nuclear clock began ticking towards doomsday.

Americans started blaming a conspiracy at home for the debacle. "Communists" were arrested, including Alger Hiss, who was accused of espionage by congressman Richard Nixon and others. In February 1950, as Mars turned stationary-retrograde in Libra (conjunct delusive Neptune and square hysterical Uranus in patriotic Cancer), Senator Joe McCarthy launched an anti-red crusade which slandered reputations and ruined careers right and left—mostly left. Anyone with any left-wing background was labeled as a communist and "blacklisted."

A climax and change of direction came in 1950–51, as Jupiter opposed Saturn. In May 1950, Mars added to the fireworks by turning stationary-direct in Virgo, aligned with Saturn (and Neptune in America's horoscope). A month later, the Cold War got hot, as the U.S. led a UN coalition to stop communist North Korea's "aggressive" invasion of South Korea. It was another "war of unification," like the one in Central Europe in 1866, exactly one cycle of Uranus before. Though fortunes see-sawed back and forth (Saturn on the cusp of Libra), the result was different from the 1860s, and unity was postponed by force. At the war's peak, General MacArthur threatened to extend the war to China, whose "volunteers" were helping the North. An outraged President Truman fired him for over-stepping his authority in a sensational episode on April 11, 1951.

A great debate then erupted over the war and the "moral decay" of America, as Jupiter in Pisces opposed Saturn in Virgo. These were the same signs in which Saturn opposed Uranus-Pluto during the similar loud debate over Vietnam, and which brought Richard Nixon to power. In 1951–52, it brought General Eisenhower ("Ike"), his mentor, to power, and Winston Churchill overturned the Labour Party in Britain. Labour's "Austerity" and Truman's "Fair Deal" (a continuation of the New Deal) were over. The political tides shifted to the right again, just like during the previous Red Scare in 1920. The thirty-year Saturn cycle took hold again, as Eisenhower's new Defense Secretary echoed Coolidge by declaring that "what's good for General Motors is good for America." Defeated Democratic candidate Adlai Stevenson replied that the Fair Dealers had been replaced by the car dealers. The Cold War reached an explosive climax when the U.S. exploded the first H-Bomb on November 1, 1952, as Saturn joined Neptune and its "Cold War square" with Uranus, and Mars T-squared the three planets. The Russians answered with their own bomb in July 1953.

By then both sides saw for the first time where this MAD arms race (Mutually Assured Destruction, the official term for atomic deterrence) would end: with the world in a grave. In 1953, Saturn joined Neptune, as it did when the Soviet Union began. Stalin died, and his more liberal successors joined Eisenhower in arranging a truce in Korea. The same conjunction also represents the "secret government" (Saturn: government; Neptune: secrecy and delusion). The CIA installed the Shah in power in Iran that year, and overturned a democracy that was too left-leaning for its liking in Guatemala the next. In October 1956, the superpowers cooperated for the first time since the Earth War. The West didn't support revolutions against Communism in Poland and Hungary, while America joined Russia in condemning aggressive actions by its own European allies against Egypt in the Suez Crisis. After that, the Cold War began to ease a bit.

In France, another "revolution" happened, as the war in colonial Algeria brought Charles De Gaulle to power under a new constitution in 1958 (the Fifth Republic). That year, both Uranus and Neptune were in the same signs (Leo and Scorpio) as in 1792 when the First Republic began. Jupiter also joined Neptune in another "Marseillaise" conjunction. This time, we were literally all going "to confront the infinite,"[13] as the Russians sent the first spacecraft into orbit in October 1957.

The Soviet launch of Sputnik was a wake-up call to Americans. They couldn't allow the Russians to conquer space, so the space race was added to the arms race. Pluto's entry into Virgo the same year represented the boom in technology which the new race unleashed.

The signal for a major regeneration sounded as Neptune entered turbulent Scorpio in 1956–57. First in Montgomery, Alabama, in December 1955 (Mars conjunct Neptune), then in Little Rock, Arkansas, in September 1957 (Mars in Virgo, conjunct Pluto), southern blacks began challenging the white supremacy laws established back in 1877, when Neptune had just gone into the opposite sign of Taurus.

The first signs of an "alternative" culture appeared, too. Beatniks like Jack Kerouac went "on the road" to escape the prevailing conformity, while others clustered in coffee houses and read poetry or argued art and literature. Pop music found a new beat: according to the cosmic clock it was time to rock. Society in the late fifties was generally more stable and secure than a decade ago; in TV terms the world of *The Honeymooners* had now been replaced by the world of *Leave it to Beaver*. But there were a few wisecracking Eddie Haskells around. Since Neptune was now in stormy, romantic Scorpio, changes were afoot, and the American public sensed that the Republican leadership under Ike was not in step with them. They narrowly elected Democrat John F. Kennedy as their new president, and readied themselves to cross what he called the "New Frontier" into the 1960s.

ASCENT TO IDEALISM: THE TRIP OF DREAMS

In his inaugural address on January 20, 1961, the new president highlighted the meaning of the next Jupiter-Saturn conjunction which occurred just three weeks later by declaring, "Let us begin!" He also aroused the revolutionary Modern Spirit among the people again by telling them, "Ask not what your country can do for you, ask what you can do for your country." That the new decade would be a bumpy "trip" of change was shown by the fact that this Jupiter-Saturn conjunction was the only major line-up in the twentieth Century that coincided with a total solar eclipse (within four days), which in turn opposed revolutionary planet Uranus (just like the 1892 eclipse). A year later, an even more remarkable eclipse happened which was joined by all the visible planets in Aquarius, a cosmic event which some say heralded "The Age of Aquarius," and others feared would bring "the end of the world."

These eclipses contained much foreboding. The first one in February 1961 also coincided with Mars stationary in Cancer, the same position that opened the Cold War in 1946 with Churchill's speech. Departing President Eisenhower gave a memorable speech warning against the growing power of the "military-industrial complex." Kennedy ignored his warning two months later by sponsoring an ill-conceived attack by exiles against Cuba (the "Bay of Pigs invasion"), as Mars opposed Saturn. (Cuba had recently gone Communist.)

On July 8, 1961, as Mars returned to Virgo (like during the first Berlin Crisis), JFK confronted Soviet leader Khruschev, who made menacing threats toward Berlin where people were escaping through the Iron Curtain. The arms race accelerated, and fallout shelters proliferated at this fearful moment. Mars now aligned with atomic Pluto, as it had done in the fall of 1949 (when the doomsday clock began ticking). Unable to get his way, Khruschev built the Berlin Wall to keep people in. The Iron Curtain had congealed into concrete. The next year, JFK discovered that the Russians had installed missiles in Cuba, ostensibly to forestall another U.S. invasion. As Mars opposed Saturn again exactly on October 22, 1962, Kennedy threatened attack if the missiles weren't removed. Nuclear confrontation made "the end of the world" seem a real possibility. The Russians finally "blinked" and removed the missiles, but then began adding to their arsenal so they wouldn't be humiliated again. The arms race continued, but the two sides now moved away from direct confrontation, sponsoring a nuclear test-ban treaty in August 1963.

A spectre also haunted the great Aquarian eclipse on February 4, 1962; it was squared by idealistic, dreamy Neptune. This made the 1960s a decade of dreams, but also of nightmares and disillusion. Our leader through this initiation was a preacher from Atlanta named Martin Luther King, Jr., whose solar degree was 25° Capricorn, the exact degree of the 1961 conjunction of Jupiter-Saturn (and Mars in the Horoscope of Modern Humanity). Leader of the Montgomery bus boycott in 1956, he adapted Gandhi's methods of non-violent civil disobedience for the civil rights movement with "sit-ins," marches, and deliberate confrontations with police. Later called "people power," it became the model for all subsequent revolts, though some of these later became violent. Dr. King asked his followers to "meet physical force with soul force," and it worked by arousing sympathy for them.

The Movement got going in 1960 with the first student sit-ins at segregated lunch counters, and continued with "freedom rides" to force integration of interstate buses. By 1963, the South was convulsed with demonstrations, and violence erupted in Montgomery, Alabama, in May. On June 11, the South's newest demagogue, Alabama Governor George Wallace, stood in the door of his state's university to bar admissions for black students. This angered Kennedy so much that he went on TV, gave his greatest speech, and proposed the Civil Rights Bill. Mars had returned to Virgo and conjoined Uranus and Pluto. On August 25, within days of the Test-Ban Treaty, hundreds of thousands of people of all races gathered in Washington to support the Civil Rights Bill. People said this march was like a divine visitation, the spirit was so high. There Martin Luther King made his famous "I have a dream" speech. It was the signal for all of us to dream again, lift our eyes above the muck and mire of the last 100 years, and remember the promise of the original Revolution. This time it was the Sun and Venus that joined the revolutionary Uranus-Pluto conjunction in Virgo.

This conjunction signaled a new revolutionary movement, spearheaded by the "humble" minorities that the sign Virgo represents. Virgo also represents students, who formulated the new Movement's goals as the New Left. Written by Tom Hayden, the Port Huron Statement of June 1962 described it as going beyond the Old Socialist Left's aim of taking over the existing industrial, consumer society to instead challenge the system itself through "participatory democracy" and "refusals of the heart."[14] Sit-ins, opposition to the war, and "dropping out" were among these "refusals" during the 1960s. When Mars returned to Virgo in early December 1964, and aligned with Uranus-Pluto again, the first New Left revolt broke out in Berkeley at the University of California, the first of many thousands of such campus revolts across the world. Using "people power," they challenged the rules against free speech left over from McCarthy's days, and won a student-faculty strike the day a partial solar eclipse squared the conjunction.

Kennedy's idealism had helped to inspire these movements, but his assassination on November 22, 1963, was a blow to the orderly progress of society. The astrological signs make clear that this seemingly senseless event was as predestined as any could ever be. We already mentioned the "coincidences" with Lincoln's death, and the twenty-year Jupiter-Saturn cycle; we need only add here that the revolutionary planets Uranus and Pluto were squaring Kennedy's Sun, and that Saturn had reached 17° Aquarius— the exact degree of the 1962 Aquarian eclipse and the Mars station in the progressed Chart of Modern Humanity, which squared JFK's Mars in his Eighth House of death.

Kennedy's popular wife Jacqueline gave his administration the name of "Camelot," because its idealism, class, and glamour became as legendary as the Knights of the Round Table. His wit and support for the arts were especially endearing. "The arts (are) close to the center of a nation's purpose, and a test of the quality of its civilization," he said.[15] By encouraging them as no president had ever done, Kennedy inaugurated the new Renaissance portended by Neptune in Scorpio. Had he lived, his administration might have become America's Augustan Age.

Kennedy's successor, Lyndon Johnson, now said, "Let us continue." As Mars reached 25° Capricorn, where Jupiter and Saturn had joined as JFK said "Let us begin," Johnson continued by declaring "war on poverty." Lyndon B. Johnson was a brilliant legislator who made JFK's ideals into realities. The Civil Rights Bill became law on June 11, 1964, one year after its proposal. Johnson went on to enact his "Great Society" program in October 1965, as the revolutionary Uranus-Pluto conjunction became exact (in his sign). Included were Head Start, the Housing Department, pollution controls, Medicare, and more. Freedom Summer in Mississippi in 1964, and riots and marches in Selma, Alabama, in early 1965 (Mars stationary in Virgo), convinced LBJ to add a Voting Rights Act. The huge socialist bureaucracy of the Second Revolution had reached its climax, not only in the U.S., but in Britain, Russia and elsewhere. But the question became, could it continue?

The 1960s were an era of "impossible dreams," and the most Quixotic of all was America's attempt to impose its will on Vietnam. Before this war ended, more bombs were dropped than in all of World War II, and millions were killed. In February 1965, as Mars in Virgo turned stationary near America's Neptune (as it had done before the Korean War), Johnson began bombing North Vietnam, then sent troops to South Vietnam in March and April as Mars opposed Saturn. The Saturn-Pluto conjunction that opened the Cold War in 1947–48 now reached its climactic opposition. America faced the limits and delusions of its foreign policy (Uranus-Pluto over delusive Neptune in Virgo in the U.S. Ninth House), and the fact that Johnson had Sun conjunct Mars in Virgo in his own horoscope made him the personification of these delusions. America was "standing up to aggressors" (the Munich Doctrine), as it had done in Korea, and in Berlin (twice), but had failed to do in Czechoslovakia (twice), all under Mars in Virgo— but as every informed student of the Vietnam War knows, it was not, as claimed, an invasion of the South by the North. South Vietnam had been created by the U.S. from part

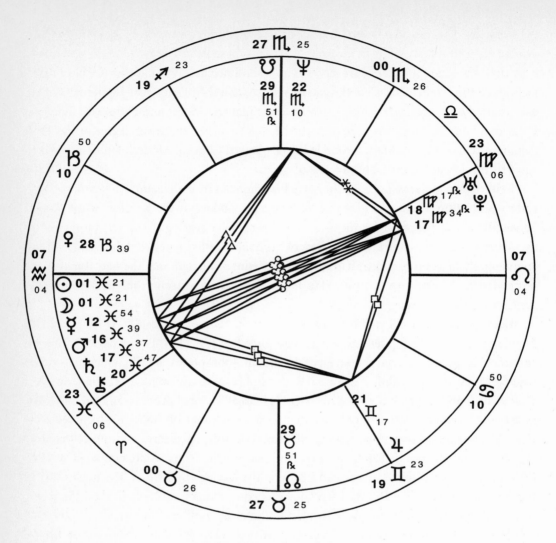

Stillness of Spirit (S.O.S.)

The "planetary pile-up" of Mercury-Mars-Saturn-Chiron opposite Uranus-Pluto at 17° Pisces-Virgo on February 20–24, 1966. This is the chart for the New Moon on February 20. Saturn in Pisces (stillness of spirit) became the key indicator of our times. The Industrial Machine that took off after the previous "pile-up" at Aries-Taurus in 1851 now started to grind to a halt. Neptune stationary at Midheaven represents the spiritual, psychedelic revolution in America. A series of revolutions and coups shook Africa at this time. Chart data: February 20, 1966, 10:49 A.M. GMT, Washington, D.C., 38N54, 77W02.

of the old French colony to forestall a communist victory in national elections. After the Americans installed Diem, a brutal dictator, to run South Vietnam in 1956 (Saturn square Pluto), the local *Viet Cong* rose against him. Supported by the North, these new enemies were nationalists who wanted to do what America itself once did—expel colonial rulers from their country.

Opposition to the war in Vietnam gave the New Left its greatest cause. It began immediately, as Mars moved over the revolutionary Uranus-Pluto conjunction in March 1965, with giant "teach-ins" at leading universities. Unfortunately, LBJ failed the class, and got even by insulting the teachers. Great marches followed, including a huge rally at Oakland's army base in October.

One of the marchers, Ken Kesey, had a different idea. "What if they gave a war and nobody came?" he asked. He and Timothy Leary believed the way to stop the war was to create a different consciousness and way of living. This idea resonated with the nonconformist "counter-culture" that had been growing since 1964, when catalytic figures like the Beatles and singer-poet Bob Dylan swept the younger generation away with their sensational music and irreverent personalities.

The psychedelic chemical LSD (or "acid") "revealed the soul," magnified the senses, and dissolved the ego—with sometimes dangerous results. Kesey, author of *One Flew Over the Cuckoo's Nest*, tried it while working at an army mental hospital. He decided to re-create the LSD experience for the multitudes with swirling light shows, day-glow paints, strobe lights, and electronic music by the Grateful Dead and others, calling it the "Acid Test." Optional acid was available too. In San Francisco in January 1966 he put on the biggest show of all, the Trips Festival, advertised as "the Acid Test without the Acid." It brought all the "trippers" and "acid heads" out of the woodwork, and soon they congealed as the "hippies" in the Haight-Ashbury district where they lived the "New Life" in an alternative community based on peace and love. A new Renaissance was born, with beads, body paint, long, natural hair styles, ecstatic dancing, vibrant clothing, and dynamic, liquid, pulsating energy. Gentle, electric mind-music called us to a flowery paisley world full of people exploring their inner selves and creating elaborate, "trippy" posters and mandalas. So much for the rat race, for a while anyhow!

The hippies did not have a program, except perhaps as much as possible to be open and share with each other and try to live without money. Their "revolution" was a quest for the spirituality missing in our materialistic wasteland, without which we would go on fighting wars and destroying ourselves. They rebelled against the long-prevailing compulsion to "succeed" and dominate the external world, preferring to "do their own thing" and follow Timothy Leary's advice to "turn on" (awaken consciousness, usually with psychedelics), "tune in" (become aware of what's happening) and "drop out" (quit the rat race and join the counter-culture).

1966 was a pivotal moment, but this call from the Spirit was felt at the same time by many others who weren't necessarily "acid heads." It was a moment of discovery in science too, leading toward the New Paradigm (the secret life of plants, the Bell Theorem, the background hum of the universe, etc.). Uranus' conjunction with Pluto in 1966 was a new signpost in the sky, awakening us to our climb, just as the 1850 conjunction had announced our descent. A New Consciousness to take us beyond war was dawning, and the fundamental issues were being defined that we still grapple with today. The ascent quickened in the

1960s, as the peak of the beckoning New Age could be seen wrapped in radiant clouds above. Although our culture has not yet reached the creative heights of past "peak experiences," our increasingly suspicious attitude toward materialism, war, and planet-plundering "progress" are evidence that we have been ascending. In time, the cultural explosion now happening in visionary art and music will be great enough to gain the recognition that it deserves. Since the outer planets have returned to high signs, the potential for a great new Renaissance is there. We need only to seize it.

The planets clumped together and focused on Washington, D.C.[16] and San Francisco[17] on February 20–24, 1966, in another tight, enormous "pile-up," like the "cosmic trigger." of 1851. If the predominant theme of the years after 1851 was "matter-in-motion," then the theme of the post-modern years after 1966 is the reverse, or "stillness of spirit." Uranus and Pluto at 17° Virgo were exactly opposed by Mars, Mercury, and Saturn (stillness) at 17° Pisces (of spirit). Since 1966, our industrial wheels have been falling still, as we heed the S.O.S. within our hearts, the message that material comforts won't fulfill us in a spiritually bankrupt and blighted society. If people can't get high in their daily lives, they will find another way. Escalating drug use since 1966 has proven that. The new danger is our own cynicism, used as the excuse to escape reality (Saturn in Pisces), including our political and social responsibilities. Since Vietnam the "credibility gap" (Pisces) has grown so much that people no longer trust their institutions or leaders (Saturn). The hope is that (through stillness of spirit) people can find the inner peace they need to create a beautiful world. The boom in holistic and human potential techniques (now called "New Age") has recruited many adult-style hippies who believe in changing themselves to change the world.

Another remarkable solar eclipse followed on November 12 that summed up all the configurations of the '60s. All the planets formed into the approximate shape of the famous peace symbol—the only time this ever happened. Venus and Neptune aligned with the eclipse in Scorpio ("peace, love and flower power," or "sex, drugs and rock'n'roll"),[18] and the ubiquitous Mars in Virgo joined the revolutionary conjunction (protest, violence). Opposing it was Saturn in Pisces, together with Chiron "the wounded healer," as society confronted all its ills and illusions. Saturn in collective, idealistic Pisces had been a powerful dissolving

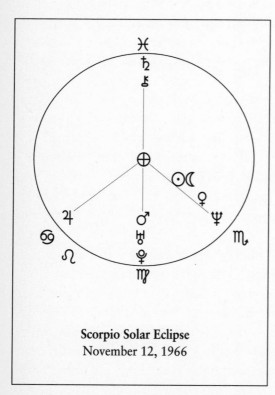

Scorpio Solar Eclipse
November 12, 1966

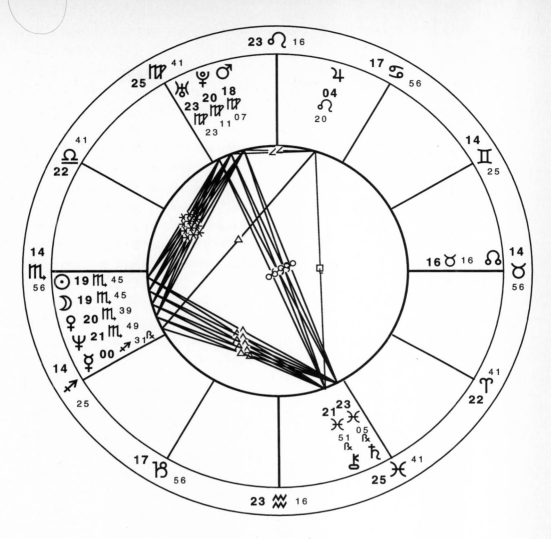

The Cosmic Peace Symbol

This chart for the total solar eclipse on November 12, 1966, is the vivid symbol of the following two years, and the "horoscope" of the flower child generation. Here all the planets (with Jupiter stationary-retrograde and just slightly out of orb) form themselves into the famous pattern of the peace symbol for the only time ever. The peace symbol is thus more than just an anti-war emblem; it's the signature of destiny. This was the chart that first inspired my research for this book. I later discovered that my own progressed Moon had been within one-half degree of the eclipse at the moment it happened. Chart data: November 12, 1966, 02:27 GMT, San Francisco, CA, 37N47, 122W25.

agent of society before: in 1789 (Fall of the Bastille), 1819 (worker and student movements), 1848 (revolutions), 1877 (violent strikes), 1905–06 (revolution in Russia), and 1936 (great worker uprisings in U.S. and France). Now it represented the artificial socio-cultural walls dissolving between us, as people "dropped out" to escape the "rat race" and tried to stop (Saturn) the war Vietnam (opposite Mars in military sign Virgo).

Two months after the cosmic peace symbol, in January 1967, the tribes gathered in San Francisco for the first "be-in" (or "love-in"); others followed, culminating in the Woodstock Festival in 1969 (Jupiter-Uranus in idealistic Libra). Once again, it seemed the "noble savages" had returned to the world. As Neptune returned to Scorpio, the Romantic Movement returned too. The liberating energy of the '60s has released us from the formal, stiff, unnatural manners of the past and allowed us to be ourselves.

In March 1967, Saturn entered Aries, and the more activist aspects in the 1966 "peace symbol" eclipse chart began to express themselves. For the first time ever, huge masses of Americans (led by Dr. King) marched to oppose a foreign war. But the war only got worse, and in June more wars broke out in the Middle East (Six-Day War) and Africa (Biafra), as stationary Mars opposed Saturn. Uranian lightning bolts also struck American cities, and the first one was called Watts (a section of Los Angeles). The riots there in August 1965, and the Mississippi March in June 1966 (Uranus-Pluto conjunction exact), inspired a militant turn in the Civil Rights Movement. "Negroes" became "blacks," and their new goal was "black power." This could also be achieved by peaceful means, and increasingly was. But agitators like H. Rap Brown used the slogan to incite more riots, which they called "the Black Revolution." "We built this country up," cried Brown, "and now we're gonna burn it down." Riots in Newark, Detroit, and elsewhere in July 1967 left dozens dead and thousands homeless.

The Revolution was approaching its climax. It went international, as campus revolts spread from the London School of Economics in November 1966 to France, Italy, Germany, Spain, Mexico, and behind the Iron Curtain in Poland and Czechoslovakia by 1968. There students spearheaded the "Prague Spring," as for the first time a Communist regime moved toward civil liberties and democracy. The Soviets still could not permit this in their own "buffer zone," though; they sent in the tanks in August. In May 1968, the French rose again, as student and worker strikes shut down the whole nation. David Caute called it "the greatest insurrection ever seen in a capitalist democracy in peacetime."[19] Such a startling event could only have happened during a revolutionary Uranus-Pluto line-up (Mars also opposed Neptune). The New Left rebels made not only such traditional demands as higher wages, but railed against consumerism and bureaucracy, and promoted "spontaneous action." De Gaulle tried proposing his own reforms, but the French were still dissatisfied, and voted down his reforms a year later, after which he resigned. Mars was then stationary and exactly squaring the new "trigger degrees" (17° Virgo-Pisces).

In spring 1968, it seemed like the world was awakening to a great liberation. In America, events boiled over after the North Vietnamese and Viet Cong mounted the huge Tet Offensive on January 30, just as Mars returned exactly to 17° Pisces for the first time since the new "pile-up." At the same time, students mounted a Democratic primary election campaign challenge to Johnson. These events helped convince LBJ to announce his resignation on March 31. The peace movement's greatest victory, it happened just three days after a solar eclipse on LBJ's natal Saturn, during his Saturn return!

Tragedy followed victory only days later. The charts in March 1968 led astrologers to predict a "full-scale insurrection." On April 4, an assassin shot Martin Luther King, the Movement's greatest prophet. It was a blow from which it has not fully recovered. the great civil rights leader. In an emotional speech given the night before he died, King shared a vision which God had given him. "He has allowed me to go up to the Mountain. I've looked over, and I've SEEN the promised land. I may not get there with you, but I want you to know tonight that we as a people will get to the promised land." The murder of the prophet of peace provoked riots in D.C., Chicago, and other cities in the largest insurrection in American history. A huge chain of campus revolts in the U.S. erupted too, starting at Columbia and accelerated around the world. In June JFK's brother Robert, who had jumped into the primary race to challenge Johnson, was also killed. After this, all hopes for an American liberation were dimmed.

Just like in 1848, the revolutions were failing. Even though the voters preferred peace candidates, Johnson's Vice President Hubert Humphrey was nominated at the Democratic Convention in Chicago in August. This betrayal provoked the loudest confrontation of the decade both inside the hall and out, as demonstrators were crushed by a "police riot." Fuming leftists called it "Czechago" (it was simultaneous with the repression of the Prague Spring). Virtually all the planets lined up in Virgo with Uranus and Pluto that month, and repressive Saturn in angry Aries became the most glaringly powerful singleton ever seen. Patriotic polarities were exploding that election season, as the violent planetary oppositions in the Cosmic Peace Symbol were played out. Those who criticized their country's misguided war policies were told to "love it or leave it" by the loyalists. Champions of this new "backlash" arose too. Running for president as an "American Independent," Gov. George Wallace taunted the demonstrators in his "Stand Up for America" campaign, warning that "any demonstrator who lies down in front of my car, it'll be the last car he ever lies down in front of!" Threatening to "throw the briefcases of all the Washington bureaucrats into the Potomac River," he was the first prophet of the reaction against "big government" which today remains more powerful than the new revolutionary movement. But an even more talented reactionary demagogue had already appeared on the scene: former actor Ronald Reagan, who had been elected Governor of California the same week as the "cosmic peace symbol."

QUIETER TIMES: THE HANGOVER

The beneficiary of all this turmoil was Ike's former Vice President Richard Nixon, who defeated Reagan, Wallace, and Humphrey in the presidential race by saying he had a secret "plan to end the war," and by appealing to what he called "the silent majority" by promising them fewer riots and demonstrations. The latter proved easier than the former, as protests continued while the war dragged on. But though things were quieting down in 1969, our vision was still expanding. We not only climbed the mountain, we flew high into space to get a Moon's eye view. On the day the first men walked on the Moon on July 20, 1969, Jupiter and Uranus were exactly in conjunction and the Earth stood high at Midheaven right over their heads. Seen from space she was "Spaceship Earth," the small, precious home without borders that we all share. The ecology movement bloomed simultaneously, climaxing on April 22, 1970, with the first Earth Day, the largest demonstration of any kind in world history. Singleton Saturn had moved into earth sign Taurus in 1969, and aligned with the Sun on Earth Day. Mars also opposed Neptune (mass action by the people).

The climax of the '60s, and a change of direction, was at hand as Jupiter opposed Saturn in 1970–71. Only days after Earth Day, President Nixon secretly sent troops from Vietnam into Cambodia, igniting yet another costly war. that still rages today. With Mars still opposing Neptune, the biggest protests yet convulsed the nation. U.S. troops stayed in Cambodia for months anyway, and in early May, student protesters were killed at Kent State and Jackson State, as the war was being "brought home." The youthful "new revolutionaries" were generally committed to non-violence, and had no more stomach for bloodshed at home than for the war abroad. Neptune entering Sagittarius in 1970 reminds us of the first great "disillusion" in the 1800s; by fall the radicals of the 1960s were disillusioned too. The radiant clouds began to darken, and the glowing vision now seemed like another deception. Even John Lennon, whose group the Beatles had broken up in 1970, confessed in one of his songs that the dream was over. Another British rock group, The Who, were singing about how they wouldn't be fooled again by the new revolution. In 1972, American songwriter Don McLean also captured the mood of the times by singing about the end of the "American Pie" and Chevies going over levies on the day the music died. The "trip of dreams" (and the Uranus-Pluto conjunction) was over; now the hangover began.

Of course, you had the literal hangovers among those burned out by counter-cultural excesses, including famous rock stars who died of drug overdoses in 1970–71 (Janis Joplin, Jimi Hendrix, Jim Morrison). An economic hangover also began in 1970, as a recession brought home the feeling that we had spent beyond our means since World War II and that the "American Pie" was diminishing. It marked the onset of decline in the industrial system which the hippies and environmentalists had criticized, and in 1972 some economists in Rome confirmed their opinion by pronouncing the "limits to growth." The great historic rebellion against technology took off—and the SST didn't. In the mid-'70s, this noisy, monstrous airplane was barred from U.S. cities. Nuclear power plants were targeted next, and all new ones were stopped. The 1970 recession also featured the first layoffs in the defense industry, and by mid-decade the first U.S. military cutbacks since World War II were made. The MAD arms race continued, but its growth was limited.

Uranus going into harmonious Libra in 1969, and Pluto in 1971, helped quiet things down; it also improved the diplomatic climate. President Nixon, the former red-baiter, took advantage by arranging a détente with Communist China and the Soviet Union in 1971–72. The same diplomatic Jupiter-Neptune conjunction that brought the UN returned too. Nixon finally achieved what he called "peace with honor" in Vietnam in January 1973, while Mars joined Neptune in diplomatic Sagittarius. LBJ died the same day. Two years later, the Vietnamese ignored this treaty and reunited their country. They celebrated their new independence on the 200th anniversary of the decision by their American enemies to declare independence (July 2, 1976). Saturn exactly squared Uranus that day (they were opposed when the war began in 1965).

The revolutions were also quieter in the '70s. Under Uranus and Pluto in Libra, a sign ruled by feminine planet Venus, the feminist movement founded in 1966 advanced, stimulated by the abortion rights decision in January 1973. Students mounted another election challenge in 1972, avenging their defeat four years ago by capturing the Democratic Party and nominating peace candidate George McGovern on July 10. But one shouldn't be nominated for president on the very day of a solar eclipse, especially if it's in your own sign (Cancer) and squaring unpredictable, shocking, electric Uranus! Two weeks later, his vice presidential nominee revealed that he had once received electric shock therapy. McGovern dropped him, but this only offended people, and he lost to Nixon by a landslide in November.

Nixon was sealing his own fate, however. Saturn in Gemini opposing Neptune in Sagittarius in 1971–72 portended the revelation of dirty secrets by the press about the government.[20] The Pentagon Papers came out the week Saturn entered Gemini in June 1971, revealing the mistakes of the Vietnam War although Nixon tried to suppress them. After failing, he set up the "plumbers unit" to spy on his enemies. In June 1972, burglars were caught in the Democratic headquarters at the Watergate Hotel in Washington. In March, they began to talk, and Nixon was implicated in a coverup. After another total eclipse in June 1973, it was revealed that all of Nixon's conversations had been recorded. The Supreme Court demanded that he turn the tapes over to Congress. The truth came out that he ordered the Watergate coverup from the start, and he was forced to resign August 9, 1974. Six weeks before, another total solar eclipse fell exactly over Nixon's Pluto in the Tenth House, symbol of his ruthless quest for power. Astrologer Dane Rudhyar had predicted the scandal, and I foresaw the timing of these events.

"I am not a crook," the new Crookback Dick explained, 493 years (one Neptune-Pluto cycle) after the original (King Richard III). In fact, he had cheated in his race with McGovern, not only through burglary but with false news leaks, forgeries, wiretaps, and illegal campaign contributions. Nixon's compulsive lying caused the credibility gap opened under Saturn in Pisces in 1966 to grow into a gaping canyon—another challenge of transition which we still haven't crossed. Singleton Jupiter in disillusioned Pisces in 1974–75, square Neptune in Sagittarius, magnified the great wave of cynicism (and more scandals) that swept across the land. It also represented a new wave of spiritual awakenings, though, and the Human Potential movement was popularized at this time along with yoga and other Eastern disciplines.

Although the people were quieter and more cynical in the '70s, big changes continued. As Saturn exactly squared Pluto, the Arabs and Israelis went to war again on Yom Kippur (October 6, 1973). The next month, as Mars turned stationary-direct in Aries (as in December 1941), the West suffered the equivalent of an economic Pearl Harbor with the Arab oil embargo. During a solar eclipse on December 24, the price of oil was doubled, and a depression ensued. Mars was in the old "trigger degree" of 0° Taurus that day, but now the oil-based, matter-in-motion economy suffered a serious blow.

In 1974–75, Neptune was back in the sign of Spain (Sagittarius), as it was during the revolt against Napoleon, and Uranus also returned to Scorpio. The old dictators of Spain and Portugal now died, and these nations finally entered the modern world of democracy. Scorpio is a turbulent sign, and Uranus (as we saw) was squaring Saturn. So major violence erupted in the mid-'70s, such as the civil war in Lebanon and the overthrow of the government of Cyprus, followed by a Turkish invasion and occupation. Saudi King Faisal was assassinated, and riots against the state-sponsored racism known as apartheid swept South Africa in August 1976, as Mars returned to Virgo.

President Jimmy Carter assumed office in 1977, the year Chiron was discovered, and indeed he was something of a "wounded healer." He was the first president to understand the limits to growth and the need to conserve energy. He also applied his healing powers to foreign policy, where he had more success. The U.S. often goes to war when Jupiter returns to Gemini and Cancer. This time, when Jupiter reached its degree in the U.S. horoscope (6° Cancer) and turned stationary there in October 1977, Egyptian President Sadat went to visit Israel at Carter's encouragement; the Camp David accords followed. The U.S. also made a treaty with Panama in which it agreed to turn over control of the Panama Canal to them.

Carter got caught up in the Neptunian currents of his time, however. Neptune in religious Sagittarius encouraged a religious revival, including "Jesus freaks" in America in 1971 and Moslem fundamentalism soon after. The Ayatollah Khomeini led a successful Islamic revolution in Iran in 1978 against the Shah, a tyrant whom the American CIA had installed in 1953. Saturn had conjoined Neptune then; now they reached their closing (or waning) square. Along with Saturn in Pisces in the 1966 "pile-up," Saturn square Neptune in the late '70s meant increasing religious influence in politics. Besides Iran, this was seen in Central America in the movement called "liberation theology," in which the Bible was used to support the goals of social justice and to challenge the U.S.-backed power of rich landlords.

All this meant trouble for America. Liberation Theology inspired socialist revolutions in Nicaragua and El Salvador, and soon the U.S. was involved in Central America, supporting the military authorities and their murderous "death squads." On November 3, 1979, as Saturn crossed the U.S. Neptune in the Ninth House (as it had before the Korean War), Iranian militants took revenge against America by seizing its embassy and taking sixty-five Americans hostage—with Khomeini's full approval. They burned American flags, while angry Americans complained loudly about being "pushed around." The Iranian Crisis caused another oil shortage, and prices skyrocketed, causing severe inflation. In December 1979, as Mars turned stationary in Virgo for the first time since Vietnam, the Soviet Union embarked on its own foolish martial adventure in Afghanistan. The communists seemed to be advancing again, just like during the red scares of thirty and sixty years before.

Carter, it seemed, could do nothing except complain about the strange "malaise" that was gripping the country. He was right, of course; Americans were cynical, nervous, and apathetic in the '70s. After all, Uranus had returned to its place in the 1890s, the previous such "age of malaise." Americans were annoyed with the truth; they wanted to hear cheerier

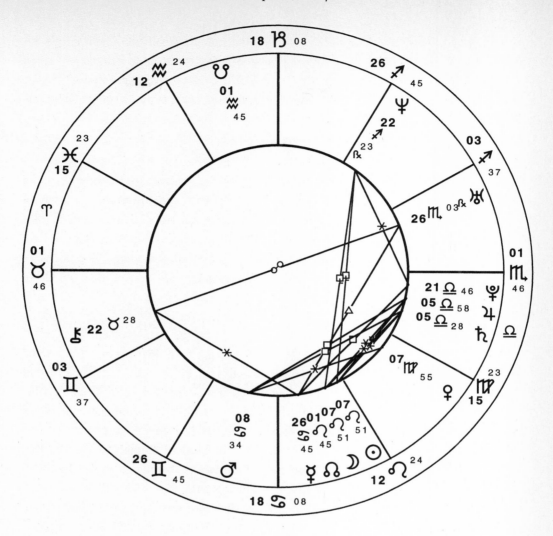

1981 Solar Eclipse

This "umbral" (not quite total) eclipse happened days after Jupiter's conjunction to Saturn on July 24, 1981. It represents the 1980s, the "decade of greed." Reaganomics was passed by Congress on July 29. The conjunction in Libra represents the diplomatic breakthroughs of the era, while Mars in Cancer squared to it shows the huge defense build-up of 1981 and the preoccupation with "family values" in these times. The conjunction in the 6th house of health (plus Venus in Virgo) shows the AIDS epidemic, while the exact Mercury-Uranus trine shows the easy advances in computer media in the 1980s. Neptune in the 8th house, sesqui-square the eclipse, reveals financial delusions. Chart data: July 31, 1981, 03:52 A.M. GMT, Washington, D.C., 38N54, 77W02.

thoughts. They wanted a new leading man, someone who talked less like Woody Allen or Dustin Hoffman (confused and uncertain), and more like Sylvester Stallone (creator of the macho characters "Rocky" and "Rambo"); someone who could make the nation feel strong again (even though it really wasn't). This was such a demanding role that only another actor could pull it off. Promising to bring back the good old days, Ronald Reagan was given the part and defeated Carter in November 1980. Other conservative rulers were elected at about this time too, such as Margaret Thatcher in Britain, and Helmut Kohl in West Germany; it was a worldwide trend.

TURNING BACK THE HOURGLASS

As the next Jupiter-Saturn conjunction arrived in 1980–81, the trip into tomorrow and its hangover ended, replaced by a retreat into yesterday. A fitting conclusion to an era whose dreams were repeatedly shot down was reached when former Beatle and peace activist John Lennon was killed on December 8, 1980. The delusional assassin said he was trying to save youth from going "over the cliff" into the living death of adulthood, claiming their leader Lennon had "sold out to commercial interests." But he killed the one person who could have kept our psychedelic, youthful dreams alive. It was truly the day the music died. Shocked and demoralized, the Beatle generation drove their Chevys off the levy, sold out their ideals to commerce, and fell under the enchanting spell of their former enemy—Ronald Reagan.

The hostages in Iran were released on the very day Reagan was inaugurated. (Questions were later raised about clandestine arms sales to Iran that began soon afterward.) Mars stood at 17° Aquarius, its exact position when the Shah was deposed—and Reagan's solar degree. Mars had also been in that degree when the Pentagon Papers came out, and when Richard Nixon decided to tape his White House conversations. Mars had turned stationary-retrograde in that degree in the progressed Chart of Modern Humanity. The "Sabian Symbol" for that degree reads, "a man whose secret motives are being publicly unmasked." Reagan would find himself in the same spotlight as his predecessor.

During their final conjunction on July 24, one week before a partial solar eclipse, Jupiter and Saturn were squared by Mars in Cancer. Symbol of the "military-industrial complex" in 1946 and 1961, now Mars in Cancer represented the biggest military expansion yet (Mars was also conjunct expansive Jupiter in the U.S. chart). The arms race now had new rules: first side to go broke loses. Cancer is the sign of the family as well as defense, and in the '80s "family values" became the new panacea for politicians who preferred not to deal with real problems. Meanwhile, monogamy made a quick comeback, because in 1981 Acquired Immune Deficiency Syndrome (AIDS) was identified. Transmitted through exchange of "precious bodily fluids," it put a real damper on sexual "deviance," and romance in general. The eighties became the AIDies, symbolized by the conjunction's place in the Sixth House of health during the eclipse in Washington on July 31, 1981.

Just two days before this eclipse, Congress passed "Reaganomics," which also made the 1980s the "decade of greed." This came exactly one cycle of Uranus after McKinley, the first conservative Republican president, instituted Wall Street-friendly policies in 1897, promising they would bring a "full dinner pail" for all the people. Spearheaded by a new wave of "tax revolts" (rebel Uranus in Scorpio, sign of taxes), the "supply-side" theory of 1981 promised that if taxes and regulations were removed from business, it would prosper, and so would we. Reagan hoped to increase military spending, reduce taxes on the rich and still balance the budget with revenue from the resulting prosperity. Comedian Rich Little said this would require keeping two sets of books. Reagan's primary election challenger (and later Vice President) George Bush called it "voodoo economics." The critics were right: the promised "prosperity" came too late, and the national debt tripled. This was quite convenient for the conservative program, though, because by bankrupting the nation it would make the Great Society social programs unaffordable.

While the New Deal had created an "urn society" where most people were in the middle class, "greed-onomics" since 1981 has created an "hourglass society" increasingly divided between rich and poor. Since "government is the problem," programs to help people are not necessary. Mothers with unsupported dependent children are called "welfare cheats" and get their benefits cut. While executive salaries soared, the minimum wage stayed flat and unions were busted—starting with the striking air traffic controllers whom Reagan fired right after the 1981 eclipse. Thatcher did the same with her coal miners in 1984. Housing subsidies were cut as home prices skyrocketed; this left millions homeless, and millions more unable to afford a home. The "prosperity" of the '80s was an illusion, because most families required two incomes, and people had to work longer hours to meet their obligations—but keeping people working all the time was a good way to stop them from engaging in all those strange, anti-materialistic social experiments from the '60s, which the conservatives hated.

Corporations took huge tax deductions for interest on their "junk bonds," which financed corporate mergers with risky debts (this was the '80s version of borrowing on margin). To pay them, they closed factories, fired their employees, and replaced them with cheap foreign labor—a strategy made easier by "free trade" and the era's increasingly global economy (in the '90s this became known as "downsizing"). Many of these companies eventually went broke, as did the banks that financed them (thanks to the deregulation of the banking industry). Then the taxpayer was handed the bill. Gone were the days of "welfare capitalism," when workers stayed with a company that looked after them; now everyone was on their own. The "corporate raiders" walked away with their pockets full, though.

Reagan and Thatcher kept their people happy with foreign distractions. As stationary Mars, Saturn, and Pluto lined up in Libra in 1982, Thatcher "glorified the British Empire" by reconquering from Argentina a small group of islands populated by a few sheep herders (the Falklands). Reagan also had to smooth over a botched attempt to protect Americans in Beirut, where 241 U.S. Marines were killed on October 23, 1983. Two days later, American soldiers invaded the tiny Caribbean island of Grenada, recently taken over by Marxists. Reagan successfully "stood up to Communist aggressors" one last time, as Mars (with Venus) returned to 17° Virgo (the 1966 "trigger degree") and squared Jupiter and Uranus. He also "rescued" American nursing students (Virgo: health).

Grenada simply wasn't a big enough enemy to feel good about pouncing on; only the Soviet Union would do. The hit science-fiction movie "Star Wars" gave the actor-president his cue. After dubbing the Soviets the "evil empire," the California cowboy presented his "Star Wars" missile defense program in spring 1983 (Jupiter-Uranus in airborne Sagittarius). He threatened them with Pershing missiles in Europe, as Mars opposed Saturn-Pluto. This made America's allies nervous: 400,000 protested in Germany. Saturn-Pluto and Jupiter-Uranus in 1983 were the same conjunctions that happened in 1914, when World War I exploded. Now we seemed on the brink again, and tensions led the "evil empire" to strike back by shooting down a South Korean airliner on September 1, killing 269 Koreans and Americans. After this disaster, both sides began to back off from the road to MAD.

Reagan had other enemies he could stand up to, though. Terrorists from Palestine had struck the Olympic Games in Munich in September 1972 and killed eleven Jewish athletes as Mars was at 15° Virgo. In 1984, now supported by Iran, they started taking American hostages in Beirut. On June 14, 1985, as Jupiter (flight) stood stationary in 17° Aquarius, they hijacked an airliner. On October 7, they commandeered an ocean liner, the *Achille Lauro*, as Mars reached 17° Virgo again, killing an American. Three days later, Colonel Oliver North, whose birthday is October 7, intercepted the plane carrying the hijackers and diverted it to Italy where they could stand trial. On April 5, 1986, U.S. soldiers were killed by a terrorist bomb in Berlin. Reagan blamed Libya's leader Moamar Qaddafi, and sent planes to bomb Libya on April 14, just five days after a solar eclipse. On that day, Mars and Neptune were exactly over Reagan's Mars and opposite America's Jupiter.

Reagan and North finally came up with a way to stick it to both of their enemies. They sold arms to Iran as ransom for the hostages, then used the proceeds to fund the Contras, who were fighting to overthrow the revolutionary socialist government in Nicaragua. The Contras were terrorists who murdered, burned villages, and attacked health clinics. In other words, Reagan and North, the self-proclaimed enemies of terrorists, had sold arms to terrorists and used the money to buy arms for other terrorists (though some was diverted to North's private estate). These decisions were made in secret, despite a Congressional ban on funding to the Contras.

On November 4, 1986, the truth came out, just as Mars reached 17° Aquarius—Reagan's "public unmasking" degree. Following Nixon's example, Reagan defended himself by lying (claiming that the arms were not sold as ransom for hostages, for example, when everyone knew they had been). His National Security Advisor John Poindexter took the rap at Senate hearings in 1987, so Reagan was not impeached. Other scandals in 1987–88 discredited junk bond traders, fundamentalist Christian preachers, and the Defense and Housing Departments of Reagan's own administration. More scandals hit his presidency than any other in history, but his Hollywood image superceded reality, and his popularity stayed high. A solar eclipse squared Neptune in March 1987, signifying this "year of scandals" as deceptive Neptune continued to oppose key planets in America's horoscope (Venus, Jupiter, Sun).

There were other terrors and errors in the air in the '80s (Uranus in airborne Sagittarius). On January 28, 1986, the space shuttle Challenger exploded after takeoff, killing seven astronauts. By coincidence the spacecraft Voyager II had flown by cataclysmic Uranus just two days before. On May 17, 1987, Iraqi missiles struck the U.S.S. Stark, killing thirty-seven. American sailors in the Persian Gulf, nervous over this incident, mistakenly shot down an Iranian airliner on July 3, 1988, as Saturn was conjunct Uranus, and was T-squared by Mercury (travel) and Mars (accidents). In revenge, Iranian/Libyan-sponsored terrorists blew up American flight Pan Am 103 over Lockerbie, Scotland in December 1988. Two months earlier, Mars had turned stationary in Aries—just like before Pearl Harbor. Other airborne errors in Bhopal, India, in 1984 and Chernobyl in the Soviet Union in 1986 helped to further discredit the chemical and nuclear industries.

A NEW ORDER UNFOLDS

Even while the old wars continued, a new global consciousness of peace was unfolding. Although Reagan credited his arms buildup for allowing him

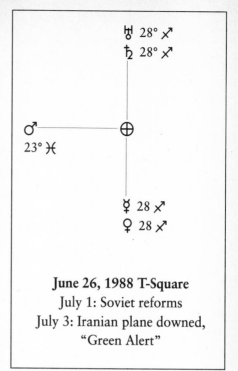

June 26, 1988 T-Square
July 1: Soviet reforms
July 3: Iranian plane downed, "Green Alert"

to seek peace with the Soviets, the nuclear freeze movement certainly pressured him. Another citizen group called Beyond War set up satellite "space bridges" between San Francisco and Moscow in the mid-1980s. When relations improved, ABC-TV adopted the technique without crediting Beyond War. (The Soviets continued to refer to it as a "space bridge," showing they remembered who it was that opened the way.)

In 1984–85, as Neptune entered Capricorn, Jupiter joined it in a conjunction that represents enthusiastic mass actions and peace breakthroughs. Horrible famines in Africa at this time inspired massive relief efforts, funded by huge benefit concerts and hit records like "We Are the World," performed together by dozens of stars. Similar events followed, such as "Hands Across America" and "Sport Aid." Millions of New Agers gathered on August 17, 1987, to celebrate the "Harmonic Convergence" (based on the Mayan Calendar), and to visualize world peace. Similar events began to be held each New Year's Eve. These events suggested that the New Consciousness might be dawning after all. Maybe we were climbing toward the peak again.

Coincidence or not, it was in the very month of the Harmonic Convergence that "peace began to break out" around the world. It could also have had something to do with the approaching conjunction of Uranus and Neptune. It began with agreements between Central American presidents and the U.S. in August 1987; the wars there ended a few years later. On September 4, the UN sent a delegation to try to stop the war raging between Iran and Iraq since 1980, and peace was achieved on 8/8/88. In 1985, new leadership in the Soviet Union under Mikhail Gorbachev began pulling back from Cold War battles. He and Reagan signed the INF Treaty, removing nuclear missiles from Europe on December 7, 1987. By 1991–92, the direct nuclear confrontation between the superpowers was over. Gorbachev also withdrew Russian troops from Afghanistan, Angola, and Southeast Asia in 1988.

Gorbachev decided his country no longer afford the Cold War, and his cumbersome bureaucracy had to be reformed. On December 16, 1986, as Mars joined Jupiter in 16° Pisces, he freed the leading Soviet dissident, Andre Sakarov. The following month he announced an official policy of *glasnost* (openness). The Prague Spring had come to Moscow in winter. *Perestroika*, or restructuring, began too, perhaps symbolized by Pluto in the "restructuring" sign Scorpio. On June 26, 1988, Saturn and Uranus, which had opposed each other when the Soviet Union was created, came into exact conjunction. On July 1, the Soviets decided to create an elected legislature and an independent presidency, taking a decisive step toward democracy.

In 1973 (in an earlier version of this book) I wrote that in 1989 "events would shift to a world stage stormed by mass movements of epic proportions." The Revolution of 1989 completed the Revolution of 1789, bringing democracy to humanity and allowing us to storm up the peak out of the Valley of Transition. The chain of events in the East began on May 22, 1988, when (as stationary Venus in Cancer opposed Saturn-Uranus) the Communists in Hungary elected a new liberal leader. In May–June 1989, millions of students and workers in China staged a mass-marathon sit-in in Tienanmen Square in Beijing and erected a miniature Statue of Liberty. It was the greatest demonstration of "people power" in history, as Mars opposed Neptune. They couldn't stop the tanks from the "People's Army," though, and a massacre ensued. One brave student showed their unbroken spirit by standing in front of a tank, a memorable image seen on world TV. (He was lucky perhaps that George Wallace wasn't driving the tank!)

Even as the Chinese democrats were crushed in Tienanmen Square in early June, the Communists were beaten in Polish elections. A new government led by the rebel party/labor union Solidarity took over in August. On May 2, the Hungarians took down the fence along the Austrian border, breaching the Iron Curtain. That day Mars entered Cancer, the sign it was in when Churchill defined it. When Jupiter reached Cancer in August, East Germans started flooding through the curtain's "hole." On October 7, as Mars T-squared Jupiter and Saturn-Neptune, huge demonstrations began throughout East Germany, forcing out the corrupt Communist leader by November.

The peak of planetary energy was now at hand. In September 1989, Pluto reached its perihelion, and a great feeling of recognition swept over us as Voyager II passed by misty, blue-green Neptune, the Planetary Ark of all

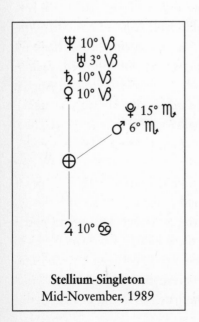

Ψ 10° ♑
♅ 3° ♑
♄ 10° ♑
♀ 10° ♑
⚳ 15° ♏
♂ 6° ♏
⊕
♃ 10° ♋

Stellium-Singleton
Mid-November, 1989

humanity, allowing us to see it close-up for the first time. In mid-November, Saturn joined Neptune exactly (with Uranus close by). Jupiter exactly opposed both Saturn and Neptune stood alone in a mammoth singleton.as the 1980s reached their climax. On November 9, young people scaled the Berlin Wall and forced the new government to dismantle it. It was a great moment for humanity—the barrier between the worlds had come down. The next year, the Russians withdrew their troops from Germany, and on October 3, 1990, the nation was reunited. On November 17, 1989, another "people power" revolution toppled the Communists in Czechoslovakia, ending fifty years of totalitarian rule. On Christmas day, the most violent upheaval deposed Ceaucescu, the brutal dictator of Romania.

The revolution continued through the first half of 1990. In January, Communists lost their hold on Bulgaria and Yugoslavia. In February, as three other planets clustered in Capricorn with Saturn-Uranus-Neptune, Communist Party rule ended in the Soviet Union itself. The movement spread to the Baltic nations, but Gorbachev tried to stop their attempt to break from the Union with oil sanctions. The "Gorbachev of South Africa," Frederik de Klerk, elected President in August 1989, freed black activist Nelson Mandela on February 11, 1990. Talks with the African National Congress began in May, and apartheid was gradually dismantled (despite horrible tribal violence). Mandela was elected President in May 1994 and held the new democracy together.

American politicians hailed the end of Soviet Communism in 1989–1990 as "victory in the Cold War," though it was the Soviets who had first realized it was leading both sides to bankruptcy. While democracy was new and liberating to Eastern nations, the switch to "free market" capitalism was a step backward in some ways, as old Communist elites became the new capitalist ones.

People also tend to forget that the West suffered its own revolutions as the Cold War ended. Many of the dictatorships that America had supported as "buffer states" against Communism were overthrown at the same time, or even earlier. It was American students who spearheaded the drive for sanctions against South Africa (passed over Reagan's veto in 1985) that forced the end of apartheid. In February 1986, "people power" helped topple U.S.-backed Filipino dictator Ferdinand Marcos. Haiti's dictator "Baby Doc" Duvalier was forced out the same month (Mars conjunct Saturn and Uranus). In June 1987, "people power" spread to South Korea, toppling the U.S.-backed government there as Mars opposed Neptune. This certainly helped inspire the Tienanmen Square uprising two years later under the same planetary aspect. In October 1988, the U.S.-installed dictator of Chile was ousted. The end of the Cold War was thus not an American victory, but the overthrow of Cold War oppression by both superpowers.

Demonstrations also began in June 1987 against dictator Manuel Noriega of Panama. Once on the CIA payroll, President Reagan and his successor George Bush now wanted to oust him for "drug trafficking." On Christmas 1989, simultaneously with the Romanian Revolution, Bush sent 25,000 troops to capture Noriega (they also killed hundreds of unarmed civilians in the effort). Jupiter was in 6° Cancer (its Declaration of Independence and

Monroe Doctrine degree), completing one cycle since our treaty with Panama had allowed us to keep troops there until 1999. It was also two Jupiter returns since Vietnam, four since World War II, and six since World War I. Certainly, its returns in 2001 and 2013 bear watching.

It seemed that the Second Revolution might be giving way to the Third. As depressing Saturn joined shocking Uranus in June 1988, a "green alert" was sounded by scientists warning that the "greenhouse effect" of pollution was causing "global warming." Serious droughts and fish kills that summer gave them credence, as did the Alaska oil spill, when Saturn joined oily Neptune in March of 1989. In 1990, Earth Day was revived, and nations agreed to halt production of chemicals that hurt the ozone layer. In June 1992, the largest conference of world leaders in history met for the "Earth Summit" in Rio De Janeiro. Saturn was stationary at 18° Aquarius, the "end of progress" degree.

On August 2, 1990, the green alert was muffled by the sounds of Iraq's invasion of Kuwait. The Democratic and Green Revolutions were put on the back burner while the industrial world worried about oil to run its front burners. Iraq and Kuwait controlled twenty percent of the world's oil, and Saddam seemed headed for Saudi Arabia, which would make it forty percent. Uncle Sam couldn't wait for sanctions against Iraq to work, so "coalition" forces rushed to Kuwait on January 16, 1991, two weeks after Mars in Taurus turned stationary, trine Saturn, and one day after a solar eclipse in 25° Capricorn (conjunct Saturn). Because the Soviet Union cooperated with this U.S.-led "UN Coalition," Bush hailed "Operation Desert Storm" as a triumph of the "New World Order." Mars in easy trine to Saturn made the war a "cakewalk." This same Mars-Saturn aspect also appeared in the charts of Bush, Hussein, America, Iraq, and the Chart of Modern Humanity, where Mars sits at 25° Capricorn. Mars in Taurus reminds us of the Yom Kippur war in 1973 that led to the first threat to the West's Middle East oil supplies. I predicted Bush's invasion in *Welcome to Planet Earth* (Libra 1990).

The New Consciousness beyond war was soon obscured by the glory of overwhelming military victory. Gung-ho citizens put yellow ribbons on their cars to "support the troops," ressponding to complaints by Vietnam veterans that they were looked down on by protestors in the '60s and '70s (which was not generally the case), and abandoned by the public and government after the war. Bush proclaimed that America had "kicked the Vietnam Syndrome," which had discouraged it from waging war, in spite of loud protests of "no blood for oil" beforehand. The president learned to wage war as forcefully and cruelly as possible in order to avoid a "long, limited war," and to stifle press coverage to lessen public opposition (following his mentor Reagan's example in Grenada).

The real "syndrome" that afflicts us the most continued, however. In *Legacy* Michael Wood pointed out that in the Gulf War, the West returned to the very place where its own civilization began—the once-thriving cities of Sumeria that had turned their land to desert through their own abuse of the Earth and its resources. Now it was fighting to defend an oil addiction which, if not broken, would eventually make the whole world look like the deserts of Sumeria.

Though Bush got a huge, temporary popularity boost from the war, the Jupiter-Saturn opposition of the time meant a change of direction was due. The war and the crisis preceding it triggered a severe recession, as Jupiter and Saturn returned to the same signs they inhabited in 1931. In late 1991, Bush's approval rating plummeted as the public grew angry over the economy. Race riots erupted in Los Angeles the following April, which were worse than the ones in 1965. Bush was not re-elected.

The currents of change that finally reached America in 1992 had already speeded up again elsewhere, as Uranus and Neptune approached their conjunction in 1993. In August 1991, after a solar eclipse in July, old Soviets ousted Gorbachev in a coup, but this sparked a revolution that led to the breakup of the Soviet Union. Mars returned to Virgo in August, its sign at the Union's founding. In early October 1993, (Saturn square Pluto) new Russian President Boris Yeltsin defeated a violent takeover bid by old-liners and instituted a new democratic constitution with a strong presidency. Peace moved ahead again, especially in the Middle East. In September 1993, as Mars and Jupiter joined in peaceful Libra, Prime Minister Yitzhak Rabin of Israel and Palestinian leader Yassir Arafat committed to peace and mutual recognition in a dramatic ceremony on the White House lawn. Israeli withdrawal from occupied Palestine began in May 1994, despite terrorist attacks, and Israel made formal peace with Jordan in October. Peace efforts further accelerated after Rabin was assassinated in November 1995, as stationary Saturn returned to critical 17° Pisces.

In the first years of the New World Order, international wars were replaced by civil wars. Yugoslavia broke up in June 1991, setting off war. In April 1992 (Mars-Saturn square Pluto), a blood bath began in Bosnia—a karmic recurrence of the crisis that toppled the old European Civilization—bringing back Nazi-like "ethnic cleansing." The West felt as helpless to resist evil as in the 1930s, two Saturn cycles before. Another blood feud struck Rwanda in Central Africa in spring 1994, killing half a million. Civil wars racked the Caucasus region of the former Soviet Union, and a bid for secession by Chechnya in January 1995 (launched as Mars turned stationary in Virgo for the first time since Afghanistan), was forcibly suppressed by the Russians. Time will tell if this leads to a breakup of Russia itself.

The U.S.A. moved in a new direction under new Democratic president Bill Clinton in February 1993. Saturn's return to Aquarius, where it symbolized Teddy Roosevelt's Square Deal in 1903, his cousin Franklin's New Deal in 1933, and JFK's New Frontier in 1963, offered hope for new reforms. But Clinton's own wavering, combined with Republican opposition, stalled all but a few of them. He did get gun control, a new Service Corps, and more taxes on the rich to help balance the budget. World trade was liberalized, but new trade battles with Japan erupted in 1995, as I had predicted. On January 11, 1994, virtually all of the planets aligned with a New Moon in conservative Capricorn. It fell in the Sixth House in Washington, representing Clinton's massive effort to reform health care that year. It failed due to pressure by the health care insurance industry, , and served only to rally the "opposition to big government" led by talk radio host Rush Limbaugh, whose birthday is January 11. In November 1994 (right after a solar eclipse), Republicans took control of

Congress in a surprise victory, and genuine reform was over—at least for the moment. The New Moon of January 11, 1994, seemed to shake up the world in other ways: six days later, a huge earthquake struck Los Angeles, leading to the largest relief effort in U.S. history (Sixth House). On its anniversary in 1995, another quake killed 5,000 in Kyoto, Japan.

On New Year's Day 1994, the revolution I had predicted for Mexico broke out in Chiapas province. Democratic reforms and economic collapse followed. In today's new "era of peace," Mars stationary often signifies the start of warlike actions by terrorists instead of by armies. In February 1993 (Mars stationary in Cancer), terrorism came to America, as eleven people were killed by a bomb at the World Trade Center in New York. The same month, a government raid on a heavily armed cult in Waco, Texas, led to a two-month stalemate, ending in the deaths of the cultists, and the destruction of their compound on April 19. Two years later, Mars turned stationary again in Leo,[21] and on April 19, 1995, the Oklahoma City Federal Building was bombed (allegedly in retaliation for Waco), killing 169 in the worst terrorist incident ever on U.S. soil. The media focused attention on right-wing "militias" intent on starting another civil war and protecting their "right to bear arms," which was under "attack" by Clinton. The Uranus-Neptune conjunction of 1993 indicates that the events in Waco and Oklahoma City were probably the start of a great American conflict that will come to its climax thirty years later. Before now my prediction that the United States might break up in 2025 seemed incredible, but by 1995, the militias, combined with determined efforts in Congress to "downsize" the federal government and "return power to the states," suddenly made it seem more plausible.

RETREAT OR REBIRTH: TOWARD THE NEW MILLENNIUM

By the mid-1990s, humanity had made great strides up the Mountain. Born in 1892, the Modern Spirit reached a young maturity as Uranus joined Neptune in 1993. Now, the Spirit of the Earth was being reborn and a global culture was developing. With the Cold War behind us and much of the world free of outright tyranny, we had an unprecedented opportunity to enter the New Age of peace and to shift our attention to creative matters.

New clouds gathered in 1995, though, obstructing our view of the peak again. Although the Dutch and Germans were transforming their economy and lifestyle in accord with Green ideals, elsewhere the progressive tides were receding. There were signs of economic recovery in Russia, but the government was becoming more repressive because of a new crime wave. Republicans in the U.S. Congress under House Speaker Newt Gingrich were redeeming promises in their "Contract with America" with lightning speed in their "First 100 Days." It is interesting that they began on January 2, 1995, as Mars turned stationary in Virgo, just like the original "100 Days" under FDR. Their version of "reform" included such things as congressional term limits, a balnced budget amendment (both of which have so far failed), and the presidential line-item veto (which succeeded). Their other measures were better termed a "Contract on America," however, outdoing even Reagan with such things as making environmentalists pay the cost of pollution control, denying welfare payments to children of unwed mothers, ending health and safety regulations, making huge cuts in Medicare, ending support for the arts—and using the savings to increase military spending and cut taxes on the rich. It's difficult to see how a "New Age" or a spiritual rebirth can happen during this retreat to the hourglass society of the 1980s. Reversing this trend and re-electing Bill Clinton seems essential in 1996 (the year of this writing). Since Uranus will be in Aquarius, as in the days of Andrew Jackson and Woodrow Wilson, this seems likely to happen.

Saturn in Pisces in 1993–96 showed society's institutions stumbling and floundering. Presidents had to be both honest and clever to get through the period unscathed, especially in foreign policy. In July 1995, as Mars in Virgo opposed stationary Saturn, a massacre in Srebrenica by the Serbs in Bosnia caused the U.S. and its allies to take action. In November, just as Saturn stood stationary in that critical seventeenth degree of Pisces (Vietnam, Tet, etc.), President Clinton committed American troops to help its European NATO allies enforce a fragile peace and transition to a coalition government there. This is an entanglement that could hardly be messier, and worse due to our early inaction. Lookm for Bosnia to come apart again in 1998–99.

Saturn in this water sign seemed to reveal itself quite literally, as floods repeatedly devastated the American Midwest, California, Europe, and other places. Such obvious signs of climate change didn't seem concerned people; they were more interested in stopping crime and immigration than saving the planet. Sensational crime stories (Pisces) disturbed and distracted the people. But in November, as Saturn stood stationary in 17° Pisces, the cosmic "stillness of spirit" trigger degree, a report by noted scientists confirmed that global warming was a fact, and that it was caused by human pollution.

As Uranus and then Neptune reach their rendezvous with America's natal Pluto in the late 1990s, economic change will be center stage. The U.S. banking and financial systems may be due for drastic change. Many corporate giants will not recover from their problems in the early '90s, and their "downsizing" will snowball toward virtual collapse. Resulting unemployment could remind people that if we are to have an intelligent, qualified work force, we can't afford to continue making college unaffordable. Young people may rally together over this issue from 1996 on. Already the spirit of liberation and expanded consciousness was rising again (Beatles revival; French worker-student strike) as Saturn returned to Pisces (as in the 1960s).

A new phase opened when Pluto entered Sagittarius on November 10, 1995, which will last through 2008. In past times, Pluto here has meant the awakening of "philosophy." It has brought vibrant expansion of the human spirit after the transformational phase under Scorpio, and there is every reason to expect this will happen again. The chart for the moment Pluto entered Sagittarius is especially promising. Harmonious Venus, passionate Mars, and expansive Jupiter were tightly linked in conjunction—and in Sagittarius to boot. All three closely squared the stationary Saturn in Pisces. This indicates that an impatient and hopeful humanity will be challenging the rotten halls of power and authority

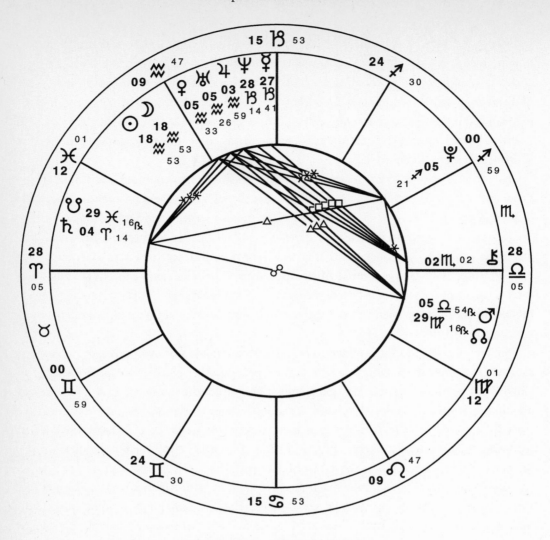

Renaissance Take-off?

This New Moon chart for February 1997 shows the powerful creative forces that we can tap into during this year. The same positions are repeated in the chart for U.S. president's Oath of Office at Noon on January 20, 1997, and in the Spring Equinox chart on March 20. In all three charts the brilliant, liberating conjunction of Jupiter-Uranus-Neptune appears on the Midheaven. In February, Mars turns stationary-retrograde at 6° Libra (President Clinton's Ascendant-Mars-Neptune). It is a great opportunity for presidential action. In April, Mars turns stationary-direct at the key degree of 17° Virgo; look for major revolts or military actions! Chart data: February 7, 1997, 03:06 P.M. GMT, Washington, D.C., 38N54, 77W02.

again in the next decade—especially in the schools and churches. Even the Pope could find himself besieged in the years following 1995. The issues of Church and State will be at the forefront— not for the first time in human history! Some astrologers say Pluto in Sagittarius indicates that the power of religious fanatics will increase. More positively, it impels us all to re-examine the philosophies that govern our lives. As Saturn returned forcefully in 1995 to the degree it occupied in the "stillness of spirit" configuration of 1966, the call was truly sounded to fulfill the challenge given us in those critical times and bring the creative spirit back into our everyday lives and public institutions. Since Uranus also entered its home territory in Aquarius in 1996, a powerful signal has been given to humanity to plunge courageously into revolutionary innovation. Unfortunately, it also means an increased danger of catastrophe (as shown in the bombings in Israel in March 1996 and the uprising in September that disrupted peace negotiations with Palestine).

Under Uranus in Aquarius, spontaneous revolutionary movements or changes in government leadership could occur in the next seven years. Innovations in communications and travel technology will revolutionize the world, and we can make it Earth-friendly for the first time (electric cars, super-conductors, etc.). Events seemed already to be confirming this prediction; the first commercial electric car came on the market as Uranus entered Aquarius in January 1996. The monolithic corporate control of our media will become a big issue. The telecommunications law of February 1, 1996, was another advance signal of Aquarius at work, and was certain to put this matter in the spotlight in the next few years (Mercury was stationary in 19° Capricorn that day, the Uranus-Neptune conjunction degree).Meanwhile, in spring 1996, people demanded that economic power be shared; an idea almost taboo for the preceding fifteen years! Again, this was a prediction of mine that came true (much to my amazement) as firings at AT&T focused attention on how corporations are "downsizing" to boost their profits.

Humanity under Sagittarius/Aquarius will be looking hopefully toward the future as we reach the end of the Millennium; and since President Clinton will be running for re-election, his 1992 theme song "Don't Stop Thinking about Tomorrow" will ring even truer this time around. Optimistic, prophetic, religious Jupiter will be turning stationary at the turn of the Millennium in our progressed Horoscope of Modern Humanity.This and Neptune's entry into Aquarius in 1998 suggests that the cynical "sobriety" of the previous years under Capricorn will finally give way to a long-overdue new burst of idealism as the century ends. As Clinton returns to office in 1997, the energy of the 1990s crests. He can be its master instead of its victim, using it to institute further reforms. Hopes will reach a boiling point along with turmoil— expectation along with exasperation. The cosmic indications for his second term are much like those for his first, although they suggest it won't be as easy for him to compromise and maneuver from 1997 on. People won't settle for less than drastic change, since Uranus is strongly accented in the charts of this period.

The significant charts of early 1997 are all strikingly similar—and similarly striking! If there is any time at which we can jump into the New Age and rise to the peak experience that will regenerate humanity, this is it! Exaltation combined with an impatience for action mark the extraordinary planetary configurations of January and February of 1997. Jupiter aligned with Uranus and Neptune may be as powerfully catalytic as Saturn's alignment with these two transcendental planets was in 1989. It's another celebration of liberty, and a demand for more, but this time liberty not only means toppling political authority

(Saturn), but a rebirth of both spirit and commerce (Jupiter). Southeast Asia may be an emerging scene of liberation.

The year 1997 may also see genuinely "New Age" values become larger than life in human affairs for the first time. It is a chance to rededicate ourselves to the true purposes of civilization and begin to create lasting monuments that represent our deepest shared experiences.[22] Many new renaissance projects can begin now, some with government support. We could see new foundations to support the arts, new religious movements, new communities, new "earthworks," new temples to God or the Goddess, new cathedrals of the spirit of global humanity. The Earth itself may come to be seen as one large temple in the years ahead. And as humanity recovers its vision, it will learn to appreciate the visionary artists and musicians whose work is already among us. We must not let this moment pass without making a major advance in human evolution, the climax of the 200-year time of transition. It is time for humanity to spread its wings and fly.

For this moment to be truly golden, reforms will also need to be made as the people demand. Corporate and government bureaucracies can no longer continue business as usual. Democracy must be reinstituted and the political power of money restricted. Alternatives must be found to massive spending on negative campaign ads. Our environment must be protected, unless we want to live in a greenhouse full of ozone holes. We must revitalize our cities and end the cycle of drug wars, drug addiction and violence. Everything from the charts suggests that our president will act effectively. For better or worse, Clinton has taken up the mantle of being the leader at the most crucial turning point in history.

It was said that no one came into office with more on his shoulders than Clinton did in 1993, but just wait until 1997—he hasn't seen anything yet! There will be more international troubles in early 1997, such as another Middle East or Far East War. The stationary Mars in Libra opposing Saturn repeats the same formation as during the "six-day war" between Israel and the Arabs in 1967. Domestic violence could still be simmering, and we could see another terrorist attack within our borders or aimed at our citizens abroad. Clinton himself could face new scandals in his new administration. Generally, though, since the aggressive, activist impulses of Mars and Saturn are harmoniously aligned with the other planets, amazingly constructive things can be accomplished quickly in early 1997. Clinton may improve his position by taking decisive anti-terrorist actions. Optimism will surround the White House as we wake up to a regenerated spirit.

Clinton presented his first program in February 1993, just as Mars turned stationary. In his second term, it turns stationary-retrograde just after he takes office. Since Mars stops exactly on his own Ascendant and natal Mars, it could truly be his golden opportunity (although he should be careful of violent attacks). Another total solar eclipse occurs in March, in the critical degree of 18° Pisces. Mars returns to 17° Virgo and turns stationary direct on April 27, 1997, exactly opposing the eclipse degree. It looks like the moment to rev up the Revolution and recover the spirit of the Marseillaise (in fact, another French uprising can't be ruled out here). It may be the time of a great riot and/or new initiatives to help the cities.

More states in the Russian Federation may try to become independent, with violent results as Russian nationalism attempts to return.

The Sixth and Twelfth Houses are emphasized in the U.S. in all the charts of the period. Will this mean that plagues and diseases reach crisis proportions, or that health care is still a great national debate? Will a cure for AIDS be announced? Perhaps new labor policies to help workers cope with downsizing and stress? Health and labor concerns challenging secret bureaucratic power structures? Another great industrial accident leading to calls for reform? A rebirth of the psychedelic culture of the sixties, begun under Uranus-Neptune in the early '90s? Whatever happens, it will be revolutionary.

We can't forget Uncle Sam's penchant for being the policeman of the New World Order; Mars turning stationary in 17° Virgo is yet another opportunity for the U.S. (or Russia) to meddle in Asia, causing the peace movement to remobilize. Another foolish action by Saddam Hussein of Iraq could be the excuse for further drastic action by the U.S. that might evoke more cries of "no blood for oil!" from the people or insults from President Clinton's critics. Transfer of power in Hong Kong to the Chinese may also prompt a dangerous attempt to unify with Taiwan in 1997, probably in February or April. The issue of Taiwan in the UN or other UN issues like the make-up of Security Council could be addressed.

The end of July may be another boiling point, as Mars makes its final opposition to a stationary Saturn. A major communications controversy, a terrorist attack, or an accident affecting transportation could dominate the news in late August or early September 1997. Early October and late December look like promising times for diplomacy and/or more progress and financial innovation on the domestic front. Since Mars joins Pluto in Sagittarius in October, it may also be a time of high adventure, such as space travel exploits or advances in long-distance travel. World trade agreements or a more enlightened religious movement may sponsor conferences that improve understanding and global cooperation on major problems. By February or March 1998, a major peace breakthrough could be announced. Ironically, the U.S. may be forced to enforce this agreement within a month, or deal with a new trouble spot.

The exuberant Pluto in Sagittarius seems to dominate the scene in early 1998, especially in its lively square to Jupiter in Pisces, which is lined up to the total solar eclipse in February. Organized religion (Jupiter) continues to be controversial, but may experience a millennial revival beginning in 1998. The high spirits of the time may contribute to a wave of mass spiritual awakenings, or perhaps New Age awareness techniques may get a boost as in 1974–75. More scandals can't be ruled out either: for example, secret misdeeds in the military may unravel. Health care reform will continue to be transformed, bringing sensational breakthroughs by century's end. The ways in which corporations and the government are keeping us unhealthy could also be exposed.

As the Twentieth Century ends, issues of justice and health in the workplace are also being combined with our growing moral and religious concerns. Perhaps the recent world trade agreements could arouse further anxiety about free trade and immigration in our increasingly global society. We may be becoming one world before we are emotionally ready,

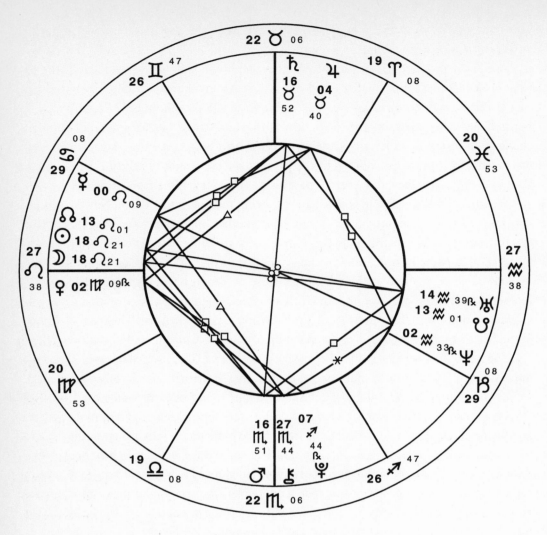

Eclipse of the Century

This total solar eclipse in Leo opposes Uranus in Aquarius, squares Saturn in Taurus, and squares Mars in Scorpio. All these planets are near the powerful mid-points of the fixed signs. Look for upheavals in the Balkans, Russia, Mexico, and Iran. A MiddleEast oil war, political terror, wild art experiments, and health innovations may also occur. Chart data: August 11,1999, 11:09 A.M. GMT, Washington, D.C., 38N54, 77W02.

and this will cause protests in 1998 and the first decades of the new century. There may be international agreements concerning ocean and space travel or pollution in 1998. Presidential diplomacy will be very active that year, and some of the President's agresssive moves in forieign affairs in the spring may be very controversial.

The exhilaration of 1997 and early 1998 may yield to increasing fear and paranoia later in the year, as depressing Saturn moves into one of its foreboding squares to nefarious

Neptune. During an eclipse in August 1998, Mars opposes Neptune and squares the stationary Saturn. There could be some violence due to religious cults or the repression of mass protest movements, or public panic over economic or environmental uncertainties. Since Saturn will be making a waxing square to Neptune in late 1998 and early 1999, we also need to look at what happened at their conjunction in 1989, such as the gigantic oil spill in Alaska that happened in March of that year or the Tienanmen Square massacre in China in June. Saturn will be returning to Taurus, just where it was when the ecology movement erupted thirty years before (after another oil spill off Santa Barbara, California). 1998–99 could see unusually severe weather.

As the new Millennium approaches, fears of the "end of the world" could grow stronger. Pluto will be opposing its position during the conjunction of 1892, just as Neptune did in the early 1970s. Disillusionment with the Pandora's box of "progress" may unleash radical change, probably in August 1998. Not only will Uranus be in radical Aquarius in 1998, Pluto will be opposing Uranus in the U.S.'s horoscope. This is on top of Neptune's continuing passage over the "corporate" Pluto in the U.S.'s second house of money, perhaps dissolving some of the old corporate power structure in America and forcing us to deal with our dependence on Middle East oil. The economy, having rebounded somewhat in the 1990s, will be generally unsettled due to radical upheavals in the first few years after 1998. Severe catastrophe, however, is not due until at least 2008.

Foreign affairs will continue to demand attention. In 1998–99, six years after their conjunction in 1993, Uranus and Neptune will be in places that correspond to those of 1914. If the Balkan conflicts are not resolved, they could explode into a major, multi-national engagement around August 1999. The chart for late 1998 suggests major diplomatic efforts by the U.S. to deal with revolutionary upheavals, not only in Eastern Europe but in Southeast Asia, too. These peace efforts will have to bear fruit if we are to avoid major catastrophe in the following three years. I also see a major religious and moral controversy breaking out in November 1998.

People of many nations will become more aggressive and belligerent in February 1999. Major religious, revolutionary upheavals are due in April and July, probably in the Middle East or the Balkans, and perhaps in Southeast Asia or Central Africa as well. Then comes the "eclipse of the century" in August, opposing cataclysmic Uranus and squaring both Mars and Saturn. Some astrologers believe that this will be the time of another great "oil war," like the Persian Gulf war of 1990–1991. There's no doubt there will also be a revolutionary civil war (Saturn square Uranus, as in 1861), and a religious war, probably in Iran. The Balkan region seems likely to explode again at this time. Uranus will soon be returning to its 1917 position (when it also opposed Saturn), and another cataclysm in Russia is a distinct possibility in August–September 1999: perhaps the break up of the federation. Mexico is due for a cyclic return of revolution, and political purges and massacres are possible in all the places we mentioned. Some of these upheavals could be tempered as early as September, when Venus turns stationary over the eclipse degree, but more upheavals could come in mid-December.

Some kind of transportation accident, violent student uprising, or terrorist bombing is possible in the U.S. after the eclipse. Though American attention will be largely directed abroad, Uranus in the Sixth House may indicate labor unrest at home, plus continued corporate and economic restructuring due to the various crises. All the upheavals around the world may cause a financial panic. In many places, such as Russia and Europe, some drastic government controls and/or restructuring of the economy could begin now. There could be wild experiments in the arts, much like the outburst of Dada shortly after the similar eclipse in February 1916. Startling new developments will occur in science and literature too, as well as fanatical student religious movements.

By December, Jupiter will be back in volatile Aries, and will turn stationary in exactly the same degree (25° Aries) where it's also turning stationary in the progressed Horoscope of Modern Humanity. One of the parties to the current troubles may now declare a "holy war," and decisive battles may be fought. As the year 2000 arrives, prophets of boom and doom alike will parade across the world stage and have people everywhere enthralled and entranced. Another eclipse on February 5, 2000, aligns with radical Uranus in 17° Aquarius. This is the degree linked to Islamic Iran and the Iran-Contra scandals (the degree whose Sabian symbol reads "a man's secret motives are being publicly unmasked"). Does this mean a new outbreak in Iran, or another Iranian clash with America in early 2000? Does it show another presidential scandal? Certainly, more troubles will erupt in the same places as they did in August.

Europe's unification will finally bear economic fruits as the New Millennium opens, but in America, all the foreign and financial uncertainties will cause people to re-evaluate and reformulate their relationship to their land and property. The two "new age planets" (or planetoids) Chiron and Pluto will be conjoined in Sagittarius on December 31, 1999. An enormous interest in prophecy (Sagittarius) is likely, but so is a great effort to heal (Chiron) and transform (Pluto) our ideas. We can hope that as we reform our economic and political system, we will learn to look to the long term and discover healing visions for our world. That is at least what the cosmic doctors Pluto and Chiron in Sagittarius prescribe as the cure to our troubles.

If we can do this, we will truly have entered a New World Order. As the New Millennium dawns in the year 2000, people will suddenly realize what great opportunities await us. If Martin Luther King were alive, he would say that we have now climbed the mountain and reached the promised land, but that our job now is to begin building our lives in Canaan. To do this, he would say, we need to live as the One People of Planet Earth we now have become. The year 2000 will be a very hopeful moment, even though dark clouds of war, revolution, and economic/ecological uncertainty continue to hang over the landscape like the morning fog. The initial troubles of the new decade will shortly pass, leaving us free to pursue the opportunities of a new golden Aquarian Age.

As we reach the pinnacle, it is important to be clear about the the current movement that bears the name "New Age." We saw it emerge in the late 1960s as the "human potential movement" and rise to fame in the 1980s during the "harmonic convergence." Astrology, and this very book, is part of it. It is important to openly support this movement toward a New Age, and not run away from the label just because of criticism from those whose minds are closed to alternate realities. It is our best chance to regain the spiritual awareness that must be put back at the center of our lives if we are to continue our journey. Everyone who pursues this quest openly and is not bound by religious or scientific dogma is a "New Ager." But the New Age must not become too limited itself, nor succumb to the ways of the Old Age. We New Agers must critically evaluate all paranormal claims that are made, and not follow gurus or "masters" blindly. We must not let money and greed become the primary motive in our work. We must remember to participate in democracy and do political as well as spiritual work, for no genuine "New Age" can flourish alongside tyranny and injustice. Our Age of Aquarius cannot remain a purely private, personal matter; it must also be reflected publicly in an emerging new civilization on a restored Earth, and expressed in inspiring works of art—ultimately our only lasting legacy to future generations.

We have made many mistakes on our journey to this New Age, for our new ways have often turned out to be more destructive than the old. From the start, our romantic journey toward the future has also been an attempt to recover the best from the past. Our journey of transition has brought deeper enlightenment, and the chance to learn what "progress" really is: not only material gain, but spiritual growth in harmony with one another and Mother Earth. Now we are reaching the Mountain Top, looking over to the Promised Land of a great new spiritual civilization. We can't afford to fall back again, or to stand pat; we must move onward and upward, into the New Millennium!

Endnotes for Chapter 15

1. Oron Hale, *The Great Illusion, 1900-1914*, 110.

2. Neptune conjunct Pluto and Uranus in Scorpio in the 1890s; Uranus conjunct Pluto and Neptune in Scorpio in the 1960s.

3. William Langer, et al, *The Expansion of Empire to Europe in the Modern World*, 578.

4. Gordon Craig, *Europe, 1815–1914*, 427.

5. Victor Hugo's "Hernani" had done the same thing one Uranus cycle before, in 1830.

6. Felix Gilbert, *The End of the European Era, 1890 to the Present*, 213–14.

7. The closing Uranus-Pluto square in 1821 corresponded to Napoleon's death; the closing Uranus-Pluto square in 1933 occurred as Hitler came to power. Perhaps Napoleon reincarnate was taking up where he left off?

8. Morrison & Commager, *The Growth of the American Republic, Vol. II*, 640.

9. Ibid.

10. William O'Neill, *American Society Since 1945*, 19; Eric Goldman, *The Crucial Decade*, 303.

11. Ibid.

12. Jupiter and Saturn joined near this point in 1821 as the Greek Revolution erupted.

13. As Kenneth Clark said about the Romantic movement and the French Revolution, when Neptune

was also entering Scorpio, in *Civilization*, 296.

14. David Caute, *The Year of the Barricades: A Journey Through 1968*, 39.

15. John Davis, *The Kennedys: Dynasty and Disaster*.

16. At the exact moment of the New Moon on October 24, 1965, the first one of three exact Uranus-Pluto conjunctions in 1965–66 was directlly overhead in Washington, D.C.

17. Most key lunation and equinox charts in 1966 put the conjunction there.

18. Perhaps the updated version of the phrase "wine, women, and song."

19. Caute. *op. cit.*, 212.

20. This was my first successful prediction of a world event. Saturn (government) and Neptune (secrets) were in the signs of journalism (Gemini and Sagittarius).

21. Mars was exactly on the Midheaven in Washington during the 1995 Spring Equinox, which is why I predicted a "season of violence" in the U.S.

22. Astrologer Mark Lerner says the "Void of Course" Moon on Inauguration Day, 1997, means that the new administration will have more success with spiritual than with practical matters. See *Welcome to Planet Earth* magazine, Aquarius-Pisces issue, page 4.

16

The Chart for the New Millennium

Now we can pick up our crystal ball and gaze into the Twenty-First Century. In fact, for many readers some of these years may no longer be ahead, but already in the past. In that case, you can see for yourself how my predictions have fared. Where they fail, the blame should probably rest with the author more than with astrology itself, although astrology also has its limitations. Barring a powerful psychic insight, predictions must necessarily be somewhat generalized, although they can be specific enough to be meaningful. Remember, however, astrological forecasts are not (nor ever shall be) sufficiently reliable to be understood as indications of unalterable fate. All an astrologer can do is outline some of the most likely possibilities; human beings will decide which (if any) of these possibilities are acted out. We can predict what may happen, or outline the conditions that may be in force, but to take anything said in this book as the absolute truth would be to set up self-fulfilling prophecies. We should also avoid predictions that are either too rosy or excessively dire. The first may merely arouse complacency; the second, fear. On the other hand, a more realistic view of where we're headed can help us navigate the path of our evolutionary journey. Much will depend on the progress of "new age" higher consciousness, and whether we seize the opportunity the New Millennium presents to build a more peaceful and creative world. That is why this is not only a book of predictions, but also a book of visions.

THE BIG QUESTIONS

There are some really basic things that concern us as we cross into the New Millennium. We should look at these before we plunge into a detailed look at the years after 2000. First of all, people wonder whether advances toward world peace and cooperation achieved in the 1990s will continue, or whether the New World Order will be even less secure than the old. On this question, the message of the planetary cycles is clear. The upheavals of the Twentieth Century were a transition to a new era. As of 2000, this transition is over. Ethnic strife will continue, and economic conflicts may replace military ones. The U.S. may even break apart or undergo a revolution. But *the great wars are past*. Every 500 years we come to a point where we can worry less about aggression by others (including the criminals across town, as well as the tyrants across the seas), and concentrate instead on creating and building a new civilization. That time has arrived. The more we realize this, the greater peace and security we will have. We may even develop One Mind as well as One World. If we choose to, we can spend fewer resources on defending ourselves, and thereby not only recover our prosperity, but expand it. Our Modern Spirit of One Humanity is becoming mature. We should keep this in mind and act like grownups—able to provide and fend for ourselves without clinging to authorities and clutching our weapons out of fear of one another.

People also wonder whether the planet itself as we know it will survive. Since even in the 1990s ecological concerns were often ignored, some hard days of reckoning lie ahead, such as the years 2008–12, which will bring many dislocations and revolutions. A flood of refugees could exacerbate ethnic fears and escapism in the following decade, but as the "Green Revolution" (begun as Uranus conjoined Pluto in the 1960s) moves toward its climax in the 2040s, the necessary changes to our way of life will probably be made. The goals of the sixties, such as peace and preserving the planet, remain our goals today as we enter the New Millennium, despite what most conservatives say. Ecology will be linked to economy (our third, ever-present concern), and the most lucrative innovations will come through learning how to preserve our resources.

The *really* big question remains: whether we will realize the opportunities our times present. Will we understand that more of us today already have more freedom and greater economic resources than any other people in history? Will we see that no one has ever had greater access to the tools of creativity than our generations do? Will we glimpse our unique time in evolution, poised as we are to become a global humanity aware for the first time of our full heritage? Will we recall how we have been inspired to do something creative with the many tools and opportunities we have been given? Will we enter the New Millennium with the sense of possibility and rebirth that is our destiny, or will we continue to be worried about money, crime, taxes, and illegal immigrants? The planets give us no real answer on this one, although they certainly offer hope. Everything depends on us. We need to remember what we are here to do before we can accomplish it.

THE CHART'S KEYNOTE: REINTEGRATION AND WHOLENESS

A world of possibilities is being projected about the New Millennium today. UFO visitors may enlighten our way or return to rule over us, helping to change our world view and way of living. Angelic Beings and Ascended Masters may arrive to become our guiding lights, taking those who follow them into a higher spiritual world. Jesus may come again to judge the living and the dead. The rate of technological change may accelerate, sweeping us all into "hyperspace." Our speed of personal "vibration" may increase, allowing us to "melt away" into higher dimensions. Our electronic high technology may be the tool for developing telepathic connections (without wires) which link us to each other and the peoples of the galaxy. We may move out to the stars and establish space colonies, as civilization on Earth is replaced by a wholesale "back to nature" movement and a "retribalization" into small communities. These are all potentialities we should keep in mind. As we move into the New Millennium, our motto should probably be: "Nothing is impossible."

The Chart for the New Millennium may give us some clues as to which way we are going. This is a chart for the moment we actually enter the New Millennium, as humanity now defines it. It is no substitute for looking at the transits (or current planetary positions) for each period, and for each year and day ahead of us, but it could give us some general insights. I have cast the chart for Washington, D.C. (currently the world's virtual capital) rather than for Greenwich, England. I have used the time of midnight, January 1, 2001—the real start of the New (or Third) Millennium (not January 1, 2000, which is the start of the last year of the Second Millennium). If you use the time of midnight all across the world, the chart will have the same rising sign and house positions in every location (with only very slight differences). The placement of the Sun at 11° Capricorn would be the same for the beginning of any new millennium, as long as January 1 at midnight is used as the starting point. The chief variables will be the positions of the Moon and planets, and the aspects between them.

The first thing we notice is the Moon's position in 22° Pisces. Does this mean the Piscean Age isn't quite over? You may remember that 22° Pisces was Saturn's degree in the Horoscope of Jesus. Christianity will not die out, as some hope and others fear. It will persevere, though in an altered form. Jesus' sacrifice on the cross will continue to be a meaningful symbol to many, and he will still be an important guide and authority figure in the New Millennium.

22° Pisces is also close to the degree (24° Pisces) which Saturn occupied in our Cosmic Peace Symbol: the degree it occupied when the Bastille fell during the French Revolution. For that reason, I call this degree "Bastille Degree." From the American Revolution to the U.S. Civil War, most revolutions broke out with a planet (usually stationary) near this degree. So you could not interpret the Moon's position in the Chart for the New Millennium as having an exclusively Christian significance.

So what does it mean? First of all, the "old paradigm" of Materialism will no longer hold true. Our movement toward "higher consciousness" and spiritual renewal begun in 1966 (year of the Cosmic Peace Symbol) will continue, and mysticism will be as important as science in shaping our lives from now on. The fact that this Pisces Moon is in the Sixth House of health is especially revealing. Health and Medicine will be the primary field in which the "New Paradigm" will manifest. What is called Alternative or Holistic medicine will make quantum leaps and will quickly become the accepted norm. Since the Sixth House also rules "work," this is also a strong indication that we will need to bring our work, our workplaces and our careers into harmony with our spiritual needs and aspirations.

Dane Rudhyar's interpretation of the "Sabian symbol" for the Moon's degree of 22° Pisces seems particularly fitting and useful. It reads: "A prophet carrying tablets of the new law is walking down the slopes of Mount Sinai." Its keynote is: "The need to bring down to the level of everyday existence the clear realizations made manifest in a great "peak experience."[1] This is much like what happened in our journey across the Valley of Transition after our "peak experience" in the French Revolution, and seems also to specifically refer to our more recent "peak experiences" in the sixties and around the turn of the Third Millennium. Our challenge will be to keep those experiences alive as we move down the Mountain and into the "Promised Land." This will require us all to follow a spiritual path, to make the divine a living reality in our daily lives, and to practice the ideas we gained while at the peak.

Although the Sabian symbol clearly refers to a Moses or Jesus figure, the "new law" seems a clear reference to the "New Paradigm." The keywords of that new paradigm are Spirit and Wholeness. Moon in Pisces in the Sixth House clearly indicates that humanity must heal and reintegrate itself after the previous millennium of destruction and conflict. In the next Millennium, we will have to fix everything we have broken in the past. We must atone for our mistakes and bridge the gaps between us to find the new unity that is now dawning among us. If we do this, we will achieve the healing we want for ourselves and the

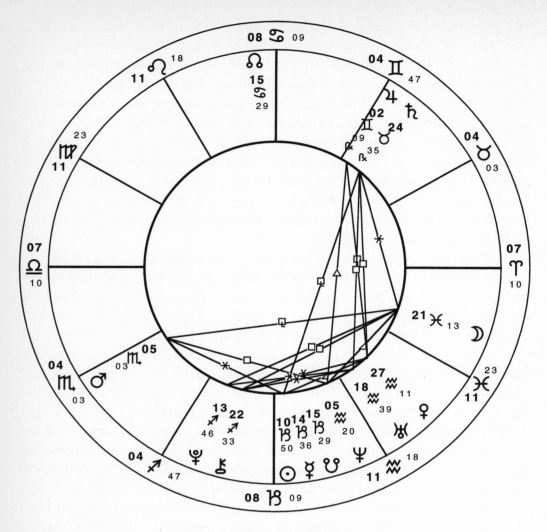

Chart for the New Millennium
Chart data: January 1, 2001, 12:00 A.M. EST, Washington, D.C., 38N54, 77W02.

planet. The importance of "healing through new ideas" in the New Millennium is confirmed by the Moon's close square to Chiron, the "wounded healer," in the sign of ideas, Sagittarius. We will need to innovate in order to live well in the Third Millennium, and we will need to clarify and follow ethical principles received from peak experiences. With Moon in the Sixth House of service, we will also learn to cooperate and help one another instead of competing with each other. This means that although compassion and social service are out of fashion now, we will soon become reawakened to the fact that we are keepers of our brothers and sisters, not only in our city and country but also around the world.

Confirming these indications of the Moon in Pisces is the fact that the closest aspect in the Millennium chart is the virtually exact square of Mars to Neptune, ruling planet of Pisces and symbol of the Ark of Humanity. Mars and Neptune form a semi-square/sesqui-square formation with the Moon. This supports prophecies of the "global mind" of one humanity. Neptune will challenge the aggressive individuality of Mars and dissolve the boundaries that keep people apart. The great task will be to integrate the needs of the individual with those of the group and the global mind. Individuals must transform themselves (Mars in Scorpio) to become conscious of larger human and divine purposes and align with them.

Mars is close to Uranus' degree in our Horoscope of Modern Humanity, which emphasizes that the threat of extinction will still hang over us if we do not continue to mature and learn to live together and share. In the Second House of finances and personal freedom, Mars shows we will continue to be challenged to change the way we earn our living if we are to survive on this planet. We must respect the rights of individuals, who will be stimulated by all the opportunities the New Millennium presents to make money through innovation and networking, but we must learn to share our resources (Scorpio). Our best opportunities to live well in one world will come from making sure that living and working standards are raised in poorer countries, not lowered in rich ones. We will need to guard against deceptive ideas (Neptune) that justify greed and desire (square Mars at 6° Scorpio). Sexual pleasures and colorful rituals will also be important to us in the next 1,000 years. These rich and ethereal experiences can help us in our paths of growth if we pursue them in the right spirit. Otherwise, they may lead us into a millennium of decadence.

Alone above the horizon are Saturn and Jupiter in the Eighth House. Although corporate power will not cease, and structure will still be important to us, our institutions will continue to be transformed in the New Millennium. Jupiter near the Ninth cusp, and Pluto in Sagittarius in the Third, suggests that travel and migration to other planets is one way to relieve the stress on our Earth's finite resources, but we must learn to live together on Earth before we can be wise enough to live in space.

Mercury conjunct the Sun and South Node in Capricorn represents the mental abilities we have already developed, and the easy access we have to them through high technology. It also suggests that "karmic readjustment" will be necessary, due to our use of science and intellect to dominate the land (Capricorn, Fourth House). The North Node in Cancer in the Tenth House means that our "direction of growth" in the New Millennium is toward developing a community of feeling. The Sabian symbol for the North Node degree of 16° Cancer reads "A man studying a mandala." Rudhyar interprets this to mean a "concern with personality integration."[2] That must become the preoccupation not only of our personal lives, but of our institutions (Tenth House). The way to wholeness and integration will be to make our highest personal values the focus of our public decisions. The way to decline would be to make pronouncements by public authorities the basis for our personal lives. Living by formulas given by others is not the way to true "personality integration," which can only come when our lives proceed outward from our own hearts and souls.

Uranus is in Aquarius in the Chart, sign of the Aquarian Age due to arrive some time during this millennium. In the chart for the previous millennium, Uranus was in Pisces. With Uranus conjunct Venus in the Fifth House, the Aquarian Age will bring greater creativity in the arts, and will challenge traditional relationships. Saturn in Taurus, however, may put a damper on some of this by squaring Venus and Uranus, and sesqui-squaring the Sun. Cultural clashes will not entirely end in the Third Millennium. Venus square Saturn, the old aspect from the Horoscope of Modern Humanity, indicates that alienation will continue to haunt us. Now, however, Uranus aligned with Venus is there to light our way out. The Venus-Saturn aspect (and mutual reception) now has become stronger and more stable, indicating that we will overcome our personal alienation by gradually learning to stabilize our lives within larger group settings and the global mind of Earth. This and all the other indications from the chart confirm that the integration of the individual within the group is the keynote of our New Millennium or Aquarian Age. Such an integration will be welcome, given the spiritual bankruptcy of both capitalist and communist collectivism in our time.

THE PROGRESSED CHART: PROGRESS AND DANGERS AHEAD

Space limitations prevent me from fully discussing all the indications of the progressed chart of the New Millennium, but we can mention a few key forecasts which gel with those to be made on the following pages. The progressed New and Full Moons happen at the same time as those of the progressed U.S. chart, and opposite those of the progressed Horoscope of Modern Humanity. The dates of the major turning points which they indicate are the same: 2009–2011, 2024–26, 2039–41, 2054–56, etc. Watch for climactic events at these times, especially the first one (2009–2011), since it is also a lunar eclipse.

Mercury squares Mars in 2020, confirming the danger of a major confrontation or war at that time. Mercury conjunct Uranus in 2022 shows the "progress" indicated by Pluto entering Aquarius that year. The increased activity of these times may lead to violent clashes around 2027 (Mars square Uranus). This is about the time Neptune will enter Aries, when the U.S. faces the danger of civil war. Saturn and Jupiter turn direct in 2024–25, indicating major institutional changes in this period. Governments may collapse or undergo fundamental reform.

In the following pages, I write of a major clash over a waterway in 2035, involving danger of nuclear confrontation. This may be confirmed by Mars opposite Saturn in the progressed chart in 2035 (as it was during the Cuban Missile Crisis), with Mercury stationary in Pisces (water sign). Mercury retrograde from the 2030s until the mid-2050s may show a period when ideas are re-evaluated and many inventions appear. Sun conjunct Uranus in 2040 and Mercury conjunct Uranus in 2046 may indicate the "Green Revolution." Another intense period of change will be around 2077, when progressed Mars conjoins Pluto.

The Chart for the New Millennium may also hold clues about how each individual can cross over "The Mountain" into the "Promised Land." If any planet in your chart is in the same degree (with a two-degree orb) as a planet in the Chart for the New Millennium, you could find new success by developing the talents which that planet represents in your nature, or you could face dangers and lessons related to the nature of that planet.

Now let us look more fully at the events of the next century. For more details about the astrological basis for these predictions, as well as the historical background of the preceding 200 years, see my book *The Horoscope of Humanity*.

ENDNOTES FOR CHAPTER 16

1. Dane Rudhyar, *An Astrological Mandala*, 282.
2. Ibid, 120.

17

Looking Over the Edge

INTO THE THIRD MILLENNIUM, 2000-2020

From atop the "Mountain" of our peak experience at the turn of the Millennium, we are now ready to peer "over the edge" into the New World of the future that stretches before us. What wonders and terrors are there to behold! Living in the New Millennium may not always be for the faint of heart, but those who have a positive, idealistic vision for tomorrow will definitely feel at home there.

The first charts for the New Millennium show bold new leadership in Washington. Since radical Uranus will be supercharged in its own sign of Aquarius, the people will be ready to support more action by the government than in the pervious period. Efforts by the Clinton administration to streamline the government may have restored a measure of confidence in it. An especially promising sign is that the Jupiter-Saturn conjunction appears on the Midheaven in Washington (see the conjunction chart for May 28, 2000). It will finally be time to re-regulate such areas as health, safety and transportation. It is difficult to conceive of a Republican administration assuming this activist role, so the U.S. president elected in 2000 will probably be either a Democrat or the standard bearer of a new progressive party.

Much will be done in the next decade to reform the financial system in many nations, but especially in the U.S. and Russia. The government will be further streamlined to better meet the needs of the people. Electronic superhighways and other planet-friendly technologies will receive government support, and a restructured mass media will be used to help democracy. Newly accepted ideas for changing the economy and society will be widely touted by government and media networks. It will be an exciting time; a great chance to make long-overdue changes. There's a great optimistic surge at the Millennium's start as we embrace New Age ideals. The first two years will see the best opportunities for political changes, because people will be more skeptical and less supportive of reforms once Uranus leaves the ground-breaking sign of Aquarius.

There may be grounds for doubt about the reforms proposed at this time. Such a revitalized government may be dangerous in ways that will only be apparent later. Just as the Federal Reserve Board, the I.R.S., and other institutions founded during the last passage of Uranus in this sign became oppressive later, so it may be with some of the new agencies founded in 2000–03. These could include new bureaucracies to "help" high technology, universal health care, or an all-powerful mass media "tsar." There may be intrusive economic controls

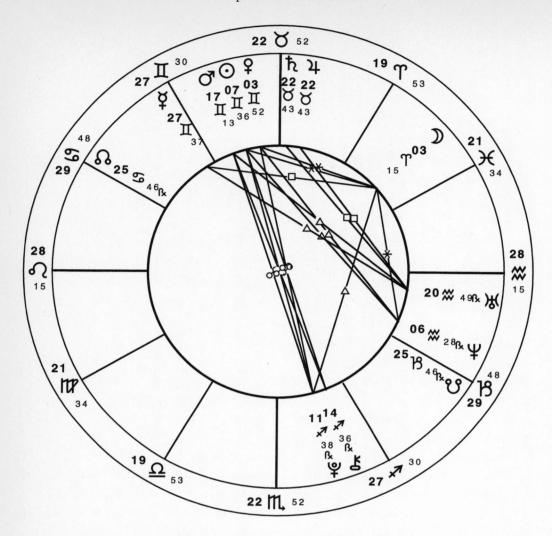

2000 Jupiter-Saturn Conjunction

The New Millennium begins boldly in Washington. This is the chart cast for the exact moment of the Jupiter-Saturn conjunction, as given in The American Ephemeris. The conjunction appears exactly on the Midheaven, pinpointing the U.S. as the center of its impact. Chart data: May 28, 2000, 04:04 P.M. GMT, Washington, D.C., 38N54, 77W02.

too. The new federal financial system will work better than the old, but, like all institutions, it could eventually become too cumbersome and restrictive. The courts may also hand down some very historic decisions on these subjects in 2001.

Other indications from the 2000 chart suggest hidden influences by powerful interests. The activities of these clandestine "string-pullers" may come to light later on, causing scandals. Another trend of this twenty-year cycle will be the rise of powerful new religious movements, and some religious groups may continue to flex their power in the political arena.

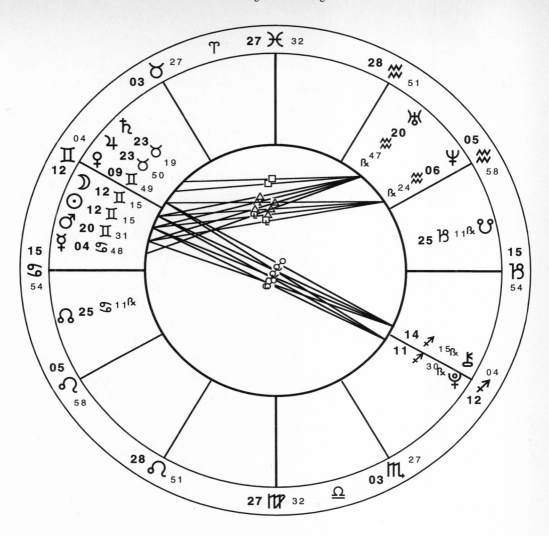

2000 Jupiter-Saturn New Moon

This is the chart for the New Moon following the Jupiter-Saturn conjunction. Uranus' square to the conjunction shows the next 20 years will be a progressive era, but prone to catastrophe. Many good reforms will be made, especially in mental health. The New Moon in the 12th house may also indicate the "poor health" of U.S. institutions. The chart shows a danger to the American president elected in 2000, and to candidates seeking the office that year. Chart data: June 2, 2000, 12:14 P.M. GMT, WAshington, D.C., 38N54, 77W02.

First and foremost, the major warning to heed concerns the safety of the new president. Since the 2000 conjunction again falls in an earth sign, the pattern of deaths in office every twenty years may return. Many other signs confirm the danger, including Mars at 20° Gemini in the Twelfth House in the chart of the New Moon of June 2, 2000 following the Jupiter-Saturn conjunction. The eclipses of November 23, 2003, April 8, 2005, October 3, 2005 and March 29, 2006 bear watching, particularly if the new president's birthday is close to these dates (or in early to mid June). If a presidential death happens, it will occur in 2001, 2003, or 2005 after re-election, if past patterns hold. Obviously, the vice- presidential candidates in 2000 must be chosen with great care—a Dan Quayle will not do! Another Aquarian Dick Gephardt, could get the nod, however—if he doesn't win the top job himself. Al Gore, an Aries, may win it, but since the Jupiter-Saturn conjunction actually precedes the election in the year 2000, candidates are in danger too before the election.

Though the first decade of the Third Millennium won't be entirely stable, it will be full of delights and opportunities. People will participate in many utopian social and political movements. Creative ferment will be higher at the beginning of the Twenty-First Century than any other time in our era; artists and inventors of all kinds should seize this golden moment and not wait for promises in the future that may never come. In these times, we will be encouraged to share all of who we are. If we as a people make this a priority, then this can be one of the most inspired periods ever for the human spirit.

STAR WARS OR HOLY WARS

Whoever is elected in 2000 will also face foreign challenges immediately, since it looks like Uncle Sam will be gearing up for war in the fall of 2000. What a way to start a Millennium! Conflicts that exploded in 1999, such as those in Russia, Iran, Mexico, or the Balkans will probably come to a head in 2001. Continuing ethnic strife in Europe seems likely. Intensive diplomatic efforts and minor interventions will try to head off trouble, especially in mid-September or early October 2000—but then comes the combative Saturn-Pluto opposition in the summer of 2001, joined by a stationary Mars in July. These planets will oppose each other across the Ascendant and Descendant of the U.S. chart. Uncle Sam will be feeling righteous again in a big way, eager to show other nations the truth. Religious issues and trade embargoes will be involved, and the U.S. may try to impose its will on its Latin neighbors. A nuclear accident can't be ruled out either during this period. It might sound strange, but it's not impossible that ETs may be contacted or involved somehow in the events of these years! We may also see the first use of "star wars" technology, or else electronic communications may be used in historic new ways to defuse the conflict.

Turning points in the confrontations come near November 2 and December 22, 2001. After the December date, the U.S. could suffer losses in a serious naval engagement. An eclipse aligned with Saturn and Pluto in May and June 2002 indicates another decisive moment. Danger to the president is shown, too. After October, 2002, the outlook for peace starts to improve. If we are even more lucky, we will escape further conflict until the decade ends. If we are even more lucky, we will enter "the millennium of peace." Many agreements (especially in the Mid-East or Balkans) may come in December. On the other hand, if there is no agreement, then late February 2003 could see another flare-up, as Mars joins Pluto and opposes Saturn.

Whether we go to war or not (and I hope we don't), the years 2001–2002 will proba-bly live up to their mythic significance. Great breakthroughs in space travel will be made, especially in satellite technology. Progress toward a manned expedition to Mars may hap-pen. Conflicts over who has the right to launch and orbit in space will have to be dealt with. From late 2002 through the spring of 2003, many significant, innovative health and wel-fare programs could be approved. Electronic media will be used to give everyone access to work and education. It will also be an excellent time to streamline the bureaucracy (Saturn trine Uranus) so that these programs will be workable for years to come and help safeguard the security of the people. Either now (2001-2003) or later (the 2020s), this could include a plan for a guaranteed annual income. This currently "unaccepted idea" could be made possible if unearned investment income were distributed more fairly.

Part of the war's aftermath in defeated nations may be new constitutions—a Saturn-Uranus trine in air signs indicates that this a great time to create them. Since one cycle of Uranus will now have passed since the First World War, these constitutional changes may come to nations established (or re-established) at that time; such as Russia, Poland and Lithuania. Iran and Vietnam may also see their first real advances toward democracy. There may be yet another clash in the Mid-East in the year 2003, which will cause more econom-ic anxiety for the U.S. and intense diplomatic efforts in the summer.

As we said before, some disaffection with change could come when Uranus enters Pisces in 2003. A war in 2001–02 should not be allowed to distract the U.S. administration from domestic reforms, or the best chance may be lost. Swelling enthusiasm among the people for reforms in late 2002 and early 2003 (Jupiter opposite Neptune) could lead to danger-ous demonstrations and government repression in February 2003. Conservatives might then cry for "law and order." But since Neptune will remain in Aquarius, this retreat from reform will be brief. The reformers may have to scale back their expectations, though. In September 2003 another great social or foreign aid program will be proposed.

ECONOMIC WOES AND RELIEF

While foreign affairs may be easier after 2002, domestic affairs will be harder. Expect a sea-son of discontent in the fall of 2003. The war, the Mid-East troubles, or the resulting fi-nancial controls could help trigger a recession. With depressing Saturn in 13 Cancer in the spotlight; it may be a reprise of 1974, with gas lines or other shortages in the U.S. What's worse, in the fall of 2003, Mars turns stationary at 0° Pisces and conjoins with Uranus. This means a severe plague or famine may hit the U.S., and strikes or protests over post-war shortages may erupt. Active efforts will be made to improve the public health. More trou-ble is due around November 23, 2003. The planets will be in critical degrees that could briefly stimulate political and social passions. Expect protests and purges to shake up the White House and Congress. Travel mishaps and naval battles may occur. In late 2003 and early 2004, the president may seem "lost at sea" and unable to handle all the troubles, es-pecially if there's an assassination attempt.

The year 2004 begins with Mars in Al Gore's solar degree—a danger signal to him if he is president. People will be demanding measures for economic recovery, and unrest is possible in Los Angeles or elsewhere in early 2004. The eclipse of April of that year could also signify renewed struggles over religious issues like abortion. In September and October 2004, members of religious or ethnic minorities will be demanding their rights (Mars-Jupiter in Virgo), and important social measures could be taken. Military altercations could occur in Asia or the Middle East in the spring or fall. After more severe economic shortages in the winter of 2004–05, new financial policies and social programs will gradually bring relief.

A Democratic (or progressive) president may well be re-elected on a close vote in 2004, despite doubts over his or her handling of the economy. Whoever wins, the planets show economic restructuring and financial reform during the next presidential term. Better ways to live on the land may receive much attention in the spring of 2005, stirring debate about the true nature of "progress" and how to improve the quality of life. We will need to remember that our high-tech society can't yet exist by itself in "cyberspace;" it still depends on our access to our dwindling basic resources on Earth and how we manage them. The American president may take strong actions to secure these resources and to open trade in 2005. The spring of that year could see breakthroughs in economic diplomacy, probably involving Europe.

In July 2005. Saturn enters Leo for a two-and-a-half year stay. This could mean serious government-supported efforts directed toward creative projects, bringing the artistic "golden age" to a climax. Education could be greatly improved after pessimistic reports. Saturn in Leo could also stand for youth acting out their cynicism, and may signify deaths of major entertainment figures. Saturn's influence in this sign will be strongest from October 2006 to May 2007. By then, the government will be focused on creative investment and long-term growth. The economy should be bouncing along again by then. It should be a stimulating and exciting time.

Mars turns stationary-retrograde in Taurus at the beginning of October 2005, with a powerful eclipse two days later. This is obviously a sign of economic restructuring. The U.S. could quarrel with other countries over land and fuel in late 2005, especially with Middle Eastern and/or Balkan nations. With Pluto transiting Sagittarius and opposing the U.S. Mars, religious fundamentalists may wage war on the U.S. in 2004–05. The U.S. will respond to this crisis by declaring its "economic independence," while intense diplomatic efforts will successfully resolve the foreign disputes. The Turks could be perturbed by economic and ethnic turmoil, and East Indian ethnic problems may explode too.

The year 2005 will be a great time for the U.S. to revamp its economic and financial system in significant ways. The president, energized by the messianic zeal of Pluto in Sagittarius, may inspire the country to "reach the unreachable star." France and other European nations will be making some exciting changes too. Let's hope, however, that we avoid dictatorial controls or crippling regulations in 2005–2006 that could come back to haunt us. Sensational crime stories involving entertainment figures in this period that could distract the people from more important matters.

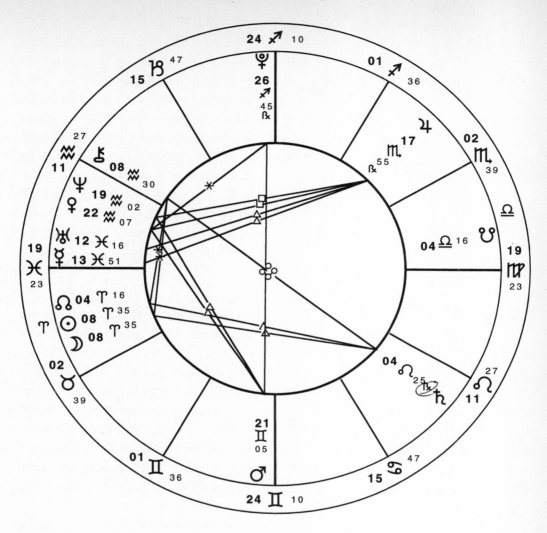

2006 Solar Eclipse

Powerful political purges will transform our legal system. Danger indicated to U.S. executive, especially if it is Gore or another Aries. The spiritual and artistic renaissance may come into focus now. Chart data: March 29, 2006, 10:16 A.M., Washington, D.C., 38N54, 77W02.

On March 29, 2006, a total solar eclipse occurs in 9° Aries that could make Al Gore a *but no — instead, his more is well received.* marked man (his Sun is at 11° Aries). Perhaps he would be wise not to run for reelection in 2004 (should he then occupy the White House), and let his vice president run instead. Even if he survives past 2006, he would fail to realize many of his exaggerated hopes during the rest of his term. The fact that Saturn in Leo will return to its own place in Gore's chart in 2006 confirms this advice. Late June 2006 also looks like a dangerous time for him, with many afflictions to his chart. If he bows out in 2004, or follows our advice very carefully, perhaps he can be the first president saved by astrological warnings. We have every right and duty to use astrology to try to avoid disasters; nowhere is it written that we can't improve upon our "destiny." As the "Aquarian Age" dawns, let's make sure the public is increasingly aware of astrology so that it can have a constructive impact on policy.

Pluto on the Midheaven. in the 2006 eclipse chart may mean America is becoming the center of the spiritual, New Age Renaissance. It could also mean a strong reform movement in the Church, and a "purge" or financial scandal in the Courts or the State Department. Powerful new proposals will be made to transform our legal system, as concern for social justice and human rights in America and elsewhere continues to accelerate. The president will probably put himself at the head of this drive. As Neptune in 2005–06 reaches 17° Aquarius, the critical 1962 eclipse degree, Americans may be reminded of the unfulfilled social dreams (Neptune) of the Kennedy era. Let's hope the idealistic president elected in 2000 doesn't suffer the same fate as Kennedy did.

SCANDAL AND PARANOIA

The aspects of late 2006 and early 2007 show increasing public concern in America over the effect of economic controls or jobs abroad on the economy. With Saturn opposing Neptune, xenophobia could begin to grow over the world trade issue, or over similar problems like immigration. The president could tap this mood to rally resurgent paranoia against Iran or other foreign enemies. In September 2007 he may have to respond to violent incidents there against Americans. The U.S. could strike out at Iran late in the year or early in 2008, when Mars turns stationary in Gemini. Also, since 2007 is the climax of the Saturn-Neptune cycle that began with their conjunction in 1989, all nations liberated that year could make major changes in their governments (especially in March 2007), powered by enormous mass movements for human rights. This may include China, where the Tienanmen Square massacre could finally be avenged.

For the U.S., partial eclipse on March 19, 2007 puts this Saturn-Neptune opposition in the spotlight. Saturn in Leo stands alone exactly on the Midheaven, and Mars opposes it in the critical degree of 17° Aquarius. This could mean our president must face an "unmasking" of his motives in a major scandal, possibly involving his actions against Iran, or the controls imposed on the economy. The recent assassination (or attempt at it) could also lead to the uncovering of a right-wing or government conspiracy with links to the JFK assassination.

Uranus in 2007 also reaches a critical degree—the "pile-up" degree of 17° Pisces. This indicates that key issues from the 1960s may resurface in a big way in the later 2000s. Environmental accidents could bring the oil and ecology issue to the fore again. The president may take bold decisive action on this issue, but any steps that seem too arrogant or tyrannical will rebound. The peace movement will loudly and successfully oppose any foolish, aggressive military moves by the U.S. (or other powerful countries). Like liberty, the price of peace in the New Millennium will be constant vigilance. The "goddess of peace" may become so important to the world by then that new statues will be erected to her, just as they once were to the "goddess of liberty."

270

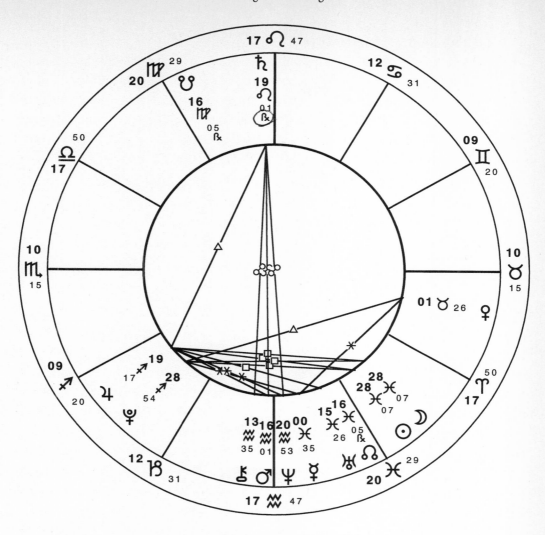

2007 Partial Eclipse

Who's being unmasked? Mars returns to critical "unmasking" degree of 16°-17° Aquarius, opposing sin-
gleton Saturn (the government) at the Midheaven during this partial solar eclipse in 2007. Tienanmen
Square may be revisited too, and "Berlin Walls" may fall again, as Saturn opposite Neptune climaxes
the cycle begun in 1989. Chart data: March 19, 2007, 02:44 A.M., Washington, D.C., 38N54, 77W02.

Jupiter's powerful conjunction with Pluto in late Sagittarius in December 2007 may
mean a realignment of foreign policy, especially concerning "fundamentalist" nations like
Iran. It may also see the climax of legal or court reforms mentioned above. With Saturn in
Virgo again, resurgent fear of foreigners may intensify in December 2007, and in the following spring. Mars stationary in Cancer in November 2007 indicates increasing anxiety
over national "defense." The total eclipse on August 1, 2008 (during which Mars in 18° Virgo opposes Uranus) may also signify shady U.S. dealings abroad in 2008, and a resurgent

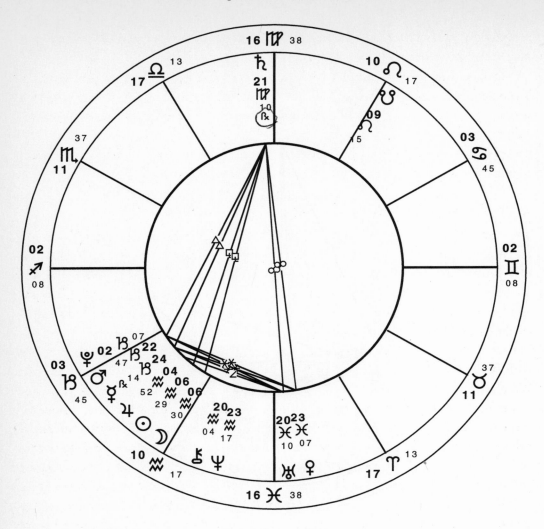

2009 Annular Eclipse

Mushrooming anxieties are shown by the Saturn in Virgo singleton at the Midheaven during this solar eclipse in 2009, just six days after a new administration is scheduled to begin in Washington D.C. (An annular eclipse is not quite total, because a ring of sunlight is left visible around the Moon's shadow.) Chart data: January 26, 2009, 07:56 A.M., Washington, D.C., 38N54, 77W02.

counter-culture at home (Venus exactly opposite Neptune). There could be unrest among the poor. This plus the other possible scandals may make it difficult for any incumbent liberal administration to hang on in the 2008 elections, despite their many accomplishments. The Republicans will probably win the election, either this year or in 2012. Indications are that 2008 will be a tight race; and since Saturn will oppose Uranus exactly on election day, the campaign will be bitter. A new demagogue may be on the rise, fomenting a fear of foreigners, deviants and bureaucrats. The old issues of science vs. religion and drugs vs.

prohibition will also be center stage in 2008–2009, as "reformers" battle "libertines." It may seem like the roaring '20s revisited.

Six days after the inauguration a startling solar eclipse happens, which puts Saturn in Virgo all alone at the Midheaven. This confirms a conservative presidency that plays on people's anxiety. It may represent a wholesale attack on the liberal programs and counter-cultural experiments of the last decade, or a determined effort to make them more efficient, probably by decentralizing them. Our technological and engineering skills will be applied to our social and financial problems.

A NEW REFORMATION

The year 2009 marks the start of an important and painful period. Pluto enters Capricorn on November 26, 2008, just before the new American president takes office. The chart for the moment Pluto enters Capricorn shows the polarizing Saturn-Uranus opposition (pitting the status quo against revolution), plus a stellium in religious sign Sagittarius. All this means another religious reformation. The previous two entries of Pluto into Capricorn set off powerful changes—the Protestant Reformation in 1517, and the Age of Democratic Revolt following the Seven Years Wars in 1762. This "reformation" will be no different, complete with the Twenty-First Century counterpart of Luther nailing his ninety-five theses to the Wittenberg Church door. Pluto in Capricorn also means that "enlightened despots" (or powerful visionary leaders) will appear in the following years who will seek to reform society. The Catholic Church is targeted for more radical change, as loud spiritual and moral debates continue to be heard. This could be the time when the well-known prophecy of the end of the Papacy could come true. A period could open in 2009 when science and religion will be forced to jettison all that is not relevant to our age of global ecological peril. There will also be passionate debates over immigrants and refugees caused by famine and revolution in many parts of the world—problems that will get much worse over the next several years. Unfortunately the peoples' fears will not help.

Fear will be somewhat superseded by philanthropy in the year 2009, as benevolent Jupiter begins a conjunction to Neptune in May. Indications are that it will be a very powerful conjunction, so idealism will reach a peak. Since Chiron will also be conjoined to it, this compassion will be directed toward healing humanity during the crisis ahead. Considering the problems, this will be welcome indeed. The challenges of these years will generate high religious enthusiasm lasting through the 2010s, giving life to the new "reformation" movement. We can expect New Age religions to offer both spiritual and practical help to an endangered world, but high expectations for political reform may be disappointed, despite ambitious efforts in 2009 to solve global problems. There may also be some major disasters at sea in early April or late May.

Europe will see spiritual and humanitarian movements in 2009, leading to increased conflict between those who want to help the starving millions and those who fear them as the year goes on. Around July 6 and/or August 19, 2009, the people's unhappiness may

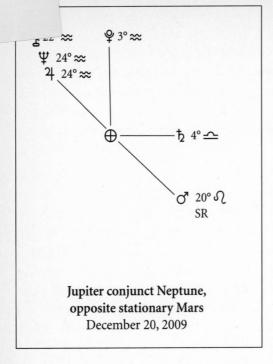

**Jupiter conjunct Neptune,
opposite stationary Mars
December 20, 2009**

break out into open conflict or civil unrest. More "unmaskings" of presidential misdeeds or terrorist actions could explode in October (Jupiter stationary in 17° Aquarius), along with more trouble with Iran; this only heightens the feelings of alienation and discontent in the land.

The ferment will rise to fever pitch in the Fall of 2009 and seriously threaten the peace among some nations. Until 2010 any conflict will probably be limited to isolated riots or terrorist bombings, and revolution will be directed toward churches and ideas; but by January it may become a major international stew. The Jupiter-Neptune conjunction in Aquarius in December 2009 will be opposed by stationary Mars in Leo (near the 1999 eclipse degree), and at the same time Saturn will square Pluto. Remember that Mars-Jupiter-Neptune is the "Marseillaise" combination from the French Revolution. So it looks as if the religious reformation will rapidly turn into a crusade, possibly another fight between Americans and Iranians. Central Asia, France, Israel or India might be involved too. California could be a center of idealistic ferment. The solar eclipse on January 15, 2010 may signal another "deadline day," like the similar one on the same date in 1991. But since peaceful Venus is joined to the eclipse, peace may have a better chance this time and the deadlock may be overcome. There will certainly be sanctions or other economic clashes, though.

DODGING AN APOCALYPSE: A TITANIC T-SQUARE

When Jupiter and Uranus enter Aries in the spring of 2010, people will be much less restrained in expressing their frustration. "Peasants" and other poor people will rise up worldwide (Mars in Virgo opposite Neptune in June), and governments will be besieged with demands for change. This will make the year 2010 the climax of this twenty-year period, as Jupiter (with Uranus) opposes Saturn. What makes this year so critical is that Pluto also moves into a tense T-square with all three planets as they enter cardinal signs. 2010 looks like a year of sudden, cataclysmic changes and drastic, forced new beginnings.

This titanic, historic T-square involves the same four planets as the T-square which coincided with the Great Depression. The solar eclipse in July could trigger a major, worldwide financial collapse. Pluto in Capricorn suggests not only that many corporations will go bankrupt, but that the economic troubles will bring down many governments with

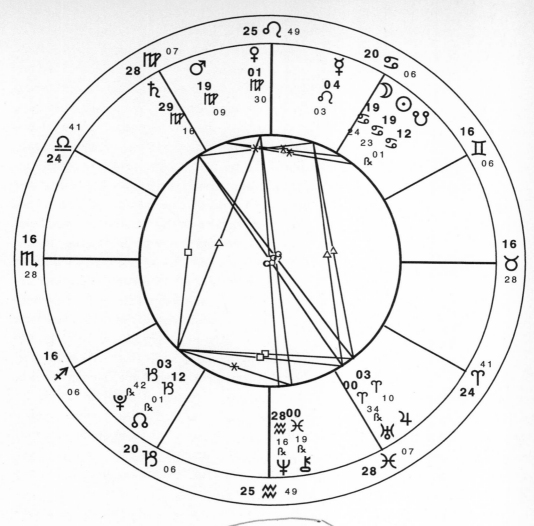

2010 Solar Eclipse

DODGING AN APOCALYPSE. A titanic T-square involving Jupiter, Saturn, Uranus and Pluto as they enter cardinal signs in 2010 is very similar to the T-square during the Great Depression of the 1930s. Economic changes are forecast for the U.S. (T-square in 2nd, 5th and 11th houses). Chiron conjunct Neptune is the "key" opening the Greater Mind of Humanity in this period, one cycle after Neptune's discovery in 1846. Chart data: July 11, 2010, 07:42 P.M. GMT, Washington, D.C., 38N54, 77W02.

dizzying speed as revolutions sweep the globe. But as we mentioned in Chapter 13, in 2010 the lunar cycles in the progressed Horoscope of Modern Humanity indicate that the common people may be in retreat. This could mean people will be easy prey to xenophobia and fear of "radicals," as in the 1920s, '50s, and '80s. This was just how Hitler eventually rose to power during the previous Great Depression. On the other hand, altruistic compassion

275

will still permeate the period as Neptune in Aquarius helps moderate the fears among the people, and may indicate that "enlightened" authorities will make constructive, revolutionary changes on behalf of the people and the planet.

The crisis of 2010 will result from the various religious conflicts around the world, magnified by serious shortages and famines; and above all, I believe, by ecological disasters. Global warming and climate change will begin to seriously affect agriculture in many places. By 2011–2012, when Neptune crosses into the chaotic waters of Pisces, all these catastrophes will produce an unprecedented stream of refugees (as Neptune in Pisces has usually indicated in the past). It is interesting that James Burke (who doesn't believe in astrology) predicted in his prophetic TV program "After the Warming" that the year 2010 would see massive waves of refugees across the borders between the First and Third Worlds, leading to many massacres. This refugee crisis will be a great moral challenge to our lingering racism.

There is no doubt in my mind that the years 2010 and 2011 will be the most difficult of any we face in the next half-century. If we survive them in reasonably good shape we will have dodged the worst bullet in our future. This prediction is a far cry from the rosy visions put forward by those who expect a New Age at the end of the Mayan Calendar in 2012. It is a bit more like the "apocalypse" forecast by psychedelic futurist Terrence McKenna, although his "transcendental object at the end of history" (due the same year) may be less lustrous than he hopes. It's another reminder that we don't have time to dawdle if we wish our golden age to unfold—the opportunities after 2010 may not be as good as those of today. Unless we learn to live harmoniously with the Earth and its diverse peoples, our standard of living may sharply decline from 2010 on, forcing us to focus on more practical matters. As Neptune enters Pisces in 2011, thus leaving the higher signs and moving into lower ones, our focus could narrow toward "worldly matters" as it did in 1520 or 1848.

Although the crisis of 2010 may retard the creative spirit of today's golden age, it won't extinguish it. The "counterculture" will certainly expand in the 2010s, as people again seek alternatives to conformity, despair and destruction. Like the "cyberpunks" of the 1990s, the new rebels will be inspired by high technology. They will also be altruistic, spiritual, and utopian like their flower child parents, though they will be more disciplined and more fully committed to realizing their spiritual visions.

A major war may break out in August 2010. If this happens, the refugee problems will be even worse. Central Asia is the most likely battle scene, but America's involvement there would be only economic. The worst war clouds will pass as the T-square dissolves.

In early 2011, there could be further scandalous breakdowns of financial institutions, and some governments which collapsed during the peak of the crisis may be forcefully reimposed. If so, mass panic could cause still more refugees and cast a pall of disillusion over the next few years. Escapist spiritual movements and conservative politicians would benefit from this turn of events.

DEPRESSION DIPLOMACY: SATURN IN LIBRA

In the fall of 2010, the charts continue to show Jupiter and Uranus together, setting off huge cosmic fireworks of change. Late 2010 and 2011 will be a great opportunity for reform movements to mobilize action. Swift progress could be made, motivated by the continuing economic crisis. The powerful, depressing Saturn singleton in Libra continues from November 2010 to August 2011, putting a damper on the chances for recovery. Saturn will be returning to Libra in the progressed Chart of Modern Humanity, though,. so the 2010s will be an opportune time to change the constitution in many countries, as leaders try to make the world's economic and political system more just and effective. Since the crisis in 2010 will be so acute, right-wing conservatives may not be able to hijack the thirty-year cyclic return of Saturn to Libra and turn it into another celebration of greed, though they'll try. The need of the people for help from their government will be too great, and while the outer planets are still in humanitarian signs Aquarius and Pisces, many people will still be idealistic. The usual "dispersion of power" under Saturn in Virgo/Libra will probably take a more compassionate and enlightened form this time, because the people will have no doubt by 2011 that humanity is locked together in a common destiny on Spaceship Earth.

A great chance to resolve some of the wars or disputes of these times will come on November 18, 2010, as both diplomatic planets Venus and Jupiter turn stationary in their own signs on the same day. But by 2011 (especially around April 23 or August 25), the American people could be calling to "Make the New World Order safe for democracy," leading to U.S. intervention by 2012. Justice and recovery at home will be linked to justice and recovery abroad in the U.S. mind. The global depression will require diplomatic solutions. As the world economy increasingly and rapidly becomes a concrete political fact, our relationship with the increasing power of the UN will be a growing issue as well. Will a new American constitution have to be integrated with a new world constitution? Will other nations bow to U.S. demands for world democracy and "global free markets?" Will "dispersion of power" mean sharing it with other developing countries? Will this mean rich nations finally agree to help poorer ones find alternative ways to develop themselves, without causing pollution and famine? Will poorer nations be asked to abide by the same regulations and standards as the rich ones do? How should the new spirituality be integrated into our institutions? These are questions that will dominate the 2010s and beyond, and which our "enlightened despots" will have to decide.

September and October 2011 may see some swift and decisive revolutionary or military actions. Right afterward, Mars begins a long stay in Virgo, inciting dissension by humble groups in society and/or action by America's or Russia's defense establishment. Indications point to U.S. intervention in Central Europe and the Middle East. During the next solar eclipse in May 2012, Mars in Virgo will be on the Midheaven in Washington. Expect military action by the U.S., as America feels again it must defend its ideals by throwing its weight around. By then, Jupiter begin its return to Gemini, and will be exactly on the Descendant in the May eclipse chart. The U.S.fulfills its role as guardian and peace keeper of the New

...er again, perhaps acting to keep a dangerous Middle East power from using nu-
...ar weapons, though not without loud protests.

Uranus makes a square to Pluto on June 2. A revolution will be happening somewhere. The U.S. will thus probably either be supporting or opposing this revolution, perhaps in the Far East. Let's hope America is not deluded again about which side is wearing the white hat. *This is a strong warning to the U.S.A. to be clear about its policy in the spring of 2012!* We don't want another Vietnam, do we???

All in all, 2012 will be a very interesting year; partly because we now expect it to be. In the spring of 2012, Mars in Virgo opposes Neptune, the planetary Ark of Humanity, as it embarks onto the vast seas of Pisces. Since the world will now be inundated with refugees from the various catastrophes during the last few years, we can expect them and their friends to demand fair treatment. As xenophobia declines, perhaps they'll get it. By the spring of 2013, we can expect a revolutionary wave similar to those of the Nineteenth Century to crash through Europe, the Middle East, and parts of the Far East, lasting throughout the year. March and July 2013 are key months. In the spring of 2012, there may be some powerful artistic and ecological projects in the works. If we have truly entered a golden age by 2012, we will understand that economics, ecology and art are all tied together.

THE GREATER MIND AWAKENS: NEPTUNE IN PISCES

In the year 2009, when the "New Reformation" begins, Neptune will return to the spot where it was discovered in 1846. In February 2012, it will enter its own sign Pisces for only the second time since then. During its first visit "home" in 1848, Neptune unleashed the power of the sleeping masses who discovered their political power and national identity. In 2012, we could see the birth of one human Great Mind related to one Planet Earth, as the masses discover their global identity. We saw the beginnings of this in the spontaneous love-ins and spiritual experiences of the 1960s, but now the ecological crisis and the flood of refugees will bring home as nothing else can how all of us are linked together. Mass communication will be powerful enough by then to solidify our experience of global unity. In 2012–2013, we can expect some kind of mass revelation, prompting people by the millions to join in communal ecstasy to experience the One Consciousness within all of us. Leaders from completely unexpected directions, perhaps even ET gurus or angels (which may have appeared in 2001) will step forward to lead humanity toward its brilliant future as the New Reformation becomes a political and spiritual revolution among the common people. Chiron's conjunction to Neptune in this period emphasizes how the new spirituality will heal humanity and become a "bridge" to higher consciousness in our daily lives. In these ways, the year 2012 will justify predictions of "the transcendental object at the end of history."

The potential for deception is also great, and many of the new cults of the time, both traditional and New Age, will mislead and take advantage of a hopeful but desperate public. The huge spiritual movements will be convenient escapes for masses of people disappointed with politics. Such disillusion would help Republicans win back the White House in November 2012. It could also lead to more mistakes in foreign policy. If the U.S. is still engaged abroad that month, many U.S. soldiers could die. During the next total eclipse in November 2013, Mars in Virgo will be on the Midheaven again in Washington, opposing Neptune. This means still more troubles for any U.S. troops abroad, causing more protests at home—the same problems that occurred during the previous eclipse in May 2012 that also put Mars in Virgo on the U.S. Midheaven.

On the other hand, lucky Jupiter will be more prominent in 2013–2014. This, together with Neptune in its own sign, indicates a reviving economy as massive new world-wide connections ease the era's chaotic conditions. International commerce will burst through the same barriers first breached by millions of refugees, and the new sense of world unity will speed this process. In July 2013, Saturn and Jupiter (with Mars) form a magnificent grand trine with Neptune. These same planets were also in grand trine when the U.S. constitution was created. People will be calling for constitutional changes in this period too, and this could be the time they happen. Many countries may agree to share scarce resources on an international basis and protect the environment. New global rules for sea, space, and electronic travel will be made. With Saturn transiting Scorpio (in powerful mutual reception to Pluto in Capricorn), the new mass mind will be firmly grounded in worldwide economic cooperation. The mos t enlightened leaders will be those who are most attuned to this new Great Mind of Humanity—and to the need to act together and save the planet we all share. July 2013 may see many people make communal experiments in their own lives, as they seek to live these ideals.

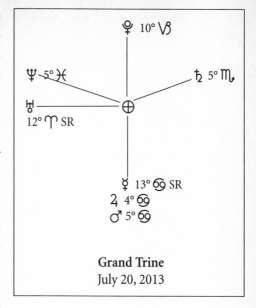

Grand Trine
July 20, 2013

RADICALS, FANATICS AND CRUSADERS

Despite all the positive responses to the crisis that began in 2010, indications are that things will remain unstable through most of the decade. Stationary Jupiter at 10° Cancer, T-squaring Uranus and Pluto, could bring discontent to a crescendo in Europe early in 2014 in ways reminiscent of the fall of 1989 (when Jupiter was also stationary at 10° Cancer). Mars will also make this T-square into a Grand Cross and turn

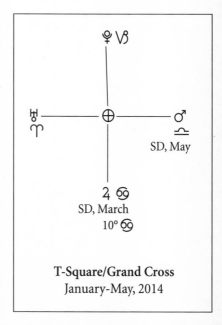

T-Square/Grand Cross
January-May, 2014

stationary in May. It certainly looks as if the revolutionary tidal wave could wash up quickly on American shores this time. Since the U.S. will still be the world's top cop and its primary immigration service as well, problems in other countries will cause problems in America. The 2014 uprisings could give further impetus to constitutional changes being debated during the decade in many nations. National reunifications (of Korea, for example) might occur as well.

Jupiter will be so prominent in late 2014 and early 2015 that it will be a signal to all of humanity to cheer up and be confident again. Its trine to Saturn in Sagittarius could indicate a breakthrough voyage in space, which might help our morale. It could be the time for a new Magellan—one civilization cycle (500 years) after the original. The rebounding economy will be strong enough to for social experimentation. Alive with a new sense of communion, we will be breaking barriers and loosening inhibitions in ways that remind us of the psychedelic '60s. Many Mercury-Neptune conjunctions in the charts of the mid-2010s suggest mind-expanding techniques (including psychedelic drugs) will be back in vogue.

There could be more trouble in the Middle East in the spring of 2015, but U.S. intervention there would be a deadly mistake. Peace agreements made in August or early September may be short-lived. By 2015, we can expect global religious reformation to cause tremendous turmoil in that explosive Middle East region, as religious reformers (Neptune in Pisces) clash with fundamentalist authorities (square Saturn in Sagittarius). Israel will be a scene of religious strife or a target of terrorist attacks. By 2016, these religious conflicts could disrupt world diplomacy again.

A furious conflict may erupt over religion and health policies, two things of vital importance to people in this period. We could see uprisings among the poor (Mars in Virgo opposing Neptune in October 2015), probably directed against church and/or health authorities. Figures reminiscent of Mother Teresa and Florence Nightingale may emerge as powerful leaders of the poor and the sick. Many moral crusaders (perhaps elder leaders from the baby boom generation) may emerge in 2015–2016 and rouse the people to tackle the issues of racism, sexism, global interdependence, ecology, and the need for creative spirituality in our society.

The government would be wise to prepare for attacks and kidnappings by religious terrorists in late September or October 2015, and again in mid-April 2016. Mars turns stationary in religious Sagittarius in April and makes dangerous aspects (conjunct Saturn, square Neptune, etc.). Authorities should heed the lessons of Waco and similar events, or needless deaths could occur.[1] The paradoxes of religious fascism and murder in God's name would

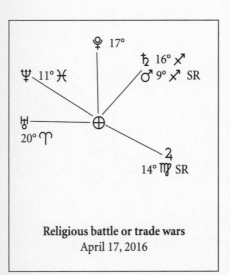

Religious battle or trade wars
April 17, 2016

seem ridiculous if they weren't so dangerous. Spain, scene of such attitudes in the past, may be subject to religious and/or separatist battles in April 2016 that threaten to tear the nation apart. Such religious upheavals could affect the U.S. economy in 2016, and the questionable finances of cults and churches in America will make headlines. These clashes will continue in the fall of 2016, and new ones may occur in Central Asia and in Latin American nations such as Brazil.

The continuing global weather crisis may cause millions more dollars worth of damage in this period (as well as in 2010–11), so governments should be prepared. By the spring of 2016, the U.S. will deal with this recurring crisis by taking major health and ecology measures in concert with other nations. The spiritual enthusiasm among the people will also move them to help others in 2016 through private agencies This crisis will be an opportunity to reorganize many of our institutions in a way that respects and serves people better. Perhaps we will understand by then that poverty will diminish only when we live in harmony with nature—and value everyone's contributions.

NEW WORLD JUSTICE

Whoever is elected U.S. president in 2016 will continue to face religious strife around the world. The U.S. in the late 2010s may offer itself again as an instrument of diplomacy and peace-keeping, but perhaps not very effectively. Small, muddled sea battles and scandals may result. Juridical Jupiter's T-square to Uranus-Pluto in 2017 also means that the religious revolution will affect the law, perhaps through court decisions. An eclipse on February 26 indicates unrest by religious rebels or the poor in many countries. The U.S. would regret any intervention in these conflicts, because it would bring many casualties. Americans will want to stay out and concentrate on their growing health and legal problems at home instead.

Many of the measures demanded by the people during the crisis of 2010 may be put into effect in 2017. These could include agricultural and ecological reforms and human rights for refugee groups. What is most significant about 2017 is Saturn's return to Libra in the progressed Chart of Modern Humanity. Whether all at once or over many years, this could mean real justice will come for those who have been denied it. Jupiter transiting Libra and Saturn passing through Jupiter's sign of Sagittarius confirms 2017 as the year when constitutional changes proposed in many lands come to fruition.

The solar eclipse of August 2017 shows a good month for international bridge building and breakthroughs in space travel. On the other hand, Israel or America could make a bombing strike or carry out a rescue attempt. Even more likely is some kind of strike or tax revolt by poor people, as Mars in Virgo once again opposes Neptune in September. No matter how many "enlightened measures" are taken, it will not be enough to quell the periodic eruptions of discontent among a people struggling to live in what may be a depleted and endangered world. We today should take pause and contemplate what our stubborn adherence to the corporate, "free market," materialistic lifestyle will mean for people in the future, who will have to live with the results. As Mercury re-enters Leo in 2017 in our progressed Horoscope of Modern Humanity, perhaps a new generation (led by some venerable baby boomer idealists) will rediscover that "making a good living" is not the same as creating a meaningful life—a lesson we all should have learned by now

REDISCOVERING NEW VALUES

The year 2018 contains more interesting cosmic events. Neptune is prominent, and reaches the critical 1966 "stillness of spirit" degree of 17° Pisces. In addition, Uranus enters Taurus in 2018–19, bringing a new phase that will be powerfully felt in the U.S. Leaders and activists will promote a new vision in the spring and summer of 2018, inspiring the people to board the train to a more prosperous, spiritual and Earth-friendly tomorrow, and work together to evade further global deterioration.

Once Uranus enters Taurus in 2018–19, spiritual reformation and concern for the Earth will be combined more often, accelerating the rebirth of nature religions. The anxious and outspoken temper of the times will ease to some extent. Better economic times should take some of the steam out of the endemic revolts. Prosperity will be helped by the new "green post-industrial revolution" being powered by all the planet-friendly technologies invented over the last two decades or so: new ways of farming, for example. Encouraged by the success of the new green and high-tech industries, people will begin to tire of riots in the streets and fanatic cult enthusiasms, preferring now to get down to business. In the summer of 2018, Mars turns stationary in Aquarius, in virtually the same degree where it also turns stationary four years later in the Horoscope of Modern Humanity! People will again be feeling the pulse of progress. There might even be a danger that global responsibility might be sacrificed to materialism again. This will be a recurring challenge in the Twenty-First Century.

Though the popular temper may be quieter after 2018, moral crusaders will still be trying to rouse the people for the looming conflicts ahead. A powerful lunar eclipse on January 21, 2019 may show more popular upheavals against the government and religious disputes between the U.S. and other nations (but not war). Many governments may be tempted to crack down on such upheavals with oppression in this period. The current "green post-industrial boom" will be at its peak in January 2019,and in this heady climate some careless entrepreneurs may lose their shirts to dishonest speculators. Investors should be very careful in this period; financial scandals are likely.

In March 2019, Uranus enters Taurus to stay. This could represent a moment when key decisions are made to encourage new lifestyles that are easier on the planet. Psychedelics are sure to be still in vogue, especially natural ones (since Uranus is entering earthy Taurus). The American people will be eager to help promote health and land reform all over the world, and to further the ideals of peace, ecology and brother/sisterhood. "Developing" countries in Africa, though, will be fighting each other over scarce natural resources such as oil. Neptune's arrival at the critical "pile-up" degree, plus Saturn's return to the 1993 conjunction degree in Capricorn, are sure signs that this year of 2019 will see the return (and possible resolution) of many key issues of our time—how all the Earth's peoples can live together in peace and preserve the planet and its resources. As Uranus passes 0° Taurus, it will also be completing exactly two cycles since the earlier "pile-up" in 1851. The two great movements of "matter-in-motion" and "stillness of spirit" will combine together in 2019, as we face the karmic results of our battle with nature and the racist, materialist delusions from our past. As the twenty-year era from 2000 to 2020 closes, we will see our true ideals and the path ahead more clearly.

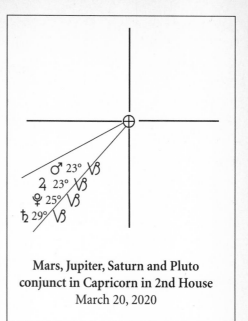

Mars, Jupiter, Saturn and Pluto conjunct in Capricorn in 2nd House
March 20, 2020

BREWING CONFLICTS

Although things will be generally quiet and stable in 2019, Mars opposing Saturn and Pluto in mid-June 2019 shows escalating ethnic conflicts over natural resources. Disturbances of this kind brewing among America's neighbors in 2019 could help to trigger the greater conflict to come in America itself in the mid-2020s. Perhaps literally "brewing": alcohol and/or drugs may be the center of contention (Neptune in Pisces). With Uranus in early Taurus, the Balkans could be unstable again, too.

In the fall of 2019, there may be more popular uprisings among the humble classes, and they may be inspired by religion. This period may see yet another great spiritual awakening. as churches become more active, and people find new ways to "get high" naturally, "get back to the land," and "rebuild nature." It may seem like 1770 all over again. Where will the new Tahiti be?

The economy may already be out of whack again by 2020. Saturn in Capricorn is always a danger signal, and a conjunction with perilous Pluto there is doubly dangerous. While things won't be nearly so bad as 2010, the fact that the next Jupiter-Saturn conjunction happens so close to the U.S. natal Pluto indicates it may trigger further economic restructuring. The spring chart for 2020 confirms this, with Mars, Jupiter, Saturn, and Pluto all conjoined in the Second House of finance. This is certain to cause the brewing conflicts throughout the world to bubble over. U.S. finances will now be so tightly bound up with those of its chief trading partners (perhaps especially in other American nations), that troubles here won't be resolved without dealing with troubles there.

Some kind of confrontation seems very likely in January 2020. Disputes will center over land, taxes, resources and liquids, and will be accompanied (as usual in these times) by religious pontifications. Diplomacy will probably postpone any conflict until June 28, but after that the danger of major war is acute. On September 9, Mars turns stationary-retrograde in Aries in square to Saturn-Pluto. If we haven't yet learned the ways of peace, this will certainly be the time for a war, and the chapter will end much the way it began.

This conflict in September 2020 will have its roots in the brewing conflicts over natural resources that erupted in January or July 2019. Since Saturn will be at 25° Capricorn (Mars degree in the chart of Modern Humanity), this confrontation may be the ultimate challenge to our desire to master and plunder the Earth and to dominate people. Saturn will have returned to the place it last occupied in January 1991, so this will also be a climactic challenge to the New World Order established thirty years before, as the U.N. tries to discipline "another Hitler" or "another Saddam." In fact, Iraq may be the culprit again, and Central Asia or India may also be a primary theater of contention. Not long after Mars turns stationary-direct in Aries (same as before Pearl Harbor) on November 14, we could see another "day of infamy."

It is likely that the U.S. will play only a supportive role in this conflict at first. American action may be limited to strikes against its "disobedient" neighbors in the fall of 2020. But whatever happens will be the opening salvo in a struggle in which the continued existence of the United States will hang in the balance. The great crisis will have opened for which the events and the "moral crusaders" of the last thirty years have been preparing us.

ENDNOTES FOR CHAPTER 17
1. Mars was in Sagittarius and making the same aspects during the cult murder-suicides in Jonestown, Guyana, in November 1978.

18

Getting Back into High Gear:

2020–2040

As we gaze ever deeper into our crystal ball, our prophetic vision will have to be 20/20 to see beyond 2020. Yet it's clear that a crucial turning point in American history lies just past that imposing marker of time. As a new score of years opens, Americans may be counting their blessings that they don't live in Asia, where rumblings of war will be disrupting the New World Order. Yet these troubles abroad will trigger troubles at home, and Americans with investments overseas may be counting their losses.

The fact that the Jupiter-Saturn conjunction on December 21, 2020, will be closely preceded by a total solar eclipse is all the indication we need that the 2020s will be a decade to remember. The chart for the eclipse shows Mars in Aries trining the eclipse itself, revealing a people confident and active again. This aggressive optimism will only increase once Neptune, the planetary Ark of Humanity, also enters Aries at mid-decade. The conjunction of 2020 is especially meaningful because it is the first one of its kind in Aquarius in over 700 years. What's more, Pluto is also aligned with it, just as this "cosmic plumber" returns to its natal position in the U.S. horoscope for the first time. The U.S. will remain in the spotlight in these times, and the America which emerges from this chapter will be greatly transformed and almost unrecognizable from the America which preceded it.

Not only will Pluto be making its karmic return in America's chart in the 2020s, so will Uranus—and Neptune will be *opposing* its natal position. This indicates that a great American crisis, another "hinge of history" comparable to the Revolution, the Civil War, and World War II, is due in the middle 2020s. The United States will pursue another "struggle for its very existence." With Neptune returning to the nadir of America's chart (the "house of home"), where it last stood in 1860, the Civil War seems the best analogy for what we can expect. But history never quite repeats itself: this time, the bone of contention and the contenders themselves will be different. The result could be the same, however—the breakup of the United States.

This time, it could be permanent. People will look at the history of the thirty years since the New World Order arrived and wonder why the "last remaining superpower" should stay standing. If the vast Soviet Union could split up, why not the United States? Has the nation become too big and cumbersome to meet our needs? Americans may also have remembered

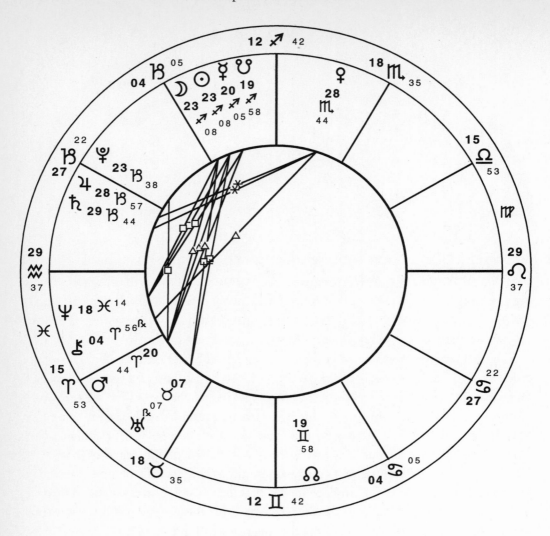

2020 Solar Eclipse

This total solar eclipse happens one week before Jupiter and Saturn join in conjunction on December 21, 2020, the first such conjunction in Aquarius in over 700 years. The following twenty years will be a true "Aquarian Age" in which we get back into high gear and witness a transformation of America. Chart data: December 14, 2020, 04:18 P.M. GMT, Washington, D.C., 38N54, 77W02.

and pondered Rodney King's question "Can we all get along?" and answered "no." The flood of refugees and immigrants over the last three decades (and especially since the great crisis of 2010–11) will have exacerbated ethnic and religious conflicts within the U.S. Asians may be dominant in the west, Mexicans in the southwest (their former territory), Blacks in the southeast, and Whites elsewhere. A "multi-cultural" nation so divided may not be able to hold together. Having ditched the old "melting pot," we may be boiling mad at each other from separate pots. The battle between feminists and family traditionalists may be one of

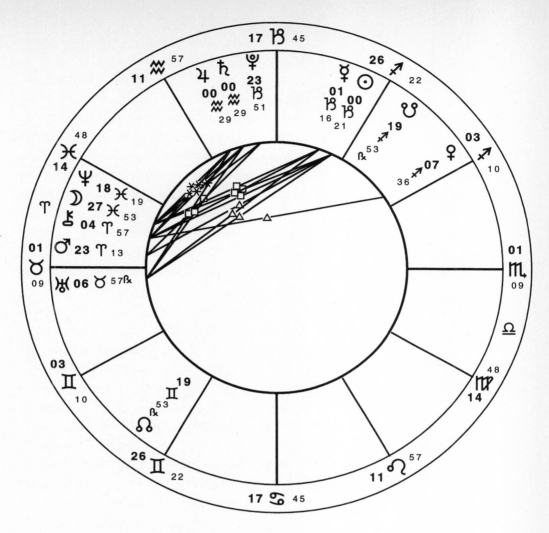

2020 Jupiter-Saturn Conjunction

This is the chart for the exact time of Jupiter's conjunction to Saturn in Aquarius, according to the American Ephemeris. The theme of change is emphasized again by the Moon conjunct Mars and Uranus on the Ascendant, and by Pluto at the Midheaven. Chart data: December 21, 2020, 06:22 P.M. GMT, Washington, D.C., 38N54, 77W02.

the issues that tears the country apart, as might the movement to preserve nature from the clutches of "progress." Militant, separatist cults will have formed and grown during the previous thirty years that could now seriously threaten the peace. Terrorists and militias talked of "civil war" in the U.S. in the 1990s—by the 2020s they may have their way. Decades-old conservative arguments about the "intrusive power of the federal government" will feed into the impulse to destroy it. Hawaiian moves for independence could trigger similar moves by other states and an attempt to preserve the union by force.

Unlike during the Civil War, when America was an island unto itself, the United States in the 2020s will find itself still the leader of the New World Order, but Americans in the 2020s will be increasingly ready to resign the position and "declare independence." National self-reliance and self-identity will be among the buzz words of the time, and all nations will prefer to look after their own affairs without having to answer to Uncle Sam. One possibility is that America will be kicked out of its superpower position, even as early as 2020; another is that the U.S. will secede from a proposed New World Government. The global environmental and refugee crisis will force us to confront the following issues: How much sovereignty should we give away, and how much should we keep? Can we become citizens of one planet Earth? Whatever we decide, the constitution and shape of America will change. The only real question is, can we make our choice without violence? The history of America says no, but by 2025 we will have entered a New Age of planetary and spiritual awareness. It won't be easy, but we can resolve our differences with a minimum of blood and desruction if enough of us are determined to do so.

In spite of the looming crisis, the first half of the decade will be relatively comfortable, peaceful, and stable. The economy will recover and surge forward, as the "green post-industrial revolution" continues. All over the world, the most difficult adjustments to the new environmental conditions will have been made. The brilliant creative ideals of the 2000s and the utopian spiritual passions of the 2010s will yield to a desire to reconstruct and rebuild the world in the 2020s. Artists and architects will seek to make their visions into imposing concrete realities. As Mars turns stationary-direct in Aquarius in the chart of Humanity in 2022, our "post-modern" aversion to progress will end. Since the 1960s, our greatest desire has been to slow down, since we instinctively knew we were on the wrong track. Now, knowing the direction of true progress, we'll be off and running full blast. The pace of inventions will skyrocket, and aggressive demands for social change will be loud, unceasing, and effective. As we expand into space, we will truly be ready to "go where no one has gone before." In the 1860s railroads spanned the continent— in this heady decade we may construct pathways to the planets, not to mention lightning-fast, giant electronic networks along which people and ideas will travel on Earth. The world will join America in seeking to attack every issue and resolve every question in the 2020s.

Because of the positive mood of the times, I think we will emerge from this "hinge of history" in the mid-to-late 2020s in better shape than before, despite many bumps and bruises along the way. The three outer planets will be forming a close, harmonious double sextile like the one during World War II—a pattern absent from the skies over the Civil War. Since the planets will be in higher signs than those occupied in the 1940s, there will be no great holocaust. All of this suggests a fortunate outcome. The aggressive pioneers of the 2020s, unlike those of the 1860s, won't be building empires of blood and iron, but arteries and capillaries through which the world's people can circulate in a global "empire" of commerce and understanding. The 2020s will also present our best chance to begin building a post-industrial economy that supports instead of destroys the Earth and offers equal opportunity to all its people.

SECRET AND SACRED POWERS

Other parts of the eclipse/conjunction chart of December 14, 2020, give us more clues about the twenty-year period that follows. Jupiter and Saturn in the troubled Twelfth House (with Pluto nearby) is a clear signal that established institutions of America may come to an end—including the presidency. The secret plutocratic potentates of the New World Order may be knocked off their silver thrones. Environmentalism will continue to expand, challenging the new developers in this era of "progress" reborn. Saturn in the Twelfth House (and its return to Pisces in 2023) further signals that we can't successfully move back out into the world and into high gear without remembering stillness of spirit. The spiritual quest will become less the province of utopian fanatics than a major task in everyone's daily lives. New cults will now become respectable institutions, especially in the early 2020s. Just as physical health care became a dominant issue in the 1980s and '90s (Jupiter and Saturn in the Sixth House in the 1981 chart), mental and spiritual health care will be a chief concern in the 2020s and '30s (Jupiter-Saturn in the Twelfth House in the 2020 chart). By the spring of 2022, some mental hospitals may be transformed into spiritual renewal centers, as "cuckoo nests" become places to "fly high."

The government will foster programs in the early 2020s to improve mental hospitals and study the healing powers of the mind and spirit. Will we finally come to grips with the effect of our cities and urban lifestyle on our mental well-being and quality of life? Will we create a new architecture that aspires to harmonize humanity and nature, rather than to dwarf and dominate both? These basic issues of our time, first broached in the Twentieth Century (and especially in the 1960s), must be taken to heart as we jump-start "progress" in the 2020s. Otherwise, we will have learned nothing from the crisis of 2010, and our civilization will be doomed.

The return of Jupiter and Saturn to their positions of sixty years before explains why the concerns of the 1960s will return too. Disillusion following the crisis of 2010 may empower the Republicans for a time, but they will be ousted again in 2020. An age of aggressive pioneers is no time for stick-in-the-mud conservatives—they'll be pushed aside in nothing flat. Indeed, both of today's major parties could bite the dust. Just as the Republicans emerged as a powerful new political party after the Civil War, so another new party (or several new parties in different regions) may rise to prominence during the 2020s as America threatens to split apart again. Uranus squaring the conjunction (as in 2000, with signs reversed) shows the period's progressive thrust, as does Jupiter-Saturn's position in Aquarius. But this time not only will the person of the president be threatened by the conjunction and the twenty-year cycle—so will the power of the presidency itself. Whoever is elected in 2020 will probably survive a violent attack "by inches," as Reagan did, but soon the presidency in America could go the way of English colonial rule—one Pluto cycle before. Internal dissension will already be high in January 2021, as revolts by environmentalists and the poor rev up and the conservative resistance grows.

THE PEOPLE PUSH FOR REFORM

In the spring of 2021, the progressive spirit among the people will be high. Broken promises will be met by marches in the streets. Mental hospitals and the secret power of corporations will be central issues by 2021. There are also warnings in the charts of a nuclear accident that contaminates the land. Uranus will be squaring Saturn closely that spring, causing confrontations between secret authorities and people who demand the truth. Since Uranus will be in Taurus, a tax revolt may come to a head. Look for June and July of 2021 to be crucial months, since the front lines in America's looming battle with itself will become very clear by then. Floods may be a serious danger that summer or in the spring of 2022.

The government will respond to the public's desire for reform with timely and effective action in 2021. Concerns over taxes and finances will become acute in the fall, when the public will be aroused to a fevered pitch by the media. The year 2022 looks even more spirited and crucial than 2021. Indications are that a new generation of radical youth will be speaking out, along with not a few older ones. Universities will be hotbeds of creative dissension and revolt in the spring of 2022, while discoveries in foreign lands or in outer space may inspire new technologies. Petroleum was discovered exactly one Neptune cycle before; could we now find another liquid energy source that won't pollute the environment?

Key economic reforms will be made in the spring of 2022, spurred on by a financial crisis as well as by the ongoing activism of the people. There could be major efforts to reform our social security system. Corporations may balk at doing their fair share (that's always an easy prediction!). Even so, reforms could be so drastic in the spring of 2022 that it will not be a good time to make risky investments. Remarkable peace efforts may be made too that spring. A benevolent spirit will encircle the world in May that diffuses many conflicts and heals religious quarrels. Much aid will be given to other nations in trouble. Overall, 2022 will be a very constructive year.

AMERICA'S KARMA

Financial speculation or accidents may make headlines in early August 2022. Then in October, Mars turns stationary-retrograde in Gemini and squares Neptune. It will be a decisive moment in American history. Neptune will oppose its location in the U.S. horoscope, while Saturn will square Uranus from the place it occupied in 1963 when Kennedy was assassinated. The current president should be careful in late 2022, and especially in early 2023 when Mars turns direct at 8° Gemini. This is not only a critical degree, but JFK's solar degree! Could the planets be trying to tell us something?

One thing they are saying is that America must now strive to complete the tasks it began under Kennedy in 1962–63. If it does not, then it may not survive the crisis which follows. Full equality and justice must be guaranteed for all, and our cities and environment must be made livable for all beings. Then and only then will our confidence in "progress" return, so that we can move forward beyond the doubts and disillusions of the previous sixty years. Pluto's return to its own place in America's horoscope is also a clear challenge to the U.S. corporate and financial structure. It won't emerge from these years without basic changes and reforms. The size and scale of companies will be reduced, and more of them will be owned by their employees. They must "share the wealth" and become more responsive to the public interest. If these changes are made, corporations can grow and thrive; otherwise, these "dinosaurs" will just decay and fall in the following years. The world's ecology issues could be addressed in a global U.N. conference in the fall of 2022, putting a spotlight on this pressing need to change our corporate system.

Mars stationary in Gemini in October, 2022, squaring Neptune as it passes a key point in America's horoscope, could indicate American involvement in another ill-advised foreign caper. The U.S. government will still be generously rescuing other peoples in trouble, but by spring 2023 more questions about Uncle Sam's role in the New World Order will already be creating divisions in the U.S. itself. How much can America take on? In March 2023, Saturn enters Pisces. The governments of the world may find themselves in over their heads, and reform movements could turn into a flood of popular unrest. More literal floods could cause trouble too. These trends may become even more visible in mid-July and mid-August of 2023. When Pluto moves from Capricorn into Aquarius in 2024, the temperature will rise even further.

In the fall of 2023, however, it looks like peace and reform will still hold sway in America, as Jupiter joins Uranus in Taurus. New institutions will be created to help green businesses, and bureaucrats will try to cure environmental and social ills more efficiently. If they don't, then the tax "reform" fever may trim back the federal money tree. Sex, romance and glamour will be rising, too. In late 2023 and early 2024, the hedonism of the Twentieth Century will emerge triumphant over the austerity of the Twenty-First. Entertainment will thrive, and new "stars" will emerge, shining through a galaxy of space-age media gadgets. So futuristic will these new gizmos be that they will make the "virtual reality" of the 1990s seem like a trip to "Jurassic Park."

THE DELUGE ARRIVES

During the next solar eclipse on April 8, 2024, Jupiter and Uranus in Taurus will be on the Midheaven in Washington. The reform trends mentioned above will still be very powerful, but now the danger of war will become acute for the U.S., and for Asia as well. Jupiter in Taurus is always a sign of possible oncoming U.S. intervention, and Uranus there is an even stronger indication. America must remind itself again about the dangers of war and violence. This time they will likely arise in a domestic quarrel, though it will be linked to international ones. America's actions toward other nations will anger their refugees here in the U.S., and revolutions in neighboring countries may trigger one at home. In October, the arrogant, expansive Jupiter will turn stationary in Gemini in the exact degree and minute of America's Mars, and will square Saturn in Pisces (just like it did during Vietnam in 1965). In December, Mars turns stationary. These are all clear signs of a possible U.S. war, and this time it may also trigger secession by several U.S. states or the expulsion of America from the UN.

Drastic internal changes will be triggered by reactions to this crisis. "Turf wars" among states and ethnic groups will sweep the nation. The people will blame the president for the crises at home and abroad and demand a change at the top. Saturn will be in the critical 1966 "pile-up" degree of 17° Pisces as the new president takes office in 2025, showing that he or she could be "adrift at sea" and beset by evaporating credibility.[1] Nevertheless, a better government is likely to emerge from this crisis. It may be a parliamentary one in which a reformed Congress has greater power. Even if the presidency survives, it will be less monolithic and more in touch with reality.

In the spring of 2025, the evangelistic, liberating energy of the people will be roused as never before by compassion for the oppressed and by expectations of a brighter tomorrow. With Neptune entering the sign Aries, as in Civil War times, the people will be ready to sacrifice themselves for a higher cause. In the 2020s, the "great secular crisis" that returns to America with every cycle of Uranus may be accompanied for the first time by a spiritual awakening. We will need to make such a spiritual regeneration if we are to successfully meet the coming years.

People will be so ready to take daring actions that there could actually be another Boston Tea Party in the spring of 2025. The symbol of that historic upheaval, Saturn conjunct Neptune, returns just as other outer planets return to their 1770s positions. Whatever the rebels throw into the sea this time, one could scarcely imagine a conjunction with greater significance for American destiny. Coming just as Neptune returns to the place it occupied during the Civil War (when the two planets were opposed), this Saturn-Neptune lineup clearly could dissolve (Neptune) the institutions (Saturn) of the United States as we now know them. The walls holding back the American people may crumble as quickly as the wall in Berlin did during the previous Saturn-Neptune conjunction. The revolutionary spirit may lead to repressive measures against the peoples' enemies, as Saturn enters Taurus in 2028. Until then, the enemies themselves, the greedy defenders of threatened institutions, will carry on a secret and treacherous campaign against the people. They will not be successful, because the people's moral concerns will win the government's favor.

People's demands will swell even more in mid-June, and crest in July, 2025, when Saturn and Neptune turn stationary at the cusp of Aries. As fate would have it, this is the exact moment of America's Jupiter return (to 6° Cancer) and of the first entry of Uranus into Gemini. A critical confrontation or momentous decision is indicated. It could be the parting of the ways for the old America and the new. In early August, Mars opposes the conjunction of Saturn-Neptune. The people will assert themselves with force, and they will be met with resistance (Saturn). It could be America's Tienanmen Square, but this time the people won't retreat.

In foreign affairs, the U.S. executive will have to preside amidst uncertain, fluctuating , and dangerous conditions in 2025 that feed the unrest or civil strife at home. Crucial, pioneering events will occur in Japan, Russia, and Central Asia which command the attention of the world. In the fall of 2025, the U.S. could suffer an historic turnabout as a result of these events, as it may have to respond to foreign intervention in *its* affairs (perhaps by Japan). This is a continuing reality the American people must reckon with if they are stupid enough to wage another civil war in the 2020s. They will also have to deal with the financial obligations caused by foreign investments.

NEW AGE PIONEERS: NEPTUNE ENTERS ARIES

On January 26, 2026, Neptune re-enters Aries for a thirteen-year stay. Since Aries is the first sign of the zodiac, this begins a new 164-year cycle for only the second time since the planet's discovery. The signs generally look very positive. The keynote of this new cycle (as opposed to the previous one that began in 1861) will be "visionary pioneering" rather than "aggression." No less than five planets will be in Aquarius, sign of the new age, on January 26, suggesting people will be idealistic and progressive during this new 164-year period. An optimistic and energetic attitude will be developing, underlined by the Sun's position in the very degree (7° Aquarius) where assertive Mars is turning stationary-direct in the progressed Chart of Modern Humanity. Uranus is exactly conjunct the Ascendant in earthy Taurus at the very moment that Neptune's new cycle begins, revealing "Nature's Revolution" on the rise, and showing progress in Earth-friendly technology. Since Saturn conjoins Neptune, the new cycle will seek to institutionalize (Saturn) the new "global awareness" (Neptune). In the 2020s, we will be in the "crescent moon" phases in all the mutual cycles of the outer planets, so this will be a very creative and optimistic time—a "flowering" of the New Age. Issues that arise in 2025–26, such as ethnic and environmental rights in an interdependent world, will be worked out over the entire 164-year cycle, just as the years 1861–62 were decisive for the 164 years that followed.

Previous "great crises" in American history every four score and four years produced breakthroughs in basic human rights. This time, its confluence with the 59-year "progressive cycle" (1789, 1848, 1906, 1965) may indicate that the crisis in 2025–26 will result in even more substantial advances in social justice, brought about by greater revolutionary energy among the people and from "muckraking" journalists. We can see this already in the charts for February and March of 2026. Humanity will march forward, as human rights become a reality everywhere for the first time in history. Resistance may continue in "the states" of America, however, since such an all-encompassing transformation as it will now be making is never easy.

HIGH SPIRITS AND SQUABBLES

The year 2026 should be an outgoing, adventurous time. People will continue to be in a rebellious mood, instigating more demonstrations and confrontations early in the year. Despite the explosive climate of unrest, "victory" may already seem in sight for the rebels. In August, negotiations will go well between authorities in the U.S. and those in other countries involved in our quarrels. Optimism may not be entirely justified, however, since Uranus will only be in its first year in Gemini, and the planets show more trouble ahead.

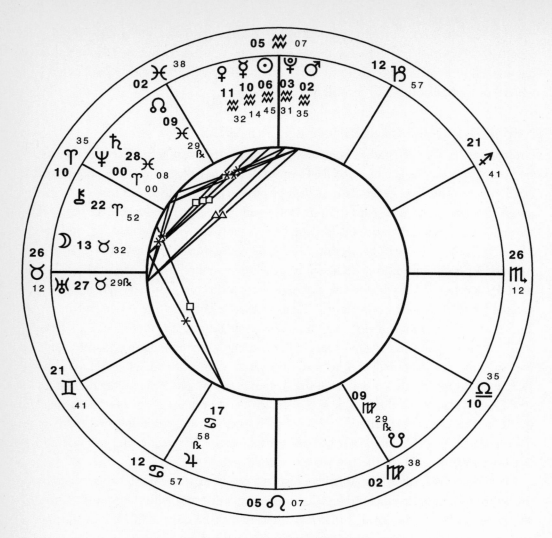

Neptune Ingress into Aries

An ingress is the moment when a planet enters a new sign of the zodiac. The chart for the moment when Neptune enters Aries on January 26, 2026, is also the start of a whole new 164-year cycle of Neptune through the signs. The chart for this moment indicates that progressive, inventive, and ecological trends will predominate in the new cycle. Nature's Revolution (Uranus in Taurus) was in the Ascendant. Note that the Sun is in the key degree of 7° Aquarius, just where Mars will be turning stationary-direct in the progressed Horoscope of Humanity. Chart data: January 26, 2026, 05:14 P.M. GMT, Washington, D.C., 38N54, 77W02.

Violent outbreaks may resume in early 2027 in the U.S. or the Middle East, as Mars in Virgo turns stationary and squares Uranus. On February 6, an eclipse will happen in the critical degree of 17° Aquarius. Fierce debates in Congress will be stirred by illegal foreign investments by authorities, and by social and health problems. Less fortunate people will be

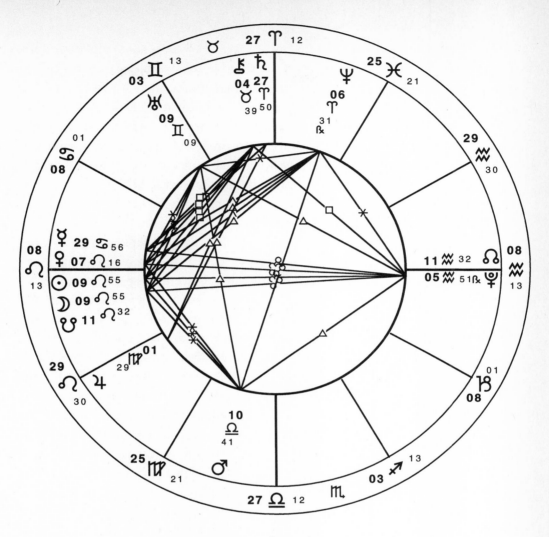

2027 Solar Eclipse
Explosions of youthful idealism after this total solar eclipse will lead to global creative projects and probably to calls for "order" from the adult establishment (Saturn in Aries at Midheaven). Chart data: August 2, 2027, 10:06 A.M. GMT, Washington, D.C., 38N54, 77W02.

in a rebellious mood, and the U.S. executive will feel pressured to act. Key battles over reforms in the Senate could challenge the president in April, as could an act of terror.

Despite these irritations and the ongoing U.S. crisis, early 2027 looks to be fairly constructive and creative. New stars will burst across the American entertainment landscape, and the arts will show greater imagination. Youthful high spirits will assert themselves in March and April 2027 as rebellious street gangs and riots at sports events grab headlines (although this may just signify a more spirited than usual spring break!) Uranus in Gemini rebellion may also take the form of computer or media sabotage by young "hackers."

The second half of 2027 may be a somewhat different story. Youthful rebellion explodes again in a big way after an August 2 eclipse in Leo that is very powerful in Washington. The eclipse is conjunct sensual Venus (in an echo of the progressed Venus in Leo in the chart of Modern Humanity), and opposing passionate Pluto in humanist Aquarius. We may see huge campus demonstrations reminiscent of the great student protests of Berkeley and Columbia, and groups of idealistic, youthful adventurers may travel the globe organizing great charitable and creative projects. When Saturn enters Aries, it always raises the temperature of the struggle; so the tide of youthful violence is likely to increase from the fall of 2027 through the spring of 2028. At the Midheaven during the August 2027 eclipse, Saturn in Aries shows adults impatient with the headstrong young rebels, and calling for "order" in the months that follow.

A crucial battle may occur around September 1, 2027. By then, Jupiter will be in Virgo, a sign of more sobering times. As Uranus crosses the "nuclear" degree of 8° Gemini, people may need to face the following sobering thought—unless the world has put an end to nuclear weapons by now (which I doubt), who will control them if the United States splits apart? Will Uncle Sam surrender them to the U.N.? Or could Americans use them or other high-tech weapons to attack each other? As Uranus returns exactly to its original position in the U.S. horoscope, this stark dilemma and others like it will rear their heads. Unless the people get answers on October 28, 2027, the military may provide one on December 23. At the same time America will also face the fundamental question: shall it have union with itself, but not the world, or shall it have union with the world, but not itself? Key confrontations and decisions will happen as Uranus reaches its home degree in America's horoscope late in 2027.

An explosion follows in early 2028, but probably not a nuclear one. Instead, a time bomb will go off in the U.S. Congress (figuratively, we hope), since a very explosive eclipse (conjunct Pluto) happens in Aquarius (legislative sign) on January 26, 2028. Perhaps the lawmakers will be dealing with the nuclear issue, or maybe with anger and crisis in the cities. Remember the riots in 1968 and 1992 when Jupiter was also in Virgo? In early 2028 (especially in May) Jupiter will be super-powerful there, so the lower classes will be demanding help, and probably getting it. An economic downturn, perhaps caused by careless speculation during the prrevious spring of 2027, may add to the urgency. These problems will inspire brilliant, landmark legislation in Congress in mid-February 2028. We may also see great advances in literature and science then, along with a danger of disasters at sea.

CONSOLIDATING CHAOS

May 8, 2028, marks a decisive moment: an important settlement could be reached in the American crisis after a major battle, perhaps spurred on by nuclear concerns. The overall turmoil will not stop, though. It will continue to swell as we reach the era's climax in 2030 (Jupiter's opposition to Saturn). Many people will be demanding individual freedom from bureaucratic repression—a very prominent theme in the Aquarius/Aries-ruled 2020s. The danger of economic confrontations in the U.S. and abroad will be acute in May and July of

2028, perhaps leading to violence. New reforms, ideas, or problems in the health field will be prominent in the news in the spring of 2028.

Although people will be high-spirited and optimistic in the late 2020s, their urge for retribution against "enemies of freedom and progress" could get carried away. Governments may respond to public unrest with repression. Congress or corporations may carry out illegal crackdowns against youthful "offenders." Japan will probably be the scene of even more cruel repressions and state economic controls, after years of trouble. If Japan tries to take advantage of the chaotic situation in America, which nation will end up stronger? In mid-November 2028, rebels will mount another challenge to federal authority (Mars in Virgo, square Uranus),while repressive economic controls may fail to tame the wild financial markets.

The partial eclipse of January 14, 2029, is in the powerful, dangerous degree of 25° Capricorn (Mars in the Horoscope of Modern Humanity) at the Midheaven in Washington. The executive branch reasserts its power forcefully, perhaps to bring order to America in the midst of its domestic crisis or civil war. A new "executive council" could take over, consistent with Pluto in Aquarius (symbolizing the power of groups). The new administration(s) will be more powerful than the old (including more power behind the scenes).

Public crusaders and their masses of rebellious followers will continue to attack poverty, pollution, disease, and corruption all around the world in the spring of 2029, as activist Mars and generous Jupiter in Libra soar into high cosmic focus.This also indicates that some quick, surprising diplomatic breakthroughs could occur in the midst of war. So could some careless, secret financial deals that may be highly embarrassing to several governments. It will be a risky time for international investing. On the brighter side, the spring of 2029 under Mars and Jupiter in Libra could be an amazingly inventive period in technology, literature and music. Mars in this Venus-ruled sign of balance and harmony recurs frequently in the charts of the later 2020s, showing many breakthroughs in diplomacy as well as intellectual and artistic achievements. Mars in Libra could also stand for air wars or intricate political maneuvering. Look for it to be significant in August 2025, August 2027, early 2029, and late 2030.

The years 2028 and 2029 could see some conflicts end and other related conflicts begin. There are dangerous signs in the spring of 2029 of more wars (Saturn square Pluto). With stationary Mars in Libra trining Uranus and Pluto in air signs, we could see some spectacular aerial battles that make Desert Storm seem like a real video game. America (or some part thereof) could find itself on the

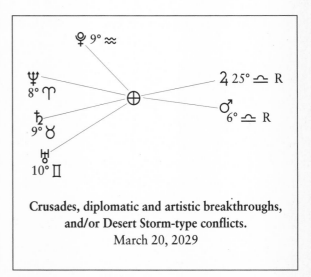

Crusades, diplomatic and artistic breakthroughs, and/or Desert Storm-type conflicts.
March 20, 2029

wrong path again, as Mars turns stationary in late Virgo in May. Suddenly, this high-tech warfare might get more difficult. Dissension will grow if American involvement in war continues, and peace would seem the better part of valor. The best path for America in the summer of 2029 would be to wage its battles on a strictly economic and diplomatic level, or better yet, to work together for peace with other nations. Such efforts would probably be very successful at this time.

AGGRESSIVE IDEALISM

In the fall of 2029, revolts over military service or health and labor matters may erupt, along with more demands to reform taxes and finances. A climactic change of direction is indicated at the decade's end, as Jupiter opposes Saturn in fixed signs. This may involve decisive actions to reorganize the world economy and make needed reforms. These financial concerns may cause some of the leaders who engaged in battles at the year's start to stop fighting by the summer, or at least turn their armed conflicts into economic ones. In 2029–2031, major efforts will be made to settle the military and economic disputes of the past ten years, the results of which may make it seem as if we have entered a greatly revised world order. In spite of these settlements, the rebellious, *"ram"*-bunctious mood of people everywhere will be at a peak in 2030, and will continue until Neptune leaves Aries " the Ram" a decade later in 2039.

In 2030, the era's headlong spirit of change will lead many people to engage in some strange experiments. Startling new developments in art may occur that will be pursued in future years, almost as if Manet were about to record another picnic in the grass. A controversial breakthrough in mind-expanding substances or mental health techniques should also occur in this period, as well as innovative new human communities and social networks.

A Mars-Mercury-Neptune conjunction in the spring of 2030 shows some kind of scandal regarding military secrets or a technological accident. Probably this will force technology into safer directions. Scandals could burst wide open in June 2030, when Saturn enters Gemini, and the press forces big institutions to change their secret policies. Such revelations could prove to be a big defeat for the forces resisting change at this climactic moment. People should travel with care this month, as severe accidents are forecast.

As Uranus returns to its Battle of Gettysburg degree (also the U.S. Mars degree), Americans may be reminded again that a nation and a world divided against itself cannot stand. Early November of 2030 could be the occasion for a sudden attack, a decisive battle, or for a decision to "stand up to aggressors" (Mars in Virgo), which may now include those who seek to undermine the world's emerging unity of mind and spirit. Success is likely in these efforts.

A REVISED WORLD ORDER: SATURN AND URANUS IN GEMINI

The new decade will be somewhat calmer than the last (meaning at least some notches below total frenzy), largely because the world will be more peaceful. After the total eclipse of

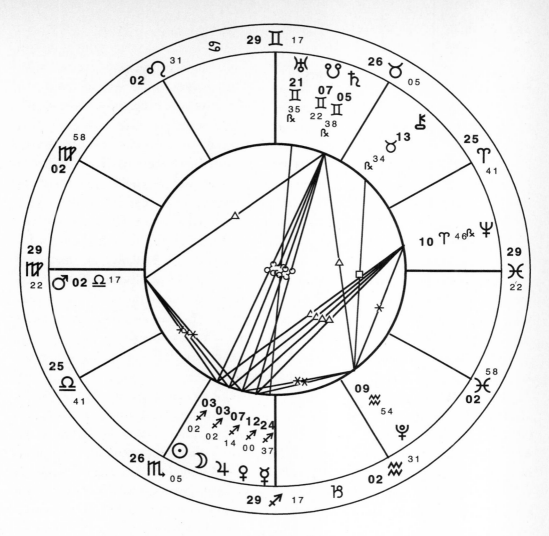

2030 Solar Eclipse

The Revised World Order. Consolidating change. Chart data: November 25, 2030, 06:48 A.M. GMT, Washington, D.C., 38N54, 77W02.

November 25, 2030, we may see some dramatic diplomatic breakthroughs like those of the earlt 1970s and 1990s, lifting hopes again that the world is coming together. Wars, mass crusades, or uprisings beginning in June–July 2029 will somehow prepare the way for these moves toward reconciliation. If not satisfied with the results, these movements could erupt again at the end of 2030. Indeed, it may sometimes seem as if the world of these years is populated almost entirely by moralizing activists. But that's not true—plenty of self-righteous intellectuals will be around too. Both figure prominently in the November 2030 eclipse, which shows Jupiter in moralizing Sagittarius opposing Saturn in intellectual Gemini. The years

2030–32 should see the climax of a six-year debate between the forces of "progress" and the forces of "obstruction," and between science and religion—one which may be characterized as a contest for the human soul. Let's hope the two sides in the debate have "evolved" a bit since Darwin's time, so that we don't make monkeys of ourselves for the next eighty years, as we did from the 1860s to the 1940s. One deadly, destructive "age of agression" is enough!

As Jupiter opposes Uranus in 2031, breakthroughs in education, travel, communication, and trade may occur. On the other hand, major financial quarrels could erupt between the U.S. and the Far East in June, when Mars turns stationary in 4° Scorpio (Uranus' degree in the chart of Modern Humanity). The outcome of this epic struggle could decide the shape of world trade for years to come. No one said building a truly interdependent world order would be easy, and it will only get harder during the late summer and fall of 2031. Americans will fight to maintain their position in this revised world order, but it looks like a difficult battle, complicated by many problems. The fall charts of 2031 show losses for American institutions, or an epidemic of deaths due to violence or disease. Plagues or floods could further erode the U.S. position, though they'll also inspire unusual outpourings of generous philanthropy. Continuing transportation problems in 2031–32 could lead to major innovations and reforms in this field. American travel workers may take advantage of this uncertain situation to wage strikes, but severe responses by the "renewed" power of government might create a climate of fear against "radicals."

The powerful total eclipse of November 14, 2031, shows that the executive branch will be acting to work out the revised world order, and this may bring some order back to America in the process. During the exact moment of the eclipse, Mars sits in the Midheaven at its Chart of Modern Humanity position of 25° Capricorn (the same degree where the eclipse of January, 2029 occurred, also on the Midheaven in Washington). The focus remains on diplomacy over the next few months, as America works out its relationship to the U.N. and other nations. Americans will resolve disputes or conclude new trade agreements within the western hemisphere now. In general, the political map may look quite different after 2032 than it did in 2028. So might the map of the (former?) United States, where a "Confederacy" may have won after all—the country may now be better described as the "Confederation of Independent States of America."

ANXIOUS ADJUSTMENTS: SATURN AND URANUS IN CANCER

The intellectual "battle" in the universities and the press will grab more headlines in the spring of 2032. Americans may still have trouble adjusting to their diminished unity and place in the world, much as they did in the 1970s. Health and welfare departments may face severe pressures. Transportation woes and air/space disasters will be in the news again in June 2032, along with technological or environmental accidents. Congress will effectively deal with these domestic adjustment problems, but in June, Americans will still be asked to render service to other peoples. The American military might no longer be top dog, but it will still be called upon to act as head nurse.

Saturn and Uranus enter emotional Cancer in the summer of 2032. A shortage of goods—and of good executive leadership—may cause much uncertainty. Anxious times will likely also be seen in Canada, the Balkans, Vietnam, the Philippines, and/or East Africa (nations ruled by Cancer). Not everyone will be pleased with the new arrangements of the revised world order. With Uranus in Cancer, some peoples may try to flex their new powers. Retribution by ethnic groups against their enemies during the recent crisis could happen. America in particular must be careful to avert another "age of hate" during this new "reconstruction" period. Trouble may be brewing in Korea too, one Uranus cycle after the Korean War. The Germans may take the opportunity to test the extent of their power in Europe, and the Scots may be ready for independence. Many nations will have to reorganize themselves in 2033–35 in the wake of all the human energy and freedom unleashed in the 2020s.

The American executive may be out to lunch, but the legislative branch will continue to make hay. In February 2033, it will tackle energy shortages and resource conservation, as these issues come back into focus under Saturn-Uranus in Cancer. Conscious of past mistakes, lawmakers will seek to improve the health of the people and the land in 2033. Progress will be made toward programs for social justice and equality too—a never-ending challenge. These Congressional actions in February and March 2033 may remind some people of the Roosevelt's "Hundred Days," exactly a hundred years before. As Pluto reaches its "point of power" in mid-Aquarius in the mid-2030s, reform fever will hit legislatures in other nations, too.

1949 REVISITED—OR IS IT 1867?

In 2033, many nations will reinvent themselves, especially those mentioned above. If Korea is still not unified, one side may open a military "campaign of unification" by June or August. Such shocking events in the Far East could stimulate American ethnic paranoia and conspiracy theories in the summer and fall. Some congressional hotheads could carry on smear campaigns reminiscent of McCarthyism in the 1950s or the reconstruction radicals of the 1860s. They may impose their will on defeated ethnic groups, passing some kind of forcible "reconstruction" law. The ACLU will have its hands full in 2033–2034 protecting the old Bill of Rights and the new social justice guarantees against all this retribution, as well as the secret repressive moves by Americans against other nations that may occur in this period. A total eclipse happens on the first day of spring in 2034, so some shocking events can be expected during that season, especially in the Far East. Shortages and recession will probably get worse in the U.S., leading to paranoid uncertainty as well as major humanitarian efforts. These tensions will probably reach their peak in late June and July 2034.

In the fall of 2033, America could also find itself waging a trade war with its recent foes, fueling the xenophobic or ethnic hysteria. The executive branch might impose trade embargoes and fuel rationing, causing trouble for the banks. Foreign trade conflicts and resulting shortages of goods may stimulate many Americans to become more aware of the need to further wean themselves and their society from their dependence on material things. As our material "prosperity" is challenged in 2033 and 2034, so also will our idea of "progress," as Pluto passes over the critical "end of progress" degree of 17° Aquarius. Religious groups may try to take advantage of this retreat from materialism to reassert themselves politically in the fall of 2033. More cult-inspired violence could result.

China could be ripe for change in 2033–2034, since one full Uranus cycle and one half of Pluto's cycle will have passed since the People's Republic was founded in 1949. The Chinese will decide if a united Republic can continue, and whether its political ideals really promote the pride, health, and prosperity of its people. It is likely that 2034 will be a revolutionary year, since Pluto will return to its position of 1789. Iraq and Iran may be targets, in addition to China. The heat of upheaval only increases in the summer and fall, as Jupiter enters Aries. People will be ready to act. In June 2034, the UN may be called upon to resolve these conflicts. If people respond positively to the cosmic challenges of this year, the rebellions will resolve themselves very constructively by year's end, leading to more campaigns for human rights in early 2035.

UNPACIFIC SEAS

Forced to reorganize itself and revise its position in the world order, the U.S. won't be in a position to intervene unilaterally in any other nation's affairs until 2035, when Uncle Sam (or one of his "children") may be ready to impose his will on others again. Let's hope he has learned how to do it peacefully. Jupiter's union with Neptune in Aries in March of 2035 shows high enthusiasm for human rights. The American people will be feeling more confident and optimistic that year, and generous social programs might alleviate the pain caused by recent shortages. Worldwide diplomatic breakthroughs may be achieved now, with American help.

As Jupiter moves into Taurus in May 2035, the U.S. may find itself over-extending and making dangerous commitments abroad. By October, the crisis will become acute, involving China, Korea, and Japan. With Pluto still in critical 17° Aquarius, and Saturn opposing it, there is danger of a violent confrontation. Mars turns stationary-direct at 17° Pisces in mid-October 2035, so this will be the crucial moment. It could involve a dispute over a waterway (a strait or canal), or ocean rights and "freedom of the seas" (which by then could also mean freedom of space travel). It could also involve oil, atomic energy or perhaps a new liquid fuel discovered around 2022. There may be battles or terrorist attacks at sea. America (or some part thereof) would probably suffer a major defeat were it to get involved at this moment, so Americans who love peace (or victory) should be vigilant. With Mars stationary in the 1966 "pile-up" degree of 17° Pisces in October 2035, cries may be heard about "another Vietnam" or "another Korea." The confrontation may have been provoked by a gigantic oil spill, or it may cause one. This would arouse further environmental protests, which would grow as we approach the "Green Revolution" of the 2040s. The crisis could also provoke more social protest in America, leading to loud confrontations in Congress over possible reforms. Upheavals could affect India or Israel beginning in the fall of 2035.

I see no letup in these crises in 2036, especially after the partial eclipses on February 27 and July 23. America will probably see its economic future at stake in this conflict, as will other nations. This will be the first year of Uranus' next square to Neptune, so it may be the start of a new kind of imperialism or another "cold war" (probably an economic one), as nations and peoples contend for resources on our increasingly finite planet. With Saturn in Leo opposing Pluto in 2036, it's a good bet that some of these nations may make moves against their neighbors. For example, Mid-East nations may try to recapture power lost because of diminishing oil revenues. The late 2030s could be the time when this region decides whether to enter the modern world or relapse into their ageless enmities.

SPIRIT IN MOTION

Nine months after Mars turns stationary in the "stillness of spirit" degree of 17° Pisces in October 2035, a partial eclipse occurs on July 23, 2036. This chart looks a lot like the "stillness of spirit" figure itself: I call it "spirit in motion." I think this chart indicates that we may now discover how to make "progress" in a more spiritual way. We can do this chiefly by making our society more fuel efficient, and thus showing respect for the Earth. With Jupiter and Saturn in the same places as during Jimmy Carter's energy proposals fifty-nine years before, 2036 will be a year to reorganize our transportation system, promote energy conservation, and develop new fuels. Spurred on by the world's conflicts over resources, Congress will probably lead the way with a generous and inventive program, finally taking on the old "big oil interests."

The "Spirit in Motion" figure could also signify revolutions and coups that ignite new conflicts, especially in Africa. In late October 2036, as Uranus in Cancer turns stationary opposite the conjunction degree of 1993, there may be new ethnic and nationalist movements in East Africa, the Balkans, or the Middle East. Conflicts in these places after 2036 (Uranus square Neptune) could be the first serious challenge to the New World Order (as recently revised), leading to further revisions in the diplomatic arrangements among peoples. The same conflicts will drag on into April 2037, when Mars joins Pluto and opposes Saturn. Middle East and Indian nationalist power struggles may continue at full tilt.

People's identification with the land will increase in 2037, and a financial crisis may lead to visionary legislative action on environmental problems. Caution is advised, though, since over-ambitious plans by liberal governments in 2036 may also engender another tax revolt the following year, fifty-nine years (two Saturn cycles) after California's famous Proposition 13. Perhaps tax rebels and environmentalists will find common ground this time, as the 2040s and the "Green Revolution" approach. In the wake of th "Spirit in Motion" figure, which will signify aroused individualism and self-confidence among the people, demands will be heard again that both government and business be smaller, less oppressive, and more accountable. As Saturn returns to Virgo on July 7, 2037, this new trend will become a political movement.

The power of Neptune in all the charts of this time suggests that an occult or spiritual revival may be stimulated by American contacts with Asia or with ETs in this period. Some visionary leaders may try to apply this spiritual knowledge to our physical fuel shortage.

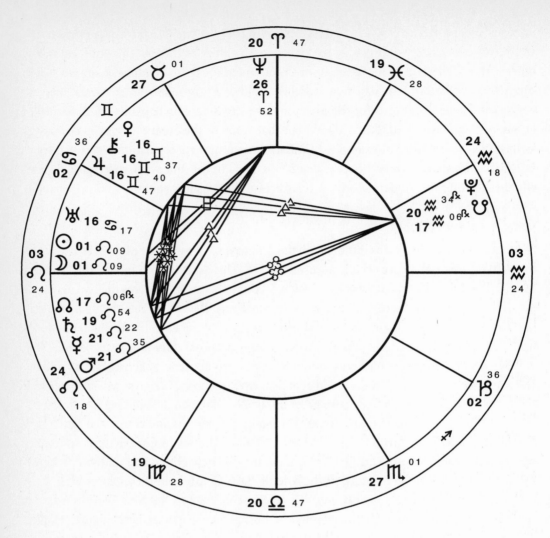

Spirit in Motion

A new energy policy and revolution in Africa are possible meanings of this powerful partial solar eclipse in 2036. Chart data: July 23, 2036, 10:38 A.M. GMT, Washington, D.C., 38N54, 77W02.

If Americans have not achieved "energy independence" by July 2037 through developing and applying new fuels, they could face more economic troubles and fights among ethnic groups. Jupiter joins Uranus in Cancer on September 8, 2037, showing further efforts to reform the corporate and financial system to make it more responsive to individuals and families. Since this conjunction is also similar to the one in 1955, it could see Congress or the courts act to uphold the civil and economic rights of ethnic groups.

BRINGING IT ALL BACK HOME

The total eclipse of July 13, 2037, in Cancer happens in the Fifth House, conjunct Uranus and Jupiter. This ordains a greater interest in children, education, and family values. Despite Uncle Sam's active involvement in the uneasy diplomatic climate, Americans will be riding a wave of domesticity. It may be the peak year of a new "baby boom." On the other hand, in the wake of the "Spirit in Motion" figure in 2036 which spotlighted the outgoing and expressive sign Leo, there could be a new wave of bohemian self-expression on the rise. New movements in art begun at the decade's start will now come into bloom. As Neptune approaches Taurus, people will be feeling more comfortable, and will want to settle down and enjoy life. This could mean a new conservative climate like that of the 1950s, perhaps magnified by xenophobia. But since Pluto will stay in Aquarius until 2043 (and afterward opposes Uranus), pressure for reform will not end. It may instead take the form of demands for "self- empowerment."

At the end of 2037, Saturn turns stationary in a familiar degree: 17° Virgo, while Mars turns stationary in Taurus, in trine to Saturn. It looks like decisive action may be applied to the conflicts over fuel and other resources that began in 2035 (probably involving Asia). On January 5, 2038, an annular eclipse forms a grand trine with Saturn and Mars. Business and government could cooperate to preserve resources and empower the people, though some wealthy businessmen may fight these measures. It will be another chance to help humanity achieve true "energy self-reliance" and make green ideals more workable. The powerful Spring Equinox chart for 2038 only confirms these indications, as Jupiter joins Uranus in Cancer exactly at the Nadir in Washington. It will bring a new thrust of environmentalism. We can now accelerate the agricultural reforms so essential to the health of people and planet alike.

Many North Americans, especially brash, outspoken youth, will ask whether their own material progress and the foreign meddlings by their government don't impair the quality of their own personal and family lives. Others will reply that they must stay active and alert to international affairs, or their rights and resources will be taken away. Americans can't preserve America without preserving the Earth—and asking other peoples to do so, too. As Jupiter returns to Leo and Neptune approaches its rendezvous with the trigger point of 0° Taurus, more crises in the Middle East will probably force the issue. The fall charts of 2038 show unusually intense diplomatic activity by Uncle Sam to resolve these crises.

ECONOMY MELTS INTO ECOLOGY: NEPTUNE IN TAURUS

Three days after the Spring Equinox of 2039, Neptune enters Taurus. This will bring a calmer, more cautious and pragmatic attitude. Revolutions will happen in the following years, but they will be focused in particular places and toward well-defined goals instead of being wild and diffuse as they were under Aries. Though radical movements will continue (Pluto in Aquarius, opposing Uranus in 2047), they will be more firmly grounded. People will want change to be slower, and in some places this might mean political conservatism. In other places (like France or California), the slower pace could mean another "Belle Epoque" in which delicate, refined arts and decadent pleasures flourish. This trend could last up to two decades, as people escape from the fast pace of city life that prevailed during the Aries age of progress, seeking instead a more pastoral lifestyle. In other words, at the end of this "high gear" era, we will change back into a lower gear.

This may not all be by choice, though. We will also be forced to slow down by deepening recession, at least in the first years of Neptune in Taurus. The international troubles and trade wars that began in 2035, plus ecological disasters, will hurt the economy. A moderate financial panic will bring about economic (Taurus) dissolution (Neptune) by 2041, as old corporate combinations melt into new ones. It will be up to us to make sure these new structures are more beneficial to the public and the planetary interest than the old ones were. The spring of 2039 will bring a chance to do this. The important reforms and international agreements begun in the new "Hundred Days" of January 2033 to improve the health of the land and its people should resume in the spring of 2039, in response to deep economic restructuring.

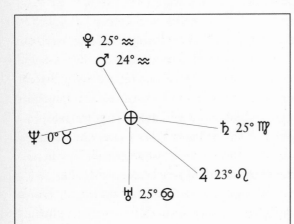

Yod figure highlights Neptune ingress into Taurus Mars-Pluto opposite Jupiter and quincunx Saturn and Uranus forms the ancient rune symbol for "protection." March 23, 2039

During the thirteen years under Neptune in Taurus, conservation and conservatism may come together at last, as economy and ecology are combined (Uranus in Cancer sextile Saturn in Virgo). International ecological problems will strongly affect world trade. A magnificent yod figure announces Neptune's entry into Taurus in March 2039. It indicates that we will have to transform the way we deal with each other, so that our personal interests and relationships are in harmony with a new global society preoccupied with protecting the planet. New Sacred Earth ideals will transmute our economic institutions over the next thirteen years as a global, ecological economy unfolds during the "Green Revolution." The shape of the yod figure itself is, incidentally, the same as the Germanic rune for "protection," and it also resembles the symbolic three-pronged staff of Neptune —now located in earth sign Taurus. We will adjust our ways of life so that we can all experience vividly our connection to the Earth Goddess, transforming our souls to better fit them for the dawning Age of Aquarius. Rich nations may now seek to protect poorer ones from the problems caused by scarce resources. Some groups will be suspicious of those in power, even believing conspiracy theories claiming that those who control access to the world's resources are plotting to destroy the planet!

The new Earth-reform diplomacy will receive its baptism in the Middle East in the summer and fall of 2039, where religious leaders may cause trouble. Another yod on July

18 will put stationary Venus in Leo at the "activating point," showing earnest attempts to solve disputes. The problems will probably arise, as suggested before, from diminishing oil revenues plus the dawning realization among Middle East peoples that they have been among the last to acheive human rights and democracy, although they were the first to achieve civilization. In mid-November, Mars in Cancer (squaring Saturn in Libra) turns stationary-retrograde, showing the new Earth diplomacy in action, and America's will to "protect" the Revised World Order. Mars in Cancer will probably also aggravate ethnic troubles, and perhaps environmental disputes. The Sagittarian total eclipse in December, 2039, may herald dramatic success in international negotiations.

In February, 2040, Mars in Cancer turns stationary-direct. Indications are that once again the Americans will feel impelled to take quick, aggressive action (probably by sea) in the Middle East. Let's hope it's not bungled like the Bay of Pigs invasion (also Mars direct in Cancer in 1961). These new Mid-East troubles may be severe enough to shift alliances within the revised world order (as in 1956, when Uranus was square Neptune, as it will be now). Saturn's position in Libra in 2040 (echoing its place in the progressed Chart of Modern Humanity) indicates that the end result of this crisis could be the arrival of genuine human justice in the landds which once invented it (Iraq, Iran, Arabia, Palestine, etc.). Six planets in Libra in September of 2040 may be the hopeful sign of this great breakthrough for human rights and justice, and in October, mass action by the Middle Eastern people (Mars opposite Neptune) may confirm it. Fall 2040 could go down in history as a time when humanity reaffirmed its commitment to the ideals of fairness and "justice for all."

The same six Libra planets can also bring justice to the American economy. They sound the keynote for the next chapter: growing economic interdependence among all peoples in a greener (meaning a more alive and prosperous) world. The period in which humanity plunged forth again into aggressive Aries will complete itself by gaining a new balance in cooperative Taurus and Libra.

ENDNOTES FOR CHAPTER 18
1. It is not unlikely that this president will, in fact, be a woman.

19

A Greener World:

2040 AND BEYOND

In many ways, the Twenty-First Century will be more peaceful and constructive than the Twentieth, despite the likelihood of ecological disasters and resulting conflicts among migrating ethnic peoples. The wars of the Twenty-First Century will be far less destructive than those of the Twentieth, and the new inventions, though equally brilliant, will not threaten our survival. If we have truly developed our new Great Mind of Humanity, in which each person senses vividly and intimately a vital connection to all people, then perhaps by 2040 we will have learned to solve our conflicts without violence. On the other hand, we may look back on the turbulence of the previous fifty years and realize how much they inspired us to do great things.

Once again, this twenty-year period is marked as significant, because the Jupiter-Saturn conjunction on October 31, 2040 is followed only five days later by a partial solar eclipse. Its chart shows both the conjunction and the eclipse in the Eighth House in Washington, with Pluto rising. This confirms that the 2040s will be a time (much like the 1880s) of dissolving economic combinations and mushrooming new ones. This is emphasized by Neptune in Taurus (economic dissolution) opposing the eclipse. Unlike the 1880s, the new combinations will be international (since the Jupiter-Saturn conjunction is in Libra, instead of also being in Taurus as in 1881). Global commerce will become truly interdependent, powered by further advances in global communications like those which began in the 1990s. Some of these new commercial combinations could be insidious in ways that make the famous "trilateral commission" seem like a friendly card game. Constant vigilance will be needed to see that organizations set up to regulate global trade aren't taken over by the corporate elites they are supposed to govern. Conservative rulers will be in power, since this sixty-year cycle will bring back the right-wing ideology of the 1920s and 1980s. Neptune will have returned to conservative Taurus, too (as in the reactionary 1880s). With Jupiter-Saturn in Libra, new executives like Reagan may appear who will manipulate the Great Mind and its tools of virtual reality communications and global institutions to enact a high-tech *1984* scenario, in which the ruler injects his/her personality into our very own subconscious and rules us from inside our own skins. These new bosses would use their powers to promote trade and pass "tax reforms" that provide enormous breaks or subsidies for

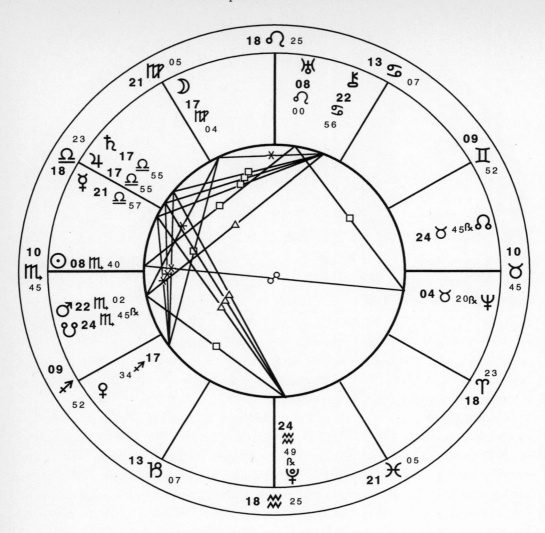

2040 Jupiter-Saturn Conjunction

This is the chart for the exact time of the conjunction, according to The American Ephemeris. *As in 2020, it puts Jupiter and Saturn in the Twelfth House when cast for America, so its institutions will face more karma and dissolution as the Green Revolution unfolds. Chart data: October 31, 2040, 11:50 A.M. GMT, Washington, D.C., 38N54, 77W02.*

the rich. Since the conjunction falls in the Eighth House in the eclipse chart, however, one of these rulers may not escape assassination "by inches" as Reagan did.

The new aristocrats have a surprise coming, though. The Green Revolution will arrive toward the end of the decade to knock them off their gilded thrones. The eclipse forecasts this by squaring Uranus. Eighth House planets are not always a good sign for the wealthy, nor for the U.S. institutions that protect them. Corporate "dinosaurs" will die or be transformed. The chart for the actual time of the conjunction itself doesn't provide any solace to the powers that be—Jupiter and Saturn join exactly on the cusp of the

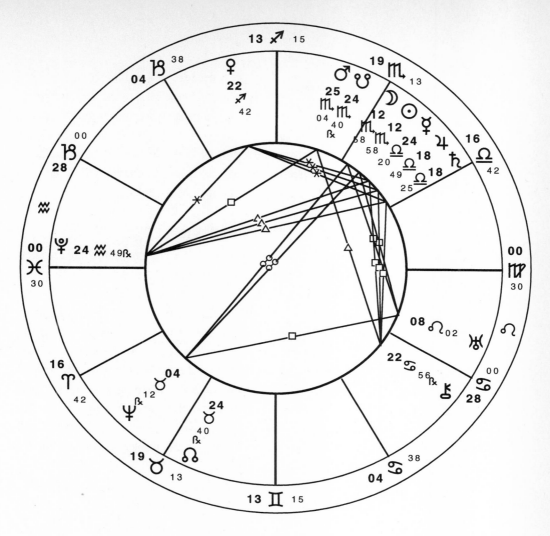

2040 Partial Eclipse

This solar eclipse follows the Jupiter-Saturn by just five days. Economic diplomacy and global market restructuring will highlight the twenty-year period beginning in 2040. Institutions will become even more international, and many American corporations will have to transform themselves or die. Chart data: November 4, 2040, 06:57 P.M. GMT, Washington, D.C., 38N54, 77W02.

Twelfth House. American institutions will face still more bad karma and dissolution as we move toward the Green Revolution, which will destroy businesses not compatible with the planet and a new life style. In the early 2040s, though, the common people will be retreating from political concerns, disillusioned by liberal excesses in the previous era and by the failure of new institutions to stop the recession in 2040. This will allow secret power grabs by the elite, fueling still more disillusion as Pluto enters Pisces in 2043. Unlike in the past, though, after 2043 disenchantment will only provoke the people to action, and humanity will emerge from the 2040s with buoyant spirits—something revolutions have seldom accomplished before.

Remember that in the Twenty-First Century, radical decades will be less radical, and reactionary decades will be less reactionary. Just as Benjamin Disraeli did in the 1870s, benevolent conservatives of the 2040s may sponsor programs to protect the people and the planet's resources, even as they enrich and protect themselves. Their secret actions and diplomatic maneuverings will go smoothly in the spring of 2041. In the fall, though, Congress may make legal reforms in the service sectors or health care financing which the corporate bosses oppose. These issues will grab the spotlight in May 2043.

THE FRENCH REORDER THE WORLD: URANUS IN LEO

There seems no doubt that every time Uranus returns to Leo, the French go through another Revolution. The early 2040s will be no exception. Uranus' continuing square to Neptune shows that this time it may come about as a result of international "cold war" tensions and conflicts, just as it did in the 1870s under the same square. We mentioned that in the later 2030s, Germany may be seeking to dominate the European Union, and this would stir up French resentment. There may even be another "war scare" in 2040, and the Germans may be singing about their "watch on the Rhine" just as they did exactly two centuries before. This rivalry may continue to be troublesome at the end of 2041, when Mars turns stationary in Napoleonic sign Leo and opposes Pluto. The contest in Europe over who will set policy will lead the French to reorganize and strengthen themselves through economic reforms. They may even follow the lead of the Americans and diminish the power of their president, perhaps creating another "directory" of five executives.

The chief goal of the French will be to become the leading economic diplomats of the world. They will command attention through their brilliant ideas on reorganizing the global economy and better integrating it with their own. The last time Uranus was in Leo, France led the way in organizing the European Common Market. This time their goal will be to create a World Common Market. This may be called GATT II, continuing the efforts of the 1990s to drop tariff barriers worldwide. They may also push for a common world currency and tax system. This is the essential step toward true world interdependence. All countries will have to adjust, including a wary Japan.

Eight planets in fixed signs (including all the outer ones) during several months of 2041 and 2042 will mean a basic restructuring of world economic institutions (including American ones). This will be needed to truly integrate them into the high-tech, global economy, so that it benefits everyone and preserves the planet. These tough matters will be hammered out as Saturn, Uranus, and Neptune form a T-square in 2042 and 2043. Trade wars could result if agreements are not reached. If only the rich benefit, or if the system is imposed by force, people will be disillusioned with it soon afterward as the planets leave the fixed signs and enter mutable ones (most notably Pluto entering Pisces in 2043). Disputes over the plans erupt as Mars turns stationary-direct and closely aligns with Uranus in Leo in the spring of

2042, or when it joins Saturn in mid-September. The whole scheme could either climax or unravel under the stressful, very exact T-square of Mars-Saturn-Uranus in May 2043.

Another thorny problem may involve Eastern Europe. The planets in the 2042–2043 T-square (Saturn, Uranus and Neptune) are the same ones that aligned in 1989. Nations that gained democracy then may erupt into social revolution and civil war in 2042–43, since their people will be impatient with their own material progress. Richer nations will have to help meet their demands in order to integrate them into the world economy. In fact, much of the world's wealth may have to be redistributed in the 2040s. The same discontents may sweep India in September 2042.

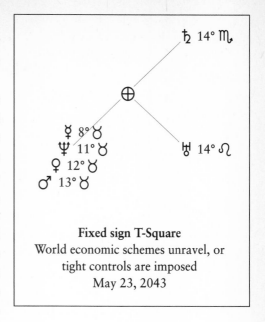

Fixed sign T-Square
World economic schemes unravel, or
tight controls are imposed
May 23, 2043

FAITHS DIE, FAITHS REBORN: PLUTO IN PISCES

The new Global Market may not be able to withstand renewed famines, natural disasters (especially severe in America in May or August 2043), and the resulting complaints. As the rich continue to try to hoard the wealth while poverty grows, the peoples' anger will encourage governments to impose draconian economic price controls (May 2042 or May 2043), while anxiety about reckless speculation by the banks and insurance companies will lead to tight regulations. Trade rivalries could bring trouble between France and other nations (especially in early 2042 and October 2043 under Mars in Leo), and may intensify in September 2044. All these events will arouse paranoia and may lead to depression by 2044, causing world leaders to make exaggerated blusterings (Saturn opposing Neptune, T-square Uranus in Leo), which will in turn discredit the economic projects of the politicians. Peoples' revolts or riots could erupt in the spring (Mars stationary in Virgo), and in the fall a corporate or economic "reign of terror" could develop as powerful leaders try to impose revolutionary changes in America or the Middle East (Mars/Saturn in Scorpio, T-square Pluto and Uranus). The Persian Gulf may see battles between contending rebel forces. All this will not only destroy (Pluto) the people's faith (Pisces) in their leaders, but incite them to look at how they can liberate themselves.

Disillusioned with charismatic leaders trying to reorganize the world forcefully and quickly in the early 2040s, people under Pluto in Pisces and Neptune in Taurus will want to see it grow greener more gradually. Smaller, unregulated communities will be built that resonate spontaneously with the Great Mind of Humanity. As Pluto crosses the point Neptune reached in 2012 , it will start to energize this Mind by purging it of obstructions and fears. First to go will be embargoes from the recent trade wars, as liquid fuels flow again in the spring of 2045. New world trade agreements and high-tech network arrangements that are easier to live with than those of the first global market in 2041–42 will arrive in October 2045, when Jupiter joins Pluto in Pisces and most outer planets shift into mutable signs. Many rulers will then start to recognize that human rights must be respected within the new Global Market, and that it doesn't need to be organized by force.

The most noticeable meaning of Pluto in Pisces will be the heightened romantic sensibility of the times. This will, in turn, stimulate Earth spirituality as represented by Neptune (ruler of Pisces) in Earth sign Taurus. By 2040, Neptune will have crossed the degree the Sun occupies each year on Earth Day. Losing faith in would-be human divinities (such as manufactured media "stars" and grandiloquent politicians), they will regain faith in nature's divinities. This will first be reflected in the performing and visual arts under Uranus in Leo from 2039 to 2046. Music, painting, drama, and poetry may be grander, more eloquent, more sensitive, more delicate, and more competently expressed in the 2040s and 2050s than during the "golden age" fifty years before. Many artists will renew themselves through Earth's rich life-giving powers, as Wordsworth did. Though based on the multimedia forms and tools invented earlier, art and culture will be "higher" than the score on the Time Line for this period suggests. The artists of the 2040s will be the Titians and Monets of their time. By mid-2047, new art forms may blaze forth which allow us to experience the spirits within nature and Earth. Under Uranus in Virgo from 2046 to 2052, the new cult of free love, pleasure and sensibility will bring back not only the 1770s "back to nature" movement, but also the La Belle Epoque of the 1880s and the counter-culture of the 1960s. It will begin to bloom profusely in the fall of 2045 from the seeds of the more blatant and wild expressions that developed under Uranus in Leo (early 2040s). The new sensibility will also be expressed in scientific and literary movements, as Uranus in Virgo opposes Pluto.

By the late 2040s, the Green Revolution will reshape science and philosophy to fit the new paradigm that says "humans are spiritual beings" and "Earth is a living Goddess," and will institute new work and health styles to fit these beliefs. Even as many people in these uncertain economic times go on dreaming (Neptune) of making money (Taurus), many materialist delusions will dissolve into a world of spirit. Spiritual techniques and psychedelic methods will resurface in a big way in the mid-2040s, and show us how to change society to conform to the New Consciousness. These impulses will burst out after solar eclipses in February 2044, August 2044 and February 2045, perhaps propelled by more health and ecological emergencies and work stoppages as well as by the ideas of nature-loving visionaries.

THE SIXTIES REVISITED

Other 1960s issues will return in the 2040s. Racism is not an easy disease to cure; in fact, it requires constant treatment. Even though much progress toward true "equal justice for all" will have been made worldwide in the 2020s, when progressed Saturn returns to Libra in the Chart of Humanity, more work will be needed as the progressed Sun joins Saturn there in 2044. In Leo, Uranus will be returning to where it was when Rosa Parks refused to go to the back of the bus in 1955, but ironically also the same sign under which Jim Crow pushed the former slaves to the back of American society in 1877. Demands for "white equality" and complaints of "reverse racism" will be heard again. These drives for "individual rights" will probably break out under the powerful Mars conjunctions with Uranus in October 2041, March 2042, and especially October 2043, when health and welfare reform may be pushed, too. The renewed civil rights thrust attains full steam once Uranus returns to Virgo (symbol of the "great society") in October 2045. At that explosive time, Mars joins it and opposes Jupiter-Pluto in Pisces. Those who feel discriminated against will flood the streets, and new laws will follow immediately. Mars and Uranus conjoin in Virgo again in October 2047, suggesting more marches and anti-discrimination legislation.

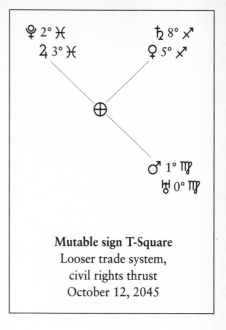

Mutable sign T-Square
Looser trade system,
civil rights thrust
October 12, 2045

As we move toward the Green Revolution's climax in 2047, the three outer planets will have returned to "feminine" signs (most notably Uranus in Virgo the Virgin), contrasting the "masculine" revival of "progress" in the 2020s, when macho Mars turned direct in the progressed Horoscope of Modern Humanity. This symbolizes the fruition of feminist trends begun at the Green Revolution's start in 1966, when all the outer planets were also in feminine signs—including Uranus in Virgo. The renewed drive for full equality will probably break out in late 2044 (Mars stationary in Libra and Virgo; Venus stationary in feminine Taurus), and other feminist issues will spring forth in December of 2045 (Venus stationary in 19° Capricorn). Our culture will be "feminized," as we learn how to nurture one another and to value Mother Earth again. We'll be less concerned with competing and climbing the ladder of success and power.

THE GREEN REVOLUTION SPROUTS

Maintaining a healthy environment will be a central issue of this era. Much will have been done by now, but it won't be enough so long as billions of human beings populate the planet and consume its resources. Technological solutions, developed so profusely during the "green post-industrial revolution" of the 2010s and 2020s, will have only delayed the needed changes in society and lifestyle: now comes the time of reckoning. The renewed natural disasters of the mid-2040s won't be as bad as those of 2010, but they'll be enough to drive home the point. The health of the planet requires not only that huge multi-national corporations and corporate farms behave themselves, but that they be eliminated. It demands not only that products which pollute our minds and bodies be regulated, but that they not be

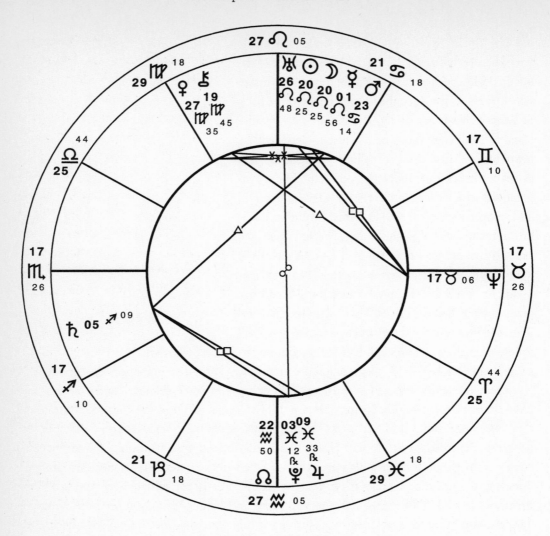

2045 Solar Eclipse

The Green Revolution is unleashed. There may be land or financial scandals that set off the re-
volt. Alternative relationships will flourish (Neptune conjunct the Descendant), and leaders may
be bold and full of bluster (Uranus in Leo at Midheaven). Chart data: August 12, 2045. 05:39 P.M.
GMT, Washington, D.C., 38N54, 77W02.

produced. It mandates not only that there be alternatives to fossil fuels, but that fossil fuels
no longer be an alternative. It requires not only that some homes, cities and nations be resource efficient, but that all of them be so. It means not only doing work we believe in, but
that this be the only "bottom line." Only a Green Revolution, anchored in the hearts and
minds of the people, can overcome resistance by greedy businessmen and consumers to these
necessary and long-delayed changes.

As Uranus opposes Pluto in 2046–48, this Third great movement of modern times will fulfill the cycle begun at their conjunction of 1966, just as the 1901 opposition fulfilled the socialist cycle begun at the 1850 conjunction and the 1793 opposition fulfilled the democratic cycle begun at the 1711 conjunction. The initiative in this Revolution may belong to enlightened executives. "Green Corporate Gorbachevs" will arrive as Pluto enters Pisces, just as the Communist one came when Pluto entered Scorpio in the 1980s. The charts in the fall of 2043 signal that one of these leaders may be an American. The growing Earth sensibility will gradually awaken more people, especially in the fall of 2045 and summer of 2047. By the mid-2040s, the connection between the increasingly bad weather and global pollution will be clearly evident, and its effects on our health will be abundantly clear and no longer tolerable. Neptune in Taurus will finally and forever dissolve the "economy" into "ecology." In the spring of 2045, America's diplomatic efforts will demonstrate that preserving the land also means dissolving barriers between nations (Saturn in Sagittarius).

Battles over land or agriculture in September 2044 may truly unleash the Green Revolution in America. Two successive eclipses in August 2044 and February 2045, both aligned with Uranus, will add fuel to the growing fire. The greatest new ecology movements will begin at the same time as the civil rights marches: August–October, 2045. The total solar eclipse in August 2045 conjoins Uranus exactly at the Midheaven in America, with Jupiter-Pluto opposing it from the Nadir (land) and Neptune at the Descendant (relationships). Important scandals or court battles over land and financial issues may stir the people.

As the revolution proceeds, it will become personal as well as political. We will be challenged to respect personal as well as biological ecology. We will understand that we heal not only the planet, but also our own alienation from work, families, and community—ills largely caused by the Industrial Age. Our values and self-esteem will be seen as crucial in our working lives. Revolutionary programs will actually encourage alternative co-housing arrangements and communes to form, and mandate that our cities be remodeled to create a sense of belonging. New public contracts will be awarded by governments for Earth-friendly businesses. The annular eclipse in the critical degree of 17° Aquarius in February 2046 echoes these indications. Since this degree recurs frequently in important charts of the later 2040s, it shows how thoroughly we will be re-evaluating the notion of "progress."

BUREAUCRATIC ADVENTURES: URANUS IN VIRGO/PLUTO IN PISCES

Of course, a backlash will develop among those who think the revolutionaries are becoming mere bureaucrats, but the reactionaries will only occasionally succeed in slowing things down. Instead of the usual sequence of events, in which revolution is followed by savage reaction, the Green Revolution may actually stimulate further reforms later in the 2050s. Much will be accomplished in this direction in the first half of 2047, when Uranus in Virgo trines Saturn in Capricorn, and in May, when Jupiter in Taurus will make that a grand trine. Saturn's position in the Sixth House in several important charts of the period emphasizes the point, but also shows that the bureaucrats may take some actions that business considers "repressive" (especially in February 2047). This will likely include not only environmental regulations, but enlightened welfare programs. By 2047, it will be an established principle that food and shelter are "civil rights" too, though maybe not "government entitlements." Uranus was also in early Virgo when Lyndon Johnson created the Great Society programs, so another "war on poverty" can be anticipated, gaining momentum when Jupiter joins Neptune in Taurus starting in June 2047. If the "revolutionary full moon" (Uranus opposite Pluto) of 2047 is to fulfill Dr. Martin Luther King's original dream of shared economic power, conceived at the "new moon" in 1966, then effective new "economic empowerment" measures can be expected. Blacks in West Africa will be on the march, completing the revolution begun in February, 1966, when many upheavals shook the continent under the potent "stillness of spirit" figure. The movements of 2035 and 2036 may set them in motion again, making Africa the scene of what could be the last successful democratic revolts in history by 2047–48. Socialist and Green ideals may also be advanced.

As in the days of Napoleon and the romantics, Pluto in Pisces will signify a lust for adventure. The equally romantic Mars in Sagittarius will T-square both Uranus and Pluto on three important occasions—on the very day of the Fall Equinox in 2046 (joined by Saturn), during the Spring Equinox of 2048, and again during the final opposition of Uranus-Pluto in June, 2048, when it will be stationary too! These cosmic lightning bolts will spur many nations to join together in vast world networks, as well as to seek out new places and fields to explore. They are also sure to set off contentious moral, philosophical, and theological debates. Approaches to population control are sure to polarize many people in the religious and secular communities.

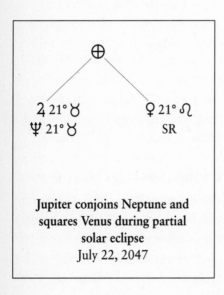

**Jupiter conjoins Neptune and squares Venus during partial solar eclipse
July 22, 2047**

The pace of international action will accelerate in late 2046 as the rebellious public temper grows. By 2047, important international financial agreements and compassionate reforms can be expected, as Jupiter and Neptune come together exactly (square Venus) during a partial solar eclipse on July 22, 2047, and again in February 2048, as they oppose Mars. In effect, the "Great Society" will be extended worldwide, despite financial difficulties in America. Knowing that poverty and conservation are incompatible, the visionaries will make rich nations pay to help the poorer ones reform their farms and industries. By the spring of 2048, the liberating spirit of the people will be at a fever pitch, and we will rise up to extend this new Green Revolution to all corners of the globe. As Jupiter joins Neptune in Taurus, just as Mars T-squares the revolutionary planets, the tide of global renewal will seem unstoppable. It will be a new worldwide Marseillaise. Powerful interests will try to stop the changes, while the people will demand still more, so things may spiral out of control by 2048.

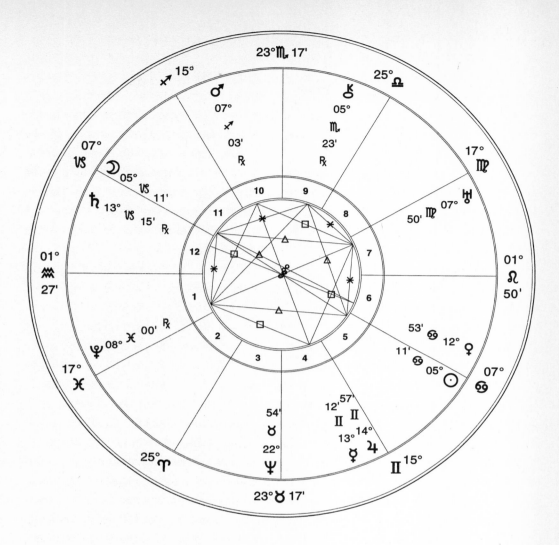

June 26, 2048 Lunar Eclipse

Final opposition of Uranus-Pluto, June 30, 2048. June 30 was the date of the final conjunction of Uranus-Pluto in 1966, and June 26 was the date of the nearest lunation in 1966. This is a powerful and wonder-filled symbol for the climax and "full moon" of the Third Revolutionary Cycle of Uranus-Pluto, happening during a lunar eclipse (itself a full moon!). This month (and also in March 2048) Mars will square Uranus-Pluto from Sagittarius, instead of from Gemini as in 1966. America will be involved abroad now as it was then, but will probably now be able to act on its true principles. The Green Revolution will be generously extended to all corners of the globe. Notice the grand square in mutable signs (dispersal) by Mars, Jupiter, Uranus and Pluto. Notice also in the eclipse chart that Venus is conjunct the U.S. Sun and the Sun is conjunct the U.S. Venus. Neptune in Taurus at the Nadir symbolizes the Green Revolution in America. Chart data: June 26, 2048, 02:09 P.M. GMT, Washington, D.C., 38N54, 77W02.

THE TRAGIC SCENARIO

Uncle Sam will be playing world cop again in the summer of 2047 or 2048 (Jupiter in Taurus/Gemini). Danger of conflict will be greatest in July, 2048 and February, 2049. America may also be directing recovery efforts along with other nations. The two roles will merge if the U.S. tries to distribute its new economic ideas by imposing them on others. America and its allies may do this by destroying outdated financial systems in many countries, and by helping indigenous peoples to secure their ethnic and ecological rights (Mars in Cancer opposite Saturn). Spain and Western Europe may be Uncle Sam's partners or rivals in this. The Spanish will be in the midst of revolution themselves in the summer of 2048, as Mars in Sagittarius (Spain's ruling sign) T-squares the opposition between Uranus and Pluto. Since these planets are also closely aspecting the degree of the 1892 conjunction, the titanic events in 2048 will either uproot or secure a lasting foundation of peace. Squaring off with America's Uranus and the "nuclear degree" (8° Gemini), Uranus and Pluto will challenge us in 2048 to end the nuclear age for good, or face a growing catastrophe in coming years.

The usual tragic scenario of revolution gone haywire could unfold after the eclipse in June 2048—the Green revolution could still turn red with blood. The score on the Time Line drops after 2050, so revolutionary events may cause civilization to decline because of the resulting crime and chaos. The destruction of old economic institutions, or debt caused by extravagant programs, could trigger financial panics and dislocations. Recession could result by 2049 as Jupiter opposes Saturn in Capricorn and shifts the direction of events. Revelations of secret medical misdeeds and financial or land fraud in the fall of 2047 could further damage public confidence. As revolutionary experiments become more radical, repression by authorities or sabotage by fanatics could follow. Uncle Sam's arrogant actions abroad could stir up the peace movement at home at the very climax of the revolutionary cycle that saw its beginning. Finally, if politics goes in a different direction from the benevolent impulses described above, unfettered attacks on bureaucracy could unleash wholesale destruction. This new libertarianism run amok could lead straight to anarchy. In that case, the great Enlightenment that promoted "individual freedom" and "free enterprise" 300 years before will finally end up releasing the tyranny of "might makes right"—destroying the binding force of our civilization.

COMPLETING THE CYCLE: THE NEXT GREAT AWAKENING

We will finally make it through our great transition and enter the New Age only if we emerge from the Green Revolution intact and avoid these pitfalls. Otherwise, we will not have created a sustainable and livable world, much less one that reflects who we are. Whatever happens, the challenges of the late 2040s will connect us to that irresistible stream of destiny that speaks to all of us in these rare moments. Pluto's powerful return to Pisces, where it launched romanticism in 1798, will be calling on us again to expand ourselves through mysticism, psychedelics, soaring visionary art, the magick of the occult—whatever comes in handy to strike fire in the spirit. Under Jupiter and Neptune in Taurus in

2047–48, Nature worship will become a leading religion on the planet, helping us to connect with Her beauty. We will make heroic, exuberant, crusading expeditions (Mars in Sagittarius) in order to preserve Her. But as the revolutionary cycle that began in the 1960s fulfills itself in its Full Moon in the late 2040s, we'll need to understand that unless we practice our spiritual knowledge while making revolution, we won't be able to avoid the usual tragic scenario.By then, we will also surely know that we can't grow a greener and more peaceful world unless our own souls (Pisces) attain a radiant glow powerful enough (Pluto) to embrace the whole world (Taurus). This time, America's periodic "Great Awakening" in the 2040s will also be humanity's. Pluto in Pisces demands that we nurture our own divinity and become whole beings on a whole Earth. We'll need to honor those brave souls who temporarily "drop out" and become spiritual seekers in 2047–48. Through their efforts, these could be very fruitful years for our Earth goddess. We will become Her, and She Herself will fully awaken through we who are Her eyes and ears.

The end of our almost-300-year journey at mid-century is marked by spectacular cosmic events, beginning with the great grand trine of Saturn, Uranus and Neptune in earth signs in November 2049. This planetary figure promises that we can make our Green ideals work, complete our painful birth trauma, and emerge as a people reborn. As the Twenty-First Century enters its second half, this grand trine shows us feeling released, and joyous times may appear over the horizon. The three planets that joined in conjunction in 1989, during the greatest victory for freedom so far in human history, will now signal an even greater triumph as they come together in grand trine. This could mean the first world democratic constitution. The Global Common Market which failed in 2043 may succeed now, since governments will have learned to respect the rights of all. Uncle Sam's return home from his adventures in 2049 may be the ultimate victory of world peace, decreed in the 1960s as the goal of this revolutionary cycle. This great moment could come when Venus turns stationary in the "stillness of spirit" degree of 17° Pisces on April 5, 2049. The unceasing wheel of untamed desire will fall silent. We will beat our swords into plowshares, and the young will learn war no more.

The second great cosmic event happens when Uranus turns stationary at 17° Virgo, its conjunction degree in 1966 (and opposite the recent Venus station), during a total eclipse with Neptune in May 2050. Uranus will thereby trigger those "strange vibrations" of eighty-four years before, and unleash the spiritual powers hidden within our commercial, scientific society. Uranus will have brought us back full circle to the 1960s. An ecstatic, psychedelic explosion of sound and color will erupt within us and around us, creating a world in which the arts of radiant light permeate and illuminate all our activities everywhere. This cyclic flashback to the 1960s also reminds us that the "Great Society" remains unfinished. In 2049, our goal will be to create such a society over the whole world. For although the 2040s are the climax and fulfillment of the Third revolutionary cycle, the Green movement itself is also the synthesis of the other two. The Modern Revolution is not over until all basic rights, including a decent standard of living and quality of life, are extended to everyone.

Today's renaissance cannot bloom if life becomes too expensive for everyone but a privileged few—we must keep services available in the community and keep costs down. No one must be left behind as we climb out of the valley of transition and enter the New World. In September 2049, Mercury, Venus, and Mars join Uranus just as it completes its first cycle since that moment in 1966 when so many of us glimpsed the New Age for the first time. The people of 2049 may be able to watch it begin to fully unfold on Earth for everyone.

The eclipse of May 2050, conjunct Neptune in Taurus, portends brilliant land reforms that will allow "progress" to continue again into the 2050s (the next "progressive decade"). Four months late comes the final great cosmic event. Mars turns stationary-direct at 17° Aquarius, the very degree where it "stalled" in 1963 in the progressed Horoscope of Modern Humanity. We are finally ready to release and "unmask" ourselves from the doubts and hesitations that have crippled us since that horrible day when President Kennedy was killed. Perhaps this mid-Twenty-first Century era will become the next Camelot, and the promise of the original one can bloom again. Watch the month of November, 2050 for decisive progressive events (or accidents).

As I finish writing this vast chronicle, Uranus and Neptune are joining together in the skies above me. I am completing a project begun when my soul awakened in 1966. When I noticed in 1968 that a Uranus-Pluto conjunction had happened simultaneously with my own awakening, it became my destiny to follow these incredible planetary movements and share what I learned about them. Now I feel wondrous anticipation as the year 2049 comes up on my "crystal ball," not only because I (and you, my readers) have now virtually completed our long and daunting journey, but because, through the magic of astrology, I have come to witness the moment, exactly one hundred years after my own birth in 1949, when the dreams which gave birth to this book may actually be fulfilled.

AFTER THE TRANSITION

Past 2050, the crystal ball begins to get dimmer. In a future edition, we will treat the rest of the Twenty-First Century in greater detail. For now, though, we can still get a pretty good view of events in this still far-off time by looking at the larger cycles.

Venus trine Jupiter in the progressed Horoscope of Modern Humanity may show exploding prosperity in 2048 due to the efforts to spread the wealth worldwide. Neptune will still be in Taurus, which usually indicates there are many good opportunities to make money. In 2053 Neptune enters Gemini, so by then the economy will be more unstable. Even before 2053, the Green Revolution will have shaken things up. The decade of the 2050s falls into the pattern of economic depressions (as do the 1870s, 1930s, and 1990s). As Jupiter opposes Saturn in 2050, therefore, expect a recession due to unstable times. The aspects in the progressed chart of Modern Humanity (and other factors) indicate that people will be in high spirits in the 2050s, so the depression will probably be mild and brief.

All depends on whether the germinating seeds planted by the Green Revolution put forth roses or only thorns. If the rosy scenario triumphs, then the new climate will be optimal for a luxuriant growth of an interconnected Green economy with help from the government. Inventors and entrepreneurs will multiply under Neptune in Gemini, especially in communications and transportation. It will be a time to celebrate exuberantly the good life on a restored planet. In fact, we may feel so good by 2060 that we may not notice how deeply the Green Revolution has dislodged us from the secure moorings of the past. In the 2060s, our new confidence will be increasingly undermined, and a new "malaise" will spread. Old and new institutions will decay and dissolve as Neptune approaches its square to Pluto in 2065. Inflation and over-expansion in 2060, followed by severe financial scandals and worker revolts in 2066, will combine to shatter the economy and threaten to make pollution so dangerous that many communities may be forced underground. It will be the usual great crisis which tests the New Civilization and challenges us to defeat "old ghosts" from the past (in this case the greed, climate change and other bad karma from the industrial age). If we have not learned the ways of peace, then a great war could explode in 2061–2062 that will involve Americans (Jupiter and Saturn in Gemini, square Pluto). If our transformation in the Green Revolution was deep enough, then we will emerge from this test even further transformed. The crisis will spur more great inventions, and the government will consolidate its power to engineer solutions to famine, disease and overpopulation. In the late 2060s, one hundred years after its beginning, the Great Society may become a working reality that ensures greater social justice for working men and women in many countries.

When Saturn joins Pluto in Pisces in 2053, it could provoke confrontations between reactionaries and reformers. When Saturn in Libra opposes Pluto in Aries in 2070, this confrontation could develop into open warfare. If state power becomes too crushing to average entrepreneurs, they could rise up to tear it down. Controls and taxes may be relaxed as prosperity returns in the 2070s. Fear of radicals could also erupt in the late 2060s or early 2070s (maybe a "green scare"). Neptune in Cancer could mean new ethnic or national rivalries, leading to further revolutions in 2075–77 (Uranus in Capricorn, square Pluto). By 2078–80, when Uranus opposes Neptune, further social upheavals could provoke a "cold war" atmosphere that severely tests the diplomatic arrangements of the Revised World Order.

The planets make some momentous alignments in 2080. Since all Jupiter-Saturn conjunctions will be in air signs for the following 140 years, the one in Aquarius in 2080 will be a "great mutation." It will line up with Uranus in Aquarius and oppose Neptune in Leo. Therefore, the following "Aquarian" decade of the 2080s, coming on the heels of the revolutions and international crises in the 2070s, may be the most "progressive" of all. New institutions will be developed to buttress the New World Order against the turmoil of the times. The Establishment will now move in complete harmony with the Green Revolution. In the early 2080s, rapid (though peaceful) upheavals in many societies could usher in a Green Great Aquarian-Age Society worldwide. Another Kennedy will inspire the world to move forward confidently toward the Twenty-Second Century. We will make plans to colonize outer space and connect with galactic networks (Neptune trine Pluto, late 2080s). Psychedelic, visionary, high-tech space art will expand into a vibrant and dynamic baroque style that infuses us with life and movement at the cellular level. Tremendous spiritual technologies and spectacular scientific discoveries will advance human potential. Under Neptune in Leo, social mores and inhibitions will crumble during a "roaring" decade that makes the 1920s look like a tea party. A reborn Broadway will stage spectacular lyric dramas that would make Shakespeare and Wagner green with envy, and the tedium of daily living will melt away in a fantastic carnival of fun and games.

Though the 2080s may be the most "progressive" decade of all time, it could also be the final one for our new society. If we don't progress *enough*, the next two decades could witness the end of civilization as we know it. Another economic or ecological crisis could begin in 2084 during a progressed lunar eclipse in the Horoscope of Modern Humanity. Political turmoil (including a foreign crisis for America) could erupt in 2085-2086 as Saturn makes a conjunction to Pluto in Aries. These events could soon shatter our confidence. Uranus dives into the chaotic waters of Pisces in 2087, inspiring a disillusioned public to throw many wonderful new social ideals out the window. A crushing blow occurs in 2090, when the next opposition of Jupiter and Saturn occurs, with a T-square to Uranus. A Jupiter-Saturn opposition usually means a "change of direction," but this time it will be a veritable earthquake. A serious depression in 2090 and/or 2092 will shut down the carnivals and close all the electronic and psychic theaters.

In the early 2090s, alienated youth will break with society, while others seek to expand in new directions. As progressed Mars in the Horoscope of Modern Humanity passes from Aquarius into Pisces in 2089, it will truly be the "end of progress," not merely an interruption as in the 1970s. From now on, merely technical innovations and novelties for their own sake will lose their charm, and political change won't seem so necessary. In the early 2090s, a new generation of neo-romantic, decadent dropouts will cluster in coffee houses, sipping acid-laden kool-aid and rediscovering the Spirit. New forms of cynical, mystic, or surrealist art will emerge, much like those of the 1920s. Humanity will experience a compassionate dedication to rescue those who are suffering during the recession (Neptune enters Virgo, 2092), and the government will consolidate its power to serve the needy. These impulses could lead us toward the next century ready to build a world that works for all.

At the turn of the century (beginning in 2095) will come another great moment of reckoning. It will truly be either the gates to hell or paradise. The Uranus-Pluto conjunction in Taurus in 2103 spells doom for all institutions not adjusted to the new reality. Swift reorganizations of power will break up bureaucracies and redistribute the wealth still hoarded by the greedy. Everything not fitted for the Aquarian Age will be eliminated. If we haven't taken heed of the prescriptions and prophecies offered by New Age and Green visionaries, including those found in these pages, we humans may have to take our leave from the stage of destiny, or at least take civilization back to the drawing board. The Revolution of 2103 will turn into another severe challenge to America's very existence by 2110, as Uranus enters Gemini.

The magnificent cosmic patterns reviewed in this book give me confidence that, in spite of all our ignorance and lethargy, we will make the right choices just in time. Throughout history, we have always made it through the transition to the golden age, 100 years after each Neptune-Pluto conjunction. The Greeks (500 B.C.), the Romans (A.D. 1), the Byzantines (500), the Chinese and medieval Christians (1000), and the Renaissance Europeans (1500) all did it. A century after our rebirth and "peak experience" in 2000, we should be quite far along on our path to the New Age, moving toward another peak of civilization and perhaps even ready to enter paradise.

CONCLUSION: PARADISE IN THE TWENTY-SECOND CENTURY

If we pass through the gates to paradise, our creativity will know no bounds. In 2100, another green post-industrial revolution will get off the ground. By 2120, we will have respiritualized our lives and entered the path to becoming gods and goddesses. We will eagerly march forward in great crusades against all enemies of the Spirit. Having preserved the planet, we can also start fully exploring and understanding the inner landscape of Earth, including ourselves, the souls who are Her consciousness. Even in 2120, the climactic moment of our New Age of Civilization will still lie ahead of us. The summit will be marked by Neptune's "Full Moon" opposition to Pluto in 2143 and by its conjunction to Uranus in Aquarius in 2165.

These will be glorious moments. Many magnificent temples to Earth and Spirit will be erected. Fervent and inspired souls will join in common bonds of love, as the great crusades in the 2120s transform Earth into Eden. Eagerly, we will receive help from more advanced people from other worlds and brighter dimensions. An irresistible, radiant, fiery energy will blaze forth within us, connecting us in communion with all beings. This glowing flame is the mature Modern Spirit, born many years ago in the fiery furnace of the French Revolution. Having survived an initiation horrific enough to test the courage and skills of the best mythic hero, our New Spirit will now be strong and wise enough to defeat any obstacle. It will shine forth in awesome glory, impelling and empowering us to leave forever behind all the conventional ways of life. Nothing but the most glorious and creative tasks will be deemed worthy of our attention; we won't have time or space for the trivial things that numb and distract us today. Seeing divinity within ourselves and Nature, we won't fail to know it in our fellow humans. Every street, town and country of Earth, at all hours of the day and night, will resonate with "noospheric effects," as the radiant One within all individual souls echoes across the landscape. No enforced code of ethics will be needed, so long as this vibrant creative spirit animates our hearts. No goal will lie before us but to replace the commercial wasteland of the Twentieth Century with a new creative spiritual civilization on a restored Earth, fertilized by the decaying remnants of all the cultures from the past. Like the citizens of Chartres once did, we will put aside all of our differences to build together this new Earth Temple. If this scenario seems rosy, the seeds for these roses have already been planted, starting over 300 years ago. This will be the flowering of true progress; not today's "progress" that leads toward an alienating and dehumanizing world, but toward the one we really want: simply a world of beauty in the fullest, deepest and profoundest sense.

Here's the best news of all: we don't have to wait for the Twenty-Second Century! The potential for Paradise lies all around us always, if we can only open our eyes. The "stars" and the planetary cycles proclaim that it is time for a New Renaissance. The New Age beckons us, according to the cosmic schedule. So let's put aside our petty doubts and fears and begin creating it now before it's too late. Only by fulfilling our destiny, so clearly written in the stars, can we truly experience the living connection between ourselves and the universe to which astrology points the way.

20

What the New Millennium
Will Mean for You

To conclude our look into the New Millennium, this chapter presents some general forecasts for each sun sign of the zodiac for the first half of the Twenty-First Century. If you think it fits you better, you can also read the section for your rising sign. If you know your birth time, find your rising sign by referring to Appendix B. Of course, the following "predictions" require the same disclaimer as do those for world events. Astrologers don't have sufficient knowledge to make forecasts of unalterable fate. Even if we did, we could not say how each person would respond. We are always free to do the best we can with what destiny gives us.

ARIES. The Millennium begins with Jupiter and Saturn joining in your Second House of finances. Apply shrewdly the great opportunities from the previous two years and you'll reap long-term rewards. In 2003–05, home and family matters or internal blocks from your childhood will concern you. Expand your relationships by dealing with these blocks. A family battle could disrupt your life in late 2007. After Pluto enters Capricorn in 2008, you will challenge authorities in order to boost your position. Long, severe power struggles could begin in 2010, especially for those Arians born in March. Uranus in your sign will make you much more rebellious for the next seven years, but also brilliant, creative and confident. Your intuitive, spiritual inclinations will also expand. In 2018, your career may peak, and you'll become more shrewd in your fights with authority. Your ambition will lead to power struggles in 2020. You will win, unless you break under the strain. In the next few years, you'll reap financial rewards and become more interested in helping society. You may get involved in conservation battles in 2025, and those born early in the sign will be infused with zealous ambition to change the world. All Arians can expect to be starry-eyed for the next fourteen years, with Neptune in your sign. Your spiritual vision will expand, freeing you from many limitations, but you may also become confused about your life direction. In early 2029, you may project your insecurity onto others through needless conflicts, and this may affect your family life by 2032–33. The effects of these disruptions in your home life in 2033–34 may linger for seven years, but these years could also present creative opportunities. More family troubles in 2039 may disrupt your finances. Jupiter and Saturn will join in your Seventh House in 2040, so your plans and fortunes will depend on your relations with others from then on. Choose your partners carefully and shore up your marriage, and don't be involved in unsure ventures in 2042. Your career may peak again in 2047–2049. The Green Revolution will primarily transform your health and spiritual life and call you to serve humanity. Quarrels in May–June 2046 could affect this.

TAURUS. The Millennium begins with a Jupiter-Saturn conjunction in your own sign. Sudden changes in your career may bring new opportunities. It's a good time to expand and solidify your goals—make them idealistic and noble. Shrewd investments of time and money now will pay off for the next twenty years, but careless, overconfident moves could cost you. Avoid hasty breaks with authority and stick to the course you believe in. Late in 2005, you'll be feeling more assertive, but stay out of trouble. Attend to matters of home and children. Around 2007, your ideals will conflict with your home life. You'll need to adjust to new realities and set long-term goals. In 2009, your faith and zeal will earn support, unless you blow it with emotional outbursts. Take care of your health and boost your confidence in 2010–11, and prepare yourself for possible legal obstacles in 2012–13. Financial battles may follow in 2016. Your fortunes will rise markedly in the next decade. Around 2020, Uranus enters your sign, and you can break out of your rut with brilliant new ideas that crown your career efforts with success. You may need to burst through the bonds of established authority, and you become an even more determined rebel late in 2024. The strain of the struggle may require you to seek refuge and renewal after 2025, however.

In 2028 a decisive turn of fate may come, as Saturn returns to Taurus. You may feel secure enough to begin new power struggles (square Pluto in Aquarius), but defeat could force you to turn inward again. Traveling and educating yourself in 2033–34 will pay off later on, and it will inspire you to break old ties and begin new goals in 2035–36. Be very clear about your new course, or those in power may defeat you right away. In 2039, Neptune enters your sign, forcing you to further clarify your goals. Your personal and home life may be unsettled and undermined in the 2040s unless you focus and expand your awareness. If you do, the next thirteen years could be very creative and inspired, especially at decade's end. The Green Revolution will free up your personal life and self-expression. You'll need to get past 2042, however, when you may be subject to intrigues, paranoid delusions, and fits of temper.

GEMINI. The Millennium begins on a note of self-study and renewal, with Jupiter-Saturn in your Twelfth House. You will emerge with greater confidence and plunge headlong into difficult conflicts. Prepare by setting and reaching goals ahead of time, and you can emerge the winner. You may face implacable foes, but dealing with them will transform you and make you powerful. Battles continue in 2003, but by later that year you may begin to reap financial benefits, especially if you invested in real estate. At the same time, you will begin to experience many sudden changes in your career, and a chance to follow your own path. You may make a painful and decisive break from authority and the past sometime in late

2007 or late 2008–2009. Don't let the crisis unbalance you, but find new goals and stick with them. Stay away from joint ventures and invest carefully or not at all in 2010, a very unstable year. In 2012, you may feel your confidence return, and you will become interested in making friends and actively helping humanity. You will be more confused than ever about your career, however. Gradually, you need to connect your work to your ideals. In 2016, the two are due to come into intense conflict, and you face real moral dilemmas and enemies you can't control. You may become a religious crusader. In the next decade, clarify your beliefs and conceive genuinely visionary goals instead of merely being outspokenly self-righteous. In late 2022 and early 2023 you could still be trying to convert the whole world to your way of thinking.

In 2023–25, you may put your ideals to work in your career and begin a brilliantly creative period. In the next seven years, you can contribute greatly to science or literature and act successfully to advance your ideals. Crucial tests could come in 2031. Your original work could pay off that year, but ideological debates could lead to breaks with others. More angry battles could erupt in late 2035, but in 2037, fruitful new paths will open up. Your creative powers will flower in the 2040s (Jupiter-Saturn in the Fifth House), but guard your health in 2042. New ideological power struggles engage you in late 2044 and 2045, as you become an obsessive crusader again, and remain so throughout the Green Revolution. Perhaps you can transform the planet, but this will also shake up your career and domestic life.

CANCER. The Millennium begins on a high note with Jupiter-Saturn in your Eleventh House. You may be involved in idealistic projects with friends. Don't let them lead you into crime, drugs or intrigue in 2001—enter a path of self-renewal instead. This will bring new confidence and success in 2002. Don't be overconfident, though, since Saturn visits your sign in 2003–04 and tests your mettle. Put your good fortune to work by investing in your own home and property, and firming up the foundations of your life. Rely on your own initiative in 2007, and don't let fears lure you into phony financial schemes. The year 2010 will be one to remember, as you face opposition on all sides. You will make decisive and revolutionary breaks from the past toward a more successful and fulfilling career, marriage, and home life all at once. The strain could break you, unless you keep a steady course. In 2014, you will feel more confident about following your goals and facing your enemies. In 2018, you must deal squarely with opposition from those in power. Discover new spiritual strength within yourself, and soon afterward your life will be more secure. Those born in the later days (or higher degrees) of Cancer will be involved in intense negotiations and partnerships in 2020 that could pay off handsomely if they are sound, though it will be a struggle to achieve them.

In 2025–26 comes a good opportunity to achieve success and satisfaction in a new career of your dreams, if you have worked diligently in the past. If not, you may be disappointed. You'll need to continually reflect on your career ideals, or you may drift aimlessly during the next seven years. Set your aims high now, and stay with them. Learn to use intuitive skills in your work. Quarrels over family investments may erupt in early 2029. Don't let pressures and upsets break you in 2032. Guard your health and sanity, penetrate to spiritual understanding, and the following years could be brilliantly creative and exciting. Make the most of Uranus in your sign from 2033–2040 to unfold your creativity and unleash your subconscious powers. Develop your original ideas about land and property, or make wonderful landscape paintings. In February 2034, you may switch career paths again if others suppress you. Stay true to your dreams, but seek better ways to realize them. This will be a test of what you began in 2025. In 2039-40, you will reach yet another milestone (Jupiter-Saturn in your Fourth House). A stable home and family will help you from now on. Original ideas pay off, but don't gamble, especially in 2042–43. Keep your sights high and help the Green Revolution by expanding your knowledge and wisdom, and sharing all you have learned on your long journey. Be transformed by renewing your mind.

LEO. The New Millennium starts out on a successful career note with Jupiter and Saturn in your Tenth House. Express creative, inspired ideas through cooperating with others. Your work may conflict with your marriage, or you may change partners (Uranus in Aquarius opposing your Sun). The early 2000s will find you impelled to help humanity, but people you know personally will baffle and confuse you (Neptune opposing your Sun until 2011). Others frequently injure your pride, and you are upset when they don't support you. Around 2003–04 will be a good time to seek inner understanding. Important struggles face you late in 2005 through 2007 (Saturn in Leo). Success comes if you are not afraid, don't back down, and are prepared for battle. Rely on yourself, since others may deceive you. Your vitality and optimism flows in late 2009 and early 2010. Opportunities mount, but maintain self-control and don't get sucked in by glamorous promises. You will need to adjust to a new phase in your life in 2012–13, but 2014 could be a very successful year. Quarrels and breaks with those in authority come in 2018–19, but this may open chances to follow a more original and satisfying line of work. It's also stressful, however, so begin a long program to shore up your health in 2020.

Once again, others oppose your plans in 2021, and you are forced to let go of many of your illusions about people and the world. After you do, opportunities will grow, though you still face implacable enemies (Pluto in Aquarius until 2043). In 2027–30, you'll be riding high with new confidence and keener vision. You'll face more attempts by foes to defeat you in 2029–2030; make them your friends by inspiring them with your radiant dreams. Domestic quarrels in the spring of 2031 may move you to seek self-understanding again. Power struggles erupt in 2035–36, and success will come only if you have transformed your attitude to others. Education is your goal in 2040, leading to lofty new career goals. With Uranus in Leo (2039–45), your new creative brilliance will help you reach them, though your own fanatic, eccentric ideals may impel you in strange and uncertain directions. During the Green Revolution, your focus improves, and you can profit through original ventures. You can help reshape the finances of society.

VIRGO. As the Millennium dawns, you are expanding your sometimes-myopic view of the world and discovering new opportunities and work styles (Jupiter-Saturn in your 9th). This will open doors to success, but may bring conflict with family. You'll find you must transform your deepest self, or you will undermine your own goals. From 2003–2010, you break away from familiar molds and work with others in creative projects that are successful in 2004. In the process, you may break many old ties and make new ones. Your creative energy may peak in 2008, as opportunities increase, but in 2009 your sense of security will be challenged, forcing you to decide what to keep and what to change. If you are shrewd, you can profit from financial structures collapsing around you in 2010–11, although those born early in the sign should be careful of deceptive promises. After 2011, the world may seem too confusing for your analytical mind. Confusion will reign off and on for fourteen years while Neptune transit in opposition to your Sun, and you'll need to adjust to new responsibilities and opportunities in 2016 that involve crucial moral choices and conflicts with your family. You may become a crusader for moral or social causes, and may feel the world doesn't understand you. Once Uranus enters your Ninth House in 2019, you may understand the world better, anyway.

A path to more creative work will open in the 2020s, but in 2023 ypou may still believe the world's out to get you. Obstacles will get in your way and force you to better understand them (Saturn in Pisces). When Uranus reaches Gemini in 2025–26, things suddenly will get clearer. You'll change your job and get a chance to do what you want. By late 2027, you may be riding high, moving toward a career peak in 2030. The following year, you'll seek to bring your home life and work into a better balance. In 2032, you'll begin to apply your success toward helping society. The year 2038 will be one of reckoning, when you'll see the results for good or ill of your previous efforts. The next year, Jupiter will join Saturn in your Second House, indicating many financial opportunities in the 2040s. In 2046, you will break ties with the past and start over, perhaps even leaving your home and job. You will then get fully caught up in the Green Revolution, becoming a charismatic, creative leader in the struggle for social justice. Still, you will suffer opposition from those who misunderstand you.

LIBRA. As the Millennium begins, you are consolidating your relationships and financial affairs (Jupiter-Saturn in Eighth House), and soon will feel free to expand your awareness of the world (as these planets move into the Ninth). The years 2003–2004 could bring a peak to your career, while 2007 may see wonderful opportunities for creative expression, as long as you can reconcile romance with reality. In 2008, Pluto begins a twenty-four-year stay in Capricorn, so there could be many gradual and unseen alterations in home and family life. By 2010–11, the changes will be quite obvious and drastic. Good results may come from past efforts, but this might impel you to break radically with those who have tied you down, and a divorce or power struggle may occur. You may then experiment boldly with alternative life and work styles or jump at exciting new opportunities. Over the next seven years (Uranus in Aries), you'll seek to realize your creative, rebellious ideas through cooperating with others, though disputes will occur. In 2014, you'll venture forth bravely and energetically to fulfill your ambitions. The year 2018 will be one of new starts and adjustment to new responsibilities. Early 2020 brings difficult struggles at home.

The new decade offers opportunities for romance and creative expression (Jupiter-Saturn in your Fifth House). Safe investments pay off. The year 2026, though full of exciting adventures and transforming friendships, will bring others into your life who may not support you as you wish (Saturn-Neptune opposing your Sun). Quarrels with those who misunderstand you may lead to neurotic suspicions. Learn to overcome your dependence on others' approval, and deal with people as they are. Mars and Jupiter in Libra will encourage a more confident attitude in 2028–29. A high worldly position may come in 2032, after which you can pursue the kind of work you believe in. In 2033, this may involve uncomfortable breaks with family or those in authority, while in 2034 you'll need to overcome fear of rivals or competitors. Once again, you will struggle to make romance into reality and reconcile your creativity with others' approval. In 2040, Jupiter and Saturn join in your sign, so you'll have a strong sense of your direction and accomplishments. You'll gain rewards, but could lose them if they aren't earned or you don't look after them. Don't invest in ideas proposed by your friends or in get rich quick schemes. Solid investments will pay off in 2042, but bad ones may cause ruin. During the Green Revolution, you'll awaken your spiritual powers, campaign for those in need, or transform work and health (yours and society's). This opens a new phase in 2047–48, with new and more lofty goals.

SCORPIO. As the Millennium begins, you are trying to build relationships with others, but finding that difficult. Obstacles will force you to seek to understand yourself and the ways of the world, leading to success in the following years. Your financial powers have expanded, but in 2002–03 you must test your acumen against the restrictive realities of a corporate structure. With Neptune in your Fourth House, you'll need a stable home base from which to work. When Uranus leaves this house in 2003, things will settle down, and you can let your home, nature and the land inspire you to creative work. A chance for a better worldly position will come in 2005, but in 2007 it may be undermined if your work disturbs your inner peace and security. Unless your dreams can be made practical, your home, career, or both could slip away. Afterward, you will be less ambitious and more interested in helping society, but the insecurity of the times may affect your health or sanity in 2010. Don't despair—pursue revolutionary methods of personal growth instead. In 2012, you may conceive practical plans to realize your creative dreams.

In 2020, Jupiter joins Saturn in (or near) your 4th house, so it could be a chance to break from others who have restricted you (Uranus in your Seventh House, 2019–26). From now on, establish your home life on firmer grounds and follow long-term, practical plans. Transform your inner life by tapping your subconscious powers and ancestral heritage (Pluto in the Fourth House from 2024 to 2043). You may be interested in natural resources, archeology, or Jungian psychology. Cooperate with family and partners to realize your worthwhile creative projects, or they may not come off. In 2028, you may want to withdraw again if financial burdens and power struggles weigh you down. Don't let depression stop you, but transform yourself by penetrating to the root of your problems. You will emerge better able to master your opponents. Travel and higher education prove good outlets to restore your health and open new opportunities from 2033 through 2040. Your career will be on a up-swing again, but your success may be limited if you haven't mastered your pride, anger, and resentment. Power struggles could undermine your security in 2035–36, just as they did in 2007. You can succeed this time, though, due to your deep inner strength. When Neptune passes Taurus from 2039–52, your magnetic charm will help you create good relationships and heighten your artistic inspirations (especially for landscape painting). Sudden, exciting, creative work opportunities open up. If you aren't strong now, though, relationships will dissolve, and once again you'll feel the world is against you. In 2042, you'll seek ideal partners for your projects, but they may prove unreliable. The Jupiter-Saturn conjunction in 2040 falls in your Twelfth House, offering you a chance to explore your mind and release past karma. The Green Revolution will impel you to heal society's alienation, which you have felt so personally. You'll find success in this in 2049. Fifty years after the year 2000, the goal for Scorpios will still be the same—finding genuine, fulfilling relationships.

SAGITTARIUS. As the Millennium begins, you'll be engaged in a quest for knowledge and illumination (as Sagittarians usually are), and trying to apply it to improving your work and health (Jupiter-Saturn in the Sixth House). You may feel that your ideas aren't appreciated, but your quest will release new powers within you. In 2001–02, opportunities to express them will be blocked, and you may exhaust yourself fighting against those who don't accept you. Impatient and indignant, your temper flares in 2003, and sometimes afterward. You'll move on, exploring wider avenues in 2005–06. Your home will be unsettled but creative, and your life will take inspiring new directions. 2007–08 will see you confidently making yourself financially independent in the years ahead through relying on your own creative career. Investments will begin to pay off in 2008–09. Invest carefully in 2010, but turn unstable times to your advantage. Conflicts with authority in 2012 may impel you toward a spiritual quest in 2013. Nature and your home life can sustain you, and good results will come around 2016 if you have earned them. If not, fears may disrupt your ambitions that year.

The 2020 Jupiter-Saturn conjunction will stir your educational interests again, and this time they will be more practical. Networking will open opportunities, and you'll set out on new courses by 2023. Analyze your dreams to release your personal power. The aspects among the planets in 2025–26 will bring many exciting relationships into your life. You will break familiar ties and become much more creative. By 2029–30 you may face opposition similar to that of 2000. Your greater charm and exuberance this time around will probably win over your foes, however. Your revolutionary, prophetic mind will be expanding, and you'll become a compelling spokesperson for your beliefs and goals (Pluto in Aquarius, 2024–43). Your career peaks in 2037–38. By 2040 (Jupiter-Saturn in your Eleventh House), you can generously devote your life to higher purposes, but in 2042–43 you will realize you must further develop yourself spiritually and physically to fully pursue them. The foundations of your being will be uprooted and vitalized. You'll find yourself at the center of action during the Green Revolution in 2045–46, and again in 2048, but avoid dangerous risks. Make the Revolution your career; it offers wide scope to remake the world over in your image. Sudden changes will be new opportunities for you.

CAPRICORN. The New Millennium finds you most concerned with creative financing— and with financing your creativity! Success will come by breaking out of old ways. Power struggles within institutions, however, could land you in another kind of "institution" in 2001–02. These could also be good years to apply your discipline to your health and spiritual path. This will help you in 2003–04, when you may feel depressed over new obstacles. Education will help you out of this and into new opportunities. Don't let powerful people lead you into financial deals in 2007, and don't be too ambitious (especially if you are born early in the sign), because the upheavals of 2010 will shake all the thrones of the powerful. If you occupy one, you will probably tumble in the catastrophe. The stress of family and career conflicts could break you at this time, but if you face the unknown, your power and confidence will grow (Pluto in Capricorn, 2008–24). If you respond creatively to the crisis, it could bring great opportunities, your view of reality will widen, and you'll become more intuitive. You will be especially enterprising (or quarrelsome) in early 2014. You can achieve financial stability and independence after 2020 (Jupiter-Saturn in your first and second house, plus Pluto in your second from 2024–43).

You will start an imaginative new course in 2025–26. Rebuild your home life, or leave it behind if it doesn't support you. Change your job if it lacks scope for your inventiveness. Your spirit of enterprise will expand in 2028–29, but by 2032 rivals or opponents may block your way (Saturn in your Seventh House). Prevail by finding more creative resources within. From 2033–40, learn to work with stubborn people and turn them into friends or partners that help you if you can. Otherwise, break with them. Working with others will release new creative and persuasive abilities, making you more successful. You'll reach a high peak in your career late in 2040. Avoid conflicts earlier in the year that could diminish your prospects, however. Look forward and prepare for the 2040s, when the highest success could be yours. Avoid risky investments suggested by friends or lovers in the tense and turbulent year of 2042, however. By 2043–44, you could become a persuasive leader for the Green Revolution with truly mystical appeal. Your confidence will expand, and by 2046 so will your consciousness. Become wise and well-traveled so you can be a prophetic catalyst for unique and spectacular accomplishments.

AQUARIUS. The New Millennium finds your creative powers at a high pitch. You'll be establishing a home base or breaking away from conditions that bind you. You'll work hard to achieve solid results in 2002. By 2005–07, however, you may think the world is turning against you. Your creativity could decline due to depression, withdrawal, or resentment, but you'll emerge from these difficult years with a more deeply inspired understanding of life. If you are a writer, you'll produce tragedies now instead of comedies. By late 2009, your flamboyant optimism may flower again, but avoid reckless adventures (especially romantic ones). The 2010 crisis will be primarily a mental one for you. You'll change your way of thinking and begin a long quest for spiritual renewal. This won't stop your career progress, which may reach a peak in 2013–14, but watch your affairs carefully and don't be complacent. In mid-2018, early Aquarians will become more rebellious or quarrelsome. Conflicts over home or finances could wreck both.

The Jupiter-Saturn conjunction will happen at the beginning of your sign in 2020. Riding a crest of success, you can embark on a unique and creative new course. Don't be careless or overconfident now, or you could suffer serious losses. In 2024–26, you may become empowered by a new urge to grow and transform your life. You'll want to learn all you can to make a truly great creative contribution to science or literature, perhaps becoming an inspired prophet helping to put humanity back on a confident, forward track. You'll be especially zealous and combative in early 2027, but you'll begin a more steady, sure-footed, responsible course in 2028–29. By 2035–36, you'll be ready to meet obstacles and power struggles head on. Difficult and depressing conflicts will arise in both periods (2028 and 2035), but they'll call forth your reserves of inner strength and resolve. The Jupiter-Saturn conjunction of 2040 in your Ninth House shows you probably will have met the tests and can move onward and outward to explore the world and its opportunities. You will also feel the need for a stable home in which to ground and anchor your wandering and creative soul. Deeper difficulties will arise in 2042, as you move toward expressing your genius during an outstanding peak in your career. You will direct or participate in vast reorganization projects to rebuild the wealth of society and the land, but trying to impose your will on others would lead to stress that could wreck your status or family life. If you can move past this temptation, you'll be able to create better financial structures for yourself and others in the mid-2040s. At that decade's end, you'll reach inward for spiritual renewal and find glorious illumination and peace.

PISCES. As the Millennium begins, you are educating yourself and exploring the deepest mysteries of life. Your quest will inspire you to break old ties and begin new goals in 2001–02, but the transition could be difficult, because you must transform your whole life purpose and break with old authorities at home, work, or church. Stress will lead to more inner work or escapism to avoid nervous breakdown. Soon, you'll emerge with greater confidence in your own creative powers (Uranus in Pisces, 2003–2010). In 2004, you'll become magnetically attractive, and your imaginative creative powers will unfold. Your spiritual quest will continue in 2006–07, as you release your hidden fears and help the less fortunate. Continue on this path while Saturn opposes your Sun in 2008–09, since attempts to push your own agenda will probably not work—avoid the frustration. Batten down the hatches and secure your finances if possible, because the crisis of 2010 will be bumpy for you. After 2011, the great task for all Pisceans is to pursue spirituality and express compassion for all beings. New career plans should reflect this. They'll work out well if they do, although financial problems may cause quarrels in early 2012. By 2016, you may have become a public figure caught up in the religious and moral controversies of the era. Rather than reflecting the fears and self-righteousness of others, lend your wise counsel and contribute your lofty vision. It will truly know no bounds now.

The conjunction of 2020 will cement your dedication to the religious life, and some of you could become monks. Expanding evangelistic zeal will lead you in late 2022 into local community crusades—or merely into family battles. You'll be feeling more buoyant and optimistic that year, so take advantage of new opportunities. In 2023–24, your career or spiritual enterprise is due to reach a milestone of success, if you have worked well. By 2026, though, you may wish to break out of confining roles and pursue a new and original course. Make sure you are financially well grounded and not deceived about what's possible. You must put your new life direction on a firmer foundation in 2031–32. Expand your creative powers in 2034, but avoid dangerous financial schemes that year. In 2035–36, you may return to diligent spiritual and humane service efforts. Avoid worldly opposition and frustration by continuing on this path through 2038–39. In the 2040s, your finances will improve through joint ventures and partnerships, although your work may conflict with your ideals in 2042. By 2043–44 you'll feel your spiritual powers expanding again. You'll break old ties and thrust yourself into the Green Revolution as an inspiring and creative agent of radical change.

APPENDIX A

SUMMARY MEANINGS OF THE PLANETS AND SIGNS

Meanings of the planets and lights: (for more complete information and symbols, see Ch. 3).

Sun: The organizing force of the solar system. Represents conscious mind, confidence, will, expression, character, ego, nobility, fatherhood, leadership, stability. Rules Leo.

Moon: The mediator between Sun and Earth. Represents change, feelings, instincts, aspirations, personality, women, motherhood, common people. Rules Cancer.

Mercury: The messenger. Represents communication, travel, ideas, the mind, youth, students, writing, speech, trade, service, humble people. Rules Gemini and Virgo.

Venus: The planet of love. Represents peace, diplomacy, pleasure, romance, the arts, the feminine, money, values, judgments, results, strategy. Rules Taurus, Libra.

Mars: The planet of war. Represents action, aggression, conflict, adventure, energy, desire, initiative, enthusiasm, machismo, pioneering. Rules Aries, Scorpio.

Jupiter: The greater fortune. Represents expansion, optimism, benevolence, good luck, prosperity, excess, pomp, organized religion, philosophy, commerce, the judiciary, foreign affairs, wide travels, universities, prophecy. Rules Sagittarius, Pisces.

Saturn: The cosmic taskmaster. Stands for restriction, authority, limitation, repression, tradition, pessimism, realism, discipline, organization, wisdom, old age, learning, ambition, the State, the Establishment, patriarchy. Rules Capricorn, Aquarius.

Uranus: The maverick. Discovered in 1781, it represents revolution, invention, liberty, progress, liberalism, independence, enlightenment, electricity, magic, the unexpected, radical change, altruism, dictators, charisma. Rules Aquarius (see Ch. 2).

Neptune: The mystic. Found in 1846, it represents spirituality, imagination, the sea, union, dissolution, chaos, delusion, deception, scandal, dreams, solvents, drugs, ESP, compassion, socialism, collectivism, nations, peoples, hospitals, asylums. Rules Pisces (see Ch. 2).

Pluto: Lord of the Underworld. Discovered in 1930, it represents death, rebirth, ecology, polarity, transformation, gangs, group power, plutocracy, atomic energy, purges, investigations, plumbing the depths. Rules Scorpio and Aries (see Ch. 2).

Meanings of the signs: (for more complete information and symbols, see Ch. 3).

Aries: ("I am") Cardinal fire sign. Represents enthusiasm, initiative, impulse, action, independence, aggression, pioneers, goals, beginnings. (Ruler: Mars.)

Taurus: ("I have") Fixed earth sign. Represents peace and plenty, stability, realism, security, stagnation, sensuality, economics, arts, architecture, nature. (Ruler: Venus.)

Gemini: ("I think") Mutable air sign. Represents intellect, ingenuity, novelty, progress, writing, youth, travel, networking, vehicles, speech. (Ruler: Mercury.)

Cancer: ("I feel") Cardinal water sign. Represents feelings, nurturing, home, defense, patriotism, conservation, family, sensitivity, moodiness, introversion. (Ruler: Moon.)

Leo: ("I will") Fixed fire sign. Represents pride, expression, nobility, leadership, gambling, speculation, games, entertainment, theater, education, youth. (Ruler: Sun.)

Virgo: ("I analyze") Mutable earth sign. Represents service, criticism, health, healing, welfare, technology, science, intellectuals, labor, the armed forces, bureaucracy, medicine, anxiety, conformity, the humble classes. (Rulers: Mercury, Chiron.)

Libra: ("I balance") Cardinal air sign. Represents diplomacy, peace, the arts, partnerships, law, politics, idealism, justice, vacillation, compromise. (Ruler: Venus.)

Scorpio: ("I desire") Fixed water sign. Represents passion, transformation, turmoil, sex, death, taxes, pooled resources, corporations, economics, communion, renewal, the occult, mysteries, psychology, investigations, awakenings. (Rulers: Mars, Pluto.)

Sagittarius: ("I see") Mutable fire sign. Represents exuberance, foreign affairs, travel, the outdoors, prophecy, higher mind, religion, clubs, philosophy. (Ruler: Jupiter.)

Capricorn: ("I use") Cardinal earth sign. Represents ambition, government, authority, tradition, pragmatism, conservatism, endurance, integrity. (Ruler: Saturn.)

Aquarius: ("I know") Fixed air sign. Represents truth, science, friendship, altruism, hope, ideals, associations, inventors, eccentricity, charisma, catastrophe. (Rulers: Uranus, Saturn.)

Pisces: ("I believe") Mutable water sign. Represents compassion, imagination, faith, mysticism, intuition, escapism, dissolution, chaos, deception, delusion, martyrdom, sacrifice, religion, Christianity. (Rulers: Neptune, Jupiter.)

APPENDIX B
ABRIDGED TABLE OF HOUSES

If you know your birth time, use this table to help you understand the meaning of the great planetary cycles in your life. These tables are cast for Washington, D.C., but are generally workable for everyone born in northern temperate longitudes. If you wish greater accuracy, have your chart cast by an astrologer or chart service.

Use the table with the date closest to your birthday, then look for the closest time listed to your own birth time. The tables will show which sign and degree is on each angle (Ascendant, Midheaven, Descendant, and Nadir) for the time listed. If you wish to, you may interpolate using your own estimates. Since these tables assume standard time, you should subtract four minutes from your birth time for each degree west your birthplace is from your standard time meridian (east: add) to get your true local time. If you were born during war or daylight savings time, don't forget to subtract an hour!

January 1

Time	Ascendant	Midheaven	Descendant	Nadir
12:42 A.M.	17 Libra	19 Cancer	17 Aries	19 Capricorn
3:08	16 Scorpio	25 Leo	16 Taurus	25 Aquarius
4:28	2 Sagittar.	16 Virgo	2 Gemini	16 Pisces
4:58	8 Sagittar.	24 Virgo	8 Gemini	24 Pisces
5:36	16 Sagittar.	5 Libra	16 Gemini	5 Aries
7:55	19 Capric.	12 Scorpio	19 Cancer	12 Taurus
9:25	16 Aquarius	4 Sagittar.	16 Leo	4 Gemini
9:42	22 Aquarius	8 Sagittar.	22 Leo	8 Gemini
10:43	16 Pisces	22 Sagittar.	16 Virgo	22 Gemini
11:55	16 Aries	9 Capricorn	16 Libra	9 Cancer
12:38 P.M.	3 Taurus	19 Capric.	3 Scorpio	19 Cancer
1:15	16 Taurus	26 Capric.	16 Scorpio	26 Cancer
2:26	8 Gemini	15 Aquarius	8 Sagittar.	15 Leo
2:57	16 Gemini	23 Aquarius	16 Sagittar.	23 Leo
4:26	7 Cancer	16 Pisces	7 Capricorn	16 Virgo
5:25	19 Cancer	2 Aries	19 Capric.	2 Libra
7:37	16 Leo	8 Taurus	16 Aquarius	8 Scorpio
9:40	11 Virgo	8 Gemini	11 Pisces	8 Sagittarius
10:06	16 Virgo	14 Gemini	16 Pisces	14 Sagittarius

January 15

Time	Ascendant	Midheaven	Descendant	Nadir
2:12 A.M.	16 Scorpio	25 Leo	16 Taurus	25 Aquarius
3:33	2 Sagittar.	16 Virgo	2 Gemini	16 Pisces
4:03	8 Sagittar.	24 Virgo	8 Gemini	24 Pisces
4:41	16 Sagittar.	5 Libra	16 Gemini	5 Aries
7:00	19 Capric.	12 Scorpio	19 Cancer	12 Taurus
8:30	16 Aquarius	4 Sagittar.	16 Leo	4 Gemini
8:47	22 Aquarius	8 Sagittar.	22 Leo	8 Gemini
9:48	16 Pisces	22 Sagittar.	16 Virgo	22 Gemini
11:01	16 Aries	9 Capricorn	16 Libra	9 Cancer
11:44	3 Taurus	19 Capric.	3 Scorpio	19 Cancer
12:21 P.M.	16 Taurus	26 Capric.	16 Scorpio	26 Cancer
1:31	8 Gemini	15 Aquarius	8 Sagittar.	15 Leo
2:02	16 Gemini	23 Aquarius	16 Sagittar.	23 Leo
3:31	7 CaIncer	16 Pisces	7 Capricorn	16 Virgo
4:30	19 Cancer	2 Aries	19 Capric.	2 Libra
6:42	16 Leo	8 Taurus	16 Aquarius	8 Scorpio
8:45	11 Virgo	8 Gemini	11 Pisces	8 Sagittar.
9:11	16 Virgo	14 Gemini	16 Pisces	14 Sagittar.
11:44	17 Libra	19 Cancer	17 Aries	19 Capric.

February 1

Time	Ascendant	Midheaven	Descendant	Nadir
1:05 A.M.	16 Scorpio	25 Leo	16 Taurus	25 Aquarius
2:26	2 Sagittar.	16 Virgo	2 Gemini	16 Pisces
2:56	8 Sagittar.	24 Virgo	8 Gemini	24 Pisces

February 15

Time	Ascendant	Midheaven	Descendant	Nadir
12:10 A.M.	16 Scorpio	25 Leo	16 Taurus	25 Aquarius
1:31	2 Sagittar.	16 Virgo	2 Gemini	16 Pisces
2:01	8 Sagittar.	24 Virgo	8 Gemini	24 Pisces

February 1

Time	Ascendant	Midheaven	Descendant	Nadir
3:34 A.M.	16 Sagittar.	5 Libra	16 Gemini	5 Aries
5:54	19 Capric.	12 Scorpio	19 Cancer	12 Taurus
7:23	16 Aquarius	4 Sagittar.	16 Leo	4 Gemini
7:40	22 Aquarius	8 Sagittar.	22 Leo	8 Gemini
8:41	16 Pisces	22 Sagittar.	16 Virgo	22 Gemini
9:54	16 Aries	9 Capricorn	16 Libra	9 Cancer
10:37	3 Taurus	19 Capric.	3 Scorpio	19 Cancer
11:15	16 Taurus	26 Capric.	16 Scorpio	26 Cancer
12:24 P.M.	8 Gemini	15 Aquarius	8 Sagittar.	15 Leo
12:55	16 Gemini	23 Aquarius	16 Sagittar.	23 Leo
2:24	7 Cancer	16 Pisces	7 Capricorn	16 Virgo
3:21	19 Cancer	2 Aries	19 Capric.	2 Libra
5:36	16 Leo	8 Taurus	16 Aquarius	8 Scorpio
7:38	11 Virgo	8 Gemini	11 Pisces	8 Sagittarius
8:04	16 Virgo	14 Gemini	16 Pisces	14 Sagittarius
10:37	17 Libra	19 Cancer	17 Aries	19 Capric.

February 15

Time	Ascendant	Midheaven	Descendant	Nadir
2:39 A.M.	16 Sagittar.	5 Libra	16 Gemini	5 Aries
4:59	19 Capric.	12 Scorpio	19 Cancer	12 Taurus
6:28	16 Aquarius	4 Sagittar.	16 Leo	4 Gemini
6:45	22 Aquarius	8 Sagittar.	22 Leo	8 Gemini
7:46	16 Pisces	22 Sagittar.	16 Virgo	22 Gemini
8:59	16 Aries	9 Capricorn	16 Libra	9 Cancer
9:42	3 Taurus	19 Capric.	3 Scorpio	19 Cancer
10:20	16 Taurus	26 Capric.	16 Scorpio	26 Cancer
11:30	8 Gemini	15 Aquarius	8 Sagittar.	15 Leo
12:00 P.M.	16 Gemini	23 Aquarius	16 Sagittar.	23 Leo
1:29	7 Cancer	16 Pisces	7 Capricorn	16 Virgo
2:26	19 Cancer	2 Aries	19 Capric.	2 Libra
4:41	16 Leo	8 Taurus	16 Aquarius	8 Scorpio
6:43	11 Virgo	8 Gemini	11 Pisces	8 Sagittarius
7:09	16 Virgo	14 Gemini	16 Pisces	14 Sagittar.
9:42	17 Libra	19 Cancer	17 Aries	19 Capric.

March 1

Time	Ascendant	Midheaven	Descendant	Nadir
12:36 A.M.	2 Sagittar.	16 Virgo	2 Gemini	16 Pisces
1:06	8 Sagittar.	24 Virgo	8 Gemini	24 Pisces
1:44	16 Sagittar.	5 Libra	16 Gemini	5 Aries
4:04	19 Capric.	12 Scorpio	19 Cancer	12 Taurus
5:34	16 Aquarius	4 Sagittar.	16 Leo	4 Gemini
5:51	22 Aquarius	8 Sagittar.	22 Leo	8 Gemini
6:51	16 Pisces	22 Sagittar.	16 Virgo	22 Gemini
8:04	16 Aries	9 Capricorn	16 Libra	9 Cancer
8:47	3 Taurus	19 Capric.	3 Scorpio	19 Cancer
9:25	16 Taurus	26 Capric.	16 Scorpio	26 Cancer
10:35	8 Gemini	15 Aquarius	8 Sagittar.	15 Leo
11:06	16 Gemini	23 Aquarius	16 Sagittar.	23 Leo
12:34 P.M.	7 Cancer	16 Pisces	7 Capricorn	16 Virgo
1:31	19 Cancer	2 Aries	19 Capric.	2 Libra
3:46	16 Leo	8 Taurus	16 Aquarius	8 Scorpio
5:49	11 Virgo	8 Gemini	11 Pisces	8 Sagittarius
6:14	16 Virgo	14 Gemini	16 Pisces	14 Sagittarius
8:47	17 Libra	19 Cancer	17 Aries	19 Capricorn
11:12	16 Scorpio	25 Leo	16 Taurus	25 Aquarius

March 15

Time	Ascendant	Midheaven	Descendant	Nadir
12:10 A.M.	8 Sagittar.	24 Virgo	8 Gemini	24 Pisces
12:48	16 Sagittar.	5 Libra	16 Gemini	5 Aries
3:08	19 Capric.	12 Scorpio	19 Cancer	12 Taurus
4:38	16 Aquarius	4 Sagittar.	16 Leo	4 Gemini
4:55	22 Aquarius	8 Sagittar.	22 Leo	8 Gemini
5:56	16 Pisces	22 Sagittar.	16 Virgo	22 Gemini
7:08	16 Aries	9 Capricorn	16 Libra	9 Cancer
7:51	3 Taurus	19 Capric.	3 Scorpio	19 Cancer
8:29	16 Taurus	26 Capric.	16 Scorpio	26 Cancer
9:39	8 Gemini	15 Aquarius	8 Sagittar.	15 Leo
10:10	16 Gemini	23 Aquarius	16 Sagittar.	23 Leo
11:39	7 Cancer	16 Pisces	7 Capricorn	16 Virgo
12:35 P.M.	19 Cancer	2 Aries	19 Capric.	2 Libra
2:50	16 Leo	8 Taurus	16 Aquarius	8 Scorpio
4:53	11 Virgo	8 Gemini	11 Pisces	8 Sagittar.
5:19	16 Virgo	14 Gemini	16 Pisces	14 Sagittar.
7:51	17 Libra	19 Cancer	17 Aries	19 Capric.
10:16	16 Scorpio	25 Leo	16 Taurus	25 Aquarius
11:37	2 Sagittar.	16 Virgo	2 Gemini	16 Pisces

April 1

Time	Ascendant	Midheaven	Descendant	Nadir
2:01 A.M.	19 Capric.	12 Scorpio	19 Cancer	12 Taurus
3:31	16 Aquarius	4 Sagittar.	16 Leo	4 Gemini
3:48	22 Aquarius	8 Sagittar.	22 Leo	8 Gemini

April 15

Time	Ascendant	Midheaven	Descendant	Nadir
1:06 A.M.	19 Capric.	12 Scorpio	19 Cancer	12 Taurus
2:36	16 Aquarius	4 Sagittar.	16 Leo	4 Gemini
2:53	22 Aquarius	8 Sagittar.	22 Leo	8 Gemini

April 1

Time	Ascendant	Midheaven	Descendant	Nadir
4:49 A.M.	16 Pisces	22 Sagittar.	16 Virgo	22 Gemini
6:01	16 Aries	9 Capricorn	16 Libra	9 Cancer
6:44	3 Taurus	19 Capric.	3 Scorpio	19 Cancer
7:22	16 Taurus	26 Capric.	16 Scorpio	26 Cancer
8:32	8 Gemini	15 Aquarius	8 Sagittar.	15 Leo
9:03	16 Gemini	23 Aquarius	16 Sagittar.	23 Leo
10:32	7 Cancer	16 Pisces	7 Capricorn	16 Virgo
11:29	19 Cancer	2 Aries	19 Capric.	2 Libra
1:44 P.M.	16 Leo	8 Taurus	16 Aquarius	8 Scorpio
3:47	11 Virgo	8 Gemini	11 Pisces	8 Sagittarius
4:13	16 Virgo	14 Gemini	16 Pisces	14Sagittarius
6:44	17 Libra	19 Cancer	17 Aries	19 Capricorn
9:09	16 Scorpio	25 Leo	16 Taurus	25 Aquarius
10:30	2 Sagittar.	16 Virgo	2 Gemini	16 Pisces
11:00	8 Sagittar.	24 Virgo	8 Gemini	24 Pisces
11:38	16 Sagittar.	5 Libra	16 Gemini	5 Aries

April 15

Time	Ascendant	Midheaven	Descendant	Nadir
3:54 A.M.	16 Pisces	22 Sagittar.	16 Virgo	22 Gemini
5:07	16 Aries	9 Capricorn	16 Libra	9 Cancer
5:50	3 Taurus	19 Capric.	3 Scorpio	19 Cancer
6:27	16 Taurus	26 Capric.	16 Scorpio	26 Cancer
7:37	8 Gemini	15 Aquarius	8 Sagittar.	15 Leo
8:08	16 Gemini	23 Aquarius	16 Sagittar.	23 Leo
9:37	7 Cancer	16 Pisces	7 Capricorn	16 Virgo
10:34	19 Cancer	2 Aries	19 Capric.	2 Libra
12:48 P.M.	16 Leo	8 Taurus	16 Aquarius	8 Scorpio
2:51	11 Virgo	8 Gemini	11 Pisces	8 Sagittar.
3:17	16 Virgo	14 Gemini	16 Pisces	14 Sagittar.
5:50	17 Libra	19 Cancer	17 Aries	19 Capric.
8:14	16 Scorpio	25 Leo	16 Taurus	25 Aquarius
9:35	2 Sagittar.	16 Virgo	2 Gemini	16 Pisces
10:05	8 Sagittar.	24 Virgo	8 Gemini	24 Pisces
10:43	16 Sagittar.	5 Libra	16 Gemini	5 Aries

May 1

Time	Ascendant	Midheaven	Descendant	Nadir
12:03 A.M.	19 Capric.	12 Scorpio	19 Cancer	12 Taurus
1:33	16 Aquarius	4 Sagittar.	16 Leo	4 Gemini
1:50	22 Aquarius	8 Sagittar.	22 Leo	8 Gemini
2:51	16 Pisces	22 Sagittar.	16 Virgo	22 Gemini
4:04	16 Aries	9 Capricorn	16 Libra	9 Cancer
4:47	3 Taurus	19 Capric.	3 Scorpio	19 Cancer
5:25	16 Taurus	26 Capric.	16 Scorpio	26 Cancer
6:34	8 Gemini	15 Aquarius	8 Sagittar.	15 Leo
7:05	16 Gemini	23 Aquarius	16 Sagittar.	23 Leo
8:34	7 Cancer	16 Pisces	7 Capricorn	16 Virgo
9:31	19 Cancer	2 Aries	19 Capric.	2 Libra
11:46	16 Leo	8 Taurus	16 Aquarius	8 Scorpio
1:48 P.M.	11 Virgo	8 Gemini	11 Pisces	8 Sagittarius
2:14	16 Virgo	14 Gemini	16 Pisces	14 Sagittarius
4:47	17 Libra	19 Cancer	17 Aries	19 Capricorn
7:11	16 Scorpio	25 Leo	16 Taurus	25 Aquarius
8:32	2 Sagittar.	16 Virgo	2 Gemini	16 Pisces
9:02	8 Sagittar.	24 Virgo	8 Gemini	24 Pisces
9:40	16 Sagittar.	5 Libra	16 Gemini	5 Aries

May 15

Time	Ascendant	Midheaven	Descendant	Nadir
12:38 A.M.	16 Aquarius	4 Sagittar.	16 Leo	4 Gemini
12:55	22 Aquarius	8 Sagittar.	22 Leo	8 Gemini
1:56	16 Pisces	22 Sagittar.	16 Virgo	22 Gemini
3:09	16 Aries	9 Capricorn	16 Libra	9 Cancer
3:52	3 Taurus	19 Capric.	3 Scorpio	19 Cancer
4:30	16 Taurus	26 Capric.	16 Scorpio	26 Cancer
5:40	8 Gemini	15 Aquarius	8 Sagittar.	15 Leo
6:10	16 Gemini	23 Aquarius	16 Sagittar.	23 Leo
7:39	7 Cancer	16 Pisces	7 Capricorn	16 Virgo
8:36	19 Cancer	2 Aries	19 Capric.	2 Libra
10:51	16 Leo	8 Taurus	16 Aquarius	8 Scorpio
12:53 P.M.	11 Virgo	8 Gemini	11 Pisces	8 Sagittar.
1:19	16 Virgo	14 Gemini	16 Pisces	14 Sagittar.
3:52	17 Libra	19 Cancer	17 Aries	19 Capric.
6:16	16 Scorpio	25 Leo	16 Taurus	25 Aquarius
7:37	2 Sagittar.	16 Virgo	2 Gemini	16 Pisces
8:07	8 Sagittar.	24 Virgo	8 Gemini	24 Pisces
8:45	16 Sagittar.	5 Libra	16 Gemini	5 Aries
11:05	19 Capric.	12 Scorpio	19 Cancer	12 Taurus

June 1

Time	Ascendant	Midheaven	Descendant	Nadir
12:49 A.M.	16 Pisces	22 Sagittar.	16 Virgo	22 Gemini
2:02	16 Aries	9 Capricorn	16 Libra	9 Cancer
2:45 A.M.	3 Taurus	19 Capric.	3 Scorpio	19 Cancer

June 15

Time	Ascendant	Midheaven	Descendant	Nadir
1:08 A.M.	16 Aries	9 Capricorn	16 Libra	9 Cancer
1:51	3 Taurus	19 Capric.	3 Scorpio	19 Cancer
2:33 A.M.	16 Taurus	26 Capric.	16 Scorpio	26 Cancer

June 1

Time	Ascendant	Midheaven	Descendant	Nadir
3:23 A.M.	16 Taurus	26 Capric.	16 Scorpio	26 Cancer
4:34	8 Gemini	15 Aquarius	8 Sagittar.	15 Leo
5:05	16 Gemini	23 Aquarius	16 Sagittar.	23 Leo
6:34	7 Cancer	16 Pisces	7 Capricorn	16 Virgo
7:31	19 Cancer	2 Aries	19 Capric.	2 Libra
9:46	16 Leo	8 Taurus	16 Aquarius	8 Scorpio
11:49	11 Virgo	8 Gemini	11 Pisces	8 Sagittarius
12:14 P.M.	16 Virgo	14 Gemini	16 Pisces	14 Sagittarius
2:48	17 Libra	19 Cancer	17 Aries	19 Capricorn
5:13	16 Scorpio	25 Leo	16 Taurus	25 Aquarius
6:33	2 Sagittar.	16 Virgo	2 Gemini	16 Pisces
7:03	8 Sagittar.	24 Virgo	8 Gemini	24 Pisces
7:42	16 Sagittar.	5 Libra	16 Gemini	5 Aries
10:02	19 Capric.	12 Scorpio	19 Cancer	12 Taurus
11:32	16 Aquarius	4 Sagittar.	16 Leo	4 Gemini
11:48	22 Aquarius	8 Sagittar.	22 Leo	8 Gemini

June 15

Time	Ascendant	Midheaven	Descendant	Nadir
3:39 A.M.	8 Gemini	15 Aquarius	8 Sagittar.	15 Leo
4:10	16 Gemini	23 Aquarius	16 Sagittar.	23 Leo
5:39	7 Cancer	16 Pisces	7 Capricorn	16 Virgo
6:36	19 Cancer	2 Aries	19 Capric.	2 Libra
8:51	16 Leo	8 Taurus	16 Aquarius	8 Scorpio
10:54	11 Virgo	8 Gemini	11 Pisces	8 Sagittar.
11:19	16 Virgo	14 Gemini	16 Pisces	14 Sagittar.
1:53 P.M.	17 Libra	19 Cancer	17 Aries	19 Capric.
4:18	16 Scorpio	25 Leo	16 Taurus	25 Aquarius
5:39	2 Sagittar.	16 Virgo	2 Gemini	16 Pisces
6:09	8 Sagittar.	24 Virgo	8 Gemini	24 Pisces
6:47	16 Sagittar.	5 Libra	16 Gemini	5 Aries
9:07	19 Capric.	12 Scorpio	19 Cancer	12 Taurus
10:37	16 Aquarius	4 Sagittar.	16 Leo	4 Gemini
10:53	22 Aquarius	8 Sagittar.	22 Leo	8 Gemini
11:56	16 Pisces	22 Sagittar.	16 Virgo	22 Gemini

July 1

Time	Ascendant	Midheaven	Descendant	Nadir
12:05 A.M.	16 Aries	9 Capricorn	16 Libra	9 Cancer
12:48	3 Taurus	19 Capric.	3 Scorpio	19 Cancer
1:26	16 Taurus	26 Capric.	16 Scorpio	26 Cancer
2:36	8 Gemini	15 Aquarius	8 Sagittar.	15 Leo
3:07	16 Gemini	23 Aquarius	16 Sagittar.	23 Leo
4:36	7 Cancer	16 Pisces	7 Capricorn	16 Virgo
5:33	19 Cancer	2 Aries	19 Capric.	2 Libra
7:48	16 Leo	8 Taurus	16 Aquarius	8 Scorpio
9:51	11 Virgo	8 Gemini	11 Pisces	8 Sagittar.
10:16	16 Virgo	14 Gemini	16 Pisces	14 Sagittar.
12:50 P.M.	17 Libra	19 Cancer	17 Aries	19 Capric.
3:15	16 Scorpio	25 Leo	16 Taurus	25 Aquarius
4:36	2 Sagittar.	16 Virgo	2 Gemini	16 Pisces
5:06	8 Sagittar.	24 Virgo	8 Gemini	24 Pisces
5:44	16 Sagittar.	5 Libra	16 Gemini	5 Aries
8:04	19 Capric.	12 Scorpio	19 Cancer	12 Taurus
9:34	16 Aquarius	4 Sagittar.	16 Leo	4 Gemini
9:51	22 Aquarius	8 Sagittar.	22 Leo	8 Gemini
10:53	16 Pisces	22 Sagittar.	16 Virgo	22 Gemini

July 15

Time	Ascendant	Midheaven	Descendant	Nadir
12:30 A.M.	16 Taurus	26 Capric.	16 Scorpio	26 Cancer
1:41	8 Gemini	15 Aquarius	8 Sagittar.	15 Leo
2:11	16 Gemini	23 Aquarius	16 Sagittar.	23 Leo
3:41	7 Cancer	16 Pisces	7 Capricorn	16 Virgo
4:37	19 Cancer	2 Aries	19 Capric.	2 Libra
6:52	16 Leo	8 Taurus	16 Aquarius	8 Scorpio
8:56	11 Virgo	8 Gemini	11 Pisces	8 Sagittar.
9:21	16 Virgo	14 Gemini	16 Pisces	14 Sagittar.
11:55	17 Libra	19 Cancer	17 Aries	19 Capric.
2:19 P.M.	16 Scorpio	25 Leo	16 Taurus	25 Aquarius
3:41	2 Sagittar.	16 Virgo	2 Gemini	16 Pisces
4:11	8 Sagittar.	24 Virgo	8 Gemini	24 Pisces
4:48	16 Sagittar.	5 Libra	16 Gemini	5 Aries
7:08	19 Capric.	12 Scorpio	19 Cancer	12 Taurus
8:38	16 Aquarius	4 Sagittar.	16 Leo	4 Gemini
8:54	22 Aquarius	8 Sagittar.	22 Leo	8 Gemini
9:57	16 Pisces	22 Sagittar.	16 Virgo	22 Gemini
11:08	16 Aries	9 Capricorn	16 Libra	9 Cancer
11:53	3 Taurus	19 Capric.	3 Scorpio	19 Cancer

August 1

Time	Ascendant	Midheaven	Descendant	Nadir
12:34 A.M.	8 Gemini	15 Aquarius	8 Sagittar.	15 Leo
1:04	16 Gemini	23 Aquarius	16 Sagittar.	23 Leo
2:33	7 Cancer	16 Pisces	7 Capricorn	16 Virgo

August 15

Time	Ascendant	Midheaven	Descendant	Nadir
12:09 A.M.	16 Gemini	23 Aquarius	16 Sagittar.	23 Leo
1:38	7 Cancer	16 Pisces	7 Capricorn	16 Virgo
2:35	19 Cancer	2 Aries	19 Capric.	2 Libra

August 1

Time	Ascendant	Midheaven	Descendant	Nadir
3:30 A.M.	19 Cancer	2 Aries	19 Capric.	2 Libra
5:45	16 Leo	8 Taurus	16 Aquarius	8 Scorpio
7:49	11 Virgo	8 Gemini	11 Pisces	8 Sagittar.
8:14	16 Virgo	14 Gemini	16 Pisces	14 Sagittar.
10:48	17 Libra	19 Cancer	17 Aries	19 Capric.
1:12 P.M.	16 Scorpio	25 Leo	16 Taurus	25 Aquarius
2:34	2 Sagittar.	16 Virgo	2 Gemini	16 Pisces
3:04	8 Sagittar.	24 Virgo	8 Gemini	24 Pisces
3:41	16 Sagittar.	5 Libra	16 Gemini	5 Aries
6:01	19 Capric.	12 Scorpio	19 Cancer	12 Taurus
7:31	16 Aquarius	4 Sagittar.	16 Leo	4 Gemini
7:48	22 Aquarius	8 Sagittar.	22 Leo	8 Gemini
8:50	16 Pisces	22 Sagittar.	16 Virgo	22 Gemini
10:02	16 Aries	9 Capricorn	16 Libra	9 Cancer
10:45	3 Taurus	19 Capric.	3 Scorpio	19 Cancer
11:23	16 Taurus	26 Capric.	16 Scorpio	26 Cancer

August 15

Time	Ascendant	Midheaven	Descendant	Nadir
4:50 A.M.	16 Leo	8 Taurus	16 Aquarius	8 Scorpio
6:53	11 Virgo	8 Gemini	11 Pisces	8 Sagittar.
7:18	16 Virgo	14 Gemini	16 Pisces	14 Sagittar.
9:52	17 Libra	19 Cancer	17 Aries	19 Capric.
12:17 P.M.	16 Scorpio	25 Leo	16 Taurus	25 Aquarius
1:38	2 Sagittar.	16 Virgo	2 Gemini	16 Pisces
2:08	8 Sagittar.	24 Virgo	8 Gemini	24 Pisces
2:46	16 Sagittar.	5 Libra	16 Gemini	5 Aries
5:06	19 Capric.	12 Scorpio	19 Cancer	12 Taurus
6:36	16 Aquarius	4 Sagittar.	16 Leo	4 Gemini
6:53	22 Aquarius	8 Sagittar.	22 Leo	8 Gemini
7:55	16 Pisces	22 Sagittar.	16 Virgo	22 Gemini
9:07	16 Aries	9 Capricorn	16 Libra	9 Cancer
9:50	3 Taurus	19 Capric.	3 Scorpio	19 Cancer
10:28	16 Taurus	26 Capric.	16 Scorpio	26 Cancer
11:38	8 Gemini	15 Aquarius	8 Sagittar.	15 Leo

September 1

Time	Ascendant	Midheaven	Descendant	Nadir
12:31 A.M.	7 Cancer	16 Pisces	7 Capricorn	16 Virgo
1:28	19 Cancer	2 Aries	19 Capric.	2 Libra
3:43	16 Leo	8 Taurus	16 Aquarius	8 Scorpio
5:46	11 Virgo	8 Gemini	11 Pisces	8 Sagittar.
6:11	16 Virgo	14 Gemini	16 Pisces	14 Sagittar.
8:45	17 Libra	19 Cancer	17 Aries	19 Capric.
11:10	16 Scorpio	25 Leo	16 Taurus	25 Aquarius
12:31 P.M.	2 Sagittar.	16 Virgo	2 Gemini	16 Pisces
1:01	8 Sagittar.	24 Virgo	8 Gemini	24 Pisces
1:39	16 Sagittar.	5 Libra	16 Gemini	5 Aries
3:59	19 Capric.	12 Scorpio	19 Cancer	12 Taurus
5:29	16 Aquarius	4 Sagittar.	16 Leo	4 Gemini
5:46	22 Aquarius	8 Sagittar.	22 Leo	8 Gemini
6:48	16 Pisces	22 Sagittar.	16 Virgo	22 Gemini
8:00	16 Aries	9 Capricorn	16 Libra	9 Cancer
8:43	3 Taurus	19 Capric.	3 Scorpio	19 Cancer
9:21	16 Taurus	26 Capric.	16 Scorpio	26 Cancer
10:31	8 Gemini	15 Aquarius	8 Sagittar.	15 Leo
11:02	16 Gemini	23 Aquarius	16 Sagittar.	23 Leo

September 15

Time	Ascendant	Midheaven	Descendant	Nadir
12:33 A.M.	19 Cancer	2 Aries	19 Capric.	2 Libra
2:48	16 Leo	8 Taurus	16 Aquarius	8 Scorpio
4:51	11 Virgo	8 Gemini	11 Pisces	8 Sagittar.
5:16	16 Virgo	14 Gemini	16 Pisces	14 Sagittar.
7:50	17 Libra	19 Cancer	17 Aries	19 Capric.
10:15	16 Scorpio	25 Leo	16 Taurus	25 Aquarius
11:36	2 Sagittar.	16 Virgo	2 Gemini	16 Pisces
12:06 P.M.	8 Sagittar.	24 Virgo	8 Gemini	24 Pisces
12:44	16 Sagittar.	5 Libra	16 Gemini	5 Aries
3:04	19 Capric.	12 Scorpio	19 Cancer	12 Taurus
4:34	16 Aquarius	4 Sagittar.	16 Leo	4 Gemini
4:51	22 Aquarius	8 Sagittar.	22 Leo	8 Gemini
5:53	16 Pisces	22 Sagittar.	16 Virgo	22 Gemini
7:05	16 Aries	9 Capricorn	16 Libra	9 Cancer
7:48	3 Taurus	19 Capric.	3 Scorpio	19 Cancer
8:25	16 Taurus	26 Capric.	16 Scorpio	26 Cancer
9:36	8 Gemini	15 Aquarius	8 Sagittar.	15 Leo
10:07	16 Gemini	23 Aquarius	16 Sagittar.	23 Leo
11:36	7 Cancer	16 Pisces	7 Capricorn	16 Virgo

October 1

Time	Ascendant	Midheaven	Descendant	Nadir
1:45 A.M.	16 Leo	8 Taurus	16 Aquarius	8 Scorpio
3:48	11 Virgo	8 Gemini	11 Pisces	8 Sagittar.
4:13	16 Virgo	14 Gemini	16 Pisces	14 Sagittar.

October 15

Time	Ascendant	Midheaven	Descendant	Nadir
12:50 A.M.	16 Leo	8 Taurus	16 Aquarius	8 Scorpio
2:53	11 Virgo	8 Gemini	11 Pisces	8 Sagittar.
3:18	16 Virgo	14 Gemini	16 Pisces	14 Sagittar.

October 1

Time	Ascendant	Midheaven	Descendant	Nadir
6:47 A.M.	17 Libra	19 Cancer	17 Aries	19 Capric.
9:12	16 Scorpio	25 Leo	16 Taurus	25 Aquarius
10:33	2 Sagittar.	16 Virgo	2 Gemini	16 Pisces
11:03	8 Sagittar.	24 Virgo	8 Gemini	24 Pisces
12:18 P.M.	16 Sagittar.	5 Libra	16 Gemini	5 Aries
2:01	19 Capric.	12 Scorpio	19 Cancer	12 Taurus
3:31	16 Aquarius	4 Sagittar.	16 Leo	4 Gemini
3:47	22 Aquarius	8 Sagittar.	22 Leo	8 Gemini
4:50	16 Pisces	22 Sagittar.	16 Virgo	22 Gemini
6:02	16 Aries	9 Capricorn	16 Libra	9 Cancer
6:45	3 Taurus	19 Capric.	3 Scorpio	19 Cancer
7:22	16 Taurus	26 Capric.	16 Scorpio	26 Cancer
8:33	8 Gemini	15 Aquarius	8 Sagittar.	15 Leo
9:04	16 Gemini	23 Aquarius	16 Sagittar.	23 Leo
10:33	7 Cancer	16 Pisces	7 Capricorn	16 Virgo
11:30	19 Cancer	2 Aries	19 Capric.	2 Libra

October 15

Time	Ascendant	Midheaven	Descendant	Nadir
5:52 A.M.	17 Libra	19 Cancer	17 Aries	19 Capric.
8:17	16 Scorpio	25 Leo	16 Taurus	25 Aquarius
9:38	2 Sagittar.	16 Virgo	2 Gemini	16 Pisces
10:08	8 Sagittar.	24 Virgo	8 Gemini	24 Pisces
10:46	16 Sagittar.	5 Libra	16 Gemini	5 Aries
1:06 P.M.	19 Capric.	12 Scorpio	19 Cancer	12 Taurus
2:36	16 Aquarius	4 Sagittar.	16 Leo	4 Gemini
2:53	22 Aquarius	8 Sagittar.	22 Leo	8 Gemini
3:55	16 Pisces	22 Sagittar.	16 Virgo	22 Gemini
5:07	16 Aries	9 Capricorn	16 Libra	9 Cancer
5:50	3 Taurus	19 Capric.	3 Scorpio	19 Cancer
6:27	16 Taurus	26 Capric.	16 Scorpio	26 Cancer
7:38	8 Gemini	15 Aquarius	8 Sagittar.	15 Leo
8:09	16 Gemini	23 Aquarius	16 Sagittar.	23 Leo
9:38	7 Cancer	16 Pisces	7 Capricorn	16 Virgo
10:35	19 Cancer	2 Aries	19 Capric.	2 Libra

November 1

Time	Ascendant	Midheaven	Descendant	Nadir
1:46 A.M.	11 Virgo	8 Gemini	11 Pisces	8 Sagittar.
2:11	16 Virgo	14 Gemini	16 Pisces	14 Sagittar.
4:45	17 Libra	19 Cancer	17 Aries	19 Capric.
7:10	16 Scorpio	25 Leo	16 Taurus	25 Aquarius
8:31	2 Sagittar.	16 Virgo	2 Gemini	16 Pisces
9:01	8 Sagittar.	24 Virgo	8 Gemini	24 Pisces
9:39	16 Sagittar.	5 Libra	16 Gemini	5 Aries
11:59	19 Capric.	12 Scorpio	19 Cancer	12 Taurus
1:29 P.M.	16 Aquarius	4 Sagittar.	16 Leo	4 Gemini
1:46	22 Aquarius	8 Sagittar.	22 Leo	8 Gemini
2:48	16 Pisces	22 Sagittar.	16 Virgo	22 Gemini
4:00	16 Aries	9 Capricorn	16 Libra	9 Cancer
4:43	3 Taurus	19 Capric.	3 Scorpio	19 Cancer
5:20	16 Taurus	26 Capric.	16 Scorpio	26 Cancer
6:31	8 Gemini	15 Aquarius	8 Sagittar.	15 Leo
7:02	16 Gemini	23 Aquarius	16 Sagittar.	23 Leo
8:31	7 Cancer	16 Pisces	7 Capricorn	16 Virgo
9:08	19 Cancer	2 Aries	19 Capric.	2 Libra
11:43	16 Leo	8 Taurus	16 Aquarius	8 Scorpio

November 15

Time	Ascendant	Midheaven	Descendant	Nadir
12:51 A.M.	11 Virgo	8 Gemini	11 Pisces	8 Sagittar.
1:16	16 Virgo	14 Gemini	16 Pisces	14 Sagittar.
3:50	17 Libra	19 Cancer	17 Aries	19 Capric.
6:14	16 Scorpio	25 Leo	16 Taurus	25 Aquarius
7:36	2 Sagittar.	16 Virgo	2 Gemini	16 Pisces
8:06	8 Sagittar.	24 Virgo	8 Gemini	24 Pisces
8:44	16 Sagittar.	5 Libra	16 Gemini	5 Aries
11:04	19 Capric.	12 Scorpio	19 Cancer	12 Taurus
12:33 P.M.	16 Aquarius	4 Sagittar.	16 Leo	4 Gemini
12:50	22 Aquarius	8 Sagittar.	22 Leo	8 Gemini
1:52	16 Pisces	22 Sagittar.	16 Virgo	22 Gemini
3:04	16 Aries	9 Capricorn	16 Libra	9 Cancer
3:48	3 Taurus	19 Capric.	3 Scorpio	19 Cancer
4:25	16 Taurus	26 Capric.	16 Scorpio	26 Cancer
5:36	8 Gemini	15 Aquarius	8 Sagittar.	15 Leo
6:06	16 Gemini	23 Aquarius	16 Sagittar.	23 Leo
7:36	7 Cancer	16 Pisces	7 Capricorn	16 Virgo
8:33	19 Cancer	2 Aries	19 Capric.	2 Libra
10:47	16 Leo	8 Taurus	16 Aquarius	8 Scorpio

December 1

Time	Ascendant	Midheaven	Descendant	Nadir
12:13 A.M.	16 Virgo	14 Gemini	16 Pisces	14 Sagittar.
2:46	17 Libra	19 Cancer	17 Aries	19 Capric.
5:11	16 Scorpio	25 Leo	16 Taurus	25 Aquarius

December 15

Time	Ascendant	MidHeaven	Descendant	Nadir
1:51 A.M.	17 Libra	19 Cancer	17 Aries	19 Capric.
4:16	16 Scorpio	25 Leo	16 Taurus	25 Aquarius
5:37	2 Sagittar.	16 Virgo	2 Gemini	16 Pisces

December 1

Time	Ascendant	Midheaven	Descendant	Nadir
6:33 A.M.	2 Sagittar.	16 Virgo	2 Gemini	16 Pisces
7:03	8 Sagittar.	24 Virgo	8 Gemini	24 Pisces
7:41	16 Sagittar.	5 Libra	16 Gemini	5 Aries
10:00	19 Capric.	12 Scorpio	19 Cancer	12 Taurus
11:30	16 Aquarius	4 Sagittar.	16 Leo	4 Gemini
11:47	22 Aquarius	8 Sagittar.	22 Leo	8 Gemini
12:49 P.M.	16 Pisces	22 Sagittar.	16 Virgo	22 Gemini
2:01	16 Aries	9 Capricorn	16 Libra	9 Cancer
2:45	3 Taurus	19 Capric.	3 Scorpio	19 Cancer
3:22	16 Taurus	26 Capric.	16 Scorpio	26 Cancer
4:33	8 Gemini	15 Aquarius	8 Sagittar.	15 Leo
5:03	16 Gemini	23 Aquarius	16 Sagittar.	23 Leo
6:32	7 Cancer	16 Pisces	7 Capricorn	16 Virgo
7:30	19 Cancer	2 Aries	19 Capric.	2 Libra
9:44	16 Leo	8 Taurus	16 Aquarius	8 Scorpio
11:48	11 Virgo	8 Gemini	11 Pisces	8 Sagittar.

December 15

Time	Ascendant	MidHeaven	Descendant	Nadir
6:07 A.M.	8 Sagittar.	24 Virgo	8 Gemini	24 Pisces
6:45	16 Sagittar.	5 Libra	16 Gemini	5 Aries
9:05	19 Capric.	12 Scorpio	19 Cancer	12 Taurus
10:35	16 Aquarius	4 Sagittar.	16 Leo	4 Gemini
10:52	22 Aquarius	8 Sagittar.	22 Leo	8 Gemini
11:54	16 Pisces	22 Sagittar.	16 Virgo	22 Gemini
1:06 P.M.	16 Aries	9 Capricorn	16 Libra	9 Cancer
1:49	3 Taurus	19 Capric.	3 Scorpio	19 Cancer
2:26	16 Taurus	26 Capric.	16 Scorpio	26 Cancer
3:37	8 Gemini	15 Aquarius	8 Sagittar.	15 Leo
4:08	16 Gemini	23 Aquarius	16 Sagittar.	23 Leo
5:37	7 Cancer	16 Pisces	7 Capricorn	16 Virgo
6:34	19 Cancer	2 Aries	19 Capric.	2 Libra
8:49	16 Leo	8 Taurus	16 Aquarius	8 Scorpio
10:52	11 Virgo	8 Gemini	11 Pisces	8 Sagittar.
11:17	16 Virgo	14 Gemini	16 Pisces	14 Sagittar.

APPENDIX C

OUTER PLANET EPHEMERIS

URANUS IN THE SIGNS (AXIS AGE TO POST-MODERN TIMES)
(accurate to +/- 1 year)

The periods of the "High Times" of Uranus are indicated in bold type.

Year	Sign	Year	Sign	Year	Sign	Year	Sign
B.C.		B.C.		B.C.		B.C.	
586	Aries	578	Taurus	571	Gemini	565	Cancer
558	Leo	552	Virgo	546	Libra	**539**	**Scorpio**
532	**Sagittarius**	**525**	**Capricorn**	**517**	**Aquarius**	509	Pisces
502	Aries	495	Taurus	488	Gemini	481	Cancer
475	Leo	468	Virgo	462	Libra	455	**Scorpio**
448	**Sagittarius**	**441**	**Capricorn**	**433**	**Aquarius**	**426**	**Pisces**
418	Aries	411	Taurus	404	Gemini	397	Cancer
391	Leo	384	Virgo	378	Libra	371	**Scorpio**
365	**Sagittarius**	357	**Capricorn**	350	**Aquarius**	342	Pisces
334	Aries	327	Taurus	320	Gemini	313	Cancer
307	Leo	301	Virgo	294	Libra	288	**Scorpio**
281	**Sagittarius**	274	**Capricorn**	**266**	**Aquarius**	258	Pisces
251	Aries	243	Taurus	236	Gemini	230	Cancer
223	Leo	217	Virgo	211	Libra	204	**Scorpio**
197	**Sagittarius**	190	**Capricorn**	182	**Aquarius**	175	Pisces
167	Aries	160	Taurus	153	Gemini	146	Cancer
140	Leo	133	Virgo	127	Libra	121	**Scorpio**
113	**Sagittarius**	106	**Capricorn**	**99**	**Aquarius**	91	Pisces
83	Aries	76	Taurus	69	Gemini	62	Cancer
56	Leo	49	Virgo	43	Libra	37	**Scorpio**
30	**Sagittarius**	**22**	**Capricorn**	**15**	**Aquarius**	7	**Pisces**
A.D.		A.D.		A.D.		A.D.	
2	Aries	9	Taurus	16	Gemini	23	Cancer
29	Leo	35	Virgo	42	Libra	48	**Scorpio**
55	**Sagittarius**	**62**	**Capricorn**	**70**	**Aquarius**	78	**Pisces**
85	Aries	92	Taurus	100	Gemini	106	Cancer
112	Leo	119	Virgo	125	Libra	132	**Scorpio**
139	**Sagittarius**	146	**Capricorn**	154	**Aquarius**	161	Pisces
169	Aries	176	Taurus	183	Gemini	190	Cancer
196	Leo	202	Virgo	209	Libra	216	**Scorpio**
223	**Sagittarius**	230	**Capricorn**	237	**Aquarius**	245	**Pisces**

Year A.D.	Sign	Year A.D.	Sign	Year A.D.	Sign	Year A.D.	Sign
253	Aries	260	Taurus	267	Gemini	273	Cancer
280	Leo	286	Virgo	293	Libra	**299**	**Scorpio**
306	**Sagittarius**	**314**	**Capricorn**	**321**	**Aquarius**	329	Pisces
336	Aries	344	Taurus	351	Gemini	357	Cancer
364	Leo	370	Virgo	377	Libra	**383**	**Scorpio**
390	**Sagittarius**	**397**	**Capricorn**	**405**	**Aquarius**	412	Pisces
420	Aries	427	Taurus	434	Gemini	441	Cancer
447	Leo	454	Virgo	460	Libra	**467**	**Scorpio**
474	**Sagittarius**	**481**	**Capricorn**	**488**	**Aquarius**	496	Pisces
504	Aries	511	Taurus	518	Gemini	525	Cancer
531	Leo	537	Virgo	544	Libra	550	**Scorpio**
557	**Sagittarius**	**565**	**Capricorn**	**572**	**Aquarius**	580	Pisces
588	Aries	595	Taurus	602	Gemini	609	Cancer
615	Leo	621	Virgo	628	Libra	**634**	**Scorpio**
641	**Sagittarius**	**648**	**Capricorn**	**656**	**Aquarius**	664	Pisces
671	Aries	679	Taurus	686	Gemini	692	Cancer
699	Leo	705	Virgo	712	Libra	**718**	**Scorpio**
725	**Sagittarius**	**732**	**Capricorn**	**740**	**Aquarius**	747	Pisces
755	Aries	762	Taurus	769	Gemini	776	Cancer
783	Leo	790	Virgo	795	Libra	**802**	**Scorpio**
809	**Sagittarius**	**816**	**Capricorn**	**823**	**Aquarius**	831	Pisces
839	Aries	846	Taurus	853	Gemini	860	Cancer
867	Leo	873	Virgo	879	Libra	**886**	**Scorpio**
893	**Sagittarius**	**900**	**Capricorn**	**907**	**Aquarius**	915	Pisces
922	Aries	930	Taurus	937	Gemini	944	Cancer
951	Leo	957	Virgo	963	Libra	**970**	**Scorpio**
976	**Sagittarius**	**984**	**Capricorn**	**991**	**Aquarius**	998	Pisces
1006	Aries	1013	Taurus	1021	Gemini	1028	Cancer
1034	Leo	1041	Virgo	1047	Libra	**1053**	**Scorpio**
1060	**Sagittarius**	**1067**	**Capricorn**	**1075**	**Aquarius**	1082	Pisces
1090	Aries	1097	Taurus	1105	Gemini	1111	Cancer
1118	Leo	1124	Virgo	1130	Libra	**1137**	**Scorpio**
1144	**Sagittarius**	**1151**	**Capricorn**	**1158**	**Aquarius**	1166	Pisces
1173	Aries	1181	Taurus	1188	Gemini	1195	Cancer
1202	Leo	1209	Virgo	1215	Libra	**1221**	**Scorpio**
1228	**Sagittarius**	**1235**	**Capricorn**	**1242**	**Aquarius**	1249	Pisces
1257	Aries	1265	Taurus	1272	Gemini	1279	Cancer
1285	Leo	1292	Virgo	1298	Libra	**1305**	**Scorpio**
1311	**Sagittarius**	**1318**	**Capricorn**	**1326**	**Aquarius**	1333	Pisces
1341	Aries	1348	Taurus	1356	Gemini	1362	Cancer
1369	Leo	1376	Virgo	1382	Libra	**1388**	**Scorpio**
1395	**Sagittarius**	**1402**	**Capricorn**	**1409**	**Aquarius**	1417	Pisces
1425	Aries	1432	Taurus	1439	Gemini	1446	Cancer
1453	Leo	1459	Virgo	1466	Libra	**1472**	**Scorpio**

Year A.D.	Sign	Year A.D.	Sign	Year A.D.	Sign	Year A.D.	Sign
1479	**Sagittarius**	**1486**	**Capricorn**	**1493**	**Aquarius**	**1501**	**Pisces**
1508	Aries	1516	Taurus	1523	Gemini	1530	Cancer
1537	Leo	1543	Virgo	1549	Libra	**1556**	**Scorpio**
1563	**Sagittarius**	**1570**	**Capricorn**	**1577**	**Aquarius**	**1584**	**Pisces**
1592	Aries	1600	Taurus	1607	Gemini	1614	Cancer
1620	Leo	1627	Virgo	1633	Libra	**1640**	**Scorpio**
1646	**Sagittarius**	**1653**	**Capricorn**	**1661**	**Aquarius**	**1668**	**Pisces**
1676	Aries	1683	Taurus	1691	Gemini	1698	Cancer
1704	Leo	1711	Virgo	1717	Libra	**1724**	**Scorpio**
1730	**Sagittarius**	**1737**	**Capricorn**	**1744**	**Aquarius**	**1752**	**Pisces**
1759	Aries	1767	Taurus	1774	Gemini	1781	Cancer
1788	Leo	1794	Virgo	1801	Libra	**1807**	**Scorpio**
1814	**Sagittarius**	**1821**	**Capricorn**	**1828**	**Aquarius**	**1835**	**Pisces**
1843	Aries	1851	Taurus	1858	Gemini	1865	Cancer
1872	Leo	1878	Virgo	1885	Libra	**1891**	**Scorpio**
1898	**Sagittarius**	**1904**	**Capricorn**	**1912**	**Aquarius**	**1919**	**Pisces**
1927	Aries	1934	Taurus	1942	Gemini	1949	Cancer
1955	Leo	1962	Virgo	1968	Libra	**1975**	**Scorpio**
1981	**Sagittarius**	**1988**	**Capricorn**	**1995**	**Aquarius**	**2003**	**Pisces**
2011	Aries	2018	Taurus	2025	Gemini	2032	Cancer
2039	Leo	2046	Virgo	2052	Libra	**2058**	**Scorpio**
2065	**Sagittarius**	**2072**	**Capricorn**	**2079**	**Aquarius**	**2087**	**Pisces**
2094	Aries	2102	Taurus	2109	Gemini	2116	Cancer
2123	Leo	2129	Virgo	2136	Libra	**2142**	**Scorpio**
2149	**Sagittarius**	**2156**	**Capricorn**	**2163**	**Aquarius**	**2170**	**Pisces**
2178	Aries	2186	Taurus	2193	Gemini	2200	Cancer
2207	Leo	2214	Virgo	2220	Libra	**2226**	**Scorpio**
2233	**Sagittarius**	**2239**	**Capricorn**	**2247**	**Aquarius**	**2254**	**Pisces**
2262	Aries	2269	Taurus	2277	Gemini	2284	Cancer
2291	Leo	2297	Virgo	2304	Libra	**2310**	**Scorpio**
2316	**Sagittarius**	**2323**	**Capricorn**	**2330**	**Aquarius**	**2338**	**Pisces**

NEPTUNE IN THE SIGNS (3000 B.C.–A.D. 2500)
(accurate to +/- 1 year)

The periods of the "High Times" of Neptune are indicated in **bold** type.

Year B.C	Sign	Year B.C	Sign	Year B.C	Sign	Year B.C	Sign
2998	Leo	2984	Virgo	2970	Libra	**2956**	**Scorpio**
2942	**Sagittarius**	**2928**	**Capricorn**	**2915**	**Aquarius**	**2902**	**Pisces**
2888	Aries	2875	Taurus	2862	Gemini	2848	Cancer
2834	Leo	2820	Virgo	2807	Libra	**2793**	**Scorpio**

Year B.C	Sign	Year B.C	Sign	Year B.C	Sign	Year B.C	Sign
2779	**Sagittarius**	**2765**	**Capricorn**	**2752**	**Aquarius**	**2738**	**Pisces**
2725	Aries	2711	Taurus	2698	Gemini	2684	Cancer
2671	Leo	2657	Virgo	2643	Libra	**2629**	**Scorpio**
2615	**Sagittarius**	**2602**	**Capricorn**	**2588**	**Aquarius**	**2574**	**Pisces**
2561	Aries	2548	Taurus	2534	Gemini	2521	Cancer
2507	Leo	2493	Virgo	2479	Libra	**2465**	**Scorpio**
2451	**Sagittarius**	**2438**	**Capricorn**	**2424**	**Aquarius**	**2411**	**Pisces**
2397	Aries	2384	Taurus	2371	Gemini	2357	Cancer
2343	Leo	2329	Virgo	2316	Libra	**2302**	**Scorpio**
2288	**Sagittarius**	**2273**	**Capricorn**	**2260**	**Aquarius**	**2247**	**Pisces**
2234	Aries	2221	Taurus	2207	Gemini	2193	Cancer
2179	Leo	2165	Virgo	2152	Libra	**2138**	**Scorpio**
2124	**Sagittarius**	**2111**	**Capricorn**	**2097**	**Aquarius**	**2083**	**Pisces**
2070	Aries	2057	Taurus	2043	Gemini	2030	Cancer
2016	Leo	2002	Virgo	1988	Libra	**1975**	**Scorpio**
1961	**Sagittarius**	**1947**	**Capricorn**	**1933**	**Aquarius**	**1920**	**Pisces**
1906	Aries	1893	Taurus	1880	Gemini	1866	Cancer
1852	Leo	1838	Virgo	1824	Libra	**1810**	**Scorpio**
1797	**Sagittarius**	**1783**	**Capricorn**	**1770**	**Aquarius**	**1756**	**Pisces**
1743	Aries	1729	Taurus	1716	Gemini	1702	Cancer
1689	Leo	1675	Virgo	1661	Libra	**1647**	**Scorpio**
1633	**Sagittarius**	**1619**	**Capricorn**	**1606**	**Aquarius**	**1592**	**Pisces**
1579	Aries	1566	Taurus	1552	Gemini	1538	Cancer
1525	Leo	1511	Virgo	1497	Libra	**1483**	**Scorpio**
1469	**Sagittarius**	**1456**	**Capricorn**	**1442**	**Aquarius**	**1428**	**Pisces**
1416	Aries	1402	Taurus	1388	Gemini	1374	Cancer
1360	Leo	1347	Virgo	1334	Libra	**1320**	**Scorpio**
1306	**Sagittarius**	**1292**	**Capricorn**	**1279**	**Aquarius**	**1265**	**Pisces**
1252	Aries	1238	Taurus	1224	Gemini	1210	Cancer
1197	Leo	1184	Virgo	1170	Libra	**1156**	**Scorpio**
1143	**Sagittarius**	**1129**	**Capricorn**	**1115**	**Aquarius**	**1102**	**Pisces**
1088	Aries	1075	Taurus	1061	Gemini	1047	Cancer
1033	Leo	1020	Virgo	1016	Libra	**992**	**Scorpio**
978	**Sagittarius**	**964**	**Capricorn**	**950**	**Aquarius**	**937**	**Pisces**
924	Aries	910	Taurus	897	Gemini	883	Cancer
869	Leo	855	Virgo	842	Libra	**828**	**Scorpio**
814	**Sagittarius**	**800**	**Capricorn**	**787**	**Aquarius**	**773**	**Pisces**
760	Aries	746	Taurus	733	Gemini	719	Cancer
706	Leo	692	Virgo	678	Libra	**664**	**Scorpio**
651	**Sagittarius**	**637**	**Capricorn**	**623**	**Aquarius**	**610**	**Pisces**
596	Aries	583	Taurus	569	Gemini	556	Cancer
542	Leo	528	Virgo	514	Libra	**501**	**Scorpio**
487	**Sagittarius**	**473**	**Capricorn**	**460**	**Aquarius**	**446**	**Pisces**
432	Aries	419	Taurus	405	Gemini	392	Cancer

Year	Sign	Year	Sign	Year	Sign	Year	Sign
B.C		B.C		B.C		B.C	
378	Leo	364	Virgo	351	Libra	**337**	**Scorpio**
323	**Sagittarius**	**309**	**Capricorn**	**296**	**Aquarius**	**282**	**Pisces**
269	Aries	255	Taurus	242	Gemini	228	Cancer
215	Leo	201	Virgo	187	Libra	**173**	**Scorpio**
159	**Sagittarius**	**146**	**Capricorn**	**132**	**Aquarius**	**118**	**Pisces**
105	Aries	92	Taurus	78	Gemini	65	Cancer
51	Leo	37	Virgo	24	Libra	**10**	**Scorpio**
A.D.		A.D.		A.D.		A.D.	
5	**Sagittarius**	**19**	**Capricorn**	**33**	**Aquarius**	**46**	**Pisces**
60	Aries	73	Taurus	87	Gemini	100	Cancer
113	Leo	127	Virgo	141	Libra	**155**	**Scorpio**
169	**Sagittarius**	**183**	**Capricorn**	**196**	**Aquarius**	**210**	**Pisces**
224	Aries	237	Taurus	250	Gemini	264	Cancer
277	Leo	291	Virgo	305	Libra	**319**	**Scorpio**
333	**Sagittarius**	**346**	**Capricorn**	**360**	**Aquarius**	**374**	**Pisces**
387	Aries	400	Taurus	414	Gemini	427	Cancer
441	Leo	455	Virgo	469	Libra	**483**	**Scorpio**
496	**Sagittarius**	**510**	**Capricorn**	**524**	**Aquarius**	**537**	**Pisces**
551	Aries	564	Taurus	578	Gemini	591	Cancer
605	Leo	619	Virgo	632	Libra	**646**	**Scorpio**
660	**Sagittarius**	**674**	**Capricorn**	**687**	**Aquarius**	**701**	**Pisces**
714	Aries	728	Taurus	741	Gemini	755	Cancer
769	Leo	783	Virgo	796	Libra	**810**	**Scorpio**
824	**Sagittarius**	**838**	**Capricorn**	**852**	**Aquarius**	**865**	**Pisces**
878	Aries	892	Taurus	906	Gemini	919	Cancer
933	Leo	946	Virgo	960	Libra	**974**	**Scorpio**
988	**Sagittarius**	**1001**	**Capricorn**	**1015**	**Aquarius**	**1029**	**Pisces**
1043	Aries	1056	Taurus	1070	Gemini	1083	Cancer
1096	Leo	1110	Virgo	1124	Libra	**1138**	**Scorpio**
1151	**Sagittarius**	**1165**	**Capricorn**	**1179**	**Aquarius**	**1193**	**Pisces**
1206	Aries	1220	Taurus	1233	Gemini	1247	Cancer
1260	Leo	1274	Virgo	1288	Libra	**1301**	**Scorpio**
1315	**Sagittarius**	**1329**	**Capricorn**	**1343**	**Aquarius**	**1356**	**Pisces**
1370	Aries	1384	Taurus	1397	Gemini	1410	Cancer
1424	Leo	1437	Virgo	1451	Libra	**1465**	**Scorpio**
1479	**Sagittarius**	**1493**	**Capricorn**	**1507**	**Aquarius**	**1520**	**Pisces**
1534	Aries	1547	Taurus	1561	Gemini	1574	Cancer
1587	Leo	1601	Virgo	1615	Libra	**1629**	**Scorpio**
1643	**Sagittarius**	**1657**	**Capricorn**	**1670**	**Aquarius**	**1684**	**Pisces**
1697	Aries	1711	Taurus	1725	Gemini	1738	Cancer
1752	Leo	1765	Virgo	1779	Libra	**1792**	**Scorpio**
1806	**Sagittarius**	**1820**	**Capricorn**	**1834**	**Aquarius**	**1848**	**Pisces**
1861	Aries	1875	Taurus	1888	Gemini	1901	Cancer
1915	Leo	1929	Virgo	1942	Libra	**1956**	**Scorpio**

Year A.D.	Sign	Year A.D.	Sign	Year A.D.	Sign	Year A.D.	Sign
1970	**Sagittarius**	**1984**	**Capricorn**	**1998**	**Aquarius**	**2011**	**Pisces**
2025	Aries	2038	Taurus	2052	Gemini	2065	Cancer
2079	Leo	2092	Virgo	2106	Libra	**2120**	**Scorpio**
2134	**Sagittarius**	**2148**	**Capricorn**	**2161**	**Aquarius**	**2175**	**Pisces**
2189	Aries	2202	Taurus	2215	Gemini	2229	Cancer
2242	Leo	2256	Virgo	2270	Libra	**2283**	**Scorpio**
2297	**Sagittarius**	**2311**	**Capricorn**	**2325**	**Aquarius**	**2339**	**Pisces**
2352	Aries	2366	Taurus	2379	Gemini	2392	Cancer
2406	Leo	2420	Virgo	2433	Libra	2447	Scorpio
2461	Sagittarius	2475	Capricorn	2488	Aquarius	2502	Pisces

PLUTO IN THE SIGNS (3000+ B.C.-A.D. 2500+)
(accurate to within +/- 1 year)

The periods of the "High Times" of Pluto are indicated in **bold** type.

Year B.C	Sign	Year B.C	Sign	Year B.C	Sign	Year B.C	Sign
3062	Aries	3034	Taurus	3010	Gemini	2993	Cancer
2980	Leo	2968	Virgo	2956	Libra	**2942**	**Scorpio**
2926	**Sagittarius**	**2904**	**Capricorn**	**2879**	**Aquarius**	**2849**	**Pisces**
2818	Aries	2789	Taurus	2765	Gemini	2746	Cancer
2733	Leo	2721	Virgo	2709	Libra	**2696**	**Scorpio**
2679	**Sagittarius**	**2659**	**Capricorn**	**2635**	**Aquarius**	**2605**	**Pisces**
2571	Aries	2544	Taurus	2519	Gemini	2501	Cancer
2487	Leo	2475	Virgo	2463	Libra	**2450**	**Scorpio**
2435	**Sagittarius**	**2414**	**Capricorn**	**2391**	**Aquarius**	**2360**	**Pisces**
2329	Aries	2299	Taurus	2274	Gemini	2256	Cancer
2241	Leo	2229	Virgo	2217	Libra	**2204**	**Scorpio**
2189	**Sagittarius**	**2169**	**Capricorn**	**2145**	**Aquarius**	**2116**	**Pisces**
2085	Aries	2055	Taurus	2029	Gemini	2010	Cancer
1995	Leo	1982	Virgo	1970	Libra	**1958**	**Scorpio**
1943	**Sagittarius**	**1924**	**Capricorn**	**1901**	**Aquarius**	**1872**	**Pisces**
1841	Aries	1811	Taurus	1784	Gemini	1765	Cancer
1749	Leo	1736	Virgo	1724	Libra	**1712**	**Scorpio**
1697	**Sagittarius**	**1678**	**Capricorn**	**1656**	**Aquarius**	**1628**	**Pisces**
1598	Aries	1566	Taurus	1540	Gemini	1519	Cancer
1502	Leo	1490	Virgo	1478	Libra	**1465**	**Scorpio**
1451	**Sagittarius**	**1433**	**Capricorn**	**1410**	**Aquarius**	**1384**	**Pisces**
1354	Aries	1322	Taurus	1294	Gemini	1272	Cancer
1256	Leo	1243	Virgo	1231	Libra	**1219**	**Scorpio**
1205	**Sagittarius**	**1187**	**Capricorn**	**1166**	**Aquarius**	**1139**	**Pisces**

Year	Sign	Year	Sign	Year	Sign	Year	Sign
B.C		B.C		B.C		B.C	
1109	Aries	1078	Taurus	1050	Gemini	1027	Cancer
1010	Leo	997	Virgo	985	Libra	973	**Scorpio**
960	**Sagittarius**	**942**	**Capricorn**	**921**	**Aquarius**	**896**	**Pisces**
865	Aries	834	Taurus	805	Gemini	781	Cancer
764	Leo	751	Virgo	739	Libra	**727**	**Scorpio**
714	**Sagittarius**	**696**	**Capricorn**	**676**	**Aquarius**	651	Pisces
621	Aries	590	Taurus	560	Gemini	537	Cancer
518	Leo	504	Virgo	493	Libra	**481**	**Scorpio**
468	**Sagittarius**	**451**	**Capricorn**	**431**	**Aquarius**	**407**	**Pisces**
376	Aries	345	Taurus	316	Gemini	291	Cancer
273	Leo	258	Virgo	246	Libra	**234**	**Scorpio**
222	**Sagittarius**	**206**	**Capricorn**	**186**	**Aquarius**	162	Pisces
132	Aries	101	Taurus	71	Gemini	46	Cancer
27	Leo	12	Virgo				
A.D.		A.D.		A.D.		A.D.	
				1	Libra	13	**Scorpio**
25	**Sagittarius**	**41**	**Capricorn**	**60**	**Aquarius**	84	Pisces
113	Aries	144	Taurus	174	Gemini	200	Cancer
219	Leo	235	Virgo	247	Libra	**259**	**Scorpio**
272	**Sagittarius**	**287**	**Capricorn**	**305**	**Aquarius**	329	Pisces
357	Aries	388	Taurus	418	Gemini	444	Cancer
465	Leo	481	Virgo	494	Libra	**505**	**Scorpio**
518	**Sagittarius**	**533**	**Capricorn**	**551**	**Aquarius**	573	Pisces
601	Aries	632	Taurus	662	Gemini	690	Cancer
711	Leo	727	Virgo	740	Libra	**752**	**Scorpio**
764	**Sagittarius**	**779**	**Capricorn**	**796**	**Aquarius**	818	Pisces
845	Aries	876	Taurus	907	Gemini	934	Cancer
957	Leo	973	Virgo	986	Libra	**998**	**Scorpio**
1010	**Sagittarius**	**1025**	**Capricorn**	**1042**	**Aquarius**	1064	Pisces
1089	Aries	1120	Taurus	1151	Gemini	1179	Cancer
1202	Leo	1219	Virgo	1233	Libra	**1244**	**Scorpio**
1257	**Sagittarius**	**1270**	**Capricorn**	**1287**	**Aquarius**	1308	Pisces
1333	Aries	1364	Taurus	1395	Gemini	1424	Cancer
1448	Leo	1465	Virgo	1479	Libra	**1491**	**Scorpio**
1503	**Sagittarius**	**1516**	**Capricorn**	**1531**	**Aquarius**	1553	Pisces
1577	Aries	1608	Taurus	1640	Gemini	1669	Cancer
1693	Leo	1712	Virgo	1725	Libra	**1737**	**Scorpio**
1749	**Sagittarius**	**1762**	**Capricorn**	**1778**	**Aquarius**	1798	Pisces
1822	Aries	1852	Taurus	1884	Gemini	1914	Cancer
1938	Leo	1957	Virgo	1971	Libra	**1984**	**Scorpio**
1995	**Sagittarius**	**2008**	**Capricorn**	**2024**	**Aquarius**	2043	Pisces
2067	Aries	2096	Taurus	2128	Gemini	2158	Cancer
2183	Leo	2202	Virgo	2217	Libra	**2230**	**Scorpio**
2241	**Sagittarius**	**2254**	**Capricorn**	**2270**	**Aquarius**	**2288**	**Pisces**

Year A.D.	Sign	Year A.D.	Sign	Year A.D.	Sign	Year A.D.	Sign
2312	Aries	2341	Taurus	2372	Gemini	2402	Cancer
2428	Leo	2450	Virgo	2463	Libra	2476	**Scorpio**
2488	**Sagittarius**	**2501**	**Capricorn**	**2516**	**Aquarius**	**2534**	**Pisces**

PLUTO AT PERIHELION (3000 B.C.–A.D. 2800)

Pluto's perihelion is the point in its orbit when it is closest to the Earth and Sun. It represents a moment of rebirth and transformation.

The occurrences in Column 1 are the most significant, since they follow the conjunction with Neptune about 100 years before.

Most degrees have been rounded up.

Column 1

Month	Year B.C.	Position
Jan.	2966	6° Virgo
May	2470	13° Virgo
Oct.	1975	20° Virgo
Feb.	1481	27° Virgo
June	984	4° Libra
Nov.	489	11° Libra
	A.D.	
Mar.	7	17° Libra
July	503	24° Libra
Dec.	998	1° Scorpio
Apr.	1494	8° Scorpio
Sept.	1989	15° Scorpio
Dec.	2484	22° Scorpio

Column 2

Month	Year B.C.	Position
Sept.	2718	9° Virgo
Feb.	2224	16° Virgo
June	1727	23° Virgo
Oct.	1232	0° Libra
Mar.	738	7° Libra
July	241	14° Libra
	A.D.	
Nov.	255	21° Libra
Mar.	751	28° Libra
Aug.	1246	5° Scorpio
Dec.	1741	12° Scorpio
May	2237	19° Scorpio
Aug.	2732	26° Scorpio

The above calculations were based on the following:

> Uranus orbit = 30,685.4 terrestrial days
> Neptune orbit = 60,189 days
> Pluto orbit = 90,465 days
> precession rate of 25,793.338374 terrestrial years
> Michelsen's *The American Ephemeris for the 20th Century*
> Michelsen's *The American Ephemeris for the 21st Century*
> *Rosicrucian Simplified Scientific Ephemeris* for 1890–1899

APPENDIX D

THE FORTUNES OF CIVILIZATION:
PHASES OF THE CYCLE

Neptune-Pluto conjunctions, discussed in Chapter 4 of this book, are only the most important milestones in the fortunes of civilization—the moments of endings and beginnings. Other aspects (also discussed in Chapter 4) mark the other important phases of rise and decay, and are accurately reflected in civilization by the arts. For example, the first sextile (sixty-degree aspect), when Neptune and Pluto are two signs apart, is a "crescent moon" phase, in which the creative energy of the new civilization is flowering and its first crises are overcome. In the arts this is called the "classical" phase, when original themes are stated in a confident but restrained and balanced style. The sextiles occurred in:

435 B.C. during the Age of Pericles in the Greek golden age.

20 B.C. (approximate aspect) and A.D. 60 during the golden age of Rome and the building of Teotihuacan. In 17 B.C. the "saeculum" was celebrated in the Augustan Age, as Virgil wrote his epic, the *Aeneid*.

A.D. 550 at the height of the Byzantine golden age under Justinian.

960–995 in the time of Otto the Great and the founding of the Sung Dynasty, and again in 1046 when the first great cathedrals were built.

1450–1500 during the creative flowering of the Renaissance and the voyages of Columbus, and again around 1537 at the time of Copernicus, Henry VIII, Suleiman the Magnificent.

1940–2040 during the crisis of our own emerging New Age

2430–2530 will be the time of the next "creative flowering" under the sextile.

The opening or waxing square (ninety-degree aspect, three signs apart) represents a serious early crisis in the new civilization. Its' foundations are tested and "ghosts from the past" are confronted. Such "first quarter" waxing squares occurred in:

405 B.C. at the end of the Peloponnesian War and the trial of Socrates.

A.D. 91 during the "reign of terror" under Roman Emperor Domitian.

583 as new barbarian invasions ended the Byzantine golden age.

1077 during the height of church-state rivalry when Holy Roman Emperor Henry IV capitulated to the Pope.

1570 during the height of the Wars of Religion and witch burnings.

2063 is the time of the next square and the next crisis.

The waxing trine or 120-degree aspect (four signs apart) is like a gibbous moon. It represents a period of confident expansion when the energies of civilization are moving toward their climax. In the arts it brings the "baroque" phase: an elaborate, lively, more rhythmic interpretation of the original classic themes. Trines occurred in:

380 B.C. in the time of Plato's dialogues, and conqueror Philip of Macedon. Greek art became less restrained and more dynamic in style.

A.D. 115 when Trajan and Hadrian expanded the Roman Empire in its "silver age," when the Pantheon was built.

607 in the time of Pope Gregory the Great, who brought Christianity to Britain. Khmer Empire was founded. Soon afterward, Mohammed founded Islam.

1100 during the First Crusade and the height of the Romanesque style. Kenneth Clark called this period "a similar outburst to the Baroque" You can see it in the lively, elaborate sculptures on southern French cathedrals.

1595 in the time of Shakespeare and the first Baroque artists and composers such as El Greco, Rubens, and Monteverdi.

2089 will bring the next lively "baroque expansion."

The opposition marks the half-way point and climax of the cycle. It is the "full moon" (or in this case a "full Neptune"), a time of expansion when the civilization is becoming fully and consciously developed. Schisms may occur, and as its ideas and formulas begin to rigidify, the civilization may begin to lose touch with its original sources of inspiration. Decline may set in afterwards. During the opposition, crucial events occur which affect the rest of the cycle. Oppositions occurred in:

330 B.C. in the time of Alexander the Great's conquests, which spread Greek culture all over Eastern Europe and Western Asia. World trade expanded in the first global economy. After Alexander died, his empire crumbled and the less secure Hellenistic Age began.

A.D. 166 in the time of Marcus Aurelius, the "philosopher-king" of Rome. After his reign, Rome began its decline and civil wars started.

660 during the conquests and expansion of Islam, when it divided into the Sunni and Shi'ite sects. The Synod of Whitby opened the way to the Northumbrian renaissance in England, climax of Dark Ages culture.

1153 during the Crusades and the first Gothic cathedrals.

1645 as imperial Europe expanded its colonies. Baroque art reached its summit in Rembrandt, Bernini and others, as well as in the reign of the "Sun King" Louis XIV. Our view of the physical cosmos was vastly expanded. The artist Jan Vermeer embodied this full moon phase as the "clear light of the fully conscious mind." The Manchu Dynasty was founded.

2140 is when the next climactic opposition is due.

The Neptune-Pluto opposition was also clearly significant in the archaic times before the Axis Age. The opposition of 823 B.C., for example, came at about the time of Homer and the start of early Greek culture. In China after 800 B.C., the strong Chou dynasty began its decline while the Upanishads (the final stage if the Vedas) were being written. Around the time of the opposition of 1320 B.C., the temple of Seti at Abados and other great temples were built during the height of New Kingdom civilization in Egypt in the reign of Ramses II. It was the last great period of ancient Egypt. The opposition of 1810 B.C. marked the fall of Egypt's Middle Kingdom to Hyksos invaders, and is close to the time of Hammurabi's law codes. At the opposition of 2305 B.C., the pharaohs' power started to decline, as authority was dispersed throughout the Old Kingdom. Civil wars began there around 2260 B.C. 2305 B.C. is also very close to the time of the first expansive Mesopotamian Empire of Sargon I (c.2325 B.C.)

The waning gibbous trine (which often lasts many years) establishes, distributes or disseminates ideas and benefits from the period of the opposition. It may mark a time of "frivolity and decadence," especially in its early years, but toward the end more decisive events and expressions occur, anticipating the square (see below). This aspect occurred in:

280-240 B.C. (approximate orb) and

190 B.C. when Rome was first inspired by Greek art and drama. Ashoka put Buddhist ideas into effect in his Mauryan Empire of India, and the Chin and Han emperors established Confucian morals in China.

A.D. 220–260 (approximate orb) and

306 in the "decadent" period of Rome and its final recovery under Constantine, when Rome converted to Christianity.

710–750 (approximate orb) when Europe repelled Moslem invaders.

796 when Charlemagne became emperor and restored European civilization.

1200–1305 (exact in 1230 and 1290) when Gothic architecture and philosophy were developed along the lines laid down during the opposition. The lighter "rayonnant" style also developed. The cults of the virgin and courtly love were popular.

1695–1795 (exact in 1712, 1730 and 1783) when the Enlightenment philosophers popularized the ideas of the new science, and applied them to help liberate society. The result was the American and French Revolutions. Art became delicate, light and decadent in the Rococo style, reflecting the frivolous attitudes in society.

2190–2280 will bring the next closing trine.

The closing, last quarter square generally follows quickly after the trine. It represents a final climax in the cycle, but also may mark the start of its final crisis or schism. Art is emotional and dramatic, as it nostalgically sums up the past, bemoans the present and/or anticipates the future. Waning squares occurred in:

155 B.C. as Rome struggled for dominance over other Mediterranean states. Rome conquered Greece in 146 B.C. Sculpture at this time consisted of dramatic, monumental, exaggerated depictions of tragic heroes.

A.D. 340 just after Constantine's reign, as schisms in the new Christian faith began to appear. The more emotional Christian art began to dominate.

830 as Charlemagne's empire declined after his death. It split up soon afterward in 843.

1325 just before the Hundred Years' War. Giotto's paintings reflected the dramatic, emotional style of this phase.

1815 during the Congress of Vienna and the defeat of Napoleon, events which resulted in nationalistic movements. Romantic artists became estranged from the new industrial society and depicted monumental disasters at sea.

2311 is the date of the next closing square.

The closing sextile or "balsamic" phase accelerates the process of dissolution and destruction, as the cycle crashes toward its close. Invasions and/or rebellions begin. It marks the period of realism, when the arts accurately depict the sufferings of the people. For example:

130 B.C. as peasant revolt in the Gracchian Revolution opened the final crisis in the Roman Republic. The troubles were reflected in the realistic sculpture of the time, like the works of the Laocoon Group.

A.D. 363 in the time of Julian the Apostate, when Christian schisms accelerated. Barbarians began their full-fledged invasions of Rome soon afterward. A.D. 857 as Viking and Saracen invasions began. Feudalism took root in Europe.

1350 as the Black Plague spread through Europe, destroying the old Medieval Christian society. Medieval art also reflected the realist trends.

1844 just before the Irish Potato Famine and the resulting revolutions, causing massive migrations from Europe. Industry expanded explosively. Realist artists and writers included Courbet, Daumier, Dickens, Marx, and others.

2338. This is the date for the closing sextile.

APPENDIX E

THE PRECESSED AND PROGRESSED CHARTS:
A FULL LISTING OF HISTORICAL MILESTONES

These major historical events are based on the Horoscope for Modern Humanity (see Chapter 12). The most important positions are noted in bold type, and corresponding transits are noted in italics. Notice that transiting positions of the outer planets are often similar or related to the progressed positions of the inner planets.

PRECESSED CHART

1760: Mars conjunct Uranus (beginning of industrial revolution/steam engine; Seven Years' War).

1784: Mercury stationary-direct at 28° Sagittarius.

1785: Saturn stationary-retrograde at 0° Libra (U.S. Constitution embodied ideals of justice).

1788: Mercury square Saturn.

1789: Sun sextile Mars; Sun in 24° Capricorn (French Revolution).

1789: Full Moon in Cancer (active awareness of common people is at its height during the Full Moon).

1791: Venus in Aquarius square Mars in Scorpio (emotions ran wild in reign of terror) *Similar to transit of Neptune entering Scorpio, 1792*

1795: Sun entered Aquarius; Venus entered Pisces (sign changes indicate shifts of energy. In this case, the reign of terror ended). *Corresponds to transit of Pluto in Pisces from 1799*

1798: Saturn re-entered Virgo (Napoleon betrayed the revolution; work began to make ideals of justice a reality).

1800: Mars entered Sagittarius (romantic age expanded) *Neptune entered Sagittarius in 1806.*

180l: Sun square Uranus (revolutionary aspect which was in orb ten years before and after 1801; it dominated the age of revolution).

1804: New Moon in Aquarius (Napoleon crowned emperor; common people in retreat at New Moon).

1810: Mars opposite Neptune-Pluto (quest of the sublime in the climax of the Napoleonic wars) *Pluto in Pisces, square Neptune.*

1811: Venus conjunct Jupiter in Pisces (another symbol of romanticism).

1813: Mercury entered Aquarius (students and soldiers [Mercury] were inspired by the "war of liberation" against Napoleon in 1813 to expand their activism.).

1815: Uranus stationary retrograde at 6° Scorpio (revolution ended with defeat of Napoleon and restoration by Vienna Concert).

1817: Mercury square Uranus (peak of student activism at Wartburg Festival, etc.). *Jupiter conjunct Uranus; Uranus square Pluto.*

1819: Full Moon in Leo (common people active, especially youth).

1819: Venus entered Aries (age of pioneers opened) *Pluto entered Aries 1822–23.*

1824: Sun entered Pisces; Neptune and Pluto stationary-direct (romantic age climaxed; dissolving industrial forces started moving us toward the modern age).

1830: Sun trine Uranus (revolutionary year) *Uranus in Aquarius opposite Saturn.*

1831: Sun square Neptune-Pluto.

1832: Mercury entered Pisces (worker unrest increased) *Uranus entered Pisces 1834.*

1834: New Moon in Pisces (post-1830 activism crushed; people retreated into disillusionment).

1844: Jupiter opposite Saturn (ongoing economic crisis in this era).

1844: Venus entered Taurus; Mars square Saturn; Sun sesqui-square Uranus

1846: Mars square Jupiter (westward ho/manifest destiny/roaring '40s enthusiasms). *Jupiter-Uranus in Aries, 1844.*

1847: Mercury entered Aries, conjunct Jupiter, square Mars (the many aspects in mid-late '40s stand for industrial expansion and crisis).

1848: Mars entered Capricorn at exact time of the beginning of the 1848 revolutions. (Revolutions' failure opened the age of realism).

1848: Full Moon in Virgo, conjunct Saturn (common people, especially workers, rose again, but had to confront reality).

1849: Venus opposite Uranus (Eureka! the gold rush, in many ways). *Uranus conj. Pluto entering Taurus, 1850.*

1851: Sun opposite Saturn (heavy hand of repression crushed the revolutions; realpolitik; industrialism) *Saturn conj. Uranus-Pluto in Taurus.*

1854: Sun entered Aries, conjunct Jupiter (Crimean War ended international cooperation; prosperity exploded as industrial revolution expanded in the 1850s) *Neptune in Pisces; Jupiter singleton.*

1863: New Moon in Aries (new beginning, as governments moved toward individualism).

1864: Sun in Aries square Mars (age of aggression; U.S. Civil War and Indian wars; Wars of German Unification; Darwinism popularized) *Neptune in Aries in 1860s.*

1865: Mercury entered Taurus (civil war ended; gilded age began) *Pluto in Taurus inaugurates age of materialism.*

1871: Venus entered Gemini (new diplomatic era [Venus] opened in the wake of the Franco-Prussian war).

1876: Mercury stationary retrograde, opposing Uranus (telephone invented, international crises were early signs of the Great War, which came when Mercury opposed Uranus again later on) *Uranus square Pluto/Saturn*

1877: Venus conjunct Neptune-Pluto (impressionism; first economic combinations and dissolutions during '70s depression). *Neptune in Taurus.*

1877: Full Moon in Libra (common people active in Granger movements, etc.; diplomatic moves by Bismarck followed).

1885: Sun entered Taurus (age of materialism continues).

1885: Sun conjunct Mercury; Mercury re-entered Aries (inventions at a peak; international crises). *Pluto entered Gemini, mercurial sign, 1884.*

1890: Sun opposite Uranus (labor unrest dominated this period).

1890: Mars trine Saturn *Mars-Saturn-Pluto T-square*

1892: Mercury square Mars (Schlieffen plan for the Great War; Populist activism). *Year of the Neptune-Pluto conjunction.*

PROGRESSED CHART:

1892: The solar eclipse in Taurus.

1893: Venus square Saturn; Sun sesqui-square Saturn (panic and depression of 1893).

1900: Mercury stationary direct at 24° Aries (Marconi invented radio; Muckrakers attacked corporations). *Uranus opposite Pluto in Gemini.*

1900: Venus entered Cancer (Freud opened subconscious; conservation movement began; nationalism heated up). *Neptune entered Cancer 1901.*

1902: Mars entered Aquarius (active progress and progressivism) *Uranus opposite Pluto, 1901*

1907: Lunar eclipse in Scorpio (increasing upheaval and activism in this era; financial panic; this eclipse was a sign of impending doom).

1909: Mars square Uranus (series of pre-war crises began in 1908) *Saturn in Aries square Uranus*

1909: Sun trine Saturn.

1911: Mercury re-entered Taurus (Balkan Wars).

1914: Mercury opposite Uranus (World War I began.) *Jupiter conjunct Uranus in Aquarius.*

1916: Sun entered Gemini.

1918: Mercury square Mars, completing T-square in fixed signs (final battles of World War I).

1918: Mars sesqui-square Saturn (final battles of World War I).

1922: New Moon in Gemini (common people in retreat during reactionary '20s; new beginning after war).

1922: Mars trine Neptune (roaring '20s enthusiasm, powered by alcohol prohibition, disillusionment). *Uranus in Pisces trine Pluto.*

1923: Saturn stationary-direct at 23° Virgo (Fascist takeovers and conservative trends world-wide). *Jupiter-Saturn conjunction at 21° Virgo in 1921.*

1925: Sun conjunct Neptune-Pluto (peak of disillusionment, gangsterism, moral decay, surrealism in arts, self-expression, and deceptive prosperity). *Neptune in Sun's sign Leo.*

1927: Sun trine Mars (energy of roaring '20s peaks; sports heroes) *Jupiter & Uranus enter Aries.*

1929: Mercury trine Saturn (depression sign).

1932: Mercury entered Gemini (materialism ends in depression).

1932: Venus sextile Saturn (depression).

1934: Sun sesqui-square Uranus (Nazism and New Deal). *Uranus square Pluto.*

1935: Sun sextile Jupiter ("happy days are here again"?).

1937: Full Moon in Sagittarius (common people active).

1937: Mercury conjunct Neptune-Pluto (worker unrest) *Saturn in Pisces opposite Neptune*

1940: Sun square Saturn (dominated entire depression/war period; peak of Nazi repression) [FDR's aspect]. *Jupiter-Saturn square Pluto.*

1940: Mercury trine Mars (World War II, a swifter moving war than World War I under Mercury-Mars square; led to aviation advances). *Uranus entered Gemini, 1941, trine Neptune.*

1945: Venus stationary retrograde at 26° Cancer (World Wars ended; U.N. and Cold War began). *Jupiter-Neptune in Libra.*

1945: Mercury square Saturn (The UN charter.)

1947: Sun conjunct Mercury (age of anxiety; first computer 1946.)

1947: Sun and Mercury entered Cancer (Cold War; Defense Dept., baby boom). *Uranus entered Cancer, 1948.*

1949: Sun trine Uranus; Sun sesqui-square Mars (Red revolution in China; atomic arms race opened). *Uranus-Pluto parallel and semi-square.*

195l: New Moon in Cancer (common people retreat into domestic concerns in conservative '50s; new beginning as post-war austerity ended).

1954: Venus sextile Saturn.

1958: Mercury square Jupiter (space race opened) *Saturn in Sagittarius.*

1958: Mercury conjunct Venus.

1959: Venus square Jupiter (this ongoing aspect of the post-war era represented exaggerated materialism and wasteful prosperity).

1962: Mercury entered Leo (youth became prominent in Kennedy years).

1963: Mercury square Uranus (youth and civil rights activism) (Kennedy's aspect).

1962-63: Mars stationary-retrograde at 17° Aquarius (Missile crisis; Kennedy assassinated; progress arrested). *Great 1962 eclipse-conjunction, 15–17° Aquarius; Saturn at 17° Aquarius Nov. 22, 1963; Neptune in Scorpio, Mars' ruling sign.*

1966: Uranus stationary-direct at 2° Scorpio (liberation movements of the '60s exploded; transcendental awakening of new consciousness, non-conformist counterculture). *Uranus conjunct Pluto.*

1966: Sun conjunct Venus (Cold War/defense establishment went haywire in Vietnam; flower children appeared; women's movement began).

1966: Full Moon in Capricorn (Activism of the people in the '60s against the all-powerful Capricornian "system" is largely defeated).

1972: Mercury opposite Mars (Nixon's aspect) (Watergate dirty tricks; currency crisis, war in Vietnam continued).

1972: Sun square Jupiter (inflation; diplomatic breakthroughs). *Jupiter conjunct Neptune in Sagittarius, 1971.*

1973: Sun semi-square Neptune (Watergate scandal; oil embargo).

1974: Sun sextile Saturn (depression brought on by events mentioned in the above two aspects).

1979: Sun entered Leo.

1980: New Moon in Leo (common people in retreat in the reactionary '80s).

1981: Sun square Uranus (revolutions in Iran and Nicaragua; Reagan counter-revolution in U.S.).

1982: Mercury entered Virgo (high-tech yuppies; computer mania; AIDS emerges).

1989: Venus stationary-direct at 10° Cancer (Cold War ended; nationalism revived; earth activism resumed). *Jupiter singleton stationary at 10° Cancer, Gorbachev's position, in fall, 1989.*

1990: Sun sextile Neptune (idealism re-awakened worldwide).

1991: Sun opposite Mars (resurgent activism; Persian Gulf War; ethnic wars in 1992–93). *Saturn square Pluto in Scorpio.*

1992: Mars sesqui-square Saturn (see above).

1992: Sun semi-square Saturn (economic panic in early '90s).

1994: Mercury sextile Venus (liberalized trade and peace breakthroughs).

1996: Full Moon in Aquarius, conjunct Mars (peak of the 1990s' resurgent activism) *Uranus enters Aquarius.*

1996: Mars trine Neptune (the creative energy of the 1990s).

1997: Mercury square Neptune (deceptive utopian ideals; occult awakenings; worker unrest; disinformation, scandal).

1999: Mercury stationary retrograde at 11° Virgo (literary, health and scientific break-throughs, religious holy war, computer age crisis).

1999: (Sun in same degree as prophetic Leo eclipse, August 11, 1999).

2001: Mercury square Neptune again.

2001-02: Jupiter stationary-retrograde in 25° Aries, conjunct Moon (Possible "holy war" cli-maxes; travel breakthroughs or ET.visits; optimism at dawn of a new millennium of peace) *Pluto in Sagittarius opposite Saturn in Gemini.*

2005: Sun trine Jupiter (prosperous period during renaissance and reform era; perhaps fi-nal end of holy war, or even of all war).

2010: Sun enters Virgo; New Moon in Virgo (people retreat again in period of disillusion-ment and economic breakdown, as medical and ecological disasters loom). *Neptune enters Pisces, Saturn in Virgo.*

2013: Sun sextile Uranus (year of revolutions). *Uranus square Pluto, 2013–14.*

2014: Sun conjunct Mercury retrograde (anxiety, inventions meet the world crisis).

2017: Saturn re-enters Libra (Dreams of justice realized).

2017: Mercury re-enters Leo (re-discovery of youthful creativity, perhaps led by elderly "baby-boomers").

2020: Venus square Jupiter (prosperity may return; diplomatic tensions).

2022-23: Mars stationary-direct at 7° Aquarius (progress resumes at full speed in its re-newed form; possible U.S. Civil War). *Pluto enters Aquarius, Neptune enters Aries).*

2022: Sun square Neptune (idealist activism*).*

2024: Mercury direct at 28° Leo (outspoken journalism, entertainment inventions) *Uranus enters Mercurial Gemini*

2025: Full Moon at 15° Pisces (people awake with compassion and a new spiritual impulse)

2026: Venus enters Leo (a new romantic expressiveness)

2028: Mercury re-enters Virgo (deeper concern with health, technology) (powerful Jupiter singleton in Virgo that year).

2028: Venus sextile Saturn (economic tensions). *Saturn enters Taurus.*

2029: Sun semi-square Uranus.

2030: Venus square Uranus.

2032: Mercury sextile Uranus (a period of reform and social adjustment). *Saturn-Uranus conjunction in Gemini/Cancer.*

2033: Neptune and Pluto turn retrograde.

2034: Sun sesqui-square Mars (more activist upheavals). *Uranus sesqui-square Pluto; Neptune in Aries.*

2035: Venus opposite Mars (pioneering and extremism; passions hot). *Jupiter-Neptune in Aries.*

2037: Mercury square Neptune *Uranus square Neptune.*

2038: Venus sextile Neptune (quieter period begins; dissolving of economic structures). *Neptune enters Taurus.*

2040: New Moon in 29° Virgo (common people in retreat).

2042: Sun enters Libra.

2044: Sun conjunct Saturn (conservatism or repression; depression; constitutional reform) *Saturn square Pluto.*

2047: Mars trine Neptune (active idealism surges). *Uranus opposite Pluto in Pisces.*

2048: Venus trine Jupiter (prosperity, diplomacy, or expansion in the arts). *Jupiter conjunct Neptune in Taurus.*

2050: Mercury conjunct Saturn (more constitutional reforms). *Saturn in Aquarius, trine Uranus and Neptune.*

2053: Sun trine Neptune (idealism). *Saturn conjunct Pluto in Pisces.*

2054: Mercury trine Neptune. *Neptune enters Gemini, 2053.*

2055: Full Moon in 14° Aries; Sun trine Mars (energetic, progressive).

2056: Mercury trine Mars; Venus enters Virgo.

2057: Sun conjunct Mercury (inventive, inquisitive).

2059: Mercury opposite Jupiter (travel, communication advances).

2061: Sun opposite Jupiter (over-optimism).

2065: Mercury enters Scorpio.

2066: Venus square Neptune (basic conflict of values, apathy and malaise). *Neptune square Pluto.*

2068: Mars sextile Jupiter.

2069: Partial eclipse at 28° Libra; Mercury conjunct Uranus.

2071: Sun enters Scorpio (Pluto enters Aries, 2067).

2073: Mars sesqui-square Saturn.

2078: Sun conjunct Uranus (revolutionary year). *Uranus opposite Neptune.*

2082: Venus enters Libra.

2084: Lunar eclipse at 13° Taurus (possible economic or ecological catastrophe). *Uranus in Aquarius.*

2084: Mercury square Mars (controversy, unrest).

2085: Mercury enters Sagittarius.

2089: Mars enters Pisces (end of "progress"; new religious enthusiasm). *Uranus enters Pisces, 2087–88.*

2090: Venus conjunct Saturn (depression threatens).

2091: Mercury sextile Saturn.

2092: Venus trine Neptune.

2096: Mercury trine Jupiter.

2097: Venus opposite Jupiter (more optimistic mood returning?).

2099: New Moon in Scorpio *Uranus in Aries, 2095–2102.*

2101: Sun enters Sagittarius (a new Baroque period).

2103: Mars trine Uranus *Uranus conjunct Pluto.*

2105: Saturn trine Neptune *Uranus trine Neptune.*

2106: Mars square Neptune.

2108: Venus enters Scorpio.

2111: Sun opposite Neptune-Pluto.

2113: Mercury retrograde at 29° Sagittarius.

2114: Full Moon In Gemini *Uranus in Gemini.*

2116: Sun trine Jupiter.

2120: Jupiter turns direct at 15° Aries (a period of crusades and expansion).

2121: Sun square Mars at 20° Pisces (religious conflicts). *Neptune enters Scorpio.*

APPENDIX F

MARS STATIONARY IN MODERN TIMES

Following is a listing of the "stations" of Mars from 1775–2050, along with its position, important aspects, and significant events. Afflictions to Saturn are shown in bold type in the "Aspects" column.

MARS STATIONARY IN THE EIGHTEENTH & NINETEENTH CENTURIES

Approximate Dates	Position	Aspects	Violent, aggressive, or crucial events
April 1–15, 1775	25 Leo		Battles of Lexington and Concord
Feb. 1777	19 Libra	Square Jupiter	Jan., Washington crossed Delaware
May 1777	1 Libra	Trine Pluto	
April 1779	29 Scorpio	**Conj. Saturn**	
June 10–July 10, 1779	13 Scorpio	**Conj. Saturn**	
June 1781	27 Capricorn		
August 1781	15 Capricorn		Oct., British surrender at Yorktown
Aug. 20–Sept. 10, 1783	16 Aries	Square Jupiter, Opp. Neptune	
Nov. 1783	2 Aries	**Square Saturn**	
Oct. 1785	16 Gemini		
Jan. 1786	27 Taurus		
Nov. 20–Dec. 10, 1787	28 Cancer	Conj. Uranus	French parliament blocks govt. loan, King arrests Orleans and others
Feb. 1788	7 Cancer		
Dec.15,1789–Jan.10,1790	2 Virgo	Conj. Jupiter	
Mar. 15–April 5, 1790	12 Leo	Conj. Jupiter	
Jan. 20–Feb. 15, 1792	6 Libra	**Opp. Saturn**	Sansculotte riots
April 1792	16 Virgo		French declare war on Austria
March 1794	13 Scorpio	**Opp. Saturn,** Conj. Neptune	Reign of Terror: execution of Hebert, Danton
June 1794	25 Libra	**Opp. Saturn,.** Conj. Nept	July, Fall of Robespierre; decisive victories for France; Whiskey Rebellion.
May 1796	2 Capricorn	Trine Uranus	Napoleon invaded Italy; battle of Lodi; Babeuf's communists arrested
July 1796	18 Sagittarius	**Opp. Saturn**	Napoleon conquered Italy
Aug. 1798	15 Pisces	Opp. Uranus, Trine Saturn	U.S. undeclared war with France; navy created; Battle of the Pyramids, battle of Aboukir
Sept. 20–Oct. 15, 1798	4 Pisces	Conj. Pluto	Tsar and Sultan declares war on France

Approximate Dates	Position	Aspects	Violent, Aggressive, or Crucial Events
Sept. 20–Oct. 10, 1800	25 Taurus	**Square Saturn**	
Dec. 1800	9 Taurus	Square Jupiter	Dec. 3, Moreau defeats Austrians; Dec. 24, bomb misses Napoleon's carriage
Nov. 1802	13 Cancer	Square Uranus	Swiss nobles revolt against Napoleon
Feb. 1803	23 Gemini	**Square Saturn**	Napoleon defeats Swiss nobles; results in war with Britain by May
Dec. 1804	20 Leo		Napoleon crowned; Russia declares war on France
March 1805	29 Cancer		
Jan. 1807	23 Virgo		Feb. 8, battle of Eylau. British close French ports
April 1807	2 Virgo	Square Neptune	Russia, Prussia declare war on France again; June, U.S.S. Chesapeake captured; June 14, Battle of Friedland
March 1809	28 Libra		Apr. 9, Austrians invade Bavaria
May 10–June 5, 1809	9 Libra	Opp. Jupiter	May 17, Napoleon captures Papal States; May 20, U.S. embargoes against Britain & France; July 5, Battle of Wagram
April 1811	11 Sagittarius	Conj. Neptune	
July 1811	25 Scorpio	Opp. Jupiter	
June 20–July 15, 1813	14 Aquarius	Opp. Jupiter	
Aug. 15–Sept. 12, 1813	3 Aquarius		Oct. 16, Battle of Leipzig
Sept. 1815	2 Taurus		Aug., political murders in France; Sept. 26, Holy Alliance
Nov. 1815	17 Aries	Opp. Venus	Quadruple Alliance
Oct. 20–Nov. 10, 1817	27 Gemini	Opp. Neptune	Oct. 18, Wartburg Festival
Jan. 1818	7 Gemini	**Square Saturn,** Opp. Uranus	Jackson invades Florida
Dec. 1819	6 Leo	Opp. Jupiter	Cato conspiracy; Jan., Spanish revolution
Feb. 15–Mar. 10, 1820	15 Cancer		Feb. 13, murder of Duke of Berry turns France to the right
Jan. 1822	10 Virgo		
April 1822	20 Leo		Massacre at Chios
Feb. 1824	14 Libra	Square Uranus	
May 1824	24 Virgo		Byron dies at Missolonghi, April 19
April 1826	23 Scorpio		Siege of Missolonghi
June 1826	5 Scorpio		
June 1828	16 Capricorn	**Opp. Saturn,** Conj. Neptune	Russia invades Turkey; tariff of abominations
August 1828	3 Capricorn		
August 1830	3 Aries	Conj. Pluto	July Revolution, Belgian revolt
Oct. 1830	20 Pisces		Polish and German revolts
Oct. 1832	8 Gemini		

Approximate Dates	Position	Aspects	Violent, Aggressive, or Crucial Events
Dec.15, 1832–Jan.5, 1833	20 Taurus	Square Uranus	Dec. 21, Egypt attacked Turks; Feb. 20, Russia defended Turks; South Carolina "nullification episode"
Nov. 1834	22 Cancer	**Square Saturn**	
Feb. 1835	1 Cancer		
Dec. 1836	27 Leo		
March 1837	7 Leo	Conj. Jupiter, Opp. Nept.	
Jan. 20–Feb. 10, 1839	1 Libra		
April 1839	10 Virgo	**Square Saturn**	Apr. 25: Chartist convention urges violence. May: Turkey attacks Mehemet Ali; Charter presented to Parliament: rejection causes violence in July
March 1841	7 Scorpio		
May 18–June 10, 1841	18 Libra		July 13, Russia agreed to Straights Convention
Apr. 20–May 10, 1843	22 Sagittarius		
July 1843	8 Sagittarius		
July 1845	2 Pisces	Conj. Neptune	Texas joins U.S.; Mexico breaks relations
Sept. 1845	21 Aquarius	Conj. Neptune	Polk sends troops to Texas
Sept. 10–Oct. 5, 1847	16 Taurus		
Nov. 24–Dec. 14, 1847	1 Taurus	Conj. Pluto	Revolutionary "banquets"; Jan., Palermo rising
Early Nov. 1849	7 Cancer	**Square Saturn**	
Jan. 15–Feb. 5, 1850	17 Gemini	Square Jupiter	Slavery debates; civil war threat
Dec. 1851	15 Leo	Square Jupiter	Napoleon III's coup d'état resisted
Feb. 20–March 15, 1852	24 Cancer	**Square Saturn**	
Jan. 1854	17 Virgo	Opp. Neptune	
April 1854	27 Leo	**Square Saturn**	Mar. 28, Britain declares war on Russia; May, Kansas-Nebraska Act
Feb. 10–March 5, 1856	22 Libra	Trine Saturn	Crimean War ends
May 1856	3 Libra	**Square Saturn,** Opp. Jupiter	Bleeding Kansas; Sumner–Brooks
April 1858	3 Sagittarius	Opp. Uranus	British seize U.S. ships
June 15–July 10, 1858	16 Scorpio		Plombieres agreement by France and Italy to attack Austria
June 1860	2 Aquarius	Opp. Jupiter	Garibaldi conquers Sicily
August 1860	20 Capricorn		Garibaldi conquers Naples; Cavour defeats Pope
Aug. 25–Sept. 20, 1862	20 Aries	Opp. Mercury, Opp. Jupiter	Aug. 26, 2nd battle of Bull Run; Sept. 17, battle of Antietam; Sept. 22, Emancipation Proclamation; Bismarck becomes Prussian president

Approximate Dates	Position	Aspects	Violent, Aggressive, or Crucial Events
Oct. 25–Nov. 15, 1862	6 Aries	**Opp. Saturn,** Conj. Neptune	Bismarck defeats liberals, militarizes
Oct. 1864	20 Gemini	Conj. Uranus, Conj. U.S.Mars	Sherman's march to the sea; Sand Creek massacre
Jan. 1865	1 Gemini		
Nov. 20–Dec. 10, 1866	1 Leo	Opp. Jupiter	U.S. confronts Napoleon III over Mexico
Feb. 1867	10 Cancer	**Sesq-Sq. Saturn,** Conj. Uranus	Mar. 2, Military Reconstruction Act
Dec. 20, 1868–Jan. 15, 1869	5 Virgo	**Square Saturn**	
Feb. 1871	8 Libra	**Square Saturn**	Prussia defeats France
April 25–May 10, 1871	18 Virgo	Square Jupiter	Mar.18–May 28, Paris Commune and fires
March 1873	16 Scorpio	Square Pluto	
May 25–June 20, 1873	28 Libra	**Square Saturn**	Spanish capture U.S.S. Virginius, murder crew
May 1875	6 Capricorn		
July 20–Aug. 10, 1875	22 Sagittarius		South Slavic revolt against Turkey
August 1877	20 Pisces	**Conj. Saturn**	Summer, violent railroad strikes in U.S.; July–Dec., battle of Plevna
Oct. 1877	8 Pisces	**Conj. Saturn**	
Sept. 20–Oct. 15, 1879	29 Taurus	Conj. Pluto	Bismarck secret alliance with Austria
Dec. 1879	12 Taurus	Conj. Neptune	
Nov. 1881	16 Cancer		
Feb. 1882	26 Gemini		
Dec. 1883	22 Leo	Square Neptune	
March 1884	2 Leo		
Jan. 15–Feb. 5, 1886	26 Virgo		
April 1886	5 Virgo	Square Neptune, Square Pluto	May 4, Haymarket square riot and bombing
Feb. 20–Mar. 15, 1888	1 Scorpio	**Square Saturn**	
May 15–June 5, 1888	12 Libra	Conj. Uranus	
April 24, 1890	14 Sagittarius	Opp. Neptune, Opp. Pluto	Mar. 15, Bismarck fired
July 5, 1890	28 Scorpio	**Square Saturn,** Opp. Neptune, Opp. Pluto	June 18: William II breaks off reinsurance treaty with Russia
July 6, 1892	18 Aquarius		Homestead Steel riots; Populist Convention
Sept. 3, 1892	8 Aquarius	Square Uranus	
Sept. 16, 1894	6 Taurus	Opp. Uranus	July 25, Sino-Japanese war; Sept. 17, battle of Yalu
Nov. 22, 1894	22 Aries		
Nov. 1, 1896	30 Gemini/0 Cancer		Greeks on Crete rebel; Greeks invade Thessaly

Approximate Dates	Position	Aspects	Violent, Aggressive, or Crucial Events
Jan. 17, 1897	12 Gemini	Square Jupiter, Conj. Neptune, Conj. Pluto	
Dec. 11, 1898	9 Leo	Square Jupiter	Strikes and riots sweep Russia
Feb. 28, 1899	20 Cancer		Feb. 4, Philippine revolt against U.S.

MARS STATIONARY IN THE TWENTIETH CENTURY

Exact Dates	Position	Aspects	Violent, Aggressive, or Crucial Events
Jan. 13, 1901	13 Virgo	Square Uranus, SquarePluto	
April 4, 1901	24 Leo		March, Platt Amendment; U.S. occupies Cuba
Feb. 18, 1903	17 Libra	Trine Pluto	Germany bombs Venezuela
May 9, 1903	28 Virgo	Square Uranus	June, Serbs revolt and execute royal family
April 2, 1905	26 Scorpio	**Square Saturn**	Mar. 31, Moroccan crisis starts
June 17, 1905	9 Scorpio		Revolution in Russia, riots in Poland
June 5, 1907	19 Capricorn	Opp. Jupiter	
Aug. 9, 1907	7 Capricorn	Conj. Uranus, Opp. Neptune	Triple Entente formed
Aug. 23, 1909	7 Aries		
Oct. 24, 1909	26 Pisces	Square Pluto	Secret Russian-Italian alliance
Oct. 18, 1911	11 Gemini	Square Mercury	Sept. 28, Italy invades Tripoli; Chinese Revolt
Dec. 29, 1911	25 Taurus	Trine Uranus	Chinese revolution; Nicaraguan disorders
Nov. 26, 1913	25 Cancer	Conj. Neptune, Opp.Jup.	Riots in Alsace-Lorraine
Feb. 12, 1914	6 Cancer	Conj. Pluto	April, U.S.-Mexican dispute
Dec. 31, 1915	30 Leo/0Virgo		Pancho Villa's raid
March 21, 1916	11 Leo	Opp. Uranus	Feb-June, battle of Verdun; Apr. 24, Easter Rebellion in Ireland; New Mexico raided by Pancho Villa; Pershing attacks Mexico
Feb. 3, 1918	4 Libra	Trine Jup., Square Pluto	Treaty of Brest-Litovsk
Apr. 25, 1918	14 Virgo	Square Jupiter	Mar., final WWI German offensive; U.S. forces arrive in Europe in May
March 15, 1920	10 Scorpio	Square Jupiter, SquareNeptune	Bavarian coup; Mar. 19, U.S. Senate rejects Versailles Treaty; Apr., war between Poland & Russia; March, Allies occupy Constantinople
May 31, 1920	22 Libra		
May 8, 1922	26 Sagittarius	**Square Saturn**	Russia's refusal to demand reparations ends Genoa conference

Exact Dates	Position	Aspects	Violent, Aggressive, or Crucial Events
July 17, 1922	12 Sagittarius	Square Uranus	Aug., Turks drove Greeks out of Turkey
July 24, 1924	6 Pisces	Square Jupiter	
Sept. 22, 1924	26 Aquarius	Opp. Neptune	
Sept. 29, 1926	20 Taurus	**Opp. Saturn,** Square Jupiter, Square Neptune	British general strike
Dec. 7, 1926	5 Taurus		
Nov. 12, 1928	10 Cancer		
Jan. 27, 1929	21 Gemini	**Opp. Saturn**	Feb. 14, St. Valentine's Day massacre
Dec. 18, 1930	17 Leo	Square Venus	
March 8, 1931	28 Cancer	**Opp. Saturn,** Conj. Pluto	April 14, Spanish revolt overthrows monarchy
Jan. 21, 1933	21 Virgo	Conj. Jupiter	Jan. 30, Hitler becomes chancellor
Apr. 12, 1933	1 Virgo	Conj. Neptune	Feb. 27, Reichstag fire
Feb. 27, 1935	25 Libra	SquarePluto, Opp.Uranus	March, Hitler resumes draft and naval buildup
May 17, 1935	7 Libra		
April 14, 1937	6 Sagittarius		Guernica bombing; Memorial Day massacre
June 27, 1937	20 Scorpio	Opp. Uranus	Japan invades China
June 22, 1939	5 Aquarius	**Square Saturn,** Opp. Pluto	
Aug. 23, 1939	24 Capricorn	**Square Saturn,** Opp. Pluto	Hitler invades Poland, World War II.
Sept. 6, 1941	24 Aries		U.S.S. Kearney hit by Germans
Nov. 10, 1941	12 Aries	**Semi-Sq. Saturn**	Dec. 7, Japan bombs Pearl Harbor
Oct. 28, 1943	23 Gemini	**Conj. Saturn,** Conj. U.S.Mars	Gilbert Islands offensive, battle of Tarawa
Jan. 10, 1944	5 Gemini	Conj. Uranus	Anzio landing; battle of Guadalcanal
Dec. 4, 1945	4 Leo	Conj. Pluto	
Feb. 21, 1946	15 Cancer	**Conj. Saturn,** Square Neptune	Churchill proclaims Cold War
Jan. 8, 1948	8 Virgo		Feb., Communists in Czechoslovakia; Gandhi assassinated
March 29, 1948	19 Leo	**Conj. Saturn,** Conj. Pluto	Berlin and Yugoslavia blockades; Marshall Plan; May, Israeli war
Feb. 12, 1950	12 Libra	Conj. Neptune	Truman orders H-bomb; McCarthy begins "Witch Hunt"
May 3, 1950	22 Virgo	**Conj. Saturn**	June 25, Korean War begins
March 25, 1952	19 Scorpio	Square Pluto	Truman seizes steel mills; Batista coup in Cuba
June 10, 1952	2 Scorpio		July 23, Nasser's revolution in Egypt
May 23, 1954	9 Capricorn		May 17, school desegregation ruling
July 29, 1954	26 Sagittarius	Trine Pluto,	Partition of Vietnam
Aug. 10, 1956	24 Pisces	Trine Saturn	Sept. 8: SEATO alliance created.

Exact Dates	Position	Aspects	Violent, Aggressive, or Crucial Events
Oct. 10, 1956	14 Pisces	Opp. Jupiter	Polish riots; Hungarian revolts; Suez Crisis
Oct. 10, 1958	3 Gemini	Square Pluto	
Dec. 20, 1958	17 Taurus	Square Uranus, Opp. Jupiter	Castro's revolution in Cuba
Nov. 20, 1960	19 Cancer	**Opp. Saturn**	
Feb. 7, 1961	30 Gemini/0 Cancer		Apr., Bay of Pigs invasion
Dec. 26, 1962	25 Leo	Square Venus	China battles India
March 16, 1963	6 Leo		
Jan. 28, 1965	28 Virgo	Conj. U.S. Neptune	LBJ begins bombing of Vietnam; Selma riots
Apr. 19, 1965	9 Virgo	**Opp. Saturn,** Conj. Uranus, Conj. Pluto	Dominican crisis
March 8, 1967	4 Scorpio		Apr. 15, Biggest anti-war protests in history
May 26, 1967	15 Libra	**Opp. Saturn**	June, 6-Day Arab-Israeli War; Biafra Civil War. July, U.S. ghetto riots
April 27, 1969	17 Sagittarius	Square Pluto	Civil War starts in No. Ireland; May 15, Berkeley riot
July 8, 1969	2 Sagittarius	Conj. Neptune	Kennedy's Chappaquiddick accident
July 11, 1971	22 Aquarius	Square Jupiter	Nixon announces China trip
Sept. 9, 1971	12 Aquarius	Trine Uranus	Attica prison riot
Sept. 19, 1973	10 Taurus	Square Jupiter, Sextile Saturn	Oct. 6, Yom Kippur War
Nov. 26, 1973	26 Aries	Opp. Uranus	Greek revolt; Arab oil embargo
Nov. 6, 1975	3 Cancer	Trine Uranus	Fall, Beirut Civil War starts
Jan. 20, 1976	15 Gemini	Opp. Neptune	South Africa invades Angola; Morocco war with Algeria; Rhodesia Civil War begins
Dec. 12, 1977	12 Leo	Square Uranus	Sadat visits Israel
March 2, 1978	23 Cancer		Israel invades Lebanon
Jan. 16, 1980	16 Virgo	Conj. Jupiter, Square Neptune	Dec. 30, Soviets invade Afghanistan
April 6, 1980	26 Leo	Square Uranus	Iran hostage rescue attempt; May, Korean riots; Miami riots; U.S. Olympic boycott; Liberia coup; Israel occupies Lebanon
Feb. 20, 1982	20 Libra	**Conj. Saturn,** Conj. Pluto	Syria crushes huge Moslem uprising
May 11, 1982	1 Libra		May, Falklands War; June, massive Israeli invasion of Lebanon
April 5, 1984	29 Scorpio		Violent British coal strike
June 19, 1984	12 Scorpio	**Conj. Saturn**	Sikh massacre; Iran bombs ships in Persian Gulf
June 8, 1986	24 Capricorn		Violent strikes in Chile and South Africa; April, U.S. bombs Libya; U.S. aid to Contras voted

Exact Dates	Position	Aspects	Violent, Aggressive, or Crucial Events
Aug. 12, 1986	12 Capricorn	Conj. Neptune	July 14, U.S. troops sent to Bolivia in "drug war"
Aug. 26, 1988	12 Aries	Square Neptune	
Oct. 28, 1988	30 Pisces/0 Aries	**Square Saturn,** SquareUranus	Dec. 21, Pan Am 103 shot down; Oct., Algerian government toppled ; Nov. 15, Palestine declares independence
Oct. 20, 1990	15 Gemini		U.S. doubles troops in Persian Gulf
Jan. 1, 1991	28 Taurus	Trine Saturn, Opp. Pluto	Persian Gulf War; Somali Civil War; Soviets invade Lithuania
Nov. 28, 1992	28 Cancer		U.S. troops sent to Somalia
Feb. 15, 1993	9 Cancer	**Sesq-Sq. Saturn,** Square Jup.	Feb. 25, World Trade Center bombed; Feb.28, shoot-out near Waco, TX between U.S. officials and religious cult
Jan. 2, 1995	3 Virgo	**Opp. Saturn,** Square Pluto	Chechnya uprising
March 24, 1995	14 Leo		April 19, Oklahoma City bombing
Feb. 6, 1997	6 Libra	**Opp. Saturn,** Trine Uranus	
Apr. 27, 1997	17 Virgo		May restimulate '60s-style protests or riots
March 18, 1999	13 Scorpio	Square Uranus	Revolution in Russia or Balkans?
June 4, 1999	25 Libra	Opp. Jupiter	Religious war?

MARS STATIONARY IN THE TWENTY-FIRST CENTURY

In this section, all of the strongest aspects are indicated in bold type.

Exact Dates	Position	Aspects
May 11, 2001	30 Sagittarius	Sextile Uranus
July 19, 2001	16 Sagittarius	**Opp. Saturn, Conj. Pluto,** Opp. Venus
July 29, 2003	11 Pisces	Trine Saturn, Square Pluto
Sept. 27, 2003	1 Pisces	**Conj. Uranus,** Opp. Jupiter
Oct. 2, 2005	24 Taurus	Opp. Venus
Dec. 10, 2005	9 Taurus	**Square Saturn, Opp. Jupiter,** Square Neptune
Nov. 15, 2007	13 Cancer	Trine Uranus, Conj. US Sun
Jan. 30, 2008	25 Gemini	Opp. Pluto, Trine Neptune/Mercury, Conj. US Mars
Dec. 20, 2009	20 Leo	**Opp. Jupiter, Opp. Neptune**
March 10, 2010	1 Leo	Sextile Saturn, Trine Venus, Trine Uranus
Jan. 24, 2012	24 Virgo	Opp. Uranus, Conj. U.S. Neptune
April 14, 2012	4 Virgo	**Conj. Neptune**
March 2, 2014	28 Libra	Square Venus
May 20, 2014	10 Libra	Opp. Uranus, Square Pluto, Conj. U.S. Saturn

Exact Dates	Position	Aspects
April 17, 2016	9 Sagittarius	**Conj. Saturn,** Square Neptune, Square Jupiter
June 29, 2016	24 Scorpio	Quincunx Uranus
June 26, 2018	10 Aquarius	Square Jupiter, Conj. 1892 prog. Mars
Aug. 27, 2018	29 Capricorn	Square Uranus, Conj. U.S. Pluto
Sept. 9, 2020	29 Aries	**Square Saturn,** Square Pluto, Venus
Nov. 14, 2020	16 Aries	Square Pluto/Jupiter, Opp. Venus
Oct. 30, 2022	26 Gemini	Square Jupiter/Neptune, Conj. US Mars
Jan. 12, 2023	9 Gemini	Sesqui-Square; Conj. U.S. Uranus, 1892 Conj.
Dec. 6, 2024	7 Leo	Opp. Pluto
Feb. 24, 2025	17 Cancer	Trine Saturn/Mercury
Jan. 10, 2027	11 Virgo	(Weak) Square Uranus/Venus
April 2, 2027	21 Leo	**Conj. Jupiter,** Trine Saturn, Conj. eclipse degree
Feb. 14, 2029	14 Libra	Trine Uranus, Pluto, Venus; Opp. Neptune; Conj. U.S. Saturn
May 5, 2029	25 Virgo	Trine Mercury, Conj. U.S. Neptune
March 29, 2031	22 Scorpio	Opp. Venus
June 13, 2031	5 Scorpio	Square Venus, Conj. 1892 Uranus
May 26, 2033	13 Capricorn	**Opp. Saturn,** Square Neptune/Venus
Aug. 2, 2033	30 Sagittarius	Opp. Uranus/Venus
Aug. 15, 2035	29 Pisces	Opp. U.S. Neptune
Oct. 15, 2035	18 Pisces	Quincunx Saturn, Trine Uranus, Opp. 1966 Conj.
Oct. 12, 2037	7 Gemini	**Square Saturn,** Opp. Venus, Conj. 1892 Conj.
Dec. 23, 2037	21 Taurus	**Square Pluto,** Trine Saturn, Venus, Sextile Uranus
Nov. 23, 2039	22 Cancer	Square Venus
Feb. 9, 2040	4 Cancer	**Square Saturn,** Square Jupiter, Sextile Uranus; Conj. U.S. Jupiter
Dec. 28, 2041	28 Leo	**Opp. Pluto,** Square Jupiter
March 18, 2042	9 Leo	**Square Saturn, Conj. Uranus, Square Neptune**
Jan. 31, 2044	1 Libra	Sextile Saturn, Trine Mercury, quincunx Pluto
April 21, 2044	12 Virgo	Semi-sextile Saturn, Trine Neptune, Square Venus, Quincunx Mercury
March 11, 2046	7 Scorpio	**Trine Mercury/Pluto,** Square Venus, Opp. Neptune
May 28, 2046	19 Libra	Sextile Saturn, Quincunx Neptune, Opp. Jupiter
April 30, 2048	21 Sagittarius	Opp. **U.S. Mars**
July 10, 2048	6 Sagittarius	**Square Uranus, Pluto**
July 15, 2050	27 Aquarius	**Square Neptune**
Sept. 13, 2050	17 Aquarius	**Conj. 1892 prog. Mars 1963,** Opp. Jupiter

Of the 114 wars from my comprehensive list, twenty-eight started near a Mars station (about two weeks before it to a month and a half after it) for an average of 24.5%. The chances of Mars being near such a Mars station are less than one in six (two months, twice, in over two years = 16.6%). That's 1.48 times the rate of chance.

Mars-Saturn aspects are another sign of war. A study of nineteen major wars involving two or more great powers shows that they started during a Mars-Saturn opposition, square or conjunction at three times the rate of chance. A study of over 100 wars shows they started under these aspects at twice the rate of chance. For more details, see E. Alan Meece, *The Horoscope of Humanity*; or contact the author c/o the publisher.

SATURN-PLUTO WAR CYCLE SINCE 1851:

Cycle	Year	Aspect	Event
1.	1851	Conj.	Dispute leading to Crimean War.
	1859	Square	France and Italy defeated Austria. Raid on Harper's Ferry.
	1866	Opp.	Prussia beat Austria. U.S.-French confrontation over Mexico.
	1875	Square	Balkan Wars, leading to Russo-Turk War and Congress of Berlin.
2.	1883	Conj.	Britain conquered Egypt from France. Upsurge of imperialism.
	1890	Square	Bismarck fired. Reinsurance Treaty broken.
	1898–9	Opp.	Spanish-American/Philippine War. Boer War. Fashoda crisis.
	1907	Square	British joined Triple Entente
3.	1914	Conj.	World War I
	1922	Square	Mussolini's March on Rome. Ruhr invasion. Greece vs. Turkey.
	1931	Opp.	Japanese invasion of Manchuria.
	1939	Square	World War II
4.	1947-8	Conj.	Cold War began. Berlin blockade. Israeli-Arab war. Kashmir War.
	1956	square	Suez War. Hungarian Revolution. Diem took over S. Vietnam.
	1965–6	Opp.	Vietnam War. Dominican civil war. 6-Day War, 1967.
	1973	Square	Yom Kippur War.
5.	1982	Conj.	Israeli invasion of Lebanon. Falklands War.
	1992-3	Square	Bosnian War. Yemen war. Georgian War. Korea nuclear crisis.
	2001	Opp.	(Aug., Nov. 2001; May 2002)
	2010	Square	(Nov. 2009, Jan. Aug. 2010)
6.	2020	Conj.	(Jan., Oct.)
	2028	Square	
	2035–6	Opp.	
	2044	Square	
7.	2053	Conj.	

APPENDIX G

U.S. WARS AND THE OUTER PLANETS

When major planets are transiting Gemini, or close to Gemini (primarily mid-Taurus to mid-Cancer, and sometimes to mid-Leo), they are passing through the U.S. Seventh House of war and over the U.S. Mars (the god of war), according to most versions of the U.S. horoscope. Uranus was also in Gemini, and Jupiter in early Cancer, at America's birth. Therefore, important in mid-Taurus to mid-Cancer tend to coincide with the start of U.S. wars. Watch for events to unfold as Jupiter turns direct in Taurus and heads toward Gemini with no further stations.

Year	War	Jupiter in:	*Uranus in Gemini	†Neptune in Gemini
Colonial era:				
1689–96	King William's War	Pisces	*	
1702	Queen Anne's War	Aries		
1739	War of Jenkins' Ear	Gemini		
1754–63	French and Indian War	Leo		
National era:				
1775–81	Revolution	Taurus	*	
1799	Naval war with France	Taurus		
1801–05	Tripoli	Leo		
1812–15	War of 1812	Cancer		
1846–48	Mexican War	Taurus		
1856–61	"Bleeding Kansas"	Aries		
1861–65	Civil War	Leo	*	
1898	Spanish-American War	Libra		†
1899	Philippine War	Scorpio		†
1917–18	World War I	Taurus		
1941–45	World War II	Gemini	*	
1950–53	Korean War	Pisces		
1965–73	Vietnam War	Taurus		
1989	Panama invasion	Cancer		
1990–91	"Desert Storm"	Cancer/Leo		
2001	?			

Below is a listing of U.S. wars fought under during Uranus in Gemini, indicated with a * in the above chart.

Period	War
1689–96	King William's War, 1689–97
1774–81	War of Independence, 1775–81
1858–65	Civil War, 1861–65
1941–48	World War II, 1941–45; plus start of Cold War, 1947
2026–33	(Another civil war, or secession from the New World Order?)

In the above chart, a † indicates when Neptune was in Gemini from 1887 to 1901, as the U.S. became an imperial world power and fought two wars. Both wars happened while Neptune was exactly conjunct Mars in America's horoscope at 22° Gemini. (Pluto was also in Gemini during this time).

Now, lets look at the transits of Jupiter through Taurus/Gemini, with corresponding events in U.S. history.

Year	Events
1775	Revolution begins
1799	Undeclared naval war with France; navy created
1811	"War hawks" agitate for war with Britain; War of 1812 follows (Cancer)
1823	Monroe Doctrine; Texas settled by Stephen Austin
1835	Texas declares independence, won in 1836 (Cancer)
1846	Mexican War
1859	Raid on Harper's Ferry sparks Civil War in 1861 (Leo)
1870	Alabama dispute with Britain
1882	Navy expands
1894–95	Cuban revolution and Venezuela crisis (led to Spanish-American War)
1905–06	Intervention by TR in Dominican Rep., Cuba, Japan, Morocco, etc.;
1917	World War I
1929	Stock market crash fuels the rise of Hitler
1941	World War II
1953–54	Korean War ends; meddling in Vietnam (Geneva Accords)
1965	Intervention in Vietnam begins
1977	Carter's negotiates Israel-Egypt treaty (Camp David Accords), 1978; Panama Canal Treaty signed (enforced during the next cycle)
1989	Panama invasion (Cancer); Desert Shield, 1990 (Cancer) Gulf War, 1991 (Leo)

Finally, we compare the cycle of Saturn-Neptune conjunctions and oppositions to pertinent events in the U.S.

Year	Aspect	Events
1774	Conjunction	Boston Tea Party, Continental Congress
1792	Opposition	French Revolution leads to political parties in U.S.
1809	Conjunction	Sea trade disputes with Britain leading to war
1827	Opposition	
1846	Conjunction	Mexican War
1862	Opposition	During Civil War
1882	Conjunction	
1900	Opposition	During Philippine revolt
1917	Conjunction	World War I
1936	Opposition	Spanish Civil War (Lincoln Brigades, U.S. neutral)
1952– 1953	Conjunction	Korean War, McCarthyism, H-bomb, Iran coup
1971– 1972	Opposition	During Vietnam; Watergate burglary
1989– 1990	Conjunction	Panama invasion; Persian Gulf crisis and war

STATISTICAL ANALYSIS

Total national wars: 15 (7% of years)
Total wars started with Jupiter between mid-Taurus and mid-Cancer (18% of zodiac): 8
15/8 = 53% (three times the chance rate of Jupiter being there)
Total wars started with Jupiter between mid-Taurus and mid-Leo (27% of zodiac): 11
15/11 = 73% (2.7 times the rate of chance).

Out of nineteen transits of Jupiter in the critical region, mid-Taurus to mid-Cancer, eight coincided with the start of U.S. wars (42%). This is six times the rate at which a U.S. war begins (7% of years from 1775 to 1990).

Eight out of thirteen conjunctions and oppositions of Saturn and Neptune from 1774 to 1989 were closely associated with U.S. wars that happened soon before, during or soon after them (61.5%). By contrast, the U.S. is at war only 23% of the time (fifty years out of 215); again 2.67 times the rate of chance.

Jupiter returns to Taurus/Gemini in (approximately) the years 2001, 2012, 2024, 2036, 2048. Look for expansive or internal U.S. wars at these times, or for efforts to promote peace through daring negotiations.

APPENDIX H

RULING SIGNS FOR COUNTRIES

Here are the signs which are associated with many of the world's most important countries, based on tradition and their most recent birthdates:

Algeria: Scorpio, Cancer
Angola: Taurus
Austria: Libra
Bahamas: Cancer
Bangladesh: Aries
Belgium: Gemini, Scorpio
Brazil: Virgo, Capricorn
Britain: Aries, Leo
Burma: Libra, Capricorn
Cambodia: Leo
Canada: Cancer
China: Libra, Aquarius
Croatia: Cancer, Scorpio
Cuba: Capricorn
Denmark: Aries
Egypt: Leo/Virgo, Gemini
Ethiopia: Scorpio, Pisces
France: Leo
Germany: Aries, Taurus, Libra, Capricorn
Greece: Capricorn, Aquarius
Holland: Aquarius, Cancer
Hungary: Sagittarius, Libra
India: Leo
Iraq: Cancer, Taurus
Iran: Aquarius
Ireland: Aries, Taurus
Israel: Leo, Taurus
Italy: Leo, Gemini
Japan: Libra, Taurus
Kenya: Sagittarius
Kuwait: Gemini
Laos: Leo, Libra
Latin countries: Sagittarius, Capricorn
Lithuania: Capricorn, Aquarius
Mexico: Libra, Capricorn, Aquarius
Morocco: Scorpio

Moslem countries: Leo, Cancer
Nigeria: Libra
Norway: Scorpio
Pakistan: Leo
Philippines: Cancer
Poland: Scorpio, Aquarius
Russia: Capricorn, Leo
Saudi Arabia: Capricorn
Scotland: Cancer
Slovenia: Cancer, Sagittarius
South Africa: Scorpio
Somalia: Cancer
Spain: Sagittarius
Sri Lanka: Aquarius
Switzerland: Virgo
Syria: Aries
Tanzania: Taurus
Turkey: Taurus, Scorpio/Libra
Ukraine: Aquarius
United States: Sagittarius, Gemini, Cancer
Vietnam: Cancer, Libra
Zaire: Cancer

BIBLIOGRAPHY

HISTORICAL REFERENCES
* Major Sources

Allen, Frederick Lewis. *The Big Change*. Bantam/Harper & Row, 1952.
————. *Only Yesterday*. Harper & Row, 1931. *
————. *Since Yesterday*. Harper & Row, 1940. *
Arnason, H. Harvard. *History of Modern Art*. H.N. Abrams, 1968.
Bailey, Thomas. *The American Pageant*. D.C. Heath & Co., 1956. *

Bell, Clive. *Art*. Capricorn Books, G.P.Putnam's Sons, 1958.
Bowra, C.M. *The Greek Experience*. New American Library, 1957.
Bronowski, J. *The Ascent of Man*. Little Brown, 1973.
Burckhardt, Jacob. *The Civilization of the Renaissance in Italy*. Harper Torchbooks, 1958.
Carlyle, Thomas. *The French Revolution*. Modern Library, 1837. *
Carman, Syrett and Wishy. *History of the American People*. Alfred A. Knopf, 1967. *
Caute, David. *The Year of the Barricades: A Journey Through 1968*. Harper & Row, 1988. *
Clark, Kenneth. *Civilization*. Harper & Row, 1969. *
Colton, Joel. *The Great Ages of Man: The Twentieth Century*. Time-Life Books, 1968.
Copelston, Frederick. *History of Philosophy*. Image Books, 1959.
Craig, Gordon A..*Europe, 1815-1914*. The Dryden Press, 1972. *
Davis, John. *The Kennedys: Dynasty and Disaster*. McGraw Hill, 1984.
De Bary, Wm. Theodore. *Sources of Indian Tradition*. Columbia University Press, 1958.
Delacroix and Tansey. *Art Through the Ages*. Harcourt, Brace & World, 1970. *
Dudley, Donald R. *The Civilization of Rome*. New American Library, 1960. *
Durant, Will. *The Story of Philosophy*. Washington Square Press, 1961.
Durant, Will and Ariel. The Story of Civilization. Simon & Schuster, 1954-1975. *
Easton, Stewart C. Brief History of the Western World. Barnes & Noble, 1966. *
————. World Since 1918. Barnes & Noble, 1966. *
Encyclopedia Britannica
Fasel, George. *Europe in Upheaval: The Revolutions of 1848*. Rand McNally, 1970. *
Furet and Richet. *The French Revolution*. MacMillan, 1970. *
Gamow, George. *Thirty Years that Shook Physics*. Doubleday Anchor, 1966.
Gershoy, Leo. *The Era of the French Revolution*. D. Van Nostrand, 1957. *
Gilbert, Felix. *The End of the European Era, 1890 to the Present*. W.W. Norton, 1970. *
Ginger, Ray. *The Age of Excess*. MacMillan, 1965.
Gips, Elizabeth. *Scrapbook of a Haight-Ashbury Pilgrim*. Changes Press, 1991.
Goldman, Eric F. *The Crucial Decade--and After*. Vintage Books, 1960. *
Goodrich, L. Carrington. *A Short History of the Chinese People*. Harper & Row, 1969. *
Hatton, Ragnhild. *Europe in the Age of Louis XIV*. Harcourt, Brace & world, 1969.
Hale, Oron J. *The Great Illusion*. Harper & Row, 1971. *

Hamilton, George Heard. *19th and 20th Century Art*. Prentice-Hall Inc.

Hayes, Carlton J. *A Generation of Materialism*. Harper & Row, 1941. *

Heer, Friedrich. *The Medieval World*. The New American Library, 1962.

Hobsbawm, E. J. *The Age of Revolution: 1789-1848*. The New American Library, 1962. *

Hollister, C. Warren. *Medieval Europe*. John Wiley & Sons, 1968.

Huizinga, J. *The Waning of the Middle Ages*. Doubleday Anchor, 1949.

Information Please Almanac. 1989, 1991 *

Lafore, Laurence. *The Long Fuse*. J. B. Lippincott, 1971. *

Lefebvre, Georges. *The Coming of the French Revolution*. Princeton University Press, 1947. *

Langer (ed.).Hexter/Pipes. *Western Civilization: The Struggle for Empire to Europe in the Modern World*. American Heritage Publishing, Harper & Row, 1968.*

Lowith, Karl. *From Hegel to Nietzsche*. Doubleday Anchor, 1967.

Machlis, Joseph. *The Art of Enjoying Music*. W. W. Norton, 1963.

Marx, Karl. *The 18 Brumaire of Louis Bonaparte*. International Publishers, 1869, 1963.

Miers, Earl Schenck. *The Golden Book of U.S. History*. Golden Press, 1963.

Miller & Gilmore. *Revolution at Berkeley*. Dell Publishing, 1965.

Morrison and Commager. *Growth of the American Republic. Vol.II*. Oxford University Press, 1950.

Mowry, George E. *The Twenties*. Prentice-Hall, 1963.

O' Neill, William L. *American Society Since 1945*. Quadrangle/New York Times Book Co., 1969.

————. *Coming Apart*. Quadrangle/New York Times Book Co., 1971. *

Roszak, Theodore. *The Making of a Counter Culture*. Anchor/Doubleday, 1969.

Sedillot, Rene. *An Outline of French History*. Alfred A. Knopf, 1953.

Southern, R. W. *The Making of the Middle Ages*. Yale University Press, 1953.

Talmon. J. L. *Romanticism and Revolt*. Harcourt. Brace & World, 1967. *

Wells, H. G. *The Outline of History*. Garden City Books/Doubleday, 1940, 1961. *

Wolfe,Tom. *The Electric Kool-Aid Acid Test*. Bantam Books, 1968. *

Woodham-Smith, Cecil. *The Reason Why*. Dutton, 1953, 1960.

World Almanac, 1977, 1982, 1986-1993.

Zinn, Howard. *A People's History of the United States,*.HarperCollins, 1980. *

CHRONOLOGIES

Bicentennial Almanac, Information Please Almanac, World Almanac,
plus references by Haydn, Langer, Little, Webster, and others

ASTROLOGY REFERENCES

Astarte. *Astrology Made Easy*. Wilshire Book Co., 1967.

Brotherhood of Light. *Mundane Astrology*

Brunhubner, Fritz. *Pluto*. American Federation of Astrologers, 1971.

Carter, C.E.O. *Astrological Aspects*. L. N. Fowler & Co., 13th edition 1975.

Davison, Ronald C. *Astrology*. Arc Books, 1963.

Dernay, Eugene. *Longitudes and Latitudes in the U.S.* American Federation of Astrologers, 1945.

————. *Longitudes and Latitudes in the World.* American Federation of Astrologers, 1945

Devore, Nicholas. *Encyclopedia of Astrology.* Philosophical Library, 1947.

Goodavage, Joseph F. *Astrology, The Space Age Science.* The New American Library, 1966.

————. *Write Your Own Horoscope.* The New American Library, 1968.

Hammond's World Atlas. Hanover House, 1962.

Hone, Margaret. *Modern Textbook of Astrology.* Fowler, 1972.

Hutin, Serge. *History of Astrology.* Pyramid Communications, 1972.

Jones, Marc Edmund. *Guide to Horoscope Interpretation.* Theosophical Publishing House, 1941.

Lerner, Mark. *Mysteries of Venus.* Great Bear Press, 1986.

Lewi, Grant. *Astrology for the Millions.* Llewellyn Publications, 1969.

Lofthus, Myrna. *A Spiritual Approach to Astrology.* CRCS Publications, 1983.

MacCraig, Hugh. *Ephemeris of the Moon.* Macoy, 1951.

MacCaffery, Ellen. *Graphic Astrology.* Macoy, 1952.

Michelsen, Neil F. *The American Ephemeris for the 20th Century.* A.C.S. Publications, 1983.

————. *The American Ephemeris for the 21st Century.* A.C.S. Publications, 1982

Parker, Derek and Julia. *The Compleat Astrologer.* Bantam Books, 1975.

Raphael's Ephemeris. 1892, 1960, 1966

Raphael's Table of Houses.

Rosicrucian Fellowship. *Simplified Scientific Ephemeris* (1890s to 1990s).

Rudhyar, Dane. *An Astrological Mandala.* Vintage Books/Random House, 1973.

————. *The Astrology of Personality.* Doubleday, 1963, 1970.

————. *Astrological Timing: The Transition to the New Age.* Harper & Row, 1969.

————. *The Astrology of America's Destiny.*

————. *Culture, Crisis and Creativity.* Theosophical Publishing House, 1977.

————. *The Lunation Cycle.* Aurora Press, 1967.

————. *The Planetarization of Consciousness.* Harper & Row, 1970.

————. *The Practice of Astrology,* Penguin Books. 1968.

————. *The Pulse of Life,* Shambhala. 1970.

————. *We Can Begin Again Together.* Omen Communications, 1974.

Stahlman and Gingerich. *Solar and Planetary Longitudes for Years -2500–2000.* Univ. of Wisconsin, 1963.

Van Norstrand, Frederic. *Precepts in Mundane Astrology.* Macoy, 1962.

ASTROLOGY MAGAZINES

American Astrology
American Federation of Astrologers Bulletin
Horoscope (Dell)
Mercury Hour
The Mountain Astrologer
Welcome to Planet Earth

HISTORICAL PHILOSOPHY, COMMENTARY, AND FICTION

Adams, *The Law of Civilization and Decay*
Bergson, *Creative Evolution*
Bergson, Larabie (ed.) *Selections from Bergson*
Blake, Penguin edition, Bronowski (ed.) *A Selection of Poems*
Blavatsky, *An Abridgment of the Secret Doctrine*
Burke, *Reflections on the Revolution in France*
Capra, *The Tao of Physics*
————. *The Turning Point*
Castellucci, *Heaven and History*
Collingwood, *The Idea of History*
Crowley, *The Book of the Law*
Dickens, *Hard Times*
————. *A Tale of Two Cities*
Ferguson, *The Aquarian Conspiracy*
Freud, *Civilization and its Discontents*
Frye, *Anatomy of Criticism*
Hardy, *Return of the Native*
Hegel, *The Philosophy of History*
————. *The Phenomenology of Mind*
Heidegger, *Being and Time*
Heisenberg, *Physics and Philosophy*
Jung, *Man and His Symbols*
Kaufmann (ed.), *The Portable Nietzsche* (includes *Thus Spake Zarathustra*)
Lewis, *Arrowsmith*
————. *Babbitt*
Lindsay, *The Late Great Planet Earth*
MacLuhan, *Understanding Media*
Mann, *The Magic Mountain*
Marx and Engels, Feuer (ed.) *Basic Writings on Politics and Philosophy*
Meece, *The Horoscope of Humanity*
Nietzsche, *Beyond Good and Evil*
————. *The Birth of Tragedy/The Geneology of Morals*
Plato, Saunders (transl.), *The Laws*
————. Davies & Vaughn (transl.), *Republic*
————. Cornford (transl.), *Plato's Cosmology; The Timeaus of Plato*
Reich, *The Greening of America*
Rousseau, Masters (ed.) *The First and Second Discourses*
————. *The Social Contract*
Rudhyar (see astrology references)
Schopenhauer, *The World as Will and Idea*
Wilbur (ed.) *Shelley. Selected by William Meredith*

Sullivan, *Beethoven: His Spiritual Development*
Teilhard de Chardin, *The Future of Man*
————. *The Phenomenon of Man*
Thompson, *At the Edge of History*
Toffler, *The Third Wave*
Turgenev, *Fathers and Sons*
Vajk, *Doomsday Has Been Cancelled*

SOURCES FROM PUBLIC TELEVISION

"A Planet for the Taking" (David Suzuki)
"A Walk Through the 20th Century" (Bill Moyers)
"An Ocean Apart" (David Dimbleby)
"America" (Alistair Cooke)
"Art of the Western World" (Perry Miller Adato, Michael Wood)
"Ascent of Man" (Jacob Bronowski)
"Berkeley in the '60s" (Susan Griffin, Mark Kitchell)
"The Civil War" (Ken Burns, Shelby Foote)
"Civilization" (Kenneth Clark)
"Columbus and the Age of Discovery" (Zvi Dor-Ner, Graham Chedd)
"Connections" (James Burke)
"The Day the Universe Changed" (James Burke)
"Europe, the Mighty Continent" (John Terraine, Peter Ustinov)
"Eyes on the Prize" (Julian Bond, Blackside Productions)
"Fame in the 20th Century" (Clive James)
"Further" (Ken Kesey, Steve Talbott)
"Legacy" (Michael Wood)
"Listening to America with Bill Moyers" (Bill Moyers)
"Making Sense of the Sixties"
McNeil-Lehrer News Hour
"Millennium" (David Maybury Lewis)
"The 1960s" (Peter Jennings)
"The Occult History of the Third Reich"
"The Power of Myth" (Joseph Campbell, Bill Moyers)
"The Presence of the Past" (Bill Moyers)
"The Prize" (Daniel Yergin)
"The Race to Save the Planet" (John Angier)
"The Romantic Rebellion" (Kenneth Clark)
"The Struggles for Poland" (Roger Mudd)
"The Unknown War" (Burt Lancaster)
"Vietnam: A Television History" (Stanley Karnow, Will Lyman)
"War and Peace in the Nuclear Age"
"The Western Tradition" (Eugene Weber)
"The World at War" (Lawrence Olivier)

SOURCES FROM COMMERCIAL TELEVISION

"CBS News" (Walter Cronkite, Dan Rather)
"Holocaust" (NBC)
"Our World" (ABC)
"NBC Nightly News" (John Chancellor, Tom Brokaw)
"Nightline" (ABC, Ted Koppel)
"The Prisoner" (Patrick McGoohan, CBS,ITC,BBC, and Scott Apel at KTEH, channel 54 in San Jose)
"World News Tonight" (Peter Jennings, ABC)

TEACHERS AND MENTORS

I acknowledge here some of my professors at San Jose State University for their outstanding and illuminating lectures on history and culture, and in some cases their help and encouragement.

Edward Black, Kathyrn Cohen, Irma Eichhorn, Marie Fox, Arturo B. Fallico, Peter Koestenbaum, Herman Shapiro, Richard Tansey

ASTROLOGY TEACHERS AND FRIENDS

Stephen Abbott, Muriel Andrews, Gavin Chester Arthur, Gregg Castelucci, Ida Chandler, Graeme Jones, Patricia Judge, Mark Lerner, Gary Lyte, Carol Joyce Moore, Steve Rasmussen, Dane Rudhyar, Loren Thornton, Carol Bowman Willis, and others.

Finally, I would like to thank my kitty, "Winky," for keeping me company.

INDEX

GLOSSARY

Affliction. A square or opposition, aspects considered to be difficult or challenging.

Air signs. Social, intellectual, inventive, diplomatic, idealistic signs Gemini, Libra and Aquarius.

Angles. The four most powerful points of the horoscope; the Ascendant, Midheaven, Descendant and Nadir. They are, respectively, the Eastern horizon (1st house cusp), the zenith or point overhead (10th house cusp), the Western horizon (7th house cusp) and the point below (4th house cusp). When planets are located on an angle at a particular place on Earth, they are most powerful at that location.

Angular. A planet on an angle, or in one of the angular houses: the 1st, 4th, 7th & 10th. These houses correspond in meaning with the cardinal signs.

Annular eclipse. A solar eclipse leaving a ring of sunlight because the Moon appears too small to block the Sun completely. It is almost as significant as a total eclipse.

Ascendant. The Eastern horizon over which the planets and signs rise every day; the rising sign; cusp of the 1st house. In a chart the Ascendant represents the personality, mood, attitude or health of a person or people.

Aspects. Angles assumed by the planets in relation to one another. The most important aspects are the conjunction (0 degrees), opposition (180 degrees), square (90 degrees), trine (120 degrees) and sextile (60 degrees).

Asteroids. Planetary fragments found between the orbits of Mars and Jupiter. Some astrologers attribute meanings to the largest ones: Ceres, Pallas, Juno and Vesta.

Cadent. The 3rd, 6th, 9th and 12th houses, whose meanings correspond to the mutable signs. They are especially concerned with travel, communication and adjustment.

Cardinal. Signs of leadership, assertion, initiative: Aries, Cancer, Libra and Capricorn.

Chart. A horoscope cast for the exact time of an earthly or heavenly event. A complete chart includes houses as well as signs and aspects.

Chiron. A small planetoid or huge comet found between the orbits of Saturn and Uranus. It represents "the wounded healer" and a bridge to the transcendent.

Conjunction. Alignment, or 0 degree angle, between two or more planets, intensifying and focusing their power and beginning a new mutual cycle.

Constellations. Mythical pictures formed by our imagination out of the patterns of the stars in the sky. The constellations of the zodiac are not the signs, although they corresponded to them about 2000 years ago and have the same names.

Cusp. The border or boundary between two signs or houses.

Cycle. A recurring period between the same or similar events in the heavens or on Earth. It can be used to predict the return of a similar event .

Degree. 1/360th of the zodiac, approximately the motion of the Sun in one day. Each sign has 30 degrees, and each degree has a Sabian Symbol that describes its meaning.

Descendant. The Western horizon where signs and planets set every day; the cusp of the 7th house. It rules relationships, war and diplomacy.

Direct (D) or (SD). A planet turns direct when it resumes forward motion after retrograding and appearing to turn stationary. When turning direct, a planet's energy is intensified and surges forth in outward expression.

Earth signs. Practical, worldly, cautious, constructive, consolidating signs Taurus, Virgo and Capricorn.

Eclipse. (1) A New Moon during which the Moon blocks the Sun's light. (2) A Full Moon during which the Earth blocks the Moon's light. Eclipses represent sudden change and can leave their mark on affairs for several years.

Elements. Basic states of the natural and psychological world: Fire, Earth, Air and Water. Each sign is associated with one of the elements. Fire signs are vital and creative. Earth signs are practical and constructive. Air signs are social and mental. Water signs are emotional and intuitive.

Ephemeris. A book which lists the zodiacal longitude of the planets.

Equinox. The 2 times during the year when the days and nights are of equal length. The first day of spring is the Vernal Equinox (equal to the first degree, or beginning, of Aries). The first day of fall is the Autumn Equinox (equal to the first degree of Libra).

Figure. (1) a chart or horoscope. (2) a pattern of aspects among the planets.

Finger of God. A powerful symbol of creative adjustment. See yod.

Fire signs. Vital, enthusiastic, outgoing signs Aries, Leo and Sagittarius.

Fixed. Representing stability, stubbornness, power and financial acumen are the signs Taurus, Leo, Scorpio and Aquarius.

Full Moon. (1) The Moon seen in the sky as a full, perfect disc. The opposition between Sun and Moon; climax of the lunation cycle. (2) The analogous point in any mutual cycle between planets.

GMT. Greenwich Mean Time. The time zone of England's Greenwich Observatory at 0 degrees longitude; the time for which the positions of the planets are listed in the ephemeris.

Grand Cross. 4 planets all squaring and opposing each other. It is a very powerful figure of maximum power, stability, control or conflict.

Grand Trine. 3 or more planets forming a mutual triangle. It is a very powerful, expansive, harmonious figure that tends to excess.

Horoscope. A view of the hour; a map of the solar system as seen from the Earth at a particular time, from which events and persons on Earth can be interpreted.

Houses. 12 segments of space as seen from any particular place on Earth. The planets and signs pass through each house each day as the Earth rotates on its axis. Each house represents a department of life or sphere of experience. See the end of chapter 3.

Ingress. A planet entering a sign, usually referring to the equinox or solstice.

Lights. The Sun and Moon.

Latitude. Position North or South of the Equator.

Longitude. (1) The point on Earth east or west of Greenwich, England. (2) The degree of the zodiac as measured from the vernal equinox, 0 degrees Aries.

Lunation cycle. The mutual cycle between the Sun and Moon, during which the Moon's light waxes and wanes through phases: New, Crescent, First Quarter, Waxing Gibbous, Full, Waning Gibbous, Last Quarter, Balsamic and back to New.

Midheaven. The zenith of the horoscope, or point overhead; top of the chart; cusp of the 10th house. It represents status, career, ambition, the executive, the government.

Modes. See Qualities.

Mutable. Adaptable, flexible, distributive, dual, mental, "common" signs: Gemini, Virgo, Sagittarius and Pisces.

Mutual cycle. The moving, recurring relationship of two planets with each other.

Mutual reception. Two or more planets each in the sign ruled by the other, magnifying the significance of both planets.

Nadir. Bottom of the horoscope wheel, or point below; cusp of the 4th house. It represents roots, home, land, the common people, farmers, weather, withdrawal from the world, rebellion against the government, spirituality, new beginnings and endings, the low point of fortune.

Natal. Of the nativity or birth; referring to the birth chart of a person or nation.

New Moon. (1) The Moon when totally dark and invisible. A conjunction between Sun and Moon, start of the lunation cycle. (2) The beginning of any mutual cycle between two planets.

Opposition. Two or more planets on opposite sides of the Earth; a 180 degree angle. It is the powerful climax and half-way point in their mutual cycle, fulfilling what began at the conjunction. It represents clarity, schism, conflicts, polarities, revisions; it is a "Full Moon" between two planets.

Orb. The amount of inexactness allowed for an aspect to be considered in effect.

Partial Eclipse. An eclipse in which the Sun or Moon's light is only partly blocked. It is not as significant as a total eclipse.

Planets. The nine major bodies of the solar system, plus the Moon; The Sun and its satellites. Each planet represents a basic human drive. When a planet is located in a sign or house it activates the qualities of that sign or house. Some astrologers also include the four main asteroids and Chiron as "planets."

Progressions. A technique to interpret the past or the future by equating one day after birth with one year of life. Precessions equate one day before birth with one year before. One day can also be equated with one month.

Qualities. Modes of behavior and action: cardinal, fixed and mutable. Cardinal signs Aries, Cancer, Libra and Capricorn represent initiative. Fixed signs Taurus, Leo, Scorpio and Aquarius represent concentration of power. Mutable signs Gemini, Virgo, Sagittarius and Pisces represent adaptability.

Quincunx. A stressful or incompatible 150 degree angle between planets, requiring adjustments to be made.

Radical. Referring to the natal or birth chart.

Retrograde (R). After turning stationary, a retrograde planet appears to move backward through the zodiac as the Earth passes it, restraining its energy or turning it inward. It symbolizes events reversing their direction.

Rising. A sign or planet on the Ascendant; coming over the horizon. In a horoscope it may signify increasing prominence or fortune.

Ruler. The planet associated with a sign or house because of its similar nature. The place where the ruler of a sign or house is will tell us more about what it means in a chart. The planet ruling the Ascendant is significant, often called the ruler of the chart.

Sabian Symbol. A mythical image that represents the meaning of each zodiacal degree.

Semi-sextile. A 30 degree angle between planets, representing a developing trend.

Semi-square. A 45 degree angle between planets; an angle of friction about half as important as a square.

Sesqui-square. A 135 degree angle similar in effect to a semi-square.

Sextile. A 60 degree angle between planets considered harmonious, constructive, mentally stimulating and artistic in effect.

Sidereal. Astrologers who use the zodiac of constellations instead of signs are called sidereal astrologers. Sidereal time refers to the daily movement of stars (or signs) instead of the sun, and is used to find the Ascendant and houses of the horoscope.

Signs. 30 degree segments of the zodiac measured from the vernal equinox. The Sun sign represents Earth's position in its yearly cycle around the Sun. The planets move "in" the signs as they move around the Sun as seen from the Earth. Each sign takes its meaning from its place on the cycle between one vernal equinox and the next. Signs are not constellations.

Singleton. (1) One planet alone in at least half the sky relative to other planets, making that planet a powerful focal point. (2) Any other way in which one planet stands out in significance from the others.

Solstice. (1) Longest day of the year, and first day of Summer (equal to 0 degrees Cancer). (2) shortest day of the year, and first day of Winter (equal to 0 degrees Capricorn).

Square. A 90 degree or right angle between planets, bringing energy and conflict between the things they represent. A Quarter phase.

Stationary (S). A planet which appears to stand still as the Earth passes close to it in space, greatly magnifying its power and significance. After turning stationary, a planet moves backward (retrograde, R) or forward (direct, D).

Suceedent. The 2nd, 5th, 8th and 11th houses, corresponding in meaning to the fixed signs. They are especially concerned with finances.

Stellium. Three or more planets in conjunction.

T-square. A planet squaring two others which are themselves in opposition, symbolizing maximum tension, energy and conflict.

Total eclipse. The most powerful kind of eclipse; light is completely blocked (see eclipse)

Transit. The current position of a planet. When it crosses another planet's original place in a horoscope, it affects everything connected with that planet in the chart.

Trine. A 120 degree angle between planets considered to be harmonious, invigorating, expansive, frivolous and/or visionary in effect.

Water signs. Emotional, nurturing, intuitive, dissolving, transforming signs Cancer, Scorpio and Pisces.

Yod. The "finger of God" pattern; a planet in quincunx to two others in sextile. It indicates adjustment through a creative outlet, adjustment through seeking of knowledge, and intuitive abilities through union of higher self and conscious mind.

Zodiac. (1) The path in space through which the planets and Earth orbit the Sun, and the 12 signs which describe this cyclic path. (2) The 12 constellations of the same name as the signs through which the planets pass as they orbit the Sun. The signs and the constellations are now about 25 degrees apart due to the precession of the equinoxes (see Chapter 2).

Stay in Touch. . .

Llewellyn publishes hundreds of books on your favorite subjects

On the following pages you will find listed some books now available on related subjects. Your local bookstore stocks most of these and will stock new Llewellyn titles as they become available. We appreciate your patronage!

Order by Phone

Call toll-free within the U.S. and Canada, 1–800–THE MOON.
In Minnesota call (612) 291–1970.
We accept Visa, MasterCard, and American Express.

Order by Mail

Send the full price of your order (MN residents add 7% sales tax) in U.S. funds to:
Llewellyn Worldwide
P.O. Box 64383, Dept. L007–9
St. Paul, MN 55164–0383, U.S.A.

Postage and Handling

- $4.00 for orders $15.00 and under
- $5.00 for orders over $15.00
- No charge for orders over $100.00

We ship UPS in the continental United States. We cannot ship to P.O. boxes. Orders shipped to Alaska, Hawaii, Canada, Mexico, and Puerto Rico will be sent first-class mail.

International orders: Airmail—add freight equal to price of each book to the total price of order, plus $5.00 for each non-book item (audiotapes, etc.). Surface mail—Add $1.00 per item.

Allow 4–6 weeks delivery on all orders. Postage and handling rates subject to change.

Group Discounts

We offer a 20% quantity discount to group leaders or agents. You must order a minimum of five copies of the same book to get our special quantity price.

Free Catalog

Get a free copy of our color catalog, *New Worlds of Mind and Spirit*. Subscribe for just $10.00 in the United States and Canada ($20.00 overseas, first class mail). Many bookstores carry New Worlds—ask for it!

Predictions for a New Millennium
Noel Tyl

He predicted the exact dates of the Gulf War and the fall of the Soviet Union. Now Noel Tyl foresees key events, with fifty-eight predictions about the dramatic political, economic, and social changes that will occur between now and the year 2012. Predictions for a New Millennium prepares us to see beyond the crisis of the moment to understand world changes strategically. Here are just a few of the momentous events that we will witness as we enter the 21st century: assassination of another U.S. president ... China abandons communism ... Saddam Hussein toppled from power ... Hitler revival in Germany. The new millennium is a pivotal time in our history. How will these events affect the economy, the world powers ... how will they affect you? The answers are here.

1-56718-737-4, 304 pp., 6 x 9, maps, graphs, index, softcover $14.95

Nostradamus 1999
Who Will Survive?
Stefan Paulus

What significant event did the 16th century prophet Nostradamus predict for the seventh month of 1999? Nostradamus predicts that a large comet will have a close encounter with the earth at that time. Could Nostradamus' "King of Terror" be lurking in that comet's tail?

Author Stefan Paulus presents Nostradamus as no one has done before. In a book that is both believable and highly readable, he pieces together the jigsaw puzzle of Nostradamus' final prophecies, correlating them to what is going on in current environmental trends. Only Paulus explores the link between the prophecies and a battle-by-battle vision of a near-future World War III. Only Paulus correlates Nostradamus' predictions with unfulfilled Biblical prophecies, particularly those from the Book of Revelation, and he explains how they could come true in ways compatible with modern scientific knowledge. In addition, Paulus compares Nostradamus' predictions with Islamic prophecies that are already being fulfilled at this time.

1-56718-515-0, 336 pp., 6 x 9, softcover $14.95

Apocalyse Now
The Challenges of Our Times
Peter Roche de Coppens

During the last two decades of the Twentieth Century, humanity is being given, collectively and individually, a very major "test" in the School of Life—true and lived initiation. Many prophecies have been made, in symbolic form, to tell us what to expect at this time, named at different times the Apocalypse, Armageddon, the Great War between the Forces of Light and Darkness, or the Coming of the Antichrist.

Most people have interpreted these prophecies and visions as pertaining to the physical world, implying the destruction of civilization and even the end of mankind and of the world itself. While it is true that our outer physical world (and culture) will be greatly affected and transformed, it is the inner world of man—consciousness—that is directly affected by this great test.

The Apocalypse really refers to an inner process of purification and transformation, not to an outer one. The battle between God-consciousness and the antichrist, our dark, unregenerated self, takes place within. How, then, do we prepare ourselves for this great change? That is the purpose of Apocalypse Now. It offers a program for not only understanding the Challenges of Our Times, but also for personal transformation and spiritual growth to fulfill the Opportunity and Potential of this New Age, now!

0-87542-677-8, 288 pp., 5¼ x 8, softcover $9.95